Financial Development, Integration and Stability

Financial Development, Integration and Stability

Evidence from Central, Eastern and South-Eastern Europe

Edited by

Klaus Liebscher

Governor of the Oesterreichische Nationalbank, Austria

Josef Christl

Member of the Governing Board of the Oesterreichische Nationalbank, Austria

Peter Mooslechner

Director of Economic Analysis and Research at the Oesterreichische Nationalbank, Austria

Doris Ritzberger-Grünwald

Head of Foreign Research at the Oesterreichische Nationalbank, Austria

Edward Elgar

Cheltenham, UK • Northampton, MA, USA

Published by
Edward Elgar Publishing Limited
Glensanda House
Montpellier Parade
Cheltenham
Glos GL50 1UA
UK

Edward Elgar Publishing, Inc.
William Pratt House
9 Dewey Court
Northampton
Massachusetts 01060
USA

A catalogue record for this book
is available from the British Library

Library of Congress Cataloging in Publication Data

Financial development, integration and stability : evidence from Central, Eastern and South-Eastern Europe / edited by Klaus Liebscher... [et al.].
p. cm.
Includes bibliographical references and index.
1. Monetary policy—European Union countries. 2. European Union countries—Economic integration. I. Liebscher, Klaus.
HG925.F555 2006
337.1′4—dc22 2006011709

ISBN-13: 978 1 84542 967 6
ISBN-10: 1 84542 967 2

Printed and bound in Great Britain by MPG Books Ltd, Bodmin, Cornwall

Contents

Contributors

Franklin Allen, Finance Department, The Wharton School, University of Pennsylvania

Ana Babus, Erasmus Universiteit Rotterdam

Laura Bartiloro, Research Department, Banca d'Italia

Frédéric Boissay, European Central Bank

Cesare Calari, Vice President for the Financial Sector, The World Bank

Oscar Calvo-Gonzalez, European Central Bank

Lorenzo Cappiello, European Central Bank

Josef Christl, Executive Director, Oesterreichische Nationalbank

Sophie Claeys, Department of Financial Economics and CERISE, Ghent University

Fabrizio Coricelli, University of Siena, University of Ljubljana and CEPR

Christoph Duenwald, International Monetary Fund

Tomas Dvorak, Department of Economics, Union College, Schenectady

Falko Fecht, Deutsche Bundesbank and European Central Bank

Gerhard Fink, Europe Institute, Vienna University of Economics and Business Administration

Zsuzsanna Fluck, Department of Finance, Eli Broad Graduate School of Management, Michigan State University, and The William Davidson Institute, University of Michigan

Tomislav Galac, Director, Financial Stability Research Department, Croatian National Bank

Bruno Gérard, Director, Mellon Capital Management

Hans Peter Grüner, University of Mannheim and CEPR

Nikolay Gueorguiev, International Monetary Fund

Christa Hainz, Department of Economics, University of Munich, CESifo and WDI

Peter Haiss, Bank Austria Creditanstalt AG and Europe Institute, Vienna University of Economics and Business Administration

Arjan Kadareja, Consultant for the European Central Bank

Matthias Köhler, Centre for European Economic Research, ZEW

Oskar Kowalewski, Finance Department, Leon Kozminski Academy of Entrepreneurship and Management, Warsaw, Poland

Tomasz Koźluk, European University Institute

Evan Kraft, Advisor to the Governor, Croatian National Bank

Alexandre Lamfalussy, Former President of the European Monetary Institute, Chairman of the Committee of Wise Men for the Regulation of the European Securities Markets

Julien Le Maux, Université Paris 1 Sorbonne

Klaus Liebscher, Governor, Oesterreichische Nationalbank

Simone Manganelli, European Central Bank

Kadri Männasoo, Research Department, Eesti Pank

Colin Mayer, Said Business School, University of Oxford, CEPR and ECGI

David G. Mayes, Advisor to the Board, Suomen Pankki-Finlands Bank, Professor of Banking and Financial Institutions at the University of Stirling

Arnaud Mehl, European Central Bank

Peter Mooslechner, Director of the Economic Analysis and Research Section, Oesterreichische Nationalbank

Fabio Mucci, New Europe Research, UniCredit Group

Dennis C. Mueller, Professor, University of Vienna

Reinhard Ortner, Member of the Managing Board, Erste Bank der Oesterreichischen Sparkassen AG

Evgeni Peev, Visiting Professor at the University of Vienna and Senior Research Fellow at the Institute of Economics, Bulgarian Academy of Sciences

Diana Pop, Laboratoire d'Economie d'Orléans

Cristian Popa, Deputy Governor, Banca Nationala a Romaniei

Alessandro Profumo, CEO, UniCredit Group

Thomas Reininger, Economist, Oesterreichische Nationalbank

Debora Revoltella, Head of New Europe Research, UniCredit Group

Doris Ritzberger-Grünwald, Head of the Foreign Research Division, Oesterreichische Nationalbank

Andrea Schaechter, International Monetary Fund

Irmfried Schwimann, Head of the Financial Services Policy Unit, DG Internal Market and Services, European Commission

René M. Stulz, Chair in Banking and Monetary Economics at the Ohio State University and Research Associate at the NBER

Gertrude Tumpel-Gugerell, Member of the Executive Board, European Central Bank

Kristin Vandenbergen, Economist, Financial Services Policy Unit, DG Internal Market and Services, European Commission

Cristina Vespro, ECARES, Université Libre de Bruxelles

Goran Vukšić, Institute of Public Finance, Zagreb

Zoltan Walko, Economist, Oesterreichische Nationalbank

Adalbert Winkler, European Central Bank

Stefan Zapotocky, Joint CEO, Wiener Börse AG

Preface

The event on which this volume is based – the Oesterreichische Nationalbank's 2005 Conference on European Economic Integration, co-organized jointly with the European Central Bank and the Center for Financial Studies – touched a wide range of issues related to financial developments, integration and stability in the enlarged European Union and its neighbouring countries in Central and Eastern Europe.

The contributors to this book pay tribute to the impressive transformation process that the countries in Central and Eastern Europe have gone through over the past decade without overlooking the risks and negative side effects involved. Among other things, the process of European integration has led to an increase in the level of per capita income and financial depth. Yet despite this success, the Central and Eastern European countries continue to lag behind Western Europe in terms of their financial development level. Also, the market structure for financial services differs between the two country groups, with perhaps the most striking difference being the high share of foreign ownership in Central and Eastern Europe. Nevertheless, the Central and Eastern European countries do not represent a homogeneous region either. These differences need to be taken into account in an in-depth analysis of financial development and integration, and in particular in economic policy assessments. While it cannot be reasonably expected that these differences will completely disappear in the near future, as such differences have not disappeared within the euro area either, domestic and European policies should continue to aim at creating an integrated European financial market. In this respect, we would like to stress the need for 'better regulation', drawing on open, transparent and evidence-based policy-making, and the need to focus on the consolidation and consistent implementation of the legislative framework for financial services, as has been proposed by the European Commission in its Green Paper on financial policies for the years 2005–2010.

Why is this important? We have seen that financial development and integration are crucial factors for economic growth in Central and Eastern Europe, and should thus benefit the economic catching-up process. This is particularly true for the new member states of the European Union, but improvements in the quality of the financial system have also been beneficial for South-Eastern European countries over the past decade.

Thus, financial development and integration should also contribute to more economic growth in the euro area. In this respect, the involvement of foreign investors in the banking systems of Central and Eastern Europe, largely pioneered by Austrian banks, has been identified as a significant beneficial factor over the past few years, despite some negative side effects. Research in this field presented in this book not only highlights a number of interesting differences between domestic and foreign banks' lending behaviour and profitability, but also shows that the entry mode of foreign banks matters for the level of interest rates they charge. Let us add here that the provision of cross-border banking services to non-bank clients is likely to have welfare-enhancing effects as well. However, this type of activity remains underdeveloped in the EU, reflecting the importance of proximity of banks to their clients.

Given relatively low financial development levels, financial sector growth in Central and Eastern Europe can be expected to remain strong over the next few years. In this respect, strong credit growth, especially of loans to households, is one of the central topics currently being discussed by policy-makers and academia. New literature presented in this book suggests that while credit growth in some countries may be characterized as excessive with signs of adverse macroeconomic effects, the financial systems have preserved overall stability in the region. Moreover, the monetary authorities are aware of the connected risks and in most countries have already moved to address the situation. However, close monitoring of the developments to detect early signs of financial sector distress and to maintain financial sector stability remains an issue. As the contributions to this volume show, important empirical research has been undertaken to identify such early warning indicators for banking crises, which should assist policy-makers in their decisions.

Financial integration in the euro area has advanced over the past few years but is not yet complete. The establishment of a legislative and institutional framework for financial integration in the European Union as a whole has been a major success. Now it is up to us all to fill this framework with life to promote European financial integration to the benefit of our economies. As evidenced by this book, the integration of Central and Eastern European financial markets with the euro area remains low, although significant cross-country differences remain. However, we believe that this situation will improve over the next couple of years. We all know that integrated and efficient financial markets enhance the smooth and effective transmission of monetary policy impulses throughout the monetary union. Financial integration is also important for the frictionless functioning of payment, clearing and settlement systems, and it also enables the banking sector to manage and diversify risks better. For all these reasons, the integration of the financial system of the new member states with that of the current euro area must be promoted already in the run-up to euro adoption. This process will continue beyond that point as well, as the developments since the start of the third stage of the economic and monetary union in 1999 have shown us.

Commercial banks and stock exchanges play a significant role in promoting financial development and integration in Central and Eastern Europe. Complementing the academic views presented in this book, the closing chapters document impressively that banks are clearly aware of the business potential which lies in the financial services sector in the region, and even banks operating on a global scale have been attracted to Central and Eastern Europe. At the same time, banks are also aware of challenges which they will likely face down this road, and they are ready to take them on. Having said this, the banking industry's natural self-interest in pursuing its business activities while keeping risks on a manageable scale will have to be complemented by adequate regulation and supervision practices. In this respect, solving outstanding issues, such as the effective supervision of financial conglomerates and of the non-bank financial sector, and finding an optimal solution to the supervision of cross-border financial institutions, will require further efforts.

Summing up, financial development and integration in Central and Eastern Europe is a key element for growth and stability not only in the region, but also for Europe as a whole. A measurable deepening of financial markets in Central and Eastern Europe has happened already, but more has still to come. This will provide an even broader variety of financial instruments to those who have been driving the catching-up process so far and will drive it further down the road. Further financial deepening is also a precondition for more stable prices for all kind of goods and services. This is where the stabilization of expectations comes in, something quite important for central banks. Therefore we do judge the ongoing integration process as vital, being an important stabilizing element for the upcoming economic and social change.

Klaus Liebscher,
Josef Christl,
Peter Mooslechner and
Doris Ritzberger-Grünwald

PART I

Achievements and challenges in European financial integration

1. Financial integration and financial deepening in the EU: mind the gap

Klaus Liebscher

The accession of ten new member states to the European Union in May 2004 was a historic milestone and a major step toward the unification of Europe. Nevertheless, the recent enlargement of the EU to the east was not the end of European integration. For one, the process toward full integration of the new member states will continue over the next few years. Then, the new member states are expected to adopt the euro at some point in the future, which will mark another milestone in the European integration process. Full economic integration between the 'old and new' member states will presumably take longer than the monetary integration process. Nevertheless, I am confident that the catching-up process, if supported by coherent macroeconomic policies, will be accomplished in the foreseeable future to the benefit of all Europeans.

Financial deepening in the new member states and further financial integration within the European Union will be essential in promoting this catching-up process. The close relationship between financial development and integration on the one hand and economic growth on the other hand has been well documented in numerous academic studies in recent years. Although the direction of causality in this finance–growth nexus is not straightforward and has to be established by empirical analysis on a case-by-case basis, nowadays the weight of evidence overwhelmingly supports the view that financial development is capable of spurring economic growth.

Let me illustrate the impact of financial development and integration on economic growth by an empirical example. A study commissioned by the European Commission (Giannetti et al., 2002) has found that raising the level of financial development in the EU to that in the USA would increase the growth rate of the manufacturing industry in Europe by slightly less than 1 percentage point per year.

According to this study, countries that currently have a comparably weak financial structure and countries with comparatively small firms would benefit most from such a step. With regard to the effects of financial integration, however, small and medium-sized enterprises are set to gain less from this process if financial integration simply brings improved access to international financial markets, since they are likely to be those that are least able to take advantage of improved external financing opportunities.

Financial integration in Europe began several decades ago, in 1957, with the Treaty of Rome, which already contained the basic principles for the creation of a single European market for financial services. In 1985, the Single Market Programme provided a general strategy based on minimum harmonization, a single passport as well as mutual recognition. The adoption of the common currency in 1999 was a major impetus for further financial integration in the European Union. In the same year, the Financial Services Action Plan (FSAP) became a top priority of EU policy. In contrast to the unfortunately slow overall progress on the Lisbon strategy of the EU, the FSAP has proved to be a success story. Almost all of the measures contained in the FSAP to promote financial integration have been agreed on in time and are now being put into practice.

And the train is rolling on. In May 2005, the European Commission put forward for public discussion a Green Paper on financial services policy for the next five years until 2010. While the FSAP has created the necessary decision-making and regulatory structure for financial integration in Europe, the major objective of the post-FSAP strategy is to complete unfinished business and finalize legislation.

All these efforts have brought measurable results for the euro area. Today, euro area money markets are nearly fully integrated. Also, the degree of integration in the government bond market has become very high since the introduction of the common currency. Euro adoption has also fuelled the development of the European corporate bond market, which has witnessed exceptional growth since 1999. However, despite a rising degree of integration and a considerable reduction in the home bias in equity portfolios of institutional investors, the euro area equity market remains the least integrated.

Integration of the euro area banking sector has also advanced since 1999. In this field, integration has largely taken the form of a considerable expansion of cross-border banking activity, such as cross-border holdings of securities and cross-border interbank loans. However, cross-border mergers and acquisitions between banks remain rare. Similarly, the volume and significance of cross-border loans to non-banks remain low in the euro area, accounting for less than 5 per cent of all loans to non-banks. Retail payment services, investment and insurance services remain highly fragmented as well, and require further integration.

With regard to financial deepening and financial integration and its beneficial effect on economic growth in the new member states of the European Union, economic growth should be understood in a broader sense, namely in the sense of closing the income gap between old and new EU member states. By raising the living standard in Central and Eastern European countries (CEECs) and reducing the income differences between member states, financial integration should also foster the political integration process and bolster political stability in a wider Europe.

The CEECs also lag behind the old member states by a large margin in terms of financial depth. On average, the ratio of domestic credit to the private sector as a percentage of GDP in the Central and Eastern European new member states stood at slightly more than 30 per cent in 2003, compared to the EU-15 average of around 120 per cent. The gap in the intermediation levels is even larger for candidate and potential candidate countries. Favourably though, we were able to observe an improvement in the degree of financial intermediation over the past decade. Strong economic growth, structural reforms in the financial sector and progress in the privatization of banks benefited this process in most countries. Similarly, bond and equity markets continue to be relatively small in the new member states in Central and Eastern Europe (CEE), both in absolute terms and in relation to GDP. Again, gaps are larger for candidate and potential candidate countries.

Notwithstanding their relatively small size, the CEECs form an active part of European financial integration. This participation started well before their formal accession to the European Union. Let me just mention the eminent role of foreign investors in the CEE banking sector, which is in clear contrast to what we can observe in the old member states. Accession to the EU in May 2004 and the principle of the EU-wide single banking licence further promoted the integration of CEE banking sectors with that of the EU-15.

CEE banks have, however, not only been targets in this integration process. Since May 2004, several banks in the new member states have notified the authorities of their intention to provide banking activities outside their home country, primarily in neighbouring EU countries, on the basis of the single EU licence. As a result, integration has begun also among CEE countries.

Furthermore, integration has advanced in the field of capital markets. In many of the countries in Central and Eastern Europe, foreign investors play a significant role in the equity and bond markets. In addition, capital market integration has also advanced at the institutional level. In this respect, stock exchanges in Central and Eastern Europe have intensified their cooperation in recent years. The most notable development in this respect has been the establishment of the Nordic and Baltic Stock Exchange through an alliance of the stock exchanges in Sweden, Finland, Estonia, Latvia, Lithuania and Denmark and there are similar considerations, led by the Vienna stock exchange, for Austria and some of its neighbouring countries.

In addition to the integration of financial intermediaries, non-financial sectors in the CEECs have gained better access to foreign financing over the past few years. This has been reflected by a steep increase in the ratio of foreign debt of the non-bank private sector to GDP over the past decade.

Financial deepening is expected to continue over the next few years, along with the expected closing of the income gap between new and old member states, and will lead to a rapid expansion of banks' balance sheets. This process of financial deepening will not only affect the banking industry, but is expected to extend into bond and equity markets and also comprise non-bank financial intermediaries, such as pension funds and insurance companies, as these are under-represented in the new member states when compared to the old member states.

At the same time, the rapid expansion of domestic credit and bank balance sheets will require close monitoring, to preserve both macroeconomic and financial stability. The integration of financial sectors will bring more complexity to the Central and Eastern European financial markets. Financial products are becoming more sophisticated, making the assessment of their risk profile more complicated. Similarly, financial integration makes financial institutions and the relationships between them, more complex and thus facilitates the shifting of risk exposure not only between individual banks, but also between economic sectors within a country and even across countries. Strong ownership links between CEE and EU-15 countries may exacerbate these channels, giving rise to a risk and crisis transmission channel.

Increased integration is likely to boost competition in the banking sector, which is undoubtedly beneficial for structural progress and efficiency. By contrast, higher competition may lead to a reduction in interest rate margins and, without a compensating rise in cost efficiency, might adversely influence banks' profitability. As a result, banks may be tempted to loosen their credit policies and take on more risk in the search for maintaining profitability. Ensuring that banks' risk monitoring capacities keep up with this process, and that additional risk is properly priced is a major challenge.

Similarly, the international integration of capital markets may give rise to portfolio capital flows and bring about more complexity. On the one hand, portfolio capital flows may be necessary for the financing of large current account deficits in some countries, or may be beneficial for the deepening of domestic capital markets. On the other hand, they also leave countries more exposed to sudden changes in investor sentiment and to global factors. Through these channels, portfolio capital flows can exert direct influence on exchange rate and interest rate developments and hence on monetary policy in the small and open economies of Central and Eastern Europe.

Financial market supervision, risk prevention and risk management, in which central banks are actively involved, have to live up to all these challenges. Monitoring the stability not only of commercial banks, but also of non-bank financial intermediaries and capital markets is therefore essential. It requires a comprehensive supervisory framework on the national level, and in those countries where financial sector supervision is not performed by a single agency, the proper flow of information between the institutions that are responsible for monitoring financial stability must be ensured.

The cross-border character of financial integration and the emergence of large, potentially systemically relevant entities under host country jurisdiction require cooperation between national supervisory agencies to ensure an effective exchange of information both from a home country and a host country perspective. In this respect, upon accession to the EU, the central banks of the new member states have joined the European System of Central Banks (ESCB) and thus adopted its financial stability monitoring, crisis prevention and crisis management framework. Their legislative and supervisory frameworks have been largely aligned with EU regulations, with the most important European banking directives having been implemented.

The new member states also joined the 2003 Memorandum of Understanding between EU banking supervisors and central banks, which accomplishes a broad set of unilateral Memoranda of Understanding. The new member states have become objects of analysis of several publications prepared by the Banking Supervision Committee of the ESCB, like the 'EU Banking Sector Stability Report', the 'Report on EU Banking Structure' or the report on the 'Banking Structures in the New EU member states'.

Naturally, they participate in the Committee of European Banking Supervisors and are involved in all stages of decision-making processes at the EU level.

Financial development and integration are important for CEE central banks also from a narrower monetary policy perspective. In order to achieve their major monetary policy goal of price stability, central banks in the region benefit from financial deepening. As we have learned, financial integration may contribute to financial deepening. In addition, since the new and future member states of the European Union are ultimately heading toward euro area membership as well, their financial sectors will have to reach a sufficient level of integration with the current euro area countries by the time the new member states wish to adopt the euro in order to ensure the smooth functioning of monetary policy in an enlarged monetary union.

REFERENCES

European Commission (2005), 'Green Paper on financial services policy (2005–2010)', Brussels.

Giannetti, Mariassunta, Luigi Guiso, Tullio Jappelli, Mario Padula and Marco Pagano (2002), 'Financial market integration, corporate financing and economic growth in the European economy', economic papers, No. 179 (November), Brussels: European Commission.

2. Benefits and risks of financial integration

Cesare Calari

In the 1990s, I had the opportunity to work on financial reform and development in Central and Eastern Europe (CEE) and the Former Soviet Union. For a while, I was based in Prague, working on the privatization of Zivnostenska Banka, the first bank privatization with foreign ownership in Central Europe. That experience, and observing transition first-hand, was one of the most exciting moments of my career.

As a European, I feel the same excitement now watching the process of financial integration as it unfolds in Europe. From this giant and innovative laboratory, I also try to draw some lessons for the developing and transition economies which are the World Bank's main concern.

The past 20 years have seen a process of financial globalization unprecedented since at least the days of the gold standard. They have also seen a reversal of the old paradigm under which finance followed trade. Now, increasingly, financial globalization precedes trade, and this affects the process of financial integration and the regulatory responses.

Among the various reasons for this phenomenon, I would like to discuss two which are of particular relevance for developing and transition economies. First, there is increasing appreciation and empirical evidence of the role of finance in promoting growth and reducing poverty. Research by Ross Levine, of the University of Minnesota, and by the World Bank,[1] for instance, has found that a doubling of the ratio of private sector credit to GDP is associated with a 2 percentage point annual increase in long-term growth. Recently, a positive association between financial development and income distribution has also been found.[2] Conversely, there is growing recognition of the costs of financial repression, including barriers to foreign entry.[3]

Second, in finance at least, 'size matters'. Many economies, including most developing ones, lack critical mass to support a broad-based, efficient and stable financial system. The drawbacks of small financial systems include: lack of diversification, excessive concentration of risks, high transaction costs due to low volume and to the need to maintain expensive financial and regulatory infrastructure. Sub-Saharan Africa is an extreme example of this.[4] If you exclude South Africa, the typical African banking system has about USD 2 billion in assets. That is the size of a small bank in Europe. Imagine, therefore, that you were running a small savings bank and had to pay for your own payments system, supervisory agency and so forth. No wonder transactions costs are high and access to financial services is limited in Africa and in many other regions. In Uganda, annual fees on a checking account are nearly 25 per cent of per capita GDP. In Malawi, 20 per cent.[5] Similar considerations apply to insurance, securities markets and pension systems.

For example, the high cost of running domestically the full infrastructure required to administer a multi-pillar pension system in a small country can be an important barrier to pension reform. Even countries larger by any other standards, such as Brazil, South Africa and Mexico, can be suboptimal when it comes to finance. Think, for example, of the disintermediation experienced by the stock markets of these countries in favour of larger and more liquid markets such as New York and London.[6] For these reasons, most countries have little alternative to some form of international financial integration, at least on a regional basis.

Integration can take many forms and present various aspects:

a. Monetary integration, either through currency unions (Europe, Western and Central Africa) or through dollarization, such as in Latin America and the Caribbean (LAC).
b. Liberalization of the capital account.
c. Subcontracting abroad of financial services or infrastructure, such as in the case of listing of securities on foreign stock exchanges.
d. Foreign entry.
e. Regulatory convergence and harmonization.

I would like to concentrate on the latter two aspects: foreign entry and regulatory convergence.

1. FOREIGN ENTRY

Foreign entry, particularly in banking, accelerated dramatically in the 1990s and still continues at a sustained, if somewhat slower, pace. Nowhere has this phenomenon been more visible than in Central and Eastern Europe. Foreign ownership now accounts for 72 per cent of the banking assets of the new EU member states and exceeds 95 per cent in Estonia, Lithuania, the Czech Republic and Slovakia.

This trend has also been remarkable in Latin America and the Caribbean, and particularly in Mexico, where US and Spanish banks have taken dominant market shares. In Africa, we are witnessing the expansion of South African banks north of the Limpopo. And in China, foreigners are bidding aggressively for minority shares in state-owned banks.

Is this trend good? By and large, the answer must be yes.

Foreign entry has brought technological and managerial improvements and economies of scale. It has also introduced more arm's length relationships between finance and industry, reducing the concentration of economic power and probably improving the quality of credit allocation. By using technology, foreign banks have sometimes been able to reach underserved market segments, such as consumers and small and medium-sized enterprises. We have evidence of this in Central Europe, with the explosion of consumer and mortgage finance, but also in other regions. Even when not serving directly the middle and retail markets, foreign banks have introduced competition that may well have forced domestic institutions to go 'downmarket'. For these reasons, by and large, foreign entry seems to have been associated with greater stability, efficiency and inclusion in financial markets. World Bank research validates this conclusion.[7]

This does not mean that there are no risks associated with foreign entry.

For one, competition and the consequent loss of franchise value of domestic banks may create moral hazard by pushing them into speculative activities in an attempt to maintain profitability. They may also find it difficult to move into new market niches because of inadequate information and contracting environments – including weak property rights. As domestic banks lose franchise value and ultimately capital, regulatory forbearance may compound losses and contribute to systemic instability.

Second, the quality of foreign entry is important.

In general, and particularly in CEE, foreign entrants have been reputable institutions from countries with sound supervisory standards. Worldwide, however, there have been various cases of dubious foreign entry, and various debacles, even without going back to BCCI. In the early 1990s, the collapse of the Zambia-based Meridien Banking network had catastrophic consequences in West Africa, where it had acquired the largest regional bank, BIAO. More recently, the acquisition of Uganda Commercial Bank by a Malaysian bank had to be reversed in part due to the deficiencies of the latter. In Albania, a major bank was privatized with participation by a Turkish bank which was later intervened. These are not isolated cases.

For the host country, risks may be compounded by the existence of domestic deposit insurance schemes, and the 'home country principle' adopted by Basel creates special coordination challenges for host country supervisors. Particularly in developing and transition economies, the capacity constraints of supervisory agencies make these coordination challenges daunting.

The situation could be further complicated by political pressures to play down prudential considerations in liberalizing foreign entry. Admittedly, it is unlikely that the Doha Round will result in a reversal of the general reservation with respect to prudential regulation included in the 1997 GATS. It may well, however, 'turn on the heat' on regulators who, particularly in developing countries, may not be in a position to assess the need to block a dubious foreign entry.

A third issue arises with respect to the risks involved in hosting too many banks from the same home country. Here, a crisis in the home country could result in systemic instability, or at least in a retrenchment in lending, in the host country. This scenario played out in the Asian crisis, where the retrenchment of Japanese banks was likely a factor. A similar scenario could materialize in Latin America and the Caribbean, if Spanish banks were to retrench.

What, then, are the policy implications for developing and transition countries that want to benefit from foreign entry without taking on excessive risk?

One recommendation is to be selective as to the quality of entrants – perhaps requiring certain minimum ratings – as well as to the quality of home country supervision. In the absence of objective rating criteria for the latter, host country supervisors should use whatever information is available, and pay attention to the type of banking markets to which the applicant has been given (or denied) entry. This criterion would have spared the Ivory Coast the BIAO/Meridien debacle, since Meridien had previously been denied entry into countries with more advanced supervisory structures.

A second recommendation is to diversify, to the extent possible, entry across several home countries. This said, many developing countries may not have much choice.

2. REGULATORY CONVERGENCE

There is growing recognition that the waves of financial instability of the 1980s and 1990s were facilitated and compounded by weaknesses in market foundations – accounting, corporate governance, insolvency regimes, property rights – and in regulatory practices.

This has led to a remarkable process of codification and dissemination of best practices in a variety of areas. The Financial Stability Forum has catalogued over 40 Financial Sector Standards and Codes, of which 12 are considered key. These standards represent a new type of international 'soft law' whose development owes much to the principle of 'minimum harmonization', which is at the core of the EU's own approach to financial integration. This principle, combined with the mutual recognition principle, and with the concept of 'reputationally induced discipline', is at the core of the effectiveness of standards and codes as a tool for regulatory harmonization. This approach can be quite effective and adapt to a fast-changing marketplace much better than the traditional law of treaties.

Given the need for rapid change and harmonization of regulatory practices, we have seen particularly strong demand for assessment of compliance with Standards and Codes in Central and Eastern Europe, and especially in the accession countries.

Compliance with Standards is assessed by the IMF and the World Bank either on a self-standing basis, or as part of a Financial Sector Assessment Program (FSAP). Thus far, we have carried out Financial Sector Assessments in 27 countries in CEE and the former Soviet Union, including all the accession countries. We are starting one in Turkey this year. One country, the Czech Republic, has undertaken assessments of all the 12 key standards. Financial Sector Assessments have evidenced much progress in the region, but still a number of areas of weakness exist, particularly in market foundations.

The Standards and Codes approach to regulatory harmonization is not without risks. For one, standards don't always travel well, and they present problems of adaptation to different legal traditions and institutional environments. Indeed, World Bank research shows that the effectiveness of Standards and Codes is crucially dependent on certain preconditions and on the domestic institutional environment. This includes the quality of the legal, judicial and regulatory process, the independence but also the accountability of regulators, the legal protection of supervisors, the role of the media, and so on.

This research – which is based on a database of 152 countries, both industrialized and developing – is summarized in a recent book by Barth, Caprio and Levine (2006) entitled *Rethinking Bank Regulation: Till Angels Govern*. One of the findings is that, in most developing countries – and in some industrialized ones as well – increasing supervisory powers is negatively co-related with stability.

The same conclusion applies to generous deposit insurance schemes, which can interfere with market discipline and be destabilizing in weak institutional environments. This is worrisome if we consider that EU deposit insurance standards will soon apply to new members with lower incomes and generally weaker institutions. EUR 20 000 is five months of average income in Luxembourg, but eight years in Romania!

An even greater concern arises from the implementation of Basel II, which is hardwired into EU law. Given the importance that Basel II attaches to supervised capital adequacy (Pillars I and II) and the demands it puts on supervisors, can we assume that accession countries, for all their progress, will be ready for its adoption?

My concern is that the combination of (a) generous deposit insurance; (b) still relatively weak institutional environments in certain accession countries; and (c) a rush to implement Basel II may increase systemic risk.

This is not a criticism of Basel II which has many excellent aspects, but simply a caution against risking to adopt it too quickly in countries that lack the preconditions.

CONCLUSIONS

In conclusion, the globalization of finance, with its aspects of financial market integration and convergence of regulatory structures, is a powerful and beneficial trend. It can lead to economies of scale and lower the cost of capital, particularly in developing and transition economies.

Perhaps the greatest benefit is that globalization can lead to a change in the political economy of finance, loosening the stranglehold of local elites and creating opportunity for broader segments of society. This aspect is masterfully described by Rajan and Zingales (2003) in their book *Saving Capitalism from the Capitalists*.[8]

For these reasons, we need more, not less, financial integration, including here in Europe where, despite a sustained and visionary effort, financial markets are still fragmented and parochial interests still prevail.

This process is not without risks. Regulatory convergence based on an appropriate mix of hard and soft law, and that recognizes the importance of local institutional environments, of incentives and of market discipline, is in my view the best response.

NOTES

1. King and Levine (1993), Levine (2005) and World Bank (2001).
2. Beck et al. (2004).
3. Barth et al. (2006).
4. Hanson et al. (2003).
5. Beck et al. (2005).
6. Claessens et al. (2005).
7. Barth et al. (2006).
8. Rajan and Zingales (2003).

REFERENCES

Barth, James R., Gerard Caprio, Jr. and Ross Levine (2006), *Rethinking Bank Regulation and Supervision: Till Angels Govern*, New York: World Bank and Cambridge University Press.

Beck, Thorsten, Asli Demirgüç-Kunt and Ross Levine (2004), 'Finance, inequality and poverty: cross-country evidence', World Bank Policy Research Working Paper 3338.

Beck, Thorsten, Asli Demirgüç-Kunt and Maria Soledad Martinez Peria (2005), 'Reaching out: Access to and use of banking services across countries', World Policy Research Working Paper 3754.

Claessens, Stijn, Daniela Klingebiel and Sergio L. Schmukler (2005), 'Stock market development and internationalization: Do economic fundamentals spur both similarly?' *Journal of Empirical Finance*, forthcoming.

Hanson, James, Patrick Honohan and Giovanni Majnoni (2003), *Globalization and National Financial Systems*, Oxford and Washington, DC: Oxford University Press and World Bank.

King, R.G. and R. Levine (1993), 'Finance and growth: Schumpeter might be right', *Quarterly Journal of Economics*, **108** (3), 717–38.

Levine, Ross (2005), 'Finance and growth: Theory, evidence, and mechanisms', in P. Aghion and S. Durlauf (eds), *Handbook of Economic Growth*, Amsterdam: North-Holland Elsevier Publishers.

Rajan, R.G. and L. Zingales (2003), *Saving Capitalism from the Capitalists: Unleashing the Power of Financial Markets to Create Wealth and Spread Opportunity*, New York: Crown Publishing.

World Bank (2001), *Finance for Growth, Policy Choices in a Volatile World*, Washington, DC: Oxford University Press.

3. Financial globalization, corporate governance and Eastern Europe

René M. Stulz*

In his recent book, Friedman (2005) makes the case that globalization leads to a flat world.[1] By that, he means that it removes obstacles that, in the past, would have prevented firms and individuals from competing with each other across the world. Such competition improves welfare not only by ensuring that goods are produced at the lowest cost but also by making sure that consumers get access to new and better goods. Assuredly, the world is not flat yet. Nevertheless, the metaphor is helpful to understand the forces that shape our world. It is even more apt to describe the financial world than the world of trade in goods.

For many countries, the most significant explicit barriers to trade in financial assets have been knocked down. Economists believe that this liberalization is extremely beneficial, because it enables investors worldwide to share risks better. Capital can be allocated more efficiently, and countries can exploit their comparative advantage better. With complete financial globalization and perfect markets within countries, welfare is maximized. Further, asset prices, portfolios, and firm financial policies are not country-dependent.

Despite a dramatic increase in cross-border trade in financial assets, the positive impact of financial globalization has been surprisingly limited. Capital does not flow to countries with low capital stocks as strongly as one would expect if the financial world were flat.[2] As Lucas (1990) points out forcefully, differences in the marginal product of capital between industrialized countries and emerging countries are large. In fact, over the recent past, capital has come rushing into the US, when one would expect it instead to flow to emerging countries. According to data from the IMF, the cumulative sum of net equity flows to less developed countries from 1996 to 2004 is a negative USD 67.4 billion.[3]

What are the obstacles left that make the financial world full of ridges and mountains, so that capital does not flow where the physical marginal product of capital is highest? The answer is what I call the twin agency problems (see Stulz, 2005): poor corporate governance and high political risk stand in the way of countries getting the full benefit of financial globalization. When the twin agency problems are serious, diffuse ownership is not feasible. Consequently, risk cannot be spread efficiently across investors throughout the world because the corporate insiders must bear much of a firm's risk. Ownership concentration limits a country's ability to benefit from financial globalization. It leads to lower financial development, more consumption volatility, stronger correlation between savings and investment, less foreign investment, lower firm valuations, smaller firms, and lower economic growth.

In this chapter, I first analyse the implications of the twin agency problems for how firms are owned and governed. I then discuss how these twin agency problems restrict firms and countries from taking full advantage of financial globalization. I finally turn to Eastern Europe and provide evidence that the twin agency problems affect these countries adversely and prevent them from capturing the full benefit of financial globalization.

1. THE TWIN AGENCY PROBLEMS

Consider a country with a high physical productivity of capital. For a marginal dollar of capital that could be spent anywhere in the world to be invested in that country, potential investors must expect to receive a return on that dollar which is, after taking into account risk, at least as high as they could get anywhere else in the world. Poor governance can make it impossible for that marginal dollar to be invested in the country because poor governance decreases the cash flows that investors can expect to receive from capital raised by the firm and hence the value of their claims on the firm. When the governance problems are sufficiently serious, the firm cannot promise a high enough dollar return to investors to raise capital to exploit its investment opportunities.

The reason a firm with poor governance cannot promise a sufficient dollar return to investors is that each firm has to resolve a fundamental agency problem rooted in the fact that corporate insiders maximize their own welfare rather than the welfare of outside investors. There are many ways for insiders to take advantage of outside investors. In countries where the rule of law is strong, the concern is often that managers choose to build empires rather than maximize shareholder wealth. In such countries, the so-called free cash-flow problem is therefore an important component of agency costs. However, in countries where the rule of law is weaker, insiders can expropriate outside investors more directly. For instance, related transactions can be used to transfer wealth from firms with outside investors to insiders. For instance, as discussed in Desai et al. (2005), a favourite approach by Russian oil companies has been to sell oil at prices substantially below world prices to privately held companies, so that outside shareholders in the oil companies received only a fraction of the cash flows generated by oil produced by these companies. When the mechanisms that prevent corporate insiders from taking advantage of outside investors are weak, a higher fraction of the return from a marginal dollar of investment is expected to be siphoned off by corporate insiders, hence the physical productivity of a marginal dollar of investment has to be large to offset the amount expected to be siphoned off and still make it worthwhile for outside investors to invest.

Besides the agency problem between corporate insiders and investors, another agency problem arises at the state level. When the state works poorly, those who control the state pursue their objectives rather than enforcing property rights and facilitating contracting among private parties. They can either expropriate investors directly or impose additional costs on investors, but either way they reduce the pay-off to those who are investing in the country. The agency problems within the firm and within the state form what I call the twin agency problems.

Pinkowitz et al. (2005) provide a useful way to understand the importance of the governance problem as an obstacle to financial globalization. One would expect a dollar of cash to be worth a dollar when a corporation is valued by the capital markets when governance works well. If a dollar of cash were worth less than a dollar, it would mean that part of the cash is wasted by managers or controlling shareholders. They investigate how capital markets assess the value of cash in 35 countries from 1988 to 1998. Their sample includes more than 6000 companies per year on average. They show that the value of a dollar of cash is worth USD 0.91 in countries with low corruption and only USD 0.33 in countries with high corruption. While the value of a dollar of cash inside the corporation is worth an amount not significantly different from one dollar in countries with low corruption, it is worth significantly less in countries with high corruption. Furthermore, they find that dividends are worth a lot more in countries with high corruption than they are in countries with low corruption. In other words, investors value cash paid out by the corporation in countries with high corruption more, because they have good reasons to expect that cash kept within the firm will be wasted or stolen.

1.1 The Firm Agency Problem and Corporate Ownership

To illustrate the implications of the twin agency problems for firm ownership and risk-bearing, let's consider an economy in which there are two types of investors, entrepreneurs and portfolio investors. While some agents can only be portfolio investors, any entrepreneur has a unique investment opportunity. If an entrepreneur takes advantage of her unique investment opportunity, she starts a firm, sells equity to outside investors, and becomes a corporate insider. If she decides to pass on the investment opportunity, she becomes a portfolio investor. At the end of a period of time, the investment opportunity pays a random cash flow. To simplify the analysis, let us assume that the firm liquidates after the random cash flow is realized.

In a world of perfect markets where the twin agency problems do not exist, the cash flow would be paid out to the investors in proportion to their agreed-upon rights. With the twin agency problems, both corporate insiders and the rulers of the sovereign state have the ability to expropriate some of the firm's cash flow. Because the corporate insiders manage the firm, they have the opportunity to expropriate cash flow first. The rulers of the sovereign state can expropriate some of the cash flow next. The cash flow left after expropriation by corporate insiders and by the state rulers is distributed as a liquidating dividend.

If an entrepreneur chooses to become a portfolio investor, her wealth at the end of the period is given by the value of her portfolio. In contrast, if she takes advantage of her investment opportunity, her wealth at the end of the period is the sum of the cash flow that she expropriates from the firm plus the liquidating dividends she receives. It is common to call the cash flow expropriated a private benefit from control. The private benefits from control can also, however, take forms other than cash. For instance, insiders may enjoy some types of investments more than others and may therefore use the resources of the firm to make the investments they enjoy even if doing so hurts outside investors.

If the state lets corporate insiders consume private benefits freely, firms would not exist unless corporate insiders could find ways to commit not to consume private benefits. So, in general, there are two sources of costs when corporate insiders consume private benefits. First, laws and regulations may punish the insiders who consume private benefits. This is the investor protection provided by the state. The extent to which it is successful in preventing excessive consumption of private benefits depends on the nature of the laws, on the quality of the judicial system, and on how well the laws are enforced. Second, corporate insiders can find ways to commit to low consumption of private benefits. This is the investor protection provided by the firm.

To understand the implications of poor investor protection, it is useful to think of the case in which corporate insiders can consume private benefits, but they pay a deadweight cost when they expropriate investors because they expend effort to do so and because they might get caught and punished. This cost varies across countries and increases with the amount of expropriation. The cost is higher in countries with better investor protection.

When insiders sell shares to the public, the capital markets reduce the share price by the present value per share of the expected consumption of private benefits. Once the shares are sold, it would make no sense for insiders not to consume the private benefits they are expected to consume since they have already paid for them by selling shares at a low price. However, because of the deadweight costs, a dollar of private benefits costs more than a dollar for insiders, so that they would prefer to find a way to commit to lower consumption of private benefits. Let's assume first that corporate insiders can commit to lower consumption of private benefits through their ownership share in the firm.

As corporate insiders consume more private benefits, the liquidating dividend paid to shareholders falls since private benefits reduce the resources available for distribution to shareholders. Consequently, corporate insiders receive a smaller liquidating dividend for the shares they own when they consume more private benefits. Since their share of the liquidating dividend is given by their ownership share of the firm's equity, the insiders incur a higher cost from consuming private benefits when they own a larger fraction of the firm's equity. Therefore, the insiders' net gain from private benefits before deadweight costs falls as their firm ownership increases. However, since the deadweight costs depend on the consumption of private benefits, they do not fall as firm ownership increases for a given amount of consumption of private benefits. Consequently, as ownership increases, the gain from consuming private benefits falls, but the cost from doing so does not, making consumption of private benefits less advantageous. The decision rule of insiders is to consume private benefits up to the point where the marginal net gain from these benefits before deadweight costs equals the increase in deadweight cost from consuming additional private benefits. Since the deadweight costs increase with the consumption of private benefits, insiders consume fewer private benefits when they own larger shares of the firm because they pay more for these private benefits themselves.

In the model described above, the only way for insiders to commit to consuming fewer private benefits is to increase their ownership of the firm's cash flow. However, insiders can own a larger stake only if they have the means to do so. As a result, if investor protection is poor, firm creation depends more on the wealth of entrepreneurs than otherwise. Further, if insiders have a larger stake in their own firm, they have to bear more firm-specific risk than if they could invest all their wealth in a well-diversified portfolio.

Firms can take steps to improve governance. For instance, they can choose to hire high-quality auditors or to have independent directors. Such steps enable corporate insiders to reduce their ownership stake in the firm's cash flows and hence make it possible to raise more capital externally.

However, a firm's costs and benefits from taking steps to improve governance depend heavily on the country in which it is located for three reasons.

First, it is much cheaper for a firm to commit to good governance if it can write contracts that are cheap to enforce. Consequently, firm-level investor protection is cheaper when a country has good laws and a judicial system that works well. For instance, firms can choose charter provisions that make it more difficult for insiders to expropriate investors. However, these provisions are only valuable to the extent that the courts can be used to enforce them.

Second, mechanisms of good governance require the availability of resources that are often scarce in countries with low economic development. For instance, it is harder for insiders to expropriate outside investors if the auditors are competent and not corrupt. Such auditors are harder to find in countries with poor economic development. Similarly, an independent and knowledgeable press is extremely valuable in monitoring corporate insiders as pointed out by Dyck and Zingales (2004), but there is no such press in many countries.

Third, good governance is valuable when a firm wants to raise capital since it lowers the cost of capital. However, if a firm is located in a country with poor financial development, the ability of firms to raise capital locally is limited, so that the incentives for good governance are low to start with.

The heavy dependence of the costs and benefits of good governance on country characteristics explains the findings of Doidge et al. (2005a). In that paper, they investigate the extent to which firm characteristics and country characteristics can explain the quality of firm governance. They use three corporate governance rankings: the S&P Transparency and Disclosure ratings, the governance ratings of Credit Lyonnais Securities Asia (CLSA), and the FT-ISS governance ratings. Their key finding is that most of the variation in corporate governance rankings can be explained by country characteristics. In particular, regressions of the S&P, CLSA and FT-ISS ratings on country dummy variables have adjusted R-squares of, respectively, 39 per cent, 73 per cent and 72 per cent. In contrast, regressions of these ratings on firm characteristics have R-squares of less than 10 per cent for the CLSA and FT-ISS ratings, and of 22 per cent for the S&P ratings.

1.2 The State Agency Problem and the Corporation

Like corporate insiders, state rulers pursue their own objectives. The institutions of the state limit the ability of state rulers to maximize their welfare at the expense of their constituents. For instance, in a democracy, state rulers who pursue their own objectives at the expense of the electorate do not get re-elected. However, state rulers who have a lot of power but do not expect to enjoy this power for a long time can find it advantageous to use the powers of the state for their own benefit.[4] Further, even when no one person monopolizes state power, coalitions can develop that find it optimal to expropriate those who do not belong to the coalition. This expropriation can take many forms. I focus on the type of expropriation that reduces the returns to outside investors.

A significant threat of expropriation by state rulers also leads to co-investment by corporate insiders. State rulers can impose redistributive taxes, confiscate assets, forbid some activities, or require bribes to enrich themselves. Even though Yukos comes to mind, it should be clear that the term 'expropriation' covers a wide range of activities, many of which are common in developed countries. For instance, Roe (2003) shows that state and union interference in corporations is frequent in European countries and affects how corporations are owned and organized.

Corporate insiders can reduce the state's proceeds from expropriation by increasing their bargaining power with the state. They can do this by making themselves more critical to the success of the firm through their choice of investment policies, its contracting policies, and its financing policies.

When management becomes more indispensable to a firm, it also decreases its cost of consuming private benefits as it becomes less subject to discipline from the market for corporate control, the labour market and shareholders. (Shleifer and Vishny, 1989, analyse this in their paper on managerial entrenchment.) Consequently, the gains that shareholders make as corporate insiders are better able to reduce the expropriation by the state may be offset by losses due to increased consumption of private benefits on the part of insiders.

Further, when management has a small stake in the firm's cash flows, it may use its entrenched position to extract the best deal from the state for itself, rather than use its power to protect shareholders. This makes the separation of ownership and control inefficient when state expropriation is significant. By having control, the corporate insiders can make decisions that limit the potential for state expropriation. By having a large stake in the firm's cash flows, they provide assurance to outside investors that they will make decisions that benefit all investors. Absent such a stake, they could let the state expropriate minority shareholders at will, in exchange for the right granted by the state to appropriate more private benefits.

Though, so far, the twin agency problems have been analysed separately, it is important to note that they can feed on each other. First, corporate insiders can be connected with state rulers, and if they are, they can use the state to steal from other investors. Rajan and Zingales (2003) show how business incumbents can use laws and regulations to tilt the playing field in their favour, thus hindering financial development that would benefit new firms. Second, state rulers can help corporate insiders protect their private benefits. Recent papers by Fisman (2001), Johnson and Mitton (2003) and Faccio (2005) illustrate the benefits corporate insiders can derive from connections with the state. Capture of these benefits generally requires opaqueness. Third, the consumption of private benefits is implicitly subsidized by the state in countries where the threat of state expropriation is economically significant. This is because the consumption of private benefits tends to be hidden from the state, so such benefits are less likely to be expropriated by the state than are firms' cash flows remaining after insiders have extracted their private benefits. Fourth, corporate insiders can use corporate resources to bribe state rulers so that they can keep and extend their private benefits. As a result, corporate insiders have few incentives to lobby for a transparent state and to fight against corruption. The state agency problem can therefore feed on the firm-level agency problem.

2. THE TWIN AGENCY PROBLEMS, CORPORATE FINANCE AND THE BENEFITS FROM FINANCIAL GLOBALIZATION

The twin agency problems have far-reaching implications for corporate finance, for financial development, and for how countries benefit from financial globalization. I discuss these implications in this section, starting with concentrated ownership.

2.1 The Implications of Ownership Concentration for Corporations

So far, I have shown theoretically that corporate insiders have to co-invest more with outside investors, and ownership becomes more concentrated as the twin agency problems become more important. The twin agency problems explain the compelling empirical evidence that corporate ownership is highly concentrated in countries where investor rights are poorly protected. La Porta et al. (1999) investigate the corporate ownership of the 20 largest firms as well as of some smaller firms in 27 countries. They find that, except in countries with good investor protection, few firms are widely held. Typically, most firms have a family as a controlling shareholder. In countries that protect shareholder rights well, they find that 47.92 per cent of firms are widely held, in that no shareholder holds more than 20 per cent of the votes. Using that criterion (p. 494), these authors find that in countries with poor shareholder rights, only 12.67 per cent of the firms are widely held. Stulz (2005) uses a measure of ownership available for more firms and countries, but somewhat less precise, namely the sum of insider and block ownership reported by Worldscope. The paper uses a proxy for each one of the twin agency problems and finds that insider ownership increases as the protection of minority shareholders becomes weaker and as political risk increases.

The twin agency problems have an adverse impact on entrepreneurship. This is because, everything else equal, the rewards from starting a firm in a country where the twin agency problems are important are much less than what they would be in a country where these problems are less important. In countries where the twin agency problems are important, there are deadweight costs from entrepreneurship that do not exist in other countries. The terms on which entrepreneurs can raise equity are inversely related to the importance of the twin agency problems. When these problems are serious, outside investors expect less of a dollar return on the firm's equity. Consequently, many firms that could get financed in countries where the twin agency problems are smaller cannot be financed in countries where they are more serious.

If it is optimal for ownership to be highly concentrated, it follows that the size of a firm is largely determined by the resources of the insiders and by their willingness to bear the firm's risk. Since the resources of insiders and their willingness to bear risk are limited, the total amount of equity of the firm is therefore limited by the insiders' capacity to acquire this equity. If the firm is successful and has to raise funds to expand, it can only do so if the capacity of insiders to subscribe to an equity issue is not exhausted. To avoid diluting ownership of cash flows, insiders can raise funds through debt. However, as a result, the firm will be more highly levered and hence more fragile. It follows that countries where the twin agency problems are more serious tend to have smaller firms and more highly levered firms.

Concentrated ownership has implications for the firm's risk management decisions. With concentrated ownership, the corporate insiders have to bear much of the risk of new projects. Since insiders are risk averse, they may therefore turn down projects because of the increased level of risk they have to bear. If, instead, ownership were dispersed, the firm could take on these projects since the risk would be shared among many investors. As John et al. (2005) show, insiders in countries with high private benefits also find it valuable to take on less risk to the extent that the claim to private benefits is more similar to a debt claim. In Jin and Myers (2006), insiders can even find it optimal to bail out the firm in bad states of the world so that they keep control of the firm. For all these reasons, one would expect firms in countries with poor investor protection to take less risky projects unless they can find ways to hedge their risks. However, countries with poor protection are often countries where the availability of hedging instruments is limited. Consequently, in such countries, firms are more likely to manage risks by diversification and through investment policy. Both of these approaches to risk management are expensive.

Consider now the impact of financial globalization on firms. In a flat financial world, the cost of capital required by outside investors would be the same everywhere in the world. Consequently, firms in any country could raise funds to finance projects that would be profitable elsewhere. With the twin agency problems, the financial world is not flat. Investors expect the same return for a given amount of risk on investments everywhere in the world. However, the expected return required by investors does not measure the cost of equity for corporate insiders. To raise equity, corporate insiders have to co-invest with outside investors in countries where the twin agency problems are significant. This co-investment is costly for corporate insiders because it forces them to bear more firm-specific risk. The twin agency costs introduce a wedge between the cost of equity required by the capital markets and the cost of equity for insiders. The extent to which a country benefits from financial globalization is inversely related to the size of this wedge.

Figure 3.1 makes this point graphically. The downward-sloping curve shows the marginal product of capital for the firm. In a world without

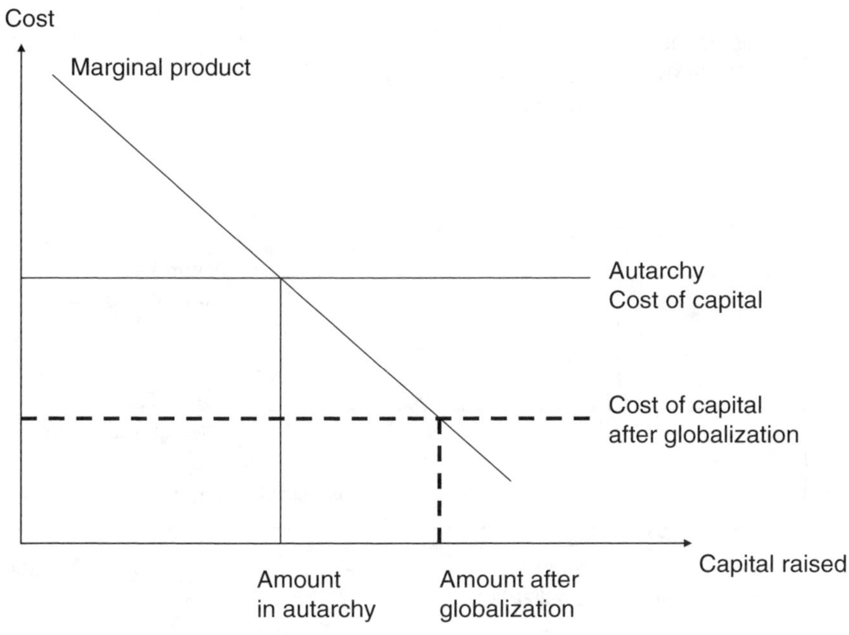

Figure 3.1 Impact of financial globalization on the amount of capital raised in the absence of the twin agency problems

financial globalization, the cost of capital would be fixed (as long as the firm is small enough) at the autarchy cost of capital. Empirical evidence on financial globalization shows that it reduces the cost of capital.[5] The reduction in the cost of capital associated with financial globalization leads to an increase in the amount of capital invested in a firm since new investment opportunities become profitable at the lower cost of capital.

Figure 3.2 takes into account the twin agency problems. With these problems, the cost of capital for corporate insiders is no longer the required expected return on capital required by outsiders. The twin agency problems introduce deadweight costs for corporate insiders that make capital more expensive. In particular, when raising external capital, corporate insiders have to bear the deadweight costs associated with the consumption of private benefits. In addition, since they have to co-invest, they have to bear more risk, which is also costly for them. The capacity of insiders to absorb more equity is limited. Consequently, if they were close to capacity before financial globalization, they cannot absorb much more equity afterwards. It follows that in this extreme case the impact of financial globalization is extremely limited. In Figure 3.2, the cost to insiders of increased capital

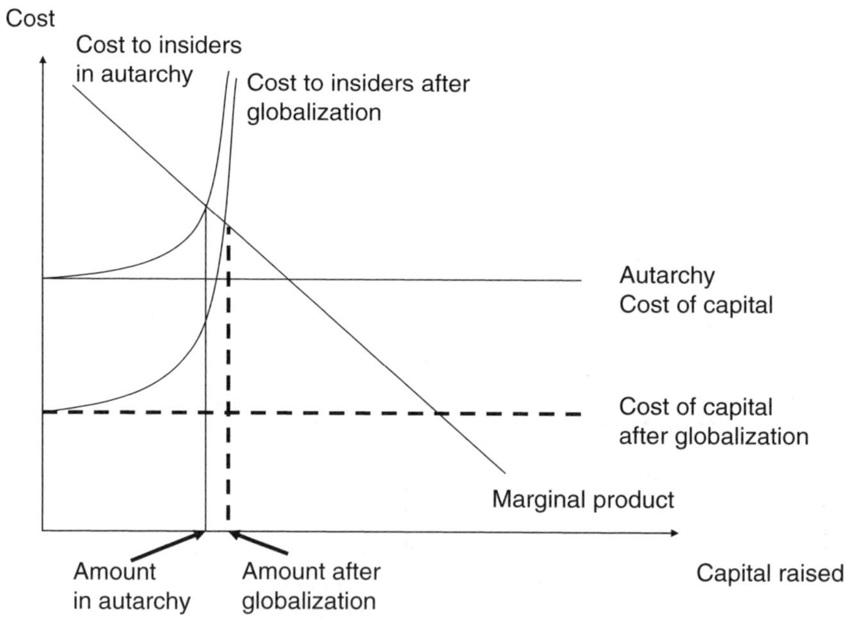

Figure 3.2 Impact of financial globalization on the amount of capital raised in the presence of the twin agency problems

raised therefore increases sharply as more capital is raised. Of course, in the case where the capacity of corporate insiders to absorb equity is large, the deadweight costs become less significant and financial globalization has much more of an impact.

So far, I have assumed that it is worthwhile for corporate insiders to start the firm. Financial globalization increases the opportunity cost of starting firms, since the expected utility of portfolio investors increases as a result of international diversification. It is therefore possible that financial globalization can lead to fewer firms being created when the twin agency problems are very serious. Further, corporate insiders may also choose not to reinvest cash flows in existing firms, because they wish to reduce their investment in their firms when portfolio investment becomes more attractive.

Unfortunately, countries with bad governance face a vicious circle. When a country protects investors poorly, financial markets are poorly developed. When financial markets are poorly developed, there are few incentives for firms to protect investors better or for politicians to reform governance. Financial globalization can help to break that vicious circle by enabling firms to access the deep capital markets of countries that protect investors well and to enable local firms to rent the institutions of these countries. With financial globalization, firms can rent institutions from countries with better institutions (see Stulz, 1999b). In particular, foreign firms that list their shares in the US benefit from some US institutions. For instance, they have to meet various disclosure requirements that US firms have to meet and their investors can rely on the US courts and benefit from the US laws and regulations.

Doidge et al. (2004) examine whether the evidence is consistent with the hypothesis that firms cross-list in the US to take advantage of the US institutions that protect investors. They find strong support for this hypothesis. They also report a large 'listing premium', that is foreign firms that list in the US are worth substantially more than foreign firms that do not. The authors examine the valuation of 712 cross-listed stocks and 4078 non-cross-listed stocks in 1997 and estimate that cross-listed firms were worth 16.5 per cent more on average than comparable firms that were not cross-listed. This cross-listing premium was even more dramatic for firms listed on NYSE, where it was 37 per cent on average. In recent work, not yet circulating as a working paper, we show that this cross-listing premium persists through time.

2.2 The Macroeconomic Implications of Concentrated Ownership

Concentrated ownership has implications for asset holdings, for the savings and investment relation, for the distribution of consumption, and for economic growth. Mean-variance portfolio investors hold their country's market portfolio when their country is completely segmented from world capital markets, and they hold the world market portfolio when their country becomes completely integrated in world markets. When concentrated ownership is optimal, insiders cannot hold a well-diversified portfolio, because they overweight their firms' shares in their portfolios.[6] It necessarily follows that outside investors must underweight the firm in their portfolios. For instance, if insiders typically hold 50 per cent of cash-flow rights in a country, this means that portfolio investors can only hold 50 per cent of a country's market portfolio. Consequently, in countries where the twin agency problems are significant, aggregate equity holdings will show a home bias as long as corporate insiders are local residents and cannot hedge their holdings, which is typically the case. The home bias induced by concentrated ownership is made worse, as shown by Giannetti and Simonov (2005), by the fact that foreign investors have less of a comparative advantage than some domestic investors in monitoring and assessing consumption of private benefits. In a recent paper, Bae et al. (2005) show that local investors have more of an information advantage in more opaque economies.

Such a home bias has important implications for the distribution of aggregate wealth, saving, investment and consumption for a country. If investors hold the world market portfolio, their wealth will be perfectly correlated with the return of that portfolio. Consequently, the wealth of investors across the world will be perfectly correlated. However, with a home bias, the wealth of investors in a country will be more correlated with the market portfolio of that country than with the world market portfolio. As wealth becomes imperfectly correlated across countries, savings and consumption are imperfectly correlated also. In particular, with the home bias, a positive shock to the local economy mostly increases domestic wealth and local savings. Presumably, the shock makes investment in the local economy attractive as well, so that shocks to the local economy induce a correlation between savings and investment. It follows that concentrated ownership can help explain the so-called Feldstein–Horioka paradox.[7]

There is a more direct link between savings and investment that results from concentrated ownership. If the local economy experiences a positive shock, so that it has better than expected investment opportunities, firms can invest in response to these improved investment opportunities only to the extent that corporate insiders can co-invest with outside investors. It follows that if corporate insiders are constrained in their ability to co-invest, domestic growth will be limited. From this perspective, local savings constrain investment in that an increase in domestic wealth makes it easier for corporate insiders to co-invest with outside investors and hence for investment to be financed.

With concentrated corporate ownership, insiders cannot diversify their portfolio as much as they would if dispersed ownership were optimal. Consequently, concentrated ownership induces a positive correlation between the corporate insiders' consumption and their firms' cash flow. In the absence of concentrated ownership, all investors' wealth would behave as if they were portfolio investors because they would have well-diversified portfolios. If we could ignore labour income or assume it can be hedged, investors' consumption would be perfectly correlated across the world. With concentrated ownership, consumption is more correlated with the country's GNP, so that domestic shocks have more of an impact on consumption.

Consider a closed economy where firms may engage in projects that carry high risks but promise high pay-offs. In a closed economy, firms will choose not to implement some of these projects because the cost of capital involved is too high given that their risks have to be borne within the domestic economy. As soon as the economy liberalizes, the cost of capital for these projects falls because their risk can be spread across the world. In a world of dispersed ownership, firms would take on these projects after liberalization.[8] Obstfeld (1994) shows that, because of this mechanism, financial liberalization leads to an increase in economic growth. With concentrated ownership, the corporate insiders may choose to reject these projects because they would have to bear more risk if they took them on. Though the cost of capital for these projects falls with financial globalization, risk-averse corporate insiders cannot diversify the risks underlying these projects because they have to co-invest with outside investors. It follows that growth will be lower on average in countries with concentrated ownership because firms will turn down good projects that firms in countries with dispersed ownership would take advantage of.

3. OWNERSHIP CONCENTRATION AND GOVERNANCE IN EASTERN EUROPE

In this section, I provide some evidence showing that the problem of poor governance significantly limits the benefits from financial globalization for Eastern European countries.

In section 2, I argued that poor governance leads to high ownership concentration. To investigate the quality of governance, I use data from the World Bank. These data represent averages of rankings across a number of governance indicators. For each category, the data gives a percentile for a country. Table 3.1 shows that in the overall governance rating, Eastern Europe increased from the 55th percentile in 1996 to the 60th percentile in 2004. The table compares the overall ranking to the ranking for

Table 3.1 Governance indicators for Eastern European countries

	Overall			Rule of law			Control of corruption		
	Percentile rank (0–100)	Income category average	Western countries average	Percentile rank (0–100)	Income category average	Western countries average	Percentile rank (0–100)	Income category average	Western countries average
Eastern Europe and Baltics									
1996	55.1	53.0	91.9	53.6	54.5	92.6	52.9	49.8	91.1
1998	55.6	53.9	92.2	55.0	54.3	93.0	55.3	53.6	93.5
2000	57.5	54.7	92.3	56.5	55.6	93.1	57.0	54.8	93.4
2002	59.7	54.5	92.2	55.4	54.8	92.9	54.6	54.0	93.3
2004	60.3	54.2	91.3	56.5	53.9	93.0	58.2	54.0	93.2
Czech Republic, Hungary, Poland and Turkey									
1996	69.7	55.3	91.9	69.3	57.3	92.6	72.2	51.5	91.1
1998	71.5	56.6	92.2	72.0	56.5	93.0	73.7	55.6	93.5
2000	68.3	57.6	92.3	70.9	58.5	93.1	69.0	57.4	93.4
2002	68.6	57.8	92.2	68.0	58.2	92.9	62.5	57.6	93.3
2004	67.0	57.8	91.3	66.8	57.7	93.0	63.2	57.2	93.2

Note: This table reports the governance indicators from Kaufmann et al. (2005) for Eastern European countries, averages across countries from their income categories and averages across Western countries (Europe, the US and Canada). Rule of law and control of corruption are the same as in Kaufmann et al. (2005). Overall is the average of the six component governance indicators – voice and accountability, political instability and violence, government effectiveness, regulatory quality, rule of law, and control of corruption.

Source: Author's compilation.

countries in the same income category. It can be seen there that the Eastern European countries rank somewhat better than they would compared to countries with similar income. At the same time, however, the ranking of the Eastern European countries is much lower than the average of the Western countries. The table also provides two additional rankings. The first one is for the rule of law and the second for corruption. For both of these rankings, Eastern European countries rank slightly better than countries with comparable income, but dramatically lower than the Western countries. The bottom line is that there is room for much progress in governance.

Figure 3.3 reports the distribution of insider ownership for Eastern European countries for which data are reported on Worldscope for blockholders. For each country, I use data reported on Worldscope to compute the average percentage of market capitalization held by corporate insiders across firms. These data have important limitations, since the reporting requirements and accuracy of firm disclosures vary widely across countries. Further, insider ownership consists of the sum of blocks of shares owned, which may include blocks unrelated to the controlling shareholders.

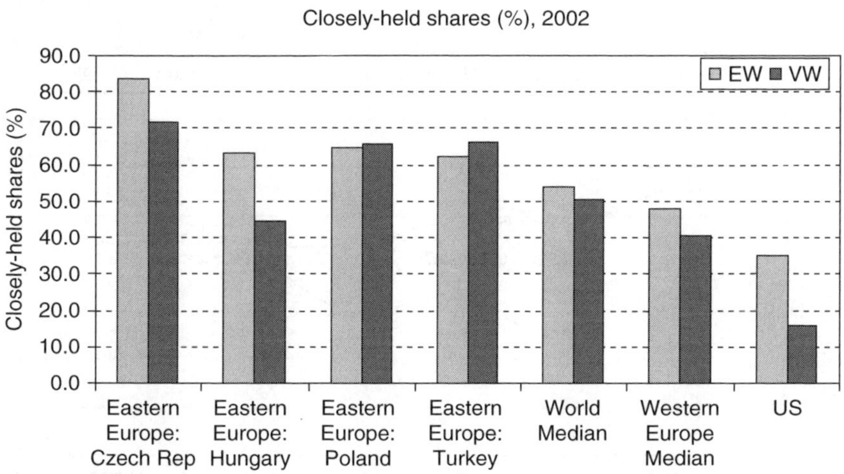

Note: The figure reports the equally-weighted (EW) average and the value-weighted (VW) average of closely-held shares reported by Worldscope for Eastern European countries in 2002.

Source: Worldscope.

Figure 3.3 Insider ownership in Eastern European countries over time (1)

Worldscope has ownership data for four Eastern European countries for 2002. It covers 25 firms from the Czech Republic, 33 from Hungary, 63 from Poland, and 315 from Turkey. Ownership is most concentrated in the Czech Republic, where the equally-weighted average of block ownership is 83.6 per cent. For each of these four countries, insider ownership is higher than for the typical Western European country. For instance, the value-weighted average block ownership has a median of 37.74 per cent among Western European countries. The value-weighted block ownership is lowest in Hungary (44.4 per cent). For the other Eastern European countries, block ownership is at least 50 per cent higher than it is in the median Western European country and is more than four times that in the US. Figure 3.4 shows the equally-weighted average of block ownership for each country in Eastern Europe starting from when data became available. The figure shows that block ownership has not decreased over time.

Other data sources indicate very high ownership concentration in Eastern European countries also. Klapper et al. (2005) report that the largest shareholder in a sample of 74 Czech firms holds 69 per cent of shares and the five largest shareholders hold 89 per cent. The equivalent numbers for Hungary are 52 per cent and 96 per cent, and for Poland they are 39 per cent and 64 per cent. Pajuste (2002) estimates that the largest

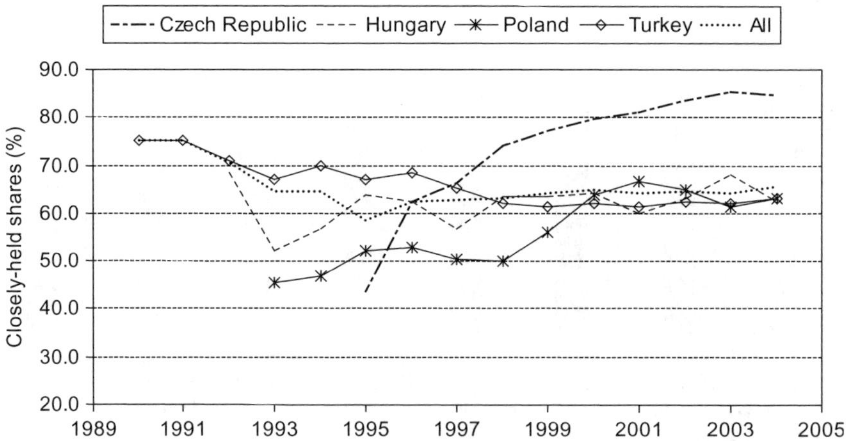

Note: The figure reports the equally-weighted average of block ownership reported by Worldscope for Eastern European countries.

Source: Worldscope.

Figure 3.4 Insider ownership in Eastern European countries over time (2)

shareholder controls 61.1 per cent of the votes on average in the Czech Republic in 2001, 44.7 per cent in Hungary in 2000, and 44.6 per cent in Poland in 2000. The study also provides information on ownership of voting rights in other Eastern European countries and finds similar numbers. Our estimates are mostly in between the Pajuste (2002) and the Klapper et al. (2005) estimates. The differences show that assessing ownership concentration is not straightforward in less than transparent countries. However, all studies show a high ownership concentration in Eastern European countries compared to Anglo-Saxon countries.

As discussed earlier, a firm's governance depends both on the governance of the country in which it is located and on firm-specific governance choices. A number of organizations rate the governance of firms. Unfortunately, the ratings of firms in Eastern Europe are extremely limited. We could only find 14 firms rated. These ratings are from Credit Lyonnais Securities Asia (CLSA).

The CLSA survey was conducted in 2001 and it rates the corporate governance practices of 495 firms from 25 countries (see Gill, 2001). This survey has been used in a number of recent papers (for instance, Chen et al., 2003; Khanna et al., 2005; Durnev and Kim, 2005; Klapper and Love, 2004; and Krishnamurti et al., 2003). The main criterion for including firms in the CLSA survey is firm size and investor interest. The CLSA corporate governance rating is based on a questionnaire given to financial analysts, who responded with 'Yes' or 'No' answers to 57 questions related to seven categories: management discipline, transparency, independence, accountability, responsibility, fairness and social responsibility. A composite governance rating is computed by giving an equal weight of 15 per cent to the first six categories and a weight of 10 per cent to social responsibility. Percentage scores on the composite governance ratings range from 13.9 to 93.5.

Figure 3.5 shows the average scores for firms in Eastern European countries as well as average scores for the other countries in which firms are rated by CLSA. We find that the average CLSA rating in all Eastern European countries is lower than the average CLSA rating across all countries. Strikingly, in the 2001 CLSA ratings, the highest rating for an Eastern European firm was 60.4 for a Hungarian firm. So, even though the CLSA ratings have a wide range, no Eastern European firm was close to the maximum. Of course, ratings of this sort are imperfect and may exhibit biases. Therefore, they have to be treated with caution.

Berglöf and Pajuste (2005) provide evidence on disclosure for Eastern Europe. They construct their own indices of disclosure. One index looks at the information reported on a firm's website. Another index looks at annual reports. Unfortunately, the indices cannot be benchmarked on

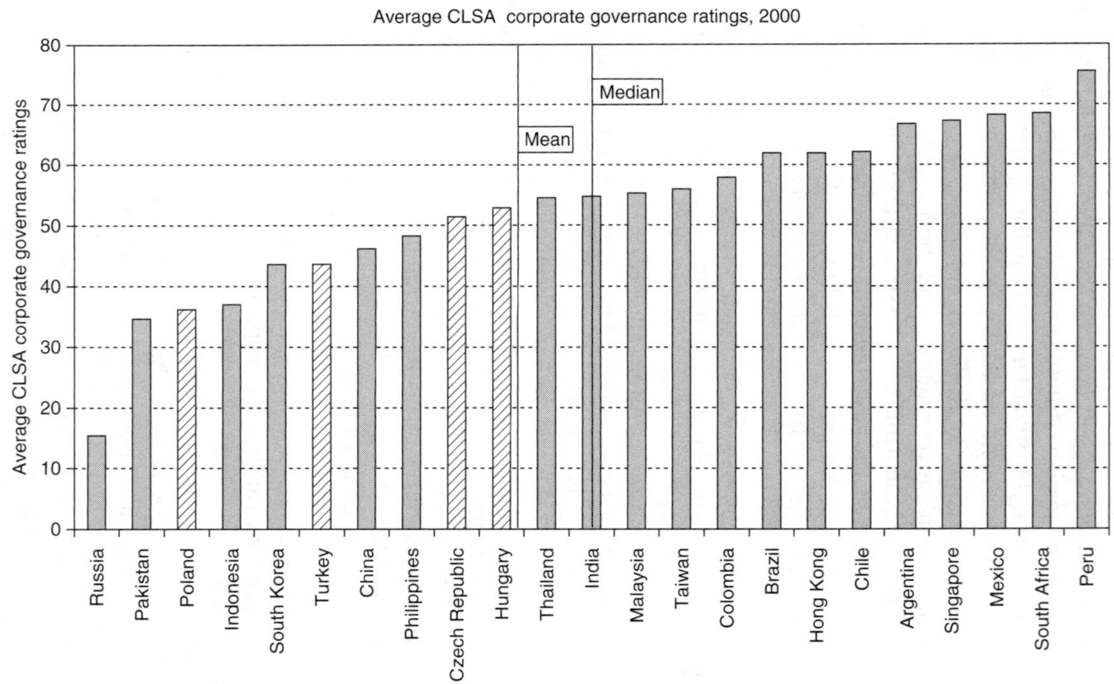

Note: The figure reports the equally-weighted average CLSA rating per country using the 2001 version of the CLSA rating.

Source: Gill (2001).

Figure 3.5 Average CLSA rating per country

other countries, which makes their interpretation difficult. However, a major result of Berglöf and Pajuste (2005) is that firms in a number of Eastern European countries disclose less than the law requires them to disclose, so that disclosure laws do not appear to be enforced well in some countries.

With the evidence so far that the twin agency problems are significant in Eastern Europe, it is perhaps not surprising that overall firm valuations are low. One way to see that is to compute Tobin's q for the firms for which data are available on Worldscope for 2004. This was done by Doidge et al. (2005b). With Tobin's q, a value below 1 indicates roughly that the value created by management is negative. Tobin's q averages to 1.06 for Hungary, 0.98 for the Czech Republic, 1.70 for Poland, and 1.20 for Turkey. (Note, however, that some of these markets experienced a very high return in 2005, which improved valuations substantially.) Doidge et al. compute Tobin's q for 9250 non-US firms. The average q for these firms is 1.45.

According to the Bank for International Settlements (BIS), no Polish firms and no Hungarian firms had an outstanding international debt issue with more than one year of maturity since 2001. While the corporate sector of the Czech Republic and of Turkey had international corporate debt outstanding, the issues took place in 2004 for a total of USD 400 million for Turkey and USD 200 million for the Czech Republic. From 2002 to 2004, the amount of international equity issues is USD 1.3 billion for the Czech Republic, USD 800 million for Hungary, USD 1.7 billion for Poland, and USD 1 billion for Turkey.[9] Only one firm from Turkey and only one firm from Hungary had a listing on a US exchange, while strikingly, however, no firm from the Czech Republic or from Poland had an ADR (American depository receipt) listed on a US exchange.

It follows from the analysis that we would expect weak financial development in Eastern European countries. Figure 3.6 shows that this is the case. Using data from the IMF, we see that the ratio of stock market capitalization to GDP is strikingly low in Eastern European countries compared even to emerging markets in general. This would still be the case after taking into account the stock market performance of these countries in 2005. The same is true for bank assets.

The analysis of section 3 implies that foreign holdings should be low in Eastern Europe. One source of data for foreign holdings is the US Treasury International Capital System (TIC) data. It reports holdings of foreign assets by US residents. Figure 3.7 shows the fraction of stock market capitalization held by US investors in each of the four Eastern European countries and for comparison shows the median fraction of market capitalization held by US investors across all countries as

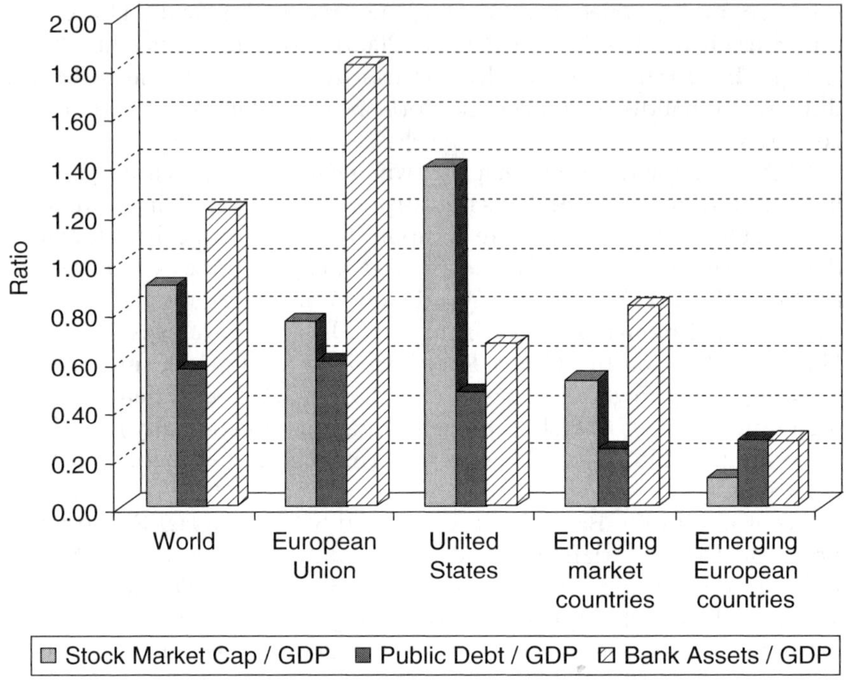

Note: The data are obtained from the IMF's Financial Stability Report, 2005.

Source: IMF (2005).

Figure 3.6 Measures of financial development for 2004

well as across Western European countries. We expect low ownership by US investors given the governance issues discussed so far and this is what we find. US investors hold a smaller fraction of market capitalization in the typical Eastern European country than they do across the world.

The story emerging from the data we have shown is that Eastern European countries have room to improve with governance at the firm level as well as at the country level. The theory discussed in section 2 predicts that poor governance leads to concentrated ownership, low valuations and reduced participation by foreign investors. The evidence from Eastern Europe is consistent with this prediction (though recent increases in the stock markets of these countries temper our conclusions with respect to valuations).

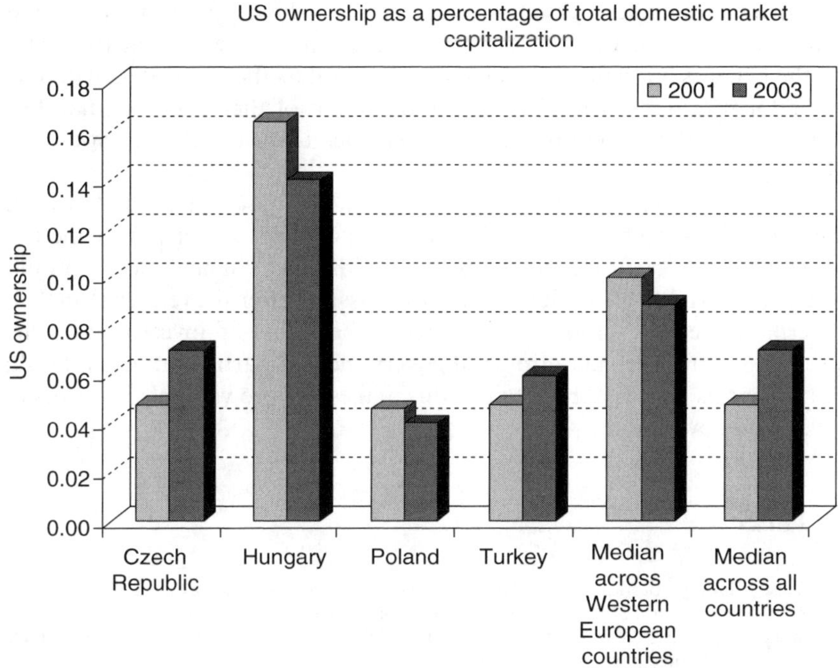

Note: This figure uses the data reported in the Report on US portfolio holdings of foreign securities of 31 December 2003, from the US Department of the Treasury.

Source: US Department of the Treasury.

Figure 3.7 US ownership in Eastern European equity markets

4. THE ROAD TO BETTER GOVERNANCE

In the analysis presented so far, ownership concentration arises because corporate insiders cannot commit not to take advantage of outside shareholders. Corporate insiders would be better off if, at the time they sell securities to the public for the first time, they could commit not to take advantage of outside shareholders. Unfortunately, their ability to make such a commitment depends on the institutions of the country in which the firm is located. In this conclusion, some issues associated with corporate governance reform are discussed.

As first stressed by Bebchuck and Roe (1999), incumbents who have already sold securities find governance reform that makes it harder for them to consume private benefits expensive. The incumbents have paid for their private benefits by selling securities at a lower price. Reform that makes it harder for them to consume these benefits means that they paid for the benefits but will not be able to extract all of them. Insiders will only find reform valuable if it allows them to sell part of their stake, so that they can diversify their holdings, and if it enables them to sell securities at a higher price.

When firms issue securities, good governance makes it possible to sell these securities at a higher price. To avoid opposition to reform from incumbents who view such reform as expropriation, governance reform should focus on the rights of holders of securities issued after the reform. Further, governance reform should both increase the rights of investors and the incentives of firms to acquire good governance. In particular, firms should be free to raise funds abroad, since this makes it more valuable for firms to have good governance.

NOTES

* Reese Chair in Banking and Monetary Economics at the Ohio State University and Research Associate at the NBER. Prepared for the Conference on European Economic Integration, Vienna, November 2005. I am grateful to Carrie Pan for research assistance and to conference participants for comments.

1. Friedman (2005).
2. For a review of issues concerning capital flows, see Stulz (1999a).
3. Data from the IMF's World Economic Outlook.
4. See McGuire and Olson (1996).
5. See, for instance, Bekaert and Harvey (2000), Henry (2000), and Stulz and Wasserfallen (1995).
6. Dahlquist et al. (2003).
7. See Feldstein and Horioka (1980).
8. See Obstfeld (1994).
9. All the BIS data are from the BIS Quarterly Review, September 2005.

REFERENCES

Bae, K.-H., R.M. Stulz and H. Tan (2005), 'Do local analysts know more? A cross-country study of the performance of local analysts and foreign analysts', unpublished working paper, Dice Center, The Ohio State University, Columbus, OH.

Bebchuck, L.A. and M.J. Roe (1999), 'A theory of path dependence in corporate ownership and governance', *Stanford Law Review*, **52**, 127–70.

Bekaert, G. and C. Harvey (2000), 'Foreign speculators and emerging equity markets', *Journal of Finance*, **55**, 565–613.

Berglöf, E. and A. Pajuste (2005), 'What do firms disclose and why? Enforcing corporate governance and transparency in Central and Eastern Europe', working paper, Stockholm School of Economics, Stockholm, Sweden.

Chen, K., Z. Chen and K. Wei (2003), 'Disclosure, corporate governance, and the cost of equity capital: Evidence from Asia's emerging markets', working paper, Hong Kong University of Science and Technology.

Dahlquist, M., L. Pinkowitz, R.M. Stulz and R. Williamson (2003), 'Corporate governance and the home bias', *Journal of Financial and Quantitative Analysis*, **38**, 87–110.

Desai, M.A., A. Dyck and L. Zingales (2005), 'Corporate governance and taxation', unpublished working paper, University of Chicago.

Doidge, C., A. Karolyi and R.M. Stulz (2004), 'Why are foreign firms listed in the US worth more?', *Journal of Financial Economics*, **71**, 205–38.

Doidge, C., A. Karolyi and R.M. Stulz (2005a), 'Why do countries matter so much for corporate governance?', unpublished working paper, Dice Center, The Ohio State University, Columbus, OH.

Doidge, C., A. Karolyi and R.M. Stulz (2005b), 'The valuation premium for non-US firms listed on US stock markets', unpublished.

Durnev, A. and E.H. Kim (2005), 'To steal or not to steal: Firm attributes, legal environment, and valuation', *Journal of Finance*, **60**, 1461–93.

Dyck, A. and L. Zingales (2004), 'Private benefits of control: An international comparison', *Journal of Finance*, **59**, 537–600.

Faccio, M. (2006), 'Politically-connected firms', *American Economic Review*, **96** (1), 369–86.

Feldstein, M. and C. Horioka (1980), 'Domestic saving and international capital flows', *Economic Journal*, **90**, 314–29.

Fisman, R. (2001), 'Estimating the value of political connections', *American Economic Review*, **91**, 1095–102.

Friedman, T.L. (2005), *The World is Flat*, New York: Farrar, Strauss, and Giroux.

Giannetti, M. and A. Simonov (2005), 'Which investors fear expropriation? Evidence from portfolio choices', *Journal of Finance*, **61** (3).

Gill, A. (2001), 'Corporate governance in emerging markets: Saints and sinners, who's got religion?', Credit Lyonnais Securities Asia.

Henry, P.B. (2000), 'Stock market liberalization, economic reform, and emerging market equity prices', *Journal of Finance*, **55**, 529–64.

Jin, L. and S.C. Myers (2006), 'R^2 around the world: New theory and new tests', *Journal of Financial Economics*, **79**, 257–92.

John, K., L. Litov and B. Yeung (2005), 'Corporate governance and corporate risk taking: Theory and evidence', unpublished working paper, New York: New York University.

Johnson, S. and T. Mitton (2003), 'Cronyism and capital controls: Evidence from Malaysia', *Journal of Financial Economics*, **67**, 351–82.

IMF (2005), Financial Stability Report.

Kaufmann, D., A. Kraay and M. Mastruzzi (2005), 'Governance matters IV: Governance indicators for 1996–2004', World Bank Policy Research Working Paper 3630, Washington, DC.

Khanna, T., J. Kogan and K. Palepu (2005), 'Globalization and similarities in corporate governance: A cross-country analysis', *Review of Economics and Statistics*, **88** (1).

Klapper, L. and I. Love (2004), 'Corporate governance, investor protection and performance in emerging markets', *Journal of Corporate Finance*, **10**, 703–28.

Klapper, L.F., L. Laeven and I. Love (2005), 'What drives corporate governance reform? Firm-level evidence from Eastern Europe', World Bank Policy Research Working Paper 3600, Washington, DC.

Krishnamurti, C., A. Sevic and Z. Sevic (2003), 'Legal environment, firm-level corporate governance, and expropriation of minority shareholders in Asia', working paper, Nanyang Technological University, Singapore.

La Porta, R., F. Lopez-De-Silanes and A. Shleifer (1999), 'Corporate ownership around the world', *Journal of Finance*, **54**, 471–517.

Lucas, R.E. Jr (1990), 'Why doesn't capital flow from rich to poor countries?', *American Economic Review*, **80**, 92–6.

McGuire, M.C. and M. Olson, Jr (1996), 'The economics of autocracy and majority rule: The invisible hand and the use of force', *Journal of Economic Literature*, **34**, 72–96.

Obstfeld, M. (1994), 'Risk-taking, global diversification, and growth', *American Economic Review*, **84**, 1310–29.

Pajuste, A. (2002), 'Corporate governance and stock market performance in Central and Eastern Europe', unpublished working paper, Stockholm School of Economics, Stockholm, Sweden.

Pinkowitz, L., R. Williamson and R.M. Stulz (2006), 'Does the contribution of corporate cash holdings and dividends to firm value depend on governance? A cross-country analysis', *Journal of Finance*, forthcoming.

Rajan, R.G. and L. Zingales (2003), 'The great reversals: The politics of financial development in the twentieth century', *Journal of Financial Economics*, **69**, 5–50.

Roe, M. (2003), *Political Determinants of Corporate Governance*, Oxford: Oxford University Press.

Shleifer, A. and R.W. Vishny (1989), 'Management entrenchment: The case of manager-specific investments', *Journal of Financial Economics*, **25**, 123–40.

Stulz, R.M. (1999a), 'International portfolio flows and security markets', in Martin Feldstein (ed.) (1999), *International Capital Flows*, Chicago, IL: University of Chicago Press, pp. 257–93.

Stulz, R.M. (1999b), 'Globalization, corporate finance and the cost of capital', *Journal of Applied Corporate Finance*, **12** (3), 8–25.

Stulz, R.M. (2005), 'The limits of financial globalization', *Journal of Finance*, **60**, 1595–638.

Stulz, R.M. and W. Wasserfallen (1995), 'Foreign equity investment restrictions, capital flight, and shareholder wealth maximization: Theory and evidence', *Review of Financial Studies*, **8**, 1019–57.

PART II

European financial structures yesterday, today and tomorrow

4. Does the financial sector need Europe?

Gertrude Tumpel-Gugerell

This chapter was originally a contribution to the 2005 Conference on European Economic Integration (CEEI), which was itself the result of joint efforts by the Oesterreichische Nationalbank (OeNB) and the research network that was launched by the European Central Bank (ECB) and the Centre for Financial Studies (CFS) in 2002. I had the privilege of participating in the East–West Conference (as the CEEI used to be called) for a number of years, and I warmly remember the intensive discussions we had on issues such as financial crises, EU membership and transition strategies. Since I left the OeNB, I have been following closely and with great interest the activities of the ECB–CFS Research Network in promoting research on capital markets and financial integration in Europe.

I would like to look at the proceedings of the first OeNB seminars in the late 1980s/early 1990s that gave rise to the East–West Conference in 1995. I think reviewing the expectations that we had at that time is important. It enables us to better assess what has been achieved since the fall of the iron curtain and it may also allow us to make some predictions about what will happen in the years to come. Adapting a famous quote by the German philosopher Friedrich Schlegel, who said 'The historian is a prophet looking backwards', I would say that anyone who dares to make prophecies about the future needs to understand the past.

1. THE EXPECTATIONS IN 1989/90

What were the expectations in 1989/90?

With regard to the transition process, the assessment at that time was very accurate. However, comparing the financial sector in Central and Eastern Europe nowadays with the situation at that time reveals that enormous progress has been achieved and that the envisaged problems did not prove insurmountable.

Significant progress has also been achieved with regard to the creation of a European single market for financial services. Yet some of the critical voices of that time have unfortunately not been proven wrong. Let me quote what they said:

> There is, however, widespread scepticism about the real opportunities which 1992 will create, at least immediately. This is related mainly to the difficulties of acquiring the necessary distribution network with which to reach customers. Acquisitions of existing networks are expensive, the development of new networks too slow as well as expensive, and the opportunities for direct cross-border sale of products and services limited. There is also a feeling that the likely continued fragmentation of national markets well after 1992, not just in language, custom and economic development but also in legal and fiscal structures and local regulatory practice (including conduct of business rules), will significantly impede foreign access.[1]

While the transition process has been successfully concluded, it is clear that the single market is not yet completed. The fact that banking markets are still far from integrated shows that all opportunities arising from the conditions in place have not been fully exploited by market forces.

In other words, I see a risk that the European financial sector will fail to reap the benefits of further integration. This issue takes on even greater importance with respect to the countries that have recently joined or will join the European Union in that full financial integration could particularly improve the welfare of these countries by achieving better income and consumption-smoothing through cross-border investment in production assets and access to external credit markets.

The main argument of this chapter will be the following: over the last 15 years, the 'old' EU member states (EU-15), on the one hand, and the 'new' EU member countries and candidates, on the other hand, have gone through two parallel transformation processes. Both groups have been converging towards a relatively similar financial system, mostly bank-based with large consolidated banks concentrating mainly on domestic (meaning national) markets – although in the case of the new member states with a high share of foreign ownership.

As a result of this convergence, both Western and Eastern European countries share the need for further progress towards financial integration. This is particularly the case where retail markets, market infrastructure, supervisory practices and aspects relating to the legal framework are concerned. Of course, the fact that the new member states had to almost entirely rebuild their financial system, which therefore underwent a rapid and profound transformation, implies that the financial systems of the 'old' and the 'new' member states also have their differences.

As a result of these differences, the new EU member states and EU candidates face their own potential obstacles to financial integration. I am thinking in particular of the potential challenges that stem from the rapid liberalization of the financial system, the high degree of foreign ownership of the banking system, and the increasing share of foreign currency-denominated loans in some countries.

Overall, as the legislative framework favourable to the creation of a single market for financial services in the EU-25 member states is basically now in place, the new challenge for public authorities is to overcome the remaining obstacles to financial integration by creating the conditions that foster and guarantee the fair, homogeneous and transparent application of the rules for all potential market participants. This is what I would like to discuss here.

2. THE PARALLEL DEVELOPMENT PROCESS

I would now like briefly to draw a parallel between the evolution of the financial systems in Western and Eastern Europe since the 1990s.

First Half of the 1990s

The first half of the 1990s was marked by the Second Banking Coordination Directive, which allowed credit institutions constituted in one EU country to establish branches or supply cross-border financial services in the other countries of the EU without further authorization. This regulation arose from the belief that the liberalization of the banking markets would increase their integration, with a beneficial impact on efficiency and profitability. In parallel, countries in Central and Eastern Europe and Baltic countries started their transition from socialist to market economy structures and institutions. Reflecting the 'big bang' nature of the reforms – meaning the profound structural changes that these countries went through – the first restructuring phase consisted of the recognition that a large share of the loans extended by state-owned banks had to be written off, the shift to the government of the related losses, and the creation of commercial banks. In most of the transition economies, the first commercial banks were carved out of the branches of the old state 'monobank'. In order to promote competition, the minimum capital requirements for a bank licence were set at low levels and the review process was rather generous, resulting in a growing number of credit institutions. In 1993 Estonia, for instance, had one foreign-owned bank and 20 small private banks, for a country of 1.5 million people.

Second Half of the 1990s

In contrast, the second half of the 1990s was characterized by a broad movement of consolidation in the banking sector, both in Western and Eastern Europe. The pattern of the consolidation process displays similarities and differences.

In the EU-15, regulator changes that were largely linked to the single market project in the first half of the 1990s triggered the wave of consolidation that followed. In the three years from 1997 to 1999 the volume of mergers and acquisitions (M&As) was multiplied threefold and the number of credit institutions in the euro area fell by roughly 8 per cent. The launch of the euro accelerated this process, and between January 1999 and June 2002 the number of monetary financial institutions (MFIs) decreased by 11.1 per cent. Transition economies followed a similar trend, although for other reasons. The lack of banking management experience caused difficulties for the new commercial banks formed from the break-up of the 'monobanks'. After a brief period, the authorities encouraged large domestic banks and also foreign investors to take over these small banks. To take the example of Estonia again, the number of banks fell from 21 in 1993 to 13 in 1999, of which four were foreign-owned, holding more than 90 per cent of the total banking assets.

These similarities hide the different natures of the consolidation processes in the EU-15 and in the new EU member states and EU candidates. Indeed, by contrast with the new EU member countries and EU candidates, the majority of the M&A deals in the EU-15 were domestic, that is to say that they were between credit institutions located in the same country.

Last Five Years

Since 2000 further progress has been achieved on financial integration, financial innovation and financial development in the EU-15 member states, thanks to the introduction of the euro, the creation of the European legislative framework for financial services and the implementation of the Financial Services Action Plan.

However, progress is more impressive on the side of the new EU member states, which have now virtually completed their transition process in terms of legal structures and institutions. In 2004 the indices of price liberalization and trade liberalization produced by the European Bank for Reconstruction and Development were close to Western European standards. On the financial side, indices on banking sector reforms are now at the levels of Bank for International Settlements standards in the case of a number of new EU member states (like the Czech Republic, Estonia, Hungary and Latvia).

As a result of this convergence process, the features displayed by the financial systems in the EU-15 countries and the new member states have become more similar. Financial deepening is still taking place at a fast pace, for instance in Estonia and Slovenia the total amount of credit to the private sector is already equal to almost 60 per cent of GDP, a level comparable to Greece and Spain.

Regarding the structure of the financial sector, commercial banks now play a prominent role in the economy of new EU member states and EU candidates. Equity and bond markets are catching up as well. Although the total stock market capitalization of new EU member states is still much lower than in the EU-15 member states – due to the fact that the markets of the former have a shorter history of development, and also to the fact that foreign investment has often been available as an alternative to domestic financing – stock market capitalization has almost doubled over the last five years in most new member states and these developments have accelerated since 2003. In the Czech Republic stock market capitalization has actually doubled since 2003 alone. However, debt securities markets in the new member states have still only achieved a third of the level of the markets in the EU-15 member states, standing at an average of 67 per cent of GDP at the end of last year.

Over and above these 'catching-up' effects, the convergence process highlights two characteristics of the new EU member states, namely flexibility and openness. The recent evolution of the banking system in the new member states testifies to its capacity to implement reforms. The rapid development of electronic communication media and services for payments related to financial institutions in the new EU member states is an example of such flexibility. The banking systems of the new EU member states seem to be more open to internationalization than those of the EU-15 member states. One example is the International Bank Account Number, an international code used for payment transactions. Of the ten new EU member states, four have already standardized the account number format for both cross-border and national payments, while of the EU-15 member states only Luxembourg has implemented it for national transactions. The high degree of foreign ownership in the banking system of the new EU member states is, of course, another example of such openness.

3. LOOKING FORWARD: THE NEXT FIVE YEARS

What are the Challenges for the Next Five Years?

The integration process of financial markets in the EU-25 member states is far from over. Despite the progress made, EU banking markets still remain rather fragmented, in particular at the retail level, in segments such as loans to households and small and medium-sized enterprises. Still less than 5 per cent of total bank loans are granted cross-border to customers in other euro area countries. I am deeply convinced that further financial integration will bring significant benefits also in retail banking. At the same time, I am certainly aware of the fact that the low level of cross-border loans reflects also – at least in parts – differences in the nature of cross-border competition in these segments. Proximity to clients, bank/customer relationships and access to information play a key role in retail banking, while they are less crucial for investment banking.

Overall, the rather modest progress in the integration of the banking sector translates into persistent differences between countries in levels of bank lending and deposit rates. In the retail sector, in particular, the low degree of integration causes differences in the pass-through of changes in monetary policy rates to retail bank rates.

The structure of the banking sector may help to explain the current situation. Despite the considerable amount of consolidation undergone by the European banking sector, the lack of progress in creating pan-European banks is hindering the realization of economies of scale and blocking the beneficial effects of increased efficiency within the EU economy. Think, for instance, of the mortgage market. If we created a single market for mortgages, home ownership could increase and further wealth could be created.

The slowdown of the financial integration process after the reforms and consolidation of the 1990s points to the risk that the integration process of financial markets and institutions has stalled, not only in Western Europe but also in Eastern Europe where the banking sector is primarily owned by West European banks.

4. WHAT CAN BE DONE TO INCREASE EUROPEAN FINANCIAL INTEGRATION FURTHER?

What can be done to increase European financial integration further? Financial integration is primarily a market-driven process. Greater financial integration can offer more opportunities for financial institutions to better manage and diversify their risks and realize economies of scale. At the same time, it is, of course, not the aim of financial integration to press one unified banking model onto Europe's banking sector. Local preferences should still be satisfied.

However, the choice between different banking products should not be artificially constrained by national restrictions and a deliberate lack of transparency.

I see it as the basic task of public authorities to create a framework whereby all potential market participants in a given financial instruments or services market are subject to a single set of rules when they decide to deal in those financial instruments or services, have equal access to this set of financial instruments or services and are treated equally when they operate in the market.

In this respect, I would like to mention a development in the field of retail payments, namely the Single Euro Payments Area (SEPA) project, an initiative of the European banking industry led by the European Payments Council.

While prices to the end-customer have been homogenized through legislation, the level of services is not influenced by legislation. A real SEPA will therefore only be achieved when payments can be made throughout the whole EU from a single bank account, using a single set of payment instruments, as easily and safely as in the national context today. The banking industry is now working to develop pan-European payment instruments and a SEPA-compliant infrastructure within the suggested timetable. The ECB is assisting this process by helping to resolve the problem of coordination and the gridlock that banks may face if they act on their own. Approximately one third of the costs and revenues of retail banks is at stake in this project.

As regards banking sector cross-border consolidation, it is important that 'home–host' coordination be developed on a robust and consistent basis for the financial groups involved to ensure that there is effective supervision, on the one hand, and to reduce compliance cost, on the other hand. I would therefore like to stress the need for the pursuit of supervisory convergence and the effective interaction between the home and host country authorities, for clarifying and harmonizing as much as possible the procedures for banks and supervisory authorities, and for making these procedures more transparent. The review of the supervisory M&A approval process presented by the Commission to the informal ECOFIN meeting in November 2005 is one step in this direction and shows greater awareness.

5. CONCLUDING REMARKS

Let me summarize the main message I would like to convey. Looking back at the last decade, financial integration has made considerable progress in the EU-25 and also in the EU candidates. The new member states and the candidate countries have successfully jumped on the European bandwagon of financial development and integration.

The legal framework to achieve one single market for financial services is now in place, and there is little doubt that the gradual introduction of the euro across the new EU member states over the next few years will further improve financial integration in Europe. However, as there is still scope for improvement in a number of sectors, such as the retail banking sector, the new challenges for public authorities over the next few years is to help market players to use European legislation and to reap all the benefits of further financial integration, by creating the conditions that foster and guarantee the fair, homogeneous and transparent application of the rules for all potential market participants.

The Commission has asked banks why there has not been greater cross-border consolidation among them. Their answers provide us with the challenges that the industry and public authorities face in the coming years, namely to:

1. Prepare the ground for cross-border consolidation, that is standardize and harmonize banking and post-trading activities.
2. Reduce complexity in the legal and supervisory framework, that is review and, where possible, abolish the hundreds of national differences in reporting and supervisory rules and types of licensing.
3. Use electronic devices for retail and corporate business.
4. Build closer customer relationships.
5. Make multicultural business environments work.

In this respect, the ECB has played and will keep on playing its role in promoting financial integration. By encouraging researchers and practitioners to undertake studies to assess the state of financial integration, the ECB–CFS Research Network on capital markets and financial integration in Europe participates in raising awareness. And this conference, in particular, helps to keep track of new developments and challenges ahead.

Research is extremely important. I would like therefore to take this opportunity of addressing top researchers in the field of financial integration to mention a number of possible topics for further research, which are of great interest to the ECB:

- On consolidation: Are there common consolidation patterns across countries in Europe? How do they compare with the United States? How much concentration is optimal in the financial sector?
- On competition: Do we have sufficient competition? Do we need to secure access to financial services for certain customer groups? What is the impact of the diversified ownership models on long-term performance and competitiveness?

- On the role of regulation and supervision: What legal framework does the financial sector need? How do legal systems affect competitiveness and performance?
- On the demarcation between the EU and the national level: How much harmonization and convergence is needed in the EU? What should remain at the national level?
- On the relationship between financial integration and economic growth: What do economies in different stages of development need?

I know these are questions for many more conferences and papers, but I am looking forward to the efforts of the research community to find the right answers and the appropriate strategies.

To conclude, the financial sector has a European framework. There was an urgent need to transform the industry: to shake up the new member states and EU candidates and to considerably reduce the number of banks in the EU-15 (by 30 per cent over a ten-year period). Measures to expand business and reduce volume costs have been taken. But more must still be done. The financial sector will be measured by European and global standards.

Special strategies and national differences will always remain. However, the financial sector needs a European perspective because Europe needs a strong single market.

NOTE

1. Price and Tower (1989).

REFERENCE

Price, L. and I. Tower (1989), 'Developments in the European Banking system in view of the unified market in the EC', in A. Wala (ed.), *New Developments in Banking and Finance in East and West*, Vienna: Oesterreichische Nationalbank, p. 75.

5. The Central and Eastern European financial sector: current state and prospects

Irmfried Schwimann and Kristin Vandenbergen[1]

On 1 May 2004, the European Union (EU) was enlarged to a union of 25 countries, the biggest single enlargement of the EU ever, with most of the new member states (NMS) coming from Central and Eastern Europe (CEE).

This enlargement was prepared by an unprecedented effort of all parties involved to ensure a smooth transition – for the new and old member states and for the European Union as a whole. The work aimed at helping the new members ease into their membership role started well before the date of accession; and it did not stop then. In parallel, the integration process was strongly helped by the reality on the markets, with market forces bridging the gap between the old and the new member states with unprecedented speed and intensity.

1. SIZE AND STRUCTURE OF THE NEW MEMBER STATES' FINANCIAL SYSTEMS

Whilst a considerable part of the European Union's population – namely 16 per cent – comes from the new EU member states, their financial sectors are comparatively very small.

A common feature of their financial systems is the relative importance of the banking sector in the new member states: all have predominantly bank-based financial systems, with the banking sector representing on average 80 per cent of total financial assets (see Figure 5.1). In relative terms, banking assets represent 77.4 per cent of GDP in the new member states, compared to 280 per cent of GDP in the EU-15. Although still small in absolute terms, insurance markets, stock exchanges and funds are developing fast.

Whilst all of the Central and Eastern European NMS countries have gone through a transition to establish functioning market economies,

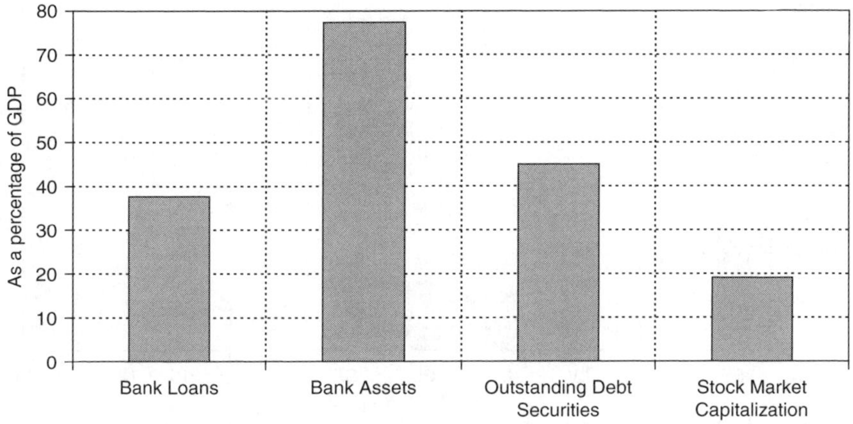

Source: ECB, Eurostat, Federation of European Securities Exchanges (FESE).

Figure 5.1 Financial structure in the NMS

developments and policy choices in the run-up to EU accession have been very different, resulting in a variety of financial systems.

1.1 Banking

Although very small in absolute size – only 1.3 per cent of total assets of EU-25 credit institutions come from the new member states – the banking sector remains the most important of the financial services sectors in all CEE-EU countries, representing 80 per cent of total financial assets. Its relative size, however, shows a considerable degree of variation: expressed as a percentage of GDP, it varies from 39.6 per cent of GDP in Latvia to 96.8 per cent in the Czech Republic.

A similar picture emerges when looking at bank loans: they represent on average 37.7 per cent of GDP in the NMS but vary from 24 per cent of GDP in Lithuania to 54 per cent of GDP in Estonia (see Figure 5.2 on p. 54).

1.2 Insurance

In the NMS, the insurance sector represents on average about 7 per cent of total financial assets. The size of their insurance markets in terms of gross premium is surprisingly small when compared to overall EU-25 markets: 1 per cent of total EU-25 life and 3 per cent of EU-25 non-life insurance markets (2003 data).

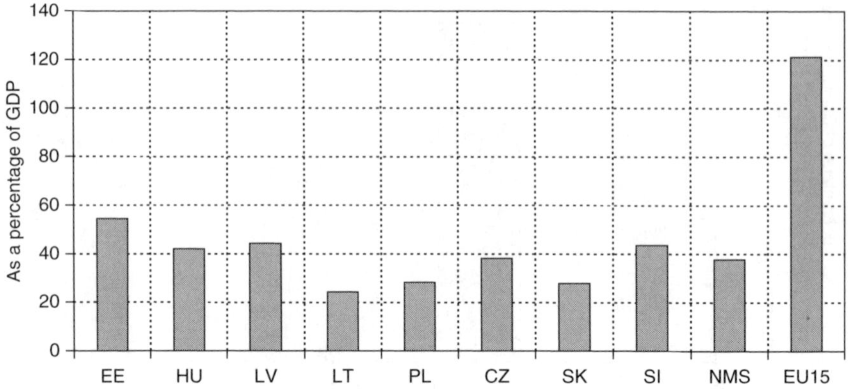

Source: ECB, Eurostat (2003 figures).

Figure 5.2 Bank loans

A picture of the situation in the individual countries can best be drawn by comparing the gross premiums per capita. Most striking in this comparison is the embryonic size of the life insurance markets in the NMS compared to the EU-15 (see Figure 5.3).

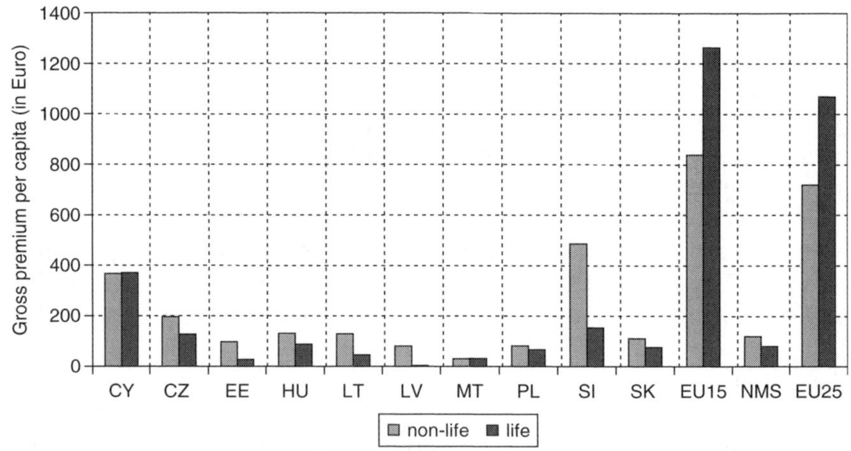

Source: European Commission, Financial Integration Monitor 2005, based on Comité Européen des Assurances (The European Federation of National Insurance Associations (CEA)) data.

Figure 5.3 Gross premium per capita in life and non-life sectors (2003 data)

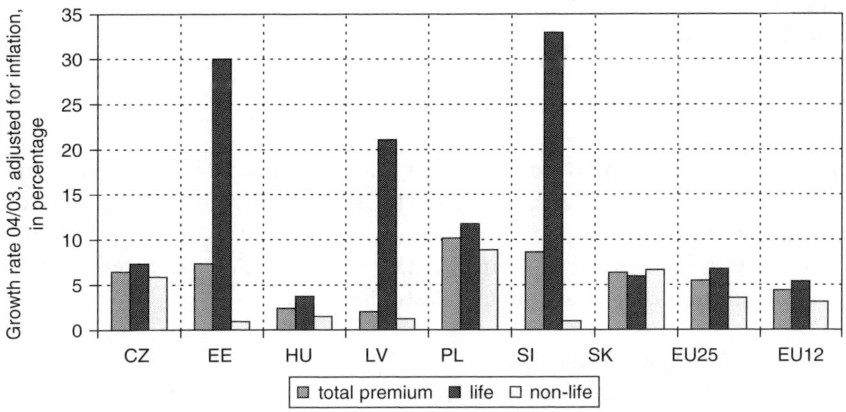

Source: Comité Européen des Assurances: The European Federation of National Insurance Associations (CEA).

Figure 5.4 Growth in insurance business

Starting levels are low, but growth rates (see Figure 5.4), particularly in the life-insurance sector, have been remarkable recently. In the life segment, this development can clearly be linked to the ongoing reform of the pensions systems, and the building up of the third pillar systems. In the non-life segment, legislative changes are contributing to growth.

1.3 Funds

Occupational pension funds, non-bank controlled funds, intermediaries and other financial entities have been or are in the process of being developed in the CEE-EU member states, but remain with less than 10 per cent of GDP well below the 90 per cent of GDP they represent in the EU-15.

Investment fund assets and the number of nationally domiciled undertakings for collective investment in transferable securities (UCITS) rose in all NMS (for which data are available)[2] in the period 1998–2004. However, volumes remain very modest in a market in which a few countries (Luxembourg, France and Germany) represent over 60 per cent of total EU activity. For the CEE countries, the strongest growth figures in UCITS were reported for Slovakia (+93.4 per cent for 2004), but the importance of the sector remains small in absolute terms, representing less than 0.1 per cent of total net assets of the European UCITS industry.

The development of pension funds is, as is the case in the EU-15, strongly dependent on the legal and fiscal context and on reforms. Even though the level of assets and participation in some countries is still modest, pension funds are growing fast.

1.4 Financial Markets

Developments in capital markets other than government bond and treasury bill markets are fairly recent in most CEE-EU member states and the smaller and less developed markets can be expected to benefit from integration with the European financial markets because of increased liquidity and choice in terms of available investment vehicles.

1.4.1 Debt securities markets

Debt securities markets have developed in all NMS, although some of them remain very small and heavily reliant on the activity of public authorities. Expressed as a percentage of GDP, their size varies strongly between 3.3 per cent for Estonia and 61 per cent for Hungary, compared to an EU average of 117 per cent (see Figure 5.5).

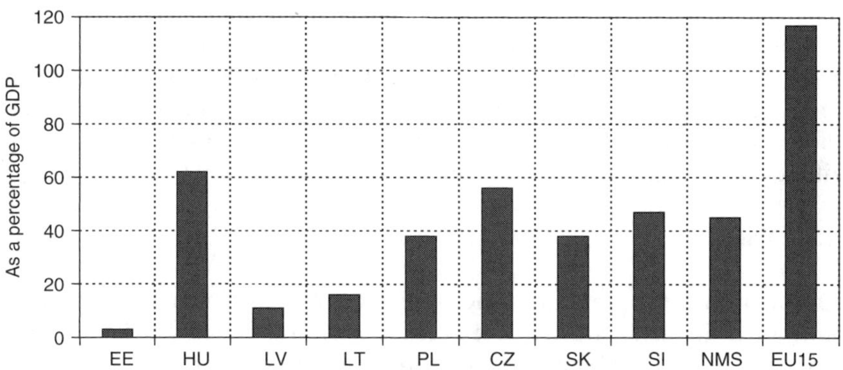

Source: ECB (2003 data).

Figure 5.5 Outstanding debt securities

1.4.2 Stock exchanges

The development of domestic stock exchanges is still at an early stage: in 2004, stock market capitalization on average amounted to 28 per cent of GDP in the NMS compared with 70 per cent in the EU-15. Estonia stands out with a market capitalization of 45 per cent of GDP. Although stock markets are still at an early stage, they have experienced strong growth rates over the past three years and are developing fast (see Figure 5.6).

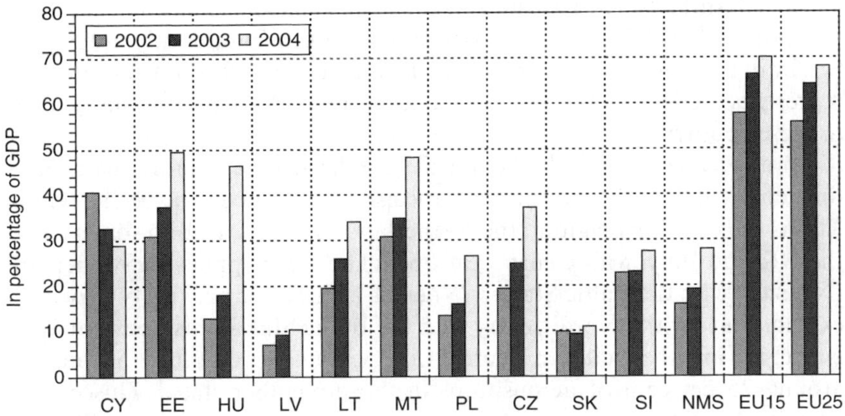

Source: European Commission, Financial Integration Monitor 2005, based on Federation of European Securities Exchanges (FESE), Eurostat-data.

Figure 5.6 Stock market capitalization (2002–2004)

2. INTEGRATION

2.1 Integration through Establishment

In most of the CEE-NMS, it has been relatively easy to buy into the banking and insurance markets. This was partly due to a considered strategy of the CEE-NMS countries to involve strategic foreign investors in their privatization processes. Foreign investors have often not only brought in technology, corporate governance expertise and know-how, but have also recapitalized the financial systems of the CEE countries in question.

The interest of the EU-15 financial institutions in buying into the financial systems of the NMS was initially motivated by the needs of their clients in these countries, and later on also by regional expansion and retail market investment strategies.

2.1.1 Foreign Direct Investment (FDI) inflows

At the end of 2003, the financial sector in the NMS accounted for 20 per cent of total foreign direct investment inflows in these countries. This is mainly attributable to bank privatizations and the sale of formerly state-owned insurance companies. In addition to the privatization processes, the prospect of the CEE countries' future EU membership as well as proximity considerations were strong incentives. FDI inflows originate mainly in the EU-15.

2.1.2 Mergers and acquisitions

The large inflows directed at NMS are clear from Figures 5.7 and 5.8: the total value of intra-EU cross-border deals from EU-15 countries into CEE represents EUR 13.4 billion, representing the bulk of non-domestic deals in these countries.

Among these flows, EU-15 countries can be grouped in three categories: first, countries whose institutions have a strategy aimed at a specific region. This is the case for Belgium, the Netherlands, Austria and, to some extent, the UK and Italy, with Central Europe[3]. The same applies to Sweden and Denmark with the Baltic States[4]. Whereas geographic proximity may be an explanation for the Nordic entry into the Baltic States, this does not apply entirely to member states in Central Europe: Benelux countries account for around 25 per cent of acquisitions in those member states. This may be explained by the relative maturity and concentration of the Benelux markets, which drive the institutions to look for new business opportunities in areas with high growth potential.

Second, some countries are home to institutions adopting a more targeted approach, with acquisitions in only one or two specific countries. This is the case for Germany with Poland and Slovakia; for France with the Czech Republic and Slovenia; and for both Ireland and Portugal with Poland.

Finally, institutions in a couple of countries (Spain and Greece) are scarcely engaged in cross-border mergers with the NMS.

2.1.3 Resulting level of foreign ownership in the NMS

In relative terms (that is, taking into account the relative size of each domestic financial sector), it becomes clear that the restructuring process has been particularly intense in those NMS where merger and acquisition activity has involved a significant proportion of the local financial sector.

Using total banking assets as a proxy for estimating the size of the financial sector, it can be seen that acquisitions have been 8 to 11 times more intense in the CEE-EU countries than in EU-15 countries (see Figure 5.9).

As a result of this consolidation process, the level of foreign ownership in the NMS' **banking sector** is on average 70 per cent of total assets, which is significantly higher than the 24 per cent in EU-15 (see Table 5.1).

In **insurance**, too, the opening up of the markets has resulted in a high level of foreign presence (among others in the form of majority holdings in former monopoly insurers). The level of foreign ownership exceeds 90 per cent of the overall market in several new member states. The market share of foreign ownership varies considerably from one country to the next as well as by market segment: in Estonia, for instance, over 93 per cent of the non-life insurance market is in the hands of foreign insurers. Similar rates apply to Lithuania, whereas foreign presence is less important in the

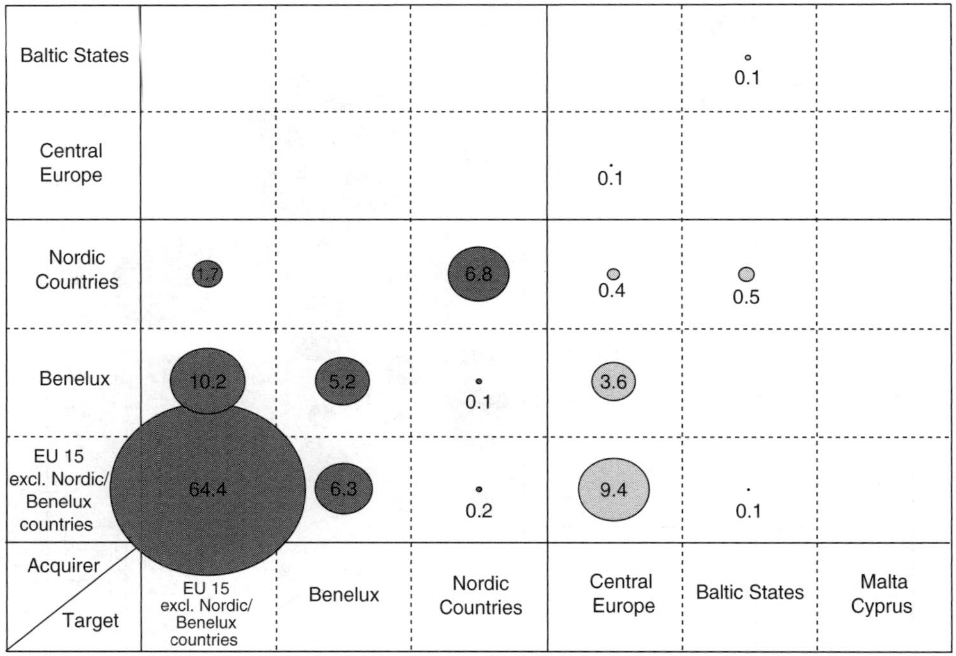

Source: European Commission, Financial Integration Monitor 2005, based on Bureau van Dijk, Zephyr database.

Figure 5.7 Total value of intra-EU deals by geographical region, excluding domestic deals (in EUR billion)

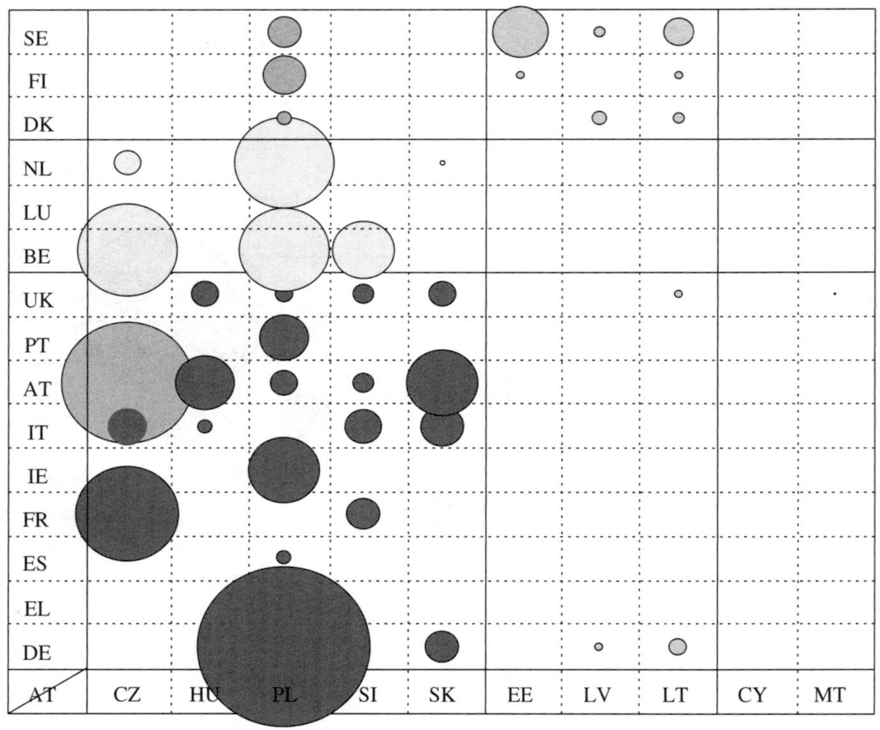

Source: European Commission, Financial Integration Monitor 2005, based on Bureau van Dijk, Zephyr database.

Figure 5.8 Total value of deals per member state from EU-15 to NMS-10 between 1999 and 2004

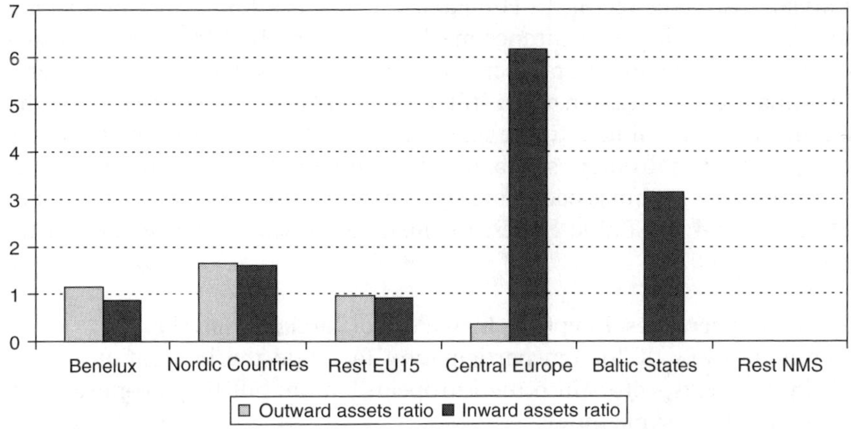

Source: European Commission, Financial Integration Monitor 2005, based on Bureau van Dijk, Zephyr database.

Figure 5.9 *Ratio of intra-EU deal values, directed towards or originating from an EU region, over national bank assets (normalized at 1 for the EU-25 as a whole)*

Table 5.1 *Share of foreign ownership in the NMS*

2003-figures	As % of total assets
CY	12.3
CZ	96
EE	97.5
HU	82.3
LT	95.6
LV	46.3
MT	67.6
PL	67.8
SI	36
SK	96.3
NMS	70
EU-15	24

Source: ECB, Bank Austria.

Latvian insurance sector. In Hungary, which was a forerunner in opening up and liberalizing its insurance markets in the early 1990s, foreign insurers now account for 90 per cent of market shares. Only in Poland and Slovenia are the largest insurers still domestically owned. In many cases the main insurers are linked to the main banks: in Estonia, two life insurance companies are subsidiaries of banks, in Lithuania three and in Latvia two.

Foreign ownership is becoming significant for **stock exchanges** as well: in Hungary and the Baltic States, for instance, stock exchanges are partly foreign owned.

2.1.4 Concerns resulting from high levels of foreign ownership

The high levels of foreign participation facilitate the integration of the NMS' financial sectors into the European Union, but they do raise some concerns at the same time.

First of all, concerns from a financial stability point of view: whilst the strong and intensive ownership links between old and new member states are an important channel for transferring expertise, product know-how and risk management practices, these benefits also come with a potential danger of transmission of external shocks. Bearing in mind the size of the NMS' financial markets, the impact of any transmission is likely to be stronger in the direction of the NMS.

In addition, the high level of foreign ownership raises some supervisory issues, in particular issues of supervisory control which emerge with increased cross-border and cross-sectoral links. So far, EU-15 companies have mainly established subsidiaries[5] in the NMS. With the possibilities offered by the EU company statute, some are considering transforming their subsidiaries into branches, a change which could have significant implications in terms of supervision of the financial system, in particular in the NMS because of their high level of foreign ownership.

2.2 Integration through EU Membership

EU membership and thus the obligation to comply with the 'acquis communautaire' have also helped the NMS to integrate quickly into the EU framework, to adapt and change their regulatory and supervisory structures and to engage in a programme of reform and change.

Correct and coherent transposition and implementation of the European financial services legislation has thus been a precondition for membership. In view of future membership, the Commission services had, together with the candidate countries, engaged in extensive screening exercises to make sure that all envisaged legislative changes were in line with European legislation. Clearly, these mandatory changes brought about a number of important changes in the legislative framework of the new member states, which in turn facilitated access and legal certainty of financial institutions and markets in these countries well before actual membership.

Since 1 May 2004, the CEE countries have been full members of the EU, with the same rights and obligations as the incumbent member states. Thus, legislative measures adopted at EU level need to be transposed, applied and enforced on time – in the same way as in the rest of the European Union. This obligation does put pressure on the legislative systems of the new members, who need to adopt all the necessary transposing laws, but also on the market participants, who need to adapt to the considerable number of new rules. However, the changes in the legislative framework of the NMS have also increased confidence from foreign investors, services providers and market participants that these markets do and will operate according to the same rules as the rest of the European Union.

Most of the NMS are doing very well in terms of transposition; some of them are even among the best performing countries (see Figure 5.10).

EU membership also brought new responsibilities to the political and administrative actors of the NMS: they now play an active role in the European regulatory and supervisory structures. In the financial services sector, these regulatory and supervisory structures are clearly defined in the four-level 'Lamfalussy approach'.[6]

As members in the European Union, the NMS are now co-responsible for EU legislation – both at 'level 1' – as members of the Council of the European Union and thus as co-legislator, together with the European Parliament – but also at 'level 2', when it comes to adopting technical implementing measures.

Of crucial importance for ensuring a well functioning European supervisory system is the active participation of the competent authorities of all member states at 'Level 3' of the Lamfalussy approach, the committees which bring together European financial supervisors and regulators.[7] The task of these Level 3 committees is two-fold: they give advice to the Commission, and they have to ensure coherent and consistent application of European rules across the European Union by cooperating closely on a day-to-day basis. This close cooperation aims at increased convergence of supervisory practices across the European Union – this is an absolute requirement if supervision is to be carried out in the same way in all 25 member states. This close cooperation also enables the member states to quickly see and adapt to best practices and to work towards a truly European culture of supervision, keeping in mind both the interests of the individual member states and their stakeholders and those of the European financial market as a whole.

Lastly, EU membership also means complying with the European

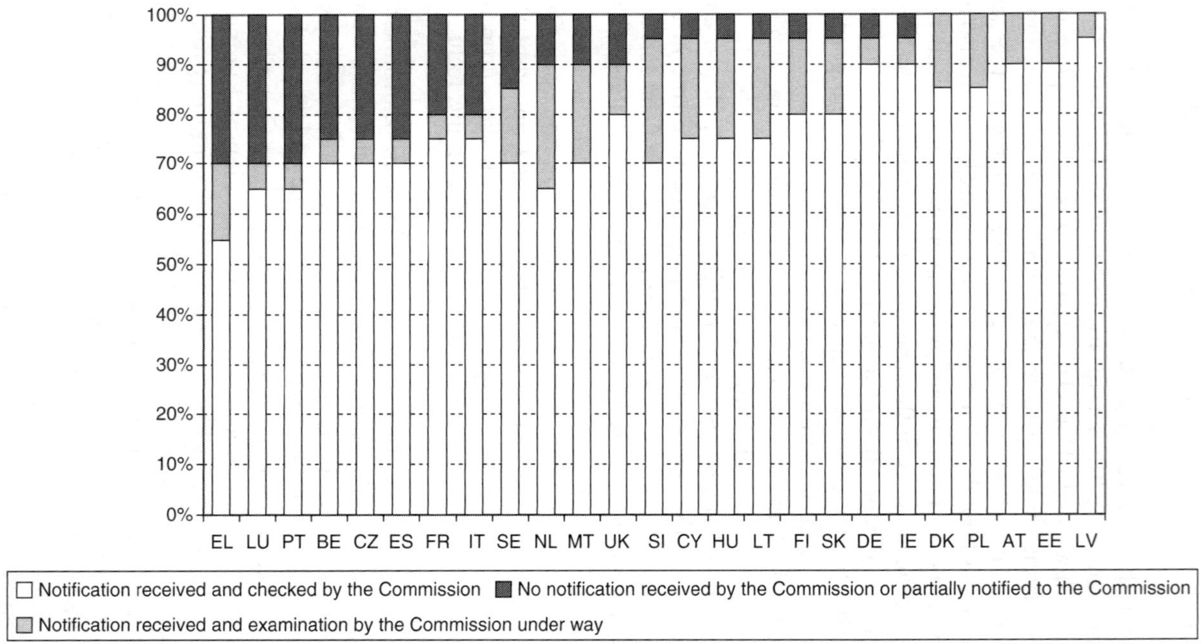

Note: [i] Regular updates (each fortnight) are published at the Commission websites: http://europa.eu.int/comm/internal_market/finances/actionplan/index_en.htm#transposition.

Source: European Commission; status: 01/02/2006.

Figure 5.10 Rate of transposition of FSAP Directives – view per member state – state of play as of 1 February 2006[i]

Union's convergence criteria in view of euro participation. In this context, measures are taken to reduce public debt, deficits and inflation to bring them in line with the criteria. As a consequence, interest rates – real and nominal – also converge.

3. POTENTIAL OF THE CEE FINANCIAL SECTOR

Comparing the current levels of development of the financial sectors of the old and new member states gives a clear picture of the situation and of the prospects. Indeed, the correlation of the development of banking, insurance markets and stock exchanges with the economic development (GDP per capita) is apparent in Figures 5.11, 5.12 and 5.13.

The comparison of NMS with EU-15 countries provides an indication of the market potential those countries represent. One could reasonably expect that this potential will be unleashed as the NMS catch up in terms of GDP.

Figure 5.11 confirms that the **banking sectors** in most of the NMS have enormous potential. Whether this potential can be translated into reality will, however, largely depend on overall economic growth and the political choices made in the development of financing. Clearly, most of the CEE countries will have to improve both labour productivity and utilization and further reform their pension systems in order to converge towards the EU-15 average. However, despite a favourable current growth environment combined with increasing demand for financial products, recent analysis suggests that it could take the CEE-EU member states years to converge to the EU-15 average.[8]

Figure 5.12 shows similar potential for the **insurance markets** in all NMS. As is the case in the banking sector, the insurance sector thrives in a 'growth environment', which creates favourable conditions. Developments in the insurance sector will also to a large extent depend on legislation, including at EU level. For instance, the introduction of compulsory third-party liability motor insurance has stimulated progress. The same can be expected for the life segment, where further developments in the regulatory environment, in particular in the area of pensions, will have an impact on the development of the market.

Likewise, the potential for the development of **stock exchanges** is positive. Market capitalization as a percentage of GDP has steadily increased over the past three years. The comparison with the situation in the EU-15 gives a clear indication where the development in the CEE countries could lead over time.

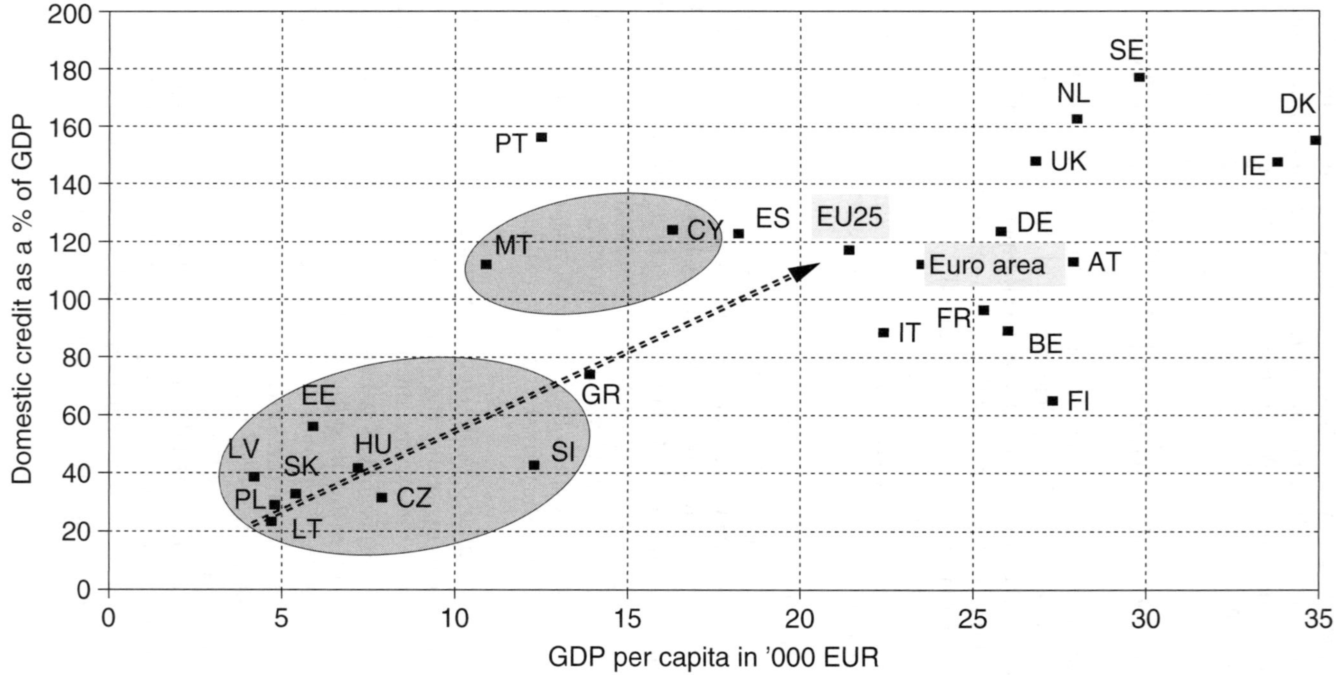

Source: European Commission, Financial Integration Monitor 2005, based on ECB and Eurostat data.

Figure 5.11 Domestic credit and economic development (2003 data)

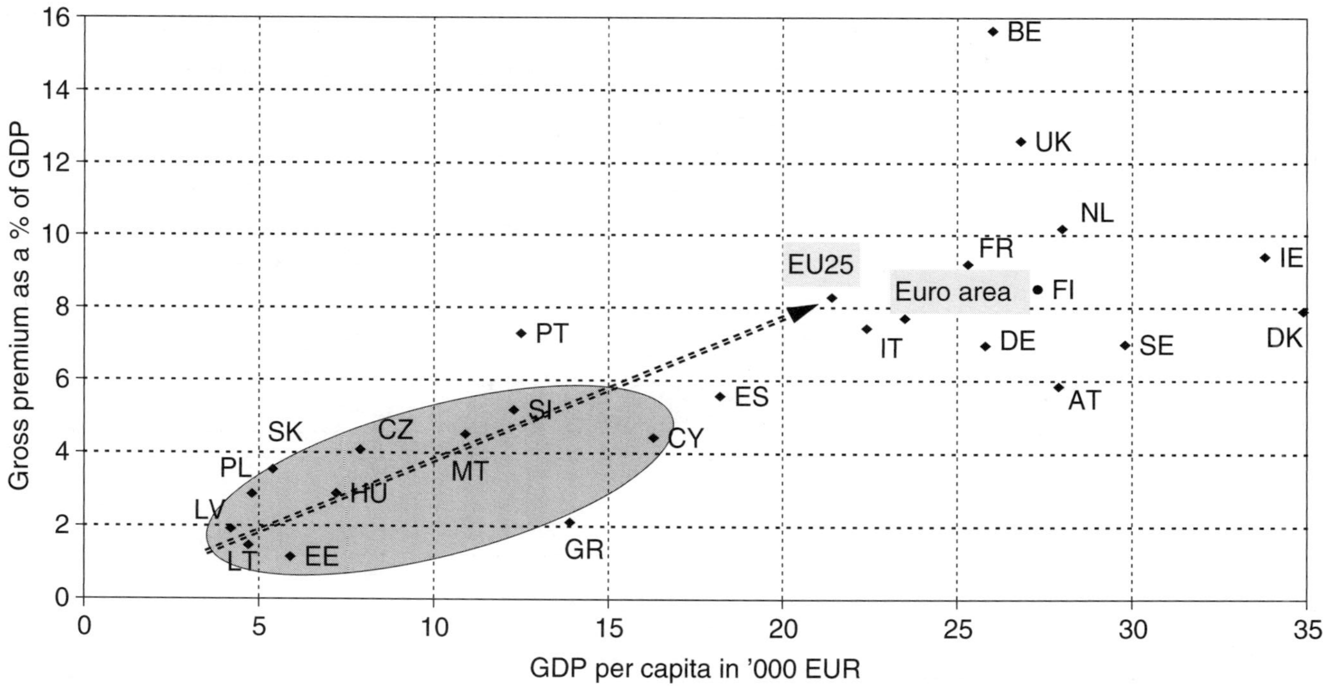

Source: European Commission, Financial Integration Monitor 2005, based on ECB and CEA-data.

Figure 5.12 Gross insurance premium and economic development (2003 data)

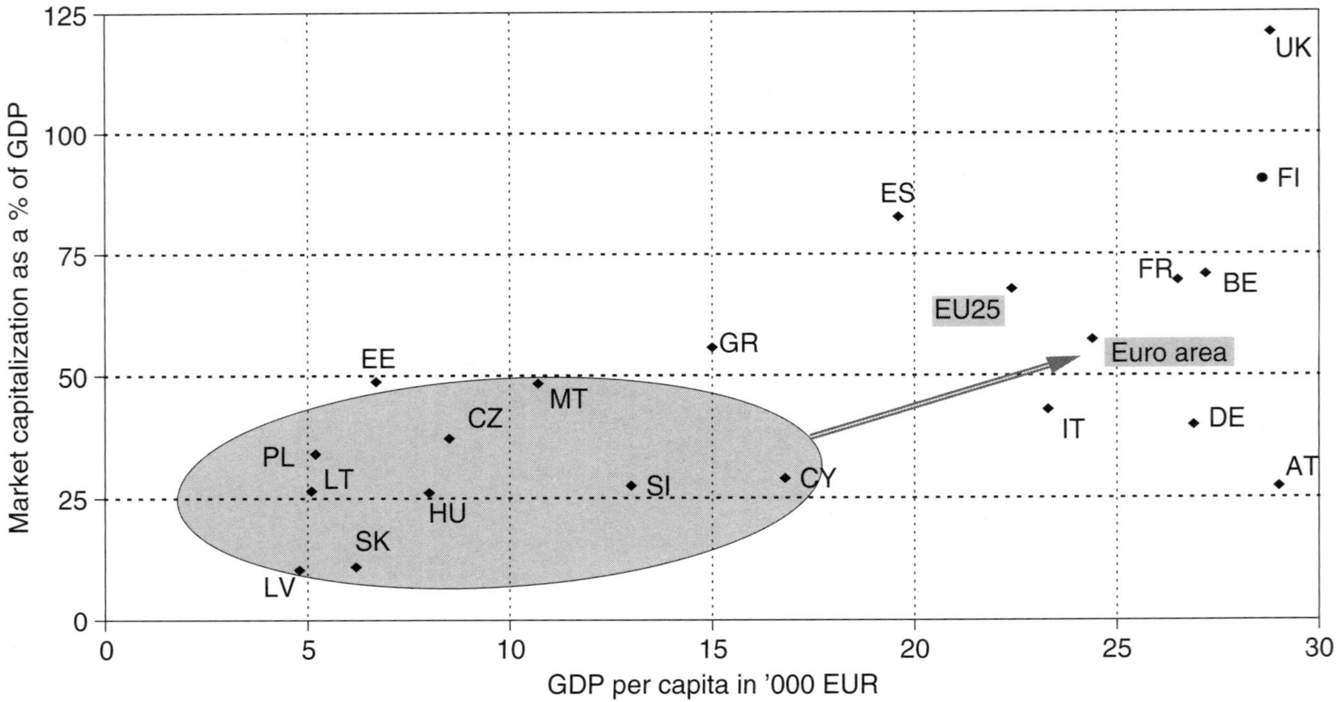

Source: European Commission, based on Eurostat and Federation of European Securities Exchanges (FESE) data.

Figure 5.13 Market capitalization and economic development (2004 data)

4. CONCLUSIONS

- On 1 May 2004, the biggest single enlargement of the European Union took place. The new member states joined with varying but significantly lower levels of financial development than is presently the case in the EU-15. Their financial systems are largely bank-based while the other financial sectors are small but growing fast.
- The transition towards market economies and to EU membership has taken place with considerable openness towards foreign, in particular EU, entry and the gradual adoption of the EU financial 'acquis communautaire'. This process has sped up the integration of their financial markets with EU-15 markets, mainly through establishment and shareholdings.
- All of the financial sectors in the new member states have an enormous growth and development potential. Whether and to what extent this potential will be realized by the different financial sectors in the individual countries will largely depend on their growth performance and on policy choices.
- Although the enhanced level of integration has opened up new possibilities, it also raises some concerns in terms of financial stability and supervision.

NOTES

1. Irmfried Schwimann is Head of the Financial Services Policy unit in DG Internal Market and Services of the European Commission. Kristin Vandenbergen is an economist in the same unit, and *inter alia* responsible for the Commission's work in tracking financial integration in the European Union. More in-depth information – also on this subject – can be found in the Commission's annual publication 'Financial Integration Monitor' (http://europa.eu.int/comm/internal_market/finances/fim/index_en.htm).
2. Hungary, Czech Republic, Slovakia and Poland.
3. Czech Republic, Hungary, Poland, Slovenia, Slovakia.
4. Estonia, Latvia, Lithuania.
5. 139 subsidiaries compared to only 23 branches.
6. Regular updates (each fortnight) are published of the Commission website: http://europa.eu.int/comm/internal_market/finances/actionplan/index_en.htm#transposition.
7. European regulatory and supervisory process via a four-level approach: (1) framework legislation adopted in co-decision (between Council and European Parliament) at 'Level 1', concentrating on the core political principles; (2) 'Level 2' implementing measures to fill in the details of 'Level 1' legislation subject to precise constraints fixed in that legislation; (3) day-to-day cooperation by national supervisors and regulators to ensure consistent implementation and enforcement; and (4) more effective enforcement of Community law.
8. CESR – Committee of European Securities Regulators; CEBS – Committee of European Banking Supervisors; CEIOPS – Committee of European Insurance and Occupational Pensions Supervisors.
9. P. Lenain, Economic Counsellor at the OECD. Presentation at the IEA conference in Prague, 29–30 November 2004.

6. CEEC financial sector issues and macroeconomic policy: a perspective from across countries

Cristian Popa

The motivation behind this chapter is to represent the perspective of economies in the region by providing a series of considerations that are valid for more than one specific country experience. This contribution is informed by research conducted in the CEEC national central banks, the BIS, and elsewhere. Furthermore, I found important in this context the discussions at the joint IMF–National Bank of Romania conference that we organized in Sinaia, Romania, in October 2005, on 'Rapid Growth of Banking Sector Credit to the Private Sector'.

Second, on a lighter note, an emotional interpretation of the well-known finding that central bankers should optimally be more inflation-averse compared to social preferences leads naturally to the conclusion that they are also prone to worry more about risks to attaining their objective, which is another way of saying that worrying more about a wide variety of prospective events is implicitly a part of central bankers' job descriptions. Given the importance of transparency and accountability in securing central bank credibility, I intend to perform this constructive worrying in a public setting. I will comment on common aspects between Central and East European countries (CEECs), the dimensions of the appropriate policy response (including, but not limited to, the monetary policy one) and challenges to the financial sector development perspective.

CEEC FINANCIAL SECTOR SALIENT FEATURES

What exactly are the salient features? First, countries in Central and Eastern Europe have relatively small financial sectors in terms of size and depth, compared to their EU-15 counterparts, or indeed to other industrialized economies (see Figures 6.1 to 6.4).

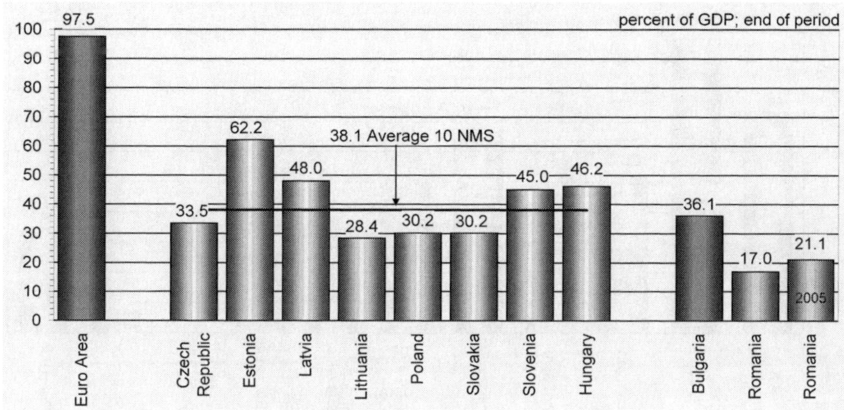

Note: 1. Non-government credit/GDP.

Source: EUROSTAT; for Romania: National Bank of Romania, National Institute of Statistics.

Figure 6.1 *Financial intermediation*[1]*, 2004*

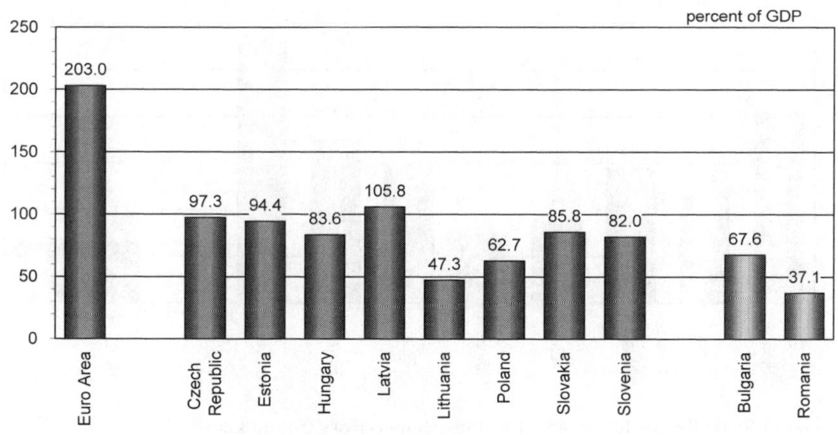

Source: Websites of central banks and EUROSTAT.

Figure 6. 2 *Bank assets, 2004*

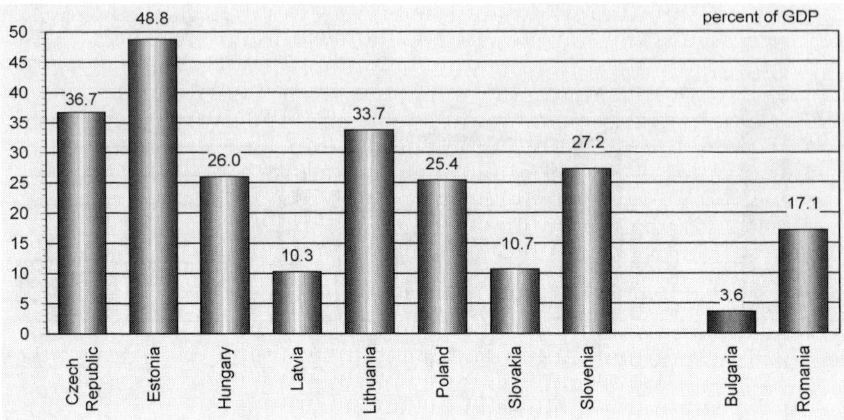

Source: EUROSTAT, NIS, BSE, RASDAQ.

Figure 6.3 Stock market capitalization, 2004

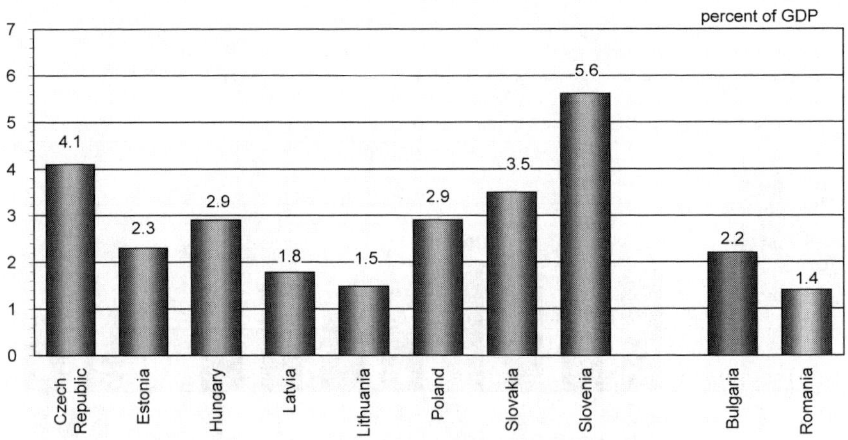

Source: Swiss Re; for Romania – Insurance Supervisory Commission.

Figure 6.4 Insurance premiums, 2004

Importantly, a relatively rapid growth of financial intermediation is also pervasive across these economies, and has been persistent over time. In part, the relatively rapid growth in intermediation (with credit growth first and foremost) arises from a base effect, given the already mentioned low starting point of economies in the region. Catching up, in the context of recent or prospective EU membership, is another powerful explanatory factor, especially for persistence, and will be considered further.

However, persuasive explanations of trajectories – ones that are rich in inference potential – seldom lie in simply describing departure and arrival coordinates. Rapid financial intermediation dynamics are an effect of the internalization over time by market players of still existing efficiency gains and niches, as well as of the opening up of entire markets – the relatively recent development of retail and mortgage lending in several of these countries comes to mind as a case in point.

In and of itself, this first characteristic of CEE economies leads to two interesting observations regarding private sector demand for financial intermediation. On the corporate side, leverage is typically lower than is the case in many more advanced economies, while recourse to domestic capital markets is also trailing behind. Therefore, besides the importance of retained earnings, direct access to foreign financing becomes an aspect to watch through the sensitive prism of private external debt, especially its short-term component.

On the household side, increasing incomes – especially important as an expectation related to improved economy-wide prospects and real convergence in the light of EU accession – also translate into larger credit demand. However, household acumen in managing substantial levels of personal indebtedness over the longer term (and I refer here especially to business cycle phases, given the strong pro-cyclicality of lending) arises also with experience and tends not to be proportional with the prospective debt levels that may be incurred over more limited spans of time. In this perspective, prolonged periods of high economic growth provide opportunities for both benefits and risks, given that, with the rapid growth of intermediation, household lending is rising the fastest, in some cases also accompanied by credit in foreign exchange.

The need for vigilance on both the macroeconomic and financial stability fronts does not derive from just the two aspects mentioned above. Another underpinning which tends to give short shrift to the benign neglect attitude possibly induced by viewing catching-up as a relatively risk-free process is the fact that many, if not all of the Central East European countries have had a history of serious difficulties in the evolution of their financial sectors, ranging from full-out crises to more moderate but still costly clean-ups. This calls for a more careful oversight and policy response connected to the development of the financial sector.

Second, all these countries – not only the new member states, but rather accession candidates and South-Eastern Europe as well – are small, open economies, which means that the importance of capital mobility, and the fact that we are part of the globalized environment is not to be neglected. There is a substantial role, indeed a dominant one of foreign private capital, because privatizations have been essentially carried out with participants outside of these economies, while many of the new greenfield financial institutions are also foreign-owned. This is important not only in the sense of an improvement in corporate governance coming through competition and increased diversification of financial products and services, but also because foreign financing is an important source of credit growth in these economies, given low domestic savings and relatively high – and, again, persistent – current account deficits.

An additional dimension related to the dominance of foreign ownership is the polarization of financial sectors, most visible in banking. The large vs. small divide (which often also reflects foreign vs. domestic ownership) is an expression of sometimes substantial concentration, which could reinforce the strength of a lending channel and therefore differently affect smaller firms compared to larger ones (Popa, 1998). However, segmentation is much less obvious when seen through the perspective of competition for the new frontier of retail banking and lending to households.

Moreover, competition in concentrated financial sectors with a substantial foreign capital presence must be viewed through the twin lens of market share and regional perspective. For the larger international financial players, competition is not carried out solely in terms of an individual CEE economy, but rather in terms of a broader regional perspective in which the competition for market share goes across countries. An important conclusion is that, while competition obviously delivers the goods in terms of governance, there is a recognizable lack of obvious stable niches for domestic players, which should be an element of preoccupation for regulators and supervisors in all of these countries, given the further concentration that should be expected to take place in analogy with current trends in the euro area and elsewhere.

Third, I would contend that important asymmetries also persist between financial sector components, given that the banking sector component is much more developed compared to securities markets or insurance markets, reflecting a certain preference – consistent with the continental model – in terms of credit finance compared to issuance of debt instruments, and of course to a certain preference for banks, as opposed to other non-bank financial intermediaries. Other asymmetries reflect the fact that longer-term credit (given the history of financial clean-ups and the persistence of high and even moderate inflation for an important number of years in these countries) has been late in arriving in a relative sense.

Finally but crucially, many of these countries still have some degree of dollarization or euroization, sometimes a substantial one. With convergence also leading to long-term appreciation of domestic currencies vis-à-vis the euro, and therefore to increases in the euro-value of both domestic-denominated assets and income streams, wealth and balance sheet effects not visible prior to the emergence of the appreciation trend may give rise to prudential problems related to banking sector asset-liability mismatches. These are not solely in terms of maturity, but in what concerns currency denomination as well (it is important to note that low levels of domestic savings and incompletely developed capital markets both reinforce the lack of longer-term resources for credit multiplication, which means foreign currency credit lines step in to fill the gap). Central bank preoccupation with this problem and its proactive tackling in some of the region's economies – including in Romania – is also coupled with the fact that even foreign players have displayed a fairly short horizon of risk perception in the approach to domestic markets, a feature not unconnected with market share prevalence in their objective functions. Also, since the central bank has a clearly specified financial stability objective, its preoccupation with issues of a systemic nature lends it an institutional perception that is inherently broader and perhaps also more risk-sensitive than that of individual financial market players.

Moreover, the monetary policy decision-making perspective mentioned at the beginning of this chapter makes it necessary to point to an added complication: in significantly euroized economies, the effectiveness of domestic interest rate signals is additionally reduced compared to the complications already posed by low levels of credit to GDP. This may even lead to perverse increases in the total volume of credit outstanding through increases in foreign exchange borrowing when aggregate demand management is approached solely through interest rate increases.

Fourth, efficiency gains and niches have been incompletely exploited as yet. In this respect, high transaction costs have been mentioned, but I would also like to point out the fact that spreads are generally higher in domestic currency banking products than in their euro market equivalents and that there is limited diversification not only of products and services, but also – and perhaps more importantly – of risks, given the still significantly constrained depth and liquidity of domestic markets. This is certainly related to the persistence of some degree of domestic market segmentation and is expected to decline over time but, in so far as it is a source of high profitability for credit institutions, risks also arise in terms of the differential transmission of domestic interest rate signals, which, in a context of spread stickiness in the short run, tend to affect deposit rates first and on the downside, before transmission reaches lending rates in the traditional manner. However, an important effect of several characteristics analysed above is the fact that newly established, smaller businesses have relatively more difficulty in accessing credit in economies where constrained risk diversification implies heavier reliance on credit histories and collateral (a stylized fact consistent with the lending channel alluded to previously).

Summing up, there are positives and risky aspects, best viewed in balance from the premises of a guarded (and pragmatic) optimism concerning the direction of future developments: characteristics such as the ones described are not necessarily new. We have seen this happening in many emerging markets reaching a certain stage of maturity, but I believe the difficulties encountered in the past in Latin America and East Asia have to be kept in mind and their lessons well and proactively heeded in terms of prevention, despite the many dissimilarities which separate CEECs from these other two groups of economies.

The good news is that there is a pole of attraction lacking in other cases: this is the prospect of EU membership or that of securing a somewhat analogous arrangement via stability and assistance agreements. Many of these economies, directly or indirectly, are looking forward to EU membership and eventual economic and monetary union integration as an end point, and therefore through regulatory convergence, the transposition of the acquis, moral suasion in a broad sense and the policy anchor of integration, the likelihood of appropriate policy adoption is higher than in cases elsewhere lacking this kind of anchor. This is due to reduced costs of model search and the heightened costs of eventual policy mistakes which may affect the accession perspective or interfere with the obligations incurred by EU membership. Generally, the quality of financial system regulation and oversight, as well as statistical disclosure is higher than was the case in the Latin American or Asian experiences at the time (standards of disclosure themselves were improved internationally as an outcome of these experiences).

THE APPROPRIATE POLICY RESPONSE

What about the appropriate policy response? What does one need to do? Well obviously intermediation is jogging along nicely. What I think policymakers as a whole need to do is to manage the very alert, very effervescent dynamics of intermediation with a view to maintaining the main macroeconomic equilibria, given of course the very high pro-cyclicality of credit development related to the business cycle. It is therefore a question not of direction, but of the safest and fastest speed in converging to that desired (and inevitable) destination, and whether that speed is attainable. How is this done? The first realization concerns the existence of limits to the use of traditional monetary and exchange rate policy instruments, owing to the presence of euroization, the stickiness of higher domestic interest rate spreads and, importantly, because many central banks in these economies are net debtors rather than net creditors, and that additionally challenges the transmission mechanism for interest rate signals. The perverse secondary effects of higher policy rates and exchange rate appreciation – both indispensable instruments in economies confronted with the need to converge to or maintain price stability in the face of a multitude of potential adverse shocks – have been mentioned previously, but I will only underline here the fact that regular assessments and stress testing of the financial system are extremely important.

Interestingly, compared to the usual bipolar approach and as already mentioned above, I see complementarities between price stability and financial stability objectives. These take the form of complementing the use of traditional monetary policy instruments with prudential and administrative measures, even if an awareness of their limited effectiveness exists *ex ante*, and keeping firmly in mind that – from the monetary policy-making perspective – the wide-scale employment of administrative measures as a substitute for monetary policy instruments is second best in the most optimistic case. The stated complementarity of objectives and of policy and prudential instruments must also be perceived realistically, which implies a certain degree of humility together with an awareness of potential risks. The important message is that there are limits to what may be achieved through traditional monetary and exchange rate policy instruments, especially *ex post* in a structurally distorted setting involving the financial sector, and there is only so much that a central bank can do even adding to that the prudential and supervisory component.

What must be achieved is to ensure that there is no large desynchronization between financial sector developments and fundamental trends taking shape in the real sector; additionally, monetary policy and measures aimed at safeguarding financial stability should act in the context of a consistent macroeconomic policy mix, which implies coherent action also through fiscal and wage policies and efforts directed at structural reform. Let me point out one simple but chilling reason for that: many of the crisis situations we have seen in the past in these countries basically arose from the fact that financial sectors were victim to incompletely hard budget constraints and an inappropriate policy response to problems in the real sector, which flowed over into the other sectors. Indeed – and the

Romanian case up to 1998–99 is testimony to this – the existence of heavy banking sector exposures towards inefficient state-owned firms led to a situation of bank captivity and moral hazard, eliminated only by a combined approach to regulatory and supervisory overhaul, financial sector liquidations and cleaning-up, as well as improvements in real sector corporate governance, including through privatization (this is why credit to majority state-owned companies has stagnated in nominal terms since 1999). Although at present the risk of such a situation re-emerging is nil, other, second generation risks exist – the analysed dual asset–liability mismatch is one of them – and should appropriately be taken into account in policy design and implementation.

FURTHER CHALLENGES IN FINANCIAL SECTOR DEVELOPMENT

What are the next challenges in the financial sector and in financial sector development? I did mention the fact that you can have perverse effects; you can also have a negative impact by slowing down credit too much compared to what is necessary in the real convergence process, and obviously that calls for an element of caution in the policy approach. The effectiveness of market-based policy instruments is dependent upon deeper financial integration and increasing sophistication of the financial sector, so you obviously need to let the process have a momentum of its own. This then becomes recursive to some extent; with higher dynamics in many of the countries under scrutiny, this is certainly bound to create a degree of discomfort in the decision-making of a central bank.

I have also mentioned the fact that administrative measures were second best in the most optimistic of cases, when contemplated to be employed in isolation. This is because in the case of almost completely open economies – and the departure point, that of small open economies, is a strong factor in this case, together with the direction of further opening up the capital account, including in light of accession – capital mobility allows banks to circumvent these measures, including by direct borrowing abroad or by resorting to non-bank financial intermediaries. In other words, what these measures do is buy you time. By themselves, they do not solve the problem, but they can help you get a better grip on the process; moreover, their effectiveness is enhanced when paired complementarily with appropriate interest rate and exchange rate settings pertaining to a necessarily prudent monetary policy stance over longer time horizons. Finally, in terms of the development of financial markets across the region's economies, I believe there is a need for diversification versus that of organic and possibly slower development of capital markets and insurance components to let those elements provide a greater freedom of choice for market players and better stability across the financial system as such.

REFERENCE

Popa, Cristian (1998), 'Nominal-real tradeoffs and the effects of monetary policy: The Romanian experience', working paper no. 244, William Davidson Institute, University of Michigan School of Business Administration, Ann Arbor, MI, December.

7. The financial system of the EU-25

Franklin Allen, Laura Bartiloro and Oskar Kowalewski[1]

1. INTRODUCTION

Despite the political and economic convergence in the European Union (EU-25), the financial structures of different members remain diverse. This chapter compares the development of EU-25 countries' financial structures from 1995–2004. We stress that the enlargement of the EU in May 2004, by changing the institutional setting, has reduced some divergences across Europe, but increased others. However, it has not significantly altered the structure of the European financial system. There is significant inertia with regard to financial structure: important and persistent transformations of financial systems can take more than a decade. At the same time, convergence in the financial systems of EU-25 countries is important, in particular for the future prospects of an eventual enlargement of the European monetary union because a common monetary policy may be hard to implement when the financial structures of member states are diverse.

We start our analysis in section 2, by outlining the economic background of the enlarged European Union (EU-25) and the main characteristics of its financial system. In section 3 we describe the banking system, while in section 4 we focus on the development of capital markets. In section 5 we present other important players in the financial system, such as the insurance industry and pension and investment funds. Finally, section 6 concludes by summarizing and making a comparison of the EU-25 financial system with that in the US and Japan.

2. THE BACKGROUND

The new EU member states (NMS), except Cyprus and Malta, have been engaged in a transition process involving institutional and structural changes that have turned former planned economies into market economies. The main economic indicators still show that significant differences exist between NMS and old member states (OMS). The level of financial development, understood as the size and efficiency of the sector, may strongly affect the pace of future economic growth.[2]

In terms of GDP the NMS are rather small compared to the OMS. At the end of 2004 the GDP at current exchange rates of the NMS was EUR 441 billion or only 5 per cent of the value of that of OMS countries with EUR 9307 billion in 2004 (Figure 7.1).

The average growth rate has been higher in the NMS than in the OMS over the years 1995–2004. As a result the NMS have made substantial progress catching up in real terms, reaching 54 per cent of the EU-25 average purchasing power per capita income in 2004. An exception is the Czech Republic, which had the lowest growth rate among the NMS. The country underwent a severe financial crisis caused by bad loan problems in 1996 (Bonin and Wachtel, 2004). The case of the Czech Republic, however, confirms the theoretical prediction that countries' economic growth and financial system development are closely linked. Thus, we believe that the financial system development of the EU-25 is essential for economic growth and for further convergence of the market structures within the EU-25.

The structure of the European financial system has changed significantly in the last few years. This change can mainly be attributed to the liberalization of international capital movements in order to create a common regulatory framework for the provision of financial services as part of the European Internal Market.

In comparison with the NMS, the OMS have a relatively deep and broad financial services industry, with total assets amounting to 558 per cent of GDP in 2002, while in the NMS it was only 170 per cent (Figure 7.2).

Credit institutions lead the EU-25 financial system, with a relative share in total assets of 52 per cent in the OMS and 73 per cent in the NMS. Apparently, the EU-25 financial structure is mainly bank-based, yet in some member states capital markets are also quite important. In the OMS other financial intermediaries have been gaining in importance in the last decade, but their position compared to credit institutions is still relatively small in terms of assets to GDP. Although the dominance of credit institutions has been declining in the NMS too, the role of insurance companies, investment funds and pension funds is still underdeveloped in comparison to the OMS. Therefore, credit institutions followed by capital markets are the main elements of the European financial system. Hence, in the next two sections we will focus on the banking system and the capital markets in the EU-25.

Within the EU-25 national differences in financial structures are significant. In the OMS, the domestic credit to GDP ratio stood at 120 per cent

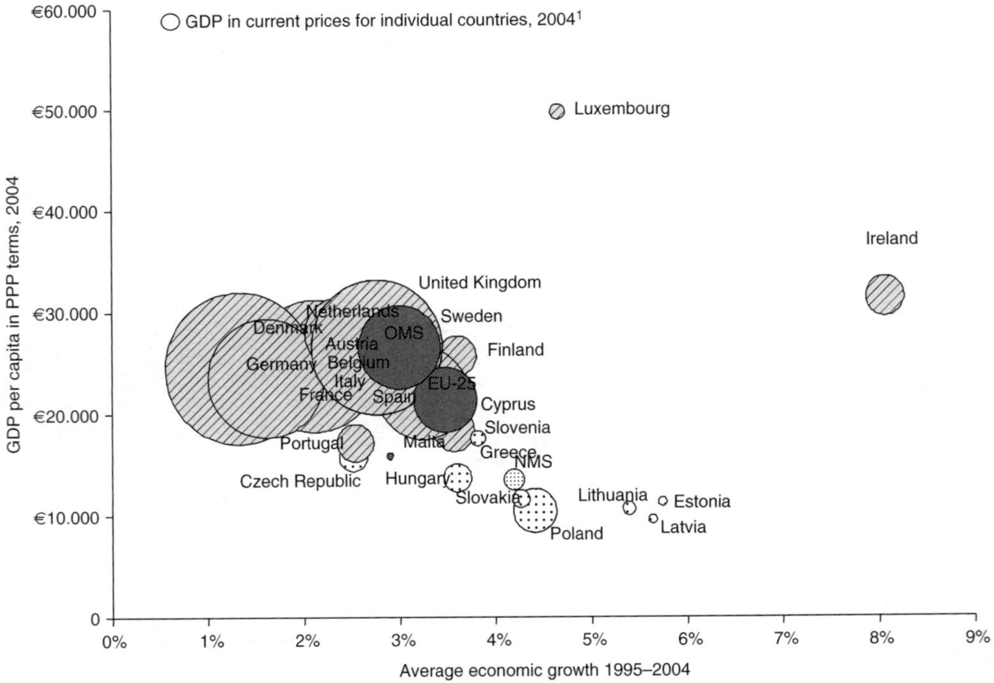

Note: 1. GDP in current prices for OMS, NMS and EU-25 is the average per country.

Source: Eurostat, ECB (2005).

Figure 7.1 Comparison of economic strength and growth

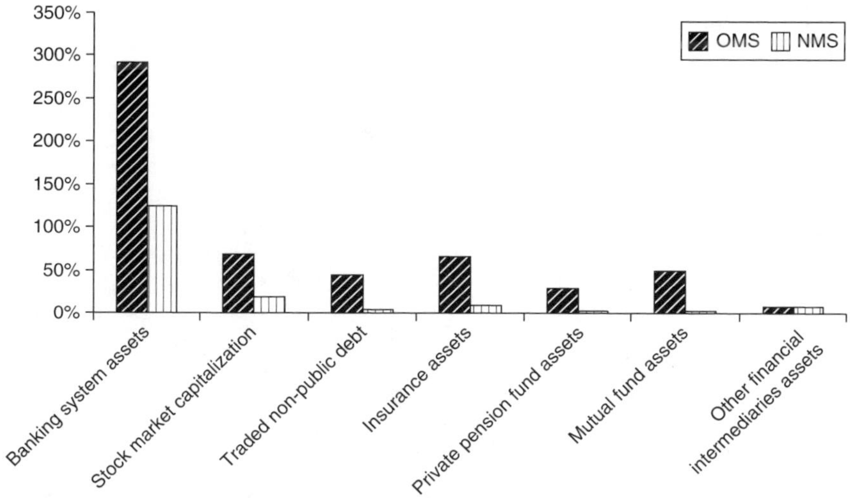

Source: ECB (2003), Eurostat, OECD, national central banks.

Figure 7.2 Assets of financial intermediaries as a percentage of GDP in 2002

in 2004, compared to a stock market capitalization to GDP ratio of around 91 per cent (Figure 7.3). NMS have significantly smaller credit to GDP and stock market capitalization ratios. Bank-based financial structures remain predominant within the EU-25, the exceptions being the United Kingdom and since recently Finland, Sweden and the Netherlands, which have moved towards market-based financial systems.

Rajan and Zingales (2003) analysed European financial system characteristics over the last two decades. Based on their findings they came to the conclusion that in the last two decades the EU-25 financial system moved away from a bank-based towards a market-based financial system. They identified the process of monetary and financial integration as the underlying cause of these changes. Rajan and Zingales (2003) argue therefore that the ongoing process will likely result in the evolution of a more market-based system over time.

Differences in financial structure are often related to divergences in countries' respective legal systems (La Porta et al., 1998). According to this theoretical prediction, a high degree of investor protection should help the development of stock markets. Conversely, a high degree of creditors' rights protection should encourage bank lending.

In the NMS improvements in the domestic legal system in the 1990s have reduced credit risk, thereby promoting credit supply since then. Apart from

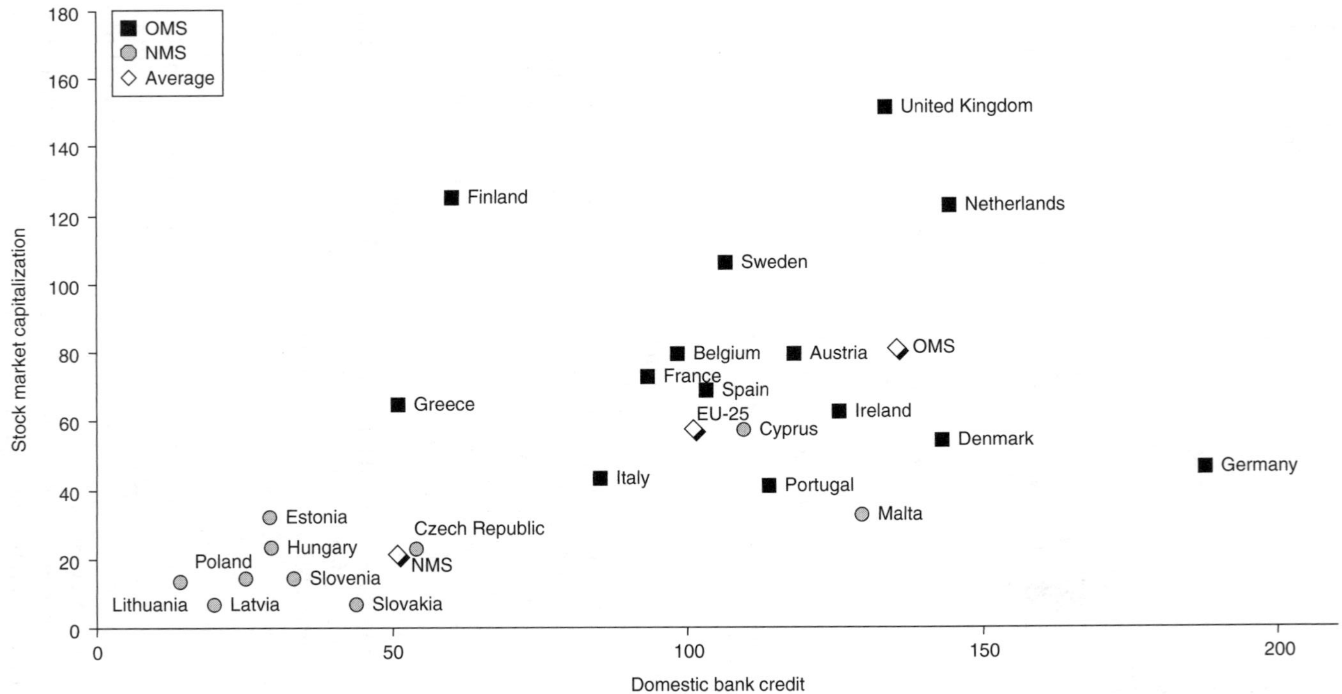

Source: ECB (2005), national central banks, World Development Indicators (WDI) and national stock exchanges.

Figure 7.3 Bank sector vs. stock market (as percentage of GDP), average 1995–2004 this, in the EU-25 the index of creditors' rights and anti-director rights protection seems not to be positively related to bank credit and market capitalization, respectively (Figure 7.4).

This situation may be explained by a weak and costly enforcement of the existing laws in some of the member states, especially in the NMS. In the OMS it takes 221 days on average to enforce a contract, while on average 305 days are needed in the NMS. Additionally the average cost of enforcing a contract as a percentage of GNI per capita is 4.45 per cent in the OMS against 5.42 per cent in NMS (Allen et al., 2005). Those numbers disclose that even as NMS have introduced high quality legal protection, they may not influence financial system development, as their enforcement remains weak and costly.

Law enforcement may play an even greater role in the future as further financial integration may result in a convergence of the legal protection of shareholders and creditors within the EU-25. The past experience shows that harmonization, integration and enforcement of the regulations affecting the financial services industry may take a long time. Therefore differences in legal protection and as a consequence in financial structures may prevail for some time in the EU-25, yet we may expect a further integration of laws and financial structures in the long run.

3. THE BANKING SYSTEM

As already shown, the financial system of the EU-25 is mainly bank-based, due to the prominent role of credit institutions (CI) in most member states. In terms of GDP, bank assets in the OMS reached 219 per cent in 2004, an increase of 17 per cent compared with 1995 (Table 7.1).

Changes in NMS bank assets were more significant and the ratio reached 85 per cent in 2004, an increase of 27 per cent since 1995. The difference in the ratio between the OMS and NMS shows a potential for development and explains the large amount of foreign bank entry in the NMS (Dermine, 2005). Data show also that credit and deposits to GDP have more than doubled over the last decade in many EU-25 countries. This means that EU-25 credit institutions were able to retain their position relative to other financial intermediaries despite the fierce competition; they even increased their importance in most economies. Only in the Czech Republic and Slovakia did the role of credit not increase; this was caused by the protracted restructuring of bad loans accumulated earlier.

Credit institutions responded to the structural changes in the financial sector and increased competition by consolidating their activities in order to

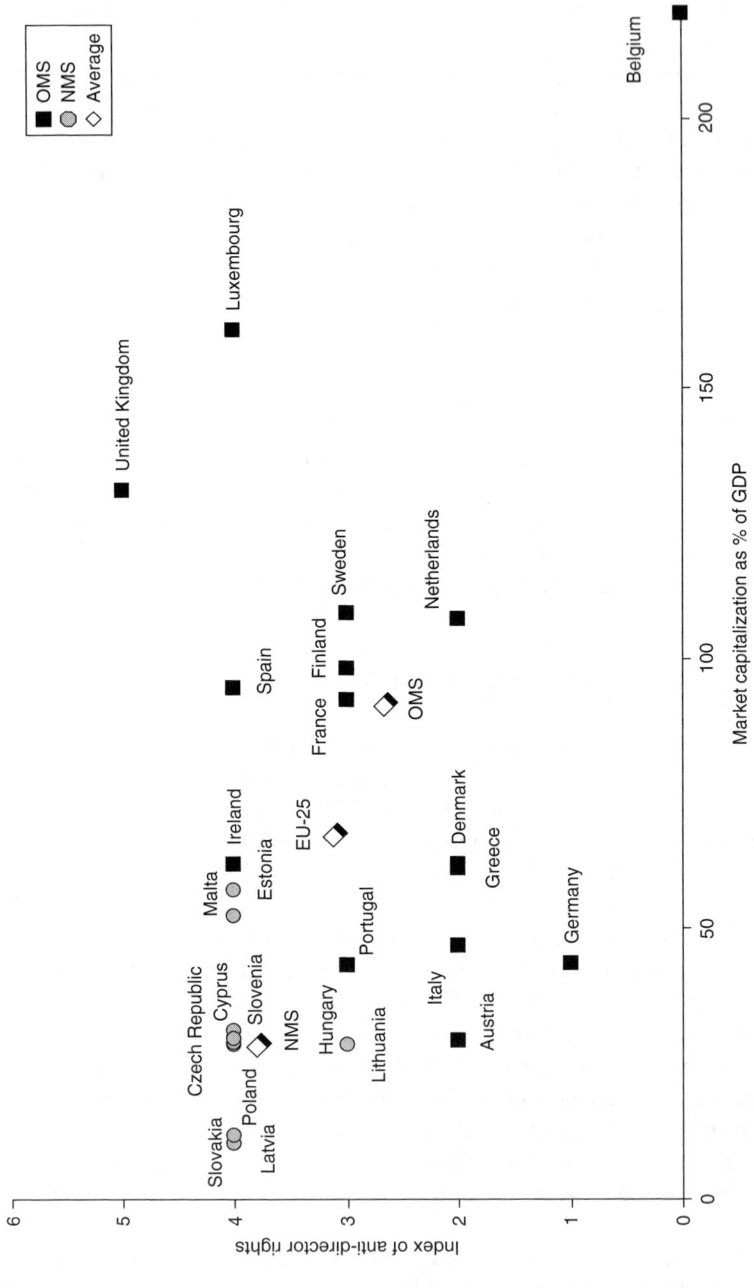

OMS
NMS
Average
Index of anti-director rights
Market capitalization as % of GDP
0
1
2
3
4
5
6
0
50
100
150
200
United Kingdom
Luxembourg
Belgium
Sweden
Netherlands
Finland
Spain
France
OMS
Ireland
EU-25
Denmark
Estonia
Malta
Greece
Germany
Portugal
Czech Republic
Cyprus
Slovenia
NMS
Hungary
Italy
Austria
Lithuania
Slovakia
Poland
Latvia

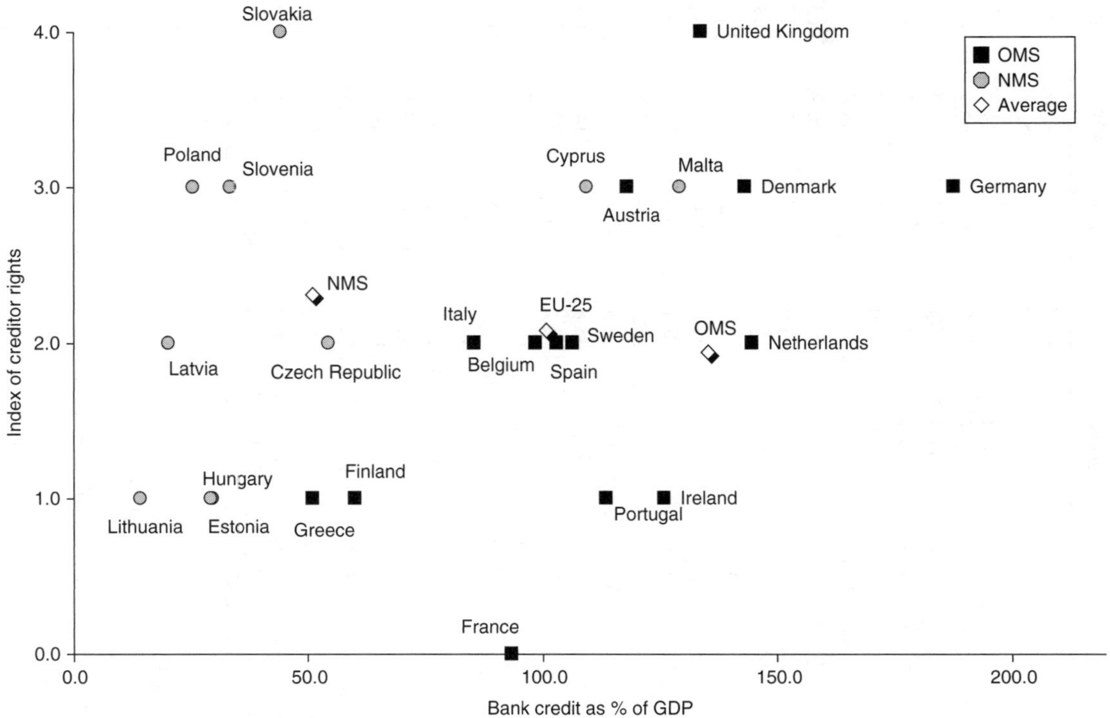

Source: ECB (2005), La Porta et al. (1998) and companies laws or commercial codes.

Figure 7.4 Legal determinants of financial activity in the EU-25

Table 7.1 Total assets, credits and deposits of CI as percentage of GDP

	Total assets		Total credits		Total deposits	
	1995	2004	1995	2004	1995	2004
Austria	213.3	268.0	94.0	125.1	85.0	97.9
Belgium	291.2	322.3	74.7	107.2	74.6	142.8
Cyprus	85.9	305.9	80.2	141.1	86.7	126.8
Czech Republic	132.1	99.7	70.7	38.7	62.2	69.2
Denmark	118.0	309.3	n/a	164.4	53.7	62.2
Estonia	35.9	94.4	14.0	65.4	16.3	45.8
Finland	117.0	141.9	66.0	69.4	54.2	53.2
France	173.1	267.9	101.9	92.9	65.8	77.0
Germany	205.0	29.7	n/a	135.8	62.4	113.3
Greece	98.0	137.9	33.6	76.4	57.1	95.6
Hungary	36.1	80.1	22.5	48.3	40.2	44.4
Ireland	129.4	486.4	70.3	176.2	65.9	122.7
Italy	139.0	168.4	95.6	88.0	57.3	58.0
Latvia	31.0	101.3	7.1	56.5	16.6	65.7
Lithuania	27.9	47.5	14.3	30.4	14.3	30.1
Luxembourg	2876.0	2708.5	n/a	467.3	n/a	859.4
Malta	177.9	476.8	95.8	200.1	114.5	204.9
Netherlands	216.0	343.3	112.5	174.1	77.9	122.4
Poland	48.8	67.6	17.3	34.8	25.7	45.6
Portugal	158.0	242.5	70.5	136.8	76.1	102.2
Slovakia	76.0	87.7	36.7	36.3	54.9	21.7
Slovenia	61.1	93.6	25.7	47.3	31.7	56.7
Spain	159.0	205.0	102.3	120.6	73.6	104.4
Sweden	152.0	208.9	114.1	114.5	40.4	51.2
United Kingdom	239.0	406.4	122.3	142.2	72.4	117.6
EU-25 average[1]	181.7	215.1	71.6	114.5	63.4	94.3
OMS average[1]	187.6	219.1	76.5	119.9	65.8	96.9
NMS average[1]	66.6	84.7	31.8	41.9	38.4	50.6

Notes:
n/a = not available.
1. GDP in PPP terms weighted averages.

Source: ECB (2002, 2005), national central banks and Eurostat.

grow in size and scope. This affected all types of credit institutions, including cooperative banks and mutual savings banks (Goddard et al., 2001). The average number of credit institutions fell from 504 in 1997 to 334 in 2004, a decrease of 34 per cent compared with 1997 (Table 7.2).

Table 7.2 Structure of the banking sector

	Number of CI		Asset share of foreign CI		CR-5		HHI	
	1997	2004	1997	2004	1997	2004	1997	2004
Austria	995	796	3.4	19.4	48.3	43.8	515	552
Belgium	131	104	30.4	23.2	54.0	84.3	669	2100
Cyprus	n/a	14	10.2	30.1	91.6	69.4	2747	1365
Czech Republic	50	74	24.0	91.8	67.0	64.0	2533	1103
Denmark	213	202	4.5	16.2	70.0	67.0	1431	1146
Estonia	12	9	29.0	98.0	83.0	98.6	4312	3887
Finland	348	363	8.4	59.5	88.0	82.7	2150	2680
France	1258	897	10.4	11.4	40.0	44.7	449	623
Germany	3420	2148	4.3	6.3	17.0	22.1	114	178
Greece	55	62	15.8	24.8	56.0	65.0	885	1069
Hungary	286	217	53.0	77.0	53.0	52.7	2101	795
Ireland	71	80	24.8	45.4	41.0	43.9	500	556
Italy	935	787	7.0	7.7	31.0	26.0	201	230
Latvia	37	23	55.0	57.8	51.0	62.4	1450	1021
Lithuania	37	74	41.0	93.0	84.0	78.9	2972	1854
Luxembourg	215	162	92.5	94.1	23.0	29.7	210	304
Malta	n/a	16	47.1	39.1	98.0	78.7	4411	2015
Netherlands	648	461	7.2	12.1	79.4	84.0	1654	1726
Poland	1378	653	15.3	67.6	46.2	50.2	859	692
Portugal	238	197	14.8	26.1	46.0	66.5	577	1093
Slovakia	29	21	30.0	97.0	63.0	66.5	2643	1154
Slovenia	34	24	5.0	38.0	62.0	64.1	2314	1425
Spain	416	346	12.5	11.5	45.0	41.9	285	482
Sweden	237	212	2.5	8.7	59.0	54.4	830	854
United Kingdom	557	413	52.2	51.3	24.0	34.5	208	376
EU-25 average[1]	504	334	20.3	29.2	33.3	44.8	389	670
OMS average[1]	640	482	15.8	19.0	33.0	44.6	370	662
NMS average[1]	233	113	23.0	70.4	61.3	60.3	2024	1087

Notes:
n/a = not available.
1. Credit institutions assets weighted averages.

Source: ECB (2002, 2005), national central banks and BankScope.

The decrease was mainly caused by a high level of mergers and acquisitions (M&A) within the EU. The large number of M&A transactions may also be a sign of convergence and integration of bank market structures of the EU-25 (Allen and Song, 2005). Within the EU-25, 438 transactions were reported involving at least one credit institution over the period 2001–2004, 68 per cent involved within border transactions, 26 per cent transactions within the European Economic Area (EEA),[3] and 6 per cent of deals were with countries outside the EEA. While in the OMS 76 per cent of transactions were domestic, in the NMS 62 per cent of deals were cross-border transactions. As a result there are significant cross-country differences in the foreign presence in the local banking sector within the EU-25.

On average 70 per cent of NMS total banking assets were controlled by foreign institutions in 2004, against only 19 per cent in the OMS. In addition foreign presence is notably high, over 90 per cent, in some of the NMS, while in some of the OMS it remains below 10 per cent of total assets.

Divergence in foreign ownership has a strong impact on the market structure in the EU. Davis and de Bandt (1999) provided evidence of monopolistic competition in a variety of European banking markets in the mid-1990s. They noted that the competitive environment in the French, German and Italian banking markets still lags behind that in the US banking sector. Data show that these markets have few outside competitors even more than a decade after the establishment of the European Economic and Monetary Union (EMU).

Significant M&A activity and a downward trend in the number of credit institutions have significantly increased the level of concentration in local markets. On average, the five largest institutions' share of total bank assets (CR-5) amounted to 45 per cent in the EU-25 in 2004, up from 33 per cent in 1997. In the OMS a similar trend is also visible from the Herfindahl-Hirschman Index (HHI), which rose from 370 in 1997 to 662 in 2004. In the NMS the HHI declined as a result of increased competition caused by foreign entry and a decrease of market share of former state-owned banks. In general, however, in NMS concentration remains high and the CR-5 ratio varies between 50 per cent and 99 per cent. Moreover in some member states the HHI coefficient also exceeds the 2000 point-high level concentration threshold.

An indication that the consolidation process and high concentration have not adversely affected competitive conditions in the EU-25 banking industry is the decline in net interest margins (NIM) (Table 7.3).

Concentration and margins are negatively related. In the NMS margins have significantly decreased despite a huge rise in concentration. In addition some of the countries with a high level of concentration have reported the lowest net interest margins within the EU-25. Apparently, concentration ratios do not necessarily reflect competitive conditions in the EU-25 banking sector.

The fall in interest margins was compensated for by a decrease in overhead costs of credit institutions. In the OMS the average overhead ratio was

Table 7.3 Indicators of banking sector performance

	NIM		Overhead costs		Cost/income		ROA	
	1997	2003	1997	2003	1997	2003	1997	2003
Austria	1.82	1.80	1.69	1.63	66.95	65.62	0.25	0.41
Belgium	1.74	1.40	1.29	1.33	66.08	67.72	0.65	0.45
Cyprus	2.24	2.51	2.13	2.29	63.37	67.39	0.75	−0.06
Czech Republic	3.61	2.54	2.66	2.52	53.37	61.48	0.44	1.28
Denmark	1.97	1.36	1.36	0.90	58.87	52.64	0.84	0.58
Estonia	6.14	4.03	3.92	2.80	53.12	52.86	3.64	2.17
Finland	3.62	1.92	1.99	2.09	57.15	59.06	1.50	1.00
France	1.62	1.15	1.73	1.47	72.01	67.37	0.31	0.40
Germany	2.31	1.86	1.67	1.44	62.48	65.93	0.30	0.18
Greece	2.5	3.51	2.63	2.59	64.66	59.89	0.71	0.94
Hungary	5.05	4.62	4.23	4.01	65.81	63.15	1.75	1.73
Ireland	2.27	1.29	1.91	0.85	60.14	51.83	0.92	0.68
Italy	2.87	2.99	2.68	2.46	73.73	69.59	0.36	0.75
Latvia	6.34	3.1	5.57	3.18	65.32	60.68	3.27	1.41
Lithuania	7.16	3.42	6.14	3.39	80.07	79.98	−0.22	1.27
Luxembourg	0.79	0.68	0.62	0.78	46.4	54.53	0.56	0.54
Malta	2.45	2.00	1.67	1.49	53.22	47.11	0.93	1.08
Netherlands	1.93	1.63	1.91	1.72	72.21	70.34	0.58	0.47
Poland	5.61	3.38	3.35	3.84	55.04	68.36	1.97	0.43
Portugal	2.79	2.23	2.22	1.79	59.88	61.06	1.05	0.79
Slovakia	2.63	3.58	3.52	3.28	79.08	70.73	−1.26	1.34
Slovenia	4.48	3.29	3.61	3.06	59.15	64.12	1.11	0.88
Spain	3.16	2.75	2.46	1.95	61.58	54.31	0.89	0.94
Sweden	1.48	1.54	0.93	0.94	50.56	49.48	0.48	0.65
United Kingdom	1.93	1.69	1.75	1.77	60.75	61.03	0.66	0.63
EU-25 average	3.14	2.41	2.55	2.14	62.44	61.85	0.90	0.84
OMS average	2.19	1.85	1.79	1.58	62.23	60.69	0.67	0.63
NMS average	4.57	3.25	3.68	2.99	62.76	63.59	1.24	1.15

Source: BankScope.

1.58 per cent in 2003 and had decreased by 13 per cent since 1997. The average ratio of overhead costs to total assets in the NMS was double that of the OMS, at 2.99 per cent in 2003, yet it had decreased already by 19 per cent since 1997. These differences suggest considerable scale inefficiencies and large potential for future improvement in the NMS banking industry.

The deterioration of interest margins and high overhead costs were responsible for the fact that the average cost-to-income ratio in the NMS, at 63.59 per cent, exceeded that of OMS. While in the NMS the average cost-to-income ratio slightly increased, in the OMS there has been an increase in efficiency. In the OMS the average cost-to-income ratio fell from 62.23 per cent in 1997 to 60.69 per cent in 2003.

The trends in income and costs are reflected in the data for profitability. However, the results for return on assets (ROA) present quite a mixed picture within the EU. The overall ROA in the EU-25 decreased moderately, to 0.84 per cent in 2003 from 0.90 per cent in 1997. On average there was, both in the OMS and NMS, a downward trend in profitability. Given that the level of return in NMS countries was quite high, the decline is understandable, while in the OMS the decrease may be related to the worsening of macroeconomic conditions. The downward trend in bank performance also reflects increased competition in the financial sector despite the overall fall in the number of credit institutions. However, the ratio shows a significant cross-country variability within the EU-25.

Concluding, even if the European financial system is mainly bank-based, there are significant cross-country differences, especially between the OMS and NMS. In the OMS the number of credit institutions is larger and thus the level of concentration is lower than in the NMS despite the continuing consolidation trend. In the last decade in the NMS most of the M&A transactions were cross-border, while in the OMS they were mainly domestic. As a consequence the level of foreign ownership in the NMS is significant, while in the OMS it remains moderately low. In general, foreign ownership had a positive impact on the risk management and performance of domestic credit institutions, as well as on the stability of the NMS financial systems.

Trends in the structure of the banking industry are reflected in the performance of credit institutions. While interest margins remained higher in the NMS over the period 1997–2003, the overhead costs were significantly lower in the OMS. Trends in performance of credit institutions suggest that the structural changes described above have not dampened competition. Differences in the credit institutions' performance reflect the persisting potential for development in the NMS, which has attracted foreign banks in the past. However, in the long term foreign banks' expectations about local bank profitability may be too high, which could induce them to compete aggressively on the local market (Dermine, 2005). Besides, a shift from subsidiaries into branches may present quite a challenge for local and host supervisors. A foreign branch may have systemic importance in the host country even though it often represents only a modest share of a foreign credit institution's total operations. As a consequence potential conflicts may emerge as far as country controls in supervision and responsibility in safeguarding financial stability are concerned. While we expect a convergence in performance and later on also of the structures of the EU-25 banking industry, we stress that enhanced coordination, regulation and information-sharing within the integrated financial system are needed in order to prevent eventual cross-border spillovers due to bank failures.

4. THE CAPITAL MARKETS

In transition economies the privatization of former state-owned companies has induced the development of equity markets: that is how the first stock exchanges appeared in the Czech Republic, Slovakia and Poland in 1991. The further development of stock markets was strongly influenced by the privatization strategies of the government in individual countries. A strategy of mass privatization schemes was employed in the Czech Republic, Slovakia and Lithuania. In these countries the stock markets quickly comprised a large number of companies. However, the extent of the equity markets restrained their liquidity. In addition the widespread ownership limited transparency and the enforcement of corporate governance mechanisms. Thus, few companies were traded and most companies were later delisted. As an example, in the Czech Republic 81 per cent of companies were delisted between 1995 and 1997, and the number of listed companies declined from 1716 in 1995 to 55 in 2004.

A different approach to privatization and stock market development was adopted in Estonia, Hungary, Latvia, Poland and Slovenia. In these countries the government decided to privatize only financially sound and recognized companies via the stock market. In addition minority stakes in the privatized companies were often sold prior to the initial public offering to a foreign strategic investor. This provided additional security for the government for the success for the planned public offer and also guaranteed a higher price for the remaining shares. As a result, the equity markets in those countries have been growing gradually and provided adequate liquidity for the listed companies. In Poland, in contrast to the Czech Republic, the number of listed companies grew steadily from 9 at the end of 1991 to 250 in 2004. However, many of those companies are currently closely held by strategic investors and therefore their equity is not always liquid. Thus, even if some market development has emerged, stock exchanges are still not very developed in Central and Eastern European countries. In fact, when we look at the average size of the stock exchange in NMS it amounts to a third of that of OMS.

Market size is rather homogeneous in NMS: the market is not very large in these countries (Figure 7.5). The evidence for OMS is more scattered, taking into account the different historical developments of all countries concerned. In those countries with a less developed stock market the ratio

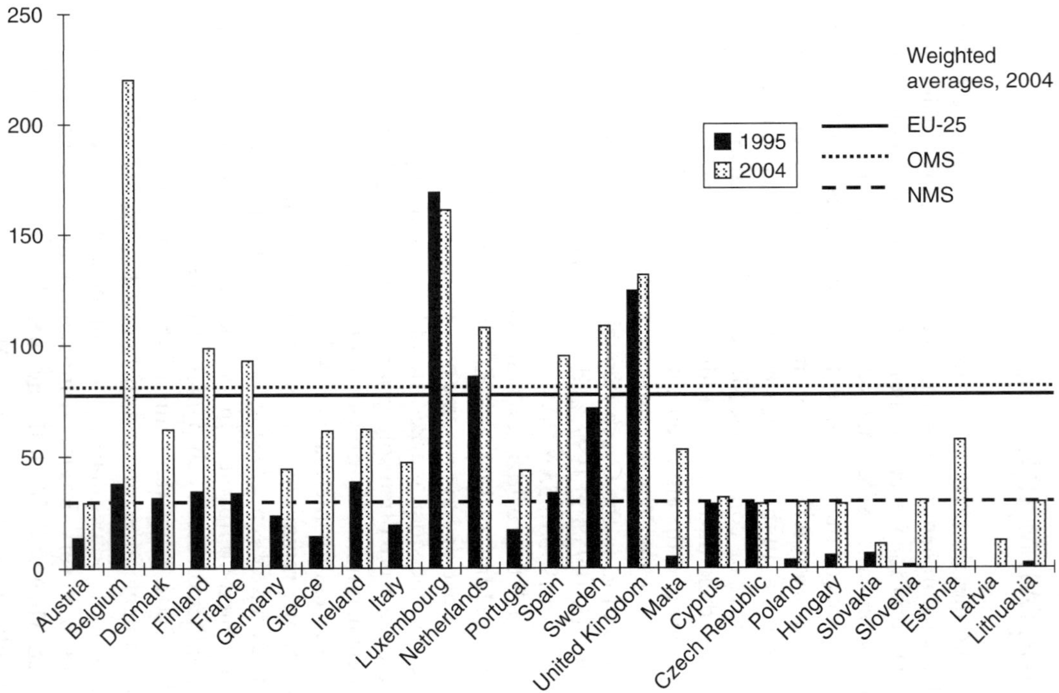

Note: 1. GDP in PPP terms weighted averages.

Source: World Development Indicators (WDI), World Federation of Stock Exchanges, national stock exchanges.

Figure 7.5 Domestic stock market capitalization as percentage of GDP[1] of market capitalization to GDP has risen a lot in the last decade. This is particularly true for NMS. For Finland it is due to the market capitalization of Nokia, which had astonishingly high values in the period 1999–2001. Now that Nokia's share values have declined to a more customary level, Finnish stock market capitalization is still high, but in line with the relatively largest European stock exchanges. The same pattern has been observed for Cyprus over the same period (1999–2001).

Considering the last decade as a whole, the largest European stock exchange markets are in Luxembourg, the United Kingdom, the Netherlands, Finland and Sweden. The London Stock Exchange is in absolute terms the largest in Europe; the Amsterdam stock exchange is large both in absolute and relative terms. The Luxembourg stock exchange, by contrast, while not very large in absolute values, is the largest in Europe when compared to GDP. The Wiener Börse is particularly small and this is probably due to the centrality of banks in the Austrian financial system. Among the new accession countries only Cyprus and the Czech Republic seem to have a market size comparable to previous EU-25 members when looking at the period 1995–2004.

On average in the last decade the most active markets have been the London and the Amsterdam stock exchanges (Figure 7.6). Transactions volumes are high in Spain, Finland and Sweden too. Despite its large size, Luxembourg has a very idle market, even more idle than that of the Wiener Börse. In NMS markets have very small trading volumes; the Czech Republic and Hungary are the only exceptions: enlarging stock exchanges seems to have been easier than having dynamic ones. Almost all markets recorded a peak in activity in 2000; after this exceptional year they have all returned to a stable level. Intra-group differences are higher for OMS.

Another important part of the domestic capital market is the market for debt securities. In the EU-25 the size of the domestic debt securities market was on average 107.6 per cent GDP in the period examined (Figure 7.7).

Debt securities markets have been growing much faster in NMS than in OMS over the period 1995–2004. However, the debt market in the NMS is still three times smaller than that of OMS with an average of 67 per cent of GDP and 146 per cent of GDP at the end of 2004, respectively. The most developed domestic bond markets were in Denmark, Italy and Belgium within the OMS,[4] and in Malta, the Czech Republic, Hungary and Cyprus among the NMS.

As we did with shares, we want to examine activity in bond trading together with the size of the market. NMS have almost no bond trading: positive trade values are recorded for Malta and Hungary, but these are quite small and much lower than the trading volumes in OMS. Data for

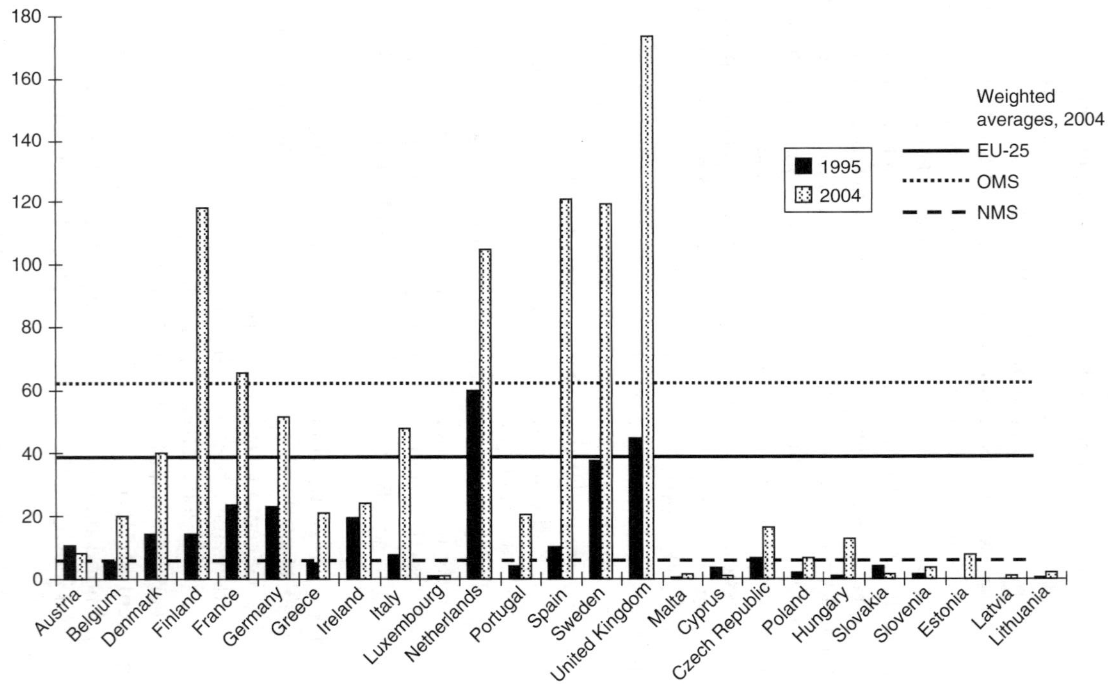

Note: 1. GDP in PPP terms weighted averages.

Source: World Development Indicators (WDI), World Federation of Stock Exchanges, national stock exchanges.

Figure 7.6 Total value equities traded as percentage of GDP[1]

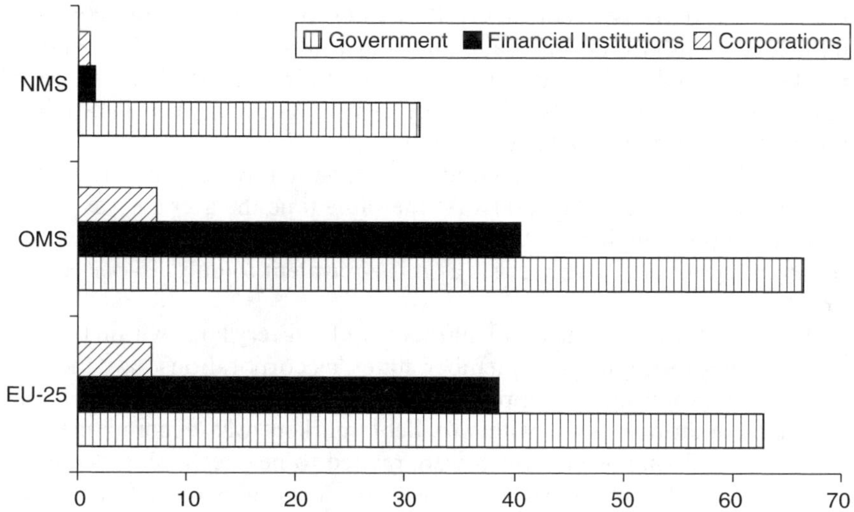

Note: 1. GDP in PPP terms weighted averages.

Source: BIS, IMF, national stock exchanges.

Figure 7.7 Domestic debt market as percentage of GDP, 1995–2004[1]

OMS are more diverse: the stock exchanges that have a higher activity in bonds are located in Denmark, Sweden and Italy. Together with the London stock exchange and the Amsterdam stock exchange, these are the only markets which record any significant activity in bonds. For Italy the reported average is influenced by the large values traded in 1996–1998; the ratio has been quite low in recent years. In the late 1990s the highest trade volumes of bonds were recorded and these years were characterized by high volatility. In recent years, trade volumes are more stable and their average level is quite low.

At first sight the EU-25 domestic debt securities market seems to be more developed than the equity market: however, the structure of the EU-25 debt markets as a whole is dominated by bonds issued by governments.

The recent increase in government debt issuance primarily reflects the financing of fiscal imbalances of member states. At the end of 2004 the value of domestic government securities as a share of GDP was 77 per cent for the EU, while for the OMS it was 82 per cent and 62 per cent for the NMS.

The amount outstanding of privately issued debt in the EU-25 is still relatively modest, while the issuance of bonds by financial institutions has increased from 41 per cent of GDP in 1995 to 47 per cent in 2004. The difference in importance of the financial institutions debt market between the OMS and the NMS is significant. While in the OMS the share of financial institution bonds was 53 per cent of GDP, in the NMS it was merely 5 per cent of GDP at the end of 2004.

In the EU-25 the corporate bond market was equivalent to only 5.6 per cent of GDP at the end of 2004. At the same time the average was over 1 percentage point higher for the OMS countries, while in the NMS the corporate bond market hardly exists as it is equivalent to only 1.5 per cent of GDP.

Although the corporate bond market is still not very large within the EU, it has been growing in most member states, as corporations have increasingly been exploring the opportunities for direct financing with better funding conditions. The switch to debt markets was accompanied by increased financing needs, which were related to new technologies and an intensive period of mergers and acquisitions. According to Hartmann et al. (2003) and Rajan and Zingales (2003) the surge in corporate bonds may also be a consequence of EMU and the introduction of the euro. Our data are consistent with this theory as they show that the largest increase in the importance of the corporate securities domestic debt market was in those member states that also introduced the euro.

Besides the introduction of the common currency, the corporate issuance of debt instruments was also encouraged by banks as a result of new BIS regulations and stronger competition in the financial system: European financial intermediaries were helping their existing customers obtain direct access to the capital market. Consequently it is hard to distinguish whether the recent changes in corporate finance towards debt securities have been driven either by market changes, corporate restructuring or the banks themselves (Pagano and Von Thadden, 2004).

In the NMS, especially in the transition economies, the bond market for non-financial corporations is still very tiny. Nevertheless, in most of these countries the government has recently made efforts to develop the debt market. For example, in Poland the legal barriers have been eased. Moreover changes in the pension system in those countries should create demand for corporate bonds, and enhance new issues in the long term.

A recent trend in European capital markets is the creation of stock exchange networks. A very large European market is forming: its main components are Euronext, connecting the Amsterdam, Paris, Brussels and Lisbon stock exchanges, and the Nordic and Baltic stock exchange, which combines the markets of Sweden, Finland, Estonia, Latvia, Lithuania and Denmark. Stock exchange networks satisfy the needs of companies seeking to broaden their shareholders' base and raise capital beyond local markets.

Together with the need of setting up a new or renewed stock exchange, this is what has probably induced the small countries of Estonia, Latvia and Lithuania to join the Nordic and Baltic alliance. It may be the only way they could avoid an almost sure decline of the local market, undermined by the migration of the best companies through cross-listing in international markets.[5]

Another characteristic of stock exchange networks is their higher efficiency, attained by extended trading hours, the possibility of remote membership, lower transaction costs and greater information. All in all, an integrated European stock exchange market should lead to greater efficiency. In the future, network externalities may contribute significantly to increasing EU-25 capital market size and activity.

5. OTHER FINANCIAL INTERMEDIARIES

The enlargement of the EU-25 accelerated the process of financial integration and is already evident in the banking industry and capital markets. The developments in each of these main areas have been summarized above, emphasizing that the extent of integration across markets is not uniform. The variation is also visible in the case of other financial intermediaries, as mentioned in section 2.

Insurance companies, investment funds and pension funds are notable features of the OMS financial system, while in the NMS these financial institutions have only marginal importance. In part this is due to the breadth of activities and the historically strong position of universal banks. The development of these financial intermediaries is strongly connected with the problem of ageing populations and ongoing pension system reforms.

Within the EU-25 the total investments of insurance companies represented 48 per cent of GDP in 2004, an increase of almost 10 per cent since 2001 (Table 7.4). In the NMS the increase was especially significant: total investments of insurance companies increased almost 30 per cent over the years 2001–2004, mainly because of an increase in spending on life insurance. The per capita life insurance premiums have increased by 37 per cent since 1996 and were equal to EUR 776 in 2003, yet there is a lot of cross-country variation in the average life insurance spending in the EU-25 (Swiss Re, 2000; 2004).

Also investment and pension funds have become a powerful factor in the financial services industry as a result of changes in saving patterns caused by demographic changes and decreasing yields on bank deposits and other traditional financial instruments.

Table 7.4 Total investments of insurance companies and total assets under management as percentage of GDP

	Insurance companies		Pension funds		Investment funds	
	1995	2004	1995	2004	1995	2004
Austria	26.6	28.8	3.7	4.3	45.3	51.7
Belgium	45.5	57.7	5.7	4.1	34.1	33.4
Cyprus	n/a	n/a	n/a	n/a	n/a	n/a
Czech Republic	7.2	9.3	2.4	3.7	4.0	4.3
Denmark	53.8	63.3	23.3	192.8	21.2	39.2
Estonia	2.3	3.4	0.0	1.9	n/a	3.5
Finland	23.7	25.5	n/a	n/a	9.0	14.4
France	55.9	59.9	0.0	0.0	43.3	48.5
Germany	44.6	49.3	n/a	11.7	37.6	38.9
Greece	9.2	7.2	0.0	0.0	13.2	9.5
Hungary	4.9	4.4	4.0	6.6	5.0	5.3
Ireland	48.2	58.2	43.7	42.0	242.7	292.5
Italy	25.2	29.4	0.5	0.9	31.5	20.8
Latvia	2.2	2.0	0.2	0.4	0.2	0.5
Lithuania	1.6	2.3	0.0	0.1	n/a	n/a
Luxembourg	130.0	130.3	n/a	n/a	3878.3	3797.9
Malta	10.9	13.9	0.0	0.0	13.0	23.5
Netherlands	66.3	65.8	100.8	106.9	25.1	20.1
Poland	5.1	7.1	2.7	7.9	1.7	4.7
Portugal	20.6	24.6	11.5	10.7	19.8	21.9
Slovakia	5.6	7.2	n/a	n/a	n/a	5.0
Slovenia	6.0	8.9	0.9	2.0	11.5	8.0
Spain	21.9	24.3	6.6	7.7	23.3	24.8
Sweden	0.1	31.3	0.0	0.0	35.6	42.1
United Kingdom	108.6	95.0	73.6	64.5	22.6	24.8
EU-25 average[1]	46.6	48.3	17.6	21.9	39.6	41.0
OMS average[1]	50.3	52.2	19.0	23.5	42.9	44.4
NMS average[1]	5.2	6.7	2.3	5.4	2.8	4.6

Notes:
n/a = not available.
1. GDP in PPP terms weighted averages.

Source: ECB (2005), national central banks and Eurostat.

Owing to favourable tax treatment the assets under management by investment and pension funds are already comparable in some countries to those of the banking industry. The growth of investment and pension funds was also encouraged by credit institutions and insurance companies as asset management makes up an important share of their non-interest income. Nevertheless, there is still significant potential for growth as weighted average assets managed within the EU-25 without Ireland and Luxembourg amount only to 29 per cent of GDP in 2004 compared to 70 per cent in the US.

6. CONCLUSIONS

In drawing our conclusions about the characteristics of the European financial system, we will briefly compare it to the financial structures in the US and in Japan.

Our first conclusion, in line with related work on financial structures (Allen et al., 2004; Hartmann et al., 2003; Allen and Gale, 2000), is that the European financial system is bank-based: in the US, on the contrary, the capital markets (including the bond markets) play the larger role in the financial system. The importance of banks in the US economy is lower than in Japan and even smaller than that of NMS. Thus, the US financial structure may be described as market-based. The Japanese financial structure can be described as bank-based, even if the size of the stock market is larger than that of the banking system: in fact the capital market is still underdeveloped, if we exclude public bonds.

Also considering the results of previous studies, we conclude that the main characteristics of the financial structure of the EU-25 have not changed in spite of the enlargement. In addition our results show that the existing differences in financial structures across the most important economic regions and countries have not been affected in the last decades.

Among the characteristics of the banking system, we have observed a high level of concentration, in particular in NMS. This has led to an increase in the European average, which is higher than the value of the concentration index for the US and Japan, probably because of a low level of integration and low foreign bank penetration in OMS. The recent wave of European cross-border mergers and acquisitions may lead to a decrease in the concentration of the banking sector in the long term.

Regardless of this high concentration, the European banking sector, in particular in OMS, is more efficient than that of the US. The factors behind the high inefficiency of the banking sector in the NMS and US are quite different: in the NMS the ratios were driven mainly by the transition economies, because of high interest rates, due to bad loans, and high overheads costs, caused by excessive employment and low application of modern technology.[6] In the US the high overhead costs are mainly due to a still large number of small banks despite the merger boom of the last decade. The significant difference in net margins between the US and other countries reflects divergences in bank activity, rather than in efficiency or competition. In the US banks are more focused on short-term and consumer financing, while in Europe and Japan they are more commercially based and long-term oriented.

In Japan the degree of concentration in the banking sector is between the level observed in the US and the EU-25. However, the efficiency of Japanese banks is close to that of the OMS. The Japanese banks have the lowest overhead costs, while net margins are comparable to the lowest in the OMS. Thus, we may deduce that the level of banks' efficiency is affected by the degree of financial development.

As anticipated, the stock and debt market in the US is more active and efficient than that in the EU-25 or Japan. The Japanese stock market is larger than the European one, but smaller, less active and efficient than the average stock market in the OMS. Moreover, the structure of the debt market varies significantly across countries: in Japan and EU-25 it is dominated by government bonds, while in the US the larger role is played by financial bonds. The European corporate debt market is the smallest when compared to the US and Japan.

We conclude the comparison examining insurance corporations and pension funds, both of which have grown in recent years in all countries. Nonetheless, insurance corporations are more important in Japan and, to a lesser extent, in the US. In the EU-25 insurance corporations and pension funds still don't play a significant role, particularly in the NMS, due to the importance of public pension schemes.

Summing up, financial systems differ a lot among countries; divergences are higher when comparing European countries with the US and Japan. Differences also emerge between OMS and NMS. The important differences between the OMS and the NMS need to be taken account of by policymakers going forward. For example, prior to the enlargement, foreign banks played an important role in very few countries. Thus policies such as supervision by a bank's home regulator could be readily justified. Now, however, with foreign banks important in so many countries this is not so clear. On the other hand, as NMS catch up and converge, differences in financial systems may decline. On the other hand they may not. We strongly believe that more research on European financial integration is needed in order to understand the structural changes in the financial system caused by the accession of new member states.

NOTES

1. Franklin Allen is from the Finance Department, The Wharton School, University of Pennsylvania, e-mail: allenf@wharton.upenn.edu (corresponding author); Laura Bartiloro is from the Research Department, Banca d'Italia, e-mail: laura.bartiloro@bancaditalia.it, Oskar Kowalewski is from the Finance Department, Leon Kozminski Academy of Entrepreneurship and Management, Warsaw, Poland, e-mail: okowale@wspiz.edu.pl. This chapter is a short version of Allen et al. (2005). We would like to thank Luc Laeven and Philipp Hartmann for useful comments.
2. For a survey of the theory and empirical research on finance and growth, see Levine (1997).
3. The EEA comprises the EU, Iceland, Liechtenstein and Norway.
4. The debt markets of Luxembourg and the United Kingdom seem small because we are only taking into account domestic securities. In fact the total bond market sizes are doubled in these countries, and hence are the greatest in EU-25, if international bonds are taken into account.
5. In the last decade, before the emergence of the European stock exchange networks, cross listing on US stock exchanges was very popular among export-oriented and high-tech European companies.
6. Recent studies present evidence that the efficiency of banks has been increasing in transition economies in recent years; see Bonin et al. (2005) and Fries and Taci (2005).

REFERENCES

Allen, Franklin and Douglas Gale (2000), *Comparing Financial Systems*, Cambridge, MA: The MIT Press.

Allen, Franklin and Wei-Ling Song (2005), 'Financial integration and EMU', *European Financial Management*, **11** (1), 7–24.

Allen, Franklin, Laura Bartiloro and Oskar Kowalewski (2005), 'The financial system of the EU 25', WFIC Working Paper 05-44, Wharton Financial Institution Center, University of Pennsylvania.

Allen, Franklin, Michael K.F. Chui and Angela Maddaloni (2004), 'Financial systems in Europe, the USA, and Asia', *Oxford Review of Economic Policy*, **20** (4), 490–508.

Bonin, John P. and Paul Wachtel (2004), 'Dealing with financial fragility in transition economies', BOFIT Discussion Paper 22, Bank of Finland.

Bonin, John P., Iftekhar Hasan and Paul Wachtel (2005), 'Bank performance, efficiency and ownership in transition countries', *Journal of Banking and Finance*, **29**, 31–53.

Davis, E. Philip and Olivier de Bandt (1999), 'A cross-country comparison of market structures in European banking', ECB Working Paper No. 7, September.

Dermine, Jean (2005), 'European banking integration: don't put the cart before the horse', paper presented at the conference on 'Cross-border banking, regulatory challenges', Federal Reserve Bank of Chicago, October.

ECB (2002), 'Structural analysis of the EU banking sector', European Central Bank, November.

ECB (2003), 'Structural analysis of the EU banking sector', European Central Bank, November.

ECB (2005), 'EU banking structures', European Central Bank, October.

Fries, Steven and Anita Taci (2005), 'Cost efficiency of banks in transition: Evidence from 289 banks in 15 post-communist countries', *Journal of Banking and Finance*, **29**, 55–81.

Goddard, John, Philip Molyneux and John O.S. Wilson (2001), *European Banking: Efficiency, Technology, and Growth*, Chichester: John Wiley and Sons.

Hartmann, Philipp, Angela Maddaloni and Simone Manganelli (2003), 'The euro-area financial system: structure, integration, and policy initiatives', *Oxford Review of Economic Policy*, **19** (1), 180–213.

La Porta, Rafael, Florencio Lopez-de-Silanes, Andrei Shleifer and Robert W. Vishny (1998), 'Law and finance', *Journal of Political Economy*, **106** (6), 1113–55.

Levine, Ross (1997), 'Financial development and economic growth: views and agenda', *Journal of Economic Literature*, **35**, 688–726.

Pagano, Marco and Ernst-Ludwig von Thadden (2004), 'The European bond markets under EMU', *Oxford Review of Economic Policy*, **20** (4), 531–54.

Rajan, Raghuram and Luigi Zingales (2003), 'Banks and markets: the changing character of European finance', in Vítor Gaspar, Philipp Hartmann and Olaf Sleijpen (eds), *The Transformation of the European Financial System*, Frankfurt: European Central Bank, pp. 123–67.

Swiss Re (2000), 'Europe in focus: Non-life markets undergoing structural change', *Sigma* No. 3/2000.

Swiss Re (2004), 'World insurance in 2003: insurance industry on the road to recovery', *Sigma* No. 3/2004.

8. Meeting the need for a regulatory framework for EU financial markets

Alexandre Lamfalussy

While I have no serious professional experience in the financial market developments of the Central and Eastern European (CEE) area, I guess that when we talk about 'financial integration' in Central, Eastern and South-Eastern Europe we also mean integration of these countries within the financial system of the European Union (EU). So I would like to use my comparative advantage to sketch how I see today the development of the regulatory framework in the EU and share my thoughts on some of the queries and challenges we face. This is likely to be of immediate interest for the ten new member countries, of a prospective interest for the countries that have entered (or hope to enter) the negotiation phase and may be of some interest even for those countries for which the EU is going to remain a large (but hopefully friendly and helpful) neighbour.

Over the past few years it has been the need to establish a Europe-wide regulatory framework which caught most of the attention; and the response to this well-identified need was the Financial Services Action Plan (FSAP), the purpose of which was to establish, by 2004, the basic regulatory framework essential for a well-functioning, integrated financial market for the EU. At a very early stage, however, it became clear that the 'traditional' legislative process would be unable to achieve this objective. (A reminder: the essence of this process was, and still is, that the Commission has the duty and the exclusive privilege of drafting a directive, which then would be submitted for decision to the Council and the European Parliament.) As a result Ecofin decided to set up in July 2000 a 'Committee of Wise Men on the Regulation of European Securities Markets', which received the mandate to identify the weaknesses of this process (not in general terms, but as it applied to the area of financial services), and to propose remedies. In February 2001 we submitted our final report to Ecofin, which approved all the major proposals of the Report, and a month later the Stockholm Summit endorsed this decision and directed the Council and Commission to implement our 'four-level' process, which carries my name – presumably as a kind of retribution for my sins.

Let me just mention a few points. First, that the 'traditional' legislative method continues to apply only to the 'core' principles (Level 1). Second, that a new body, the 'Committee of the European Securities Regulators' (CESR), acting as adviser to the Commission, is entrusted with the elaboration of the implementation details (Level 2); this distinction, which exists in all member countries, did not exist at the European level. The Commission then submits these details for decision to another new institution, the 'Securities Committee'. Third, that CESR, wearing a different hat, provides guidelines for consistent national transpositions (Level 3). Finally, at Level 4 the Commission exercises its enforcement powers.

So much for the novelties of the new institutional set-up. But for this structure to ensure a significant improvement in the speed, consistency and most of all the quality of directives, three innovations are expected to play a major role: throughout the whole process, and even before the Commission embarks on a legislative initiative, there is thorough consultation of all stakeholders; the process is fully transparent; and not least, an inter-institutional body monitors the working of the process.

The new process has by now been operational for more than four years at the time of writing. Has it managed to deliver what our Committee hoped it would do? Yes – up to a point. In one important sense the FSAP is in place: the targeted 'core' or framework legislation has been adopted, and the directives related to technical implementation details are well advanced. I also believe that the quality of the regulations has substantially improved: gone are the complaints heard four-to-five years ago about a 'top down' approach and ignorance how markets are 'really' working. I have not noticed one single instance of stakeholders complaining about lack of transparency, or inadequate consultation. In my judgement, all key institutional participants – CESR, the European Commission, the governments and the European Parliament – played the game correctly, despite the fact that they had ample opportunities to wreck the process. But having said this, judgement has still to be suspended. Level 3 – national transposition – is just only beginning. And remember: inconsistent or even contradictory transposition of the directives was one of the main complaints about the working of the 'traditional' system. More important, new concerns and challenges have emerged, to which I now turn.

One major concern, voiced by almost all market participants, is about – how times have changed! – 'excessive' consultation. Consultation is indeed a time-consuming, labour-intensive and costly procedure. This applies, incidentally, both to the consulting institutions – CESR and the Commission – and to the consulted stakeholders. It requires highly qualified staff and, at the end of the day, full involvement at the highest level of responsibility. But you can't have it both ways: defending your legitimate interests without making the necessary efforts to have your voice heard.

Far more important, to my mind, is the need to properly respond to the complaint about 'regulatory overload', which means, in substance, that the super-imposition of European regulations on national ones adds up to an unbearable, very costly, total regulatory burden which moreover paralyses innovative business initiatives. Hence the insistence on carrying out a cost/benefit analysis before launching a new regulatory initiative, on the ground that not all activities need to be regulated at the European level, or indeed at all. This request seems to me fully justified, and by now has been accepted by the Commission. But beware of two pitfalls. One, believing that all costs and benefits can be reliably quantified. A lot can be – hence the justification of cost/benefit analysis. But not everything. So let us push the analysis as far as it can go, but not beyond. The other pitfall is accepting the simplistic ideological divide between those for whom the main justification for regulation is to protect the 'weak' against what they perceive to be the abusive practices of the 'powerful' and those who believe that unregulated competition would solve all our problems by promoting growth. I do not believe that a debate at this level of generalization could lead us anywhere. In financial services, where the pace of change is so spectacular, we have to look at specific market segments to decide whether the result of a cost/benefit analysis should be qualified by resorting to arguments that defy quantification.

A third concern arises from the fact that Ecofin decided in December 2002 to extend the four-level regulatory process to the whole financial services industry, notably to banking. When I was consulted on the desirability of this initiative, my reaction was in two parts. On the one hand, I found this to be a good move – not simply because it was a flattering initiative – but because I believed, and still believe, that the inability of the 'traditional' legislative process to cope with highly technical matters in a fast-changing environment applied just as much to banking as to the securities markets. Just think of the horrendous complexity of Basel II. On the other hand, I pointed out that the focus of regulatory interest in banking is on prudential matters (which is not the case in the securities markets), and this will inevitably throw up the controversial question of the operational involvement, or the lack of it, of central banks in regulation and supervision. Which it duly did.

A fourth, and very recent concern has to do with the potentially disturbing consequences of the constitutional treaty debacle for the efficient working of the four-level approach. This requires a short reminder. In 2001 the European Parliament, while accepting the principle of splitting the legislative process into Level 1 and Level 2, requested the right to 'call back' elements of the implementation details which, in their view clashed with the dispositions of the 'core' principles laid down in Level 1, and which had been approved by the MPs. Not an unreasonable request, given that a lot of substance can be hidden in the implementation details. But the satisfaction of this right could in practice lead to substantial delays and undermine the efficiency of the whole process. The risk of this happening was not negligible: market participants have the deplorable habit of missing the opportunity to voice their concern when core principles are under distinction; but they wake up when they see the fine print of the implementation details. Why not ask in this case the help of their MPs? After a long and difficult negotiation between the Commission and the Parliament an agreement was reached, and the new process could start operating in February 2002. A key factor which helped achieving this agreement was the perspective for the European Parliament to achieve an unquestionable co-legislator status; an expectation which would have become reality after the ratification of the constitutional treaty. I can only express my hope that our MPs and the Commission are aware of their responsibility in keeping alive the spirit of the agreement hammered out in late 2001.

By way of conclusion, I would like to put the undoubtable progress in the implementation of the Financial Services Action Plan, and the help given in this respect by the four-level regulatory process, in proper perspective. A regulatory framework is just that – a framework. And even if this framework can be deemed satisfactory, it remains a framework. It does not, by itself, lead to the realization of a single, deep, liquid, innovative financial market within the European Union. It is one of the preconditions for allowing genuine financial integration to happen. There are, however, other preconditions as well: adjusting supervisory structures to the progress in financial integration; harmonizing supervisory practices; improving the post-trading infrastructure; lifting the obstacles to integration arising out of differences in taxation and legal systems; coming to grips with accounting standards; and, most of all, tempering the deep-seated protectionist instincts of our authorities. And even if we move towards the realization of all these preconditions, the final say is going to be in the hands of market participants: they are the actors of integration.

PART III

The European financial system as an economic driving force

9. Finance and growth: the legacy of Schumpeter to be rediscovered?

Peter Mooslechner

1. GENERAL INTRODUCTION

Joseph A. Schumpeter, born in 1883[1] in the small city of Triesch[2] about 170 kilometres north of Vienna, at that time the important capital of the Austrian-Hungarian Empire, is one of the outstanding economists of the 20th century. The works of J.A. Schumpeter truly belong to the great intellectual achievements in economics; his ideas – like those of Adam Smith, John Maynard Keynes or outstanding thinkers in economics – re-appear on the scene from time to time in new context and in new cloth. Had his work not been crowded out by Keynes' path-breaking and directly policy-related work, Schumpeter very likely would have qualified for the most influential economist of the 20th century or of modern economics in general.[3]

As has also been typical of outstanding economists, Schumpeter's work covers an extremely broad range of issues, thereby crossing the narrow borders of economics as a science as well, to include political, sociological and, in particular, institutional aspects. At the same time, his thinking was very 'pragmatic' and 'reality-oriented' in many respects. His direct interest in both practical policy-making and business is reflected by episodes as Austrian Minister of Finance (as which Schumpeter served for little more than half a year in 1919) and manager of a small private bank in Vienna (Biedermann Bank, where he was appointed president in 1921). Both episodes, in politics as well as in banking, turned out to be not very successful, but they are particularly fascinating in relation to his theoretical work. Schumpeter's willingness to become a banker can only be understood against the background that in Schumpeter's Vienna the banker was seen as the only really respectable businessman (Streissler, 1982). Banking and financing was the dominating perspective left in the former capital of the Austrian-Hungarian Empire, which was transformed into a (much too big) capital of a rather small country as a result of World War I (Ausch, 1968).

In Schumpeter's writings, all these elements are present in his thought on the interaction of financial markets and growth, that is the importance of financing related to economic development in general and investment in particular:

- this specific aspect of Schumpeter's work is one of the most popular elements of his thought taken up in the recent literature;
- similarities as well as differences in Schumpeter's and Keynes' work belong to the most fascinating episodes in the history of economics at the beginning of the twentieth century;
- Schumpeter's entrepreneur, well known to concentrate on 'creative destruction' and 'innovation', also faces the challenge of putting together a suitable financing package for his activities.

Last but not least, it has to be mentioned that the topic of financial sector development, financing and growth is by no means a Schumpeterian or Viennese topic only. It is of utmost importance for emerging markets in general and catching-up countries in particular, where growth is a key issue. Obviously, the Central and Eastern European (CEE) countries and even more the countries in South-Eastern Europe (SEE) are representative examples in this respect. Starting from a position of underdeveloped financial markets and institutions, many of the central questions related to the financing–growth nexus have to be dealt with right from the beginning in these countries, as an important pre-requisite for their catching-up process.

2. HOW SCHUMPETER'S IDEAS ON FINANCE RE-APPEAR IN THE RECENT LITERATURE

Pinning down the theme 'finance for growth' to set the stage for the contributions published in this issue is a tall order, particularly in the face of many comprehensive papers and literature surveys shedding light on the theory and empirics of finance and growth (for example Pagano, 1993; Giovannini, 1993; Levine, 1997; Leahy et al., 2001; Thiel, 2001; Wachtel, 2001; Dolar and Meh, 2002; Giannetti et al., 2002). From the wide range of aspects related to finance and growth three selected issues deserve particular attention because they are fundamental for finding adequate policy prescriptions for economic policy decision-making and at the same time key to the current discussion (Arestis and Stein, 2005). First of all, from a rather theoretical-historical perspective the basic question is 'Does finance matter?' (Davidson, 1978); next, the essential functions of financial markets and the important characteristics of financial market transactions are crucial; and, finally, the perennial debate of different financial systems is definitely among the most influential topics in current economic discussions. In the end, the state of our knowledge on possible economic policy and institutional consequences for countries in various stages of transformation is at the core of the debate (Demirgüç-Kunt and Levine, 2001; Demirgüç-Kunt and Maksimovic, 2002).

When analysing financial markets explicitly in a macroeconomic context, a number of interesting gaps emerge related to the role that financial markets and financial institutions play in the economy. Over the past decades economic reality has to a large extent been shaped by financial market shocks. The European monetary union and the greater importance attached to financial stability in the hierarchy of economic goals have been direct consequences of this situation. Today, economic policy-makers all over the world regard financial market developments as a permanent economic policy challenge. Questions like how to design an adequate regulatory framework for the supervision of financial markets and institutions, effective early warning systems for financial crises and the implications of asset market instabilities are of utmost importance for financial regulation issues. In a long-term perspective the existence of a relevant relationship – both in a positive and negative sense – between financial markets and macroeconomic developments is one important, if not the most important question in economics. This link was and is crucial during particular historical phases. In contrast, in economic theory it is by no means clear whether financial markets and the real economy are indeed related and, if so, in what form, and how such a relationship ties in with our understanding of macroeconomic developments.

The most recent wave of Schumpeter's re-appearance in economics concentrates on the importance of financing, financial markets and financial institutions for economic development. Perhaps not necessarily the most prominent aspect of Schumpeter's work, the influence financial market developments gained since Schumpeter's times without doubt justifies increased attention on this particular element of his legacy. The definite renaissance of 'Schumpeterian finance' in modern economics started with King and Levine (1993). They motivate the Schumpeterian connection of their empirical work by pointing out that Joseph Schumpeter in 1911[4] argued that the services provided by financial intermediaries – mobilizing savings, evaluating projects, managing risk, monitoring managers, and facilitating transactions – are essential for technological innovation and economic progress. In fact, this line of reasoning was by no means new when it was re-introduced by King and Levine in the early 1990s. Extensive empirical and institutional work on topics such as financial development, financial deepening or financial repression by Gurley and Shaw (1955), Gerschenkron (1963), Goldsmith (1969) and McKinnon (1973) had already illustrated the interaction between financial and economic development for a broad range of countries at different stages of development. But it seems to be a fair qualification that all this work took place outside the mainstream in economics.

Schumpeter assigned specific importance to the role of financial intermediation for economic development. Up to his time economics had mostly completely ignored the role of financial intermediation for real activities; almost all models of development and growth gave no role to financing. Contrary to this view, elements of both sides can be found in the writings of Schumpeter. Today, 'financial development' is empirically measured and defined by a series of indicators to be used in traditional cross-country studies on the relationship between financial development and long-run output growth. At the same time possible channels creating this link are examined, ranging from an impact on physical capital accumulation to an increase in the efficiency in allocating capital. King and Levine (1993) conclude that Schumpeter might have been right about the importance of finance for economic development.[5] This finance–development link, however, is typically not the economic mechanism most closely associated with Schumpeter. The popular standard statement of the Schumpeterian vision is one of 'creative destruction', a process by which invention and innovation replace old production methods and goods with better procedures. Yet, an integral part of the Schumpeterian story is that financial intermediaries make possible technological innovation and economic development: 'The banker . . . authorizes people, in the name of society as it were, to . . . (innovate)' (Schumpeter, 1911).

3. SCHUMPETER ON FINANCING INNOVATION AND ECONOMIC DEVELOPMENT

Schumpeter's view of how financing and financial markets have a direct impact on growth is easily explained. Schumpeter explicitly opposes himself to the classical view that money and finance have to be seen as a 'veil' only, and that nothing essential will be lost by analysing the economic sphere without dealing with money and finance. His thinking on the role of finance is broadly related to his views on the dynamics of the process of development, in particular how innovation and new investment opportunities can be realized. The importance of financing – as well as the monetary system – in Schumpeter's world is closely connected to his famous concepts of 'creative destruction' and the 'entrepreneur'.

Schumpeter's central aim is to explain how in his view long-term economic dynamics require a particular type of genius, 'entrepreneurs' who break through the stability of (static) equilibrium with innovations, that is with new methods of production and/or new goods. Schumpeter's entrepreneurial innovations are financed by credit creation (and not by savings). The social function of money and credit creation is to permit entrepreneurs to take resources out of the income stream before they have put resources into it (and before the respective savings could have been created).

Schumpeter's model is dynamic in nature. His dynamic mechanism is driven by powerful forces that shape the long-run characteristics of an economy, of development.[6] The nature of these forces (technological and organizational innovations, entrepreneurial activity, and the credit mechanism) is well known in the literature. However, there are two aspects that may deserve specific attention. First, the big changes which shape the course of economic development cannot be understood to take place gradually and continuously. Second, the theory of money, credit and banking is, of course, an integral part of his theory of economic development and its dynamic aspects.

Schumpeter considers the concept of innovation – which means new products, new methods of production and new markets and sources of supply – not timed to the business cycle, but a cause of change outside the business cycle, which can then shape it. Schumpeter uses the term 'gales of creative destruction' when he speaks of innovation, because he thinks of innovation hitting the economy as an exogenous force. Innovations are the economic applications of inventions and discoveries which cause fundamental change to the entire economy. Of course, other phenomena can also affect movement in the cycle, but innovation is the most important causal factor.

The starting point in this analysis is 'the stationary state'. There is no innovation going on, and savings are used only to replace depreciated capital. The 'entrepreneur' in the sense of Schumpeter does not exist. 'The entrepreneurial function' is to disturb the stationary state, to create change, to seek new profit opportunities and to try to establish monopoly positions in the market. To succeed in this, entrepreneurs need debt financing. They need finance to gain command over inputs engaged in 'old-style' productions in order to recombine resources, and they need command of finance first. Savings from the ordinary circular flow are seen as inadequate; entrepreneurs cannot afford to finance their purchases of inputs out of traditional business savings (profit) from current production.

As entrepreneurial activity increases, so does the level of income and output. Innovating occurs in periodic clusters of activity. The activity of the first innovators and the profits that they gain attract imitators, which increases the amount of innovative activity first and, as a consequence, later on starts to dampen the profits of the innovators. 'Creative destruction' means that resources are reallocated from old to new industries and output in traditional industries is reduced. Then the expansion gets ready for a new stage of development. The increase in capital goods increases productive capacity, and now incomes are rising, especially incomes connected with the new innovative part of the economy. Driven by this, the whole economy is growing.

To make this whole process feasible, innovative entrepreneurs rely on bankers and financial investors willing to shift their funds in their direction. But this willingness as well as the opportunity for more and more new investment is not going to last forever. At some point there is an exhaustion of opportunities for new investment and/or households and firms start to reduce their spending, partly because they are squeezed by debt as the boom fades away. Once again a static equilibrium will evolve as long as no new wave of innovation pushes the economy.

In sum, what Schumpeter had in mind as the main force of economic change and what is more specifically called 'progress' consists mainly in a change in method of production. This is what changes most powerfully the surface and structure of economic life. Examples of this are 'revolutions' like the introduction of electricity, of the motor car or the personal computer, things we would call nowadays the introduction of new 'general purpose technologies'. These events entail quite a different kind of risk or uncertainty, the risk of carrying out processes that have not been tried by experience. As a matter of fact most of these attempts fail, but those which succeed create a 'rush'. This is Schumpeter's explanation of why progress comes in rushes. From his extensive studies in economic history he concluded that the upswings of a cycle are usually dominated by some new industry or product. They create prosperity and after prosperity, depression. But to understand the entire Schumpeterian mechanism in detail one has to go one step further and to take credit into account.

The financing of a new industry means expansion of bank credit. Naturally, an entrepreneur investing in new things has not yet at his command the receipts from future sales. He will generally have to rely on credit. Banks meet this demand by credit creation, they expand credit by granting new loans. This is what Schumpeter made so popular among bankers and, at the same time, is what explains to some extent his personal interest in the banking business. Although stressing the role of entrepreneurs in the economic process, he always held the view that successful entrepreneurs must be backed by bankers. They finance the innovation process and bear the risk incorporated in innovation, and in the end Schumpeter labels credit creation through the banking system as one of the crucial elements of his definition of capitalism.

It has to be kept in mind that the connection between finance and economic growth was of almost no importance in the thinking of classical economists. Schumpeter (1911) put the role of financial intermediaries and financial markets at the centre of economic development. He thereby forcefully contributed to the revolution already under way in economics at that time that in the end completely changed the understanding of how a modern capitalist economy is supposed to function. Strangely enough, the English translation of Schumpeter's *Theorie der Wirtschaftlichen Entwicklung* (published in 1911) did not appear until 1934 (*The Theory of Economic Development*). Therefore, it reached the English-speaking community of economists with a considerable lag, and its reception was considerably limited, first by the First World War and, second, by the Great Depression. And in the end, Keynes contributed to this 'ignorance' of Schumpeter's ideas by his publication of the *General Theory* in 1936, which right from the beginning dominated economic discussions.

Financial intermediation is key in the tradition of Schumpeter. Financial intermediaries contribute significantly to growth in modern models of new growth theory, an element which can already be found in Schumpeter's writings. Of course, he did not use the modern jargon of financial markets but he concentrated on the role of the banker as an example:

> The banker stands between those who wish to form new combinations and the possessors of productive means. He is essentially a phenomenon of development, though only when no central authority directs the social process. He makes possible the carrying out of new combinations, authorises people, in the name of the society as it were, to form them. He is the ephor of the exchange economy. (Schumpeter, 1934)

Schumpeter returned to the role of financing for development many times in his later writings. In fact, his view of the issue tends to become stronger and stronger: 'the relation between credit creation by banks and innovation is fundamental to the understanding of the capitalist engine' (Schumpeter, 1939).

To stress the importance of credit as such was no novelty in Schumpeter's Vienna; it merely pointed out a fact of general belief, that banks (and, in particular, bankers) not only hold a singular (social) position in the economy but that important economic power is concentrated in them as well. The at that time rising importance of the accumulation of financial capital considerably contributed to the economic importance of credit. For example, Mises (1980) in his well-known monetary treatise published in 1912 devoted a substantial passage on the cyclical process determined by credit creation; Wieser (1914) even mentioned the role of credit for creating progress. Schumpeter transformed credit into a necessary prerequisite for innovation, which in turn is the fundamental source of economic expansion. In particular new entrepreneurs and their new enterprises, new products or new processes, which are the main sources of innovation, rely on bank credit as the main source of financing in his understanding.

One of the most fascinating little stories to tell in this context of monetary thinking at the beginning of the last century is that of Schumpeter's unpublished book on money *Das Wesen des Geldes*. As we have seen, Schumpeter during his whole lifetime was – in theoretical and practical terms – very much interested in the monetary system and he incorporated many elements stemming from this interest in several of his works. Despite this prominent role in his economic thinking he always felt that his work on these issues was not received well by the profession (Busch, 2003). In fact, he did work on a big volume on money and finance since his early years as an economist (Schumpeter, 1970) and published several pieces of this work separately, for example *Das Sozialprodukt und die Rechenpfennige* (1917). Finally, the completed manuscript was planned to become published in 1929, when Schumpeter, returning from a trip to the US, decided that it would 'never' become published. The true reasons for this remain somehow in the dark, but there are several nice stories why this could have been the case. One is that he became familiar with Keynes' *Treatise* and feared not being able to compete with it; another story concentrates on the failure of his *Theorie der Wirtschaftlichen Entwicklung* to gain widespread attention because it was available in German only. In fact, there are some indications that he did work on an English translation of the manuscript afterwards but, in the end, the book was published only posthumously in 1970. Whatever the true reason for not publishing it during his lifetime, what the book clearly documents is Schumpeter's encompassing knowledge of the status of the international academic discussion regarding money, banking and finance in the 1920s, including Wicksell, Keynes, the Austrians and the entire discussion that took place in Germany.

Schumpeter used the relationship between banker and industrialist to illustrate the importance of the financial system in choosing and adopting new technologies. He contends that well-functioning banks spur technological innovation by identifying and funding those entrepreneurs with the best chances of successfully implementing innovative products and production processes. Schumpeter (1911) accords the banking system a more important role, since it is the banking system which facilitates an economic upswing through its financing of innovative entrepreneurs, thus paving the way for a higher level of equilibrium output. He saw financing and the financial intermediary as agents of change that spur new methods of production. Thus, the pivotal role of a financial intermediary was supposed to bring in radical changes by combining different activities.

4. FROM SCHUMPETER AND HIS CONTEMPORARIES TO KEYNES AND BEYOND . . .

As already mentioned, apart from a very specific type of monetary analysis focusing on precious metals and an extremely brief discussion of bank lending, classical economists did not cover financial markets and their macroeconomic importance (Blaugh, 1978; Spiegel, 1983). In their view, efficiency and macroeconomic equilibrium were determined by the real economy, and the classical concepts concentrated on the behaviour of market participants and market structure on goods markets; financial transactions did not systematically impact the economic situation.

In general, mainstream economic doctrines ranging from classical theories via Keynesian and neoclassical views to real business cycles are characterized by merely rudimentary efforts to integrate financial markets explicitly into analysis. Banks, which dominate the financial systems of advanced market economies, are only very rarely modelled as a separate component in macroeconomic models. A case in point is the IS–LM model, which for decades mirrored the textbook consensus on macroeconomic thinking. While this model lacks many essential Keynesian principles, it differs from classical orthodoxy in that monetary factors are seen to have an influence on the real economy via the determination of the interest rate. Yet, even though a rudimentary securities market is thus implied in the model, it ignores any independent effect of non-monetary financial markets on the real sector, for instance associated with investment financing by financial intermediaries. In most macroeconomic models implicit financial markets merely accommodate real sector decisions passively, even in such cases where the model allows for a relationship between monetary conditions and the real economy. In addition, it is important to note that modelling the interaction between monetary policy and the real economy does not yet imply that financial markets play a role of their own.

However, the picture would be incomplete without at least naming some economists who held diverging views and who placed a particular emphasis on the relationship between finance and growth. Nevertheless, such theories have somehow never figured broadly in mainstream textbooks. At least, it seems interesting to note that a significant part of this non-mainstream view is – as Schumpeter – related to the turn of the century and the early decades of the 20th century.

Knut Wicksell, born in 1851 in Stockholm, published his *Geldzins und Güterpreise* (*Interest and Prices*) in German in 1898, thus boosting the impact of his work in Germany and Austria. Moreover, his decision to become an economist was also considerably influenced by a three-year grant he received in 1887 to study economics in Germany and Austria. In Vienna, he attended lectures by Carl Menger and he also spent some time in Berlin. When he died in Stockholm in 1926 he was working on a contribution for a book honouring Friedrich von Wieser. In general, Wicksell's publications did not receive widespread attention during his lifetime but the ties between him and Austrian economic thinking were obvious.

Wicksell (1913, 1922, 1934), who never followed mainstream economic beliefs, postulates the existence of two distinct rates of interest. The natural rate of interest as the expected return on new capital is determined by the real sector, while the loan rate of interest is affected by the banking market. Divergence between these two interest rates sets in motion a cumulative process of expansion or contraction of income and prices (via investment decisions). In the light of the active role of the loan interest rate, the financial markets have a pivotal function in Wicksell's model and introduce a direct connection between the monetary system and real economic developments. Money and the entire financial system become an indispensable part of how he understood the functioning of the economy (Formaini, 2005).

In Great Britain the publication of Keynes' *A Treatise on Money* in 1930 summarized the status of the discussion on monetary issues since the beginning of the century. Intended to become the 'domestic counterpart' of his *Tract on Monetary Reform* (1923) the *Treatise* consists of seven books in two volumes, definitively covering the monetary and financial knowledge of the time – in a traditional 'non-Keynesian' way. Although early knowledge of its content may have caused Schumpeter's decision not to publish his volume on money, the impact of the *Treatise* in history remained limited as well. It was soon overshadowed by the publication of the *General Theory* in 1936, although it was at that time the most comprehensive exposition of the current debate on monetary, banking and financial market issues. Keynes did refer to the most recent works by Wicksell and the Austrians also, but the substantive integration of these approaches into his work happened in the transition from the *Treatise* to the *General Theory* only, in the process of 'how Keynes became Keynesian' (Screpanti and Zamagni, 2005, p. 249ff). Interestingly enough, Keynes in his 'Monetary theory of production' (1933) as well as in 'The general theory of employment' (1937) very much stressed the importance of (*ex ante*) finance for the dynamics of a monetary economy. In Keynes' thought after the *Treatise* banks hold the key position in the transition from a lower to a higher scale of activity and only a rise in investment financed by credit expansion increases income

(Arestis et al., 2002). After the *General Theory* the question of the need for funding did force Keynes to make explicit two important interrelated issues barely touched on in the *General Theory*. On the one hand, the existence of mechanisms to finance, and in particular to fund investment, was a condition for sustained growth of investment. On the other hand, this conclusion forced him to make explicit the importance of the institutional setting (financial institutions and markets) for macroeconomic performance – a question he almost entirely left aside in the *General Theory* but dealt with in detail in the *Treatise*.

Very similar to Schumpeter, Keynes clearly had in mind the procedures to be followed by a producer in order to secure the necessary supply of finance for his undertaking. He first has to secure short-term liquidity covering the cost of production, and second needs to fund the short-term obligations by a long-term issue. This two-step provision of finance envisaged by Keynes is exactly the required device faced by entrepreneurs in deciding on new investment. The initial provision of bank credit makes the production of new capital goods possible, and at the same time increases the money stock. When investment has been carried out with the consequent increase in income and saving, long-term finance is accommodated by the outcome of a successful wave of new investment.

Incorporating financial markets, Minsky's theory of investment makes an effort to give an authentic interpretation of Keynes and to adapt his model to the modern world of financial markets. His theory, which explicitly accounts for budgetary constraints and financing conditions, builds on the financial framework of consistent sectoral balance sheets by definition underlying all economic activity. Minsky (1976) distinguishes a mix of fragile financing constellations and at the same time considers cash flows and obligations incurred in the process of building up capital stock. This puts the spotlight on the issue of how to finance investments and on the prevailing financial market situation. Here, Minsky not only extends Keynes, but also Irving Fisher's (Fisher, 1933) debt deflation theory, which, under the influence of the Great Depression, tackles very similar mechanisms.

Overall, when studying the work of Wicksell, of Keynes beyond the *General Theory* and Minsky from the point of view of how financial markets and institutions are integrated into the process of innovation and investment, it comes as a surprise how similar many of their thoughts are to Schumpeter's view. Of course, there are many differences in detail and in the scope of the analysis, in particular the time horizon covered – cyclical or more long-term – creates a clear distinction. But, at the same time, all three examples stress the same kind of mechanism: the importance of financing and financial behaviour for economic growth.

5. SOMETHING TO LEARN FOR THE PATH OF ECONOMIC DEVELOPMENT IN CEE AND SEE COUNTRIES?

The link between financial developments and economic growth has now reappeared in the economic literature, with pioneering work done by Levine and others starting in the early 1990s. As usual, the results of empirical research available so far are not fully unambiguous, but today the generally held perspective is much closer to Schumpeter's view that financial development is connected to and indeed supports economic activity than it was for decades in mainstream economics.

Three major channels for this interaction are mainly held to be important from a modern point of view: first, financial development can spur economic growth by reducing the cost of capital. To the extent that financial development is associated with the entry of new financial intermediaries, competition in financial markets is likely to intensify, which can be expected to lead to a reduction in the cost of financial intermediation and an enhanced availability of credit. In addition, increased competition can be expected to contribute to an increase in the efficiency of the overall financial system.

Second, financial development can also enhance growth by allocating capital more efficiently across alternative investments. By facilitating the trading, hedging and pooling of risks, a more developed financial sector allows investors to fund risky but profitable investment projects that would otherwise be forgone. Furthermore, to the extent that more sophisticated financial intermediaries are more effective in distinguishing good and bad projects, funds are allocated to more profitable projects, enhancing the productivity of the economy as a whole. Also, more developed financial markets may reduce the cost of financial intermediation since they can deal better with the problems caused by asymmetric information.

Finally, financial development may affect households' savings rate. Nevertheless, the direction of this effect is not straightforward. On the one hand, financial development and integration may have a positive impact on the savings ratio, by offering households a broader and more secure range of vehicles for savings. On the other hand, financial development may also provide households with better insurance against shocks, and offer them better and cheaper access to credit. Therefore, the impact on households' net savings may turn negative. However, it should be borne in mind that especially in economies with open capital accounts, to which the countries in Central and Eastern Europe belong, domestic investment activity may decouple from domestic savings, weakening the relationship between the domestic savings rate and economic growth.

In parallel, empirical research has concluded that further financial development and integration in the euro area could spur economic growth, at least to some extent and if not compensated by other negative impacts. Countries with initially weak financial structures and countries with the dominance of small and medium-sized enterprises (SMEs) have been found to be the main beneficiaries of financial development. These results have clear implications for the countries in CEE and SEE, particularly, as they currently have relatively underdeveloped financial structures and a strong share of SMEs. Therefore, if the validity of the finance–growth nexus was to be found in these countries, it would strongly benefit the economic catching-up process. This makes research in this field – along the avenue described by Schumpeter and others – a very interesting issue with far-reaching implications.

Based on these results, the development of financial markets and financial institutions is seen now as an important prerequisite for successful transformation. Adequate payment facilities, sufficient mobilizing of funds, efficient channelling of domestic savings into productive investment and raising an appropriate amount of risk capital are widely accepted as important features for the development of a market economy and to exploit the growth potential of a country. At the same time, to avoid financial fragility and macroeconomic instability it is also necessary to address potential problems of the liberalization and the development of the financial sector. These efforts must be in line with the needs of transformation in the real sector of the economy.

Whereas traditional pure economic theory quickly leads to fairly clear-cut conclusions about the advantages of a fully liberalized financial environment, one has to learn from history that these comparative static results, derived under conditions of perfect markets and rational economic agents, are not automatically applicable to any stage of economic development or any market structure in the real world (Shiller, 2002). It should, for example, be remembered that the Western European market economies were allowed to realize their successful economic development after World War II under a different regime.

Perhaps the most important historical lesson from comparing the preconditions and experiences of financial market development in different countries can be that transformation, development and the process of establishing sufficient market structures and institutions require quite a long time. To establish a financial setting appropriate for transformation and economic development and to avoid the risk of financial instability and crisis is a very tricky exercise, in particular at a very early stage of economic development when substantial institutional adaptation is necessary.

6. CONCLUSIONS

Without doubt, financial market developments, in particular financial market growth and a marked differentiation of financial products, have shaped the economic situation of the twentieth century to an enormous extent. Although the framework conditions for this development after World War II may have been very specific, historical experience makes it rather unlikely that there is no interrelationship between financial market developments and the real economy, or only a negligible one. This brings us back to Schumpeter who dedicated particular importance to financing and financial intermediation in determining the growth rate.

Surprisingly enough, and rather contrary to Schumpeter and some others, mainstream economic theory as well as financial economics have considerable problems in sufficiently integrating financial markets into macroeconomic analysis. At the same time, economic policy-makers had and have to regard financial market developments as a growing and permanent economic policy challenge. More recent theoretical developments (for example Behavioral Finance), try to react to this challenge and to give financial markets an independent new role. The role financial markets are allowed to play in the context of macroeconomic thinking, and consequently in policy suggestions based thereon, implicitly hinges first and foremost on the underlying theoretical model.

One specific aspect of the debate is that nowadays the overall degree of development of a financial system is seen to be the important factor instead of the extensively discussed differences between bank-based and market-based financial systems (Levine, 2000). This seems to be very likely in line with Schumpeter's approach, if he were in a position to adapt his argumentation to modern circumstances. Well-developed financial markets can be expected to have a positive influence on economic performance, to a large extent independently of a specific structure of a financial system (Levine, 2003; Manning, 2003). In addition, institutional differences – for example in the legal system – are considered to explain the main differences in how financial systems work and how efficient they are. Structural features of financial systems do also play a role for the efficiency of financial systems, but these are primarily related to specific distributive effects of financing depending on the type of firm (for example a small versus a large firm) or the type of financing (for example financing of innovations versus financing of traditional sectors).

In the end, the functional efficiency of a financial system, centring on the efficient transfer of funds with a view to financing investment and innovation, directly relates financial markets to the real economy and Schumpeterian economic development. Almost by definition, functional efficiency takes the priority a financial system needs to fulfil from a macroeconomic point of view. Factors determining the transfer of financial funds to 'entrepreneurs' and 'innovators' are essential for the potential level of investment and the dynamics of the growth path of the economy to be realized. Combining historical, economic policy and financial market perspectives, there seems to be a clear need for a re-orientation in Schumpeter's direction of a macroeconomic theory integrating financing and its impact on economic development into the core of the analysis.

NOTES

1. Interestingly enough, 1883 is also the year in which Karl Marx died and John Maynard Keynes was born.
2. Today the name of the city is Trest and it is situated in Moravia, Czech Republic.
3. See Backhaus (2003), Frisch (1982), Haberler (1950) and/or Swedberg (1994) for a comprehensive account of Schumpeter's life and scientific work.
4. To avoid any confusion: the first issue of Schumpeter's *Theorie der Wirtschaftlichen Entwicklung*, while dated 1912, had in fact been published already in 1911 (Swedberg, 1994).
5. Other authors explicitly mentioning the Schumpeterian context of their work are, for example, Fernandez and Galetovic (1994) or Sinha (2001).
6. In modern economics Schumpeter's argumentation would possibly relate to the potential growth path of an economy.

BIBLIOGRAPHY

Arestis, Ph., M. Deai and S. Dow (eds) (2002), *Money, Macroeconomics and Keynes*, London: Routledge.

Arestis, Ph. and H. Stein (2005), 'Finance and development: the role of institutions', *International Review of Applied Economics*, Special Issue, **19** (4).

Ausch, K. (1968), *Als die Banken Fielen*, Vienna: Europa Verlag.

Backhaus, J. (2003), *Joseph Alois Schumpeter*, Dordrecht: Kluwer Academic Publishers.

Blaugh, M. (1978), *Economic Theory in Retrospect*, Cambridge: Cambridge University Press.

Busch, U. (2003), 'Joseph A. Schumpeter's "Soziologie des Geldes"', in J. Backhaus (ed.), *Joseph Alois Schumpeter*, Dordrecht: Kluwer Academic Publishers.

Davidson, P. (1978), *Money and the Real World*, London: Wiley.

Demirgüç-Kunt, A. and R. Levine (2001), '*Financial Structure and Economic Growth: A Cross-Country Comparison of Banks, Markets, and Development*', Cambridge, MA: MIT Press.

Demirgüç-Kunt, A. and V. Maksimovic (2002), 'Funding growth in bank-based and market-based financial systems: Evidence from firm-level data', in *Journal of Financial Economics*, **65** (3), 337–63.

Dolar, V. and C. Meh (2002), 'Financial structure and economic growth: A non-technical survey', in Bank of Canada Working Paper 2002–2024.

Fernandez, D. and A. Galetovic (1994), *Schumpeter Might be Right – But Why?*, SAIS, John Hopkins University Working Paper (96-01).
Fisher, I. (1933), 'The debt-deflation theory of great depressions', *Econometrica*, **1**.
Formaini, R.L. (2005), 'Knut Wicksell, The birth of modern monetary policy', Federal Reserve Bank of Dallas, *Economic Insights*, **9** (1).
Frisch, H. (1982), *Schumpeterian Economics*, New York: Praeger.
Gerschenkron, A. (1963), *Economic Backwardness in Historical Perspective*, Cambridge, MA: Harvard University Press.
Giannetti, M., L. Guiso, T. Japelli, M. Padula and M. Pagano (2002), 'Financial market integration, corporate financing and economic growth', in *Economic Papers* No. 179, European Commission.
Giovannini, A. (ed.) (1993), *Finance and Development: Issues and Experiences*, Cambridge: Cambridge University Press.
Goldsmith, R. (1969), *Financial Structure and Development*, New Haven: Yale University Press.
Gurley, J. and E. Shaw (1955), 'Financial aspects of economic development', *American Economic Review*, **XLV**.
Haberler, G. (1950), 'Joseph Alois Schumpeter 1883–1950', *The Quarterly Journal of Economics*, **3**.
Keynes, J.M. (1923), *A Tract on Monetary Reform*, London: The Macmillan Press.
Keynes, J.M. (1930), *A Treatise on Money*, London: The Macmillan Press.
Keynes, J.M. (1933), 'A monetary theory of production', in D. Moggridge (1987), *John Maynard Keynes, The General Theory and After*, London: The Macmillan Press.
Keynes, J.M. (1936), *The General Theory of Employment, Interest and Money*, London: The Macmillan Press.
Keynes, J.M. (1937), 'The general theory of employment', in D. Moggridge (1987), *John Maynard Keynes, The General Theory and After*, London: The Macmillan Press.
King, R. and R. Levine (1993), 'Finance and growth: Schumpeter might be right', in *Quarterly Journal of Economics*, **CVIII**.
Leahy, M., S. Schich, G. Wehinger, F. Pelgrin and Th. Thorgeirsson (2001), 'Contributions of financial systems to growth in OECD countries', in Economics Department Working Papers No. 280, OECD.
Levine, R. (1997), 'Financial development and economic growth: Views and agenda', *Journal of Economic Literature*, **35,** 688–726.
Levine, R. (2000), *Bank-Based or Market-Based Financial Systems: Which is Better?* University of Minnesota, Department of Finance Working Papar (0005), June.
Levine, R. (2003), 'More on finance and growth: More finance, more growth?' *Federal Reserve Bank of St. Louis Review*, July/August.
Manning, M. (2003), 'Finance causes growth: Can we be so sure?', *Contributions to Macroeconomics*, **1**.
McKinnon, R. (1973), *Money and Capital in Economic Development*, Washington: Brookings Institution.
Minsky, H. (1976), *John Maynard Keynes*, London: Palgrave Macmillan.
Mises, L. (1980), *The Theory of Money and Credit*, Indianapolis: Liberty Classics.
Moggridge, D. (1987), *John Maynard Keynes, The General Theory and After*, London: The Macmillan Press.
Pagano, M. (1993), 'Financial markets and growth: An overview', *European Economic Review*, **37** (2/3).

Schumpeter, J. (1911), *Theorie der Wirtschaftlichen Entwicklung*, Leipzig: Duncker and Humblot.

Schumpeter, J. (1917), *Das Sozialprodukt und die Rechenpfennige*, Archiv für Sozialwissenschaft und Sozialpolitik, **44**.

Schumpeter, J. (1934), *The Theory of Economic Development*, Cambridge, MA: Harvard University Press.

Schumpeter, J. (1939), *Business Cycles: A Theoretical, Historical and Statistical Analysis of the Capitalist Process*, New York and London: Macgraw Hill.

Schumpeter, J.A. (1970), *Das Wesen des Geldes* (the nature of money), Göttingen (aus dem Nachlass herausgegeben von F.K. Mann), Vandenhoek & Ruprecht.

Screpanti, E. and S. Zamagni (2005), *An Outline of the History of Economic Thought*, Oxford: Oxford University Press.

Shiller, R. (2002), 'From efficient market theory to behavioral finance', in Cowles Foundation Discussion Paper No. 1385, October.

Sinha, T. (2001), 'The role of financial intermediation in economic growth: Schumpeter revisited', in S. Dahiya and V. Orati (eds), *Economic Theory in the Light of Schumpeter's Scientific Heritage*, Rohtak, India: Spellbound Publishers.

Spiegel, H. (1983), *The Growth of Economic Thought*, Durham: Duke University Press.

Streissler, E. (1982), 'Schumpeter's Vienna and the role of credit in innovation', in H. Frisch (1982), *Schumpeterian Economics*, New York: Praeger.

Swedberg, R. (1994), *Joseph A. Schumpeter*, Stuttgart: Klett Cotta.

Thiel, M. (2001), 'Finance and economic growth – A review of theory and the available evidence', in *Economic Papers*, No. 158, European Commission, July.

Wachtel, P. (2001), 'Growth and finance', *International Finance*, **4** (3).

Wicksell, K. (1913 and 1922), *Vorlesungen über Nationalökonomie*, Jena: Gustav Fischer.

Wicksell, K. (1934), *Lectures on Political Economy*, London: Macmillan.

Wicksell, K. (1965), *Interest and Prices*, New York (English translation of 'Geldzins und Güterpreise', 1898).

Wieser, F. (1914), *Theorie der gesellschaftlichen Wirtschaft*, Tübingen: JCB Mohr (Paul Siebeck).

10. The impact of the euro on investment: sectoral evidence

Tomas Dvorak*

1. INTRODUCTION

There is overwhelming evidence that European financial markets are becoming more integrated, and that a great deal of this integration has been facilitated by the common currency (for a survey see Baele et al., 2004, or Cappiello et al., 2005). However, evidence that this integration has any real effect on resource allocation is scarce. Economists expect that financial integration will lead to more investment and to a more efficient allocation of capital. More investment is expected as a result of the lower cost of capital. More efficient allocation of capital is expected because integrated financial markets should be better at identifying investment opportunities. Financial integration is not an end in itself but rather a means to achieve higher economic growth. Greater investment and its more efficient allocation are the two principal channels through which financial integration will lead to growth. The purpose of this chapter is to investigate these two channels. Specifically, I ask whether the introduction of the euro led to more investment and caused the additional funds to be allocated more efficiently.

That financial integration will ultimately lead to growth seems to be generally accepted. A document describing the financial policy of the European Commission states that 'The economic benefits of European financial integration are beyond doubt' (European Commission, 2005, p. 5). As evidence, the European Commission points to two studies. The first study is London Economics (2002), which simulates the effects of the reduced cost of capital in a macro model and finds a significant increase in GDP. The key mechanism is that a lower cost of capital increases investment, which in turn raises GDP. The second study is Guiso et al. (2004), who try to quantify the effect of financial integration on growth. They argue that financial integration facilitates financial development for the less financially developed countries. They draw on the large 'finance and growth' literature that established a positive link between financial development and growth.[1] Using a number of simulations they find that the 'growth dividend' from financial integration in

Europe is substantial – especially for the currently less financially developed countries. Guiso et al. are, however, silent on the exact channels through which financial integration affects growth.

My strategy is to look at the two channels through which financial integration is expected to lead to growth. My approach is therefore more structural than that of the two studies above. If financial integration does not lead to either more investment or to its better allocation, then there is little hope for financial integration to lead to growth through other channels. Another aspect of my strategy is to use the euro's introduction as a one-time increase in the degree of financial integration. Financial integration is normally a gradual process, but the introduction of the euro is an event which may provide the statistical power to estimate its effects. The adoption of the common currency has eliminated exchange rate risk, lowered information barriers and increased liquidity in financial markets. Since the euro facilitates financial integration, I, in part, interpret its effects as the effects of financial integration.

I use panel data on 27 industries in 17 countries for ten yeas. The time period covers five years prior to and five years following the introduction of the euro. It includes countries that adopted the euro as well as those that did not. In my baseline specification I regress the growth rate of investment on time, country and industry fixed effects and a dummy indicating the years and countries in which the euro was used as the official currency. The coefficient on the euro is the difference-in-differences estimator of the effect of the euro on the growth rate of investment. I find that the euro is associated with an increase in the growth rate of investment of about five percentage points. This effect is extremely robust and persists even after controlling for aggregate stock returns, changes in interest rates, GDP growth and other factors. The effect also appears to be greatest immediately following the euro's introduction in 1999 and then gradually declines.

The impact of the euro on investment should not be uniform across countries and across industries. If the euro opens the door to large and liquid financial markets, then countries with previously low levels of financial development should benefit more than countries that already had developed financial markets. I find that the impact of the euro is no greater in countries with previously low levels of financial development. This suggests that the euro enhances the workings of financial markets in *all* countries – not just in those that are financially less developed. Thus, one of the main predictions of Guiso et al. (2004) that the growth dividend will be larger in financially less developed countries is not supported by my findings on the euro's effect on investment.

The impact of the euro also varies by industry. Financial integration particularly benefits financially constrained firms or firms which depend heavily on external finance. If these characteristics vary across industries, then the euro's impact should also vary across industries. I use a number of industry characteristics including an index of dependence on external finance, average establishment size, investment, R&D and export intensities. I find that the euro's impact is greater in industries that depend on external finance – evidence that is consistent with the finding that the euro facilitates financial development, and with the prediction of Guiso et al. (2004) that financially dependent industries benefit most from financial integration.

I find no evidence that the euro has led to a more efficient allocation of capital. I do find that investment tends to flow to industries with high multi-factor and capital productivity growth. This tendency, however, does not change after the introduction of the euro. This is inconsistent with the hypothesis that the euro and the associated financial market integration will improve the efficiency of capital allocation.

My contribution is closely related to Bris et al. (2005), who show that after 1999 firms in euro countries invested more than firms in non-euro countries. The difference is that I use sectoral instead of firm-level data, and that in addition to investigating the effect of the euro on investment, I examine the euro's effect on the efficiency of investment. Also, while they focus on the difference between the effect of the euro in weak and strong currency countries, I emphasize the variation of the euro's effect according to different levels of financial development and industry dependence on external finance. My results confirm those of Bris et al. that the euro has led to a substantial increase in investment.

Another paper on real effects of the euro is Blanchard and Giavazzi (2002), who find that the link between national investment and savings has recently weakened in Europe, and especially in the Economic and Monetary Union (EMU). This confirms that the EMU countries are becoming financially integrated, and that this integration has real effects on choices of consumers and investors.

I also build on the literature documenting the financial integration in Europe and the role played by the common currency in facilitating this integration. For example, Sentana (2002) and Hardouvelis et al. (2002) find that financial integration leads to a lower cost of capital. It is reasonable to ask if the lower cost of capital had any real effects and spurred investment. Similarly, the boom in corporate bond issuance reported by Pagano (2004) or the reduction in underwriting fees reported by Santos and Tsatsaronis (2003) is expected to allow firms to raise more funds for investment. In addition, the competition and shifts in portfolio allocation as reported by Adam et al. (2002, pp. 36–7) would lead investment to its most productive use. Whether these developments led to higher and more efficient investment is the subject of this chapter.

2. DATA

I use data from the STAN database published by the OECD. STAN includes annual industry level data for most of the OECD countries. The available information includes production, value added, labour input and investment. I use data on 10 euro and 7 non-euro countries. Of the euro countries Ireland is excluded because Irish data are not available in STAN, and Luxembourg is excluded because it does not publish data on investment. Also excluded due to insufficient investment data are New Zealand and Japan. The industry breakdown varies across countries ranging from two- to four-digit detail of the ISIC rev. 3 classification. In order to form a sample of independent observations I use only non-overlapping industries. For example, if I include transport equipment (ISIC 34-35) I do not include motor vehicles (ISIC 34) because it is contained within the former. Since the industry detail varies across countries and across different sectors, I choose a combination of two-digit industries to maximize the number of observations.

The dependent variable throughout this chapter is the growth rate of real gross fixed capital formation (STAN code GFCFK).[2] It includes net acquisition of new tangible (for example machinery and equipment, livestock, constructions) as well as non-tangible assets (for example software, mineral exploration) which are intended to be used for more than one year. It excludes acquisition of land and military outlays by government. Table 10.1 shows the descriptive statistics of investment growth for the entire sample as well as the breakdown by euro vs. non-euro country and pre-euro vs. post-euro years. For the entire sample average investment growth was 4 per cent per year, with the median growth of 3.6 per cent. There are 3790 observations on investment growth in the entire sample. On average, investment grew faster in the pre-euro years than in post-euro years and it grew faster in euro countries than in non-euro countries.

As a measure of industry output I use the growth rate of real value-added (STAN code VALUK). I also calculate three measures of productivity growth. Labour productivity growth is the difference between the growth of real value-added and the growth of total employment (STAN code EMPN). The second measure of productivity growth is the difference between the growth of real value and the growth rate of real net capital stock (STAN code NCAPK). I call this capital productivity growth. Finally, multi-factor productivity growth is the difference between the growth of real value-added and the weighted average of employment and real capital stock growth. The weight on employment growth is the labour's share in value-added (LABR/VALU). One minus the labour's share is the weight on the growth of real capital stock. It is important to note that the

Table 10.1 Descriptive statistics of investment growth

	All years	Pre-euro (1993–1998)	Post-euro (1999–2003)
All countries			
Mean	0.040	0.067	0.010
Median	0.036	0.057	0.015
Standard deviation	0.205	0.231	0.168
Number of observations	3790	1982	1808
Non-euro countries			
Mean	0.057	0.098	0.001
Median	0.051	0.081	0.014
Standard deviation	0.233	0.260	0.176
Number of observations	1437	825	612
Euro countries			
Mean	0.030	0.045	0.016
Median	0.028	0.042	0.015
Standard deviation	0.185	0.204	0.163
Number of observations	2353	1157	1196

Note: Investment growth is the growth rate of real gross fixed capital formation. The non-euro countries are Australia, Canada, Denmark, Sweden, the United Kingdom and the United States. The euro countries include Austria, Belgium, Finland, France, Germany, Greece, Italy, the Netherlands and Portugal.

Source: Author's calculations.

data on capital stock in STAN have many missing observations and are currently under review by the OECD.

I also use a number of industry characteristics. The first is an index of dependence on external finance (*RZ*) as constructed by Rajan and Zingales (1998). It is designed to measure technological demand for external financing – it is high when an industry depends on external financing (such as drugs and pharmaceuticals) and low if an industry does not require a lot of external financing (such as tobacco). The *RZ* measure is available in the ISIC rev. 2 industry classification, whereas the STAN data uses ISIC rev. 3 classification. In addition, *RZ* is available only for manufacturing. Using rev. 2 to rev. 3 concordance, I was able to match the *RZ* measure to 11 out of 27 of my industries. The second industry characteristic is investment intensity (*Inv*), calculated as the share of gross fixed capital formation in value-added (GFCK/VALU in STAN codes). The third characteristic is export intensity, calculated as the share of exports in value-added (EXP/VALU in STAN codes). The fourth characteristic is research and development intensity (*R&D*) calculated as the share of R&D expenditures in value-added. The data on R&D expenditures come from the OECD's *Science and Technology* database, which uses the same industry classification as STAN. Finally, *Size* is measured as total employment divided by the number of establishments. This comes from an older OECD database entitled *Structural Statistics for Industry and Services*.

Finally, I include a number of macroeconomic variables. Aggregate stock returns are logarithmic returns of the dollar MSCI price index for each country. Real GDP growth and the log of GDP per capita (in 2000 US dollars) come from the *World Development Indicators*. As long-term interest rates I used 10-year government bond yields from the *International Financial Statistics* (for Canada, Austria and Norway) and Eurostat (all other countries).

3. ESTIMATION

3.1 Does the Euro Lead to More Investment?

My goal is to measure the effect of the common currency on investment. We see in Table 10.1 that average investment growth before the euro's introduction was *lower* than in the years after. It is possible that the high investment growth prior to 1999 was driven by the worldwide investment boom of the late 1990s and that the decline in investment afterwards had nothing to do with the euro's introduction. Clearly, investment is in large part driven by business cycles. Also, in Table 10.1 we see that on average, investment growth in euro countries was *lower* than in non-euro countries. It is possible that the euro countries typically invest less that the non-euro countries. For example, Germany has had a low investment growth for the past decade – both before and after the euro's introduction.

In order to measure the effect of the euro on investment growth, we need to evaluate the change in the investment growth in euro countries *relative* to the change in the investment growth in non-euro countries. In other words, we need a difference-in-differences estimator. The panel nature of my data is ideally suited for this task. First, I include fixed year effects to control for factors that vary over time but which are common across countries (for example the worldwide investment boom in the late 1990s). Second, I include country fixed effects to control for factors that vary across countries but which are constant over time (for example the sluggish investment growth in Germany). Finally, I include industry effects to control for the fact that some industries (for example telecommunications) grow faster than others. The baseline specification is as follows:

$$I_{i,j,t} = \phi_i + \psi_j + \omega_t + \beta Euro_{j,t} + \varepsilon_{i,j,t} \tag{10.1}$$

where $I_{i,j,t}$ is the growth rate of investment in industry i, country j and year t, ϕ_i, ψ_j and ω_t are industry, country and year fixed effects, and *Euro* is a dummy variable equal to one in years and countries in which the euro is the official currency. The coefficient of interest is β. It is the difference between the expected growth rate of investment after and before the introduction of the euro conditional on a typical investment in a given country, year and industry. If the euro spurs investment, then β should be positive and significant. I assume that the error terms $\varepsilon_{i,j,t}$ are independent across countries but may be correlated within countries – across industries and over time. This addresses the possible serial correlation in residuals that often plagues the difference-in-differences estimates as pointed out by Bertrand et al. (2004).

I expand the baseline specification to control for a number of macroeconomic factors that typically appear in investment equations. First, I include lagged GDP growth to capture aggregate business cycle fluctuations as in accelerator models of investment of Clark (1979) or Acemoglu (1993). Second, I include aggregate stock market returns which serve both as a proxy for Tobin's q and a financial accelerator. Third, I include lagged interest rates and lagged changes in interest rates. Finally, following Bris et al. (2005) I include GDP per capita. Unfortunately, STAN does not include any balance sheet data and therefore I am unable to include cash flow, cash holdings or leverage. I am also unable to calculate industry level q. However, if variables such as q or cash flow vary over time and across industries but not across countries, they could be controlled for by including interactions between the industry and year dummies. Therefore, I include these interactions in nearly all of the specifications in this contribution.[3] Including the interactions controls for other industry- and year-specific factors, for example the plunge in investment in telecommunications in 2002. To control for all industry- and country-specific factors (for example the surge in infrastructure investment in Greece prior to the 2004 Olympic Games) I include the interactions between industry and country dummies.[4]

Table 10.2 shows the results. The first column shows the estimates of equation (10.1). The estimate of β is positive and statistically significant. It shows that investment growth in countries that adopted the euro is 6.7 percentage points higher than it would have been otherwise. Given the average value of investment growth of 4 per cent, I regard this effect as large and economically significant. The effect is also about 4 percentage points larger

Table 10.2 Does the euro lead to more investment?

	(1)	(2)	(3)	(4)	(5)	(6)	(7)	(8)
Euro	0.067**	0.057**	0.068**	0.058*	0.069**	0.058**	0.070**	0.059*
	(3.61)	(2.65)	(3.42)	(2.53)	(3.75)	(2.84)	(3.52)	(2.67)
Aggregate stock returns		−0.001		0.000		−0.003		−0.003
		(–0.03)		0.01		(–0.14)		(–0.11)
Lagged interest rate		−0.002		−0.002		−0.002		−0.002
		(–0.52)		(–0.44)		(–0.62)		(–0.55)
Lagged change in int. rate		−0.013**		−0.011*		−0.012**		−0.011**
		(–2.72)		(–2.54)		(–3.11)		(–2.97)
Lagged GDP per capita		−0.643**		−0.654**		−0.646**		−0.654**
		(–4.87)		(–4.55)		(–4.87)		(–4.61)
Lagged GDP growth		0.664		0.607		0.699		0.640
		(1.03)		(0.84)		(1.12)		(0.91)
Country*industry dummies	No	No	Yes	Yes	No	No	Yes	Yes
Year*industry dummies	No	No	No	No	Yes	Yes	Yes	Yes
N	3790	3790	3790	3790	3790	3790	3790	3790
R-squared	0.066	0.071	0.123	0.128	0.146	0.151	0.203	0.208

Notes: The dependent variable is the growth rate of real investment. *Euro* is a dummy variable equal to one for years and countries in which the euro is used as the official currency. All specifications include year, country and industry fixed effects. Macroeconomic controls include aggregate stock returns, lagged GDP growth, lagged interest rates, lagged change in interest rates and per capita GDP. T-statistics calculated using robust and country 'clustered' standard errors are in parentheses. * and ** indicate significance at 5 and 1 per cent levels.

Source: Author's calculations.

than that found in Bris et al. (2005). In specification (2) I control for the macroeconomic variables: aggregate stock returns, lagged interest rates, lagged changes in interest rates, lagged log of GDP per capita and lagged GDP growth. With these controls the magnitude of β drops somewhat but remains statistically and economically significant.

In specifications (3) and (4) I include interaction terms between the year and industry dummies. The coefficient on the euro dummy remains statistically significant and of similar magnitude. The magnitude drops when macroeconomic controls are added, but the coefficient again remains statistically and economically significant. The inclusion of the interaction terms increases the R-squared to 0.12. In specifications (5) and (6) I include interaction terms between the industry and country dummies. The results regarding the effect of the euro remain unchanged. The same is true when both sets of interactions are included.

In order to check if the effect of the euro on investment is robust, in Table 10.3 I re-estimate some of the specifications from Table 10.2 using four sub-samples. The first sub-sample includes only manufacturing industries. I include only the specifications with macroeconomic controls. The effect of the euro remains highly statistically significant with a magnitude ranging from 5.3 to 9.6 percentage points. The second sub-sample is the non-manufacturing sector. The effect is again statistically significant with a magnitude of around 6.5 percentage points as shown in panel b. The third sub-sample, estimated in panel c, excludes the three non-European countries (Australia, Canada and the US) from the sample. Once again, I find the effect of the euro statistically significant and of a similar magnitude as before. Finally, in panel d I eliminate observations that fall into the top and bottom 1 per cent of observations of investment growth. This eliminates any outliers. The magnitude of the effect of the euro now appears somewhat smaller – around 4.2 percentage points – but the t-statistics are much higher. Clearly, the elimination of extreme values of investment growth improved the precision of my estimates. In addition to these four reported robustness checks I tried excluding the UK, excluding electrical equipment and telecommunications, excluding public administration, education and health. In all cases the effect of the euro remains both statistically and economically significant.

3.2 Does the Impact of the Euro Vary over Time?

I examine if the effects of the euro are different in different years. Instead of including one *Euro* dummy as in equation (10.1), I include a set of five interactions between the *Euro* dummy and five dummies, each indicating one of the five post-euro years. For example, *Euro* Year* 2002 equals one for

Table 10.3 *Does the euro lead to more investment? Robustness check*

	(1)	(2)	(3)	(4)
Panel a: Manufacturing only				
Euro	0.053**	0.053**	0.054**	0.054**
	(3.04)	(2.85)	(3.02)	(2.81)
Country*industry dummies	No	Yes	No	Yes
Year*industry dummies	No	No	Yes	Yes
R-squared	0.142	0.176	0.222	0.256
N	1572	1572	1572	1572
Panel b: Non-manufacturing only				
Euro	0.063*	0.064*	0.061*	0.063*
	(2.26)	(2.20)	(2.28)	(2.18)
Country*industry dummies	No	Yes	No	Yes
Year*industry dummies	No	No	Yes	Yes
R-squared	0.057	0.120	0.122	0.184
N	2218	2218	2218	2218
Panel c: Europe only				
Euro	0.067*	0.069*	0.066*	0.069*
	(2.35)	(2.26)	(2.42)	(2.30)
Country*industry dummies	No	Yes	No	Yes
Year*industry dummies	No	No	Yes	Yes
R-squared	0.071	0.129	0.151	0.209
N	3240	3240	3240	3240
Panel d: Without bottom and top 1 per cent				
Euro	0.042**	0.042**	0.043**	0.042**
	(3.93)	(3.67)	(4.15)	(3.85)
Country*industry dummies	No	Yes	No	Yes
Year*industry dummies	No	No	Yes	Yes
R-squared	0.095	0.155	0.195	0.253
N	3715	3715	3715	3715

Notes: The dependent variable is the growth rate of real investment. *Euro* is a dummy variable equal to one for years and countries in which the euro is used as the official currency. All specifications include year, country and industry fixed effects. Macroeconomic controls include aggregate stock returns, lagged GDP growth, lagged interest rates, lagged change in interest rates and per capita GDP. T-statistics calculated using robust and country 'clustered' standard errors are in parentheses. * and ** indicate significance at 5 and 1 per cent levels.

Source: Author's calculations.

all EMU countries in 2002 and zero otherwise. The baseline specification can be written as:

$$I_{i,j,t} = \phi_i + \psi_j + \omega_t + \beta_s EURO_{j,t} * \omega_s + \varepsilon_{i,j,t} \tag{10.2}$$

where s=1999, . . ., 2003; and β_s is the effect of the euro in year s.

The results appear in Table 10.4. I show the results with and without the macroeconomic controls and with or without the country/industry and industry/year interaction terms. All specifications include year, country and industry dummies. It appears that the effect of the euro is greatest immediately following its introduction in 1999. The coefficient on the *Euro* Year* 1999 dummy is robustly significant and ranges from 8.6 to 9.8 percentage points. The effect is also robustly significant in 2000, but the magnitude of the effect is somewhat smaller, ranging from 6 to 6.8 percentage points. The effects of the euro in 2001 and in 2002 are significant at 5 per cent when macro controls are not included, but only at 10 per cent when macro

Table 10.4 Does the impact of the euro vary over time?

	(1)	(2)	(3)	(4)
Euro*Year 1999	0.089**	0.086**	0.098**	0.087**
	(3.04)	(3.00)	(3.23)	(3.37)
Euro*Year 2000	0.060*	0.064*	0.068*	0.060*
	(2.16)	(2.17)	(2.13)	(2.26)
Euro*Year 2001	0.062*	0.071	0.073*	0.066
	(2.36)	(1.90)	(2.56)	(1.75)
Euro*Year 2002	0.081*	0.077	0.071**	0.052
	(2.57)	(2.01)	(2.89)	(1.65)
Euro*Year 2003	−0.010	−0.005	−0.016	−0.032
	(−0.36)	(−0.17)	(−0.55)	(−1.16)
Macroeconomic controls	No	Yes	No	Yes
Country*industry dummies	No	No	Yes	Yes
Year*industry dummies	No	No	Yes	Yes
R-squared	0.101	0.104	0.235	0.239
N	3790	3790	3790	3790

Notes: The dependent variable is the growth rate of real investment. *Euro* is a dummy variable equal to one for years and countries in which the euro is used as the official currency. All specifications include year, country and industry dummies. Macroeconomic controls include aggregate stock returns, lagged GDP growth, lagged interest rates, lagged change in interest rates and per capita GDP. T-statistics calculated using robust and country 'clustered' standard errors are in parentheses. * and ** indicate significance at 5 and 1 per cent levels.

Source: Author's calculations.

controls are included. In 2003, the effect of the euro is statistically insignificant. Euro area firms invested more than non-euro area firms in 1999 and 2000, perhaps even in 2001 and 2002. However, by 2003 investment growth in the euro area is no greater than in the non-euro countries.

The gradual decline in the impact of the euro on investment growth stands in contrast with the euro's effect on trade. Both Micco et al. (2003) and Flam and Nordstrom (2003) find that the euro's positive effect on trade is greater in later years than immediately following the euro's introduction. The immediate impact of the euro is consistent with a rapid transformation of financial markets in the euro countries. Perhaps the elimination of exchange rate risk and the instant emergence of a booming corporate bond market spurred investment immediately following the euro's introduction. I find no evidence of reversals in investment. While investment growth in euro countries slows after 1999 it never turns negative. Thus, the euro's initial effect on investment is permanent. If the nearly 10 percentage points larger investment growth in euro countries was partly a result of euphoria over the common currency, firms do not appear to have scaled back investment once the euphoria passed.

3.3 Does the Impact of the Euro Vary across Countries?

To investigate whether the effect of the euro varies across countries I replace the single *Euro* dummy with a set of ten interactions between the euro dummy and the ten euro countries. For example, *Euro*Austria* equals one if the observation is for Austria and between 1999 and 2003. The baseline specification can be written as:

$$I_{i,j,t} = \phi_i + \psi_j + \omega_t + \beta_k EURO_{j,t} * \psi_k + \varepsilon_{i,j,t} \tag{10.3}$$

where k indexes the 10 EMU countries and β_k is the euro's effect in country k.

The results are presented in Table 10.5. The effect of the euro is statistically significant in most countries whether or not I include the macroeconomic controls or year/country/industry dummy interactions. The largest effect appears in Austria and France, ranging from 9.9 to 11.8 percentage points. The effects are also strong and robust in Germany, Belgium, Spain and the Netherlands. In Portugal the effect is significant only at the 10 per cent level when macroeconomic controls are included. The effect of the euro is significant in Italy and Greece only when macro controls are excluded. In Finland, the effect of the euro appears insignificant.

If the euro facilitates financial development in the less financially developed countries, its effect should be higher in those countries. Euro countries with historically low levels of financial development should experience

Table 10.5 Does the impact of the euro vary across countries?

	Euro's impact				Country characteristics		
	(1)	(2)	(3)	(4)	Market cap.	Claims fin. inst.	Acc't stand.
Euro*Austria	0.118**	0.099**	0.119**	0.100**	0.07	0.87	54
	(7.70)	(4.43)	(8.07)	(4.49)			
Euro*Belgium	0.057**	0.038*	0.063**	0.044*	0.26	0.37	61
	(3.73)	(2.14)	(3.83)	(2.23)			
Euro*Germany	0.094**	0.053*	0.095**	0.055*	0.19	0.92	62
	(6.40)	(2.10)	(6.07)	(2.01)			
Euro*Spain	0.072**	0.065*	0.076**	0.068*	0.18	0.72	64
	(4.94)	(2.20)	(4.54)	(2.14)			
Euro*Finland	0.018	0.056	0.021	0.058	0.18	0.67	77
	(1.19)	(1.73)	(1.27)	(1.70)			
Euro*France	0.118**	0.091**	0.118**	0.091**	0.20	0.91	69
	(8.06)	(3.26)	(9.86)	(3.40)			
Euro*Greece	0.047**	0.052	0.047**	0.045	0.08	0.40	55
	(3.07)	(0.99)	(3.03)	(0.88)			
Euro*Italy	0.073**	0.031	0.077**	0.031	0.12	0.51	62
	(4.75)	(1.15)	(4.39)	(1.14)			
Euro*Netherlands	0.040**	0.040**	0.044**	0.045**	0.41	1.28	64
	(2.65)	(2.66)	(2.64)	(2.63)			
Euro*Portugal	0.039*	0.046	0.042*	0.047	0.08	0.63	36
	(2.52)	(1.73)	(2.48)	(1.75)			
Macro controls	No	Yes	No	Yes			
Country*industry	No	No	Yes	Yes			
Year*industry	No	No	Yes	Yes			
R-squared	0.104	0.107	0.236	0.238			
N	3790	3790	3790	3790			

Notes: The dependent variable is the growth rate of real investment. *Euro* is a dummy variable equal to one for years and countries in which the euro is used as the official currency. All specifications include year, country and industry fixed effects. Macroeconomic controls include aggregate stock returns, lagged GDP growth, lagged interest rates, lagged change in interest rates and per capita GDP. T-statistics calculated using robust and country 'clustered' standard errors are in parentheses. * and ** indicate significance at 5 and 1 per cent levels.

Source: Author's calculations.

higher growth than countries with historically well developed financial markets. The last three columns of Table 10.5 show three measures of financial development. These data come from Demirgüç-Kunt and Levine (2001) and include market capitalization as a percentage of GDP, claims of banks and other financial institutions as a percentage of GDP and an index of accounting standards. All values are averages from 1980 to 1995.[5]

Comparing the estimated effects of the euro on investment and the characteristics of the financial systems prior to EMU, there does not appear to be a systematic relationship. If anything, the effect of the euro appears to be smaller in countries that are less financially developed. For example, the effect of the euro is less robust in Italy, Greece and Portugal, all of which rank in the bottom half on all three measures of financial development.

In order to systematically investigate the variation in the euro's impact I estimate another set of regressions. I create a dummy variable, *LowFD*, which is equal to one for the four countries that ranked in the bottom half on all three measures of financial development. These countries are Spain, Portugal, Greece and Italy. I interact the *LowFD* dummy with the *Euro* dummy. In addition, I interact the *Euro* dummy with each of the three specific financial development measures. Given that there are only ten EMU countries in my data, the *Euro* dummy and each of the interaction terms are highly correlated. For example, the correlation coefficient between the *Euro* dummy and the interaction between the *Euro* and accounting standards is nearly 0.99. Therefore, it may be difficult to estimate how the effect of the euro varies with financial development measures.

The results are reported in Table 10.6. The first two columns show that the coefficient on the interaction between *Euro* and *LowFD* is not statistically significant. This means that the difference between the impact of the euro in more or less financially developed countries is not statistically significant. When I interact the *Euro* dummy with the specific financial development measures, the coefficients are statistically insignificant at the 5 per cent level in all cases. Therefore, I do not find evidence that the effect of the euro varies with the level of financial development. However, this may be due to high collinearity rather than to the absence of structural differences. Only the interaction between *Euro* and market capitalization is statistically significant at 10 per cent when country/industry and year/industry interactions are excluded. The coefficient is negative, providing suggestive evidence that the effect of the euro is larger in countries with a low level of stock market development.

3.4 Does the Impact of the Euro Vary across Industries?

There is ample evidence that the effects of financial development vary across firm or industry characteristics. Most notably, Rajan and Zingales (1998) show that financial development affects industries that depend on external finance. If the euro facilitates financial development, its effects should also vary across industries. Similarly to the previous two subsections, I replace the *Euro* dummy with a set of 27 interactions between the *Euro* dummy and an industry dummy indicator. For example, *Euro*Agriculture* equals one if

Table 10.6 Does the impact of the euro vary by financial development?

	(1)	(2)	(3)	(4)	(5)	(6)	(7)	(8)
Euro	0.060**	0.062**	0.079**	0.078*	0.045	0.047	0.064	0.064
	(2.93)	(3.00)	(2.63)	(2.57)	(1.26)	(1.27)	(1.68)	(1.51)
Euro*low FD	−0.011	−0.013						
	(–0.55)	(–0.60)						
Euro*market cap.			−0.110	−0.095				
			(–1.86)	(–1.50)				
Euro*claims of fin. inst.					0.015	0.016		
					(0.43)	(0.43)		
Euro*acc't stand.							−0.000	−0.000
							(–0.23)	(–0.13)
Macro controls	Yes	Yes	Yes	Yes	Yes	Yes	Yes	Yes
Country*industry	No	Yes	No	Yes	No	Yes	No	Yes
Year*industry	No	Yes	No	Yes	No	Yes	No	Yes
R-squared	0.071	0.208	0.072	0.208	0.071	0.208	0.071	0.208
N	3790	3790	3790	3790	3790	3790	3790	3790

Notes: The dependent variable is the growth rate of real investment. *Euro* is a dummy variable equal to one for years and countries in which the euro is used as the official currency. *LowFD* is a dummy variable that equals one for Greece, Italy, Spain, and Portugal. All specifications include country, year and industry fixed effects and the interactions between industry and year effects, and industry and country effects. Each specification also includes macroeconomic controls: aggregate stock returns, lagged GDP growth, lagged interest rates, lagged change in interest rates and per capita GDP. T-statistics calculated using robust and country 'clustered' standard errors are in parentheses. * and ** indicate significance at 5 and 1 per cent levels.

Source: Author's calculations.

the observation is for agriculture in years and countries in which the euro is the official currency. The baseline specification can be written as:

$$I_{i,j,t} = \phi_i + \psi_j + \omega_t + \beta_i EURO_{j,t} {}^* \phi_i + \varepsilon_{i,j,t} \tag{10.4}$$

where β_i is the effect of the euro on investment in industry *i*.

Table 10.7 shows the results. I present only results with the macroeconomic controls included and with or without country/industry and industry/year interaction terms. It appears that the effect of the euro varies greatly across industries. This is especially true when I include the country/industry and industry/year interactions. Of the 27 industries, the effect is significant in 12 industries when interactions are excluded and in 7 when interactions are included.[6] Looking at the specification when country/industry and industry/year interactions are included, the effect of the euro appears particularly large in non-energy mining, machinery and

Table 10.7 Does the impact of the euro vary across industries?

	ISIC	β	t-stat	β	t-stat
Agriculture	1–2	0.026	3.11	−0.001	−0.04
Fishing	5	0.061	−0.45	0.208	0.83
Mining – energy	10–12	0.027	3.98	0.153	1.31
Mining – non-energy	13–14	0.039	2.70	0.151	2.77
Food and tobacco	15–16	0.025	3.62	0.070	2.80
Textiles, leather	17–19	0.028	−0.05	−0.015	−0.33
Wood	20	0.035	1.04	0.000	0.01
Paper and printing	21–22	0.034	1.78	0.059	0.83
Chemical products	23–25	0.030	1.86	0.046	1.07
Non-metal products	26	0.029	0.59	0.130	4.03
Basic metals	27–28	0.032	0.34	0.070	1.03
Machinery	29	0.031	1.69	0.099	2.71
Electrical equipment	30–33	0.039	1.31	0.151	4.31
Transport equipment	34–35	0.046	1.11	0.077	1.76
Manufacturing nec	36–37	0.029	0.42	0.047	1.30
Elec., gas, water	40–41	0.052	1.99	−0.008	−0.11
Construction	45	0.030	1.33	0.010	0.20
Wholesale, retail	50–52	0.024	1.95	0.013	0.48
Hotels, restaurants	55	0.029	2.16	0.095	1.89
Transport, storage	60–63	0.027	3.86	0.112	2.66
Telecommunications	64	0.037	1.76	0.087	1.73
Finance	65–67	0.038	1.36	0.113	2.32
Real estate	70–74	0.029	1.87	−0.007	−0.24
Public administration	75	0.025	4.25	−0.028	−0.99
Education	80	0.028	2.55	−0.037	−0.62
Health	85	0.028	2.89	−0.021	−0.52
Personal services	90–93	0.025	2.95	0.099	1.79
Macro controls		Yes		Yes	
Country*industry		No		Yes	
Year*industry		No		Yes	
R-squared		0.01		0.5	
N		3790		3790	

Notes: The dependent variable is the growth rate of real investment. *Euro* is a dummy variable equal to one for years and countries in which the euro is used as the official currency. All specifications include country, year and industry fixed effects and the interactions between industry and year effects, and industry and country effects. Each specification also includes macroeconomic controls: aggregate stock returns, lagged GDP growth, lagged interest rates, lagged change in interest rates and per capita GDP. T-statistics are calculated using robust and country 'clustered' standard errors. * and ** indicate significance at 5 and 1 per cent levels.

Source: Author's calculations.

equipment, electrical and optical equipment, finance, and transport and storage.

I examine the above effects in a systematic way by considering five industry characteristics: an index of industry's dependence on external finance constructed by Rajan and Zingales (1998) (*RZ*), share of research and development expenditures in value-added (*R&D*); share of investment in value-added (*Inv*); size measured as employment per establishment (*Size*); and share of exports in value-added (*Exp*). I interact these five industry characteristics with the *Euro* dummy so that I can estimate how the euro's impact varies with each characteristic. The baseline specification can be written as

$$I_{i,j,t} = \phi_i + \psi_j + \omega_t + \beta EURO_{j,t} + \gamma_X EURO_{j,t} {}^* X_{i,j} + \varepsilon_{i,j,t} \qquad (10.5)$$

where $X_{i,j}$ is the value of one of the five industry characteristics in industry i and country j, and γ_X measures how the effect of the euro varies with industry characteristic X.

The rationale for including the *RZ* measure is straightforward: if the euro improves the workings of financial markets, it should primarily help industries that depend on external finance. I include the *R&D* measure partly because it is correlated with the *RZ* measure and is available for more industries than *RZ*. Industries with the need for large R&D investment depend on financial markets to finance this investment. Of course, an industry's need for R&D does not mean that it will have high R&D expenditures, especially if external finance is unavailable.[7] Nonetheless, I expect the euro to spur investment in R&D intensive industries. Similarly, I also expect the euro to spur investment in investment-intensive industries as measured by *Inv*. I also examine if the effect of the euro varies by size. On the one hand, it is well known that small firms tend to be financially constrained (Gertler and Gilchrist, 1994). If the euro improves the workings of the financial market it should allow small firms which were previously financially constrained to invest more. On the other hand, Bartram and Karolyi (2005) find that the reduction in market risk following the introduction of the euro is greatest for large firms – hence larger firms should benefit more. In addition, the financial integration spurred by the euro has been more intense in equity and bond markets than in banking (Vives, 2001; Schoenmaker and Oosterloo, 2005). Since it is primarily large firms that tap equity and bond markets, it could again be large firms that benefit from the euro. Therefore, how size affects the euro's impact is ambiguous. Finally, I look at the effect of export intensity on the euro's impact on investment. I expect the export-intensive industries to invest more since a common currency reduces the cost of international trade.

The *RZ* measure is constant over time and across countries. For example, the *RZ* index is the same for the basic metals industry in all countries. The assumption is that an industry's technological need for external finance does not change with time and is the same across countries. The other four measures I average over time so that they vary only across industries and countries. For example, the share of *R&D* expenditures in the telecommunications industry is different in Germany than in Portugal, but in each case it is constant over time. I did this in part because *Size* and *R&D* expenditures have many missing values, and by averaging over time I am able to use more observations. I assume that the average size of an industry and its R&D intensity remain constant over time.

The results are shown in Table 10.8. I present only the results where country/industry and industry/year interactions, and macroeconomic controls are included. The coefficient on the interaction between *Euro* and *RZ* is positive and statistically significant. This means that the effect of the euro is greater in industries that depend on external finance. This is consistent with the euro facilitating financial development and allowing financially dependent firms to grow faster. It shows that industries in euro countries and years with an average value of *RZ* of about 0.36 are expected to invest about 4.5 percentage points more than industries in non-euro countries and years. However, the industries in euro countries and years with a maximum value of *RZ* index of 0.96 are expected to grow about 12 percentage points faster. I also examine if the impact of financial dependence on the effect of the euro is different in financially less developed countries. If the euro primarily enhances financial markets in countries with low financial development, then financial dependence should matter more in those countries. I interact the *Euro***RZ* term with the low financial development dummy *LowFD*. The coefficient on this (triple) interaction is statistically insignificant, suggesting that the euro enhances investment in financially dependent industries in *all* countries – not just those that are financially less developed.

The coefficients on the interactions between *Euro* and other industry characteristics are insignificant. Therefore, the euro seems to boost investment equally in industries with various R&D and investment intensities as well as in industries with various sizes of establishments. The coefficient on the interaction between the *Euro* and export intensity *Exp* is negative and statistically significant at the 10 per cent level. This suggests that the effect of the euro is lower in export intensive industries. This is puzzling since there is evidence that the euro increased trade both within and outside of EMU countries (Micco et al., 2003; Flam and Nordstrom, 2003). If the euro increases trade it should also increase investment in export intensive industries. One possibility, suggested by Bris et al. (2004) is that a common

Table 10.8 Does the impact of the euro vary by industry characteristics?

	(1)	(2)	(3)	(4)	(5)	(6)	(7)	(8)	(9)	(10)
Euro	0.009	0.011	0.048**	0.047**	0.050*	0.052*	0.092**	0.086**	0.091*	0.091*
	(0.33)	(0.40)	(3.49)	(3.40)	(2.09)	(2.06)	(7.64)	(7.37)	(2.59)	(2.42)
Euro*RZ	0.126**	0.107*								
	(2.69)	(2.02)								
Euro*RZ*LowFD		0.048								
		(1.04)								
Euro*RD			0.001	0.001						
			(0.56)	(0.56)						
Euro*RD*LowFD				0.008						
				(1.39)						
Euro*Inv					0.041	0.024				
					(0.88)	(0.37)				
Euro*Inv*LowFD						0.035				
						(0.60)				
Euro*Size							−0.000	−0.000		
							(–1.6)9	(–1.3)2		
Euro*Size*LowFD								0.001		
								(1.42)		
Euro*Exp									−0.008	−0.008
									(–1.96)	(–1.94)

Euro*Exp*LowFD										0.003
										(0.14)
R-squared	0.258	0.258	0.284	0.285	0.208	0.208	0.265	0.267	0.208	0.208
N	1572	1572	1886	1886	3790	3790	2176	2176	2341	2341

Notes: The dependent variable is the growth rate of real investment. *Euro* is a dummy variable equal to one for years and countries in which the euro is used as the official currency. *RZ* is a measure of industry dependence on external finance from Rajan and Zinglaes (1998). *RD*, *Inv* and *Exp* are the shares of R&D expenditures, investment and exports in value-added. *LowFD* is a dummy variable that equals one for Greece, Italy, Spain, and Portugal. All specifications include country, year and industry fixed effects and the interactions between industry and year effects, and industry and country effects. Each specification also includes macroeconomic controls: aggregate stock returns, lagged GDP growth, lagged interest rates, lagged change in interest rates and per capita GDP. T-statistics calculated using robust and country 'clustered' standard errors are in parentheses. * and ** indicate significance at 5 and 1 per cent levels.

Source: Author's calculations.

currency eliminates the possibility of competitive depreciations and therefore export industries in weak currency countries may invest less as a result.

3.5 Does the Euro lead to a more Efficient Allocation of Capital?

Measuring the efficiency of investment allocation is difficult. Capital is allocated efficiently if its marginal product is equal across all firms. The difficulty lies in measuring the marginal product of capital and also in the presence of adjustment costs. Various approaches have been adopted in the existing literature. Abiad et al. (2004) use the dispersion of Tobin's q as a measure of the efficiency of capital allocation. To the extent that q measures the marginal product of capital, a lower dispersion in q implies a more efficient allocation of capital. Galindo et al. (2003) measure the marginal return to capital as the ratio of sales to capital or profits to capital, and investigate if investment flows to firms with higher marginal return. Claessens and Laeven (2003) consider the efficiency of investment allocation across tangible and non-tangible assets. They find that in countries with poor property rights, firms under-invest in non-tangible assets. They emphasize the link between property rights, financing and growth. Another approach to measuring the efficiency of investment is in Chari and Henry (2004). They view investment as efficient when it takes place in firms that provide the most risk-sharing benefits.

In assessing the efficiency of investment I estimate the elasticity of investment with respect to value-added and three different measures of productivity. This strategy follows that of Wurgler (2000) and Maksimovic and Phillips (2002). Wurgler calculates the elasticity of investment with respect to output in order to evaluate the efficiency of financial markets across countries. Maksimovic and Phillips calculate the elasticity of investment with respect to shipments and different productivity measures in order to evaluate the efficiency of investment allocation within conglomerates.[8] These approaches are non-structural but have the advantage of being simple, intuitive and transparent. In contrast, the approaches that use Tobin's q critically depend on our ability to estimate q accurately. In order to evaluate the impact of the euro on investment efficiency I estimate the elasticities of investment with respect to value-added and productivity measures before and after the introduction of the euro. If the euro leads to more efficient investment, elasticities after its introduction should be higher than before. The baseline specification can be written as follows:

$$I_{i,j,t} = \phi_i + \psi_j + \omega_t + \beta EURO_{j,t} + \eta Q_{i,j,t} + \theta Q_{i,j,t} * EURO_{j,t} + \varepsilon_{i,j,t} \quad (10.6)$$

where $Q_{i,j,t}$ is either value-added growth, labour, capital or multi-factor growth, η is the elasticity of investment with respect to value-added growth or the three productivity measures before the euro. The coefficient of interest is θ. It is the difference between the elasticities before and after the introduction of the euro. If the euro improves efficiency of investment, θ should be positive.

The results appear in Table 10.9. I only present the results when country/industry and year/industry dummy interactions and macroeconomic controls are included. The estimated elasticities of investment with respect to multi-factor and labour productivities are positive and significant at the 5 per cent level. The elasticity with respect to value-added is also positive, but significant only at the 10 per cent level. The elasticity is insignificant with respect to labour productivity. Therefore, investment tends to flow to industries that experience high output and productivity growth. However, the coefficients on the interactions of value-added and the productivity measures with the *Euro* dummy are statistically insignificant in all cases. This suggests that the tendency for investment to flow to the most productive and expanding industries is no different when the euro is the official currency. Thus, the euro does not appear to lead to more efficient allocation of capital. I also examine if the euro improves investment allocation only in countries with low financial development. To do so, I interact value-added and the productivity measures with the *Euro* dummy and with the *LowFD* dummy indicating countries with low financial development. Again, the coefficients on this triple interaction are statistically insignificant, indicating that even in countries with previously low levels of financial development there is no change in investment efficiency when the euro became the official currency.

4. CONCLUSION

I find strong evidence that the introduction of the euro is associated with a significant increase in the growth rate of physical investment. While investment growth fell everywhere after 1999, firms in the euro area reduced investment growth by about five percentage points less than in other countries. This suggests that the well documented transformation of financial markets in EMU has real effects on resource allocation. The evidence supports the predictions that financial integration will lead to a substantial 'growth dividend'. This should give further impetus to financial integration efforts as outlined by the financial policy of the European Commission and the ECB. The result also suggests that higher investment growth may be expected for future members of EMU – a factor that may be important

Table 10.9 Does the euro lead to more efficient investment?

	(1)	(2)	(3)	(4)	(5)	(6)	(7)	(8)
Euro	0.056*	0.057*	0.046*	0.047**	0.042**	0.043**	0.043*	0.045*
	(2.47)	(2.53)	(2.51)	(2.63)	(3.15)	(3.26)	(2.24)	(2.41)
Value-added	0.187	0.187						
growth	(1.68)	(1.67)						
Value add.*	0.136	0.167						
Euro	(0.55)	(0.66)						
Value*Euro*		−0.246						
LowFD		(−1.02)						
Multi. prod.			0.554*	0.553*				
growth			(2.50)	(2.50)				
Multi. prod.*			−0.279	−0.339				
Euro			(−0.64)	(−0.71)				
Multi.*Euro*				0.481				
LowFD				(1.08)				
Labour prod.					0.038	0.039		
growth					(0.38)	(0.39)		
Labour prod.*					0.248	0.278		
Euro					(1.19)	(1.22)		
Labour*Euro*						−0.195		
LowFD						(−0.86)		
Capital prod.							0.601*	0.603*
growth							(2.11)	(2.12)
Cap. prod.*							−0.432	−0.456
Euro							(−1.25)	(−1.24)
Cap.*Euro*								0.274
LowFD								(0.86)
R-squared	0.217	0.217	0.387	0.388	0.218	0.218	0.393	0.393
Number of observations	3764	3764	1254	1254	3618	3618	1254	1254

Notes: The dependent variable is the growth rate of real investment. *Euro* is a dummy variable equal to one for years and countries in which the euro is used as the official currency. *LowFD* is a dummy variable that equals one for Greece, Italy, Spain and Portugal. All specifications include country, year and industry fixed effects and the interactions between industry and year effects, and industry and country effects. Each specification also includes macroeconomic controls: aggregate stock returns, lagged GDP growth, lagged interest rates, lagged change in interest rates and per capita GDP. T-statistics calculated using robust and country 'clustered' standard errors are in parentheses. * and ** indicate significance at 5 and 1 per cent levels.

Source: Author's calculations.

when considering the decision whether or when to adopt the common currency.

The effect of the euro does not appear larger in countries with previously low levels of financial development. This goes against some of the conclusions of Guiso et al. (2004) who predicted that countries with low levels of financial development would benefit most. The euro seems to enhance investment growth in *all* euro countries, even those with already well developed financial markets. The prediction of Guiso et al. (2004) that the euro would benefit industries that depend on external finance is supported by my data. I find that the impact of the euro is stronger in industries that depend on external finance.

The euro's impact on investment may not have been due only to better workings of financial markets. An alternative interpretation is that firms increased investment because they expected their earnings to grow with increased trade. While this may be part of the explanation, there are at least three strikes against it. First, I find no evidence that export-intensive industries increased their investment more than other industries. Second, I do find that the euro had a bigger impact in industries that depend on external finance. This suggests that the euro's impact had something to do with financial markets rather than trade. Finally, Bris et al. (2004) find that expected earnings of companies in the euro area did not increase following the euro's introduction.

NOTES

* Department of Economics, Union College, Schenectady, NY 12308.

1. Levine (2005) provides a comprehensive survey of this literature.
2. The exception is Great Britain, which had missing values for real capital formation (GFCFK) but non-missing values for nominal capital formation (GFCF). I divided GFCF by the British value-added deflator of the manufacturing sector to create real capital formation GFCFK.
3. Indeed, in their firm-level study, Bris et al. (2005) use lagged industry level q rather than firm level q.
4. I cannot include the interaction between the year and country dummies as these would be perfectly collinear with the *Euro* dummy.
5. These statistics have mcap, privo, account codes in the Demirgüç-Kunt and Levine dataset.
6. When macroeconomic controls are excluded the number of significant industries is 16 and 9.
7. For this reason the *RZ* measure is calculated using US data – assuming that the financial markets in the US are near frictionless.
8. This approach is also similar in spirit to Fisman and Love (2004) who find that countries with well developed financial markets respond to sectoral shocks better than in less developed financial markets.

REFERENCES

Abiad, Abdul, Nienke Oomes and Kenichi Ueda (2004), 'The quality effect: does financial liberalization improve the allocation of capital?', IMF Working Paper 04/112.

Acemoglu, Daron (1993), 'Learning about others' actions and investment accelerator', *Economic Journal*, **103** (417), 318–28.

Adam, Klaus, Tullio Jappelli, Annamaria Menichini, Mario Padula and Marco Pagano (2002), 'Analyse, compare, and apply alternative indicators and monitoring methodologies to measure the evolution of capital market integration in the European Union', Centre for Studies in Economics and Finance (CSEF) working paper.

Baele, Lieven, Annalisa Ferrando, Peter Hordahl, Elizaveta Krylova and Cyril Monnet (2004), 'Measuring European financial integration', *Oxford Review Of Economic Policy*, **20** (4), 509–30.

Bartram, Söhnke and Andrew Karolyi (2005), 'The impact of foreign exchange rate risk on firm value evidence from the introduction of the euro', working paper, Ohio State University.

Bertrand, Marianne, Esther Duflo and Sendhil Mullainathan (2004), 'How much should I trust difference in differences estimates?', *Quarterly Journal of Economics*, **119** (1), 249–75.

Blanchard, Olivier J. and Francesco Giavazzi (2002), 'Current account deficits in the euro area: the end of the Feldstein Horioka puzzle?', *Brookings Papers on Economics Activity*, **2**, 147–86.

Bris, Arturo, Yrjö Koskinen and Mattias Nilsson (2004), 'The euro and corporate valuations', working paper.

Bris, Arturo, Yrjö Koskinen and Mattias Nilsson (2005), 'The real effects of the euro: evidence from corporate investments', *Review of Finance*, **9**, 1–37.

Cappiello, Lorenzo, Philipp Hartmann, Peter Hördahl, Arjan Kadareja and Simone Manganelli (2005), 'The impact of the euro on financial markets', paper presented at the ECB conference, Frankfurt, June 2005.

Chari, Anusha and Peter Blair Henry (2004), 'Is the invisible hand discerning or indiscriminate? Investment and Stock Prices in the Aftermath of Capital Account Liberalizations', working paper.

Claessens, Stijn and Luc Laeven (2003), 'Financial development, property rights, and growth', *The Journal of Finance*, **58**, 2401–36.

Clark, Peter (1979), 'Investment in the 1970s: theory, performance and prediction', *Brookings Papers on Economic Activity*, **1** (79), 73–113.

Demirgüç-Kunt, Asli and Ross Levine (2001), *Financial Structure and Economic Growth: A Cross-Country Comparison of Banks, Markets and Development*, Cambridge, Mass.: MIT Press.

European Commission (2004), 'EMU after five years, Special Report no. 1', Directorate-General for Economic and Financial Affairs.

European Commission (2005), 'Green Paper on Financial Services Policy (2005–2010)', http://europa.eu.int/comm/internal_market/finances/actionplan/index_en.htm.

Fisman, Raymond and Inessa Love (2004), 'Financial development and intersectoral allocation: a new approach', *The Journal of Finance*, **59,** 2785–807.

Flam, Harry and Hakan Nordstrom (2003), 'Trade volume effects of the euro: aggregate and sector estimates', working paper.

Galati, Gabriele and Kostas Tsatsaronis (2003), 'The impact of the euro on Europe's financial markets', *Financial Markets, Institutions and Instruments*, **12**, 165–222.
Galindo, Arturo, Fabio Schiantarelli and Andrew Weiss (2003), 'Does financial liberalization improve the allocation of investment? Micro evidence from developing countries', Boston University working paper.
Gertler, Mark and Simon Gilchrist (1994), 'Monetary policy, business cycles and the behavior of small manufacturing firms', *Quarterly Journal of Economics*, **109**, 309–40.
Guiso, Luigi, Tullio Jappelli, Mario Padula and Marco Pagano (2004), 'Financial market integration and economic growth in the EU', *Economic Policy*, **19**, 523–77.
Hardouvelis, Gikas A., Dimitrios Malliaropulos and Richard Priestley (2002), 'The impact of globalization on the equity cost of capital', mimeo.
Levine, Ross (2005), 'Finance and growth' in Philippe Aghion and Steven Durlauf (eds), *Handbook of Economic Growth*, The Netherlands: Elsevier Science.
London Economics (2002), 'Quantification of the macroeconomic impact of integration of EU financial markets', available in the EU Commission website.
Maksimovic, Vojislav and Gordon Phillips (2002), 'Do conglomerate firms allocate resources inefficiently across industries? Theory and evidence', *Journal of Finance*, **57**, 721–67.
Micco, A., E. Stein and G. Ordoñez (2003), 'The currency union effect on trade: early evidence from the European Union', *Economic Policy*, **18**, 315–56.
Pagano, Marco (2004), 'The European bond markets under EMU', *Oxford Review of Economic Policy*, **20** (4), 531–49.
Rajan, Raghuram G. and Luigi Zingales (1998), 'Financial dependence and growth', *The American Economic Review*, **88**, 559–86.
Santos, Joao and Kostas Tsatsaronis (2003), 'The cost of barriers to entry: evidence from the market for corporate bond underwriting', Federal Reserve Bank of New York and Bank for International Settlements, working paper.
Schoenmaker, Dirk and Sander Oosterloo (2005), 'Financial supervision in an integrating Europe: measuring cross-border externalities', *International Finance*, **8**, 1–27.
Sentana, Enrique (2002), 'Did EMS reduce the cost of capital?', *The Economic Journal*, **112**, 786–809.
Vives, Xavier (2001), 'Restructuring financial regulation in the European Monetary Union', *Journal of Financial Services Research*, **19**, 57–82.
Wurgler, Jeffrey (2000), 'Financial markets and the allocation of capital', *Journal of Financial Economics*, **58**, 187–214.

11. Importance of financial sectors for growth in accession countries

Gerhard Fink, Peter Haiss and Goran Vukšić*

1. INTRODUCTION

Over the last decade the role of financial sector development in economic growth has become a major topic in empirical research. Most cross-section-oriented studies (for example Rousseau and Wachtel, 2000; Levine et al., 2000; Singh et al., 2000; Demirgüç-Kunt and Levine, 1999) base their analyses on broad samples of industrial and developing countries. Most of them find a positive interrelation between financial development and economic growth. But as Ahmed (1998) argues with respect to bank development:

> there are reasons to expect that [. . .] the effect of bank development on growth may not be the same in magnitude in developing countries and industrial economies [. . .]. Thus due to country aggregation we cannot answer interesting questions such as: how do the effects of banking development in a country such as the United States differ from those in Zimbabwe, say?

A recent study by Rousseau and Wachtel (2005) also shows that the analysis of a possibly different impact of finance on growth in different countries or periods becomes increasingly important. They find that the finance–growth nexus seems to be significant for middle income countries (between USD 3000 and 12000 per capita), but not for low and high income countries. In addition, if countries are grouped according to the relative development of their financial sectors they find evidence for positive and significant effect on growth only for the group of countries in the middle range (countries with M3-to-GDP ratios between 45 and 60 per cent). Rousseau and Wachtel (2005) conclude that: 'the correlations between finance and growth found in cross-country data may well reflect differences in country characteristics rather than any dynamic cause–effect relationship from finance to growth'. They call for more studies on individual countries' experiences and the relationship between finance and growth.

Picking up this thought, our chapter addresses two research questions: first, has financial development played a significant role for the growth performance of 'emerging market' transition and accession countries? Second, do different financial segments (that is banking intermediation, stock markets, bond markets) affect real growth differently in these countries?

We use a production function approach to investigate the relationship between financial markets and economic growth during the 1996–2000 transition period of nine EU accession and new EU member countries.[1] First we use an aggregate measure of financial development covering credit, bond and stock markets, which is less influenced by differences in financial market structures between countries, and changes of financial market structures within countries. The following analysis of causal links between single financial market segments and economic development is a first step in determining interdependencies between the structure of financial markets and economic growth, an issue rather ignored by the literature so far. In the context of accession countries, bond markets are, to our knowledge, taken explicitly into account for the first time. Methodologically, we rely on a panel data approach. As for the specification of growth regressions, we follow the standard approach by Mankiw et al. (1992), who use physical capital stock, labour and human capital as explanatory variables of economic growth. We add different financial market variables: two different measures of total financial intermediation, domestic credit, private credit, stock market capitalization and bonds outstanding. Such extensions of a standard growth model are the most common approach in the literature.

We find that the overall financial sector development, and especially two single segments – domestic credit expansion and development of bond markets – stimulate economic growth in our sample. In contrast to earlier studies in other regions (for example Atje and Jovanovic, 1993; and Levine and Zervos, 1998), we find no significant influence of private credit and stock markets on growth for accession countries. As for the other growth determinants, real capital stock growth turned out to be an important factor contributing to economic development, while labour participation and educational attainment did not play a significant role. The results indicate a clear distinction between the growth effects of the financial funds channelled to/through the public sector and those directed to the private sector at this stage of development. It turns out that in order for the private sector to be more effective in promoting growth different potential obstacles need to be removed. The results are especially relevant in the context of EU enlargement – for securing rapid development and real convergence of new EU member states, but also of other accession countries and emerging markets.

The remainder of the chapter is organized as follows. Section 2 reviews relevant empirical literature that deals with the nature of the finance–growth link in accession countries. Section 3 outlines the basic theory, discusses some methodological issues and states the econometric model. Section 4 analyses summary statistics of data and gives an overview of the econometric results. In the fifth section the results are discussed and interpreted.

2. FINANCE AND GROWTH IN ACCESSION COUNTRIES: EARLIER RESULTS

Since most (but not all) of the accession countries considered in this study were transition economies of Central and Eastern Europe during the period covered here, this section will concentrate on reviewing the literature on finance and growth in transition. In discussing the previous evidence on the impact of financial intermediation on growth, it is useful to analyse the effects of individual financial sectors separately. We mostly rely on the study by Bonin and Wachtel (2003) who give an extensive review of developments in banking sectors and capital markets. Other literature on this topic has mostly been concerned with the banking sector only, given its dominant role in the financial sectors of these countries.

Banks in the former socialist countries prior to the 1990s were largely inefficient and characterized by a large amount of bad loans and preferential allocation of credit (Drakos, 2003; Eller and Haiss, 2003; Fink et al., 1998). The inherited, mostly monobank systems were eliminated in the late 1980s and early 1990s. The banking sectors have experienced a large number of new entries and declining state ownership due to privatization. However, soon it turned out that liberalization and privatization alone are not enough to create a strong and stable banking sector. It became clear that it will take longer to achieve higher independence from the state and to restructure the banks – that is to remove the mostly inherited bad loans from their balance sheets, but also to stop the continuing bad lending practices (Bonin and Wachtel, 2003; Fink and Haiss, 1999).[2] In addition, although the regulatory framework was created rather early, bank supervision was not effective because of the lack of trained and experienced personnel and infrastructure. This problem was especially profound in the countries that chose to promote competition by imposing very soft initial licensing conditions on banks, leading to entry of many 'small weak banks engaged in risky, and sometimes fraudulent activities' (Bonin and Wachtel, 2003; see also Fink et al., 1998). All these reasons led to banking crises in many transition economies, forcing the governments to intervene and often recapitalize the banks. More and more, the governments were turning to foreign participation in the bank privatization process as an effective and possibly necessary way to promote competition, enhance the efficiency and strengthen the independence of the banking sector. Five issues still stick out with regard to the microeconomic safety and soundness of the new member states' financial sectors: the small size of the financial sector in absolute and relative terms; large foreign bank ownership; the level of concentration and competition; bad debt; and the product range (Breuss et al., 2004).

Drakos (2003) finds that the banking sector improved its efficiency as measured by the net interest margins in the period between 1993 and 1999. He showed that foreign banks contributed to this improvement by intensifying competition and by producing positive externalities to the banking sector through demonstration effects. In addition, selling the controlling shares to foreign banks helped the governments to credibly signal the end of bank bailouts. The result that foreign ownership of banks in transition countries increases the overall efficiency of the banking sector is confirmed by Weill (2003) for the Czech Republic and Poland.[3] Fries et al. (2002) give some evidence that bank performance and increased efficiency depends on the reform environment as well as the competitive conditions in which they operate. They conclude that an appropriate regulatory framework may be a necessary condition for an efficient banking system. Pistor et al. (2000) analyse the impact of legal change in the protection of shareholder and creditor rights in transition countries and of the effectiveness of legal institutions on the propensity of firms to raise external finance. Their results clearly emphasize the role of effective institutions. Bonin and Wachtel (2003) argue that although more order and better business practices in banking sectors of the transition economies have been established, although there have been fewer and fewer non-performing loans in the banks' balance sheets, and although regulation and supervision have become much more effective, banks are not necessarily effectively serving the economy: in some transition countries banks still may be lacking the willingness or ability to lend to enterprises.

Koivu (2002) performed an econometric investigation, using a fixed-effects panel model to see whether relatively larger and more efficient banking sectors have promoted economic growth in 25 transition economies. The efficiency is measured by the margin between lending and deposit interest rate, and the size of the banking sector is defined as the share of bank credits to the private sector in GDP. She concludes that the interest rate margin is a significant determinant of growth, and that lower margins promote growth. Yet the size of the banking sector is not found to be growth enhancing. Actually, when used in a regression, its lagged value is found to have a significant negative influence on growth.

Stock markets in transition economies developed relatively quickly on average, but unevenly across countries, driven above all by the privatization process, especially in countries that relied on voucher methods (for example the Czech Republic). The ratio of market capitalization to GDP (a common measure of the development of stock markets) tends to be highest where privatization has gone the furthest, but it is still comparatively low. This measure, however, is not always a good indicator of how well stock markets perform their function as financial intermediaries. Their effectiveness may be limited by illiquidity and lack of transparency, as is often the case in transition countries (Bonin and Wachtel, 2003). Although the number of listed companies kept increasing due to further mass privatization programmes, the value-traded ratio remained relatively low,[4] given very diffuse ownership structures and little trade in the stocks of many small companies (Bonin and Wachtel, 2003). As was the case for banks, institutional frameworks and infrastructures became effective only with a time lag, causing many problems with transparent transfer of ownership and price manipulations, thus further reducing the effectiveness of stock markets as financial intermediaries. Another important issue is that larger companies which were successfully privatized in more advanced transition countries have access to international capital markets.[5] This is an indicator of the attractiveness of these companies and achievement of accounting and disclosure standards. Yet it may represent an obstacle to further development of local capital markets, which may remain restricted to small and illiquid issues. This problem is not specific to transition countries. Virtually all emerging economies (except for the very large ones) and even some of the small developed countries face similar problems (Bonin and Wachtel, 2003).

Given that the described circumstances affect the development of stock markets and their effectiveness as financial intermediaries, it is hard to expect that stock markets could have significantly promoted economic growth in transition economies. Kominek (2003) analyses the likely effect of stock markets on growth in the Czech Republic and Poland. A major finding is that the less favourable conditions and circumstances of the Czech stock market have not caused any important disadvantages to industries traditionally regarded as financially dependent on external financing, but firms listed in Poland (not only those considered financially dependent) have outperformed their counterparts in the Czech Republic. In general, quoted companies developed better than the non-listed firms in both countries. Still, the direction of causality does not seem to be from stock markets to industry growth.

Another potentially important segment of the financial sector is the bond market. In the transition economies bond markets are mostly small, only governments and few large companies are potential issuers (ECB, 2003; Haiss and Marin, 2003), which also have direct access to international markets. Although large government deficits have also led to the sale of debt to the local public, there are rarely secondary markets for bonds, since these are mostly bought and held by banks. An additional reason for lacking secondary market activity is that other institutional market participants, such as pension funds and insurance companies, have been underdeveloped as well. The situation is even worse with private bond markets in transition countries, which are so rare that they have been considered 'a missing element of capital market development' (Bonin and Wachtel, 2003). Yet there are some corporate issues on domestic markets, especially in more advanced transition economies. Further development of institutional investors can contribute to faster development of the bond markets by strengthening the demand side of the market. With progress in enterprise restructuring, regulatory frameworks, accounting and disclosure standards, the supply side of the bond markets can also start developing more rapidly since the restructured larger companies, which are able to issue bonds, have access to finance at more favourable rates than bank loans. This segment of financial intermediation, although relatively small, can be expected to have had stronger positive consequences for economies in transition than bank credits or stock markets. As described earlier, among other difficulties, bank credits have been afflicted with a significant portion of non-performing loans. At the same time, stock market capitalization has been inflated with many listed companies whose shares were not actually traded. In other words, they have been illiquid. By contrast, bonds are either issued by governments and are therefore of very low default probability, or by restructured, large and sound companies, which have achieved higher accounting and disclosure standards therefore increasing transparency.

While Bonin and Wachtel (2003) ask whether the capital raised by the government, either through bond issues or, more importantly through privatization, represents an improvement in resource allocation, since it rarely increases private capital stock,[6] this is not the crucial question here, as the improved access to finance for the public sector does not have to improve growth only by increasing private capital stock. Public infrastructure expenditures, education expenditures, or implementing efficiency-enhancing public administration reforms may lead to higher growth rates as well. Another important remark by Bonin and Wachtel (2003) should not be left out here. In conclusion, they argue that many problems faced by the financial sectors of transition countries at the end of 1990s are also typical problems of other emerging market countries. This justifies adding two emerging economies, Malta and Turkey, to our sample.

3. THEORY, METHODOLOGY AND THE PRODUCTION FUNCTION APPROACH

3.1 Theory

Schumpeter had already emphasized the importance of financial intermediaries and financial markets in the process of economic development. In the 1960s and 1970s this interest was renewed and later, with the development of endogenous growth theory, for the first time the functions of financial systems and the positive impact they exert on economic development could be modelled. Berthelemy and Varoudakis (1996b), Becsi and Wang (1997), Pagano (1993) and especially Levine (1997) give excellent surveys of the functions of financial markets and how they help to improve economic development.[7] Fink et al. (2004b) provide an extension to financial sector macro efficiency.

Financial intermediaries and markets arise because of market frictions including information costs, costs of enforcing contracts, and exchanging goods and financial claims (Levine, 1997). The primary function of financial systems is to facilitate the allocation of resources. More specifically, financial systems may facilitate risk management – they help to diversify liquidity risks (Greenwood and Smith, 1997; Bencivenga and Smith, 1991; Levine, 1991) and idiosyncratic investment and demand risks (Greenwood and Jovanovic, 1990; Levine, 1991; Saint-Paul, 1992; Obstfeld, 1994). At the same time, diversification makes possible the financing of riskier, but more productive investments and innovations (Greenwood and Jovanovic, 1990; Greenwood and Smith, 1997; Levine, 1991; Bencivenga and Smith, 1991; Obstfeld, 1994; Saint-Paul, 1992; King and Levine, 1993a).

Financial intermediaries and financial markets also decide directly on the allocation of resources, gather information and exert corporate governance (Greenwood and Jovanovic, 1990; King and Levine, 1993b). Intermediaries may be seen as specialized economic agents in performing these tasks, which lowers the information costs for the whole economy. They may mobilize savings and facilitate the exchange of goods, services and contracts. In addition, financial markets are a necessary condition for the increasing specialization of the economy (for example Saint-Paul, 1996; Greenwood and Smith, 1997) and build the basis for an efficient payment system. By reducing market imperfections and frictions, the development of financial markets promotes economic growth ('supply leading approach', Patrick, 1966), but simultaneously there exists a reverse channel from economic growth to financial development: economic growth produces an increased demand for financial services; thus, financial development must be understood as a 'demand driven approach' (Patrick, 1966). It is possible to analyse theoretically both causal channels within a single model and allow for feedbacks among them if we assume that the development of financial systems is – similar to other networks – expensive and characterized by large fixed costs. Economic growth increases the amount of savings; savings will be intermediated more and more efficiently in a financial system characterized by increasing returns to scale; thus, an increasing amount of investments can be financed, which further stimulates economic growth.

It must be noted that although the theoretical literature is mostly concerned with two channels of influence from finance to growth; private capital accumulation and technological innovation, there may be other channels as well. It is not necessarily the level of (private) capital stock in the economy that is affected, but its quality with respect to expected returns on investment, because some of the functions of financial systems mentioned above, such as gathering information and deciding directly on resource allocation, may affect the choice of projects to be financed and carried out. It has also been a widely accepted fact that investing in human capital, public infrastructure or efficiency enhancing reforms in public administration may also be growth-promoting although not through the above channels. Still, all of these investments must be financed and are therefore reinforced by the well-functioning financial system.

3.2 Methodology and the Model

According to Temple (1999), the most popular method among economists exploring economic growth are cross-section growth regressions. Still, there are many problems associated with this approach, such as for example parameter heterogeneity, unobserved fixed effects, measurement errors, or endogeneity. Economists have used different techniques to mitigate some of these potential problems (for example using initial and not average values of variables to alleviate endogeneity), so that the popularity of cross-section regressions is still rather high. Temple (1999) argues that the use of panel data models has some advantages.[8]

Wachtel (2001) believes that although the above techniques (using the initial or lagged variables) are commonly used to ameliorate the effects of simultaneity, they do not completely solve the problem. He argues that the dynamic panel data methods (panel VARs) do a much better job. In contrast, Temple (1999) believes that the 'finite sample properties of most dynamic panel data estimators are not yet well understood'. He gives a detailed discussion of advantages and disadvantages of different approaches and argues that conventional panel data regression, used to supplement (or supplemented with) cross-section results, is a better method than the dynamic panel data approach. Researchers are not unanimous in deciding what kind of data to use, either. Since the underlying relationship is a long-run one, some argue that five- or ten-year averages of variables should be used in regressions, preventing short-term macroeconomic effects from influencing the results. Research by Rousseau and Wachtel (2000), Hahn (2003) and Beck and Levine (2004) follows this approach. Yet averages lower the number of observations that can be used in estimations. Furthermore, panel data techniques require time series to span two decades or more. Finally, if the number of cross-section units is not large enough, one may not have enough observations for a meaningful estimation. In this case, switching to annual data and applying the panel data method is probably a much better choice.

For example, Koivu (2002) and Mencinger (2003) follow this approach in similar settings for transition countries. Admittedly, in such cases, one actually addresses the short-run economic activity or performance, rather than long-run economic growth or development. Another open question is whether fixed or time effects, both or none of those, should be used in panel data specifications. While fixed effects may account for omitted variables, many researchers believe that these effects are lost with the differencing, that is in derivation of the estimated equation from a production function relationship, and that they should not be used in regression. Some economists think that they should be used if they enter the equation significantly, but one needs to be cautious because they may cause problems in the context of financial intermediation and growth research (Wachtel, 2001). After all, the measures of financial development vary significantly across countries, but in a single country very slowly over time.[9]

Here, we rely on a panel data approach because our sample is small: we have only nine cross-section observations for accession countries. Our findings reconfirm preliminary results based on simple cross-country regressions (Fink et al., 2006). By using the panel data approach with annual data, we get more observations. That the results of two approaches are not very different is often the case when applying different techniques in finance and growth research (even when applying different panel data methods: see Wachtel, 2001, or Rousseau and Wachtel, 2005). As for the specification of growth regressions, we rely on the modification of the approach formally derived in Mankiw et al. (1992). They use capital stock, labour and human capital as explanatory variables, modelled as inputs in the production function.[10] We augment their production function by adding different financial market variables in our empirical specifications. So basically, we run a regression, controlling for the sources of growth other than financial intermediation, which were formally derived from the standard model of Mankiw et al. (1992) and empirically confirmed. As argued by Temple (1999), extensions of this kind are not perfect, and make the interpretation of the results difficult. Nevertheless, Temple states that informal regressions, whose specification is mostly driven by earlier results rather than by a formal model, are the most common approach in the literature.[11]

It must be noted that in many cross-section and panel data studies dealing with the finance–growth nexus (for example King and Levine, 1993a and 1993b; Levine and Zervos, 1998; see also Wachtel, 2001) change in capital stock is used as an alternative dependent variable, and does not enter the regression as an explanatory variable. This is motivated by the theory described above, which asserts that an important, but not the only, channel of influence to growth is capital accumulation. While it is likely (as many empirical studies confirm) that this is an important channel, we believe that the capital stock variable must be taken into account as an explanatory variable as well when analysing output growth. The reason is that financial intermediation, as captured by the most commonly used variables, may not be the only factor behind capital accumulation.[12] Thus, omitting the capital accumulation variable, if it is significant, would lead to inconsistent estimates (unless fixed effects are used in panel data model specification). In addition, in such an approach, the effect of capital accumulation on growth could possibly be (partly) picked up by the financial intermediation variable, but in this case, it is not the impact of the financial variable on growth that is (possibly) found, but the effect of capital accumulation. Comparable situations arise in studies dealing with the effect of foreign direct investment (FDI) on growth (see for example Borensztein et al., 1998; Campos and Kinoshita, 2002; or Mencinger, 2003). FDI can also contribute to capital formation, but is usually used in regressions in addition to the capital accumulation variable in an augmented production function approach, similar to ours. In the approach by Atje and Jovanovic (1993) the investment rate and financial variables enter the regression together. They use a similar argument that we have mentioned earlier; that there may be effects of financial intermediation on growth which do not necessarily affect the level of capital stock in an economy.[13]

For our regressions, we use the following model specifications:

$$\Delta y_{i,t}/y_{i,t-1} = \alpha + \beta_1 \Delta k_{i,t}/k_{i,t-1} + \beta_2 \Delta part_{i,t} + \beta_3 \ln(e_{i,t}) + \beta_4 FI_{i,t} \quad (11.1)$$

$$\Delta y_{i,t}/y_{i,t-1} = \alpha + \beta_1 \Delta k_{i,t}/k_{i,t-1} + \beta_2 \Delta part_{i,t} + \beta_3 \ln(e_{i,t}) + \beta_4 FI_{i,t-1} \quad (11.2)$$

$$\Delta y_{i,t}/y_{i,t-1} = \alpha + \beta_1 \Delta k_{i,t}/k_{i,t-1} + \beta_2 \Delta part_{i,t} + \beta_3 \ln(e_{i,t}) + \beta_4 FI_{i,t-2} \quad (11.3)$$

where $y_{i,t}$ denotes real output per capita in country i at time t and $\Delta y_{i,t}$ stands for $y_{i,t} - y_{i,t-1}$. Thus, the dependent variable $\Delta y_{i,t}/y_{i,t-1}$ is real output growth per capita, in per cent. As for the explanatory variables, $k_{i,t}$ denotes real capital stock per capita in country i at time t and $\Delta k_{i,t}$ stands for $k_{i,t} - k_{i,t-1}$. Thus, $\Delta k_{i,t}/k_{i,t-1}$ stands for real growth rate of per capita capital stock. Change in the labour participation rate (*Δpart*) is defined as a percentage change of the ratio of the number of employed persons to the total population. The natural logarithm of a constructed indicator for educational attainment ($\ln(e_i)$) is used to describe the quality of human capital. *FI* stands for the different financial intermediation variables which are expressed in relationship to GDP. More detailed definitions of variables as well as the data sources are given in the data section that follows, as well as in the Appendix. Subscript i stands for cross-section units, that is countries ($i = 1 \ldots 9$), while t denotes years ($t = 1996 \ldots 2000$).

In the second and third specifications, the financial intermediation variables with one-year and two-year lags are used, in order to alleviate the potential simultaneity problem between financial development and output growth and to check for the direction of this relationship (that is for the predictive power of financial intermediation for future growth rates; see Levine and Zervos, 1998, or Wachtel, 2001, for an in-depth discussion).[14] Since, in our case, neither fixed nor time effects turned out to be significant, we present the results of the pooled data regressions with common intercepts.[15] It must be stressed that such a procedure also excludes taking into account different initial conditions (especially initial income), which may be important for future growth rates according to the convergence discussion in growth theory. Since the time horizon under study here is relatively short, this problem should not be very serious (which is possibly already reflected in insignificant fixed effects).

4. IMPACT OF FINANCE ON GROWTH

4.1 Data

Our sample consists of nine countries.[16] The time period considered is 1996 to 2000, for all countries and financial market segments.[17] We use data on real per capita output growth, real growth of capital stock per capita, change of labour participation rate, educational attainment as a proxy for the quality of human capital, and the following financial development indicators: two measures of total financial intermediation, domestic credit, private credit, stock market capitalization and bonds outstanding. The *first measure* of total financial intermediation (TFI 1) is a sum of the following individual segments: domestic credit, stock market capitalization and bonds. The *second measure* (TFI 2) uses private credit instead of domestic credit. Exact definitions of variables are given in the Appendix.

Table 11.1 presents summary statistics on output and capital stock growth, changes in labour participation, educational attainment and six financial

Table 11.1 Summary statistics: annual data 1996–2000

	Output	Capital stock	Labour	Education	TFI 1	TFI 2	Domestic credit	Private credit	Stock markets	Bonds
Mean	2.42	3.11	−0.85	4.13	100.19	84.98	50.86	35.65	17.87	31.47
Median	3.9	2.96	−0.45	4.10	79.11	65.36	41.17	24.43	12.84	21.47
Maximum	10.32	8.21	3.52	4.40	311.72	285.66	143.15	117.09	111.67	63.22
Minimum	−9.56	−3	−8.41	3.81	20.17	9.34	11.82	4.97	0.04	0.47
Standard deviation	4.16	3.1	2.66	0.15	62.46	58.61	34.24	31.61	23.11	19.13
Observations	45	45	45	45	45	45	45	45	45	45

Notes: Output growth, capital stock growth and change in participation – in %; educational attainment – logarithm of constructed indicator (see Appendix); all financial variables – in % of GDP.

Source: Own calculations, data source: see Appendix.

intermediation indicators. For the first three variables, we observe relatively high variability. For example, maximal value of output growth in the sample amounted to 10.32 per cent, while the lowest value was –9.56 per cent.

The standard deviation of educational attainment over time and across countries was comparatively low. At the same time, the variability of all financial variables, relative to the highest values, was comparatively high in these accession countries.

At the first glance, one might conclude that this reflects rapid development of the financial system in these countries over the period under study.

Although this might be true for some countries, average development of the financial variables for the whole region was not much, if at all, faster than in developed countries, as shown in Figure 11.1, where the development of the averages of these variables is compared to other country groups.

The values of financial intermediation relative to GDP are, as expected, much lower in accession countries than in the more developed ones.

The summary statistics for single countries in Table 11.2 show a relatively high degree of heterogeneity in the sample. TFI 1 averages range from only 22.85 per cent of GDP (Romania) to 236.75 per cent of GDP (Malta). Banking intermediation dominates the financial sectors in most of these economies, with domestic credit being considerably higher than stock market capitalization and bonds outstanding. Exceptions include Bulgaria and Hungary with amounts on bonds outstanding substantially higher than the average (more than 50 per cent of GDP), and Turkey, where the amounts of funds intermediated in each of the segments of capital markets are close to the amount of domestic credit.

Table 11.3 shows the simple correlation coefficients between all the variables used in panel estimations. As expected, the coefficients between single financial market segments and the two measures of total financial intermediation are relatively high, ranging between 0.6452 and 0.8945. Output growth, on the other hand, is strongly positively correlated with capital stock growth (0.5586); less strongly, but still positively with change in labour participation (0.1873); and barely with educational attainment (0.0236). The correlation coefficients between output growth and other explanatory variables are also positive (except for bonds outstanding), albeit at times rather small, except for domestic and private credit for which the correlation coefficients are 0.1358 and 0.1101 respectively.

4.2 Results

This section presents the results of our panel data regressions. Findings reconfirm preliminary results derived from simple cross-country regressions

(Fink et al., 2006). The strongest positive and significant effect on growth stems from the capital stock growth (see Tables 11.4 and 11.5).

This is true for all model specifications, using both measures of total financial intermediation. In addition, we find some evidence that total financial intermediation has positively affected economic development in accession countries when it enters in regression with a one-year (for both measures) or two-year lag (for TFI 2). Change in labour participation was always insignificant, and educational attainment was significant with the predicted positive sign only in the specifications where financial variables entered with a two-year lag.

Tables 11.6 and 11.7 contain the results of panel estimations of regressions using domestic and private credit as financial variables. Findings with respect to capital stock growth, change in participation and educational attainment remain basically unchanged. We find evidence that domestic credit expansion was a significant engine of growth in those specifications into which it entered the regression with one- or two-year lags. Private credit was never significant.

As for the findings of regressions with stock market capitalization and bonds outstanding (Tables 11.8 and 11.9), again capital stock growth was a significant factor strongly contributing to the economic development. Change in participation, educational attainment and stock markets turned out to be insignificant in all specifications. Bond markets, on the other hand, significantly and relatively strongly promoted growth with a time lag.

5. SUMMARY AND CONCLUSIONS

As a summary, we can state that there is some evidence that total financial intermediation contributed to economic growth in accession countries. This positive and partially significant relationship between finance and growth is confirmed in our regressions with single financial market segments. Unlike private credit, which was never significant, domestic credit made an important contribution to economic growth. In addition, there is solid evidence that bond markets played an important role in promoting growth, while stock market capitalization turned out to be insignificant in all of the specifications. This is an important finding, as addressing financing needs efficiently through bond markets has been rather neglected during transition in most countries.

That private credit expansion was not significant coincides with the results of Koivu (2002). One of the possible explanations for different findings for two measures of bank credit for transition countries is that

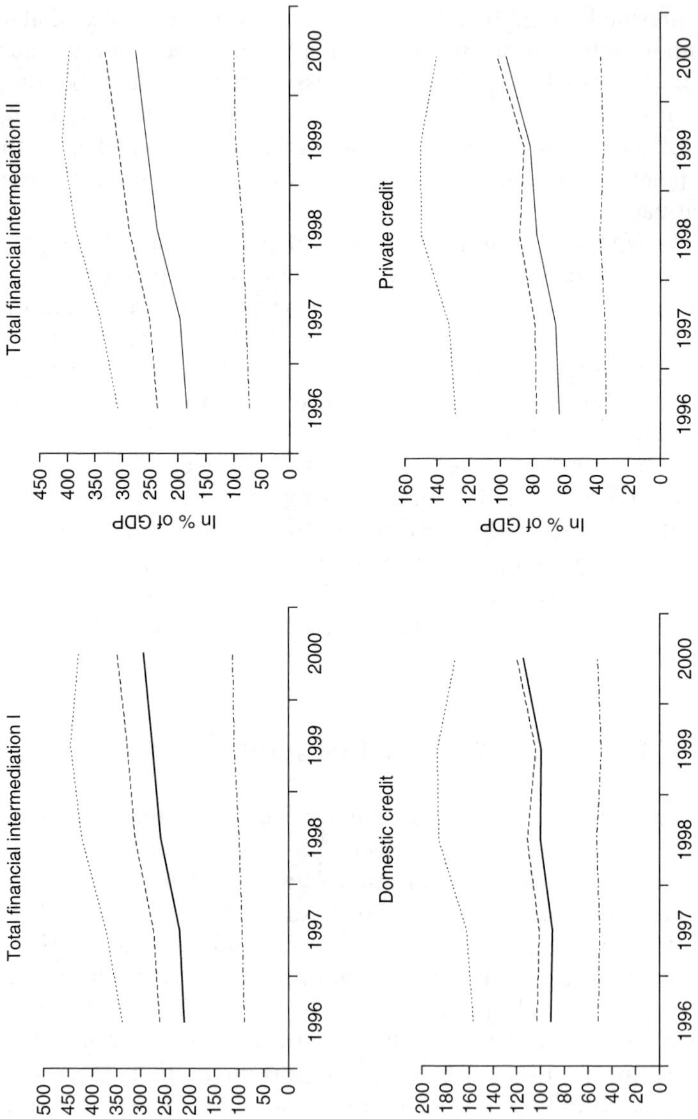
Total financial intermediation I
In % of GDP
500
450
400
350
300
250
200
150
100
50
0
1996
1997
1998
1999
2000
Total financial intermediation II
In % of GDP
450
400
350
300
250
200
150
100
50
0
1996
1997
1998
1999
2000
Domestic credit
In % of GDP
200
180
160
140
120
100
80
60
40
20
0
1996
1997
1998
1999
2000
Private credit
In % of GDP
160
140
120
100
80
60
40
20
0
1996
1997
1998
1999
2000

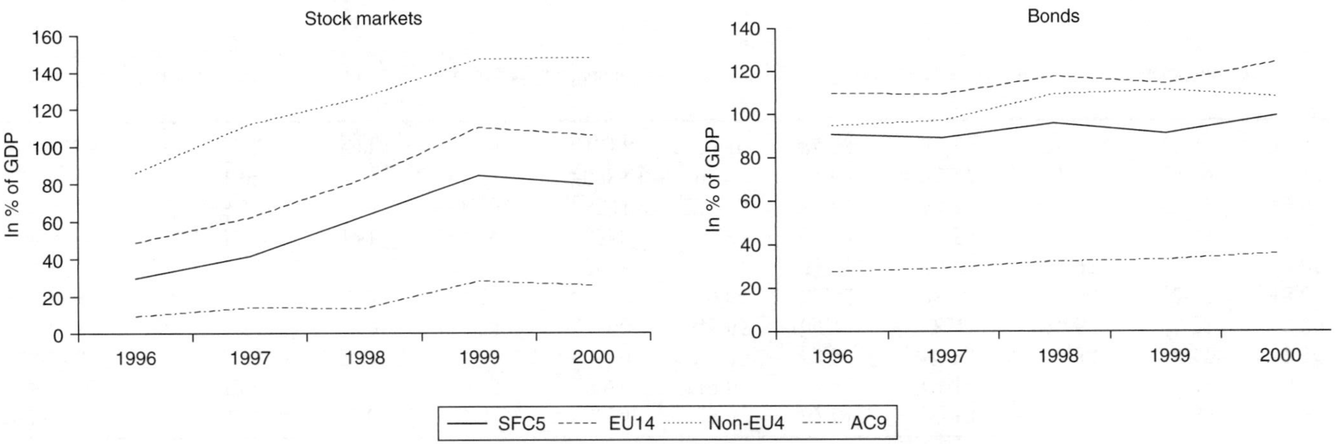

Notes: SFC5 = Structural fund countries: Greece, Ireland, Italy, Portugal and Spain; EU14 = EU countries without Luxembourg and new member states; Non-EU4 = USA, Japan, Norway and Switzerland; AC9 = Accession countries.

Source: Own calculations, data source: see Appendix.

Figure 11.1 Financial sectors in different groups of countries

Table 11.2 Data for all countries: 1996–2000 averages

	Output	Capital stock	Labour	Education	TFI 1	TFI 2	Domestic credit	Private credit	Stock markets	Bonds
Bulgaria	−0.07	−0.96	−2.31	4.3854	73.6	62.61	20.18	9.19	0.66	52.77
Czech Republic	1.09	2.39	−1.95	4.0989	119.61	121.25	64.11	65.75	20.34	35.15
Slovakia	3.97	5.73	−1.88	4.0979	77.26	53.27	59.33	35.34	4.17	13.76
Hungary	3.56	2.29	1.34	4.1490	143.65	109.73	58.43	24.52	26.22	58.99
Slovenia	4.34	6.28	1.2	4.1208	69.61	62.32	38.94	31.66	12.27	18.4
Poland	5.15	7.25	−0.28	4.3643	66.41	51.21	34.16	18.97	13.2	19.05
Romania	−1.3	−0.51	−0.49	4.0558	22.85	13.94	16.56	7.65	0.93	5.36
Malta	3.1	1.79	−1.56	3.8291	236.75	212.81	133.75	109.81	53.01	49.98
Turkey	1.93	3.69	−1.74	4.0783	92	77.67	32.27	17.95	29.99	29.73
Average	2.42	3.11	−0.85	4.1311	100.19	84.98	50.86	35.65	17.87	31.47

Notes: Output growth, capital stock growth and change in participation – in %; educational attainment – logarithm of constructed indicator (see Appendix); all financial variables – in % of GDP.

Source: Own calculations, data source: see Appendix.

Table 11.3 Correlations

	Capital stock	Labour	Education	TFI 1	TFI 2	Domestic credit	Private credit	Stock markets	Bonds
Output	0.5586	0.1873	0.0236	0.0884	0.0742	0.1358	0.1101	0.0705	−0.0397
Capital stock	–	0.3003	0.1092	−0.1046	−0.1075	0.0276	0.0372	0.0199	−0.4149
Labour	–	–	0.0234	0.0244	0.0097	−0.0720	−0.1081	0.2326	−0.0724
Educational attainment	–	–	–	−0.5462	−0.5511	−0.6997	−0.7007	−0.4490	0.0114
TFI 1	–	–	–	–	0.9852	0.8945	0.8198	0.8185	0.6753
TFI 2	–	–	–	–	–	0.8793	0.8602	0.8258	0.6452
Domestic credit	–	–	–	–	–	–	0.9462	0.5986	0.4078
Private credit	–	–	–	–	–	–	–	0.5625	0.3038
Stock markets	–	–	–	–	–	–	–	–	0.3930

Source: Own calculations, data source: see Appendix.

Table 11.4 Results: total financial intermediation 1

	Dependent variable is output growth					
	Financial variable with 2-year lag		Financial variable with 1-year lag		Financial variable with no lag	
Constant	−0.4309**	(0.1978)	−0.3240	(0.2082)	−0.0759	(0.2058)
Capital stock growth	0.3204**	(0.1380)	0.6358***	(0.1910)	0.7636***	(0.1923)
Change in participation	0.1118	(0.2345)	0.0039	(0.2074)	0.0173	(0.1868)
Educational attainment	0.1016**	(0.0458)	0.0728	(0.0496)	0.0156	(0.0491)
Total financial intermediation 1	0.0277	(0.0167)	0.0268**	(0.0115)	0.0120	(0.0094)
R^2	0.166		0.294		0.270	
Observations	27		36		45	

Notes: Heteroskedasticity-consistent standard errors in parentheses, *** significant at 1% level, ** significant at 5% level and * significant at 10% level.

Source: Own calculations.

Table 11.5 Results: total financial intermediation 2

	Dependent variable is output growth					
	Financial variable with 2-year lag		Financial variable with 1-year lag		Financial variable with no lag	
Constant	−0.4243**	(0.1842)	−0.3019	(0.2031)	−0.0647	(0.2040)
Capital stock growth	0.3220**	(0.1392)	0.6329***	(0.1876)	0.7616***	(0.1913)
Change in participation	0.1370	(0.2564)	0.0219	(0.2191)	0.0227	(0.1897)
Educational attainment	0.1012**	(0.0433)	0.0688	(0.0486)	0.0135	(0.0488)
Total financial intermediation 2	0.0275*	(0.0153)	0.0256**	(0.0117)	0.0116	(0.0098)
R^2	0.144		0.268		0.266	
Observations	27		36		45	

Notes: Heteroskedasticity-consistent standard errors in parentheses, *** significant at 1% level, ** significant at 5% level and * significant at 10% level.

Source: Own calculations.

Table 11.6 Results: domestic credit

	Dependent variable is output growth					
	Financial variable with 2-year lag		Financial variable with 1-year lag		Financial variable with no lag	
Constant	−0.6035**	(0.2400)	−0.4036	(0.2641)	−0.1187	(0.2540)
Capital stock growth	0.2279	(0.1375)	0.5671***	(0.2062)	0.7133***	(0.1987)
Change in participation	0.2031	(0.2788)	0.0743	(0.2390)	0.0622	(0.1951)
Educational attainment	0.1439**	(0.0560)	0.0935	(0.0628)	0.0264	(0.0604)
Domestic credit	0.0536**	(0.0245)	0.0454*	(0.0223)	0.0237	(0.0204)
R^2	0.191		0.257		0.266	
Observations	27		36		45	

Notes: Heteroskedasticity-consistent standard errors in parentheses, *** significant at 1% level, ** significant at 5% level and * significant at 10% level.

Source: Own calculations.

Table 11.7 Results: private credit

	Dependent variable is output growth					
	Financial variable with 2-year lag		Financial variable with 1-year lag		Financial variable with no lag	
Constant	−0.5372**	(0.2315)	−0.2873	(0.2585)	−0.0688	(0.2507)
Capital stock growth	0.2438*	(0.1320)	0.5805***	(0.1935)	0.7196***	(0.1940)
Change in participation	0.2441	(0.2970)	0.0858	(0.2445)	0.0626	(0.1956)
Educational attainment	0.1306**	(0.0540)	0.0682	(0.0615)	0.0157	(0.0600)
Private credit	0.0451	(0.0276)	0.0303	(0.0258)	0.0180	(0.0227)
R^2	0.133		0.206		0.255	
Observations	27		36		45	

Notes: Heteroskedasticity-consistent standard errors in parentheses, *** significant at 1% level, ** significant at 5% level and * significant at 10% level.

Source: Own calculations.

Table 11.8 Results: stock markets capitalization

	Dependent variable is output growth					
	Financial variable with 2-year lag		Financial variable with 1-year lag		Financial variable with no lag	
Constant	−0.1816	(0.1939)	−0.1520	(0.1804)	0.0152	(0.1673)
Capital stock growth	0.3408*	(0.1834)	0.5932***	(0.1895)	0.7487***	(0.1907)
Change in participation	0.2515	(0.2574)	0.0311	(0.2218)	0.0136	(0.1970)
Educational attainment	0.0497	(0.0461)	0.0368	(0.0444)	−0.0038	(0.0413)
Stock markets capitalization	−0.0698	(0.1256)	0.0282	(0.0220)	0.0092	(0.0216)
R^2	0.081		0.193		0.247	
Observations	27		36		45	

Notes: Heteroskedasticity-consistent standard errors in parentheses, *** significant at 1% level, ** significant at 5% level and * significant at 10% level.

Source: Own calculations.

Table 11.9 Results: bonds outstanding

	Dependent variable is output growth					
	Financial variable with 2-year lag		Financial variable with 1-year lag		Financial variable with no lag	
Constant	−0.1734*	(0.0974)	−0.0636	(0.1258)	0.0361	(0.1448)
Capital stock growth	0.5063***	(0.1721)	0.8592***	(0.1961)	0.8871***	(0.2168)
Change in participation	−0.0201	(0.2124)	−0.0916	(0.1870)	0.0117	(0.1676)
Educational attainment	0.0379	(0.0242)	0.0073	(0.0310)	−0.0134	(0.0352)
Bonds outstanding	0.0844*	(0.0446)	0.0949**	(0.0377)	0.0512	(0.0364)
R^2	0.223		0.362		0.295	
Observations	27		36		45	

Notes: Heteroskedasticity-consistent standard errors in parentheses, *** significant at 1% level, ** significant at 5% level and * significant at 10% level.

Source: Own calculations.

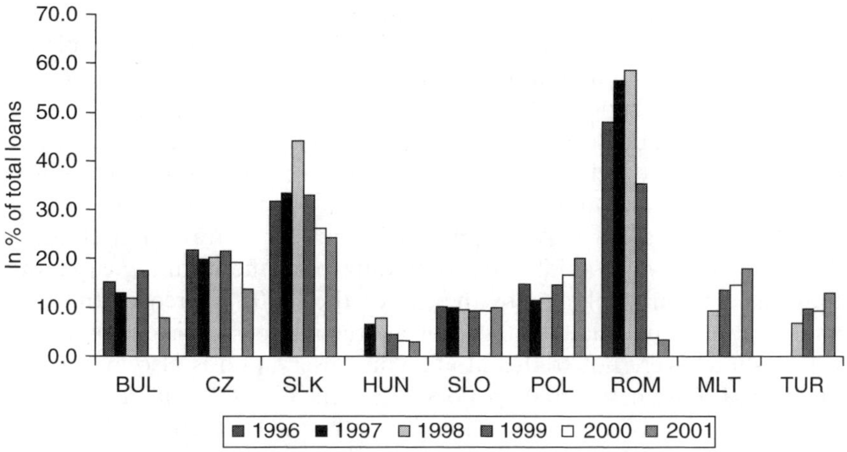

Source: EBRD Transition Report 2003; MLT and TUR: European Commission (2002).

Figure 11.2 Non-performing loans

there have been many bad loans to the private sector (see Figure 11.2), which were only gradually removed from the banks' balance sheets.

This made the contribution of private credit to growth relatively weak compared with domestic credit, which also included bank credits to central and local government, for which there is very low default probability. In addition, as stated by Berglöf and Bolton (2002), banks, which tend to dominate the financial sectors of the transition economies, mostly provide working capital finance to enterprises, while investment finance mostly comes from retained earnings and foreign direct investment.

Similar arguments about a different impact of financing the private and the public sector can possibly be applied in interpreting the results of the impact of bond markets on growth, since these markets are heavily dominated by government issues in all accession countries. This is because only the near-monopoly public sector and a few larger and sound companies can issue bonds and expect the market participants to actually buy these. In addition, interest rates on long-term government bonds are an important reference value for the whole financial sector, therefore facilitating the efficiency of financial intermediation and improving the risk diversification possibilities of other market participants. As a consequence, bond markets have had the strongest, positive and significant impact on output growth in accession countries among all financial segments.[18] Taken together, these results indicate a different relationship between bond issuance and GDP growth depending on the level of development.

Stock markets, in contrast, turned out not to have had any significant influence on growth in accession countries. This can possibly be explained with their relative underdevelopment. Minier (2003) showed that the positive relationship between finance intermediation (as measured by stock market turnover, but also by private credit) and growth depends on the level of stock market development. According to her findings, finance is not a significant determinant of growth for the group of countries with low stock market capitalization.[19] Although stock markets in transition countries developed relatively rapidly due to privatization, the resulting capitalization was comparatively low by the end of the 1990s. Moreover, these low amounts were 'artificially' inflated by a large number of listed companies, whose shares were not traded at all. This observation is also in line with findings of Kominek (2003) for Poland and the Czech Republic.

The above line of argumentation is in contrast to the theoretical literature on channels of influence from financial intermediation to growth, which emphasizes the role of the private sector. We believe that some of the specific problems in transition countries, discussed earlier, sufficiently explain the difficulties of financing the private sector, which then lead to our results (for example low accounting and disclosure standards in business practices of many enterprises, poor business practices in the banking sector and questionable criteria of credit allocation, weak law standards in general, inefficient legal institutions and so on).[20] According to Bonin and Wachtel (2003) banks in some of these countries maintained very conservative liquid portfolios and were largely unwilling or unable to lend to enterprises during the transition period. In contrast, as mentioned earlier, it has been recognized that public expenditure (or at least some segments) may also be growth promoting (see for example Shioji, 2001, for recent evidence). The increase of consumption (private and public) financed by expanding bank credit may also have contributed to higher growth rates over the relatively short period of five years. It is important to mention that Berglöf and Bolton (2002), who conclude that there is little evidence that financial expansion has promoted growth in transition, also stress the important limiting role of soft budget constraints, weak rule of law and lack of fiscal and monetary discipline. Although their conclusions imply that stronger fiscal discipline would contribute to strengthening the finance-growth nexus, they do not consider possible positive growth effects of public expenditure, especially if it is not financed by higher tax rates. Relations between banks and central and local governments can be assumed to be less sensitive to, for example, weak contract enforcement and some other obstacles typical for financing the private sector of accession countries. Therefore, it is not unexpected that the financial funds channelled through/to public sectors turn out to be more effective in promoting economic development.

As for the other three potential sources of growth, only capital accumulation turned out to be significant and a positive predictor. We believe that this can be explained by the relatively large capital scarcity in transition countries, making its accumulation crucial for development (UNECE, 2000a). This has also led to large capital inflows into these countries. In the context of transition economies Lipschitz et al. (2002) state that: 'Capital flows to economies undergoing far-reaching structural change are expected, as they reflect investment opportunities in excess of those that can be financed by domestic savings.' These flows included both large portfolio and foreign direct investment. Such international capital flows may have played an important role for the economic growth of transition countries, but the empirical evidence on their impact on growth (for FDI) is mixed. While Mencinger (2003) finds no significant positive relationship (but only negative for some specifications), Campos and Kinoshita (2002) report a significant positive impact of FDI on growth. In addition, UNECE (2000b) reports that FDI inflows may have relaxed balance of payment constraints and contributed to output growth 'by increasing the availability of resources for development'. Further research will be necessary to verify the finding that access to bond markets is important for development and growth in transition economies reported here.

We conclude that our results confirm the paradigm of the growth-supporting role of the financial sector also for transition countries. However, our findings about the role of different financial market sectors deviate from the expectations that free stock markets are a major growth driver: bond markets and total domestic credit expansion – both of which include public finance – stimulated economic growth in our sample, whereas private credit and stock market capitalization (that is solely private finance) had no significant influence on growth. For transition economies, financial funds channelled through the combination of public and private sectors seem to provide stronger growth triggers than those channelled solely through the private sector in the intermediate stage of development. In emerging markets bond markets play a far more important role than hitherto assumed. We argue that possible obstacles hindering private credit and stock markets to exploit their full potential need to be explored further. As long as corporate governance in the private sector is weak, the risk of financial investment in this sector may be considered to be far too high, and thus, providing finance to an efficient state can be a major way to reasonably foster economic growth during transition. While we are by no means arguing that the private sector is unimportant for economic development in emerging markets, our findings support Rousseau and Wachtel (2005) in arguing that the widely accepted aggregate effect of finance on growth varies with the level of economic development and, therefore, country characteristics need to be considered. This draws renewed attention to the role of individual financial market segments and to specific effects of economic transition onto the ability of these segments to foster real economic growth in transition and emerging market economies.

APPENDIX: DEFINITIONS OF VARIABLES

Output growth growth rate of real gross domestic product per capita. (Source: primarily International Financial Statistics (IFS) of the IMF, 2004; where necessary time series were supplemented with data from the OECD Historical Statistics, OECD, 2004a, and OECD National Accounts of OECD Countries, OECD, 2004b.)

Capital stock growth growth rate of real physical capital stock per capita; time series on physical capital stock (K) were calculated by using perpetual inventory methods:

$$K_t = K_{t-1} \cdot (1 - d) + I_t$$

whereby I denotes gross fixed capital formation and d represents the constant rate of depreciation that is assumed to be 0.07; the initial capital stock values (K_0) were calculated following Easterly and Levine (2001) by

$$\frac{K_0}{Y_0} = \frac{(I/Y)^{\varnothing}}{(g_y^{\varnothing} + d)}$$

where $(I/Y)^{\varnothing}$ represents annual average investment rates over a ten-year period and $g_y^{\varnothing}$ denotes output growth averaged over a ten-year period. Since data for transition countries are only available for some years, we use for calculations the longest period available for each country. (Source: Real gross fixed capital formation data mainly from OECD Historical Statistics (OECD, 2004a), and National Accounts of OECD Countries (OECD, 2004b), for transition economies from UNECE (2000a), and International Financial Statistics of the IMF (2004).)

Change in participation rate changes of the ratio of the number of employed persons to total population (Source: OECD Quarterly Labour Force Statistics (OECD, 2004c), OECD Main Economic Indicators (OECD, 2004d), and UNECE Economic Survey of Europe, UNECE (2004).)

Educational attainment logarithm of the following measure: weighted population fraction under 25 years of age having completed 3 levels of education, attainment rates: primary education (weight: 1), secondary education (weight: 1.4), post-secondary education (weight 2). (Source: Barro and Lee, 2000; Human Capital Updated Files, April 2000, available at: http://web.korea.ac.kr/~jwlee/).

Domestic credit volume of loans of deposit money banks and monetary authorities to all residents divided by GDP. (Source: International Financial Statistics of the IMF, 2004.) In general we use line 32 ('Domestic Credit') of the IFS monetary survey, which only contains deposit money banks and monetary authorities. For some countries with a different institutional set-up (for example, Malta and Turkey), we use IFS data from the banking survey (line 52) which additionally contains 'other banking institutions' and 'non-bank financial institutions'. For details, see Blum et al. (2002, p. 51f).

Private credit volume of loans of deposit money banks and monetary authorities to the private sector divided by GDP. (Source: International Financial Statistics of the IMF.) In general we use line 32d ('claims on the Private Sector') of the IFS monetary survey (IMF, 2004), which only contains deposit money banks and monetary authorities. For some countries with a different institutional set-up (for example Malta and Turkey), we use IFS data from the banking survey (line 52d; IMF, 2004) which additionally contains 'other banking institutions' and 'non-bank financial institutions'.

Stock market capitalization value of listed domestic stocks on domestic exchanges divided by GDP. (Source: for most countries Federation of International Stock exchanges, FIBV (2004); additional data of national stock exchanges are used for Slovakia, Hungary and Romania.)

Bonds outstanding value of outstanding amounts of both domestic and international debt securities divided by GDP. (Source: Bank for International Settlements/Securities Statistics, BIS 2004; for countries other than Poland, Hungary, Czech Republic data are just available for the size of public bond markets; as it seems that total bond market size is almost identical with public bond market size in these countries, we use data on public bond markets to proxy total market size.)

Total financial intermediation 1 sum of domestic credit, stock market capitalization and bonds outstanding. (Source: See sources for domestic credit, stock market capitalization and bonds outstanding.)

Total financial intermediation 2 sum of private credit, stock market capitalization and bonds outstanding (Source: See sources for private credit, stock market capitalization and bonds outstanding.)

NOTES

* Gerhard Fink is Jean Monnet Professor at the Europe Institute, Vienna University of Economics and Business Administration, Austria. Peter Haiss is lecturer at the Europe Institute, Vienna University of Economics and Business Administration and project manager with Bank Austria Creditanstalt, Austria. Goran Vukšić is research fellow at the Institute of Public Finance, Zagreb, Croatia. The authors gratefully acknowledge the support granted by the Jubiläumsfonds of the Oesterreichische Nationalbank (OeNB) (project no. 8868). For more details and related research see http://fgr.wu-wien.ac.at/institut/ef/nexus.html. We also thank Aurel Schubert, OeNB, for helpful comments. The opinions expressed are the authors' personal views.

1. The group of countries labelled as EU accession countries includes: Bulgaria, the Czech Republic, Slovakia, Hungary, Slovenia, Poland, Romania, Malta and Turkey. This group largely consists of transition economies, and we therefore, although not completely correctly, use both terms: transition and accession countries.
2. The quality of the existing relationships in state-owned banks could only be recognized gradually. It is also worth noting that the approach to cleaning up bank balance sheets differed across countries (Berglöf and Bolton, 2002).
3. Bonin et al. (2004) provide some more evidence that foreign banks are more efficient than domestic banks, and especially more than those owned by the government. In addition, they find that the method and timing of privatization matters for bank efficiency.
4. While there are less than 10 000 firms listed on the national exchanges in the United States and about 3000 on the New York Stock Exchange, 8748 companies were listed in transition stock exchanges in 1999 (Bonin and Wachtel, 2003).
5. At the end of 1999 there were 72 companies from transition countries listed at the New York Stock Exchange or Nasdaq (Berglöf and Bolton, 2002).
6. Krkoska (2001) finds that FDI, capital market financing and domestic credit have made a significant contribution to overall gross fixed capital formation in transition countries. Capital market liquidity (defined by turnover ratio), in contrast, has played no significant role.
7. A survey of the theoretical literature is out of the scope of this chapter. We only give a very brief overview of the basic theoretical insights together with the most important references. Interested readers are advised to consult the above surveys. We mostly rely on Levine (1997).
8. For example, panel data techniques may automatically account for omitted variables and heterogeneity of the initial conditions. Or, when longer spans of data are available, one can use several lags of regressors as instruments, when needed, and thus alleviate problems of potential measurement error and endogeneity.
9. Koivu (2002) disagrees with this argument in the context of transition economies and allows for the fixed effects.
10. This model has become a textbook model, and will not be formally derived here. An explanation of the model is also available, for example, from Temple (1999), or Romer (1996). In addition, our approach is an informal modification and extension of the model that reduces the relevance of its formal derivation and exposition.
11. Specifically, standard specifications used in the empirical finance–growth studies (see Wachtel, 2001) can also be regarded as informal.

12. Capital accumulation may, for example, be promoted by entrepreneurial finance (Bonin and Wachtel, 2003) or international capital flows (see Krkoska, 2001, for evidence on this in the context of transition countries).
13. It should be noted here that we also implemented simple regressions testing the impact of financial intermediation on capital accumulation, and the results were almost always insignificant.
14. We realize that using lagged values of some variables may not completely solve the endogeneity problem, but we would like to point out that the relationship between investment and growth (as well as between human capital and growth, Temple, 1999) may be problematic in this respect as well. As shown by Blomstrom et al. (1996): 'economic growth induces subsequent capital formation more than capital formation induces subsequent growth'. Still, most growth regressions, including ours, are carried out with devoting even less attention to this simultaneity problem. Rarely, some authors use instrumental variables (Temple, 1999). As stated by Rousseau and Wachtel (2005), the choice of method for dealing with potential simultaneity problems is not crucial – using instrumental variables or lagged values for financial variables yields remarkably similar results.
15. In addition, including fixed effects would further reduce the number of degrees of freedom which is already rather low for some specifications because the number of observations is not very big, especially in regressions with lagged financial variables.
16. Bulgaria, Czech Republic, Slovakia, Hungary, Slovenia, Poland, Romania, Malta and Turkey.
17. Although our initial sample contained another five countries, we had to exclude them from estimations because of more severe data limitations: there are no (or not enough) data on human capital (educational attainment) for three Baltic countries and Croatia. In addition, Cyprus was excluded from the sample because of insufficient numbers of observations on outstanding bonds.
18. Fink et al. (2004a) report a less clear-cut relationship between bonds outstanding and GDP growth for EU countries. Applying a sectoral split, Fink et al. (2005) provide preliminary evidence for reverse Granger causality from GDP growth to public bond issues in the EU. They also report some evidence for Granger causality from bond issues by corporations and financial institutions to GDP growth for EU countries.
19. This argument applies to stock markets and private credit. Bank credit to public sector and bond markets was not considered in the study by Minier (2003).
20. For a detailed discussion see Fink et al. (1998) or more recently Eller and Haiss (2003).

REFERENCES

Ahmed, S. (1998), 'Comment on: The legal environment, banks, and long-run economic growth', *Journal of Money, Credit, and Banking*, **30** (2), 614–20.

Arnold, L. (1998), 'Poverty traps and financial development in a model of finance and growth', *Zeitschrift für Wirtschafts- und Sozialwissenschaften*, **118**, 415–24.

Atje, R. and B. Jovanovic (1993), 'Stock markets and development', *European Economic Review*, **43**, 632–40.

Barro, R.J. and J. Lee (2000), 'International data on educational attainment: Updates and implications', CID Working Paper No. 42.

Beck, T. and R. Levine (2004), 'Stock markets, banks, and growth: Panel evidence', *Journal of Banking and Finance*, **28**, 423–42.

Becsi, Z. and P. Wang (1997), 'Financial development and growth', *Economic Review of the Federal Reserve Bank of Atlanta*, **82** (4), 46–62.

Bencivenga, V.R. and B.D. Smith (1991), 'Financial intermediation and economic growth', *Review of Economic Studies*, **58**, 195–209.

Berglöf, E. and P. Bolton (2002), 'The great divide and beyond – financial architecture in transition', *Journal of Economic Perspectives*, **16** (1), 77–100.
Berthelemy, J.C. and A. Varoudakis (1996a), 'Economic growth, convergence clubs, and the role of financial development', *Oxford Economic Papers*, **48**, 300–28.
Berthelemy, J.C. and A. Varoudakis (1996b), 'Models of financial development and growth: A survey of recent literature', in N. Hermes and R. Lensink (eds) (1991), *Financial Development and Economic Growth*, Routledge, pp. 7–35.
BIS – Bank for International Settlements (2004), *Securities Statistics*, Bank for International Settlements, Basel.
Blomstrom, M., R.E. Lipsey and M. Zejan (1996), 'Is fixed investment the key to economic growth?', *The Quarterly Journal of Economics*, **111** (1), 269–76.
Blum, D., K. Federmair, G. Fink and P. Haiss (2002), 'The financial-real sector nexus – Theory and empirical evidence', IEF Working Paper No. 43, Europe Institute WU-Wien.
Bonin, J. and P. Wachtel (2003), 'Financial sector development in transition economies: Lessons from the first decade', *Financial Markets, Institutions & Instruments*, **12** (1), 1–66.
Bonin, J., I. Hasan and P. Wachtel (2004), 'Privatisation matters: Bank efficiency in transition countries', BOFIT Discussion Papers No. 8.
Borensztein, E., J. De Gregorio and J.-W. Lee (1998), 'How does foreign direct investment affect economic growth?', *Journal of International Economics*, **45** (1), 115–35.
Breuss, F., G. Fink and P. Haiss (2004), 'How well prepared are the new member states for the European Monetary Union?', *Journal of Policy Modeling*, **26**, 769–91.
Campos, N.F. and Y. Kinoshita (2002), 'Foreign Direct Investment as technology transferred: Some panel evidence from the transition economies', *The Manchester School*, **70** (3), 398–419.
Demirgüç-Kunt, A. and R. Levine (1999), 'Bank-based and market-based financial systems: Cross-country comparisons', World Bank Working Paper No. 2143.
Drakos, K. (2003), 'Assessing the success of reform in transition banking 10 years later: an interest margins analysis', *Journal of Policy Modeling*, **25**, 309–17.
Durlauf, S.N. and D.T. Quah (1998), 'The new empirics of economic growth', NBER Working Paper No. 6422.
Easterly, W. and R. Levine (2001), 'What have we learned from a decade of empirical research on growth? It's not factor accumulation: Stylized facts and growth models', *The World Bank Economic Review*, **15** (2), 177–219.
EBRD (2003), Transition Report 2003: Integration and regional cooperation, London: EBRD.
ECB – European Central Bank (2003), 'Bond markets and long-term interest rates in European Union accession countries', European Central Bank, Frankfurt.
ECB – European Central Bank (2004), 'The acceding countries' economies on the threshold of European Union', *ECB Monthly Bulletin*, 2/2004, 45–56.
Eller, M. and P. Haiss (2003), Strukturschwächen im Finanzsektor der Bewerberstaaten als Verstärker spekulativer Blasen: Implikationen für die EU-Erweiterung', *Bankarchiv*, **50** (3), 253–64.
European Commission (2002), 'Update of the report on macroeconomic and financial sector stability developments in candidate countries', European Economy – Enlargement Papers No. 111.
FIBV (2004), *Stock Market Capitalization Statistics*, Federation of International Stock Exchanges.

Fink, G. and P. Haiss (1999), 'Central European financial markets from an EU perspective: Theoretical aspects and statistical analyses', IEF Working Paper No. 34, Europe Institute WU-Wien.
Fink, G., P. Haiss and S. Hristoforova (2004a), 'Growth triggers in the European Union', in C. Dreger and G. Hansen (eds), *Advances in Macroeconometric Modeling*, Baden-Baden, pp. 205–37.
Fink, G., P. Haiss and H. Kirchner (2005), 'Die Finanzierung über Anleihenemissionen und Zusammenhänge zum Wirtschaftswachstum', *Kredit und Kapital*, **38** (3), 351–76.
Fink, G., P. Haiss and H. Mantler (2004b), 'Financial sector macro-efficiency', in M. Balling, F. Lierman and A. Mullineux (eds), *Financial Markets in Central and Eastern Europe*, London, pp. 61–98.
Fink, G., P. Haiss and G. Vukšić (2007), 'Preliminary conjectures on the finance and growth nexus in Eastern Europe', *Osteuropa Wirtschaft*, 51 (forthcoming).
Fink, G., P. Haiss, L. Orlowski and D. Salvatore (1998), 'Central European banks and stock exchanges: Capacity-building and institutional development', *European Management Journal*, **16** (4), 433–46.
Fries, S., D. Neven and P. Seabright (2002), 'Bank performance in transition economies', EBRD Working Paper No. 76.
Greenwood, J. and B. Jovanovic (1990), 'Financial development, growth and the distribution of income', *Journal of Political Economy*, **98**, 1076–107.
Greenwood, J. and B.D. Smith (1997), 'Financial development and the development of financial markets', *Journal of Economic Dynamics and Control*, **21**, 145–81.
Hahn, F.R. (2003), 'Financial development and macroeconomic volatility: Evidence from OECD countries', WIFO Working Paper No. 198.
Haiss, P. and S. Marin (2003), 'Corporate bonds as financing vehicle in Central and Eastern Europe', in P. Chadraba and R. Springer (eds), *Proceedings of the 11th Annual Conference on Marketing and Business Strategies for Central and Eastern Europe, Vienna*, pp. 196–204.
IMF (2004), International Financial Statistics, Washington, DC.
King, R.G. and R. Levine (1993a), 'Finance and growth: Schumpeter might be right', *Quarterly Journal of Economics*, **108** (3), 717–37.
King, R.G. and R. Levine (1993b), 'Finance, entrepreneurship and growth: Theory and evidence', *Journal of Monetary Economics*, **32**, 513–42.
Koivu, T. (2002), 'Do efficient banking sectors accelerate economic growth in transition countries?' BOFIT Discussion Papers No. 14.
Kominek, Z. (2003), 'Stock markets and industry growth: an eastern European perspective', EBRD Working Paper No. 81.
Krkoska, L. (2001), 'Foreign Direct Investment financing of capital formation in Central and Eastern Europe', EBRD Working Paper No. 67.
Levine, R. (1991), 'Stock markets, growth and tax policy', *Journal of Finance*, **46** (4), 1445–65.
Levine, R. (1997), 'Financial development and economic growth: Views and agenda', *Journal of Economic Literature*, **35**, 688–726.
Levine, R. and S. Zervos (1998), 'Stock markets, banks and economic growth', *American Economic Review*, **88** (3), 537–58.
Levine, R., N. Loayza and T. Beck (2000), 'Financial intermediation and growth: Causality and causes', *Journal of Monetary Economics*, **46**, 31–77.
Lipschitz, L., T. Lane and A. Mourmouras (2002), 'Capital flows to transition economies: Master or servant?', IMF Working Paper WP/02/11.

Mankiw, G., D. Romer and D. Weil (1992), 'A contribution to the empirics of economic growth', *Quarterly Journal of Economics*, **197**, 407–34.
Mencinger, J. (2003), 'Does Foreign Direct Investment always enhance economic growth?', *Kyklos*, **56**, 493–510.
Minier, J.A. (2003), 'Are small stock markets different?', *Journal of Monetary Economics*, **50**, 1593–602.
Obstfeld, M. (1994), 'Risk trading, global diversification and growth', *American Economic Review*, **84** (5), 1310–29.
OECD (2004a), OECD Historical Statistics, Paris.
OECD (2004b), National Accounts of OECD Countries, Paris.
OECD (2004c), Quarterly Labour Force Statistics, Paris.
OECD (2004d), OECD Main Economic Indicators, Paris.
Pagano, M. (1993), 'Financial markets and growth: An overview', *European Economic Review*, **37**, 613–22.
Patrick, H.T. (1966), 'Financial development and economic growth in underdeveloped countries', *Economic Development and Cultural Change*, **15**, 174–89.
Pistor, K., M. Raiser and S. Gelfer (2000), 'Law and finance in transition economies', *Economics of Transition*, **8** (2), 325–68.
Romer, D. (1996), *Advanced Macroeconomics*, New York: McGraw-Hill.
Rousseau, P.L. and P. Wachtel (2000), 'Equity markets and growth: Cross-country evidence on timing and outcomes, 1980–95', *Journal of Banking and Finance*, **24**, 1933–57.
Rousseau, P.L. and P. Wachtel (2001), 'Inflation, financial development and growth', in T. Negishi, R. Ramachandran and K. Mino (eds) (2001), *Economic Theory, Dynamics and Markets: Essays in Honor of Ryuzo Sato*, Deventer: Kluwer Academic Publishers, pp. 309–24.
Rousseau, P.L. and P. Wachtel (2002), 'Inflation thresholds and the finance–growth nexus', *Journal of International Money and Finance*, **21**, 777–93.
Rousseau, P.L. and P. Wachtel (2005), 'Economic growth and financial depth: Is the relation extinct already?' UNU/WIDER conference on Financial Sector Development for Growth and Poverty Reduction, July, Helsinki.
Saint-Paul, G. (1992), 'Technological choice, financial markets and economic development', *European Economic Review*, **36**, 763–81.
Saint-Paul, G. (1996), 'Demand-driven financial development', in N. Hermes and R. Lensink (eds) (1996), *Financial Development and Economic Growth*, Routledge, pp. 37–52.
Shioji, E. (2001), 'Public capital and economic growth: A convergence approach', *Journal of Economic Growth*, **6**, 205–27.
Singh, A., A. Singh and B. Weisse (2000), 'Information technology, venture capital and the stock market', University of Cambridge Accounting and Finance Discussion Papers No. 00-AF47.
Temple, J. (1999), 'The new growth evidence', *Journal of Economic Literature*, **37** (1), 112–56.
UNECE (2000a), 'Financing growth and development in the transition economies: The role of domestic savings'. Background paper by the Economic Analysis Division for the UNECE Regional Conference 'Financing for Development'.
UNECE (2000b), 'FDI and the macroeconomy in the transition economies'. Background paper by the Economic Analysis Division for the UNECE Regional Conference 'Financing for Development'.

UNECE (2004), *Economic Survey of Europe*, 2004/2, Geneva.
Wachtel, P. (2001), 'Growth and finance: What do we know and how do we know it?', *International Finance*, **4** (3), 335–62.
Wachtel, P. (2003), 'How much do we really know about growth and finance', *Economic Review of the Federal Reserve Bank of Atlanta*, **88** (3), 33–47.
Weill, L. (2003), 'Banking efficiency in transition economies', *Economics of Transition*, **11** (3), 569–92.

12. Financial sector development in South-Eastern Europe: quality matters

Arnaud Mehl, Cristina Vespro and Adalbert Winkler*

1. INTRODUCTION

Transition economies inherited from the socialist era financial sectors that did not allocate resources on a market basis. Banks passively accommodated and monitored payment flows between socially-owned enterprises. In the early 1990s, there was widespread consensus that financial sector reform could contribute to the transition from plan to market and foster growth (Blommestein and Spencer, 1993; Fries and Lane, 1994). This view was also supported by a large body of literature (surveyed in Levine, 1997, for instance) which finds a positive and causal link between financial development and long-run economic growth in large country samples.

This chapter sheds further light on the finance–growth nexus, focusing on South-Eastern Europe, namely Bulgaria, Romania and the countries located in the Western Balkans (Albania, Bosnia and Herzegovina, Croatia, FYR of Macedonia, Serbia and Montenegro). Such a focus is relevant for a number of reasons. First, although there is a vast literature on the role of the financial sector in transition economies (EBRD, 1998; Bonin and Wachtel, 2002; Winkler, 2002), empirical studies on the finance–growth nexus have been relatively scarce.[1] Second, many financial sector studies have focused on the new EU member states (see for example Caviglia et al., 2002), leaving South-Eastern European countries in the shadow. Third, in the last decade, the environment of the financial sector, identified as key to the finance–growth relation (Wachtel, 2001), went through significant changes in this region. Last, from an institutional perspective, South-Eastern European countries embarked on a process of integration into EU structures, either through accession negotiations (for Bulgaria, Croatia and Romania) or within the so-called 'Stabilisation and Association' process (for the remaining countries), which, in light of the acquis communautaire, has some implications on banking sector reform.

About 15 years after the start of transition, it is of course still too early to draw definitive conclusions. Having said that, preliminary empirical results suggest that the improved quality of the financial sector and its environment has been favourable to growth, more than financial deepening per se. Indeed, as the quality of the financial sector environment remained poor in the first half of the 1990s, financial deepening resulted in inflationary finance in many countries, ultimately contributing to crises and large output losses. Only since the late 1990s, have tightened regulations and supervision as well as the opening of domestic banking sectors to foreign investors changed the environment of the financial sector in South-Eastern Europe positively, and these have been going hand in hand with macroeconomic stabilization and economic growth.

The remainder of the chapter is set out as follows. Section 2 provides a conceptual framework to interpret the empirical evidence. Section 3 applies this framework to the experience of South-Eastern European countries. Section 4 presents some empirical evidence on the finance–growth nexus in South-Eastern Europe. Section 5 concludes.

2. A CONCEPTUAL FRAMEWORK TO INTERPRET FINANCIAL DEVELOPMENT IN SOUTH-EASTERN EUROPE

Financial sector development is usually measured by quantitative indicators such as the monetization ratio or the financial intermediation ratio (McKinnon, 1973; Shaw, 1973). The monetization ratio (broad money to GDP) measures the transfer of financial resources from the household and corporate sector to the financial sector. The financial intermediation ratio (credit to the private sector to GDP) measures the backflow of financial resources to the household and corporate sector.

These indicators are supposed to measure the financial system's capacity to perform its main functions, namely to overcome information asymmetry, to reduce transaction costs, manage liquidity and idiosyncratic risks, monitor managers and to facilitate the allocation of resources, across space and time, in an uncertain environment (Merton and Bodie, 1995). By fulfilling these functions, financial systems can affect growth by promoting capital accumulation and/or by exerting a positive impact on the pace of productivity growth (Levine, 1997).

The financial sector only fulfils these functions properly and thus supports growth if financial institutions are subject to proper governance so that banks' incentives are compatible with those of depositors or borrowers. In this case, banks resort to signalling, screening, monitoring and self-selection as key instruments to overcome asymmetric information problems. In practice, on the assets side of the balance sheets of banks, these instruments include the requirement that loans are extended only after borrowers have provided proper information (such as balance sheet data, business plans or data on market and socio-economic position) and/or assets (including collateral, reputation or own funds) to the bank (Gertler and Rose, 1994). Moreover, loan portfolios need to be sufficiently diversified (Diamond, 1984). However, banks may be subject to moral hazard and adverse selection behaviour, which has been found to be at the core of 'poor' banking practices, including the granting of bad loans, which themselves are conducive to resource misallocation, inflationary finance, bank failures, financial crises and ultimately significant output losses (Sundararajan and Balino, 1991; Caprio and Klingebiel, 1996; Caprio, 1997; Ingves, 2003).

This is why the quality of the financial sector environment may also be crucial in ensuring growth-promoting effects of financial development. In particular, banking regulation and supervision are key in setting out and enforcing standards that require banks to resort to mechanisms that mitigate moral hazard and adverse selection (Dewatripont and Tirole, 1994). The main instruments – as laid down in the Basel standards, for instance – include capital adequacy, loan classification, provision requirements, limits on large exposures and connected lending, as well as requirements for liquidity, credit and market risk management. Moreover, an adequate legal and accounting framework is needed to establish and enforce property rights and provide reliable information. Econometric evidence suggests that countries with legal systems that give a high priority to secured creditors' rights, rigorous contract enforcement and high-quality accounting standards tend to have better-developed financial intermediaries (Levine et al., 2000).

To wrap up, qualitative indicators need to complement quantitative indicators to assess financial development. This is illustrated in the four quadrants of Table 12.1. The top left quadrant describes an economy where the financial sector is not developed, both in quantitative and qualitative terms, that is shallow and with a poor environment. The top right quadrant describes a financially deep economy with a poor environment. In a market economy, this situation is not sustainable, as banks would end up overburdened with bad loans, which would lead either to a financial crisis and bank failures or to inflationary finance if bank recapitalization is financed by money printing. The lower left quadrant describes an economy with a stable financial sector, with a good environment, but too shallow to actively support growth. The lower right quadrant depicts the optimal situation: the financial sector is both deep and characterized by a good environment.

Table 12.1 Financial development: quantity and quality

		Financial depth	
		Shallow	Deep
Quality of the environment	Poor	*Non-developed financial sector*	*Socialist financial system* *Financial sector prone to inflation and crises*
	Good	*Stable financial sector, but not actively growth-supportive*	*Developed and growth-supportive financial sector*

Source: Authors' compilation.

In this framework, growth-supportive financial development can be considered as an evolution whereby the economy's financial deepening is either based on a good environment (from the lower left to the lower right quadrant), or is at least going hand in hand with its improvement (from the top left to the lower right quadrant), as indicated by the arrows.

3. FINANCIAL DEVELOPMENT AND GROWTH IN SOUTH-EASTERN EUROPE: THE DESCRIPTIVE EVIDENCE

3.1 Up to the late 1990s: Deep Financial Sector, but Poor Environment

In the planned economy environment, financial sectors played hardly a part in the allocation of resources. Thus, before 1990, there was no need for banking supervision and regulation, or for an appropriate legal framework. In quantitative terms, however, financial sectors were relatively deep at the outset of transition, with monetization ratios above 70 per cent of GDP in Albania, Bulgaria and Moldova and 50 per cent in Romania (EBRD, 1998). In the early 1990s, however, many countries in the regions failed to design and implement reforms that would have led to a better quality of the financial sector environment. The main deficiencies were:

- *Poor institutional and legal environment*. Although parliaments passed legislation and governments adopted regulations on financial contracts, their effectiveness was diminished by inconsistencies with other legislation, often inherited from the socialist rule, and not fully implemented by courts, mainly in the areas of insolvency, bankruptcy and collateral.

- *Inadequate banking supervision.* Given that banking regulation and supervision had to be created from scratch, most supervisory departments were not able to set out and enforce international standards that guarantee sound finance, regarding loan loss provisioning, limits to exposure and connected lending, in particular. Staff was limited in number, often neither experienced nor adequately trained, and unable to deal with an increasing number of banks. Finally, since state-owned banks remained dominant players, governments were reluctant that supervisors act decisively to liquidate troubled banks, which weakened banking supervision even further.
- *Insufficient restructuring and poor governance of state-owned banks.* The consensus in the early 1990s was to give priority to the restructuring and privatization of state-owned commercial banks. However, due to political economy reasons, in particular (Bokros, 2002), reforms were delayed or did not improve the governance of banks (Keren and Ofer, 2002). The latter continued to be subject to political pressure with a view to extending loans to non-profitable state-owned enterprises in so-called 'priority sectors'. This contributed to resource misallocation and bad loans (EBRD, 1998).
- *Lax regulation on licensing new private banks and connected lending.* Authorities opened the banking market to private-owned institutions to strengthen competition and efficiency. However, this led to an unregulated free-for-all in a number of countries, as minimum capital requirements were either set at very low levels deliberately or became low in real terms due to high inflation. Companies misused this situation by establishing banks that served as their financial department (so-called 'agent' or 'pocket' banks; see World Bank, 1989 and 1993). This increased inefficiency costs relating to resources misallocation and reputation costs as 'pocket' banks severely undermined private sector confidence in the banking sector as a whole.
- *Lack of human capital and credit technology.* Banks overall were not accustomed to credit risk assessment, risk management, resorting to loan security or credit monitoring (Gelb and Honohan, 1991; Caprio, 1995). As a result, most institutions were unable to use best practices.

3.2 The Crises Years: Shallower Financial Sector, Persistently Poor Environment

When the first attempts of macroeconomic stabilization took hold in the mid-1990s, the low quality of the financial sector environment became visible, as the granting of 'false credit' (McKinnon, 1993) led to a rise in non-performing loans and financial crises, ultimately. Some countries, such as Bulgaria in 1997 and Croatia in 1998/1999, faced outright banking crises. A number of banks went bankrupt and were eventually closed down or sold (Gomel, 2002). Other countries, such as Romania and Serbia under the Milosevic regime, managed to avoid outright crises thanks to high inflation rates fuelled by central bank and government interventions. Somewhat different, the 1997 financial crisis in Albania was triggered outside the financial sector, with a run on pyramid schemes by enterprises and households.

Financial crises in South-Eastern European countries were associated with financial shrinkage. The monetization ratio in Bulgaria, the most spectacular example, halved in one year from about 70 per cent of GDP in 1996 to 30 per cent in 1997. The impact of the financial crisis in Croatia was milder, with a levelling-off in financial deepening for about one year. Financial crises were also accompanied by substantial output losses and a large investment decline. Real GDP decreased in Bulgaria by 9 per cent in 1996 and by 7 per cent in Albania in 1997. Output losses in Croatia were more limited, at 1 per cent in 1999, although the recession was the only one the country had experienced since the end of the war in the mid-1990s. Likewise, Romania went through three years of recession between 1997 and 1999, while struggling with several bank failures and crises. Finally, in FYR of Macedonia, where an outright crisis did not occur, major weaknesses in the banking sector were identified as a cause for slow growth (Drummond, 2000).

3.3 The late 1990s: a Better Environment

Output and budgetary costs of financial crises were instrumental in bringing about a decisive change in financial sector reform policies in the most recent years. Reforms have successfully improved the environment of the financial sector by focusing on three dimensions:

1. *Hardening of budget constraints.* Central banks in the region have reduced or ceased to lend to commercial banks, thereby putting harder constraints on their refinancing opportunities. As early as late 2000, central bank lending to commercial banks was virtually nil in most countries of the region. Conversely, central banks have accumulated foreign assets, which in most countries cover more than 100 per cent of reserve money.
2. *Tightening of banking supervision and regulation.* Authorities have endeavoured to adopt international standards on banking supervision and even more stringent requirements, in some cases (Talley et al., 1998).

Table 12.2 Capital adequacy in South-East Europe, 2000–2004

	2000	2001	2002	2003	2004
Albania	42.0	35.3	31.6	28.5	21.6
Bosnia	28.4	25.1	20.5	20.3	18.2
Bulgaria	35.5	31.1	25.2	22.2	16.6
Croatia	21.3	18.5	17.2	16.2	14.1
FYR of Macedonia	36.7	34.3	28.1	25.8	23.1
Romania	23.8	28.8	25.0	21.1	18.7
Serbia	0.7	21.9	30.4	31.3	27.9
Turkey	9.0	15.3	25.3	30.9	28.8

Source: National authorities.

Regulatory and supervisory reforms have touched many areas, but the main focus has been on capital adequacy requirements (Table 12.2). The amount of capital needed to obtain a banking licence has increased substantially and some countries have raised capital adequacy ratios above the 8 per cent-Cooke reference value. Regulations on classification and provisioning of loans have been strengthened. Many countries in the region have introduced international accounting standards to improve transparency. Banking supervision has been strengthened in terms of both on-site and off-site inspection.

3. *Consolidation of the banking sector and opening to foreign investors.* Financial crises and higher minimum capital requirements have led to consolidation. Since the mid-1990s, the number of banks in countries which had a relatively large number of licenced banks, such as Bosnia and Herzegovina, Croatia or Serbia, has decreased significantly (see Figure 12.1). In line with developments observed in the new EU member states, authorities have opened banking sectors to foreign investors, mainly by privatizing the remaining state-owned banks. Banks owned by foreign investors, mainly from the euro area, have become the dominant players in all banking sectors of the region, in terms of number of banks operating and banking sector assets. Foreign bank entry has contributed to improve the financial sector environment for two reasons. First, it has allowed 'reputational capital' (Hellman and Murdock, 1998) to be imported and the interest of banks and depositors to be aligned. Euro area banks would indeed lose money if they lent badly. Second, foreign banks are less likely to engage in connected lending as reputable foreign shareholders do not borrow from the local banks in which they have invested (EBRD, 1998). As a result, foreign bank entry further hardens budget constraints imposed on the real sector.

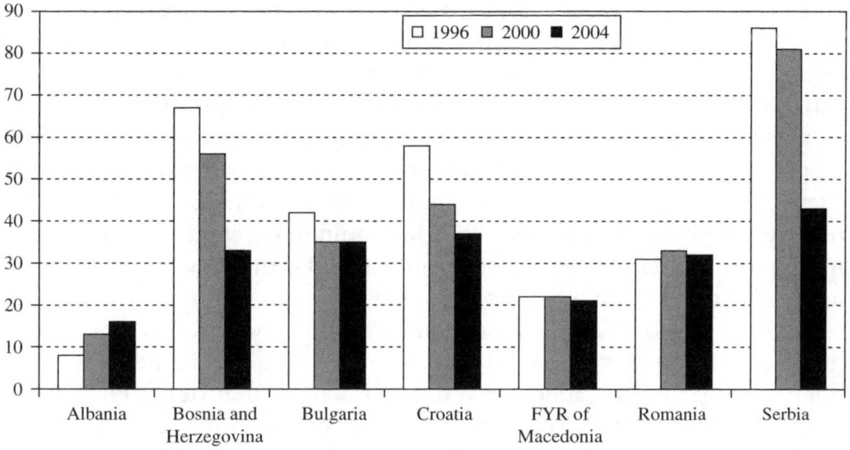

Source: EBRD.

Figure 12.1 *Number of banks*

3.4 Most Recent Years: from Consolidation Efforts to Credit Boom

Against the background of a catching-up process in terms of financial sector quality, financial depth has significantly increased in recent years. Monetization has grown for three reasons: (a) higher macroeconomic stability, as reflected in low or declining inflation rates and rather stable exchange rates; (b) the presence of reputable foreign-owned banks; (c) the impact of the euro cash changeover, mostly in former Yugoslavia countries, where legacy currency cash, in particular Deutschmark bank notes, was circulating. In this respect, credit institutions widely advertised euro-denominated accounts at attractive conditions. Households and firms deposited their holdings of legacy currency cash 'under the mattress' to minimize risks and cost relating to the cash changeover, giving a large boost to the volume of deposits (Padoa-Schioppa, 2003; ECB, 2002).

In contrast, financial intermediation remained subdued temporarily, as banks lent more cautiously. They were indeed reluctant to expand their lending activities to the new private sector as most micro, small and medium-sized enterprises were fairly young, fragile and offered a limited borrowing track-record (Klapper et al., 2002). Moreover, there has been anecdotal evidence that when entering the respective markets some foreign-owned banks endeavoured to 'cherry-pick the best borrowers available on the market (especially those from their own countries of origin)' (Grigorian and Manole, 2002). Banks also focused on wholesale banking and on activities that generate fees and commissions, such as international payment transactions, short-term trade credits and issuance of securities (Buch, 2002). Cautiousness also reflected the need to change procedures and risk management tools, which took time to implement, as banks lacked adequately trained staff with experience in selecting, analysing and monitoring clients. As a consequence, credit quality rose substantially or remained at relatively high levels. Together with high minimum capital requirements, recapitalization efforts and foreign investments, this has led to a strong increase in capital adequacy ratios.

Since the turn of the millennium, however, improvements in credit quality have been followed by a robust credit expansion, albeit its initial starting point, timing and dynamics have differed across countries (Figure 12.2). Real GDP growth has accelerated in tandem, driven by domestic consumption and investment. Strong credit growth was first observed in Croatia (Kraft and Jankov, 2005), most pronounced in Bulgaria, while reaching the 'sleeping beauties' (Albania, FYR of Macedonia and Romania) in 2003/2004 (Cottarelli et al., 2005).

Lending to households in some instances doubled within a year, reflecting booming housing and consumer credit. Banks financed the expansion by reducing reserves and foreign assets, using the deposits inherited from the cash changeover and increasingly relying on loans from banks abroad, mainly from their parent banks in the euro area. In many countries of the region, a large and increasing share of lending has been in foreign currency,

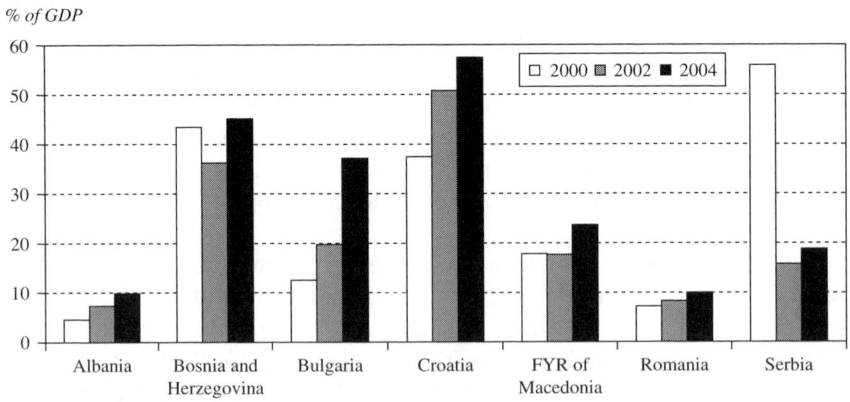

Source: IMF, national authorities, authors' compilation.

Figure 12.2 Private sector credit by the banking sector

thereby creating potential risks of currency mismatches, as households and many corporations do not have appropriate hedges. Authorities in the region have taken administrative and regulatory measures to curb credit growth, by *inter alia* tightening eligibility criteria for consumer and mortgage loans as well as reserve requirements, for example by introducing special requirements on foreign liabilities, or by announcing outright credit ceilings.

4. EMPIRICAL EVIDENCE ON THE FINANCE–GROWTH NEXUS IN SOUTH-EASTERN EUROPE

The descriptive evidence suggests that financial deepening in South-Eastern Europe has been a bumpy road, as decisive measures to ensure a high degree of quality in the financial sector environment have only been implemented since the late 1990s. The importance of the quality of the financial sector environment is, however, also confirmed by econometric evidence, based on the standard empirical framework pioneered by King and Levine (1993a; 1993b), testing for the impact of financial sector development on growth in the region over the 1993–2003 period.

To this end, we regress real GDP per capita growth for the seven South-Eastern European countries on the two quantitative measures of financial development (the monetization and intermediation ratios) and a standard set of conditioning variables. We also try to capture more qualitative aspects of financial development with the foreign bank penetration ratio, which has been used in the literature to measure competition and efficiency in the banking sector (Demirgüç-Kunt and Levine, 1999).

The set of conditioning variables includes the log of initial real GDP per capita, to capture convergence effects, the initial secondary school enrolment rate, to proxy human capital investment, as well as government size and openness (see Wachtel, 2001; Rousseau and Wachtel, 2000). More importantly, growth in transition economies seems to be related to the timing of macroeconomic stabilization and the extent of structural reform (Fischer and Sahay, 2000). We therefore use inflation as a proxy for macroeconomic stability and allow it to have a non-linear effect, so that only inflation above a certain threshold (set here at 4 per cent) can have a negative impact on growth (Khan et al., 2001; Cottarelli et al., 2005). As regards structural reforms, we place a particular emphasis on the quality of the financial environment and use the EBRD indicator of banking sector reform. We additionally account for the role of the legal environment, whose impact on finance has been highlighted by La Porta et al. (1997; 1998) by including an index of creditor right protection for transition economies as compiled by Pistor et al. (2000). Last, we include in the set of conditioning variables time dummies, to control for global factors and the war periods which have marked part of the region's recent history.

Turning to the choice of estimator, we resort to two-stage least squares (2SLS) due to potential reverse causality between growth and financial depth, as well as between growth and inflation, using lags as instruments. We do not include fixed effects, given that financial systems develop slowly, financial depth ratios are highly autocorrelated and may be collinear to a constant term (Wachtel, 2001).

4.1 Results

Regressions results are reported in Table 12.3. Overall, they suggest that financial deepening did not have a significant impact on the growth performance of South-Eastern European countries over the last decade. The financial intermediation and monetization ratios are found to have a negative effect on growth, which is significant in most specifications. These findings are at odds with the standard results from the literature on the finance–growth nexus but in line with the experience of South-Eastern European countries. In particular, they mirror the string of banking crises of the 1990s and their adverse impact on economic activity. Conversely, the foreign bank penetration ratio, which captures financial sector evolutions that are more qualitative in nature, exerts a positive impact on growth, even if it is not always significant. As could be expected from the conclusions of Fischer and Sahay (2000), initial GDP per capita and human capital are wrongly-signed and insignificant in all specifications. This confirms that traditional determinants of long-run growth are not well suited to explain transition from planned to market economy.

On the other hand, and in line with results found in previous literature, macroeconomic instability, as proxied by inflation higher than a 4 per cent-threshold, has a significant and detrimental impact on growth in all specifications (note that a positive sign means negative association with growth, as we take here the *inverse* of the deviation from the threshold; hence, the higher inflation, the more negative the deviation; see also Cottarelli et al., 2005). Also in line with results found in the literature, the impact of inflation on growth is non-linear. Lower inflation than the threshold is not significant in all specifications. Somewhat weaker is the evidence on the impact of structural reforms in the banking sector, as proxied by the EBRD indicator. In most regressions, they have a positive – albeit not significant – effect on growth. Conversely, higher creditor right protection almost always exerts a positive and significant impact on

Table 12.3 Regression results

Financial intermediation ratio	−0.026**	−0.030				
Monetization ratio			−0.070**	−0.083***		
Foreign bank penetration					0.057*	−0.079
Banking sector reform	0.038**	0.033		−0.071	0.005	0.056
Creditor rights protection	0.011**	0.036***	0.044***	0.079***	0.010	0.045***
1/(Inflation above 4% threshold)	0.001***	0.002**	0.005**	0.005**	0.001***	0.001
Inflation below 4% threshold	0.000	0.000	−0.001	−0.001	−0.000	0.000
1995 dummy	0.040**	0.050**	0.043*	0.020	0.031	0.001
Log (initial GDP)		0.037		0.032		0.008
Log (initial secondary school enrolment)		−0.117		−0.215		−0.178
Government expenditure to GDP		−0.079		−0.054		−0.149**
Openness to GDP		0.029*		0.142**		0.051
Constant term	−0.148**	−0.586**	−0.125**	−0.186	−0.033	−0.456*
Number of observations	53	53	59	64	50	50
R^2	0.47	0.53	0.41	0.61	0.38	0.36

Notes: Robust standard errors. (*) significant at 10%; (**) significant at 5%; (***) significant at 1%.

Source: Authors' calculations.

growth. This suggests that improvements in the financial sector environment, in particular with regard to contract enforcement, matters. These results are in line with those of Levine et al. (2000), who had also underscored the crucial role played by the overall institutional and legal framework governing contractual relations. Overall the evidence seems to suggest that better quality of the financial sector and its environment, together with higher macroeconomic stability, accelerates growth, rather than financial deepening per se.

5. CONCLUSIONS

Earlier literature on the finance–growth nexus found evidence that financial deepening is good for growth. The experience of South-Eastern European countries since the 1990s, however, provides weaker evidence for such a link. This chapter has tried to offer a conceptual framework to interpret this experience based on the following considerations:

- In the early years of transition, financial sectors in South-Eastern Europe were characterized by relative depth, partly due to the socialist legacy and partly to reforms that largely failed to improve the quality of their environment.
- After the outbreak of financial crises, the financial sector environment improved substantially, with harder budget constraints, tighter banking supervision and regulation and the opening to foreign banks.
- Since 2000 there have been signs that financial development in a proper sense, that is based on financial deepening and a good environment, may have started in the region, alongside strong credit growth.

To wrap up, in terms of our conceptual framework, financial sectors in South-Eastern Europe remained throughout most of the 1990s in the top right quadrant of Table 12.4, moved shortly to the top left quadrant in the crises years, then to the lower left quadrant with the improvement in their environment, and seem to be now on their way to the lower right quadrant.

To confront this conceptual framework with the data, we used a standard econometric framework and indeed did not find evidence that financial deepening impacted growth positvely in South-Eastern Europe. There are several possible explanations for this result. Admittedly, available time series may still be too short to uncover such an impact. Morever, the specific

Table 12.4 The evolution of financial sectors in South-Eastern Europe since the start of transition

		Financial depth	
		Shallow	Deep
Quality of the environment	Poor	*Non-developed financial sector*	*Socialist financial system* *Financial sector prone to inflation and crises*
	Good	*Stable financial sector, but not actively growth-supportive*	*Developed and growth-supportive financial sector*

Source: Authors' compilation.

nature of the transition process may make the standard growth regression framework ill-suited to model the evolution of output in the region. This is suggested by the fact that the initial level of development and stock of human capital are found to be insignificant or wrongly-signed. However, a third interpretation is that it is the quality of the financial sector and its environment that mattered for growth, rather than financial deepening per se. Indeed, together with higher macroeconomic stability, higher creditor right protection and increasing foreign bank penetration are found to have a positive and statistically significant impact on growth.

Looking ahead, our results suggest that, together with stability-oriented policies, a sound legal environment, in particular when it comes to contract enforcement, and the continuation of the opening up of the financial sector are instrumental in ensuring that the ongoing credit expansion in the region goes hand in hand with growth.

DATA APPENDIX TO THE EMPIRICAL ESTIMATES

- EBRD banking sector reform indicator: EBRD indicator of structural reform in the banking sector. Source: EBRD, *Transition Report* (2002, 2003 and 2004 issues). Data available from 1993 to 2003.
- Foreign bank share: number of foreign banks in total number of banks as a measure of foreign bank penetration. Source: EBRD, *Transition Report* (2002, 2003 and 2004 issues). Data available from 1993 to 2003, except for Albania, Macedonia, Serbia and Montenegro (1994–2003), Croatia (1995–2003), Bosnia and Herzegovina (1999–2003).
- GDP per capita growth: log difference of GDP per capita, in constant local currency. Source: IMF, *World Economic Outlook*; data available from 1993 to 2004. However, for Serbia and Montenegro, data from this source were available from 1998.
- Government size: natural logarithm of general government expenditure as share of GDP. Source: EBRD (2001, 2002, 2003, 2004), data available from 1993 to 2003. However, for Bosnia and Herzegovina and Serbia and Montenegro, data from this source were available from 1995 and from 2000, respectively.
- Inflation: log difference of the GDP deflator. Sources: IMF, *World Economic Outlook*; data available from 1993 to 2004. However, for Bosnia and Herzegovina and Serbia and Montenegro, data from this source were available from 1995 and 1999, respectively.
- Initial human capital: 1993 gross secondary school enrolment rate, as a percentage. Source: *World Development Indicators*, World Bank.

- Initial real GDP per capita: GPD per capita in 1993 (1995 for Bosnia and Herzegovina and Serbia and Montenegro, due to data unavailability), in constant 1995 US dollars. Source: *World Development Indicators*, World Bank.
- Intermediation ratio: credit to the private sector as a percentage of GDP. Source: EBRD (2002, 2003, 2004). Data available from 1993 to 2003, except for Albania (1994–2003), Bosnia and Herzegovina (1999–2003), Serbia and Montenegro (1996–2001).
- Creditor right protection indices for the year 1998 specifically constructed for transition economies. Source: Pistor et al. (2000).
- Monetization ratio: broad money as a percentage of GDP. Source: EBRD (2001, 2002, 2003, 2004). Data available from 1993 to 2003, except for Bosnia and Herzegovina (1994–2003) and Serbia and Montenegro (1998–2003).
- Openness: natural logarithm of trade in goods as share of real GDP. Source: *World Development Indicators*, World Bank, data available from 1993 to 2004. However, for Bosnia and Herzegovina data from this source were available from 1994 and for Serbia and Montenegro from 1995.

NOTES

* Arnaud Mehl and Adalbert Winkler: European Central Bank and Cristina Vespro: Ecares, Université Libre de Bruxelles. The chapter builds on earlier versions of papers presented at the KfW conference on 'Innovative approaches to financial sector development in volatile environments', Berlin, November 2002, and at the 9th Dubrovnik Economic Conference on 'Banking and the Financial Sector in Transition and Emerging Market Economies', Dubrovnik, June 2003. The authors are grateful to the conference participants, Roland Beck, Matthieu Bussière, François Gurtner, Oscar Calvo-Gonzalez, Francesco Mazzaferro, Tomasz Michalski, Georges Pineau, Ralph Süppel, Franziska Schobert, Nikolaus Siegfried, Christian Thimann and Andrea Wölfel for helpful comments on earlier drafts. Research assistance from André Geis and Calin Arcalean is gratefully acknowledged. The views expressed in the chapter do not necessarily represent those of the European Central Bank. E-mail for correspondence: adalbert.winkler@ecb.int.

1. Empirical studies on the finance–growth nexus in transition economies, albeit with no specific focus on Southeast Europe, include Berglöf and Bolton (2002), Koivu (2002) and more recently Fink et al. (2005).

REFERENCES

Berglöf, E. and P. Bolton (2002), 'The great divide and beyond. Financial architecture in transition', *Journal of Economic Perspectives*, **16** (1), 77–100.

Blommestein, H.J. and M.G. Spencer (1993), 'The role of financial institutions in the transition to a market economy', IMF Working Paper, Washington DC.
Bokros, L. (2002), 'Financial sector development in Central and Eastern Europe', in A. Winkler (ed.), *Banking and Monetary Policy in Eastern Europe. The First Ten Years*, Houndmills and New York: Palgrave Publishing, pp. 11–42.
Bonin, J. and P. Wachtel (2002), 'Financial sector development in transition economies: Lessons from the first decade', paper originally presented at the Fifth Dubrovnik Conference on Transition Economics, Dubrovnik, Croatia, available at http://pages.stern.nyu.edu/%7Epwachtel/DubrvnkVJun02.pdf.
Buch, C. (2002), 'Governance and restructuring of commercial banks', in A. Winkler (ed.), *Banking and Monetary Policy in Eastern Europe. The First Ten Years*, Houndmills and New York: Palgrave Publishing, pp. 43–71.
Caprio, G. (1995), 'The role of financial intermediaries in transitional economies', *Carnegie-Rochester Conference Series on Public Policy*, **42**, 257–302.
Caprio, G., Jr (1997), 'Safe and sound banking in developing countries – We're not in Kansas anymore', World Bank Working Paper, No. 1739, Washington DC.
Caprio, G. and D. Klingebiel (1996), 'Bank insolvencies – cross country experience', World Bank Policy Research Paper, No. 1620, Washington DC.
Caviglia, C., G. Krause and C. Thimann (2002), 'Key features of the financial sectors in EU accession countries', in C. Thimann (ed.), *Financial Sectors in EU Accession Countries*, Frankfurt: European Central Bank.
Cottarelli, C., G. Dell'Ariccia and I. Vladkova-Hollar (2005), 'Early birds, late risers, and sleeping beauties: Bank credit growth to the private sector in Central and Eastern Europe and in the Balkans', *Journal of Banking and Finance*, **29** (1), 83–104.
Demirgüç-Kunt, A. and R. Levine (1999), 'Bank-based and market-based financial systems – cross-country comparisons', Policy Research Working Paper, No. 2143, The World Bank.
Dewatripont, M. and J. Tirole (1994), *The Prudential Regulation of Banks*, Cambridge and London: MIT Press.
Diamond, D. (1984), 'Financial intermediation and delegated monitoring', *Review of Economic Studies*, **51**, 393–414.
Drummond, P. (2000), 'Former Yugoslav Republic of Macedonia – Banking soundness and recent lessons', IMF Working paper, WP/00/145, Washington DC.
EBRD (1998), *Transition Report*, London.
EBRD (2001), *Transition Report*, London.
EBRD (2002), *Transition Report*, London.
EBRD (2003), *Transition Report*, London.
EBRD (2004), *Transition Report*, London.
European Central Bank – ECB (2002), *Review of the International Role of the Euro*, Frankfurt-am-Main.
Fink, G., P. Haiss and G. Vukšić (2005), 'Importance of financial sectors for growth in accession countries', paper presented at the conference on European Economic Integration organized by the ECB, OeNB and CFS, Vienna, 14–15 November 2005.
Fischer, S. and R. Sahay (2000), 'The transition economies after ten years', IMF Working Paper, WP/00/30, Washington DC.
Fries, S.M. and T.D. Lane (1994), 'Financial and enterprise restructuring in emerging market economies', IMF Working Paper, Washington DC.

Gelb, A. and P. Honohan (1991), 'Financial sector reform', in V. Thomas, A. Chhibber, M. Dailami and J. de Melo (eds), *Restructuring Economies in Distress, Policy Reform and the World Bank*, Washington DC.

Gertler, M. and A. Rose (1994), 'Finance, public policy and growth', in G. Caprio, J. Atiyas and J.A. Hanson (eds), *Financial Reform, Theory and Experience*, Cambridge University Press, pp. 13–48.

Gomel, G. (2002), 'Banking and financial sector in transition countries and convergence towards European integration', mimeo, http://eaces.gelso.unitn.it/Eaces/work/Papers/Gomel-eaces_080502-rev.pdf.

Grigorian, D.A. and V. Manole (2002), 'Determinants of commercial bank performance in transition. An application of data envelopment analysis', IMF Working Paper, WP/02/146, Washington DC.

Hellmann, T. and K. Murdock (1998), 'Financial sector development policy: The importance of reputational capital and governance', in R. Sabot and I.P. Székely (eds), *Development Strategy and Management of the Market Economy, 2*, Oxford: Clarendon Press.

Ingves, S. (2003), 'Banking crisis from an international perspective', speech given at the Seminar on Financial Safety Nets, SEDESA Seguro de Depósitos Sociedad Anónima), Buenos Aires, 8 April, 2003, http://www.imf.org/external/np/speeches/2003/040803.htm.

Keren, M. and G. Ofer (2002), 'Globalization and the role of foreign banks in economies in transition', mimeo, http://eaces.gelso.unitn.it/Eaces/work/Papers/Globalization%20and%20the%20Role.pdf.

Khan, M., A. Senhadji and B. Smith (2001), 'Inflation and financial depth', IMF Working Paper, No. 01/44, Washington DC.

King, R.G. and R. Levine (1993a), 'Finance, entrepreneurship and growth', *Journal of Monetary Economics*, **32**, 513–42.

King, R. and R. Levine (1993b), 'Finance and growth. Schumpeter might be right', *Quarterly Journal of Economics*, August, **108** (3), 717–37.

Klapper, L.F., V. Sarria-Allende and V. Sulla (2002), 'Small- and medium-size enterprise financing in Eastern Europe', World Bank Policy Research Paper, No. 2933, Washington DC.

Koivu, T. (2002), 'Does financial development affect economic growth in transition countries?', paper presented at the BOFIT seminar, Bank of Finland, 20 May 2002.

Kraft, E. and L. Jankov (2005), 'Does speed kill? Lending booms and their consequences in Croatia', *Journal of Banking and Finance*, **29** (1), 105–21.

La Porta, R., F. Lopez-de-Silanes, A. Shleifer and R.W. Vishny (1997), 'Legal determinants of external finance', *Journal of Finance*, **LII** (3), 1131–50.

La Porta, R., F. Lopez-de-Silanes, A. Shleifer and R.W. Vishny (1998), 'Law and finance', *Journal of Political Economy*, **106** (6), 1113–55.

Levine, R. (1997), 'Financial development and economic growth. Views and agenda', *Journal of Economic Literature*, **35**, June, 688–726.

Levine, R., N. Loayza and T. Beck (2000), 'Financial intermediation and growth. Causality and causes', *Journal of Monetary Economics*, **46**, 31–77.

McKinnon, R.I. (1973), *Money and Capital in Economic Development*, Washington DC: The Brookings Institution.

McKinnon, R.I. (1993), *The Order of Economic Liberalization, Financial Control in the Transition to a Market Economy*, 2nd edn, Baltimore and London: John Hopkins University.

Merton, R. and Z. Bodie (1995), 'A conceptual framework for analysing the financial environment', in D.B. Crane (ed.), *The Global Financial System: A Functional Perspective*, Boston: Harvard Business School Press.
Padoa-Schioppa, T. (2003), 'The euro goes east', *Comparative Economic Studies*, **45**, 215–31.
Pistor, K., M. Raiser and S. Gelfer (2000), 'Law and finance in transition economies', *Economics of Transition Journal*, **8** (2), 325–68.
Rousseau, P. and P. Wachtel (2000), 'Inflation, financial development and growth', in T. Negishi, R. Ramachandran and K. Mino (eds), *Economic Theory, Dynamics and Markets: Essays in Honor of Ryuzo Sato*, Kluwer, 2001.
Shaw, E.S. (1973), *Financial Deepening in Economic Development*, New York, London, Toronto: Oxford University Press.
Sundararajan, V. and T.J.T. Balino (1991), 'Issues in recent banking crises', in V. Sundararajan and T.J.T. Balino (eds), *Banking Crises. Cases and Issues*, Washington DC, International Monetary Fund, pp. 1–57.
Talley, S., M. Giugale and R. Polastri (1998), 'Capital inflow reversals, banking stability, and prudential regulation in Eastern Europe', World Bank Policy Research Paper, No. 2023, Washington DC.
Wachtel, P. (2001), 'Growth and finance: What do we know and how do we know it?', *International Finance*, **4** (3), 335–62.
Winkler, A. (2002), *Banking and Monetary Policy in Eastern Europe – The First Ten Years*, Houndmills and New York: Palgrave Publishing.
World Bank (1989), *World Development Report*, Washington DC.
World Bank (1993), *Russia – The Banking System in Transition*, Washington DC.

PART IV

Credit growth in Central and Eastern Europe: a cause for concern?

13. Happy, sad and open endings: a comparison of credit growth in CEECs with past experiences and ongoing developments in Austria, Finland and Spain

Doris Ritzberger-Grünwald

1. THE SCEPTICISM CONCERNING FAST CREDIT GROWTH IN CEECs

Today any discussion of ongoing concerns about Central and Eastern European countries (CEECs) will inevitably include the high credit growth rates which characterize most of these economies. Very often this leads to a debate in which some find this development quite natural or even necessary, linking it to the still ongoing catching-up process,[1] whereas others are worried, as credit overexpansion is used as an indicator for up-coming banking crises.[2]

In looking for benchmarks, several studies have tried to find the 'optimal path for credit growth' or 'the equilibrium growth rate of credit'.[3] This growth rate should neither over-liquidize the economy, nor should it hamper the healthy development of investment and consumption. To find such an equilibrium for an industrialized economy is not at all an easy task. It is even more complicated for a transition country, where private credits have started to emerge only recently, as credit to the private sector was more or less non-existent in planned economies. As a fully-fledged financial market is characterized by a certain level of banking intermediation, one also has to acknowledge a need for catching-up in this respect. Therefore a country may easily end up with credit growth in double-digits (see Figure 13.1).

In the period 2002 up to 2005, cumulative growth of private sector credit exceeded 300 per cent in half of the 16 countries in the region, with Romania and Serbia-Montenegro reporting outstanding high credit growth rates. In a further five countries the growth rate ranged from 170

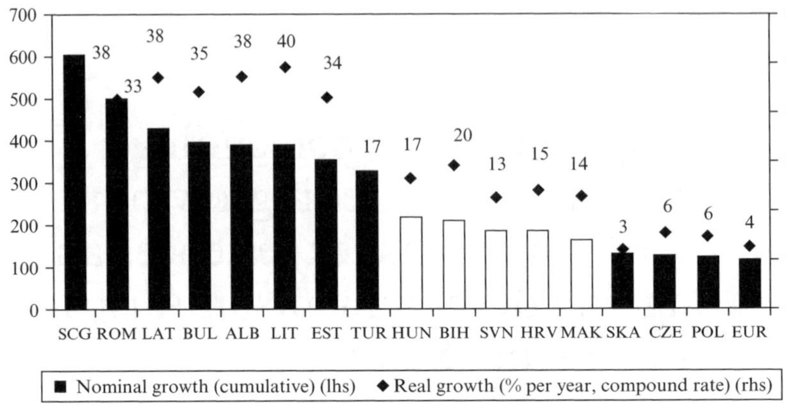

Notes: ALB = Albania, BIH = Bosnia-Herzegovina, BUL = Bulgaria, CZE = Czech Republic; EST = Estonia, EUR = Euro area, HRV = Croatia, HUN = Hungary, LAT = Latvia, LIT = Lithuania, MAK = Macedonia, POL = Poland, ROM = Romania, SCG = Serbia-Montenegro, SVK = Slovakia, SVN = Slovenia, TUR = Turkey.

Sources: IMF; International Financial Statistics; national data; author's estimates; Mihaljek (2006).

Figure 13.1 Bank credit to the private sector 2002–2005

to 230 per cent in nominal terms. In the Czech Republic, Poland and Slovakia, the expansion was considerably slower. Overall, the pace of credit growth seen in CEECs was above the euro area in all countries. In real terms credit growth exceeded 30 per cent per annum in seven out of 16 countries, with Lithuania in the lead; and in a further six countries it ranged between 10 and 20 per cent. Although financial intermediation levels in the region are still low compared to the euro area, credit-to-GDP ratios have increased significantly in several countries in recent years (Backé and Zumer, 2005).

Mainly driven by housing loans, lending to households has continued to expand much faster than corporate lending. Housing loans expanded on average by over 50 per cent per annum and contributed 42 per cent to the growth of total private sector credit during 2003 to 2005 (Table 13.1). While increases in house prices have not been excessive so far, there are signs that the construction industry in several countries may have started to hit capacity constraints. There are two exceptions worth noting: first, in Lithuania and in Slovenia, corporate lending (and not lending to households) was the main driver of credit growth of this period. Second, in Bulgaria and Croatia, consumer loans, especially car and credit card loans, predominated

Table 13.1 *Housing sector loans and private sector credit growth 2003–2005*

Countries	Growth of private sector credit[1]				Contribution to growth of private sector credit[2]			
	Corporate	Household			Corporate	Household		
		Total	Housing	Consumer		Total	Housing	Consumer
Bulgaria	28.7	63.3	114.8	51.5	50.5	49.5	17.3	32.1
Croatia	8.4	16.7	23.3	13.7	22.4	62.7	24.9	37.9
Czech Republic	11.1	32.3	39.6	23.3	10.7	89.3	69.9	19.4
Estonia	30.6	37.4	41.8	20.5	45.5	54.5	48.9	5.6
Hungary	12.3	28.5	26.1	44.2	40.8	59.2	43.9	15.8
Latvia	16.4	53.2	60.0	42.4	43.0	57.0	35.5	6.4
Lithuania	27.6	67.1	68.9	3.3	59.0	41.0	40.7	0.3
Romania	30.8	64.8	67.8	42.9	50.7	49.3	46.1	3.2
Serbia	25.2	61.4	–	–	48.4	51.6	–	–
Slovakia	3.7	35.4	34.9	15.6	27.0	73.0	51.7	15.2
Slovenia	40.0	105.0	–	–	78.0	22.0	–	–
Average	**21.3**	**51.4**	**53.0**	**28.6**	**48.3**	**55.4**	**42.1**	**15.1**

Notes:
1. Annual growth rate of private sector credit (excluding credit to financial intermediaries), 2003–05; in percent. Data for 2005 are for the latest month available.
2. Percentage contribution to the annual growth rate of private sector credit; average for 2003–05 (for Slovakia, 2004–05). Based on monthly data.

Sources: Central Banks; BIS estimates; Mihaljek (2006).

over housing loans (Kraft and Jankov, 2005). The more detailed analysis of the driving forces behind credit development is not only useful in assessing the potential risk involved for the banking sector, but also helps to judge current account deficits, being quite large in some countries.

In 2004, foreign-owned banks accounted on average for almost 70 per cent of total banking sector assets in the region. Obviously they are quite heavily involved in the development of private sector growth. At the same time, one can also observe high credit growth rates in countries in which foreign-owned banks play only a minor role, such as Latvia, Serbia and Montenegro, and Turkey. This may serve as an indicator that high credit growth is a more general phenomenon of catching-up, not necessarily caused by structural factors like foreign banks' dominance.

2. CAN CEECs BE COMPARED WITH OTHERS?

Very often the phenomenon of high credit growth rates in CEECs is described as something unique. In an international comparison, emerging market economies located in Latin America or East Asia are often taken as examples. A complementary approach would be to learn from the experiences made by different EU countries in the context of financial market liberalization.[4] For some of them this was a long-lasting process, whereas others liberalized their markets more quickly. But all of them faced the problem of high credit growth rates at a certain point of time. The interesting question is how EU countries reacted to that, and how successful they had been in preventing either an overheating of the economy or a banking crisis.

In the following, three cases are under special consideration: Austria in the late 1970s and early 1980s, Finland in the late 1980s and early 1990s, and Spain nowadays. Austria as a case in point for a country which managed the situation well; Finland as an example of a country that ended up in a considerable financial crisis; and Spain, the euro area country with the second highest private credit growth rate, being a case on which the jury is still out. Although neither Austria, Finland, nor Spain had been transition economies, all of them had to cope with elements of catching-up in the analysed period.

In a nutshell, Austria ranked only eighth among the present EU-15 in terms of GDP per capita at PPP in 1975. Yet the country managed to catch up fast with real GDP growth rates exceeding the EU average by 1 percentage point during the 1970s, thus progressing to fifth place in the EU ranking by 2005. In the period under consideration, the late 1970s and early 1980s, the Austrian economy was heavily dependent on its neighbouring country, Germany. Privatization of state-owned industries and in the banking sector was still in its infancy. At the same time, linkages between the two sectors were strong, as Austrian banks held a significant share of the state-owned industry, which was actually not very diversified, producing mainly steel and petrochemicals.

Finland was also lagging behind. The financial markets were curbed by a high degree of concentration in the banking sector, modest borrowing requirements of the central government, and several peculiarities in the tax system. The real side of the economy, relying mainly on the paper industry, specialized in barter trade with Russia. The catching-up process, spurred by the liberalization of financial markets, was stopped abruptly when the breakdown of the USSR swept export markets away and the country went into a deep recession, in which its total GDP loss amounted to nearly 12 percentage points.[5]

Spain, finally, has been catching up quickly since its EU entry in 1986. The drastic change in the political system (end of the Franco era), the broad effort to overcome the huge regional differences (for example infrastructure investments), and a liberal immigration policy enhanced this catching-up process. Driving in the fast lane was only interrupted once by the ERM crisis, which resulted in unusually low real GDP rates (1992: 0.9 per cent; 1993: −1.0 per cent). Euro area membership or, more precisely, the sharp drop of real interest rates gave an additional push to internal demand, resulting in extraordinarily high real GDP growth rates.

During the periods under consideration credit growth to the private sector increased significantly in all three countries. The national authorities reacted differently: whereas Austria was relatively strict, willing to turn back the wheel and going so far as to re-implement credit limits when things started to get out of control, the Finnish authorities were keen on deepening the financial markets quickly and actively supported the fast increase of the relatively low debt level of households. In Spain, the hands of the national authorities were tied by EU membership, respectively the common market and the already existing monetary union. Moral suasion and some minor measures were used when overheating became obvious. Overall there was a common change in the attitude towards credits to the private sector. Starting from stringent, highly regulated financing conditions, a more market-orientated approach took over, which resulted in completely liberalized, but strictly supervised credit granting banks.

3. A HAPPY ENDING: THE STEP BY STEP LIBERALIZATION IN AUSTRIA

There are many different ways in which to liberalize a financial market. It can happen relatively quickly or slowly step by step, it can be implemented counter-cyclically or in parallel with the business cycle. Braumann (2002) describes the Austrian story of financial markets' liberalization, looking for key variables which were responsible for the fact that the process of liberalization did not lead to a financial crisis, as was the case in many other countries.

Austria liberalized its financial markets quite slowly. In fact it took the country nearly 25 years to eliminate all restrictions. Starting with the lifting of restrictions on the establishment of branch offices in 1977, continuing with the liberalization of interest rates in 1980, the reform of banking supervision in 1987, the removal of capital controls from 1988 to 1991, the introduction of free market entry in 1994 and the privatization of state-owned banks from 1992 to 2000, the overall process was very protracted. One of the key elements was the abolition of credit controls in 1981.

In Austria credit control agreements were implemented for the first time in 1951. Initially, the agreement was quite basic, but several extensions turned it into a sophisticated instrument, which became an important element in monetary and credit policy. Three parties were involved: banks, the central bank and the ministry of finance. The general aim was to limit credit to the private sector.

Initially, the credit controls consisted of a set of qualitative and quantitative measures. Qualitative ones tried to channel credit to the productive sector of the economy,[6] whereas quantitative ones limited the amount of credit. Banks had to hold a certain liquidity reserve under a framework established in parallel with reserve requirements and therefore criticized widely (Neudörfer, 1986). The liquidity reserve framework was complemented by the obligation that credits were not allowed to grow more quickly than deposits. In 1957 a so-called credit ceiling, which was based on the bank's own capital and liabilities, was implemented. This was a much more direct and therefore much more effective instrument, although it also had its limits: increasing the credit ceiling in a recession does not mean that the demand for credit follows accordingly. Whenever a bank exceeded this ceiling, it was fined. This sort of agreement was extended to the entire sector (Klauhs, 1971).

In 1973 this passive[7] credit control mechanism was – against several critical voices (for instance Klauhs, 1971, who stressed the sectoral unfairness of such an instrument) – complemented by an active credit control mechanism. This new instrument foresaw an upper limit for the monthly growth rate of loans, the so-called Limes.[8] Complying with the Limes was a precondition for access to the central bank's refinancing instruments (Androsch, 1985).

With the exception of a temporary weakening in 1975 and 1976, these rules were kept in place until 1981, when active and passive credit controls were lifted. Interestingly, they were lifted separately and with different arguments: most of the active measures were abandoned in February 1981, as the central bank blamed them for competitive distortions between credit institutions (and therefore indirectly confirmed all the criticism). The passive measures were abandoned in June 1981, when the ministry of finance, the central bank and credit institutions were not able to agree how these measures might go along with the new Banking Act of 1979. In May 1982 the very few remaining active measures which restricted credit growth for households (Limes on consumer credit) were abolished. And from September 1982 banks were even allowed to advertise such loans.

Only in 1975 (and 1976), when the oil crises led to a European-wide recession, the Austrian real GDP shrunk by 2.0 per cent[9] and the demand for private credit was low, were credit controls weakened.[10] Interestingly,

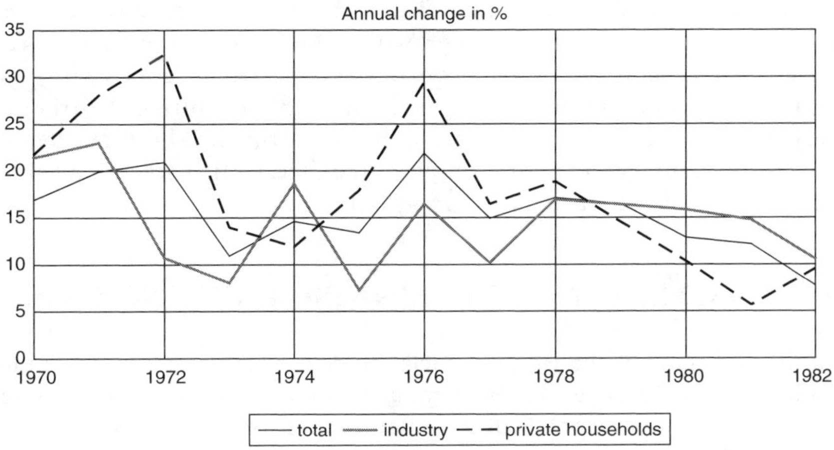

Source: OeKB, OeNB.

Figure 13.2 Credit growth to the private sector in Austria 1970–1982

the measures were not abolished completely. In fact they were kept in place for the next upswing. Financial institutions were hardly affected by the recession. This was not only because of the countercyclical reaction of the credit controls. The need to finance the rising budget deficit and several financial needs of state-owned firms also ensured the constant expansion of banks' balance sheets (Handler and Mooslechner, 1986; Mooslechner, 2005).

In fact, in the late 1970s, when the Austrian economy rebounded and real GDP growth peaked at 5.5 per cent in 1979, private credit growth rates remained subdued (see Figure 13.2). As capital controls remained in place, no additional foreign capital was attracted, and the rising demand for credit was successfully counteracted with high real interest rates and credit limits. Later on, at the end of the 1980s, capital controls were lifted, and capital inflows increased sharply. Asset prices boomed, but credit growth remained moderate, as banks had to fulfil new and much higher supervisory standards. In addition, banks' collateral, while quite diversified, included only a low share of housing (Braumann, 2002). After 1991, when capital markets were liberalized completely, the integration of the Austrian financial market with its European counterparts intensified, and all segments became much more competitive. Today, there is no evidence that private-sector credits from banks to firms are restricted (Waschiczek, 2005).

The Austrian success story reflects several elements: liberalization was very slow, the Austrian authorities cooperated, there was no direct connection between asset prices and credit growth, and the timing of the liberalization steps was countercyclical. The pace of liberalization was accelerated in periods with slower growth, caused by the oil price shocks or the global recession, but slowed down or even reversed in periods with high GDP growth rates. Overall, compared with other countries, Austria did very well. At the same time, financial market structures both inside and outside the country were fairly simple at the time, so that some challenges which others have to face today simply did not exist.

4. A SAD ENDING: THE FINNISH BANKING CRISIS

At the beginning of the 1980s financial markets in Finland were still quite undeveloped. Banks owed their dominance[11] mainly to the tax-exemption of deposits and to the policy of low interest rates conducted by the authorities as well as the credit rationing and the exchange control associated with it. Bank–customer relationships and prior savings were key criteria for access to credit. As a result the debt level of households was low in international comparisons. Nonetheless, Finland serves as an example for being a quick reformer of financial markets (Braumann, 2002). This was enhanced by a quite favourable economic background: in the 1980s Finland was on a catching-up route, with GDP growth rates above OECD averages, resulting in a permanent increase of households' real income and wealth. During this period the deregulation of domestic financial markets and capital movements took place (see Figure 13.3).

Finland operated extensive interest rate regulations but, in contrast to Austria, imposed no direct ceiling on bank lending. In 1983 the Bank of Finland started a step-by-step dismantling of average lending rate controls. This was followed by a sharp increase in the importance of competitively-determined interest rates, making bank lending more profitable. Credit growth was spurred by the tax deductibility of interest payments, a peculiarity quite common in Nordic countries at that time.[12]

The removal of interest rate regulation, together with a relatively loose fiscal policy and a rapid growth in the economy from 1987 onwards, led to a credit boom. Housing and consumption loans were rising very fast, driving up real bank lending by 55 per cent in the period 1986 to 1988. Although the economy showed several signs of overheating, with the current account deficit widening to 5.0 per cent of GDP in 1989, and inflation rates climbing to 6.8 per cent, the Finnish authorities were extremely reluctant to implement restrictive measures because of international forecasts of a recession. The central bank's attempts to put a brake on the lending increase by imposing higher reserve requirements on banks was to little avail. In retrospect it was easy to see that collateral was

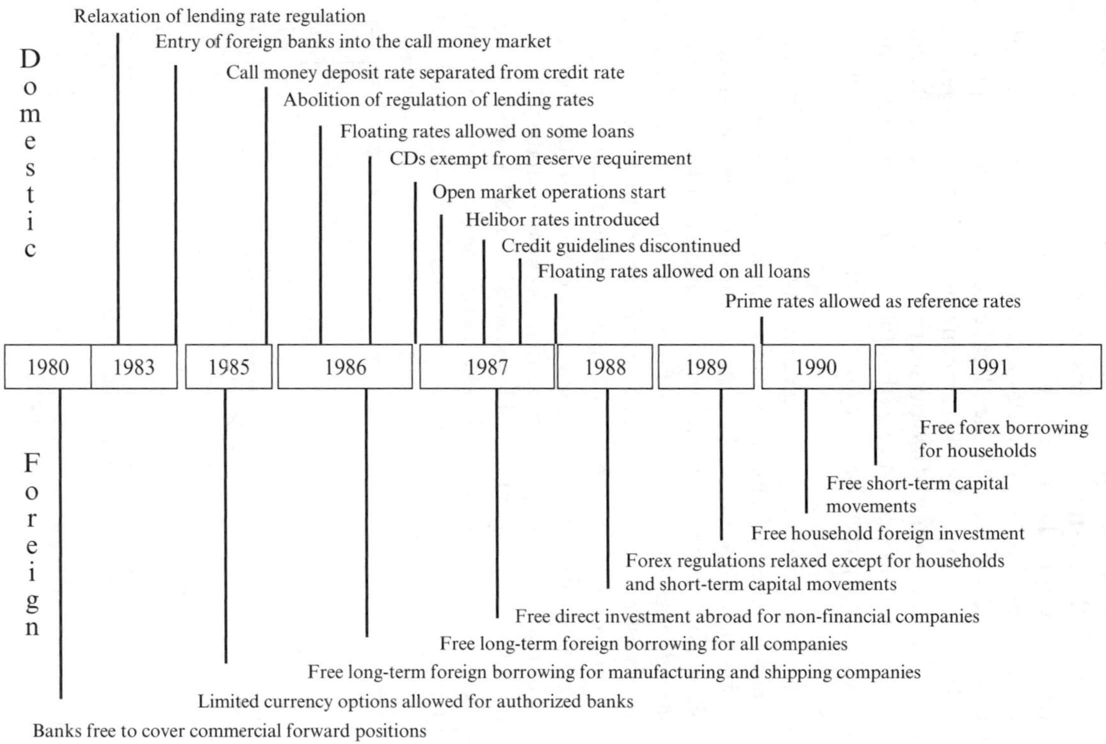

Source: Vihriälä (1997).

Figure 13.3 The deregulation of financial markets in Finland inadequate for many loans and that assessments of borrowers' creditworthiness were lax (Commission on the Banking Crisis, 1992).

In parallel to the already mentioned credit boom there was a boom in asset prices. In 1986 capital transfers were fully liberalized. Strong capital inflows, together with investors' yield awareness, overly optimistic expectations, driven up by speculation, resulted in increased asset prices, especially those for shares[13] and for houses. As both are widely accepted as collateral, credits became even cheaper. Real estate prices rose appreciably in 1988 and 1989, only to fall by the same margin in 1990 and 1991 when the bubble burst (see Figure 13.4). Also share prices fell drastically, partly because of the increase in interest rates that followed the abolition of interest rate controls, and partly because of the deterioration of corporate profitability.

Subsequently monetary policy was tightened. With the onset of the 1990s, domestic demand began to decline as a result of a sharp increase of interest rates and adjustment to over-indebtedness. Unfortunately this coincided with the collapse of the trade with the Soviet Union and Eastern Europe, which accounted for 20 to 25 per cent of Finland's total exports. Because of low competitiveness and weak external demand, exports to western markets were not able to compensate the loss of market shares. Output began to decline and firms realized that they had been overoptimistic. Collateral values started to fall and non-performing loans increased sharply.

The decline in bank profitability, which started in 1989, came to a head in 1992 when banking groups' combined losses amounted to more than FIM 20 billion. The prime reasons for the losses were write-downs on loans

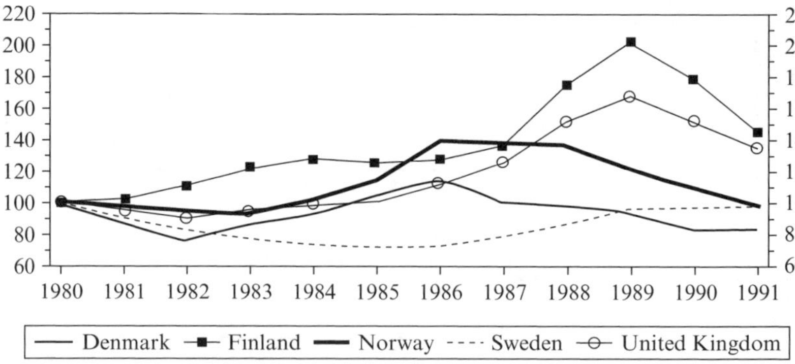

Note: 1980 = 100.

Sources: Norges Bank and the Bank of England.

Figure 13.4 House prices in selected countries

and guarantees as well as lower net income from financial operations due to the increase in non-performing assets. Obviously, in competing for market shares, banks relaxed their credit-granting standards and partly lost control of the credit risks (Pensala and Solttila, 1993). In addition, a large share of the loan portfolio comprised housing loans, carrying an interest rate which was tied to a base rate prescribed by the authorities and therefore was much too low to be profitable.

These developments led to a veritable banking crisis, which incidentally did not come as a surprise, as all other Nordic countries had been affected by similar crises in a 'clockwise' fashion immediately before Finland, starting with Denmark, followed by Norway and Sweden (Grünwald, 1993). In spring 1992 the authorities presented a package of measures designed to help the banking system weather the crisis. The above-mentioned link to the base rate for housing loans was removed. Moreover the package contained government subsidies in the form of loans carrying particularly low interest rates, and an opening for increased foreign and government investment in the banking sector. In addition a government insurance fund was set up for the banks, and the worst loans were hived off into special management companies in the central bank.

Overall, financial deregulation reinforced banks' dominant position. The release of households' pent-up demand for credit led to a sharp increase in household indebtedness in relation to disposable income. In 1988 the household net savings rate even became negative. Loans were mostly being raised from banks. Moreover, the increase in companies' foreign currency loans intermediated by banks further consolidated the role of banks in financial intermediation (Malkamäki and Solttila, 1991).

The analysis of the boom period of 1986 to 1990 supports strongly the hypothesis of moral hazard behaviour of banks. Lending growth was, *ceteris paribus*, negatively associated with bank capital and positively associated with bank costs. That this was not just a matter of underestimating the risks is suggested by the fact that banks that had opted for a growth strategy initially, did not change their behaviour even though external conditions worsened in the middle of the boom period (Vihriälä, 1997).

External advisors (for instance, Bordes, 1993) made the following overall assessment: on the whole, financial deregulation was implemented in accordance with the general principles of finance. But, two aspects of the process met with criticism. First, the banking legislation was not sufficiently adapted to the new financial environment. Second, legislation prevented deregulation on tax-exempt accounts, whereas the regulation of average lending rates and the upper limits on lending rates were abolished. Therefore, the spread on bank lending rose during the liberalization phase and the deregulation led to an excessive surge in the supply of credit and in private indebtedness.

Interestingly, in trying to get the crisis under control, prudential measures were not an issue, and turning back the wheel of financial liberalization was out of the question, too. Instead mainly macroeconomic policy measures were discussed[14] and finally implemented. Somehow this is surprising, as Finland, not even being a member of the EU at the time, would have had a much broader variety of instruments at its disposal. At the same time, it shows that the liberalization of financial markets, while being irrevocable, can easily get out of control, as no one is going to stop the party.

5. AN OPEN ENDING – THE HOUSING BOOM IN SPAIN

Although one has to admit that credit growth rates in euro area countries are far below those of the CEECs, for some countries they are surprisingly high. This is overlooked quite often, as monetary policy in the euro area does not take into account national developments, even though they influence overall euro area figures. But for financial stability, credit growth rates on a national level are still an important indicator, and therefore worth being analysed more deeply.

In December 2005, three out of 12 countries reported exceptionally high annual growth rates of credit to the private sector (Spain 28 per cent, Ireland 27 per cent, Greece 18 per cent; see Table 13.2.). Because of its 11 per cent share of euro area GDP, Spain contributed 41 per cent to the total euro area credit growth rate. Therefore, credit growth in Spain influenced the development in the euro area quite heavily, and whereas credit growth rates in Ireland and Greece – although still at a high level – are already on a declining path, they are still increasing in Spain (see Figure 13.5).[15] These facts make it worthwhile having a closer look.

Spain is one of the fastest growing economies in the euro area. It has not only profited from entering the EU and the preferred access to EU regional and cohesion funds but has also benefited from the drop in real interest rates going hand in hand with entering monetary union (European Commission, 2005). The favourable financing conditions resulted in high public and private investments. Since the mid-1980s there has been an overwhelming demand for housing, reflecting demographic factors, immigration, a permanent increase of income, an increasing participation rate, purchases of second homes by non-residents, and speculative behaviour. Actually, between 1997 and 2004, the number of new dwellings initiated annually more than doubled. In 2004 it was 700 000, and projections for 2005 and 2006 suggest that the figure could be around 800 000 annually. This is more than the number of new residences initiated in Germany, France and the UK together (Yaniz Igal, 2006).

This housing boom led to a constant increase in housing prices, which has accelerated since the end of the 1990s. Since 1998, real estate prices have risen by about 90 per cent in real terms, which is more than in most other OECD countries. Households have increased borrowing sharply, debt as a percentage of disposable income doubling since 1995 to 100 per cent, thus exceeding the EU average now. In trying to judge whether the steep rise in household debt[16] and property prices is sustainable, Ayuso et al. (2003) estimated a – relatively small – overvaluation of house prices between 10 and 20 per cent in 2003. But because of the ongoing high increase of house prices[17] (at a rate of more than 15 per cent in 2004) the Spanish authorities saw a need for action. In 2004 the Bank of Spain urged banks to exercise caution in their mortgage lending and to avoid granting loans amounting to more than 80 per cent of the house value, even though solvency ratios and provisions in the financial sector remained high (OECD, 2005). To reduce the vulnerability of borrowers to a rise in interest rates, the Ministry of Economy and Finance announced measures lowering the conversion cost of a variable rate to a fixed rate loan.

The housing boom was and still is mostly financed by mortgage loans. These loans continued to increase at a high rate. In December 2005 credits for housing increased by 34 per cent annually, followed by credits to private firms and credits for private consumption that increased by 27 per cent and 22 per cent respectively (see Table 13.2).[18] This was spurred by several factors: mortgage interest rates fell from around 10 per cent in the mid-1990s to around 3 per cent in 2005. Therefore, real mortgage interest rates are close to zero or even negative. This fall in interest rates was combined with sustained disposable income growth of 3 per cent in real terms. Finally, after the 1999 reform of the personal income tax, tax incentives to housing acquisition increased further by around 8 per cent in effective terms, partially offsetting the effect of price increases (Yaniz Igal, 2006). This expansionary housing policy[19] is quite a contradiction to the much more cautious signals of other Spanish authorities.

Financial sector development has also played its role. One of the supply-side explanations for the upward trend in house prices is the relaxation of credit restrictions. As a result, the housing credit to household income ratio has grown continuously since the mid-1980s, as has the housing credit to value of property assets ratio since the early 1990s. There are several supply-side factors supporting the growing indebtedness of households. First, greater competition and more flexible regulations may have

Table 13.2 Nominal annual loan growth, share in national outstanding amounts and in national loan growth (%) (December 2005)

	Consumer credit					Lending for house purchase				
		Share in					Share in			
	Growth rate	outstanding amounts		annual growth rates		Growth rate	outstanding amounts		annual growth rates	
		national level	Euro area	national level	Euro area		national level	Euro area	national level	Euro area
Belgium	6	4	2	3	1	18	45	3	72	4
Austria	13	12	5	14	9	12	23	2	24	2
Germany	−2	8	31	34	−9	1	43	33	−116	4
Spain	22	6	14	5	37	34	37	15	43	35
Finland	17	9	2	11	4	17	44	2	56	2
France	6	11	26	7	21	14	38	17	56	19
Greece	22	15	4	19	10	31	32	1	50	3
Ireland	18	8	3	6	7	29	41	3	43	6
Italy	16	4	8	8	17	17	21	7	44	10
Netherlands	5	4	4	2	3	12	56	13	67	12
Portugal	−2	5	2	−1	0	12	42	3	66	3
Euro area	7	7	100	6	100	13	38	100	51	100

	Other lending					Loans to non-financial corporations					Total		
		Share in					Share in						
	Growth rate	outstanding amounts		annual growth rates		Growth rate	outstanding amounts		annual growth rates		Growth rate	Share of the euro area in	
		national level	Euro area	national level	Euro area		national level	Euro area	national level	Euro area		out-standing amounts	annual growth rates
Belgium	6	9	3	5	5	5	43	3	20	2	10	3	3
Austria	32	12	4	29	34	7	53	4	33	3	11	3	4
Germany	−2	14	43	56	−28	−2	35	23	126	−5	0	29	−2
Spain	13	8	13	4	55	27	48	17	48	49	28	16	41
Finland	7	10	2	6	4	9	37	1	28	1	13	1	2
France	0	6	10	0	1	7	46	18	37	16	9	17	17
Greece	13	1	0	1	1	10	51	2	30	2	18	2	3
Ireland	28	3	1	3	8	28	48	3	48	9	27	3	8
Italy	2	13	18	4	14	5	62	19	44	13	8	14	12
Netherlands	2	3	3	1	2	8	37	7	31	7	10	9	9
Portugal	7	6	2	6	4	4	47	3	29	1	7	2	2
Euro area	3	9	100	3	99	8	45	100	40	99	9	100	99

Source: ECB, data based on outstanding amounts, national shares do not add up to 100% due to rounding differences.

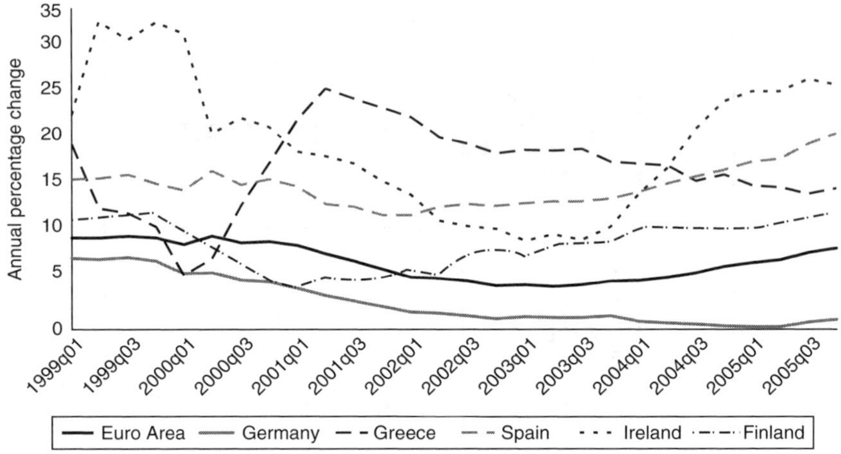

Source: ECB.

Figure 13.5 Growth of loans to the private sector in selected countries

encouraged greater availability of financing for housing. Moreover, the decline in inflation rates should have further stimulated loan supply by reducing the financial burden in the first years of the loan's life. Nonetheless, another part of the growing indebtedness can also be endogenous, as the rise in real estate prices tended to favour an increase in debt to the extent that it provided higher collateral for loans (Martinez Pages and Maza, 2003).

The banks still seem to do good, as only 0.8 per cent of total loans are doubtful, and the default rate at credit institutions in general, and at banks and savings banks in particular, have been at or close to all-time lows in 2004 and 2005 (La Caixa, 2005). Nevertheless, during the last years more and more critical voices entered the stage, predicting a burst of the bubble in the housing market, which could be followed by a severe financial crisis, as the collateral for most of the credits would be downgraded significantly. However, the most recent study on the Spanish housing market, applying the concept of accessibility, predicts a soft landing: the annual financial effort, which is the proportion of the household nominal gross disposable income devoted to repayments in the first year of the loan, tells the story of the Spanish housing market outcomes over the last two decades perfectly. This indicator halved during the 1990s (from 45 to 18 per cent) and has grown only slightly since 1999. In other words, the high price increases have been offset by higher income and – even more so – better financial conditions, so that the annual financial effort has declined significantly for the single household. As a result, rising house prices have not had any significant impact on households' purchasing power (Yaniz Igal, 2006).

This concept of accessibility not only explains the high demand for dwellings, it also explains the lending boom: the decrease in interest rates, stemming not only from monetary union, but also from higher integrated financial markets, which led to more competition between Spanish banks, made credits affordable to a much higher extent. As monetary conditions are going to be tightened, but several other, expanding factors will remain, the activities in the housing market – inclusively high credit growth – will be restrained only slightly, and the already existing signs for overheating will bottom out. Whether this argumentation outweighs the concerns of the OECD (2005), which has recently pointed out the risks related to the steep rise in households' mortgage debt (usually contracted at variable rates), and the consequences of an increase in interest payments should interest rates go up, is still to be seen.

6. WHAT CAN CEECs LEARN FROM OTHERS?

While being quite different, the three more or less historical examples of Austria, Finland and Spain, would appear to have been cornerstones on the path of financial market liberalization in Europe, starting with a heavily regulated economy and ending up with a completely deregulated market. They reflect the broad variety of possible measures which can be applied to limit the amount of credit growth, starting with the very strong setting of credit ceilings, ending up with nothing more than moral suasion. Therefore these examples mirror perfectly the three different institutional stages: not being an EU-member, being an EU member, and being a member of monetary union. In this respect those CEECs which are not a member of the EU yet have the highest leeway in creating and setting measures that rein in high credit growth (Hilbers et al., 2005).

Not surprisingly, circumvention was an issue in all three examples. Perhaps the amount of circumvention was negatively correlated with the intensity of financial market regulation, but in the end the inefficiency was even obvious in Austria, bringing the whole concept of quite heavy regulations to an end. Also the measures taken by the Finnish authorities have not been successful. A lot of circumvention was seen, for instance newly created financial institutions stepped in when banks' lending business was restricted. This is not very encouraging for the policy options available in the CEECs today.

Another lesson which can be learned is that especially in a liberalized financial market, strong supervision authorities, working together not only across sectors but also across national borders, make a difference. Basel II, which sets new common standards for capital requirement ratios, is also an effort into this direction. Obviously supervision is even more important when real estate values are on a persistent rising trend. Very few people can conceive that these 'tangible' values could fall abruptly, even more so as investment calculations are based on historical events. Only after the turnaround does it become clear that their forecast relied on a hazardous assumption.

In steering private credits, central banks used their monetary policy instruments (especially the reserve requirement ratio) to support overall credit policy. In a monetary union, where monetary policy targets the aggregate, credit growth on a national level is no longer an issue. Catching-up developments seen in Spain, but also in Portugal, Ireland and Greece, are left to national housing policies and fiscal measures. Therefore, to adopt adequate policies, it is important to know the factors and the channels which are responsible for high credit growth. Is it demand-driven, as private consumption increases, based on increasing wealth, increasing house prices, or constantly rising income expectations? Or is it more supply-driven, as growing competition forces the banking sector to look out for new customers or to sell newly created financial products?

Foreign ownership of banks has several implications, too, for instance for the possibilities for relying on sources of the parent bank, or for the possibilities to circumvent prudential measures taken by the local authorities. In fact, some CEECs show a significantly faster growth of foreign liabilities than residents' deposits, implying a rising external debt by the private sector. Whether this phenomenon increases the risk of a financial crisis is not clear. Obviously the answer also depends on the kind of exchange rate regime in place. It is therefore not surprising that central banks outside the euro area, including those in Bulgaria, Croatia and Romania, have significantly raised reserve requirements to restrict the growth of consumer and mortgage loans over the past two years.[20]

A comparison with the Austrian story shows that financial market liberalization evolved much more quickly in the CEECs. The process, for which Austria had needed nearly 25 years, giving banks and customers time to adapt slowly, was finished in a couple of years.[21] By definition there was no time to implement those changes counter-cyclically. Quite to the contrary, the lifting of credit controls coincided with above-average GDP growth rates climbing up the catching-up route. In addition, in many CEECs new legal regulations changed the situation concerning owning a house or assets privately.

All in all, one can learn a lot from the deregulation experiences made by several EU countries in the context of how to deal with high credit growth. The problem is not so much credit growth as such, as several countries have dealt with it quite successfully. The inadequate management of credit risk by the institutions involved seems to be much more important. Obviously, each country has to find its own way – not only because of different stages of financial market integration, but also because the CEECs are passing quite different institutional milestones along the catching-up route at the moment. Nevertheless one may hope that the still open endings take the right turn to end up as happy ones.

NOTES

1. Regarding convergence times to 80 per cent of the income level of the EU-14, the results of Wagner and Hlouskova (2005) range from a mean convergence time of 9.4 years (standard deviation 4.3 years) for Slovenia to 71.4 years (standard deviation 18.9 years) for Romania.
2. For instance Kaminsky et al. (1997) came to the conclusion that five out of seven studies dealing with this issue find credit growth to be an important determinant of banking and/or currency crisis. More recently, Ball and Pain (2000) and Terrones and Mendoza (2004) came to similar conclusions.
3. The findings of Backé et al. (2006) give a mixed picture. While some countries such as Lithuania and Romania have private credit-to-GDP ratios which are well below the level that would be justified by fundamentals, others had already come close to equilibrium by 2004. The rapid adjustment observed in Croatia, Estonia, Latvia and possibly Bulgaria might lead to the emergence of (over)shooting instances in the near future.
4. Brzoza-Brzezina (2005) compares the ongoing lending booms in the Czech Republic, Hungary and Poland with the – at least until now harmless ones – in Greece, Ireland and Portugal, which took place in the forefront of euro adoption, mainly caused by the substantial fall in real interest rates.
5. In Finland, real GDP growth was negative for four years in a row (1990: −0.3 per cent; 1991: −6.4 per cent; 1992: −3.8 per cent; 1993: −1.2 per cent).
6. Non-productive was a synonym for 'economically not justified' and included credits which (i) allow an extraordinary amount of stocks, (ii) are for speculative purposes, or (iii) finance over-extensive consumption (Klauhs, 1971).
7. The terms 'active' and 'passive' relate to the sides of the balance sheet.
8. Limes I, which was followed by several adaptations, stated a maximum growth rate of 1 per cent.
9. The 2.0 per cent are real time data which were revised afterwards.
10. For instance the recommendations of 1972, to restrict credits for private consumption and to make no advertisement for consumer credits, were lifted.
11. The breakdown of total assets at the end of 1986 into 15.2 per cent cash and deposits, 67.6 per cent loans and 8.3 per cent securities shows that Finnish financial institutions were quite heavily loan-based and under-securitized at this time (Nyberg, 1991).
12. In 1991 an amendment to tax law entered into force, under which a flat level tax was levied on interest earnings at source. At the same time, the tax deductibility of interest was reduced (Malkamäki and Solttila, 1991).
13. Share prices rose sevenfold in the period from the beginning of 1980 until the end of 1989.
14. See for instance Bordes, 1993, who suggested a restrictive fiscal policy combined with a loosened monetary policy with a floating markka, and the intermediate return to a fixed exchange rate regime inside a Nordic monetary union or eventually inside the EMU.
15. Bank credit, loan losses and provisions for loan losses in Spain are – as in many other countries – strongly cyclical (Fernandez de Lis et al., 2000). Therefore the – for euro area

standards – very high real GDP growth rates, lying constantly above 3 per cent in recent years, explain part of the ongoing behaviour of credit growth.
16. Household indebtedness at the end of 2004 stood at EUR 595.18 billion, which meant EUR 13.534 per capita, some 15.4 per cent more than in the year before (la Caixa, 2005).
17. Although the growth rate of the Spanish HICP constantly lies above the euro average, there is almost no connection with the boom in house prices, as owner-occupied housing is not reflected by the indicator.
18. In Spain, the share of credits to private firms is 48 per cent, and the share of credits for housing is 37 per cent, whereas credits for private consumption and other purposes play only a minor role in the overall amount of credits.
19. For many years the prevailing goal has been 'home ownership assistance', a housing policy which was set up to increase the proportion of owner-occupiers in recent decades, and which contained the following measures: (i) income tax relief on the purchase of a main residence, without any means test, granted both by the central and many regional governments; (ii) assistance to help the least-well off households purchase a home via housing plans; (iii) the application of a reduced value added tax (VAT) rate on residential construction (7 per cent instead of 16 per cent); (iv) no taxation of the imputed rents of owner-occupiers. In the meantime the proportion of owner-occupiers reached 85 per cent in 2001, the highest in the OECD (OECD, 2005).
20. Hilbers et al. (2005) give a detailed overview about all measures taken to rein in high credit growth in the following countries: Bosnia, Bulgaria, Croatia, Estonia, Greece, Iceland, Latvia, Moldova, Poland, Portugal, Romania, Serbia, Spain and Ukraine.
21. In Austria, the ratio of credits to the private sector to GDP more than doubled between 1973 (60 per cent) and 2000 (126 per cent), which was one of the highest growth rates worldwide (Braumann, 2002), exceeded by Malaysia only. This steep increase was outperformed by most CEECs, in which this ratio grew even more quickly.

REFERENCES

Androsch, H. (1985), *Die Politische Ökonomie der Österreichischen Währung. Ein Überblick über die Österreichische Währungspolitik von 1760 bis 1984 vor dem Hintergrund der Internationalen Entwicklung*, Vienna: Verlag Orac.

Ayuso, J., J. Martinez, L.A. Maza and F. Restoy (2003), 'House prices in Spain', *Economic Bulletin*, Bank of Spain, October.

Backé, P. and T. Zumer (2005), 'Developments in credit to the private sector in Central and Eastern European EU member states: Emerging from financial repression – A comparative overview', in *Focus on European Economic Integration* **2**, OeNB.

Backé, P., B. Egert and T. Zumer (2006), 'Credit growth in Central and Eastern Europe: New (over)shooting stars?', in *Focus on European Economic Integration* **1**.

Ball, J. and D. Pain (2000), 'Leading indicator models of banking crisis', *Financial Stability Review*, Bank of England, December, London.

Bordes, Ch. (1993), 'The Finnish economy – the boom, the debt, the crisis and the prospects', mimeo, June.

Braumann, B. (2002), 'Die Liberalisierung des österreichischen Finanzsektors – eine Analyse des Erfolgs', Oesterreichische Nationalbank, *Finanzmarktstabilitätsbericht* **4** (also available in English language).

Brzoza-Brzezina, M. (2005), 'Lending booms in the new EU member states, Will euro adoption matter?', *ECB Working Paper Series* No. 543, November.

European Commission (2005), 'Country study: Spain in EMU: A virtuous long-lasting cycle?', Directorate-General for Economic and Financial affairs, European Economy, *Occasional Papers* No. 14.
Fernandez de Lis, S., J. Martinez Pages and J. Saurina (2000), 'Credit growth, problem loans and credit risk provisioning in Spain', Banco de España – Servicio de Estudios, Working Paper No. 0018.
Grünwald, D. (1993), 'Die Bankenkrise in Finnland und anderen nordischen Ländern', mimeo.
Handler, H. and P. Mooslechner (1986), 'Hintergründe und ökonomische Aspekte der Novellierung des Kreditwesengesetzes 1986', WIFO Monatsberichte 12.
Hilbers, P., I. Otker-Robe, C. Pazarbasioglu and G. Johnsen (2005), 'Assessing and managing rapid credit growth and the role of supervisory and prudential policies', IMF Working Paper No. WP/05/151.
Kaminsky, G., S. Lizondo and C. Reinhart (1997), 'Leading indicators of currency crises', IMF Working Paper No. WP/97/79.
Klauhs, H. (1971), 'Mindestreserven und Kreditkontrollabkommen als Instrumente der österreichischen Konjunkturpolitik', in W. Schmitz (ed.), Geldwertstabilität und Wirtschaftswachstum, Festschrift für Andreas Korp, Vienna: Springer-Verlag.
Kraft, E. and L. Jankov (2005), 'Does speed kill? Lending Booms and Their Consequences in Croatia', *Journal of Banking and Finance*, **29**.
'La Caixa' Research Department (2005), 'Considerable increase in household indebtedness in 2004', The Spanish Economy: Monthly Report June.
Malkamäki, M. and H. Solttila (1991), 'Developments in financial markets in the 1980s', *Bank of Finland Bulletin*, Special Issue on Financial Markets in Finland.
Martinez Pages, J. and L.A. Maza (2003), 'Analysis of house prices in Spain', Working Paper No. 0307, Banco de España, Madrid.
Mihaljek, D. (2006), 'The role of housing markets and foreign-owned banks in credit growth in central and eastern Europe', in C. Enoch and I. Otker-Robe (eds), *Rapid Growth of Bank Credit to the Private Sector in Central and Eastern Europe*, Proceedings of a conference held in Sinaia, Romania, 7–8 October 2005, Washington, DC: International Monetary Fund (forthcoming).
Mooslechner, P. (2005), 'Vom "ruinösen Wettbewerb" zur wettbewerbsfähigen Position auf einem um Osteuropa erweiterten Heimmarkt. Banken und Bankenpolitik in Österreich seit den 1970er Jahren', in O. Rathkolb, Th. Venus, U. Zimmerl (eds), *Bank Austria Creditanstalt. 150 Jahre österreichische Bankengeschichte im Zentrum Europas*, Vienna.
Neudörfer, W. (1986), 'Die Kreditkontrollabkommen und ihre Problematik', in Österreichische Bankwissenschaftliche Gesellschaft (ed.), *Das Kreditwesen in Österreich, Festschrift für Hans Krasensky*, Vienna, Verlag Manz.
Nyberg, P. (1991), 'The Finnish financial markets in international perspective', Bank of Finland Bulletin, Special Issue on Financial Markets in Finland.
OECD (2005), Spain, OECD Economic Surveys, Volume 2005/6 – April.
Pensala, J. and H. Solttila (1993), 'Banks' nonperforming assets and write-offs in 1992', Bank of Finland Discussion Papers 10.
Report by the Commission on the Banking Crisis (1992), Norwegian Official Reports NOR 1992:30E, Oslo.
Terrones, M. and E. Mendoza (2004), 'Are credit booms in emerging markets a concern?', in *World Economic Outlook*, IMF, Washington.
Vihriälä, V. (1997), 'Banks and the Finnish credit cycle 1986–1995', Bank of Finland Studies E, 7.

Wagner, M. and J. Hlouskova (2005), 'CEEC growth projections: Certainly necessary and necessarily uncertain', *The Economics of Transition*, **13** (2).
Waschiczek, W. (2005), '10 Jahre EU-Beitritt: Auswirkungen auf die Finanzmarktstruktur', in *Geldpolitik & Wirtschaft* 2, Oesterreichische Nationalbank.
Yaniz Igal, J. (2006), 'The Spanish housing market: are we in for a soft landing?', *ECFIN Country Focus*, **3** (1).

14. Is lending in Central and Eastern Europe developing too fast?

Frédéric Boissay, Oscar Calvo-Gonzalez and Tomasz Koźluk

1. INTRODUCTION

Bank credit to the private sector has seen a significant increase among many Central and (South)-Eastern European countries (CEECs). However, the speed of credit growth in the region has been far from homogeneous. The average annual credit growth in real terms over the last five years has been above 20 per cent in four of the countries under consideration here (Latvia, Bulgaria, Lithuania and Estonia) while three other countries have exhibited average annual real growth rates above 10 per cent (Hungary, Croatia and Romania). By contrast, real credit growth has been somewhat slower in Slovenia and has been below 5 per cent or even negative in Poland, the Czech Republic and Slovakia. However, real GDP growth has also been particularly fast among the very countries that have experienced very fast credit expansions.[1] Real per capita GDP in purchasing power terms increased by more than 50 per cent from 1999 to 2004 in each of the Baltic states and was close to that figure in Bulgaria. Moreover, despite a fast increase in GDP, there has also been a notable increase in the GDP ratio of credit to the private sector in most CEECs (see Backé and Zumer, 2005). This increase is all the more notable if one considers that the corresponding ratio for other emerging regions of the world economy has not increased notably or even decreased. This suggests that some factors specific to the region may be at play.

To what extent can this credit expansion be explained by the rapid transition from a centrally-planned to a market-based economy in just over a decade? This question brings to the fore the importance of the developmental path that these countries have followed since the 1990s. The early years of the transition usually exhibited a significant slump in GDP followed by a period of rapid economic growth. In some cases, during the turbulent early 1990s rapid privatization of the banking sector and expansion of the undeveloped financial markets, which were basically set up from scratch, resulted in excessive lending booms followed by credit crunches and bank runs and crises that in some cases spilled over to the entire economy. Perhaps the most illustrative example is that of Bulgaria, where problems in the banking sector were at the heart of the macroeconomic crisis that would see the annual inflation rate reaching 2000 per cent in March 1997. The largely state-owned Bulgarian banking system had been financing for years the mounting losses from non-restructured enterprises, leading to a gradual erosion of the balance sheets of banks. By the time the crisis broke out, nine out of the ten state-owned banks, which accounted for 80 per cent of banking assets, had negative capital, and around half of the private banks were technically bankrupt. The Bulgarian National Bank increased liquidity to support the ailing banking sector, attempting to sterilize it through open market transactions. In the end, the crisis led to the closure of 17 banks, which accounted for around one-third of total banking assets (Yotzov, 2002). Across the region, the immature banking system was often flawed by inadequate regulation, corruption and simple lack of experience of the agents involved.

Financial liberalization during that first phase of transition may have in some cases undermined real sector development (Berglöf and Bolton, 2002). This turbulent recent history, together with the low levels of financial intermediation at the beginning of transition, helps to explain why the CEECs still exhibit significantly lower levels of lending in terms of GDP compared not only to developed countries but also to countries in a similar state of economic development. As shown in Figure 14.1, all CEECs with the exception of Croatia stood in 2003 below a simple regression line fitted for the correlation between private credit to GDP and per capita GDP across all countries in the world for which data was available.

Figure 14.1 suggests that there may indeed be sound reasons to expect credit growth in CEECs to be faster than in both developed countries and other emerging regions of the world. While in the early and mid-1990s banks were often engaged in connected lending to a rather restrictive number of corporate borrowers or lending into arrears to state-owned enterprises that faced soft budget constraints, progress in the transition process has done away with those practices (Bokros, 2002; Mehl et al., 2005).

Assuming that catching up in incomes will proceed and that it will be accompanied by financial deepening, as suggested by the simple correlation shown above, credit will necessarily have to grow faster than GDP in the CEECs. There are numerous sound reasons that may help to explain the recent acceleration of credit growth in the region. A non-comprehensive list of such factors would include foreign bank entry (which may have brought both improved risk management techniques as well as increased access to funding from parent banks); a more competitive environment in the

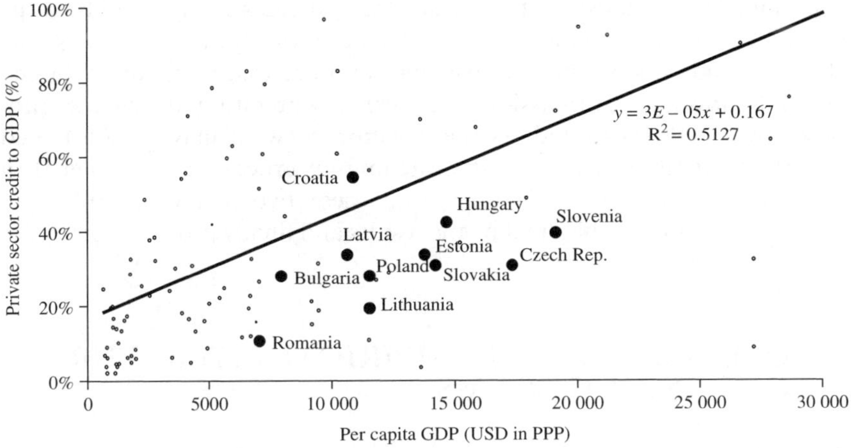

Source: IMF (IFS and WEO).

Figure 14.1 Credit to the private sector to GDP and per capita GDP, 2003 (124 countries)

banking sector (which may have contributed to declining interest rates); improvements in the institutional environment; improvements in the credit-worthiness of borrowers on the back of improved economic prospects; as well as growing property prices (which may have led to higher financing needs). The reform of the banking sector is also a key development among these transition countries. Privatization may have led to faster financial deepening through foreign bank entry but this is not the only channel through which banking sector reform may affect the pace of financial deepening. Banking sector reform brought about both new market segments and increased competition, thus increasing the range of products available to potential borrowers and reducing the costs. This would lead to faster financial deepening. However, while credit growth can be seen as a natural adjustment due to recent banking system reforms, improved bank efficiency, and capital inflows from western European countries, some concerns have been raised with regard to the speed of these adjustments. As Borio and Lowe (2002) put it, 'one of the relatively few robust findings to emerge from the literature on leading indicators of banking crisis is that rapid domestic credit growth increases the likelihood of a problem', and in some CEECs the growth rate of the credit-to-GDP ratio is close to that observed in, for instance, Indonesia, Korea or Sweden, prior to their financial crises in the 1990s.

The purpose of this chapter is to incorporate this key characteristic among CEECs of catching up in both real incomes and in financial deepening into a statistical framework that provides a way to address the question of whether credit may be growing excessively fast. In doing so the chapter builds upon a limited existing literature that is discussed briefly below. Following the discussion of the existing literature, the chapter proposes two methods to address the question of what may be considered 'excessive' credit growth given the catching-up process. The chapter then cross-checks the results obtained from these two methods, explores a number of themes highlighted by the results and finally provides some concluding comments.

2. OVERVIEW OF THE EMPIRICAL LITERATURE ON LENDING BOOMS

The empirical literature on lending booms faces the enormous challenge of having to provide a working definition of what can be considered to be an 'excessive' rate of credit growth. In theory an episode of credit growth can be thought of as 'excessive' if either (i) it endangers financial stability via financing undeserving projects that will eventually turn into bad loans; or, (ii) it leads to unsustainable macroeconomic developments, such as a deteriorating external position leading to an unsustainable build-up of external debt. None of these two effects can be easily measured or forecast. It is thus unsurprising that the empirical literature on the measurement of 'excessiveness' has been very limited.

Despite this intrinsic difficulty, policy-makers and market participants alike are faced with the need to assess credit growth developments. From an operational point of view an episode of rapid credit growth is typically labelled 'excessive' or as an unsustainable 'credit boom' when the observed growth rates exceed a given threshold. This threshold is usually estimated on the basis of the country's trend in credit growth, using a Hodrick-Prescott filter. For example, IMF (2004a) labels a credit expansion a 'credit boom' if it exceeds 1.75 times the standard deviation of the country's average credit fluctuation around the trend. The threshold value in this case is selected because, assuming the observations of credit growth were drawn from a normal distribution, there would only be a 5 per cent probability that they would lie more than 1.75 times outside the standard deviation. While the specific thresholds may differ, it is common in this literature to focus on deviations from an estimated trend (Gourinchas et al., 2001; Tornell and Westermann, 2002; Ottens et al., 2005). However, as has often been pointed out in the literature, in the context of transition this is particularly difficult given both the short time series and the likely structural breaks in the series (Duenwald et al., 2005). This difficulty is particularly unsatisfactory given the acceleration in the pace of credit in the region in recent years.

There has been in fact a growing literature on lending booms in European transition economies. However, most of these papers describe credit developments and their implications on the rest of the economy (Cottarelli et al., 2005; Duenwald et al., 2005; Kraft and Jankov, 2005). While extremely valuable in themselves, none of these papers provide an econometric analysis of the growth of the credit-to-GDP ratio. In particular, Cottarelli et al. (2005) explicitly refrain from exploring this question, focusing instead on deriving a static model of the expected credit-to-GDP ratio on the basis of economic fundamentals. Their conclusion that many countries in the region exhibited credit-to-GDP ratios below the level that would be warranted by their economic fundamentals only serves to underscore the importance of exploring what can be said about the different paths followed by these countries in their approach towards their credit-to-GDP equilibrium levels.

Schadler et al. (2004) provides a useful approach to the question of measuring excessive credit growth, even though the paper deals mainly with the issue of whether rapid credit growth should affect plans for euro adoption in new member states. Acknowledging the challenges posed by the transition, their approach is to draw on the experience of existing members of the euro area to infer likely trends in the new member states since 'historical data from the CECs would not be relevant to predicting future credit developments' (Schadler et al., 2004, p. 4). The paper estimates a vector error correction model (VECM) on quarterly euro area data for 1991–2002. The VECM of the demand for credit includes three variables: (i) the credit-to-GDP ratio; (ii) a proxy for the cost of credit (long-run real interest rate on government bonds); and (iii) per capita income. A co-integrating relationship between these variables is then found, which can be used to draw some inferences about likely future developments in the CEECs. For example, a 10 per cent increase in per capita income raises the credit-to-GDP ratio by around 3 percentage points in the long run.

3. DETECTING EXCESSIVE CREDIT GROWTH

In the absence of a generally-accepted way of determining what rate of credit growth may be deemed to be 'excessive' we propose to focus on both macroeconomic fundamentals as well as on the gap between the actual credit-to-GDP ratio and an equilibrium level. The latter is important for the analysis since the countries in the region have been experiencing major structural changes related to the transition process. Our approach is to model credit growth as a simple function of its main macroeconomic determinants, namely GDP growth and interest rate, as well as the gap between the observed credit-to-GDP ratio and its equilibrium level. This allows us to estimate the elasticity of credit with regard to those variables and to derive estimates of expected credit growth in the countries of the region. The comparison between observed and expected credit growth provides us with a measure of 'excessive' credit growth. We will consider that *credit growth is 'excessive'* when it is higher than the level implied by its three main determinants given the estimated elasticities. Two key steps in this simple approach are the determination of the equilibrium credit-to-GDP ratio and the estimation of the credit elasticities.

3.1 Equilibrium Credit-to-GDP Ratios

For CEECs, the equilibrium credit-to-GDP ratio is difficult to measure because it has to account for the effects of the transition from a centrally-planned to a market-based economy, which are not straightforwardly measurable. Credit not only depends on its traditional macroeconomic determinants, but also on the new circumstances arising from the financial liberalization during the transition process. These new circumstances may affect the banking sector and credit supply in various ways. For example, free entry into the banking sector, the opportunity for foreign banks to own local banks or create local branches, and the gradual expansion of these banks in the retail credit markets have certainly worked to increase credit supply and lower lending rates (De Haas and Naaborg, 2005). On the other hand, however, stricter supervisory requirements might have had opposite effects. The fact that the overall impact of financial liberalization on credit supply is probably gradual and perhaps ambiguous makes it difficult to measure and, *a fortiori*, to model. For simplicity, however, we will assume that the effects over time of financial liberalization on aggregate credit supply can be approximated by a deterministic non-linear time trend (see below).

Our formal definition of the equilibrium level of credit builds on the following credit demand/supply nexus:

$$\begin{cases} C^s = C^s((+)R^\ell - R, (+)Y, (?)Z) \\ C^d = C^d((-)R^\ell, (+)Y) \end{cases} \Rightarrow C^* = C((+)Y, (-)R, (?)Z)$$

where C^s, C^d and C^* denote the aggregate real credit supply, demand and equilibrium levels respectively, Y is real GDP, R is the real interbank rate, R^ℓ is the real retail lending rate, and Z captures the effects of financial liberalization on credit supply. While Y and R are the main standard determinants of aggregate credit, the Z factor is specific to transition economies. As is common practice in the literature, at this stage we will model the equilibrium credit-to-GDP ratio rather than credit itself. For transition economies the evolution of the credit-to-GDP ratio can be seen as depending not only on the real interest rate but also on the transition path to a market-based economy, which we will model as a gradual time trend:

$$\begin{cases} \dfrac{C_{it}}{Y_{it}} = \alpha_i + \beta_i R_{it} + \gamma_i Z_{it} = \left(\dfrac{C}{Y}\right)^*_{it} + \varepsilon_{it} \\ Z_{it} = \gamma_{i1} \cdot t + \gamma_{2i} \cdot t^2 \end{cases} \quad (14.1)$$

where t stands for time (quarters) and i for the country, $(\frac{C}{Y})^*_{it}$ denotes the equilibrium credit-to-GDP ratio, and ε_{it} is the gap between the observed credit-to-GDP ratio and its equilibrium level. This equilibrium ratio represents the credit-to-GDP ratio that we would expect to observe in the absence of short-term shocks, given the interest rate, R_{it}, and the position of the economy on its way to a market-based economy, Z_{it}. To overcome the issue of the non-measurability of financial liberalization, and in line with the observation, we model the Z factor as a deterministic and non-linear time trend, so that the residual ε_{it} obtained in equation (14.1) is a mean stationary.

3.2 Estimates of Credit Elasticities

We estimate elasticities on the basis of the following short-run dynamic equation of credit growth:

$$\Delta \log C_{it} = \beta + \beta_c \Delta \log C_{it-k} + \beta_y \Delta \log Y_{it-l} + \beta_r \Delta R_{it-j}$$

$$+ \lambda \left[\log\left(\frac{C_{it-m}}{Y_{it-m}}\right) - \log\left(\left(\frac{C}{Y}\right)^*_{it-m}\right) \right] + \gamma_i \cdot 1_\Delta + \varepsilon_{it} \quad (14.2)$$

where 1_Δ is a dummy variable equal to one during period Δ and to zero otherwise, the coefficients (β, β_c, β_y, β_r, λ) are credit elasticities and ε_{it} is the residual. The dummy variable 1_Δ allows us to design a test for 'excessive' credit growth since the coefficient on this dummy variable is, by construction, the difference between the observed credit growth and the credit growth implied by the macroenomic variables (GDP and interest rates) and the gap between the observed credit-to-GDP ratio and its equilibrium level.

The limited availability of data poses, however, a challenge to estimate these elasticities for each of the countries in the region. To circumvent this issue, and to gain some comfort that the results are not driven exclusively by the choice of methodology, we will estimate two sets of elasticities:

- First, we will estimate the credit elasticities for a number of benchmark countries where the credit-to-GDP ratio had been relatively stable over a long period of time. These countries are chosen for two main reasons. First, the long time series available for these countries makes it possible to derive robust estimates of the elasticities for each of these countries. Second, precisely because we use countries with stable credit-to-GDP ratios as benchmarks, we are likely to obtain lower elasticities than may be expected for catching-up countries. Since we use these elasticities to derive the expected credit growth in the CEECs, and the measure of 'excessive' credit growth is the difference between the actual and the expected credit growth, we are likely to bias the results towards making it more likely that we will detect 'excessive' credit growth. This gives us an upper bound for our measure of 'excessive' credit growth.
- Second, we will estimate the credit elasticities using data for the countries in the region. Given the limited length of the time series of data available for each country we will estimate relation (14.2) using a data panel but constraining the elasticities to be identical across all CEECs. We thus estimate elasticities for the 'average' country in our panel. In contrast with the benchmark countries, most of the countries in the panel experience rising credit-to-GDP ratios. Therefore, we are likely to obtain higher elasticities than with the benchmark countries and to bias our results towards making it less likely that we will detect 'excessive' credit growth. This gives us a lower bound for our measure of 'excessive' credit growth.

3.3 Test Strategy

Our *test for excessive credit growth* during a period Δ focuses on parameter γ_i, which is the only country-specific parameter in relation (14.2). A strictly positive γ_i means that credit in country i grew faster during period Δ than what its standard determinants would have implied. In this case, we conclude that credit growth was excessive by γ_i per cent on average through the period Δ. Note that an appealing feature of our test strategy is the comparability of the coefficient γ_i across countries, which enables us to *rank countries according to the excessiveness* of their credit growth: the higher γ_i, the higher excessive credit growth during period Δ. To sum up, the steps to perform our test are the following:

- Estimate relation (14.1) and compute the implied equilibrium credit-to-GDP ratio $(\frac{C}{Y})^*_{it}$ for each country;
- For the test using the elasticities of the benchmark countries:
  - Estimate the short-run elasticities (β, β_c, β_y, β_r, λ) for each benchmark country (relation (14.2));
  - Use these estimates and the data from CEECs to compute the implied growth rates of credit for each CEEC;
  - Compute the average difference γ_i between observed and implied growth rates of credit for each CEEC;
  - Discuss whether $\gamma_i > 0$ or not and rank the countries according to their γ_i.
- For the test using the elasticities of the average CEEC:
  - Estimate the short-run elasticities (β, β_c, β_y, β_r, λ) common to all CEECs as well as the country-specific coefficients γ_i (relation (14.2));
  - Test whether $\gamma_i > 0$ or not and rank the countries according to their γ_i.

The above test for 'excessive' credit growth must be interpreted with caution since our working definition of 'excessiveness' is necessarily conditional on the model that we use. In particular, macroeconomic variables other than those considered here (GDP and interest rates) could also influence credit growth. In addition, our test is also conditional on the equilibrium level of the credit-to-GDP ratio, which is estimated to fit the data. While the increase in the latter may reflect the nature of the transition process, it cannot be ruled out that it may lead to unsustainable developments and financial and/or macroeconomic instability.

3.4 Data

The CEECs had levels significantly lower than the EU average throughout the sample period (1996–2004). By 1998 all 8 of the countries considered in the study had *total outstanding loans*-to-yearly GDP ratios below 40 per cent, the lowest being Bulgaria (which was still coping with the aftermath of the banking crisis), Latvia, Lithuania and Romania. All four of these countries had a ratio below 20 per cent. Croatia had the highest stock of loans at around 40 per cent of GDP. By 1996–1997, a vast majority of loans was *denominated in domestic currencies* (DC loans), except in Latvia and

Table 14.1 Share of loans in total lending to the private non-financial sector in 2004 (in per cent)

	Domestic currency	Long-term loans	Credit to households
Bulgaria	53.5	86.5	32.1
Croatia	88.0	–	54.5
Estonia	20.0	91.4	47.0
Hungary	56.0	62.3	44.6
Latvia	40.8	85.3	35.4
Lithuania	36.5	–	–
Romania[1]	39.1	49.9	46.2
Slovenia	69.3	69.1	28.9

Note: [1]As the breakdown short-term/long-term and households/corporates is available only for domestic currency denominated loans, the figures are in percentage of domestic currency denominated loans.

Source: Authors' calculations.

Romania. In Estonia, Hungary, Lithuania, Slovenia and Croatia, the share of DC loans was around 70 to 80 per cent. In 2004 however, the Baltic states and Romania all had a share of DC loans below 50 per cent, while Croatia and Slovenia remained at around 70 to 80 per cent. In 1996 only Estonia and Slovenia had a share of *long-term* loans (that is with more than one year of maturity) higher than 50 per cent, while in 2004 this share was above 50 per cent in practically all the countries. Regarding the share of *loans to households*, only Hungary and Slovenia reported shares above 20 per cent in 1997, while by 2004 this share was around 30 per cent in Slovenia and Bulgaria, slightly higher in Latvia and around 45 to 55 per cent in Croatia, Estonia, Hungary and Romania (see Table 14.1).

As a result of the banking crisis, total loans to GDP ratio dropped from levels reaching 70 per cent to below 10 per cent in *Bulgaria* in 1996–1997. Subsequent years brought a gradual recovery, growth picked up especially after 2000 and total loans reached levels above half of the ones preceding the crisis. Before the crash, a vast majority of loans were denominated in foreign currencies while this ratio is now more balanced. About half of the loans before the crisis were loans to private enterprises, while households had a share of about 20 per cent. Most of the loans to these two sectors were short-term loans. This changed during the recovery, as most loans went to the private sector and now have a longer maturity. *Croatia* was characterized by a fairly steady growth of loans, mainly to households and denominated in domestic currency. Loans to corporations constituted the majority of loans in 1998 and about half of loans in 2004 while loans in foreign currency were far lower than domestic currency loans. Both of the latter categories remained fairly constant in comparison to GDP. In the case of *Hungary*, total loans have doubled in the last 9 years, reaching 45 per cent of GDP. Most of this growth was imputable to long-term loans, foreign currency denominated loans, and loans to households, while domestic currency loans and short-term loans stayed fairly stable and loans to enterprises grew at a relatively slow pace. In *Romania* total loans (as percentage of GDP) fell from 1998 to 2000, and picked up from 2000 onwards to double in the following four years and reach about 20 per cent of GDP. While credit to corporations was not as severely affected by the fall, most of the recovery was due to a rise in credit to households. The currency composition was almost unaffected by these movements. Total loans in *Slovenia* doubled with respect to GDP from about 28 per cent in 1996 to almost 50 per cent in 2004. Foreign currency-denominated loans grew faster than those denominated in domestic currency, growing from 5 per cent of GDP in 1996 to 33.1 per cent in 2004. Overall the fastest expansion of credit relative to GDP took place in the *Baltic states*. Starting from the lowest levels in our sample in 1996, Estonia and Latvia now have the highest credit-to-GDP ratios of our sample. In the case of Lithuania, the credit-to-GDP ratio doubled over the last decade.

3.5 Test Using Benchmarks

We estimated relations (14.1) and (14.2) for 11 benchmark countries whose credit-to-GDP ratio had been stable over a long period of time (on average 19 years) since 1960. These countries are Australia (1960Q2–1984Q3), Belgium (1989Q4–2004Q4), Finland (1960Q2–1980Q4), France (1974Q1–1986Q4), Germany (1968Q1–1983Q4), Greece (1960Q2–1978Q4 and 1981Q2–1995Q4), Ireland (1979Q2–1995Q4), Norway (1960Q2–1983Q4), Spain (1973Q1–1996Q4), Sweden (1970Q1–1988Q1), and United States (1981Q2–1995Q4). For comparison purposes and given the availability of data, we considered total lending to the private sector only.

We also estimated relation (14.1) for the 8 CEECs in order to compute their equilibrium credit-to-GDP ratio. As the interbank interest rate was not available for all these countries, and given that a large fraction of the CEEC banking system is owned by foreign (European) banks, we used the Euribor in the estimations. The estimates of relation (14.1) are reported in Table 14.2.

The quadratic time trend is significant in all countries but Slovenia and the comparison of the equilibrium with the realized credit-to-GDP ratios shows that the quadratic time trends capture a great deal of the evolution

Table 14.2 Estimates of relation (14.1): total lending

	Outstanding loans of MFI sector (excluding NCB) to non-MFIs end of quarter, as a ratio of yearly GDP							
	Bulgaria	Croatia	Estonia	Hungary	Latvia	Lithuania	Romania	Slovenia
time²	0.0006	0.0004	0.0005	0.0002	0.0005	0.0003	0.0002	−0.0000
	(14.58)*	(5.76)*	(11.79)*	(13.22)*	(16.24)*	(5.73)*	(2.45)**	(−0.97)
time	−0.0064	−0.0032	−0.0042	−0.0001	−0.0010	−0.0070	−0.0110	0.0074
	(−5.82)*	(−1.51)	(−3.42)*	(−0.23)	(−1.19)	(−3.95)*	(−4.24)*	(7.28)*
RIR	0.26	0.77	1.02	0.89	−0.21	−0.91	−1.62	−0.26
	(0.82)	(0.72)	(1.77)***	(3.61)*	(−0.9)	(−1.24)	(−1.74)***	(−0.9)
const	0.11	0.37	0.31	0.21	0.14	0.17	0.31	0.40
	(15.06)*	(11.16)*	(16.84)*	(27.45)*	(25.71)*	(7.78)*	(10.59)*	(42.49)*
obs.	24	28	28	28	28	28	28	28

Notes:
Numbers in brackets are t-statistic values.
*, **, *** denote 1%, 5%, 10% significance respectively.

Source: Authors' compilation.

of credit in CEECs over the past seven years. As this trend is assumed to control for the effects of transition-related processes such as banking sector reform, we therefore implicitly assume that the latter explains a large part of the acceleration of credit observed over the past seven years.

The growth rates of credit implied by the standard elasticities and three main determinants are reported in Figure 14.2, and the average differences between these growth rates over the period 2001–2004 for each CEEC are reported in Table 14.3. We find that Slovenia and Romania are the only two countries where aggregate credit grew in line with its main determinants. In contrast, the quarterly growth rate of credit in Bulgaria and Latvia was on average more than 7 percentage points higher than what the evolution of GDP, interest rates, and financial liberalization would have implied. Although to a lower extent, we find that Lithuania, Estonia, Hungary and Croatia have also experienced excessive credit growth since 2001.

3.6 Test Using CEEC Data

We now turn to our second test and use our panel of quarterly observations for the countries in the region starting in 1998. We will consider various credit aggregates; in particular, total lending (outstanding stock of total loans of MFIs to the non-MFIs), loans broken down by currency denomination (domestic and foreign), maturity (short and long term) and by type (to households or corporations). Table 14.4 sums up the results (the detailed results of the estimations are available from the authors on request).

The results of Table 14.4 broadly confirm those of Table 14.3. The growth of total lending in Slovenia and Romania has not been excessive since 2001, while for Bulgaria and Latvia it has exceeded the level implied by fundamentals by more than 5 percentage points. The two tests also give similar results regarding the ranking of the countries, as Bulgaria and the Baltic countries still appear to have the highest excessive growth rate of total lending. Moreover, for these countries, our results suggest that most credit sub-components have grown too fast, which is not the case for the other countries. Notably, excessive credit growth seems to originate from loans denominated in domestic currency (which still represent a low proportion of total credit) in Croatia,[2] and from credit to households in Hungary (where they represent 44.6 per cent of total loans). That total lending has grown in line with its main determinants in Slovenia and Romania should not mask the fact that some sub-components of lending have recently developed fast in these countries. Our results indeed suggest that lending in foreign currency and in domestic currency have on average grown by 4.1 percentage points and 4.2 percentage points too fast per quarter in Slovenia and Romania respectively since 2001. These developments may however be interpreted as a catch-up effect to the extent that these two types of loans were still representing a very low percentage of total lending in Slovenia and Romania in 2004.

4. SELECTED ISSUES: EXCHANGE RATE REGIMES AND COMPOSITION OF CREDIT

A key result from the disaggregated analysis is that credit growth in countries with relatively fixed exchange rate regimes is faster than what may be reasonably explained by the macroeconomic fundamentals considered and the gap to the equilibrium credit-to-GDP ratio. Bulgaria, Estonia and Lithuania all feature currency boards whereby the exchange rate is fixed to the euro.[3] In addition to these countries with hard pegs, both Croatia and Slovenia have followed tightly managed exchange rate regimes, and hence fluctuations of the real exchange rate have been limited, as shown in the top panel of Figure 14.3. In fact, despite pursuing a managed float, the fluctuations of the real exchange rate of both Croatia and Slovenia have been particularly limited. In contrast, countries which have typically exhibited more limited credit expansions have also seen greater flexibility of their real exchange rate, as shown in the bottom panel of Figure 14.3.

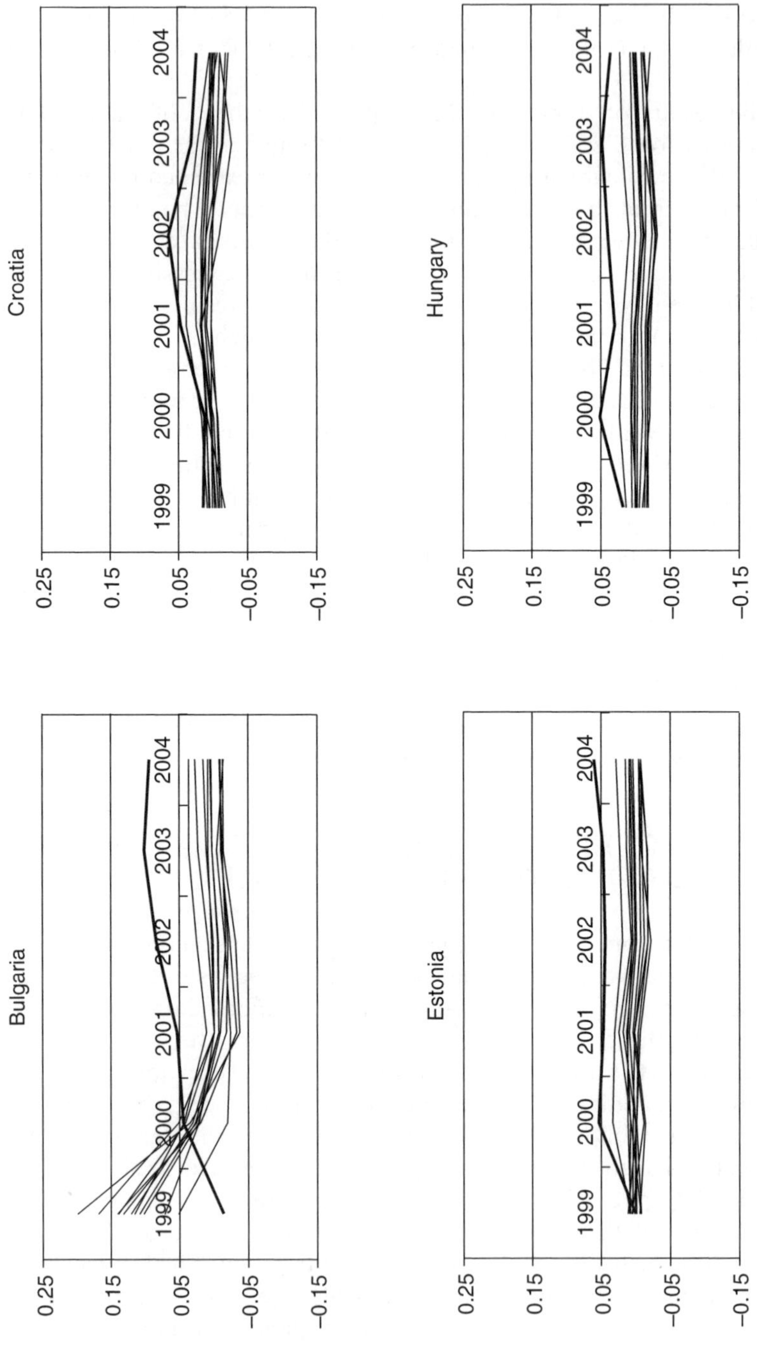
Bulgaria
Croatia
Estonia
Hungary
0.25
0.15
0.05
−0.05
−0.15
1999
2000
2001
2002
2003
2004

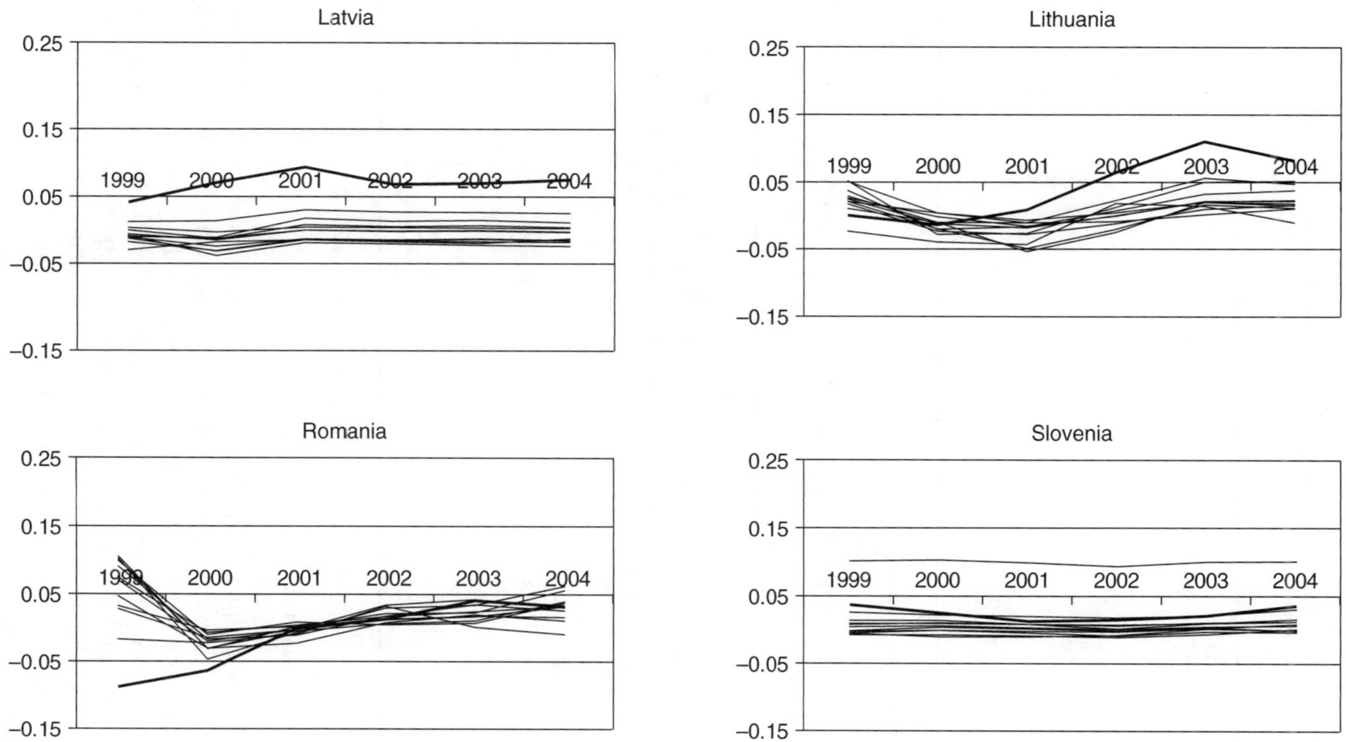

Source: Authors' compilation.

Figure 14.2 Observed (bold lines) versus projected (thin lines) growth rates of total lending

Table 14.3 Average quarterly excessive credit growth over the period 2001–2004 (1) (in per cent)

Countries *i* (ranked)	Coefficients γ_i
Bulgaria	7.8
Latvia	7.4
Lithuania	5.5
Estonia	4.1
Hungary	3.9
Croatia	2.9
Slovenia	0.3
Romania	0.0

Source: Authors' compilation.

Table 14.4 Average quarterly excessive credit growth over the period 2001–2004 (2) (in per cent)

	Coefficients γ_i						
Countries *i* (ranked)	Total loans	Foreign currency	Domestic currency	Short term	Long term	Credit to HHs	Credit to corp.
Bulgaria	5.6*	6.4*	5.6*	3.4**	2.1***	4.8*	5.5*
Latvia	5.4*	5.2*	5.1*	4.8*	0.5	4.5*	5.0*
Lithuania	4.0*	2.0	6.0*	–	–	–	4.9*
Estonia	2.9*	2.5**	3.8*	2.1	–3.1	2.5**	1.6
Croatia	2.2*	0.9	3.3*	–	–	0.9	1.0
Hungary	2.0*	0.1	0.6	0.3	0.4	3.1**	0.0
Slovenia	0.4	4.1*	0.4	1.1	−0.2	−1.8	1.7**
Romania	0.0	2.1	4.2**	1.4	1.2*	5.6***	0.5

Note: *,**,*** denote 1%, 5%, and 10% significance respectively.

Source: Authors' compilation.

This prompts the question of whether the exchange rate regime may have influenced credit developments. One possible mechanism through which the exchange rate regime may lead to higher credit growth is through encouraging lending in foreign currency. As borrowing in foreign currency is usually associated with lower interest rates, perhaps borrowers in those countries are taking increasing amounts of debt denominated in foreign currency in the belief that there is no foreign exchange rate risk associated with such borrowing. Perhaps lenders in those countries are content with

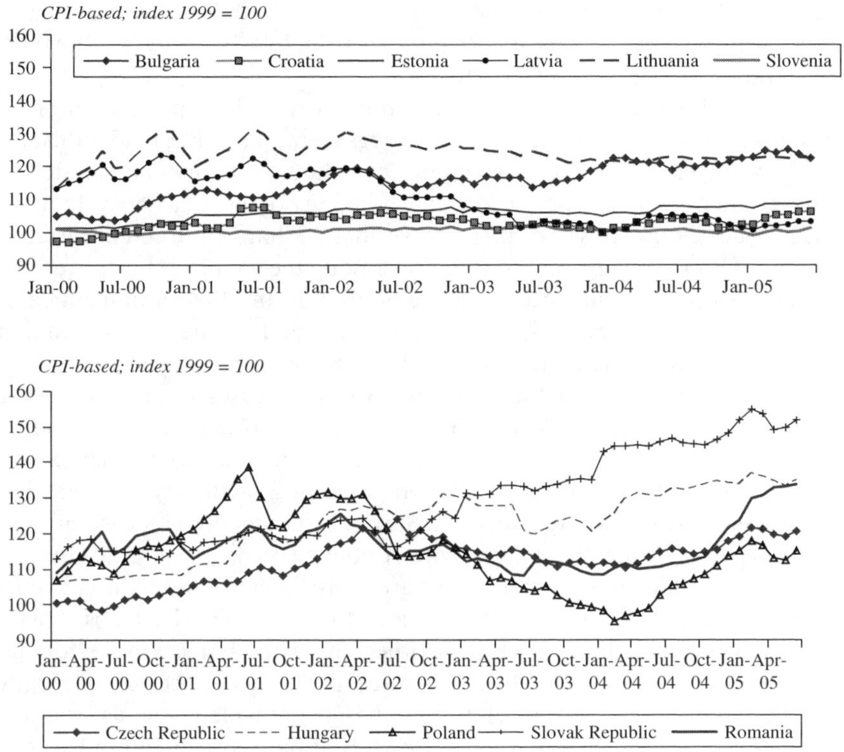

Source: IMF, authors' calculations.

Figure 14.3 Real exchange rate developments (versus euro)

lending in foreign currency to non-foreign currency earners, thus transforming the exchange rate risk into credit risk. This may be the case if lenders also share the view that countries with hard pegs such as the currency boards to the euro (Bulgaria, Estonia and Lithuania) do not in fact pose a significant exchange rate risk. Moreover, the regulations in some of these countries allow in fact that lending in euros may not be considered as foreign currency exposure when calculating the net open foreign position of banks,[4] as in Estonia, where the share of loans in foreign currency is indeed very high (80 per cent of total loans in 2003). Other countries such as Croatia and, to a lesser extent, Latvia, Lithuania, Romania and Bulgaria also have relatively high shares of foreign loans in total loans. Moreover, in some cases there is a very large discrepancy between the share of loans in foreign currency and the corresponding share for deposits, which is possibly explained by the lack of a need to match open positions in foreign currency. According to this view, the presence of foreign banks would also play an important role as they would in principle be more comfortable extending loans in their own currency.

Overall, this scenario of fast credit growth driven by a perception of no exchange rate risk in the context of hard pegs seems plausible. Under this scenario, however, lending in foreign currency should not only accelerate but also should do so at a faster pace than lending in domestic currency. In other terms, one should observe an increase in the share of foreign currency lending. This is only the case in Bulgaria among the countries that have been detected as experiencing 'excessive' credit growth. In other prominent cases such as Estonia, Latvia or Lithuania no clear trend can be observed and in the case of Croatia the share has actually decreased in recent years. This suggests that, while lending in foreign currency in some cases may be proceeding at too fast a pace, this is not a distinctive feature of foreign currency lending only. Moreover, while Bulgaria, Estonia, Lithuania and, to a lesser extent, Croatia have been identified as cases where credit growth may be deemed to be 'excessive' according to our tests, Slovenia stands out as a case of very limited exchange rate fluctuations with contained credit growth thus far.

Beyond the idea that foreign banks are more likely to lend in foreign currency than domestic banks, the presence of foreign banks also helps explain fast credit growth through various other channels. For example, foreign banks may have access to additional sources of finance as they can typically tap the parent bank. Moreover, foreign banks are widely seen as bringing know-how. Empirical studies have shown that bank privatization leads to efficiency gains especially in the case of privatization to foreign strategic investors.[5] A more efficient banking sector will increase financial intermediation. In fact, as shown in the lower panel of Figure 14.4, there is some indication that foreign bank presence in these countries has been associated with higher credit growth.

The upper panel of Figure 14.4 shows how, with the exception of Slovenia, the average share of banking assets owned by foreign banks' subsidiaries or branches has been above 50 per cent for all countries in the region. It is also worth highlighting the relatively limited foreign bank penetration of the Slovenian banking system since, if confirmed that foreign bank entry is associated with a faster financial deepening, it would help explain why, among the CEECs with relatively fixed exchange rate regimes Slovenia stands out as having seen the slowest growth of credit. At the other extreme, Croatia and Estonia stand out as having the highest penetration rate of foreign banks. Regarding Croatia, the other CEEC with a relatively fixed exchange rate that has not seen such a fast credit growth, it is worth noting that the Croatian National Bank (CNB) already took measures in 2003 to curb credit growth. In particular, banks were made to hold CNB

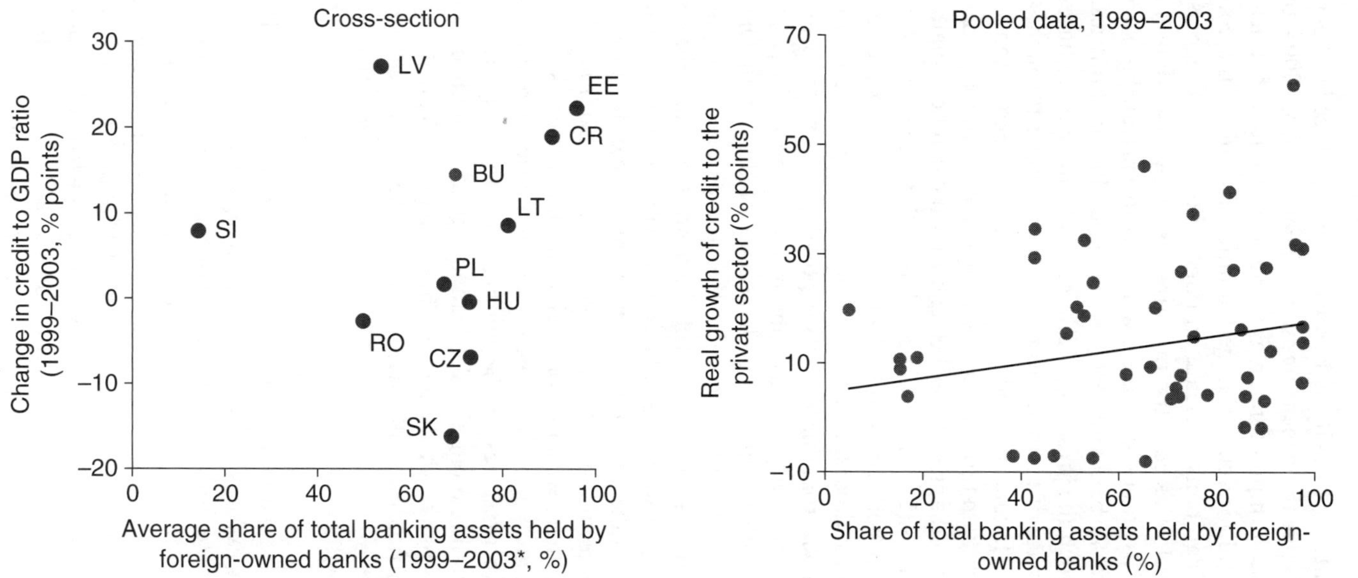

Note: * available years, time-span differs for some countries.

Source: EBRD, authors' calculations.

Figure 14.4 Credit growth and foreign ownership of the banking system paper bearing low interest rates if their growth of assets exceeded 4 per cent in a given quarter. While these measures were repealed as from 2004, banks were then made to hold liquid foreign exchange assets equal to at least 35 per cent of their total foreign exchange liabilities. Estonia is the country with the largest foreign bank presence and one of the largest increases in financial deepening. In this country, privatization and consolidation took place in the mid-1990s and by 1998 there were only five private banks in the country, down from 42 banks in 1992. As in other Baltic countries, one channel through which the presence of foreign banks appears to have contributed to the fast pace of financial deepening in Estonia is through access to foreign sources of finance to fund the domestic credit expansion.

Overall, it is precisely in those countries for which our proposed methodologies suggest that credit growth has been above what can be explained by economic fundamentals (Estonia, Bulgaria, Latvia, Lithuania and Croatia), that we see either sharp increases in (and/or high levels of) the ratio of foreign liabilities to total banking assets. In this regard, Slovenia, Slovakia and Romania stand out from this analysis as possible cases where, while our methodologies have not yet detected abnormal developments, external funding may be currently fuelling an acceleration of credit growth. One possible explanation for these phenomena is that the perception of limited foreign exchange rate risk not only affects borrowers but also the foreign bank subsidiaries, which would be induced to expand their loan portfolios in local currencies to take advantage of an interest rate differential that is perceived to come with no or little exchange rate risk. In addition, foreign bank entry and a limited perception of foreign exchange rate risk could lead to 'excessive' credit growth of *both* foreign and domestic currency lending through competitive pressures in the marketplace. Increased lending in foreign currencies could potentially also lead to a greater supply of domestic currency loans by banks which, perhaps more reliant on deposits or other domestic sources of funding, still strive to keep market share.

4.1 Credit Composition

A second key result from our disaggregated tests on credit growth is that, for countries exhibiting 'excessive' credit growth at the aggregate level, the result also typically applies to both credit to households and credit to corporates. This is the case for both Bulgaria and Latvia, while data were not available for Lithuania. In Estonia, however, credit growth was only deemed to be 'excessive' in the case of lending to households. That credit growth to corporates appears to be 'excessive' is somewhat surprising to analysts of developments in the region, which often refer to the appearance of new products such as mortgages and the launch of consumer credit as key factors in explaining credit growth. In fact, credit growth in certain retail segments has grown spectacularly high. Moreover, this rapid credit growth has been accompanied hand in hand by rising house prices (Papademos, 2005).

As shown in the upper panel of Figure 14.5 for the case of Bulgaria, there has been a recent acceleration in the mortgages segment, which may have repercussions for real estate prices in the near future. The lower panel of Figure 14.5 illustrates the close connection between house prices and the development of mortgage lending for Estonia.

In the case of Estonia, where as we have seen credit growth appears to be 'excessive' in the case of lending to households but not to corporates, a number of policy measures help to explain the prominent growth of home mortgage loans. In particular, through a state-owned credit guarantee foundation, KredEx, Estonian families and young adults can get a guarantee of up to 24 per cent of the value of the collateral provided they have their own funds equivalent to 10 per cent of the value of the property being purchased. Set up in 2000, the activity of KredEx as a provider of mortgage loan guarantees has increased significantly in recent years, also through the introduction in 2003 of a new KredEx service aimed at providing grants for revamping Soviet housing. In addition, tax deductibility of mortgage payments may have helped to increase demand for mortgage loans and housing, which has seen an increase in prices since mid-2003 far above the growth of wages.

However, while the mortgage and consumer credit markets have been undoubtedly developing fast in the region, interpreting the rates of growth of credit in these market segments needs to take account of the low starting levels.[6] As shown in Figure 14.6, the case of Croatia provides a clear example of the trend of shifting from loans to enterprises to loans to households. Data for Latvia also show how, while gaining ground at the expense of industrial credit, consumer credit is still limited.

5. CONCLUSIONS

The experience of many emerging market countries suggests that episodes of fast credit growth often, though by no means always, end in financial and currency crises. Given the high output costs of such crises, policy-makers in Central and South-Eastern European countries have been paying increasing attention to developments of credit to the private sector in the region. Increased attention has also been followed by a number of policy measures aimed at slowing down the pace of credit growth. Curbing credit growth is not, however, without welfare costs as financial deepening is in principle associated with increased economic growth and efficiency. In this context, empirical work on the nature of the observed credit growth in the

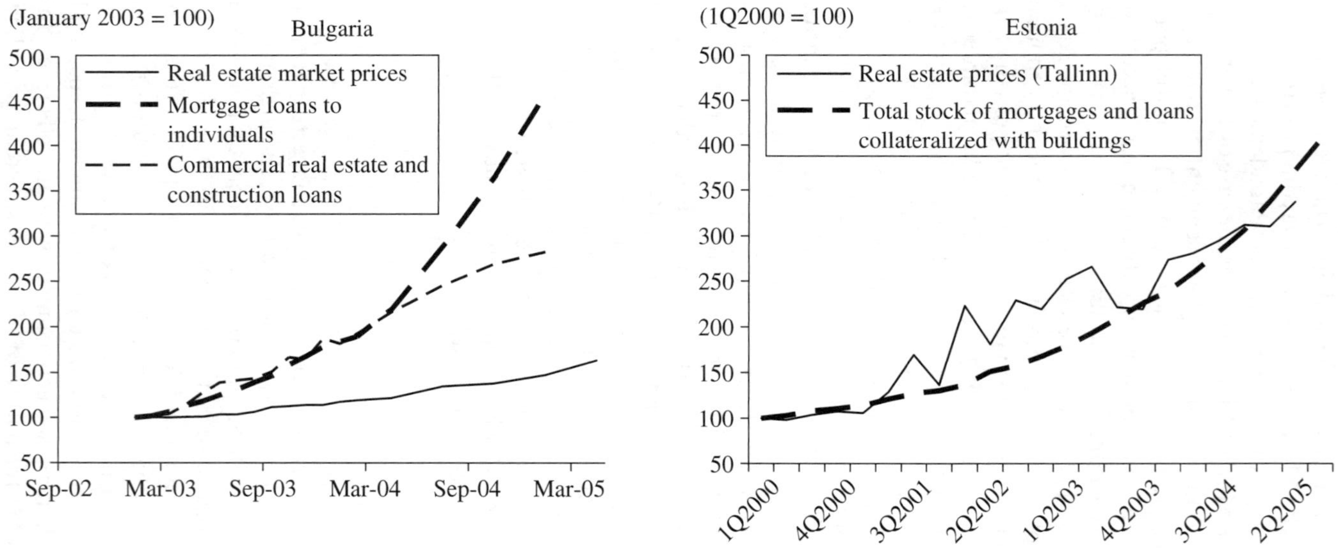

Sources: IMF, BNB and NRPA.

Sources: Bank of Estonia and Estonia's statistical office.

Figure 14.5 Mortgage loans and real estate prices in Bulgaria and Estonia

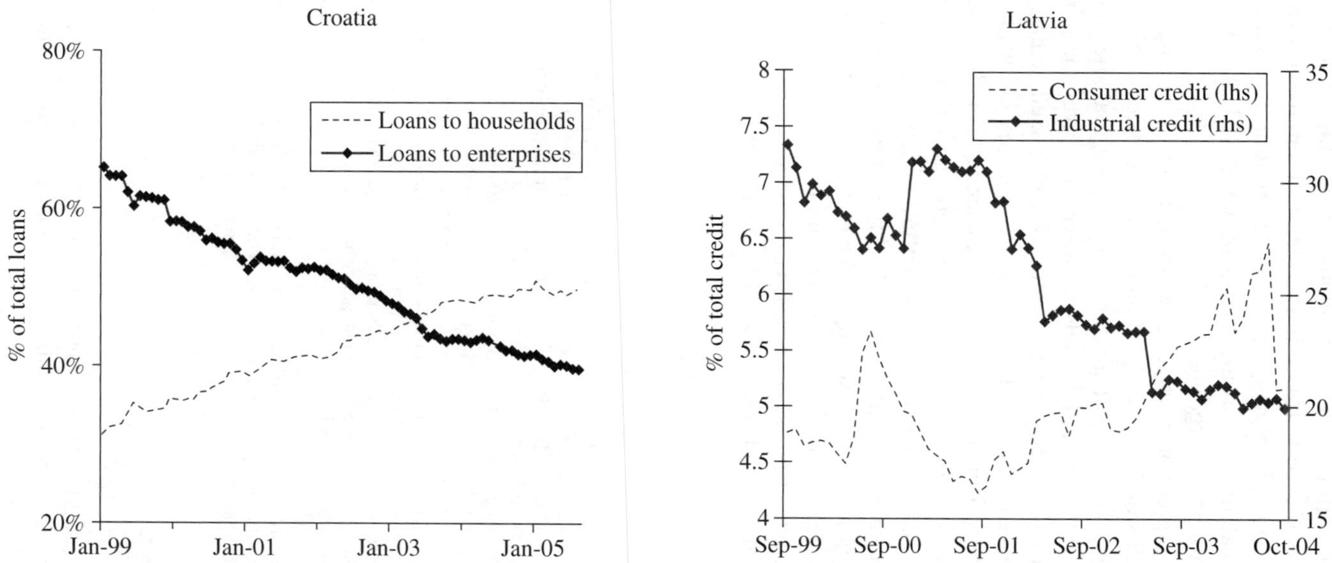

Sources: Hrvatska Narodna Banka, Latvijas Banka.

Figure 14.6 Evolution of credit composition

region can be a useful input for the policy-maker. This chapter provides one such empirical study of credit growth in the region. Its main contribution is to suggest a methodology for assessing credit growth in the region while accounting for the catching up in incomes associated with the transition process that the region is undergoing.

A key result from this chapter is that, even accounting for a rising trend in the equilibrium credit-to-GDP ratio, a number of countries in the region have experienced 'excessive' credit growth in the sense that the observed credit growth is higher than what we would have expected given the evolution of macroeconomic variables. In particular, countries with fixed exchange rate regimes appear to have experienced credit growth well beyond what would have been expected according to our model. However, tests on disaggregated credit data by currency suggest that 'excessive' credit growth is not limited to lending in foreign currency but is also a feature of lending in domestic currency. This somewhat puzzling result calls for further research on the mechanisms through which the exchange rate regime may impact credit developments in the region. While the results from this exercise necessarily depend on our narrow definition of 'excessive' credit growth, they bring a new perspective to understand credit developments in the region.

NOTES

1. For an overview of developments in credit to the private sector among the new member states from Central and Eastern Europe see Backé and Zumer (2005).
2. Data on which the estimations for the foreign/domestic currency are based are not corrected for indexed loans and therefore results are less informative.
3. The Lithuanian litas was pegged to the US dollar prior to 2002.
4. For example, in the case of Bulgaria the limits on open foreign exchange positions are such that each bank must maintain daily (i) a maximum ratio of up to 15 per cent between its open position in any particular currency and the amount of its own funds, excluding the euro and (ii) a maximum ratio of up to 30 per cent between its net open foreign currency position and the amount of its own funds, excluding the euro (IMF 2004b, p. 164).
5. See, for example, Clarke et al. (2005) overview paper in the special issue on bank privatization in developing countries (including emerging Europe) in the *Journal of Banking & Finance*.
6. The difficulty in interpreting growth rates given low starting levels of credit to the private sector in general, has recently prompted some researchers to shift their focus of analysis to credit flows, rather than stocks. See, for example, Arpa et al. (2005).

REFERENCES

Arpa, M., T. Reininger and Z. Walko (2005), 'Can banking intermediation in the Central and Eastern European Countries ever catch up with the euro area?', Mimeo, Oesterreichische Nationalbank.

Backé, P. and T. Zumer (2005), 'Developments in credit to the private sector in Central and Eastern European EU member states: Emerging from financial repression – A comparative overview', *Focus on European Economic Integration*, **2** (05), Oesterreichische Nationalbank, October.

Berglöf, E. and P. Bolton (2002), 'The great divide and beyond: Financial architecture in transition', *Journal of Economic Perspectives*, **16** (1), Winter, 77–100.

Bokros, L. (2002), 'Financial sector development in Central and Eastern Europe', in A. Winkler (ed.), *Banking and Monetary Policy in Eastern Europe. The First Ten Years*, Houndmills and New York: Palgrave Publishing, pp. 11–42.

Borio, C. and P. Lowe (2002), 'Asset prices, financial and monetary stability: exploring the nexus', *BIS Working Paper* No. 114, Bank for International Settlements, July.

Clarke, G.R., R.C. Cull and M. Shirley (2005), 'Bank privatization in developing countries: A summary of lessons and findings', *Journal of Banking & Finance*, **29**, 1905–30.

Cottarelli, C., G. Dell'Ariccia and I. Vladkova-Hollar (2005), 'Early birds, late risers, and sleeping beauties: Bank credit growth to the private sector in Central and Eastern Europe and in the Balkans', *Journal of Banking & Finance*, **29** (1), 83–104.

De Haas, R. and I. van Lelyveld (2006), 'Foreign banks and credit stability in Central and Eastern Europe. A panel data analysis', *Journal of Banking & Finance*, **30** (7), 1927–52.

De Haas, R. and I. Naaborg (2005), 'Foreign banks in transition economies: Small business lending and internal capital markets', *International Finance working paper* 0504004, Economics Working Paper Archive at WUSTL.

Duenwald, C., N. Gueorguiev and A. Schaechter (2005), 'Too much of a good thing? Credit booms in transition economies: The cases of Bulgaria, Romania and Ukraine', *IMF working paper* no. 05/128.

EBRD (2004), Transition Report, London.

Gourinchas, P., O. Landerretche and R. Valdes (2001), 'Lending booms, Latin America and the world', *NBER Working Paper* 8249.

Hilbers, P., I. Ötker, G. Johnsen and C. Pazarbasioglu (2005), 'Assessing and managing rapid credit growth and the role of supervisory and prudential policies', *IMF Working Paper* no. 05/ 151.

IMF (2004a), 'World Economic Outlook', April.

IMF (2004b), 'Annual Report on Exchange Arrangements and Exchange Restrictions', August.

IMF (2005), 'Global Financial Stability Report', September.

Kraft, E. and L. Jankov (2005), 'Does speed kill? Lending booms and their consequences in Croatia', *Journal of Banking & Finance*, **29**, 105–21.

Lepik, I. and J. Tõrs (2002), 'Structure and performance of Estonia's financial sector', in C. Thimann (ed.), *Financial Sectors in EU Accession Countries*, European Central Bank, Frankfurt.

Mehl, Arnaud, Cristina Vespro and Adalbert Winkler (2005), 'The Finance–Growth Nexus and Financial Sector Environment: New Evidence from South-Eastern Europe', paper for the Conference on Financial Development, Integration and Stability in Central, Eastern and South-Eastern Europe, Oesterreichische Nationalbank, 14–15, November 2005.

Ottens, D., E. Lambregts and S. Poelhekke (2005), 'Credit booms in emerging market economies: A recipe for banking crises?', *DNB Working Paper* No. 46, De Nederlandsche Bank, June.

Papademos, L. (2005), 'Financial structures, credit growth and house prices in the new EU member states: Policy challenges on the road to the euro', Speech at the Conference held by Latvijas Banka, Riga, 19 September 2005; www.ecb.int.
Schadler, S., Z. Murgasova and R. van Elkan (2004), 'Credit booms, demand booms, and euro adoption', paper for the Conference on Challenges for Central Banks in an Enlarged EMU, Oesterreichische Nationalbank, 20–21 February 2004.
Tornell, A. and F. Westermann (2002), 'Boom-bust cycles: Facts and explanation', *IMF Staff Papers*, **49** (Special Issue), 111–55.
Yotzov, V. (2002), 'The financial sector in Bulgaria: structure, functioning and trends', in C. Thimann (ed.), *Financial Sectors in EU Accession Countries*, European Central Bank, Frankfurt.

15. Too much of a good thing? Credit booms in transition economies: the cases of Bulgaria, Romania and Ukraine

Christoph Duenwald, Nikolay Gueorguiev and Andrea Schaechter[1]

1. INTRODUCTION AND CONCLUSIONS

Rapid private sector credit growth has been among the most notable economic phenomena across many transition economies – particularly in the Central and Eastern European countries (CEECs) – over the past few years.[2] Such lending booms have presented both opportunities and challenges to economic policy-makers. On the one hand, the surge in financial intermediation reflects a welcome catch-up from low levels, and financial deepening is generally associated with increased growth and efficiency. On the other hand, rapid credit growth has been associated with macroeconomic and financial crises, emanating from macroeconomic imbalances and banking sector distress. Policy-makers therefore face the dilemma of how to minimize the risks of financial crisis while still allowing bank lending to contribute to higher growth and efficiency.

The recent experiences of three transition economies – Bulgaria, Romania and Ukraine – provide useful case studies of credit booms in different macroeconomic and institutional settings. Recent papers on credit booms have focused on large cross-country data sets. In contrast, this chapter seeks to zero in on the experiences of a small set of countries with similar developmental characteristics. Rapid increases in bank credit to the private sector in Bulgaria, Romania and Ukraine reflect a mix of demand- and supply-side factors. On the demand side, macroeconomic stabilization and robust growth have lifted households' confidence that rises in income will be permanent and have boosted businesses' willingness to invest. As for credit supply, bank privatization and increased competition in particular in banking systems dominated by foreign-owned banks, improved creditor rights, and large capital inflows have increased banks' propensity to lend.

The credit expansion in all three countries has been excessive. In Bulgaria and Romania, credit booms have since 2002 contributed importantly to widening macroeconomic imbalances, in particular large trade and current account deficits, and heightened external vulnerability. With limited monetary tools at their disposal, policy-makers in these countries have tightened fiscal policy to offset the sharp increase in private sector consumption and investment. Nevertheless, the larger external current account deficits – albeit financed to a large extent by foreign direct investment (FDI) inflows – have generated concerns about external vulnerability, and the need to persevere with tight fiscal policies remains. In contrast, the credit boom in Ukraine was accompanied by strong output growth and large external current account surpluses, although inflation has picked up. Risks in terms of loan quality and the impact on banking sector stability are thus the predominant concerns rather than macroeconomic imbalances.

Policy responses in the three countries have been tailored to address the identified risks, but further action is probably necessary. In Bulgaria and Romania, such action will probably continue to emphasize tighter macroeconomic policies, although supervisors will need to remain vigilant to ensure continued financial sector health, particularly as credit may be diverted to less supervised channels. In Ukraine, stronger prudential and supervisory policies will remain at the heart of efforts to reduce financial vulnerabilities. In all three countries, these efforts to maintain macroeconomic and financial sector stability will be part of a broader framework of prudent fiscal and incomes policies and structural reform.

The plan of the chapter is as follows. The next section discusses the causes and characteristics of the credit booms, emphasizing the similarities and differences between the three countries. Section 3 outlines both the opportunities and the risks arising from the rapid credit expansions, followed in section 4 by a discussion of the possible and actual policy responses.

2. CAUSES AND CHARACTERISTICS OF THE CREDIT BOOMS

2.1 Background

Credit has expanded rapidly in all three countries in an environment of strong GDP growth and generally falling inflation (Table 15.1). Driven by strong external and domestic demand, growth has averaged between 5 and

Table 15.1 Basic economic indicators, 2000–2004 (Annual per cent change, unless otherwise indicated)

	2000	2001	2002	2003	2004	Average
Bulgaria						
GDP growth	5.4	4.1	4.9	4.5	5.6	4.9
Inflation (end of period)	11.4	4.8	3.8	5.6	4.0	5.9
Current account balance (% of GDP)	−5.6	−7.3	−5.6	−9.2	−7.5	−7.0
Budget balance (% of GDP)	−1.0	−0.9	−0.6	−0.4	1.8	−0.2
Romania						
GDP growth	2.1	5.7	5.1	5.2	8.3	5.3
Inflation (end of period)	40.7	30.3	17.8	14.1	9.3	22.5
Current account balance (% of GDP)	−4.6	−6.5	−4.4	−6.0	−7.5	−5.8
Budget balance (% of GDP)	−4.0	−3.2	−2.6	−2.3	−1.1	−2.6
Ukraine						
GDP growth	5.9	9.2	5.2	9.6	12.1	8.4
Inflation (end of period)	25.8	6.1	−0.6	8.2	12.3	10.6
Current account balance (% of GDP)	4.7	3.7	7.5	5.8	10.5	6.4
Budget balance (% of GDP)	−1.3	−1.6	0.5	−0.9	−4.5	−1.6

Sources: National authorities, IMF staff estimates.

8 per cent from 2000 to 2004. A generally countercyclical fiscal stance, as evidenced by the improving fiscal balances, and prudent monetary frameworks have led to single-digit or near-single-digit inflation. However, the external current account deficits have expanded considerably in Bulgaria and Romania, driven by strong domestic demand. In contrast, Ukraine has maintained large current account surpluses, largely driven by favourable terms of trade shocks and an undervalued exchange rate.

The three countries are at different stages of the transition process. Bulgaria and Romania are on the verge of European Union (EU) membership and have largely caught up with the central European transition economies in terms of structural reform indicators, although progress in corporate governance still lags behind. Structural reforms in Ukraine, on the other hand, have been much slower, and particularly accounting and reporting standards for corporates as well as corporate governance need to be strengthened for FDI to pick up.

Developments in credit dynamics in all three countries have followed a bust–boom pattern. After a sharp drop in financial intermediation during a deep macroeconomic/banking crisis, credit growth was initially subdued, reflecting low credit demand and banks' risk aversion. The subsequent stabilization and return of sound growth, together with banks' restructuring and balance sheet rehabilitation, has rekindled credit demand and encouraged banks to reassess positively their borrowers' creditworthiness, find new lending opportunities, and eventually even to engage in a race for market share, pushing up credit sharply.

As elsewhere in the region, credit has grown rapidly in the three countries in the acceleration phase, albeit from a small base. While credit-to-GDP ratios were in the teens when credit began to accelerate, real growth rates have been in the 30–50 per cent range (Table 15.2). Annual flows, perhaps a better measure of the macroeconomic impact of credit, have ranged from 3 to 12 per cent of GDP. Such credit dynamics are part of a region-wide trend. As Figure 15.1 illustrates, credit has been growing quickly in most CEECs in the past three years as well.

The banking sector is still relatively small in all three countries despite the large number of banks and rapid asset growth over the past four years (Table 15.3). Relative to GDP, Bulgaria's banking system – consisting of 29 banks and 6 branches of foreign banks – is the largest, with total assets of 46 per cent of GDP. The assets of Ukraine's 158 banks amount to 37 per cent of GDP. However, many of the banks are small, and most are affiliated with corporates. Romania has 32 banks and 7 branches, with assets of 35 per cent of GDP.

Most banks are private now in these countries, and foreign ownership dominates in Bulgaria and Romania. State ownership is limited to two or three banks in each country, including the state savings banks in Romania and Ukraine, which have state guarantees for their deposits. In both countries, these institutions are being restructured, and Romania is aiming to privatize its bank by mid-2006. Through the privatization process, large European banks acquired most of the banking system assets in Bulgaria and Romania. However, the share of foreign-owned banks is much smaller in Ukraine, reflecting the difficult business environment, but interest in foreign banks has picked up strongly from late 2005.

The institutional framework of the financial sector is generally adequate in Bulgaria and Romania, but still exhibits weaknesses in Ukraine despite recent progress. The joint IMF–World Bank Financial Sector Assessment Programs (FSAPs) conducted in the three countries in 2002–03 gave generally good marks to the authorities' regulatory framework and supervisory activity in Bulgaria and Romania but pointed out various shortcomings in Ukraine. Recommendations for Bulgaria and Romania included strengthening supervision on a consolidated basis and training bank supervisors in international accounting standards. For Ukraine, the

Table 15.2 Basic credit indicators, 2000–2004

	2000	2001	2002	2003	2004
Bulgaria					
Real credit growth (in %, year-on-year, deflated by CPI)	4.5	26.3	37.2	39.5	40.4
In local currency	11.9	26.6	23.7	37.7	27.9
In foreign currency	−6.6	25.9	61.8	42.1	57.3
Credit flows in % of GDP	1.7	3.6	5.7	8.4	11.5
By currency: local	1.6	2.3	2.5	4.7	4.8
By currency: foreign currencies	0.2	1.2	3.2	3.7	6.7
By borrower: households	0.4	1.1	1.4	3.2	4.9
By borrower: companies	1.4	2.5	4.3	5.2	6.6
Credit stock in % of GDP (year-end)	12.2	14.5	19.0	26.3	35.4
By currency: local	7.9	9.4	11.1	15.1	18.5
By currency: foreign currencies	4.3	5.2	8.0	11.2	16.9
By borrower: households	2.3	3.1	4.3	7.2	11.5
By borrower: private companies	9.3	10.8	14.1	18.4	23.2
Share of foreign currency deposits as % of total	54.0	52.8	49.6	48.0	43.1
Share of foreign currency loans as % of total	35.5	35.4	41.8	42.5	47.6
Romania					
Real credit growth (in %, year-on-year, deflated by CPI), composite	7.9	28.0	32.4	56.8	40.5
In local currency	−5.4	20.0	19.1	77.4	11.2
In foreign currency (in EUR)	15.8	33.2	40.4	38.1	60.5
Credit flows in % of GDP	0.6	2.9	3.3	6.2	5.6
By currency: local	0.8	1.5	1.3	3.6	1.0
By currency: foreign currencies	−0.2	1.5	2.1	2.6	4.2
By borrower: households	0.1	0.3	0.8	2.9	1.9
By borrower: companies	0.4	2.6	2.5	3.4	3.3
Credit stock in % of GDP (year-end)	9.3	10.1	11.8	15.9	17.5
By currency: local	3.8	4.1	4.4	7.1	6.9
By currency: foreign currencies	5.5	6.1	7.4	8.8	10.6
By borrower: households	0.5	0.7	1.4	3.9	5.0
By borrower: private companies	7.5	8.0	8.9	10.5	11.2
Share of foreign currency deposits as % of total	47.0	49.3	44.7	42.5	41.2
Share of foreign currency loans as % of total	59.5	59.8	62.7	55.4	60.8
Ukraine[1]					
Real credit growth (in %, year-on-year, deflated by CPI)	28.6	32.7	48.4	51.2	16.9

Table 15.2 (continued)

	2000	2001	2002	2003	2004
In local currency	37.4	32.7	52.9	53.4	15.7
In foreign currency (in USD)	17.9	32.8	41.9	47.8	18.7
Credit flows in % of GDP	4.7	4.2	6.2	10.5	6.4
By currency: local	3.1	2.5	4.0	6.6	3.8
By currency: foreign currencies	1.5	1.8	2.2	3.9	2.7
By borrower: households	0.2	0.2	0.8	2.1	1.7
By borrower: companies	4.5	4.0	5.4	8.4	4.8
Credit stock in % of GDP (year-end)	12.3	14.4	19.3	27.0	27.0
By currency: local	7.3	8.5	11.7	16.6	16.5
By currency: foreign currencies	5.1	5.9	7.6	10.4	10.5
By borrower: households	0.6	0.7	1.5	3.3	4.2
By borrower: private companies	10.6	12.3	16.2	21.5	21.0
Share of foreign currency deposits as % of total	41.4	41.3	39.5	38.5	39.1
Share of foreign currency loans as % of total	38.5	32.9	32.6	32.2	36.5

Note: 1. Ukraine: During the tumultuous presidential elections in late 2004, the banking sector lost substantial amounts of deposits and had to temporarily reduce lending.

Sources: Bulgarian National Bank, National Bank of Romania, National Bank of Ukraine and IMF staff estimates.

advice focused on the need to achieve international standards, in particular in terms of related-party lending, identification of bank owners, banks' risk management practices as well as the need to raise capital requirements and tighten the definition of capital. While progress on the last two suggestions was made, including by raising the minimum capital adequacy ratio from 8 per cent to 10 per cent, the first three issues have not yet been appropriately tackled. These remaining institutional weaknesses, as well as the prominence of domestic bank ownership, make Ukraine's banking sector weaker than Bulgaria's and Romania's.

Episodes of economic instability in the past have caused dollarization, which has proved difficult to reverse. Even though confidence in local currencies has been partly restored following successful inflation stabilization, and real local currency deposit interest rates have been high in Romania and Ukraine, the share of foreign currency-denominated deposits remains large in all three countries. At the same time, borrowers, mindful of the lower effective cost of foreign currency-denominated loans, have maintained about 40–60 per cent of their loans in foreign currency, thereby exposing the banking sector to indirect foreign exchange risk (Table 15.2).

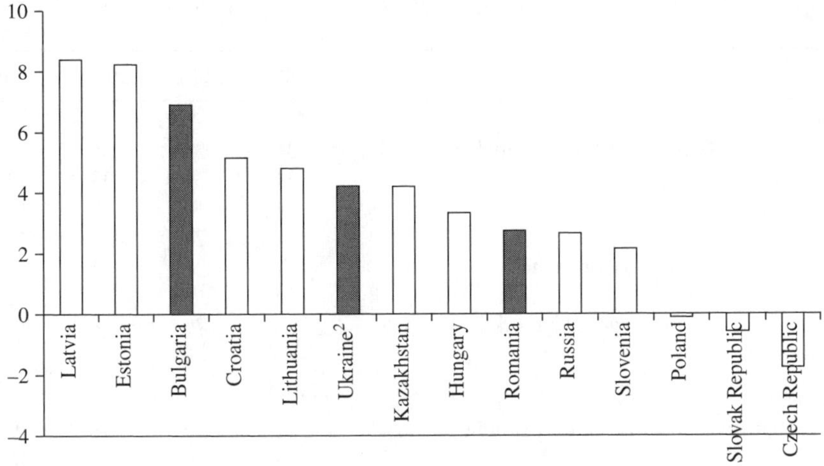

Notes:
1. Bank credit to the private sector.
2. During the tumultuous presidential elections in Ukraine in late 2004, the banking sector lost substantial amounts of deposits and had to temporarily reduce lending.

Sources: IMF, *International Financial Statistics*, *World Economic Outlook*; and IMF staff estimates.

Figure 15.1 Credit growth in transition economies, 2001–2004[1] *(average annual change in the credit-to-GDP ratio)*

By aiming, explicitly or implicitly, at some measure of exchange rate stability throughout most of the period analysed (Box 15.1), monetary policy frameworks have inadvertently encouraged demand for foreign currency-denominated loans.

2.2 Causes of Credit Booms

The common factors behind the sharp credit acceleration in all three countries are successful post-crisis macroeconomic stabilization and robust growth, restoration of confidence in the banking sector, institutional changes, and sizeable foreign exchange inflows. All three countries went through deep macroeconomic and financial crises in the second half of the 1990s, which all but halted financial intermediation for a while. Prudent macroeconomic policies, leading to fast disinflation, quickly rebounding GDP, and rapidly rising profits and incomes, whetted appetite for borrowing and improved banks' perception of the borrowers' creditworthiness. The entry of reputable international banks and strengthening of the

Table 15.3 Ownership structure of the banking sector, 2000–2004

	2000	2001	2002	2003	2004
Bulgaria					
Number of banks and bank branches	35	35	34	35	35
Private	31	31	31	33	33
Domestic	8	6	7	8	9
Foreign[1]	23	25	24	25	24
o/w: foreign bank branches	8	7	6	6	6
State-owned[2]	4	4	3	2	2
Share of assets of largest 10 banks in total assets	83	78	79	78	78
Romania					
Number of banks and bank branches	41	41	39	38	39
Private	37	38	36	35	36
Domestic	8	6	4	7	6
Foreign[1]	29	32	32	29	30
o/w: foreign bank branches	8	8	8	8	7
State-owned[2]	4	3	3	3	3
Share of assets of largest 10 banks in total assets	–	–	–	80	80
Ukraine					
Number of banks and bank branches	153	152	157	158	160
Private	151	150	155	156	158
Domestic	120	122	135	137	139
Foreign[1]	31	28	20	19	19
o/w: foreign bank branches	0	0	0	0	0
State-owned[2]	2	2	2	2	2
Share of assets of largest 10 banks in total assets	55	53	54	54	53

Notes:
1. Banks where foreign parties hold more than 50% of the total outstanding share value.
2. Banks where state institutions yield effective control.

Sources: Bulgarian National Bank, National Bank of Romania, National Bank of Ukraine and IMF staff estimates.

institutional frameworks – including through strengthened banking regulation and supervision, higher minimum capital adequacy requirements, stronger creditors' rights, and the introduction of international accounting standards – restored the population's confidence in the banking sector, leading to a quick rise in deposits and pressure to find profitable asset placements. At the same time, sharply declining budget deficits and ample

BOX 15.1 EXCHANGE RATE REGIMES

The Bulgarian National Bank (BNB) operates a currency board arrangement, which has three key features: (i) a fixed exchange rate peg to the euro; (ii) automatic convertibility, a commitment on the part of the BNB to buy and sell foreign currency at the fixed rate; and (iii) a prohibition on domestic credit creation by the BNB. The latter implies that the BNB cannot affect the money supply through open market operations or the extension of domestic credit.

The National Bank of Romania (NBR) is in transition from exchange-rate targeting to inflation targeting. Until November 2004, the NBR relied on the exchange rate as an implicit nominal anchor for monetary policy, guiding it broadly in line with the annual disinflation target and moderate real effective appreciation. The existing restrictions on capital flows afforded the NBR a degree of autonomy in setting its policy interest rate, which it used mainly to support the targeted exchange rate dynamics and reserves accumulation. In view of its transition to inflation targeting in 2005, the NBR recently stopped announcing real appreciation targets, limited its interventions in the foreign currency market, and allowed some nominal effective appreciation.

The National Bank of Ukraine (NBU) has operated a de facto peg of the hryvnia to the US dollar but is contemplating a move to more exchange rate flexibility and inflation targeting. While the exchange rate against the US dollar was de facto fixed from 2000, the NBU allowed the hryvnia to appreciate by about 5 per cent in April 2005. Since then it has targeted it within a narrow band of 1 per cent but reduced its presence on the foreign exchange market. Moving to a new regime that would allow more exchange rate flexibility and ultimately to a framework of inflation targeting is being contemplated.

external budgetary financing limited government paper issuance. Finally, a fall in the country risk premia and improved business conditions gave and still give rise to large capital inflows, coming mainly through the mostly foreign-owned banking sector, and adding to supply-side pressures to lend.

The ongoing credit boom reflects a mix of supply- and demand-side factors. In broad terms, the credit boom reflects a catching up from depressed levels of post-crisis bank lending and is thus part of a process of financial deepening. The following factors are especially important:

- The newly privatized banks have been keen to boost profitability and market share. With high capital adequacy ratios, banks managed to increase profitability by shifting the composition of their assets toward loans. In Bulgaria and Romania, this more aggressive stance has been actively encouraged by the banks' foreign parents. Many of the banks' foreign owners are domiciled in less profitable mature markets, so parents have encouraged their subsidiaries and branches to pursue aggressive loan portfolio expansion to gain market share and improve consolidated results, thereby contributing to the acceleration of credit. In Ukraine, where foreign banks are less prominent, the lack of other investment opportunities has forced banks to expand their loan portfolios in pursuit of higher profits.
- Banks' ability to fund loan expansion has been boosted by strong capital inflows, mostly through the banking system, amid high global liquidity, low interest rates, and increased confidence associated with Bulgaria's and Romania's prospective EU accession and Ukraine's large current account surpluses.
- The greater supply of credit has been matched by increased demand from both businesses and households. For the former, a newfound confidence in the future – prompted by rising profits and, for Bulgaria and Romania, strong EU accession prospects – has boosted investment intentions and demand for credit. For the latter, consumer and mortgage credit has taken off partly because household demand for durables and real estate has increased from previously depressed levels as households have felt more confident in their ability to service debt, and partly because the banks have offered new products with more flexible terms.
- Finally, an additional factor explaining the credit boom may be crowding in: bank credit to the public sector has declined substantially, reflecting small general government fiscal deficits or even surpluses and the availability of ample external financing and privatization revenue.

2.3 Characteristics of Credit Booms

A fast expansion of credit to households and lengthening of maturities are common in all three countries (Table 15.2). Households have converted their confidence in a permanently rising disposable income into a sharp rise in consumer and mortgage loans. In Bulgaria and Romania, the share of household loans has surged to one-third of total loans while it is still much lower in Ukraine (16 per cent) despite a rapid acceleration over the past years. The increase in credits to households has been matched by a declining share of state-owned enterprises in non-government credit, partly reflecting major progress in privatization. In all three countries, business credit remains the largest component of total credit, with services and industry still getting the lion's share of credit in all three countries (80–90 per cent). Reflecting increased confidence of both creditors and debtors, a marked shift from short- to medium- and long-term credit has occurred reducing the share of short-term credit (maturity less than one year) to 46 per cent in Ukraine, 42 per cent in Romania, and 24 per cent in Bulgaria.

Widespread lending in foreign currencies is another common feature (Table 15.2). Despite different exchange rate regimes (Box 15.1), the expected cost of foreign currency credit is perceived to be lower than local currency loans in all three countries (a belief validated *ex post* for the time being as well). In Bulgaria, the currency board has assured borrowers of exchange rate stability, while banks still charge higher rates for loans in domestic currency. In Romania, the sharp drop in the risk premium after EU accession became a near certainty has led to strong and persistent inflows, which has significantly lowered the effective cost of foreign currency credit. In Ukraine, the de facto exchange rate peg has also provided an incentive for a rise in foreign currency credit, closely associated with the boom in loans to households; however, local currency loans in Ukraine have expanded even faster, in contrast to the other two countries. In all three countries, most enterprises that borrow in foreign currency do not appear to be hedged, except for the natural hedge enjoyed by exporters.

In all three countries, banks have extended loans at very high, though falling, real interest rates and intermediation spreads in local currency. A dearth of alternative sources of corporate financing (for example, corporate bonds and stock market initial public offerings) has led the banks to compete on terms like the range and fees for services rather than on deposit and loan rates. In Romania, the high reserve requirements have also contributed to the spread. Ukraine is an exception, as lower operating and provisioning costs have enabled banks to cut lending rates, causing an 18 percentage point fall in the deposit loan interest rate spread since end-2000.

Banks have funded the expansion of credit mostly through mobilization of deposits. Deposit growth has been relatively quick, owing to improved confidence, remittances from abroad, and, in Romania, high real leu deposit rates. In addition, a reduction of placements abroad, reflecting low global interest rates and a rapid accumulation of foreign liabilities, has resulted in a sharp drop in banks' net foreign assets.

3. OPPORTUNITIES AND RISKS

3.1 Opportunities

An increase in the level of financial intermediation is associated with an increase in the long-run growth rate of the economy. The theoretical and empirical literature generally supports the view that financial sector development increases economic growth.[3] There are various channels through which financial development can contribute to economic growth, including by collecting information and thereby improving the allocation of capital; sharing risk; and pooling savings and raising the efficiency of financial intermediation. Indeed, by easing financing constraints, increased bank lending can contribute to higher investment and consumption, and, ultimately, a higher standard of living.

From a structural perspective, the increase in financial intermediation in the three countries can therefore be considered beneficial. Per capita GDP in Bulgaria, Romania and Ukraine is still well below the average of EU countries and CEECs. To the extent that financial deepening raises the country's potential growth rate – through increases in the marginal productivity of capital and higher private savings and investment – recent developments in these countries should in principle be welcomed.

At the same time, episodes of rapid bank lending also entail risks. The risks can be broadly grouped into two categories: (a) the emergence or worsening of macroeconomic imbalances ('macro risk'); and (b) risks to financial sector stability owing to deteriorating bank asset quality ('credit risk'). When they materialize, these two risks are typically mutually reinforcing, creating boom–bust cycles in credit and asset markets and large swings in macroeconomic fundamentals. Moreover, the two types of risk may also be causally linked: abrupt corrections of macroeconomic imbalances have in some instances triggered financial sector distress, while the latter has caused economic disruptions.

3.2 Macroeconomic Risks

Rapid credit growth poses potential risks for macroeconomic stability. Increased credit availability eases liquidity constraints on households and firms, leading to higher consumption and investment. Given short-run supply constraints, this upward shift in credit-financed domestic demand would tend to exert upward pressure on prices in asset, goods and labour markets. Concurrently, demand for foreign goods – both consumption and investment – will rise, causing a deterioration in the trade balance. Thus, if left unchecked, a rapid increase in credit can boost domestic prices and wages – which at an unchanged nominal exchange rate could reduce international competitiveness – and heighten external vulnerabilities. Indeed, in characterizing emerging market credit booms, IMF (2004) notes that there is almost a 70 per cent probability that a credit boom coincides with either a consumption or investment boom, and that credit booms are often associated with banking and currency crises. The same paper also concludes that emerging market credit booms have not, on average, resulted in higher inflation – partly reflecting the high degree of trade openness in these economies – but rather have led to a deterioration of the current account and nominal exchange rate appreciation.

The experience of Bulgaria and Romania accords well with these priors (Figure 15.2). Both countries have seen domestic demand contributions to real GDP growth rise sharply, while net export contributions have turned negative. These shifts have coincided with the rapid increase in bank lending documented in section 2. Consumer price inflation has remained relatively tame in both countries, partly reflecting lower food prices due, in turn, to strong agricultural output, and nominal effective exchange rate appreciation in Bulgaria has offset the impact of higher oil prices. Thus, overheating has so far largely been manifested in widening trade deficits, owing to rapid growth in imports.[4] In contrast, Ukraine's macroeconomic imbalances are of a different nature as Ukraine has registered large current account surpluses in recent years on the back of strong export commodity prices and an undervalued currency. The pickup of inflationary pressures since 2004 can be attributed mainly to expansionary fiscal policy, emerging capacity bottlenecks, rapidly rising wages and pensions, and an accommodative monetary policy stance.

Econometric analysis suggests that rapid credit expansion in Bulgaria and Romania has been a significant factor in explaining the deteriorating trade balance, although tighter fiscal policy has helped moderate the impact (Table 15.4). The estimation results suggest that each percentage point of GDP of additional credit leads to a deterioration in the balance of goods and non-factor services (with a one-quarter lag) of about 0.4 percentage point of GDP for Bulgaria and 0.7 percentage point of GDP for Romania. The change in the fiscal stance is also an important determinant of changes in the trade balance: a 1 percentage point increase in the fiscal balance improves the trade balance by 0.2 percentage point (with a one-quarter lag). The same-size response in both countries probably reflects the broad similarity in the use of the exchange rate as a nominal anchor during the analysed period, despite the different monetary policy frameworks. The results also suggest that private savings provide a significant but incomplete Ricardian offset to changes in public savings, albeit somewhat above what

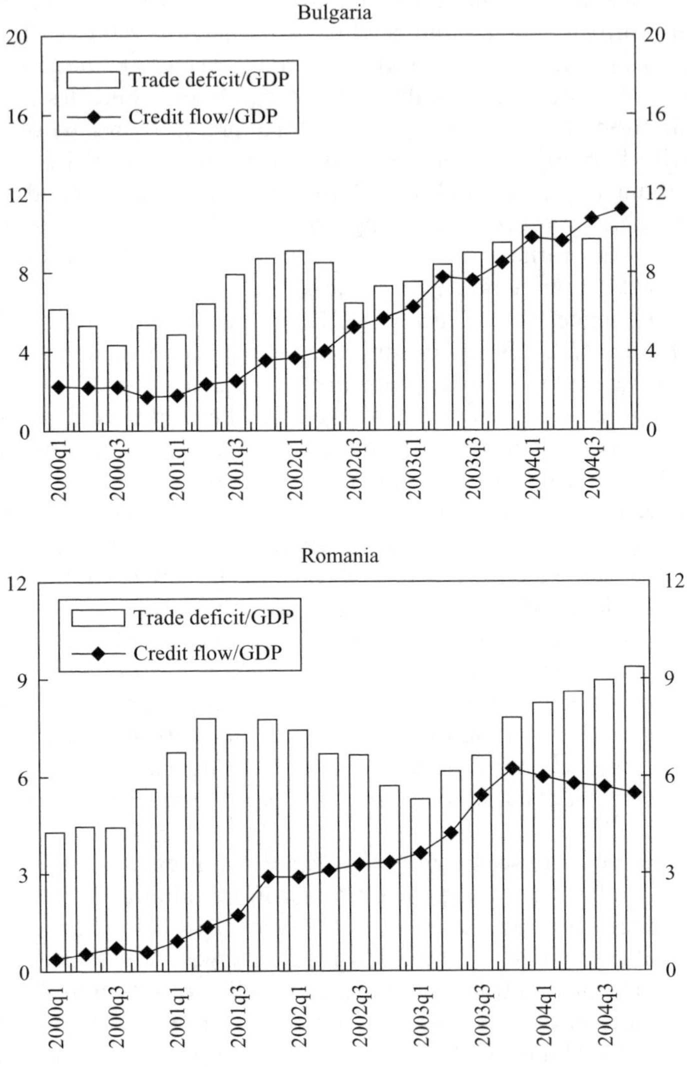

Sources: National authorities; IMF, International Financial Statistics; and IMF staff estimates.

Figure 15.2 Credit flows and trade deficit, 2000–2004 (in per cent of GDP)

Table 15.4 Impact of credit growth on the trade balance (Dependent variable: trade balance-to-GDP ratio)

	Coefficient	Std. Error	*t*-Stat	Prob.
Constant	−0.031	0.010	−3.043	0.004
Fixed effects				
Bulgaria	−0.008			
Romania	0.008			
Lagged trade balance	0.197	0.156	1.262	0.214
Lagged fiscal balance	0.190	0.097	1.952	0.058
Lagged credit flow				
Bulgaria	−0.442	0.151	−2.930	0.006
Romania	−0.706	0.189	−3.735	0.001
Change in GDP	−0.050	0.051	−0.982	0.332
Memo items:				
Sample: 1999Q2–2004Q4		Durbin Watson stat		1.975
Total pool (balanced) observations	46	*F*-stat		13.312
Adjusted *R*-squared	0.621		Prob (*F*-stat)	0.000

Source: IMF staff estimates based on data from national authorities.

is typical for a developing country (Chinn and Prasad, 2003). Finally, it seems that, in terms of the efficiency of policy instruments, moderating credit growth in these two countries is more powerful than attempts to offset it by tightening the fiscal stance (see section 4).

3.3 Risks for Banking Sector Stability

Rapid credit growth can trigger banking sector distress not only through macroeconomic imbalances but also through excessive risk taking and a deterioration of loan quality. Risk assessments may suffer due to the vast amount of new loans extended. Loan officers may be overburdened and agree to riskier loans that are not appropriately priced. Moreover, lending booms can facilitate 'evergreening' when new loans are used to service existing debt. At the same time, banks may neglect to further diversify their loan portfolios in an environment in which they can service existing clients. And finally, the perceived risk of loans may be underestimated during lending booms because the risk assessments are based on the current strong economy and rising values of underlying collateral.

Thus, rapid credit growth has been one of the most robust leading indicators for banking distress even though the majority of lending booms have not resulted in banking crises. Numerous studies have found that periods of significant and accelerating credit growth often preceded banking crises.[5] The likelihood of a banking crisis following a lending boom is estimated to be as high as 20 per cent, depending on the data set and methodology used. Prominent examples include the Scandinavian banking crises in the early 1990s, Mexico's banking crisis in 1994, and the Asian financial crisis in 1997–98. The ratio of credit to GDP increased rapidly in those countries, averaging 5.2 percentage points per year in the five years leading up to the crisis and dropping precipitously afterward. While the level of credit in Bulgaria, Romania and Ukraine is still much below that of many prominent crisis countries, the speed of credit expansion is approaching levels comparable to them (Table 15.2).

Prudential indicators point to the strength of banks in Bulgaria and Romania, while Ukraine's banking system seems plagued by structural weaknesses (Table 15.5). Despite the ongoing credit acceleration, banks in Bulgaria and Romania are well capitalized and liquid. Moreover, these countries' institutional frameworks are considered relatively well developed, driven by the EU accession process and the large share of foreign bank ownership. In contrast, Ukrainian banks suffer from widespread related-party lending practices, relatively high non-performing loans (NPLs), poor asset diversification, weaknesses in banks' risk management and loan practices, in particular in light of low transparency in the enterprise sector, and low bank profitability. In the EBRD's index on banking sector reform, Ukraine lags both countries while its credit-to-GDP ratio is already at a level of more advanced transition economies (Figure 15.3).[6]

4. POLICY OPTIONS AND AUTHORITIES' RESPONSES

Policy-makers face a number of difficult questions in deciding how to respond to a credit boom:

- On what basis should the judgment be made as to whether credit is expanding too quickly? Are there speed limits?
- Assuming it is decided that credit is growing too quickly, how should the policy response be apportioned between (a) offsetting the effects of the credit boom with other policy instruments and (b) moderating the credit boom itself?
- Is it advisable to use prudential measures for macroeconomic objectives?

Table 15.5 Prudential indicators of the banking sector, 2000–2004 (in per cent)

	2000	2001	2002	2003	2004
Bulgaria					
Capital adequacy ratios	35.6	31.3	25.2	22.0	16.1
Non-performing loans/total loans	17.3	13.1	8.6	7.3	6.9
Return on assets	3.1	2.9	2.1	2.4	2.1
Return on equity	22.5	22.0	16.4	22.8	20.6
Liquid assets/total assets	26.0	25.5	29.3	25.5	31.6
Romania					
Capital adequacy ratios	23.8	28.8	24.6	20.0	18.8
Non-performing loans/total loans	6.4	3.9	2.8	8.3	8.1
Return on assets	1.5	3.1	2.7	2.4	2.5
Return on equity	12.5	21.8	18.8	18.2	19.3
Liquid assets/total assets[1]	–	–	78.6	62.7	63.6
Ukraine					
Capital adequacy ratios	15.5	20.7	18.0	15.2	16.8
Non-performing loans/total loans[2]	29.6	25.1	21.9	28.3	30.0
Return on assets	−0.1	1.2	1.2	1.0	1.1
Return on equity	−0.5	7.5	8.0	7.6	8.4
Liquid assets/total assets	20.8	15.3	13.5	15.3	16.7

Notes:
1. Liquid assets are assets with residual maturity of up to three months.
2. The NBU estimates that about 94% of loans classified as substandard are being paid on time.

Sources: Bulgarian National Bank, National Bank of Romania, National Bank of Ukraine and IMF staff estimates.

Deciding whether a credit expansion is excessive or not is difficult both in general and for the three countries. During the convergence process, a certain degree of re-intermediation, higher consumption and investment growth, and wider external current account deficits is to be expected. Unfortunately, the academic literature provides few reliable guideposts in answering the question of 'how fast is too fast'. In principle, an equilibrium level of credit could be calculated, based on a country's economic and institutional fundamentals.[7] This can then be compared with the current level of credit. However, while such a calculation might provide a 'target', it does

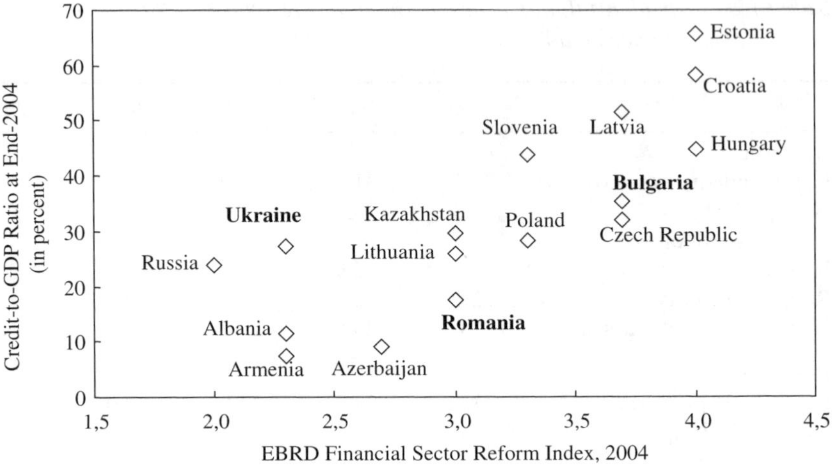

Note: 1. Private sector credit.

Sources: IMF, International Financial Statistics; EBRD Transition Report 2004 and IMF staff estimates.

Figure 15.3 Transition economies: credit-to-GDP ratio and institutional reform, 2004[1]

not provide any guidance on how rapidly a country should move to that equilibrium level.

The test of whether credit is growing too rapidly should be based on the extent to which the risks identified earlier – macroeconomic and prudential – appear to be materializing. On the domestic side, is inflation (in goods, assets and labour markets) rising, and if so, is this linked to the credit boom? On the external side, are trade/current account balances deteriorating beyond what could be deemed sustainable? In assessing the current account position, two questions are critical: (a) to what extent is rapid credit growth responsible for the deterioration in the current account balance, and (b) what is the level of the current account balance that stabilizes the external debt-to-GDP ratio over the medium term?[8] Answering the latter question depends crucially on assumptions regarding the future size of non-debt-creating inflows.[9] Finally, an assessment of prudential risks would involve monitoring closely indicators of banking system health, such as NPL ratios, capital adequacy ratios, loan concentration ratios, and balance sheet mismatches (especially maturity and currency). Assessing such risks is a complicated task for supervisors, as it is difficult to disentangle boom excesses from equilibrium trends. In addition, certain indicators – for instance, NPL ratios – are lagging indicators of emerging risks, and reliable early warning indicators for banking fragility remain largely elusive.

The menu of available policy options depends on the country's policy framework and institutional setting. The tools include macroeconomic policies (fiscal, monetary, and exchange rate policies), regulatory and supervisory policies, administrative measures (such as controls on capital inflows), and market development measures.[10] Many credit boom countries have used a combination of the above policies. Constraints on policy options relate to the type of monetary/exchange rate policy framework and to the institutional setting: with a fixed exchange rate regime, traditional monetary policy tools (for example, changes in interest rates, open market operations) are ineffective, particularly in cases with open capital accounts. In such a setting, efforts to drain liquidity from the domestic banking system to reduce funding sources will be frustrated: as long as returns on lending remain high, non-bank/cross-border flows will quickly replenish funding sources. Regulatory and supervisory policies aim to ensure banking sector health; their effectiveness in moderating credit growth has not yet been established, and there is a general consensus that such measures cannot substitute for monetary policy. Thus, if supervisors try to reduce credit growth, they may in fact divert it to less supervised channels (for example, leasing companies). However, in combination with monetary policy, changes in the prudential regime can help avoid excessive credit growth. Administrative measures – for instance, general or bank-by-bank credit ceilings, or capital inflow controls – are generally viewed as a last resort, owing to their bluntness and distortionary effects. Finally, market development measures – including establishment of credit registries to improve the credit culture and development of securities markets to reduce dependence on bank credit – may help, but the impact is likely to be marginal and of a more medium-term nature.

The authorities in the three countries understand the risks associated with the credit booms and have responded in varying ways and degrees to both offset and moderate rapid credit growth:

- In **Bulgaria**, policy options are constrained by the currency board arrangement. The main response has been a tightening of fiscal policy, both through higher revenue – reflecting mostly cyclical factors and improved compliance in the face of lower taxes – and expenditure restraint. A host of monetary measures – notably moral suasion, a tightening of reserve requirements and prudential supervision, and, most recently, quantitative restrictions on credit (enforced with the help of marginal reserve requirements for banks exceeding the limits) – have been implemented. The tightening of reserve requirements last year does not appear to have reduced credit growth, although such growth may have been even higher otherwise. It is too early to assess the impact of the quantitative limits on credit expansion that took effect on 1 April 2005, but first signs indicate a significant diversion to other forms of financing (non-bank/cross border). Going forward, it is possible that further fiscal tightening would be necessary should the monetary measures prove ineffective in preventing a further widening of external imbalances.

- In **Romania**, a combination of fiscal policy, monetary policy, and prudential measures has been used to both moderate and offset credit growth. Fiscal policy has been consistently tightened, with the general government deficit narrowing from 3.2 per cent of GDP in 2001 to 1.1 per cent in 2004. The NBR tried interest rate hikes in 2003 but had to reverse course in 2004, as falling inflation and large capital inflows made high real interest rates both unjustifiable and untenable. Moreover, these hikes merely changed the composition of credit in favour of foreign currency loans without reducing the overall credit flow. As the boom occurred mostly in loans to households, the NBR tightened households' eligibility for credit by lowering the ceiling on the maximum monthly payment-to-net income ratios, standardizing the down-payment for mortgage loans at 25 per cent, and strengthening the required guarantees/collateral. Finally, the reserve requirement on foreign currency-denominated bank liabilities was increased and extended to liabilities with residual maturity longer than two years. These measures did reduce credit growth somewhat, but a further fiscal tightening is likely to be necessary in the period ahead to support efforts on the monetary side.
- In **Ukraine**, the focus was on bank regulatory and supervisory measures. The NBU raised the minimum capital adequacy ratio, strengthened the definition of capital, tightened loan classification rules, raised provisioning requirements for foreign-currency-denominated loans, tightened related-party lending regulations, and put in place a new risk assessment methodology for its supervisors. These measures were aimed at strengthening banks' resilience to shocks. Credit growth decelerated during 2004 (even when the sharp drop during the political crisis is excluded), but it is unclear to what extent this can be attributed to the NBU's responses. Going forward, further progress in strengthening bank regulation and supervision, as well as the institutional environment, is needed, with particular focus on related-party lending.

NOTES

1. The views expressed in this chapter are those of the authors and should not be attributed to the International Monetary Fund, its Executive Board, or its management.
2. IMF (2004) makes a distinction between rapid credit growth and a credit boom. The former can occur as part of financial deepening (trend) and normal cyclical upturns, while the latter represents an excessive and therefore unsustainable cyclical movement. While such a distinction may be sensible for advanced economies, the short time series and likelihood of a structural break in the series make such a distinction less meaningful for economies in transition. We therefore use the terms 'rapid credit growth' and 'credit boom' interchangeably in this chapter.
3. IMF (2004) summarizes the state of play in the literature; a more extensive discussion of both the theory and empirics regarding finance and growth can be found in Levine (2003).
4. Developments in bank credit are probably more closely mirrored in the trade rather than the current account. In Bulgaria, for example, the current account deficit narrowed in 2004 despite an acceleration in credit growth as the invisibles strengthened substantially; the trade deficit, meanwhile, remained at a very high level (14 per cent of GDP) despite favourable movements in the terms of trade. Competitiveness does not appear to have been a significant factor in the deterioration of trade balances in Bulgaria and Romania.
5. Eichengreen and Arteta (2001) find robustness in these results by testing the findings of earlier studies. See also IMF (2004) and the references there.
6. The EBRD (2005) comes to a similar conclusion by constructing a vulnerability indicator based on credit growth and stock market prices changes on the one hand, and banking sector institutional weaknesses on the other hand. For more details on Ukraine's banking sector see Ong et al. (2005) and Schaechter (2005).
7. Given the ongoing structural changes in such transition economies, however, these estimates of equilibrium credit must be taken with a grain of salt. A recent attempt at such estimates is Cottarelli et al. (2005), who calculate equilibrium credit-to-GDP ratios for a number of CEECs. For Bulgaria and Romania, the estimated ratios are 52.6 per cent and 58 per cent, compared with ratios of 34.4 per cent and 17.9 per cent, respectively, at end-2004. These estimates are based on 2002 data and are now somewhat dated. Boissay et al. (2005) also attempt to find a measure of excessiveness of credit growth by modelling credit growth as a function of macroeconomic fundamentals and the gap between the actual credit-to-GDP ratio and an equilibrium level. Their estimations yield that credit growth has been excessive in Bulgaria, while in Romania only loans to households have risen too fast. They do not include estimations for Ukraine.
8. Aside from medium-term considerations, prudence suggests keeping the current account at manageable levels to reduce vulnerability to sudden reversals in capital. A recent survey of early warning system models by Berg et al. (2004) reports widespread use of the current account as one of the predictive variables. For instance, Goldstein et al. (2000) find the current account deficit to be among the best predictors of currency crises.
9. In this context, imports related to FDI are often thought to be self-financing as they generate future exports; however, to the extent investment is made in non-traded sectors, this argument cannot be made.
10. For a fuller discussion of policy options, see Hilbers et al. (2005).

REFERENCES

Berg, Andrew, Eduardo Borensztein and Catherine Pattillo (2004), 'Assessing early warnings systems: How have they worked in practice?' IMF Working Paper 04/52, Washington: International Monetary Fund.

Boissay, Frédéric, Oscar Calvo-Gonzalez and Tomasz Kozluk (2005), 'Is lending in Central and Eastern Europe developing too fast?' Chapter 14, this volume.

Chinn, Menzie D. and Eswar S. Prasad (2003), 'Medium-term determinants of current accounts in industrial and developing countries: An empirical exploration', *Journal of International Economics*, **59** (1), 47–76.

Cottarelli, Carlo, Giovanni Dell'Ariccia and Ivanna Vladkova-Hollar (2005), 'Early birds, late risers, and sleeping beauties: Bank credit growth to the private sector in Central and Eastern Europe and in the Balkans', *Journal of Banking and Finance*, **29**, 83–104.

Duenwald, Christoph and Bikas Joshi (2004), 'Bulgaria's credit boom: Characteristics, consequences, and policy options', *Bulgaria: Selected Issues and Statistical Appendix*, Country Report No. 04/177, Washington: International Monetary Fund, pp. 6–25.

Eichengreen, Barry and Carlos Arteta (2001), 'Banking crises in emerging markets: presumptions and evidence', CIDER Working Paper No. C00-115, Berkeley, California: University of California Center for International and Development Economics Research.

European Bank for Reconstruction and Development (2005), *Transition Report*, London.

Goldstein, Morris, Graciela Kaminsky and Carmen Reinhart (2000), *Assessing Financial Vulnerability: An Early Warning System for Emerging Markets*, Washington: Institute for International Economics.

Hilbers, Paul, Inci Otker-Robe, Ceyla Pazarbasioglu and Gudrun Johnsen (2005), 'Assessing and managing rapid credit growth and the role of supervisory and prudential policies', IMF Working Paper 05/151, Washington: International Monetary Fund.

International Monetary Fund (2004), 'World Economic Outlook: Advancing Structural Reforms', Washington.

Levine, Ross (2003), 'Finance and growth: theory, evidence, and mechanisms', mimeo, Washington: World Bank.

Ong, Li Lian, Andrea Schaechter and Dimitry Sologub (2005), 'Developments in Ukraine's financial sector – FSAP Follow-Up Report', in *Ukraine: Selected Issues*, Country Report No. 05/416, Washington: International Monetary Fund, pp. 69–100.

Schaechter, Andrea (2005), 'Credit boom in Ukraine: Risks for banking sector stability', *Ukraine: Selected Issues*, Country Report No. 05/20, Washington: International Monetary Fund, pp. 14–35.

16. The 'New Europe' household lending market

Fabrizio Coricelli, Fabio Mucci and Debora Revoltella[1]

1. INTRODUCTION

In the last few years, household credit has been the most dynamic component of credit flows, both in advanced European countries and in the New Europe region,[2] despite a significant difference in the depth of the financial sector in the two groups of countries.

In the New Europe, household credit was practically absent until the year 2000 or so. With the ongoing economic and institutional convergence towards the EU, rapid growth of household loans was thus to be expected and considered a natural phenomenon. Real convergence, associated with expectations of fast income growth, is bound to increase the propensity to fall into debt by households that aim at smoothing their consumption over time. Moreover, households in the New Europe have low levels of financial wealth and are thus subject to severe liquidity constraints. The potential demand for loans by these liquidity constrained households is very large. Moreover, ambitious growth and development strategies of all banks and other financial intermediaries in the market have triggered a rise in supply, helping to relax, to a large extent, households' liquidity constraints. The emergence of cross-border competition, whether direct or indirect, has prompted a gradual standardization of products and market conditions. In summary, examining both demand and supply factors, the chapter concludes that the rapid expansion of household debt in New Europe is by and large an equilibrium phenomenon, even though the process is not necessarily sustainable or immune from serious risks, both at the macroeconomic level and at the level of financial institutions.

Section 2 of the chapter provides a snapshot of the New Europe household lending market. We have built a new database, which allows a comparison among countries, adding up different forms of household debt, both from banking and non-banking financial institutions. Using as a benchmark the euro area experience, we compare the most recent developments at the regional and at the individual country level.

To obtain a clearer view of current trends in the New Europe, section 3 examines the factors behind growth in household debt. In particular, we try to understand if the current level of credit growth throughout the region is compatible with a new equilibrium, in the context of gradually relaxing credit rationing conditions.

Section 4 discusses whether the current level of household debt is sustainable in the medium to long run, distinguishing between microeconomic and macroeconomic implications of rising household debt. Section 5 concludes.

2. HOUSEHOLD DEBT MARKET IN THE ENLARGED EUROPE

Over the last ten years, the household lending market has grown considerably at the international level, reflecting structural changes in the financial sector. The increase in households' gross financial and non-financial assets has gone hand in hand with an increasing financial deepening of the liability side of their balance sheets. Retail has become increasingly relevant for banking and non-banking financial institutions, not only in the most developed financial systems (the US and UK), but also in the main European and EU converging countries, albeit in different ways.

In the euro area, households' loans increased from around 40 per cent of total loans in 1995 to 45 per cent in 2004. The increase in household indebtedness has mainly been driven by mortgage lending, sustained by extremely favourable financial conditions and rising property prices, which have generated greater wealth for home owners and increased the value of properties used to secure loans. On the other side, increasing cross-border competition (direct or indirect) enhanced the quality of products and more generally supply conditions. In the euro area, mortgages have risen sharply. In 2004 mortgages accounted for 68 per cent of the total, compared with 59 per cent in 1998. Overall, total credit to households increased from 45.5 per cent of GDP in 1995 to 50 per cent in 2004.

Although it would be inappropriate to speak about a unique euro area retail lending model, as market maturity and supply conditions vary significantly across euro area countries, there have been common trends (Aleati et al., 2005).

The experience of countries of the previous accessions, Greece, Ireland, Portugal and Spain, is particularly relevant for New Europe countries (Brzoza-Brzezina, 2005; HNB Financial Stability Report, 2005). Indeed, in the wake of their accession to the euro area started in the mid-1990s, those countries experienced an accelerated pattern of credit growth, with real annual rates close to 30 per cent, largely driven by the mortgage market. In Portugal, credit growth accelerated starting from 1995–96, with a peak in 1999 and a subsequent stabilization, which led to a bust in economic performance. In Ireland the upward trend started in 1995, with a peak in 1998 and subsequent revival in recent years, while in Greece, the pick-up recorded in 1995 still has to guarantee long-lasting effects in terms of financial market development, with the level of household debt to GDP in the country, at 31 per cent, well below the euro area average.

Accelerated growth in household debt has characterized all New Europe countries as well (see Table 16.1). Despite the much lower financial penetration in the region, compared to the euro area level, the observed patterns of development largely resemble those of the more advanced neighbouring countries: a fast growth of retail, which thus becomes the most dynamic segment for banking and non-banking institutions, was driven first by the consumer sector and, since 2000, by the mortgage market. Structural as well as cyclical factors might explain such growth.

Credit expansion has been grounded all over the New Europe countries in an environment of strong economic growth and generally falling inflation and interest rates. Driven in most cases by strong domestic demand, economic growth has averaged between around 3 per cent and

Table 16.1 Forms of debt (in %)

	Euro area		New Europe[1]	
	2000	2004	2000	2004
Growth in debt (% annual average 2000–2004)	7		23	
Growth in mortgages	8		43	
Growth in consumer credit	2		13	
Growth in other loans	4		21	
Debt/gross disposable income (%)	68	75	9	18
Debt/GDP (%), of which:	46	50	7	12
Mortgages (% of GDP)	29	34	1	4
Consumer credit (% of GDP)	7	7	4	5
Other loans (% of GDP)	9	9	2	3

Note: 1. The total for New Europe does not include Lithuania and Slovenia as data are not available; other loans include current account overdrafts, credit cards, financial leasing and other loans.

Source: UniCredit New Europe Research Network database, based on ECB, national central banks and Eurostat.

8 per cent in the last four years, approaching 4 per cent at the regional level. High-inflation countries, like Turkey and Romania, have experienced a very successful stabilization process in recent years, which has allowed inflation to finally pass to one-digit levels in 2005. All the other countries have also seen a normalization of the inflation pattern. Interest rates have been on a generally decreasing trend (or at absolute low levels).

The transition process and EU convergence suggest increasing demand for both consumer and investment goods, as income growth expectations lead to an inter-temporal consumption smoothing. At the same time, despite the average regional home ownership rate being quite high (69 per cent, compared to 70 per cent at the euro area level), house investment demand (new or restructuring) is increasing as income increases and rates decline, with old apartments, mostly coming from the socialist era, being generally small and poor quality. On top of that, there is a positive on-off in demographical trends, with the baby boom generation now adding to housing demand.

The supply side has also played a strong role in supporting market growth. At the beginning of the 1990s, banks' book portfolios were mainly targeting the corporate sector, while the retail lending market was virtually inexistent. In the last few years all the local banks, most being under foreign control, started to develop aggressive growth strategies in the market, by providing new services and products. Competition, even if still focused, has increased rapidly, driving down margins. Household loans are the fastest growing market in the region's financial sector: in 2004 they accounted for 38 per cent of total bank loans, compared to 23 per cent in 2000.

Thanks to both demand and supply, as a percentage of GDP, household loans have practically doubled, from 7 per cent in 2000 to 12 per cent in 2004. Obviously, growth of retail loans has been particularly fast in those countries which had a small market, such as Bulgaria, which experienced a real growth rate of retail credit of about 58 per cent in 2000–2004, or Romania (106 per cent) (see Table 16.2). In terms of composition, household debt was mainly in the form of consumer credit in the 1990s (consumer credit and other loans represented 80 per cent of household debt in 2000). The expansion of the last few years has led to a radical shift. In line with developments in the euro area, mortgages have been the main driver behind the boom and have grown by an average 43 per cent a year, fuelled by both demand- and supply-side factors. Mortgages now represent 36 per cent of the total retail lending market, while consumer and other credit account for the remaining 64 per cent.

The most peculiar retail lending market throughout the region is the Turkish one. Turkey has a small retail lending market (corresponding to only 6 per cent of GDP), but quite sophisticated and innovative, in terms

Table 16.2 Structural indicators (in %)

	Household debt/GDP 2004[5]	Mortgage/ household debt 2004	Real lending growth (CAGR 2000–2004)	Mortgage growth – Consumer growth (CAGR 2000–2004)	Avg int. rate level (2000)[1]	Avg int. rate level (2004)[1]	Avg inflation 2000[3]	Avg inflation 2004[3]	Avg economic growth 2000–2004 (CAGR)
Romania	5	29	106	11	52	26	46	12	6
Latvia	19	64	68	32	13	9	3	6	7
Bulgaria	12	22	58	21	17	13	10	6	5
Hungary	20	48	45	43	22	15	10	7	4
Estonia	24	70	39	17	11	6	4	3	7
Croatia	32	37	26	5	12	8	6	2	4
Czech Rep.	14	55	25	10[2]	9	8	4	3	3
Slovakia	10	55	21	−32[4]	14	7	12	8	4
Poland	13	31	10	32	14	7	10	4	3
Turkey	6	10	4	10	49	34	53	10	4

Notes:
1. Figures refer to interest rates on local currency credits applied to retail customers. In Croatia, interest rates on long-term Kuna credits indexed to foreign currency.
2. CAGR 2001–2004.
3. Harmonized indices of consumer prices, annual average rate of change.
4. In Slovakia, the less dynamic growth in the mortgage lending in 2000–2004 is mainly related to the building societies component, due to decrease of subsidies. Loans granted by non-bank financial institutions excluded from total individuals' liabilities.
5. For Hungary, Estonia and Latvia, total liabilities exclude other accounts payable (AF.7).

Source: UniCredit New Europe Research Network database, based on Eurostat, national central banks.

of services and products, even if still targeting only the small financially active share of the population. With stabilizing economic patterns and rapidly decreasing interest rates, demand for credit has grown fast, while at the same time, reducing inflation and income potential from securities and other capital market operations, banks have turned towards the retail market, relaxing supply conditions. Consumer credit still represents the dominant share in households' debt portfolio, with credit card services being particularly developed. The proper mortgage market is still on a development phase and is expected soon (most probably in 2006) to add to the non-mortgage-backed housing market. It should be noted that the bulk of housing and mortgage loans accounts for only 1 per cent of the Turkish GDP, compared to 5 per cent at the aggregate New Europe level and 34 per cent at the euro area level, suggesting there is definitely room for growth.

Bulgaria and Romania are experiencing strong economic growth as well, while ranking at the lowest position in the region in terms of per capita income and per capita wealth. Credit demand is increasing fast, while supply heavily targets the household segment. While the stock of corporate loans still prevails on aggregate, indeed, the main driver for future development is definitely on the retail side. With a weight of more than 70 per cent, consumer credit represents the most significant share of household debt. The mortgage market continues to grow fast, as testified by strong growth rates in the last couple of years averaging 158 per cent and 108 per cent for Romania and Bulgaria, respectively.[3] Interesting to note, the distance between the two markets remains high, with Bulgaria most probably being ahead of Romania in terms of market development. Romania is also giving somewhat more reason for concern, given the recently experienced declining trend in households' financial wealth over GDP and relevance of foreign currency (FX) lending.

The other New Europe countries form a more homogeneous group and are more similar to the more financially advanced neighbours.

Poland, with a 13.2 per cent household debt over GDP ratio and a 9.5 per cent average yearly real growth of credit, shows a gradually developing retail lending market, with some phases of bust, such as the one generated by FX exposure in 2000. The consumer credit market has been growing fast in recent years and still accounts for roughly 70 per cent of the total household debt portfolio. Throughout the 1990s, Poland experimented with various types of loan products and housing programmes designed to promote the development of a market-based housing finance and production system. Legislative reforms and the expansion of the banking system, including the creation of mortgage banks, broadened the access to capital, increased competition and enhanced the diversity of products. In spite of these positive developments in the housing finance system, the use of mortgages has started to expand rapidly only in recent years, following more favourable financial conditions. More generally, the acceleration of lending growth in both mortgage and consumer components is also associated with a relaxation of credit conditions, with banks and other financial intermediaries fast enlarging their clients' pool.

Slovakia and the Czech Republic feature a relatively developed retail lending market, with the mortgage and the consumer component having almost equal weight. Mortgage finance and housing subsidy schemes were introduced in the first half of the 1990s, relatively early compared to the rest of region. A further increase in volume in the mortgage market was observed in the latest few years triggered by a lowering of interest rates and the high non-saturation of the residential market.

Croatia shows a rather developed retail lending market, with prevalence of the consumer credit component, but strong growth of the mortgage component. The Croatian banking sector is characterized by strong competition, with foreign-owned banks dominating the market. In the context of a 'fixed on average' commitment on the exchange rate, the banking sector is to a large extent 'euroized', with both loans and deposits being largely denominated in euros. It should be noted that Croatian households continue to show increasing net financial wealth-to-GDP ratios, despite the strong debt burden, in the context of relatively high income and standard of living levels.

Hungary, Latvia and Estonia show a relatively high level of financial deepening and a strict prevalence of the mortgage component in households' debt portfolios, which is confirmed by the rapid growth in mortgages during the period 2000–2004. In Hungary the development of the mortgage market has been affected by government subsidies for house purchase, which also prevented a contraction in market rates (as the actual price paid by the client was equal to the face interest rate minus the subsidy). Between 2000 and 2003 there was a significant housing boom in the country, stimulated by housing shortages, economic growth and the above-mentioned subsidy programme. Borrowing boomed, and by the end of 2003 outstanding mortgage loans had risen sharply to 8 per cent of GDP from 1 per cent in 2000. Curtailment of the subsidy scheme discouraged further borrowings and the loans market fell rapidly in 2004, partially depressing the housing market. Lending growth in Estonia and Latvia has instead been associated with low interest rates. In Estonia, mortgage interest rates deductibility was also allowed. Moreover, in all three countries, substantial growth has also characterized the consumer credit share of the market, with some evidence, particularly in Hungary and Estonia, of a direct relationship between credit growth and consumption performance.

3. MAIN DETERMINANTS OF HOUSEHOLD DEBT

As anticipated, the rapid expansion of household credit in New Europe is likely to reflect both supply and demand factors. Expectation of sustained growth, as a result of integration in the EU, raised consumer demand. At the same time, entry of foreign banks, competition for a growing retail market and a more stable macroeconomic environment have reduced the cost of loans. Moreover, a large proportion of households in New Europe are likely to be liquidity-constrained, as they have low levels of current income and financial wealth and the stock of consumer credit is very low. If this is the case, a large component of expansion in household credit can be associated with the loosening of liquidity constraints.

3.1 Relevance of Liquidity Constraints

We investigate the relationship between the dynamics of consumption and that of household credit, to have a first indirect test for the relevance of liquidity constraints in the New Europe. Our sample consists of 42 quarterly observations for each country on real consumption during the interval from 1995:01 to 2005:02, and 26 observations on real credit to individuals from 1999:01 to 2005:02. The cyclical component for both series has been extracted using a Hodrick and Prescott (HP) filter with a smoothing parameter of 1600 (the standard choice for quarterly data).[4] Note that, as in Bacchetta and Gerlach (1997), we consider both housing credit and consumer credit as determinants of consumption. By accessing credit markets for mortgages, households can indeed free resources for consumption.

A first interesting result comes from the analysis of the trends, which appear to be positive in all countries for both consumption and household credit with the only exception of Poland, where the slight downward slope of credit trend reflects the boom/bust cycle following the marked economic slow-down in the second half of 2000. Overall, this confirms structural developments in terms of convergence in standards of living of the population towards the EU, and increasing financial deepening.

To gain some insights into the role of liquidity constraints, we focus on consumption, income and credit. In a world with perfect financial markets and no liquidity constraints for individuals, households would be free to smooth consumption over time. The volatility of consumption would be low and possibly lower than the volatility of real GDP.[5] By contrast, when households face liquidity constraints and limited access to lending markets, consumption would be more volatile and its dynamics would follow changes in the availability of credit.

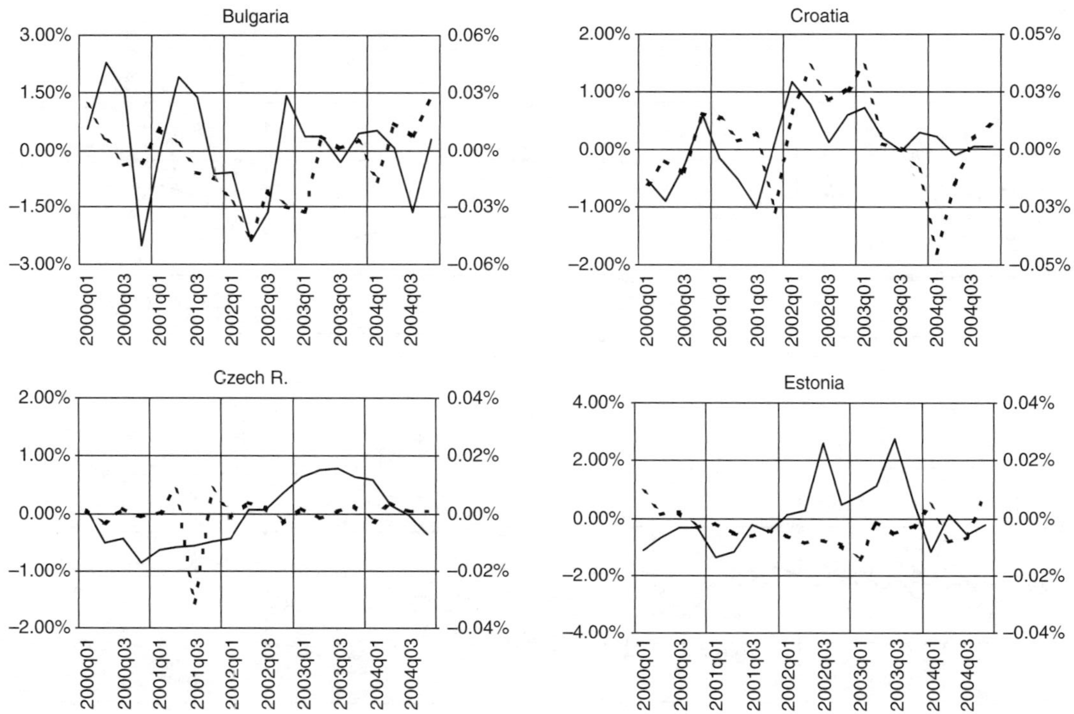
Bulgaria
3.00%
1.50%
0.00%
–1.50%
–3.00%
0.06%
0.03%
0.00%
–0.03%
–0.06%
Croatia
2.00%
1.00%
0.00%
–1.00%
–2.00%
0.05%
0.03%
0.00%
–0.03%
–0.05%
Czech R.
2.00%
1.00%
0.00%
–1.00%
–2.00%
0.04%
0.02%
0.00%
–0.02%
–0.04%
Estonia
4.00%
2.00%
0.00%
–2.00%
–4.00%
0.04%
0.02%
0.00%
–0.02%
–0.04%
2000q01
2000q03
2001q01
2001q03
2002q01
2002q03
2003q01
2003q03
2004q01
2004q03

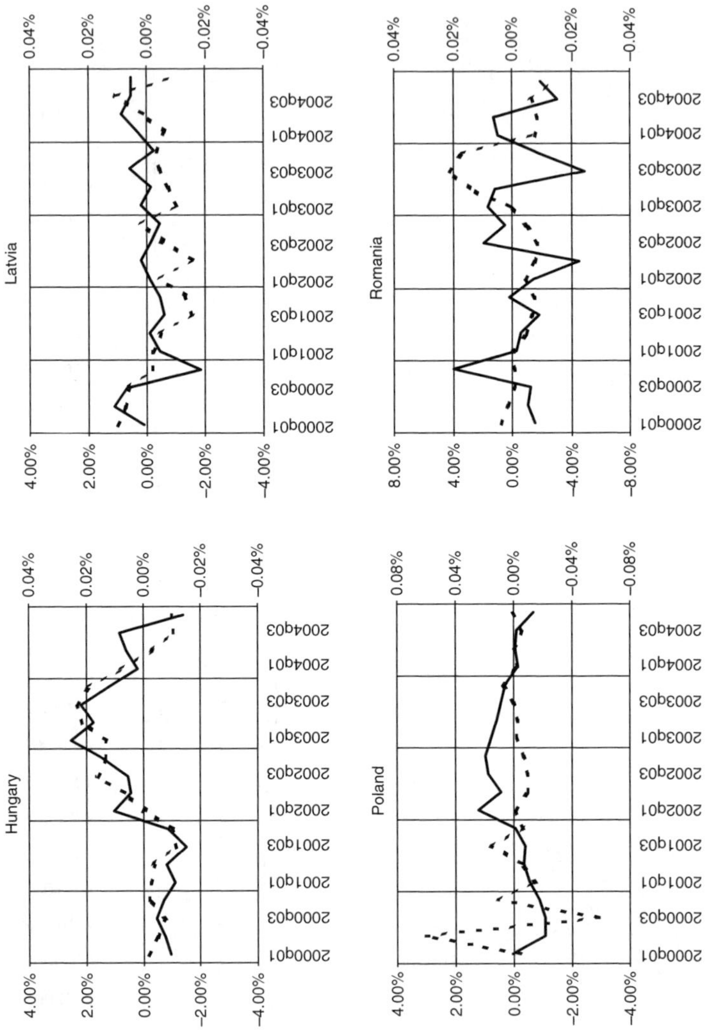
Hungary
Latvia
Poland
Romania
4.00%
2.00%
0.00%
−2.00%
−4.00%
8.00%
4.00%
0.00%
−4.00%
−8.00%
0.04%
0.02%
0.00%
−0.02%
−0.04%
0.08%
0.04%
0.00%
−0.04%
−0.08%
2000q01
2000q03
2001q01
2001q03
2002q01
2002q03
2003q01
2003q03
2004q01
2004q03

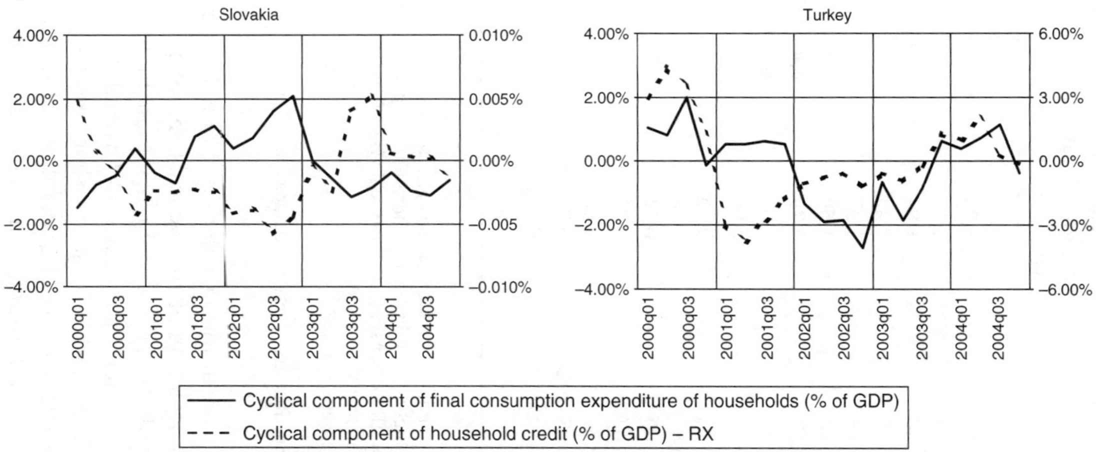

Notes: Dotted lines represent in all figures the cyclical component of real credit to individuals as a percentage of GDP while solid lines depict the cyclical component of real final expenditure of individuals (as a percentage of GDP) extracted using an HP filter. Credit series have been deflated using the harmonized indices of consumer prices and are shown on the RX axis.

Source: UniCredit New Europe Research Network database, based on Eurostat and national central banks.

Figure 16.1 Cyclical component of consumption and credit

Table 16.3 Consumption and real GDP volatility[1] and credit–consumption correlation

	Coefficient of variation of real consumption (in %)	Coefficient of variation of real GDP (in %)	Corr (cons, credit)[2]
Bulgaria	**4.76**	**3.39**	**0.3**
Czech Republic	2.64	1.76	0.1
Croatia	1.28	1.14	0.4
Estonia	**3.00**	**1.94**	**−0.5 (0.1 five lags)**
Hungary	**1.85**	**0.40**	**0.8**
Latvia	1.80	1.37	0.04
Poland	1.18	1.59	−0.1 (0.1 three lags)
Romania	**4.83**	**2.79**	**0.02 (0.2 two lags)**
Slovakia	1.98	1.01	−0.3 (0.2 three lags)
Turkey	**4.76**	**3.90**	**0.4**
Belgium	0.77	0.75	0.2
Germany	0.87	0.76	0.3
Spain	1.00	0.54	0.4
France	0.67	0.72	0.3
Greece	0.67	1.00	–
Italy	0.68	0.71	0.5
Netherlands	1.19	0.92	−0.2
Portugal	1.09	1.08	−0.1

Notes:
1. Volatility is computed as the standard deviation of the cycle, divided by the mean of the trend. Countries with relatively higher volatility of consumption compared to real GDP have been highlighted in bold. Both for consumption and real GDP, the cyclical component have been extracted from series in levels.
2. Based on series taken as percentage of GDP.

Sources: UniCredit New Europe Research Network database and Eurostat.

Table 16.3 shows that consumption volatility throughout the region, measured as the standard deviation of the cyclical component normalized by the series average, tends to be much higher than in the euro area economies and generally higher than real GDP volatility. Despite fast growth of the retail lending market, it seems that credit is not able to smooth consumption. In some cases, strong volatility is also combined with a relevant correlation between consumption and credit, providing some first evidence of the existence of liquidity constraints.

We find evidence of liquidity constraints in Turkey, where on top of high volatility of consumption, a significant correlation between the credit and the consumption dynamics is detected (0.4). Most probably a high share of

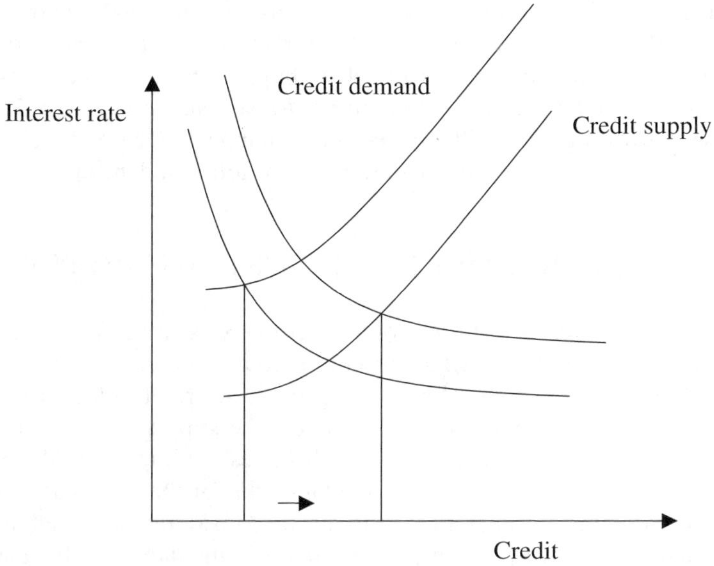

Figure 16.2 *Credit demand and supply*

the population in the country needs credit to satisfy its consumption pattern. A similar pattern is clear in Bulgaria (with slightly lower correlation), and in Romania and Estonia, although high consumption volatility is combined with lower contemporary correlation among credit and consumption. A strong correlation between consumption and credit patterns emerges in Hungary, being also very clear from the graph. Consumption volatility in the country is not particularly high in absolute terms, but much higher than income volatility, confirming that individuals are not able to follow a smooth path. A 0.4 correlation between consumption and credit is observed in Croatia, however, matched to low volatility of consumption. Less clear evidence of liquidity constraints is detected in other countries, but volatility of consumption is always confirmed much above the euro area levels.[6]

A clear implication of the relevance of liquidity constraints is that the current fast increase in household credit can be ascribed to a supply-side relaxation. Declining lending rates, as well as declining spreads between lending and deposit rates, are signals of such a dominant role of supply factors, as illustrated in Figure 16.2.

Looking forward, the dynamics in lending rates will, however, also be affected by shifts in demand and by risk factors. Liquidity constraints broadly reflect the risk associated with the borrower, with the best group of clients today having access to the market and the most risky ones being excluded. In such a context, competition is today fairly high for the clients already in the market, leading to a fast contraction in interest rates. A relaxation of credit constraints is most likely to happen through an expansion of the customer pool, by allowing new clients to have access to credit. If this is the case, the average risk will increase and pricing will have to take account of this, thus leading to a much less rapid contraction in lending margins.

4. HOUSEHOLD DEBT AND SUSTAINABILITY

Overall, current trends in household credit markets can reflect an equilibrium phenomenon in which household credit increases rapidly from extremely low initial levels. The rate of growth of credit indeed appears to respond to changing market conditions on the supply side and to good prospects for income growth. However, this does not imply that the process is free from macroeconomic risks and from risks for the financial sector. In order to understand if current trends can be considered sustainable in the medium to long term, we develop an analysis involving both microeconomic (credit risk) and macroeconomic considerations.

4.1 Microeconomic Sustainability – Credit Risk

Analysing credit risk issues involves two different aspects: sustainability of debt for the household sector and potential vulnerabilities for the banking sector.

Household sector

First we consider the current financial position of households (see Table 16.4). With expectations of rapid income growth and inter-temporal consumption smoothing, it is rational for individuals to increase their indebtedness propensity. Moreover, improved supply conditions and a gradual decrease in credit rationing support an increasing indebtedness of households. But to what extent is this sustainable?

A first indicator to consider is simply the ratio between household debt and GDP, which is still low, especially in comparison with the euro area and the US/UK.[7] Croatia is the country with the highest ratio households debt-to-GDP ratio, which lies at 32 per cent in 2004, followed by Estonia, with a 24 per cent ratio. Still those figures are much lower than the 50 per cent average reported for the euro area countries, even if above those of some more financially developed countries, such as Italy. If we correct indebtedness data for the mortgage component, which is fully backed by real estate values as long as there are no bubbles in the market, indebtedness levels

Table 16.4 Households' indebtedness and degree of leverage

	Household debt/GDP (in %)		(Consumer + other credit)/ GDP (in %)	Household debt/ financial assets[3] (in %)	
	2000	2004	2004	2000	2004
Euro area	46	50	16	23	25[1]
New Europe	7	12	8	15	23
Bulgaria	2	12	9	8	28
Croatia	15	32	20	27	46
Czech Republic	7	14	6	11	21
Estonia	9	24	7	37	83
Hungary	6	20	10	11	36
Latvia	3	19	7	11	29[2]
Poland	10	13	9	23	24
Romania	1	5	4	4	31
Slovakia	5	10	5	10	22
Turkey	6	6	6	11	13

Notes:
1. Figures on gross financial wealth for the euro area are Bank of Italy estimates and relate to 2003.
2. As of 2003.
3. For Estonia, Hungary and Latvia, non-quoted shares, other equity and other account receivables have been excluded from gross financial wealth for homogeneity.

Source: UniCredit New Europe Research Network database, based on national central banks.

range between 4 per cent and 10 per cent, with the only exception being Croatia, which is still above 20 per cent, against 16 per cent at the euro area level. We believe such values are affordable as a whole and do not raise concerns in terms of systemic risks. Problems might arise for specific households, particularly if one considers that debt is not homogeneously distributed at the country and at the regional level, but tends to be concentrated in a small share of the population which is financially active.[8]

Another important indicator is the degree of leverage – that is, the ratio of debt to financial assets. The degree of leverage has risen significantly in converging Europe, jumping from 15 per cent in 2000 to 23 per cent in 2004, very close to the 25 per cent euro area level. Although this is largely due to the wealth gap between the two regions and thus a consequence of historical problems, it points to a potential source of vulnerability. Indeed, New Europe households do not have a financial wealth 'cushion' in the event of adverse macroeconomic events affecting income levels, thus being more vulnerable to potential shocks.

Households moreover tend to be more subject to potential risks arising from interest rate shocks. Note that in every country of the converging Europe group, the cost of debt service shows a clear upward trend, indicating that the impact of growing volumes of debt has more than offset the drop in interest rates.

Another possible area of concern is rising debt in foreign currency (which exposes consumers to heightened exchange rate risks). This is particularly evident in countries where rapid expansion in foreign currency borrowing has been due chiefly to consumers' desire for advantageous interest rates, which they have obtained without considering the speculative implications. Some banks specifically target FX lending products, as they manage to keep margins higher in the context of lower funding costs.

Table 16.5 presents quantitative/qualitative information on households' FX exposure to the FX risk. In particular, we combine data on the percentage of retail lending in FX, qualitative information on the prevalence of euro-denominated or alternative forms of denomination (following households' search for the lowest possible rate), on the relative stability of

Table 16.5 Vulnerabilities to interest rates and FX risk

	Debt servicing payments as a percentage of gross disposable income[1]		Exposure to FX risk			
	2000	2004	% FX over total	Main currency of denomination	Exchange rate risk	Mismatch
Bulgaria	1%	3%	7%	Euro	No – CB	No
Croatia	5%	7%	72%	Euro	Moderate	Yes
Czech Republic	1%	3%	0%	–	–	–
Estonia	1%	2%	56%	Euro	No – CB	Yes
Hungary	2%	5%	9%[2]	Swiss F	Volatile	Yes
Latvia	1%	3%	53%	Euro	No – CB	Yes
Poland	1%	1%	23%	Swiss F	Volatile	Yes
Romania	2%	3%	46%	Euro	Volatile	Yes
Slovakia	1%	2%	0%	–	–	–
Turkey	5%	2%	3%	–	–	–

Notes:
1. Based on own estimates of GDI for all countries except the Czech Republic and Slovakia.
2. If both bank and non-bank lending are included, the ratio is close to 30%.

Source: Own calculation on national central banks' and experts' evaluation for qualitative information.

the national exchange rate against the euro and on households' currency mismatch (measured as matching of deposit denomination to loan denomination). Interestingly, the qualitative information shows that the risk may in fact be slightly lower than the FX exposure figures would imply. This is the case for Croatia, where despite a huge share of FX-indexed loans, households actually also have a large share of deposits in FX and the exchange rate tends to be stable on average against the euro, following a rather strong central bank commitment.[9] In Estonia and Latvia, the existence of a currency board (CB) prevents oscillations of the exchange rate against the euro, in which FX loans tend to be denominated. Risks may be somewhat higher in the Polish, Hungarian and the Romanian case. In Poland, more and more mortgages are denominated in Swiss francs, with individuals clearly taking unhedged speculative positions.

Another source of vulnerability is housing market exposure, in the context of fast increasing debt and fast rising house prices. Despite the clear correlation between house price growth and credit growth, we do not see signals of a potential real estate bubble in the New Europe, with prices still much below those recorded in the neighbouring countries and demand to a large extent being above supply (thus suggesting potential for future growth). A survey of the last issues of the Financial Stability Reports by the supervision authorities of all the markets analysed confirms our idea. Only in Hungary is the central bank actually concerned about a possible excess supply.

On the positive side, one note on financial and real wealth accumulation of households. If we deduct from household debt the mortgage component, assuming that mortgage is largely financing house purchase and thus represents a shift from financial to real wealth, the 'corrected net financial wealth' (measured as financial wealth as a ratio of GDP minus consumer and other credit as a ratio of GDP), is on an increasing path at the regional level on aggregate and in almost all countries (see Figure 16.3). This means that while household debt is rising on aggregate, households at the same time continue to accumulate financial wealth, and the wealth accumulation effect masks the indebtedness effect. This result would imply that households are now facing improving financial conditions, which make debt more convenient. Of course, the sector performance can also hide intra-country differences, with those households getting indebted being different from those able to save. Interestingly, this result is fully consistent with our analysis on liquidity constraints. The corrected net financial wealth figures show negative developments only in a few countries, namely Hungary, Slovakia and Romania.[10]

Banking sector

Finally one consideration coming from the credit supply side, where market conditions have widely improved in the last years. Banks, to a large

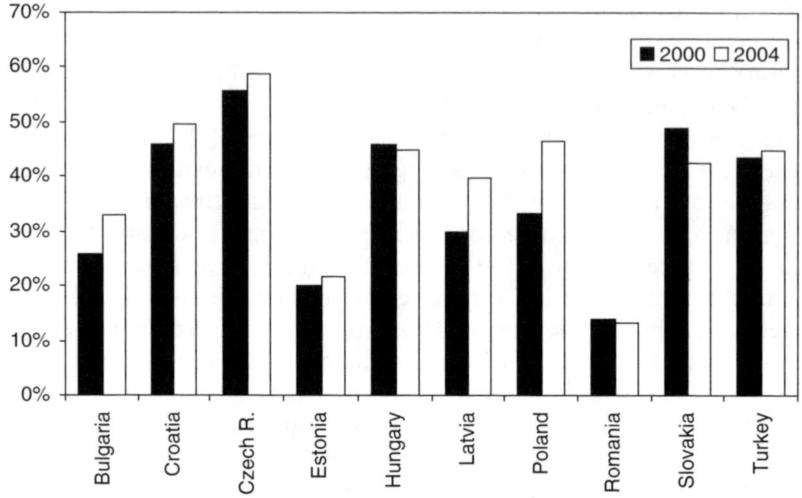

Note: (*) Corrected net financial wealth represents the difference between gross financial wealth of individuals and total liabilities excluding those connected to mortgage loans as a percentage of GDP. For Estonia, Hungary and Latvia, non-quoted shares, other equity and other accounts receivable have been excluded from gross financial wealth for homogeneity.

Source: UniCredit New Europe Research Network database.

*Figure 16.3 'Corrected' net financial wealth as a ratio of GDP**

extent foreign owned, are well managed, credit risk control procedures are clearly in place, banking supervision is strong in all the analysed markets and prudential requirements are strict. Most of the countries have implemented and are implementing credit bureau (see Table 16.6), also providing information on small credits, which allows a monitoring of credit risk both at an aggregate and at the single counterpart level. In such a context, we do not see any potential major problem for the banking sector arising from households' financial behaviour. The only possible source of risk is the external debt financing strategy of banks in some countries. In most cases, such debt is raised from parent companies, which should provide for adequate guarantees. Still, those habits could generate disequilibrium on the macroeconomic side, with banks helping to fuel excessive lending growth and thus with a potential second-round effect on banks.

Overall, while we do not have a final answer to our question on retail lending growth sustainability, we have some evidence showing that on aggregate we do not see major risks on the horizon. Yet we see a potential vulnerability to shocks, both for households and for the financial sector.

Table 16.6 Banking sector stability

	Capital ratios[1]	Credit bureau	ROA[3]	ROE[4]	Banks' external financing[5]
Bulgaria	16.1	Credit bureau system in place, recording all retail loans above BGN 1000 + private run.	2.4	17.3	19.3
Croatia	15.3	In place, recording all loans; reports from credit cards and leasing companies to be introduced soon. First 'positive register' reports expected in January 2006.	1.7	16.1	29.2
Czech Republic	12.6	In place; 3 registers including one for households.	1.7	23.3	Not relevant
Estonia	11.5	In place	2.0[4]	24.3	48.0
Hungary	12.2	In place	1.9[4]	24.9	20.0
Latvia	11.4	In place	1.5[4]	22.8	54.4
Poland	15.5	Two bureau, both private, of which one registers only banking loans, while the second registers any outstanding debt above PLN 200.	1.5	17.6	9.8
Romania	12.0	In place since 2004, with full coverage. 'Positive info' recording – expected to be implemented.	3.1	18	15.8
Slovakia	18.7	In place, recording retail loans of all relevant banks.	1.4[2]	16.4	14.4
Turkey	28.8	In place for consumer credits.	3.0	14.2[3]	11.0

Notes:
1. Overall Solvency Ratio, national central banks and ECB.
2. NPL reports include only loss and substandard categories.
3. Before tax.
4. After tax.
5. External financing is calculated as ratio of foreign liabilities (liabilities to non-residents) to total liabilities as they appear in the Analytical Reporting of Commercial Banks.

Sources: National central banks and UniCredit New Europe Research Network.

4.2 Macroeconomic Sustainability

From a macroeconomic point of view, the main problem is to understand if the current strong and sustained pattern of retail lending growth in the New Europe reflects structural factors or cyclical dynamics, or rather a credit boom fuelling a consumption boom. Understanding this is particularly relevant for designing appropriate policy responses. A permanent expansion of credit beyond the equilibrium level might (but not always does) contribute to the appearance of asset prices bubbles, overheating of the economy, deterioration of the external balance and inflationary pressures, increasing as well credit risk. Most likely this will be the case, when the credit expansion is associated with an irrational consumption boom (Hungarian National Bank, 2005). However, bursting a credit bubble can lead to economic stagnation, with equally long-term negative effects. In such circumstances, and given the fact that it is very difficult to properly identify 'dangerous booms', there are no straightforward policy responses to high credit growth.

We continue to focus only on household consumption and household credit. In order to identify consumption and retail credit booms in our sample, we assume that such episodes arise when consumption/credit is above 1.5 standard deviations from its respective trend. With this measure we identify (Table 16.7) 8 quarters of consumption booms in 4 New Europe countries in the 2000–2004 period, and 13 quarters of credit booms in 5 countries. Only in 2 cases (Hungary 2003 and Turkey 2000), do we see combined credit and consumption booms.[11]

Starting from the above analysis we also investigate the relationship between consumption and credit growth and trade balance deterioration.

Table 16.7 Retail credit and consumption booms

Country	Household credit boom	Consumption boom
Bulgaria	–	–
Croatia	2002q2 and 2003q1	–
Czech Republic	–	–
Estonia	–	2002q3 and 2003q3
Hungary	2002q3, 2003q2 and 2003H2	2003H1and q3
Latvia	–	–
Poland	2000q2	–
Romania	2003q2 and H2	–
Slovakia	–	2002q3 and q4
Turkey	2000H1 and q3	2000q3

Source: Authors' compilation.

Figure 16.4 shows periods of consumption boom (highlighted with a vertical column), the cyclical component of household credit and the threshold for identifying a household credit boom and the trade balance as a ratio of GDP for the country. In the two cases in which a consumption boom is accompanied by a credit boom (Hungary in 2003 and Turkey in 2000), the trade balance is also showing a clear contemporary deterioration, suggesting a possible direct link. In all the other cases we do not detect coincident cases of consumption and credit booms, and the relationship between accelerated growth of the above-mentioned variables and trade balance performance is less straightforward, with some clearer evidence in Romania, Turkey and Latvia.

Our graphical analysis obviously cannot be exhaustive to clarify such important issues. Nevertheless, it suggests interesting future areas of research. We believe it is important to more formally test the relationship and the causality between trade balances and credit growth, splitting between households and corporate credits. To properly design policy responses, we believe it is crucial to clearly understand if the current account deterioration is a consequence of households' or companies' (even small companies') behaviour.

5. CONCLUSIONS

Retail lending grew very fast in the New Europe region in recent years, prompting a debate on whether such a rapid growth can be considered sustainable. We have investigated the main determinants of retail lending growth throughout the region, highlighting the role of liquidity constraints. In particular, we have shown that consumption volatility in New Europe countries tends to be higher than in the euro area and generally higher than income volatility. In some cases, strong volatility is also combined with a strong correlation between consumption and credit, providing first evidence of the existence of liquidity constraints. If this is the case, current trends in household credit markets can reflect an equilibrium phenomenon in which household credit increases rapidly from extremely low initial levels, in the context of a relaxation of liquidity constraints. The rate of growth of credit responds to changing market conditions on the supply side and to good prospects for income growth. In such an environment loosening credit market conditions can have sizeable effects on consumption, which, in some cases, may create macroeconomic imbalances, both in terms of current account deficits and inflationary pressures.

As concerns sustainability, we distinguished micro/banking risks and macro effects. On the micro side, while we do not have a final answer on whether the current phase of retail lending growth is sustainable for

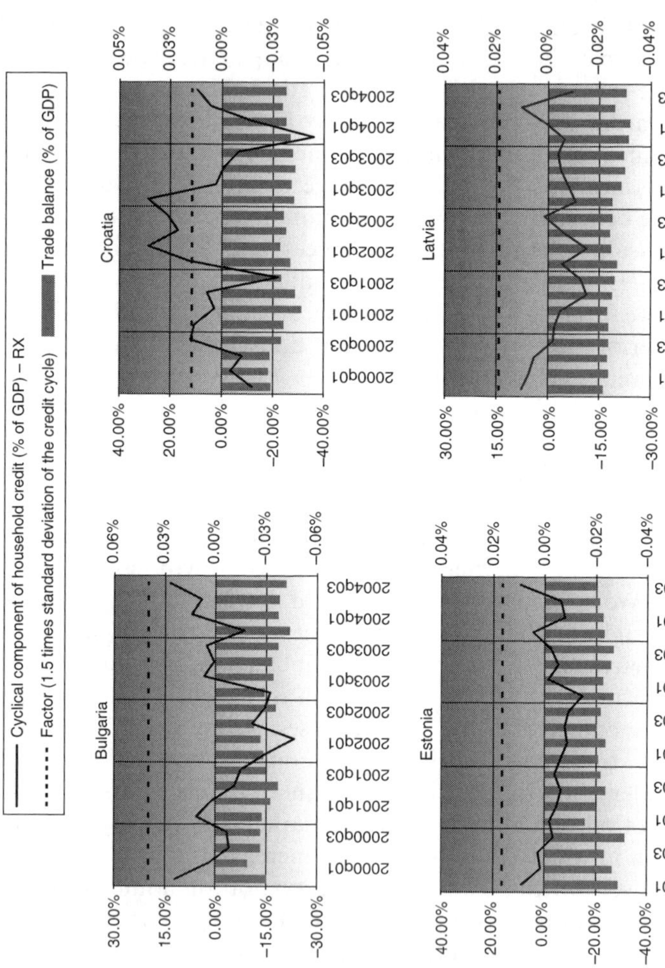

Cyclical component of household credit (% of GDP) – RX
Factor (1.5 times standard deviation of the credit cycle)
Trade balance (% of GDP)
Bulgaria
Croatia
Estonia
Latvia

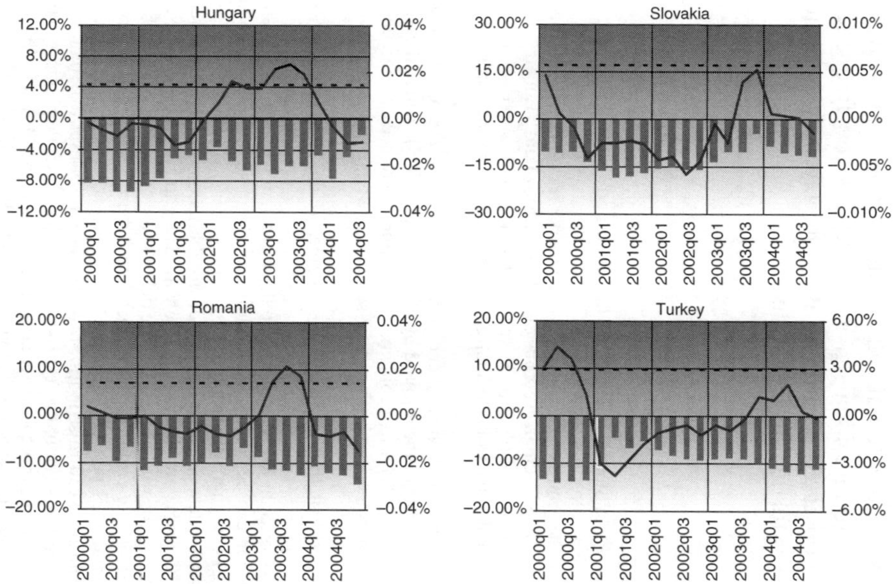

Notes: The series on real credits to individuals and trade balance have been seasonally adjusted using the census X11 additive method. The trend has been extracted using an HP filter with a smoothing parameter of 1600. The dotted line represents in all graphs the absolute threshold used to identify credit boom episodes equivalent to 1.5 times the standard deviation of that country's credit fluctuations around trend. Such a threshold is motivated by the fact that, if credit deviations were normally distributed, there would be a 5 per cent probability of observing these extreme values. Consumption booms have been identified using the same criteria and are represented in all graphs by shadowed areas.

Sources: Trade data: IMF – DOTS based on country's declarations of exports and imports. Credit Data: UniCredit New Europe Research Network database.

Figure 16.4 Credit booms and trade deficit

households, we have some evidence showing that on aggregate we do not see major risks on the horizon. However, we see a higher potential vulnerability to shocks for certain groups of households. On the macro side, the causality link between credit expansion and external balance deterioration is not clear, although our analysis of credit/consumption boom episodes provides in some cases evidence on the relevance of recent boom phases in fuelling a worsening of the trade balance. We believe such evidence is not sufficient to conclude that most external vulnerability problems arise from sustained growth of credit to individuals given the relative low frequency of boom episodes in the observed period and the role played by credit to enterprises, which deserves further investigation.

NOTES

1. Fabrizio Coricelli, University of Siena, University of Ljubljana and CEPR. Fabio Mucci and Debora Revoltella, New Europe Research, UniCredit.
2. We define as New Europe the group of CEE new EU members plus other EU acceding or converging economies. In particular, we consider Poland, Slovakia, Hungary, the Czech Republic, Estonia, Latvia, Bulgaria, Romania, Croatia and Turkey. Due to unavailability of data, Slovenia and Lithuania have been excluded from the analysis.
3. CAGR 2002–2004.
4. The HP filter is sensitive to the beginning and end values of the series. The results highlighted are, however, quite similar to those found by Hilbers et al. (2005), using different methodologies, which accounts for this problem. As a standard remedy to the end-point bias, we ignore two quarters from both ends of samples (that is, every sample ends at 2004).
5. Better if comparison is with volatility of disposable income, which, however, was not available.
6. A forthcoming paper by Coricelli, Mucci and Revoltella shows that roughly 53 per cent of households in the region can be considered liquidity constrained, and among them only a small share (13 per cent) actually has access to credit.
7. It would be better to consider debt as a ratio of gross disposable income (GDI). However, data for gross disposable income are always available with delay and for most countries we only have an estimate. By the way, using GDI, the debt ratio would be 18 per cent for New Europe, compared to 75 per cent in the euro area. Single countries range from 7 per cent (Turkey and Romania) to 51 per cent (Croatia).
8. We do not have data for debt and wealth distribution at the single country level, to be matched with data on income distribution, so actually we do not know if debt is weighting more than average on wealth and income for those who actually have access to credit. However, the cross-country variability suggests some areas of attention, like Bulgaria and Romania, where due to low average per capita income and higher than average credit rationing, as well as lower 'free income', once basic needs are satisfied, the real indebtedness level of those households having access to the credit market could be higher than the average suggests.
9. Note that borrowers may be different from savers. Moreover, we cannot evaluate how much gross disposable income is indexed to FX (some correlation can be assured by the tourism industry, which is quite significant for the Croatian economy).
10. Another thing to note is that households in New Europe can expect a sort of wealth effect, as a consequence of convergence in real assets prices towards those prevailing at the euro area level.

11. Very similar results have been obtained using two alternative criteria. In the first one, real flows of consumption and credit (in level) have been used and deviations from the trend were taken as a percentage of the trend itself. In the second one, flows as a percentage of GDP were used with deviations from the trend measured in percentage terms.

BIBLIOGRAPHY

Aleati, A., M. Consalvi, A. Moneta, F. Mucci and D. Revoltella (2005), 'Households lending market in the enlarged Europe', in G. Bracchi and D. Masciandaro (eds), *Le Banche Italiane e la Finanza per lo Sviluppo*, Edibank.

Bacchetta, P. and S. Gerlach (1997), 'Consumption and credit constraints: International evidence', *Journal of Monetary Economics*, **40**, 207–38.

Bethlendi, A. and Vas E. Nagy (2004), 'Dynamic expansion in the Hungarian consumer lending market in the light of international trends', in *Report on Financial Stability*, Hungarian National Bank, December.

Bokor, L. and G. Pellényi (2005), *Foreign Currency Denominated Borrowing in Central Europe: Trends, Factors and Consequences*, International Center for Economic Growth.

Brzoza-Brzezina, M. (2005), 'Lending booms in Europe's periphery: South-Western lessons for Central-Eastern members', http://akson.sgh.waw.pl/~mbrzez/english/index.htm.

Croatian National Bank (2005), *Macroprudential Analysis*, No. 1, July.

Crook, J. (2003), *The Demand and Supply for Household Debt: A Cross Country Comparison*, Credit Research Centre, University of Edinburgh.

Czech National Bank, *Financial Stability Report*, various issues.

Debelle, Guy (2004), 'Household-debt and the macro economy', *BIS Quarterly Review*, March, pp. 51–64.

De Bondt, G. (1999), 'Credit channels and consumption in Europe: Empirical evidence', *BIS Working Paper*, No. 69, June.

Duenwald, C., N. Gueorguiev and A. Schaechter (2005), 'Too much of a good thing? Credit booms in transition economies: The cases of Bulgaria, Romania, and Ukraine', *IMF Working Paper*, June.

European Central Bank (2003), *Structural Factors in the EU Housing Markets*, March.

European Central Bank (2004a), 'EU measuring financial integration', *Occasional Paper Series*, No. 14, April.

European Central Bank (2004b), *Capital Markets and Financial Integration in Europe*, December.

European Central Bank, *Financial Stability Review*, various issues.

European Central Bank, *EU Banking Sector Stability*, various issues.

Hilbers, P., I. Otker-Robe, C. Pazarbasioglu and G. Johnsen (2005), 'Assessing and managing rapid credit growth and the role of supervisory and prudential policies', IMF WP/05/151, July.

Hungarian National Bank (HNB), *Report on Financial Stability*, various issues.

Mihaljek, D. (2005), 'Rapid expansion of credit in South Eastern Europe: a cause of concern?' Presentation at ICEG EC conference, April.

Polish Central Bank (2004), *Financial Stability Report*.

Uluskula, L., P. Luikmel and J. Kask (2005), 'Critical Levels of Debt?' Bank of Estonia.

PART V

Foreign bank entry and corporate ownership structures: implications for business, competition and profitability

17. Foreign banks in Eastern Europe: mode of entry and effects on bank interest rates

Sophie Claeys and Christa Hainz*

INTRODUCTION

Many emerging countries are hesitant about letting foreign banks enter their market. When deciding on the liberalization of the banking sector, policy-makers weigh the costs and benefits of foreign bank entry on the domestic banks and on the corporate sector. On the one hand, governments fear that foreign banks will engage in *cherry picking*, leaving the domestic banks with bad loans in their portfolio. On the other hand, the local banking market can benefit from the better technologies that foreign banks use through learning and spill-over effects. Through an increase in bank competition, domestic firms may gain by paying lower interest rates for their loans.

The empirical facts about bank market entry differ substantially between regions. In Europe, for instance, foreign bank market share in total banking sector assets amounted to about 55 per cent in 2003 in the new EU member states, while being almost absent in the large EU-15 countries (ECB, 2005). This is surprising, because there are no formal restrictions on market entry. Interestingly, the foreign-owned banks in more developed countries have a lower profitability than domestic banks (Claessens et al., 2001).

Rather the opposite situation is found in emerging markets. In these markets, foreign banks are often more profitable and efficient than domestic banks (Demirgüç-Kunt and Huizinga, 2000; Bonin et al., 2005; Martinez Peria and Mody, 2004). More importantly, foreign bank presence may improve access to credit for creditworthy firms (Giannetti and Ongena, 2005). In Eastern Europe, foreign bank entry has increased competition and improved lending technologies such that lending to small and medium-sized enterprises and retail markets gradually increased (De Haas and Naaborg, 2005).

Policy-makers decide not only on the liberalization of bank entry but often also on the mode of entry. Depending on their evaluation of the entry mode, governments provide incentives that encourage foreign bank entry either through a greenfield investment, by establishing a foreign *de novo* bank, or through acquisition. However, while empirical evidence shows that foreign *de novo* banks are more profitable and efficient than foreign acquired banks (Martinez Peria and Mody, 2004; Majnoni et al., 2003), the differential impact of the mode of entry on domestic bank lending conditions and competition remains unclear.

In this chapter, we shed light on how the impact of foreign bank entry on the host country depends on the *entry mode*. We analyse the impact of the mode of entry on competition. Specifically, we investigate the effects of the mode of foreign bank entry on the lending rate in markets where firms heavily depend on bank financing: are lending rates higher if foreign entry predominantly happens through the establishment of a *de novo* bank or through the acquisition of a domestic bank? Neither the theoretical nor the empirical literature provides complete answers to this question.

We focus on the transition economies of Central and Eastern Europe, where foreign banks are now dominating the market (foreign bank market shares went up from approximately 10 per cent in 1995 to almost 64 per cent in 2003, on average). Furthermore, these markets are characterized by heterogeneous forms of market entry, which moreover vary over time. This allows scope to analyse the direct or initial impact of foreign entry.

THE IMPACT OF THE MODE OF FOREIGN BANK ENTRY ON CREDITOR INFORMATION

In Claeys and Hainz (2006), we develop a theoretical model in which domestic banks possess private information about their incumbent clients but foreign banks have better screening skills. We argue that, after foreign bank entry, information on old and new firms' creditworthiness is unevenly distributed between the foreign and the domestic bank. First, the domestic bank has access to *soft* information on those firms with which it has already established a relationship in the past. This generates an absolute information advantage for the domestic bank about these old firms' creditworthiness. Second, in an emerging market context, the foreign bank is assumed to possess better screening skills than the domestic bank. This implies that the foreign bank will be able to better process *hard* information about new firms that apply for credit through credit evaluation. We show that this information advantage allows the foreign bank to offer slightly lower rates than the domestic bank. However, the information advantage also enables the foreign bank to extract rents from firms that apply for credit for the first time when offering credit contracts. Foreign banks will therefore be able to offer new applicants more competitive rates than the domestic bank. As a result, foreign bank entry will drive down a country's average interest rate for new loans.

However, the foreign bank's scope for extracting rents from new applicants depends on the mode of entry. A foreign *de novo* bank will only enter the market if its advantage in screening new firms compensates for the disadvantage it has compared to the domestic banks with respect to *soft* information about old firms. If a foreign bank acquires a domestic bank, it also acquires the credit portfolio which contains information about the quality of client firms. In addition to this acquired information, the bank possesses superior screening skills compared to domestic banks. The distribution of information between domestic and foreign banks and consequently the degree of competition depend on the mode of entry. We refer to this differential effect as a 'competition effect' that depends on the mode of entry.

This argument indicates that interest rates for new creditors will be lower when the foreign bank enters the market by establishing a foreign *de novo* bank compared to acquiring a domestic bank. However, the average interest rate that a bank demands depends on a bank's portfolio composition of newly applying and old firms. Therefore, we additionally analyse what we refer to as the 'portfolio composition effect'. Old firms might get more favourable rates from their incumbent bank, such that the average lending rate demanded by acquired banks may still be lower than the one from a foreign *de novo* bank.

ENTRY POLICY IN CENTRAL AND EASTERN EUROPE

The diverse process of deregulation in the countries of Central and Eastern Europe led to an uneven reduction of the barriers to entry. The countries that we analyse are Bulgaria, Croatia, the Czech Republic, Estonia, Hungary, Latvia, Lithuania, Poland, the Slovak Republic and Slovenia for the period 1995–2003. These countries have shown widely different policies towards the mode of foreign bank entry.[1] Foreign bank entry was sometimes allowed early in transition – with changing restrictions on the mode of entry.

The example of Poland illustrates how government policy has changed during the last 15 years. In the very beginning of the transition process, bank entry was not regulated. Foreign banks were even given tax holidays. After many small, undercapitalized banks had entered, the minimum capital requirement increased and tax holidays for foreign banks were eliminated. Starting in 1992, the Polish government preferred selling its domestic banks to foreign owners over issuing new bank licences to foreign banks. The aim of the politicians was to sell (often weak) domestic banks to foreign banks, which brought in new capital and had the expertise to restructure these banks. A few banks were privatized between 1993 and 1997, but at the time the government was mainly selling minority shares to foreign investors. In 1999 the government started to sell majority shares of the state-owned banks to foreign investors and allowed foreign banks to open branches without restraints (NBP, 2001).

DATA ON OWNERSHIP STRUCTURE

We want to determine and compare what average lending rates look like if a foreign bank enters either through a *de novo* investment or through acquisition. For this purpose, we create a database that captures the time-varying ownership structure of individual banks in Central and Eastern Europe.

We use yearly data of about 200 individual banks in 10 Eastern European transition countries, for the period 1995–2003. For each country, we gather commercial banks' balance sheets and income and loss accounts from the BankScope database maintained by Fitch/IBCA/Bureau Van Dijk. Consolidated statements were preferred but unconsolidated statements were used when the consolidated one was not available. We obtain historical bank-specific ownership data from central and commercial banks' annual reports. Each bank is classified as either domestically or foreign owned, whereby a foreign bank can be the result of a cross-border acquisition or a greenfield investment. A bank is classified as foreign when at least 50 per cent of its shares are foreign owned. We distinguish between banks that are foreign owned since the start of the sample in the year 1995 and banks that become foreign owned from 1995 onwards. Each foreign bank can enter the sample either as a foreign *de novo* bank or as a foreign acquired bank.

In order to capture the differences in information distribution and screening skills as described above, we assume that for each bank the following events related to acquisition can occur during the sample period:

1. foreign *de novo* bank acquires a domestic bank;
2. foreign acquired bank acquires domestic, foreign acquired or foreign *de novo* bank;
3. foreign *de novo* bank acquires foreign *de novo* bank;
4. domestic bank acquires domestic bank.

For case (1), the merged bank is classified as having entered via acquisition from the date of acquisition onwards. For case (2), banks remain classified as foreign acquired banks. This classification enables us to distinguish between banks which have (a) access to *soft* information but have inferior screening skills (domestic banks), (b) *soft* information and a superior screening ability (foreign acquired banks) and (c) a superior screening ability only (foreign *de novo* banks). For cases (3) and (4) we assume that these mergers simply lead to bigger banks, without generating an impact on information distribution.

SUMMARY STATISTICS

Table 17.1 presents the average percentage of foreign bank presence and market share in total loans by mode of entry for the period 1992–2003.

Foreign bank participation has increased dramatically. In 1992, about 16 per cent of the banks in our sample were foreign owned. Foreign bank presence rose to 57 per cent in 2003, in which year they represent a market share

Table 17.1 Foreign bank presence and market share by mode of entry (%)

Year	Foreign Bank		Foreign MA		Foreign de novo	
	Foreign bank presence (%)	Market share (%)	Foreign bank presence (%)	Market share (%)	Foreign bank presence (%)	Market share (%)
1992	15.96		2.66		13.30	
1993	18.47		3.15		15.32	
1994	20.73		2.85		17.89	
1995	22.39	10.82	3.47	0.82	18.92	10.00
1996	27.05	8.02	5.00	2.48	22.14	5.54
1997	32.75	16.28	10.14	9.76	22.73	6.53
1998	36.65	25.36	12.59	16.74	24.46	8.62
1999	41.25	35.23	15.75	25.38	25.98	9.85
2000	47.03	45.48	21.79	34.18	25.64	11.30
2001	50.66	55.37	25.33	40.64	25.78	14.73
2002	52.63	62.36	29.47	46.65	23.67	15.71
2003	56.93	63.94	33.00	48.34	24.50	15.61
Average	35.21	35.87	13.77	25.00	21.69	10.88

Notes: Foreign MA: a foreign bank that acquires a domestic bank and obtains a majority ownership share. Foreign *de novo*: a foreign bank that enters the market as a *de novo* bank that has a majority foreign ownership share. Foreign bank presence (%) is the relative number of foreign to the total number of banks. Foreign bank market share (%) is the ratio of foreign loans to the country total. The sum of values for Foreign MA and Foreign *de novo* can differ from the value for Foreign Bank due to rounding differences.

Source: Own calculations based on Bankscope, central bank and bank annual reports.

of 64 per cent. In the beginning of the 1990s, the majority of foreign bank entry is via the establishment of a *de novo* bank. While foreign *de novo* banks represent on average 22 per cent, foreign bank acquisitions account for 14 per cent. However, foreign acquired banks gradually increase their presence over the years and represent 33 per cent of all banks in our sample by 2003. Foreign acquisitions eventually become the dominant mode of entry: banks that were foreign acquired between 1992 and 2003 have a market share of 25 per cent, on average, while foreign banks that entered the Central and Eastern European banking markets through a *de novo* investment have on average a market share of 11 per cent. Since foreign acquired banks buy a customer base, their market share grows much faster than that of *de novo* banks. In 2003, foreign acquired banks possess a market share of 48 per cent whereas foreign *de novo* banks only have 16 per cent of the credit market.

Figures 17.1 and 17.2 show how foreign bank presence varies over countries and over time, by mode of entry. Figure 17.1 presents the percentage of foreign bank presence; Figure 17.2 shows market shares starting from 1995.

The figures reveal some important differences between the countries. The figures show that countries that had already joined the European Union in May 2004 differ from those applying for membership in 2007. In Bulgaria and Croatia, the neighbours of the enlarged European Union, the market share of foreign banks is about 46 per cent and 36 per cent respectively in 2003 and thereby remains significantly lower than in the other eight countries.

In Hungary, foreign banks already outnumbered domestic banks in 1993. Due to the Hungarian liberalization strategy that started in the early 1980s, the share of foreign banks has gradually risen and now represents more than 70 per cent of the market. In the beginning of the 1990s, the Czech Republic and the Polish banking sector were also characterized by a large inflow of foreign *de novo* banks. The cumulative market share for *de novo* banks is, however, relatively small (7 and 17 per cent) compared to the market share for *de novo* banks in Hungary (24 per cent). In 1999 the Polish government started to sell majority shares of domestic banks to foreign investors. This led the number of foreign banks in Poland to exceed the number of domestic banks in 1999 and to dominate the market in terms of market share from 2000.

The Baltic countries started liberalizing market entry into the banking sector relatively late. Therefore, the changes observed are even more dramatic. Estonia, for example, has only three foreign-owned banks (AS Sampo Pank, Hansabank and Eesti Uhispank), but Hansabank alone accounts for over 70 per cent of assets from 2001 (Claeys and Hainz, 2005). Thus, banking in Estonia can be considered as predominantly a foreign affair.

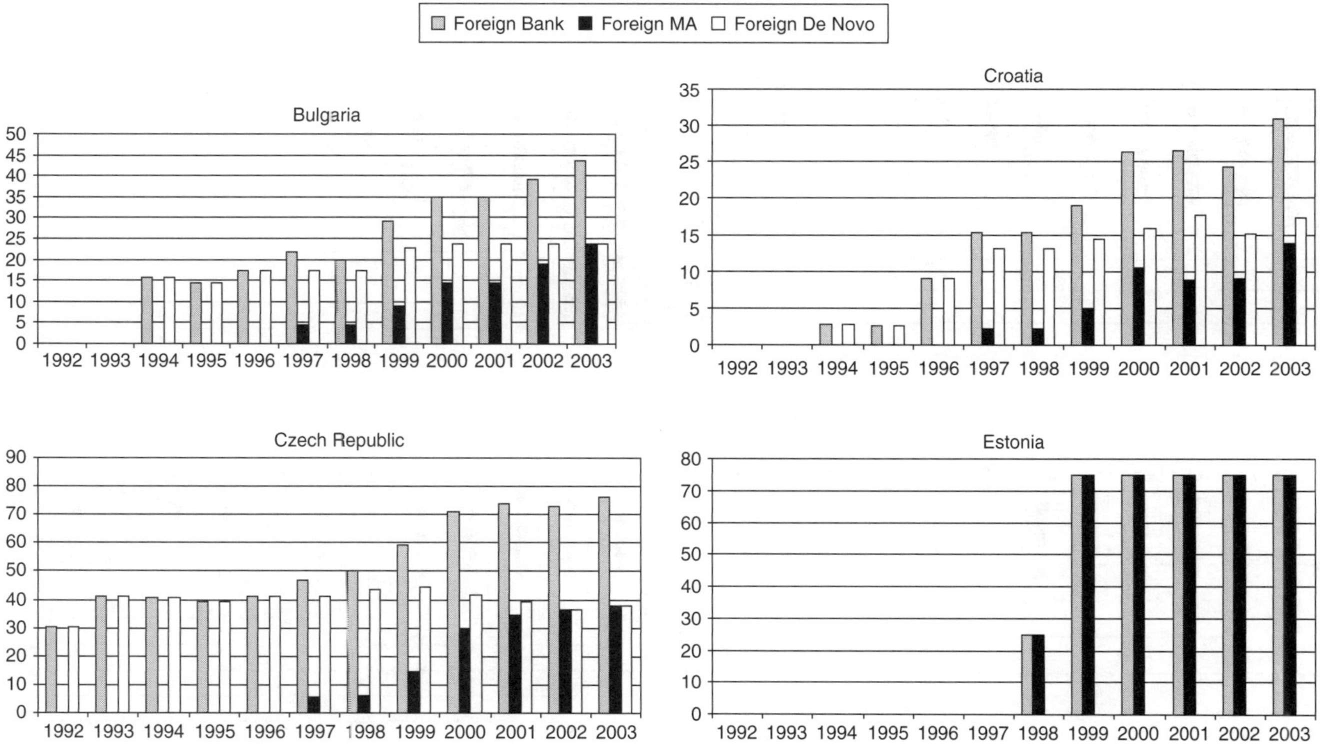

Foreign Bank
Foreign MA
Foreign De Novo
Bulgaria
Croatia
Czech Republic
Estonia

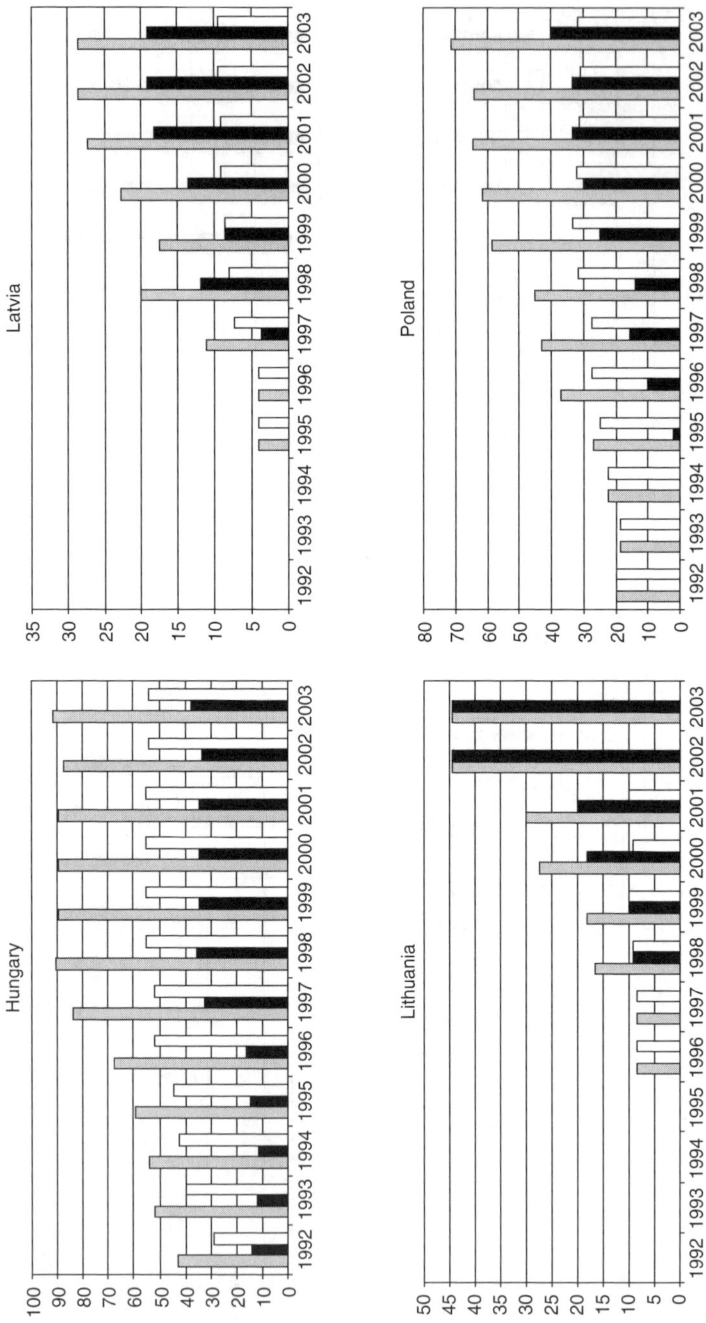
Hungary
100 90 80 70 60 50 40 30 20 10 0
1992 1993 1994 1995 1996 1997 1998 1999 2000 2001 2002 2003
Latvia
35 30 25 20 15 10 5 0
1992 1993 1994 1995 1996 1997 1998 1999 2000 2001 2002 2003
Lithuania
50 45 40 35 30 25 20 15 10 5 0
1992 1993 1994 1995 1996 1997 1998 1999 2000 2001 2002 2003
Poland
80 70 60 50 40 30 20 10 0
1992 1993 1994 1995 1996 1997 1998 1999 2000 2001 2002 2003

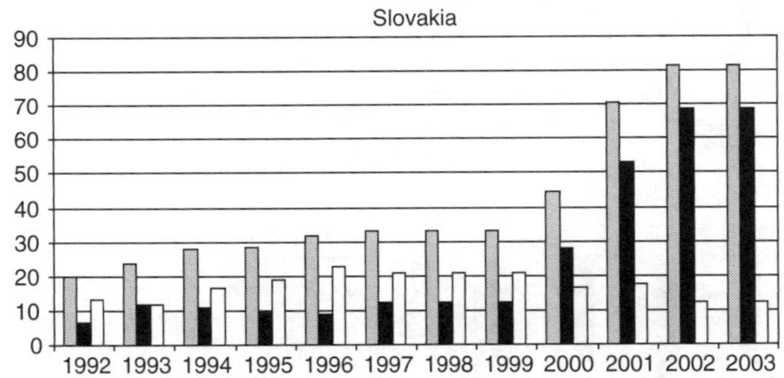

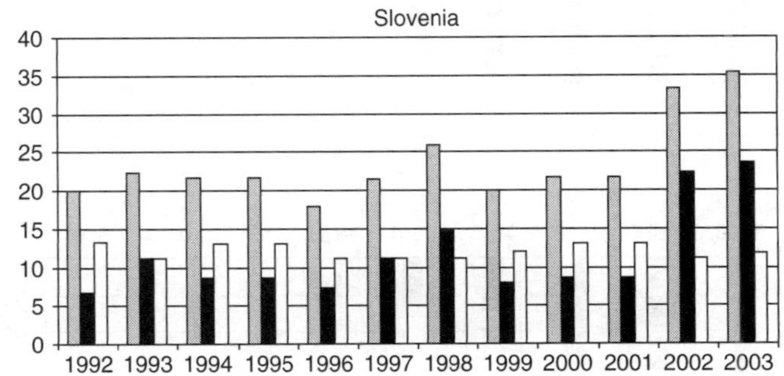

Source: Own calculations based on Bankscope, central banks and bank annual reports.

Figure 17.1 Foreign bank presence by mode of entry (%)

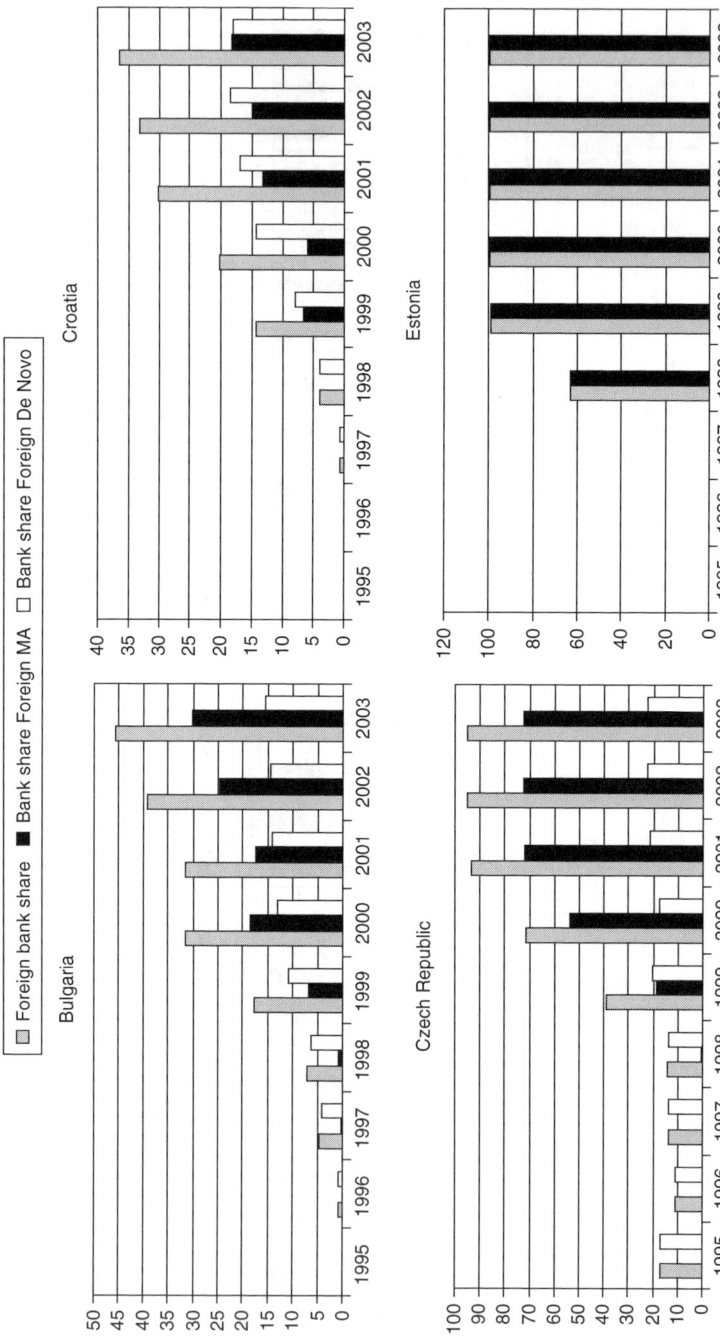

Foreign bank share
Bank share Foreign MA
Bank share Foreign De Novo
Bulgaria
Croatia
Czech Republic
Estonia

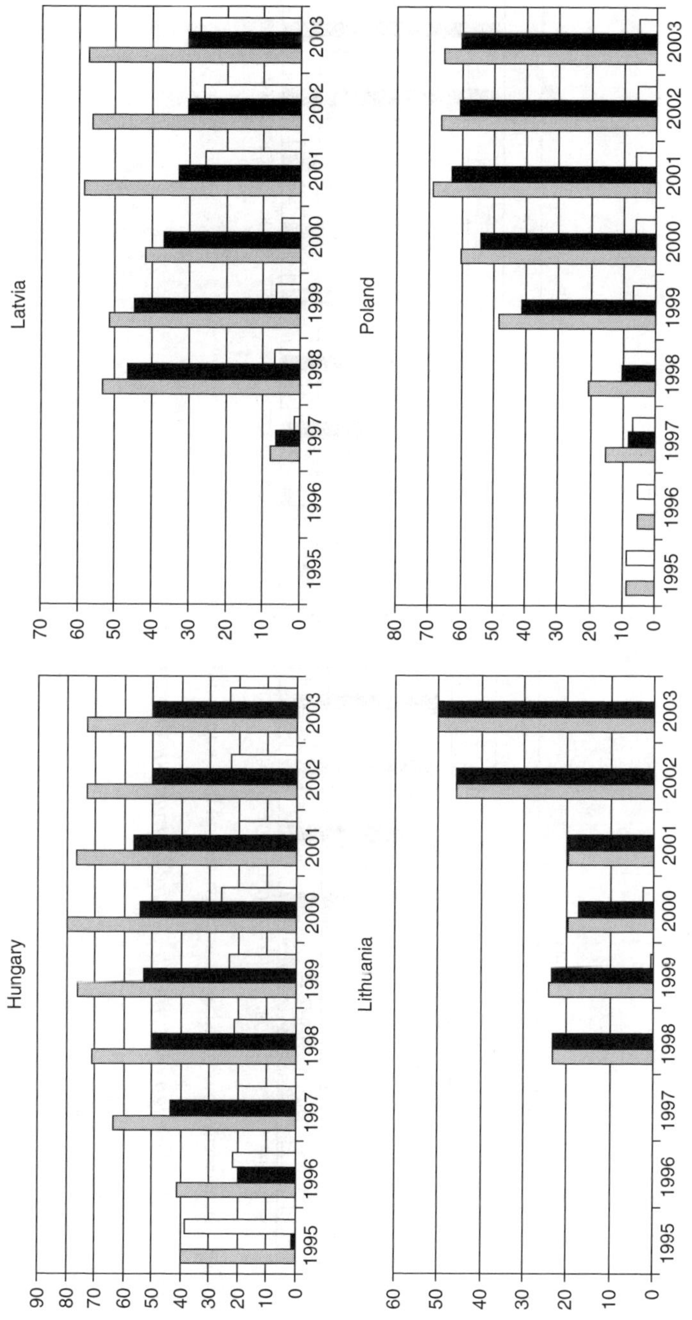
Hungary
Latvia
Lithuania
Poland
1995
1996
1997
1998
1999
2000
2001
2002
2003

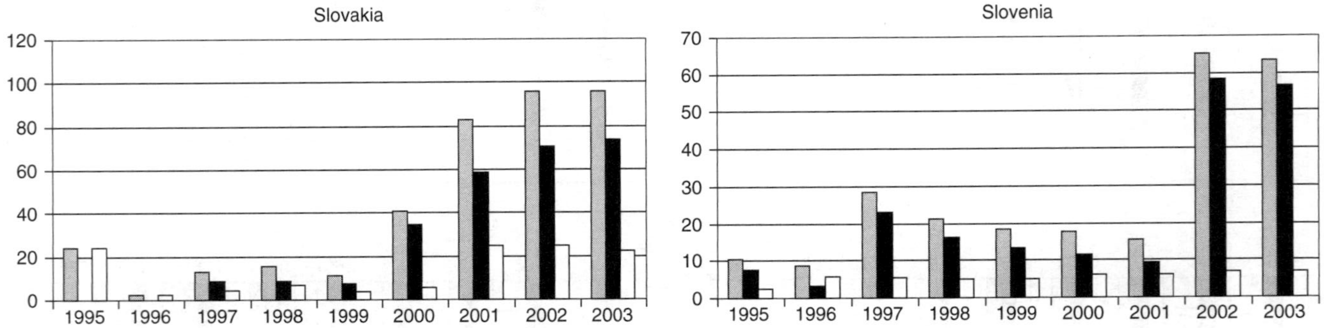

Source: Own calculations based on Bankscope, central banks and bank annual reports.

Figure 17.2 Foreign bank market share by mode of entry (%)

In Slovakia, foreign banks had already entered in the early 1990s but they did not become significant players before the year 2000. Although Slovenia is characterized by a relatively low percentage of foreign bank presence, foreign banks obtained over 60 per cent of bank loans by 2002. These loans are almost exclusively granted by foreign acquired banks. Foreign *de novo* banks hardly play a role on the credit market in Slovenia.

Figures 17.1 and 17.2 illustrate that there is a considerable amount of foreign entry occurring in most countries included in our sample. Furthermore, the market shares of foreign banks have gradually risen and are starting to dominate the market. Together with the increase in foreign acquisitions, banking markets became more and more concentrated. This resulted in an average market share of almost 60 per cent held by the top three banks per country.

EVOLUTION OF BANK LENDING RATES BY OWNERSHIP STRUCTURE

Figure 17.3 presents the evolution of average bank lending rates and foreign bank market shares between 1995 and 2003. Compared to Western Europe, bank interest rates are still relatively high, but decreased significantly from 22 per cent in 1995 to 13 per cent in 2003. At the same time, foreign bank market shares increased dramatically to about 64 per cent.

In Claeys and Hainz (2006), we perform a regression analysis which confirms that a higher foreign bank share in loans negatively impacts the average lending rate, which supports the competition effect that we describe above. Moreover, we document that an increase in foreign *de novo* market share leads to a bigger reduction in *domestic* bank average lending rates compared to the reduction following an increase in foreign acquired market share. This indicates that competition is more intense when entry predominantly happened through foreign *de novo* investments.

Since we cannot disentangle individual bank–firm relationships through bank balances, we cannot observe the share of old and new firms that apply for credit at the bank. We do, however, observe the average interest rate that banks charge to both types of customers. Figure 17.4 graphically illustrates how the average lending rate evolves per year after the foreign bank has entered the market, by mode of entry. Figure 17.4 also shows the evolution of domestic bank interest rates over the years after entry. From the figure it is clear that on average, foreign banks charge lower interest rates than domestic banks (15.5 and 18.5 per cent respectively). However, in the first year after entry, foreign and domestic bank lending rates do not differ

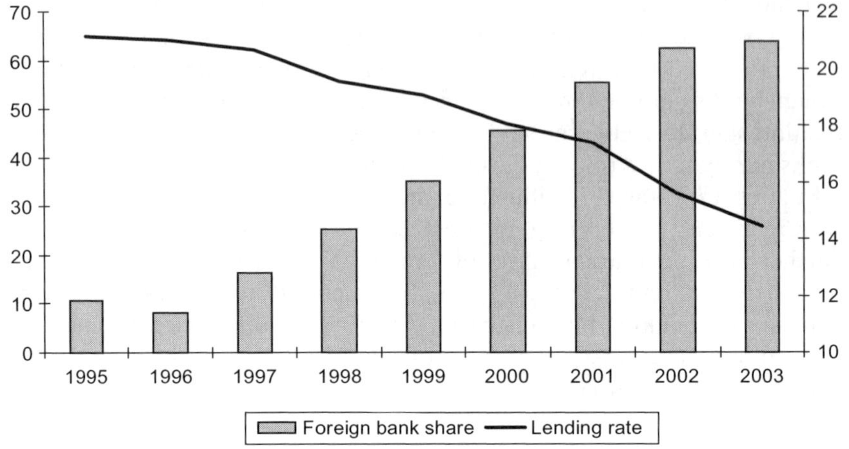

Note: Bank lending rates (%) are calculated as interest income over (2-year) average loans (3-year moving average). Foreign bank market share (%) is the ratio of foreign loans to the country total.

Source: Own calculations based on Bankscope, central banks and bank annual reports.

Figure 17.3 Evolution of bank lending rates (right scale) and foreign bank market share (left scale) (%)

significantly. Furthermore, domestic banks have been operating longer in the market compared to foreign banks. One corollary of this is that in the first year after entry, foreign banks may be charging higher rates than domestic banks that have been in the market longer at that time. However, foreign banks reduce their lending rates much faster compared to domestic banks after entry.

Indeed, using regression analysis, we find that foreign acquired banks charge between 1 and 2 per cent less than domestic banks, while foreign *de novo* banks charge, on average, almost 1 per cent more than domestic banks. Furthermore, while foreign acquired banks already charge less in the first year after acquisition, foreign *de novo* banks initially charge higher lending rates than domestic banks, but quickly reduce their interest rate in the first years after entry. Finally, our results point out that foreign *de novo* banks charge higher lending rates than foreign acquired banks, which indicates that the loan portfolio composition effect dominates the competition effect. The loan portfolio composition effect allows both the domestic and the foreign acquired banks to charge lower average lending rates.

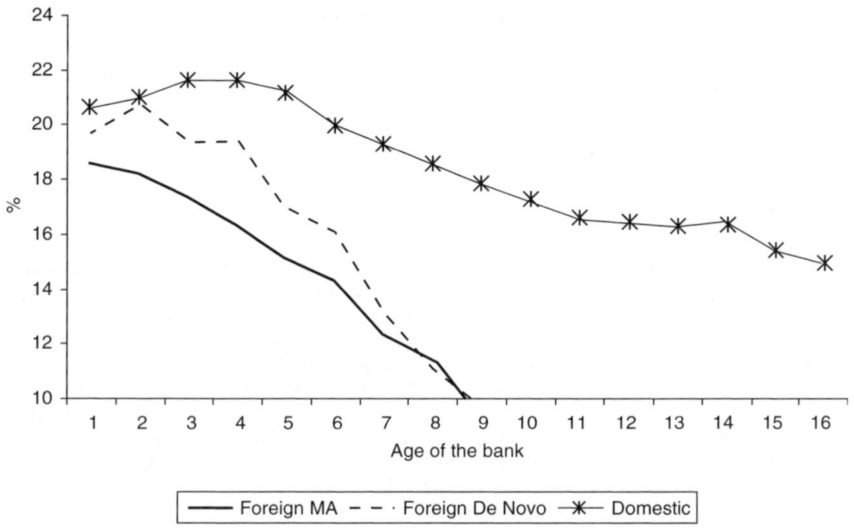

Notes: Bank lending rates (%) are calculated as interest income over (2-year) average loans (3-year moving average). *Foreign MA:* a foreign bank that acquires a domestic bank and obtains a majority ownership share. *Foreign De Novo*: a foreign bank that enters the market as a *de novo* bank that has a majority foreign ownership share. *Domestic*: a domestic bank.

Source: Own calculations based on Bankscope, central banks and bank annual reports.

Figure 17.4 Average lending rates by mode of entry: evolution per year after entry

CONCLUSION

Credit markets in many Eastern European countries are now dominated by foreign-owned banks. This ownership structure resulted from the liberalization of foreign bank entry in the early 1990s and the privatization of state-owned banks, mainly by selling majority shares to foreign investors. The majority of loans from foreign banks are granted by acquired banks. The presence of foreign acquired banks as measured by their relative number among the banks in our dataset increased somewhat more slowly than that of foreign *de novo* banks. However, since market entry through acquisition allows acquiring a credit portfolio and a customer base, acquired banks were able to expand their market share much faster than the foreign *de novo* banks. Our results also show that the interest rate decreased after foreign bank entry. Moreover, while the reduction in domestic interest rates is more pronounced in the case of foreign entry through a *de novo* investment, foreign *de novo* banks charge higher interest rates than foreign acquired banks. This result is consistent with the prediction of our theoretical analysis according to which competition increases more if the foreign bank enters as a *de novo* bank.

NOTES

* Sophie Claeys: Department of Financial Economics and CERISE, Ghent University, W. Wilsonplein 5D, B-9000 Ghent, Tel. 32-9-264 34 91, Fax. 32-9-264 89 95, e-mail: sophie.claeys@ugent.be. Sophie Claeys gratefully acknowledges financial support from the Programme on Interuniversity Poles of Attraction of the Belgian Federal Office for Scientific, Technical and Cultural Affairs, contract No. P5/21. Christa Hainz: Department of Economics, University of Munich, Akademiestraße 1/III, 80799 Munich, Tel.: 49-89-2180 3232, Fax. 49-89-2180 2767, e-mail: christa.hainz@lrz.uni-muenchen.de. Christa Hainz gratefully acknowledges financial support from the European Central Bank under the Lamfalussy Fellowship Program and from the Deutsche Forschungsgemeinschaft through SFB/TR 15 Governance and the Efficiency of Economic Systems. Any views expressed are only those of the authors and do not necessarily represent the views of the ECB or the Eurosystem.

1. For an overview, see Bonin et al. (1998). For a detailed listing on foreign *de novo* entry, foreign and domestic mergers and acquisitions between 1990 and 2003 in Central and Eastern Europe, we refer to Claeys and Hainz (2005).

REFERENCES

Bonin, John P., Iftekhar Hasan and Paul Wachtel (2005), 'Privatization matters: Bank efficiency in transition countries', *Journal of Banking and Finance*, **29** (1), 31–53.

Bonin, John P., Kalman Miszei, István P. Székely and Paul Wachtel (1998), *Banking in transition economies: Developing market-oriented banking sectors in Eastern Europe*, Cheltenham, UK and Northampton, MA, USA: Edward Elgar.

Claessens, Stijn, Asli Demirgüç-Kunt and Harry Huizinga (2001), 'How does foreign entry affect domestic banking markets', *Journal of Banking and Finance*, **25**, 891–911.

Claeys, Sophie and Christa Hainz (2005), 'Acquisition versus Greenfield: The mode of foreign bank entry in Central and Eastern Europe: Data appendix', mimeo.

Claeys, Sophie and Christa Hainz (2006), 'Acquisition versus Greenfield: The impact of the mode of foreign bank entry on information and bank lending rates', mimeo.

De Haas, Ralph and Ilko Naaborg (2005), 'Does foreign bank entry reduce small firms access to credit? Evidence from European transition economies', *De Nederlandsche Bank Working Paper*, No. 50, August 2005.

Demirgüç-Kunt, Asli and Harry Huizinga (2000), 'Determinants of commercial bank interest margins and profitability: Some international evidence', *World Bank Economic Review*, **13**, 379–408.

European Central Bank (ECB) (2005), *EU Banking Structures*, October 2005.

Giannetti, Mariassunta and Steven Ongena (2005), 'Financial integration and entrepreneurial activity: Evidence from foreign bank entry in emerging markets', mimeo, Stockholm School of Economics.

Majnoni, Giovanni, Rashmi Shankar and Eva Vàrhegyi (2003), 'The dynamics of foreign bank ownership: Evidence from Hungary', *World Bank Policy Research Working Paper*, 3114, August.
Martinez Peria, Maria Soledad and Ashoka Mody (2004), 'How foreign participation and market concentration impact bank spreads: Evidence from Latin America', *Journal of Money, Credit and Banking*, **36** (3), 511–37.
National Bank of Poland (NBP) (2001), 'The Polish Banking System in the Nineties', NBP Research Paper.

18. Ownership structures and investment in transition economies

Dennis C. Mueller and Evgeni Peev*

1. INTRODUCTION

In Eastern Europe, the modernization of privatized firms (former state socialist enterprises) and the growth of newly established private firms depend on efficient investment policies.[1] Some recent studies have examined the effects of corporate governance on investment performance in Western countries.[2] However, only a few studies focus on the effects of ownership structures on investment in transition countries.[3] This chapter has two major goals: (a) to measure the returns on company investment across Central and Eastern Europe (CEE) and compare them with companies in the 'old' European Union countries (EU-15); (b) to compare ownership structures of public firms in CEE and EU countries and measure investment performance by ownership groups in CEE countries. In the next section, we discuss the main hypotheses of the study. Section 3 presents the methodology employed for estimating returns on investment and the data used to test the hypotheses. The empirical results are analysed in section 4 and discussion on the key findings is presented in the last section.

2. HYPOTHESES

In Eastern Europe, the institutional environment has three key characteristics.

1. All transition economies have a civil-law tradition as in continental Europe. Candidates for EU membership have adopted civil-law type institutions to facilitate their adjustment to the EU legal environment. In many CEE countries, however, there still exists a gap between law development and law enforcement. The written laws are similar to or even better than those in the EU-15 countries, but law enforcement is rather inefficient.[4]

2. Some studies show that despite major differences in privatization policies, the striking outcome after more than ten years of transition process is the emerging ownership concentration and convergence of financial and legal systems in CEE countries (Berglöf and Bolton, 2002). Ownership structures of non-financial firms measured by the share of the largest owner have become fairly concentrated. The major corporate governance conflict is between the controlling shareholder and minority shareholders (Berglöf and Pajuste, 2003).
3. Bank-based financial systems have emerged with foreign-owned commercial banks prevailing. Most stock exchanges are very illiquid and only a small number of firms are actively traded. The number of firms listed on local stock exchanges after mass privatization has steadily decreased and market capitalization is very low. This has occurred despite both the global tendency toward corporate governance convergence on the Anglo-American system, and efforts in the 1990s to develop the capital market in CEE countries.

We maintain that the civil law legal system, more fragile capital markets and emerging concentrated ownership in Eastern Europe lead to country corporate governance systems with weak protection of shareholders' rights. In these corporate governance systems, managers usually have high discretion over cash flows; they pay out less in dividends and pursue growth strategies investing in unprofitable projects. We test for CEE countries whether the average firm has poorer investment performance measured by its returns on investment relative to its cost of capital than the average firm in both Western Europe and Anglo-American countries.

The profitability of investment opportunities varies both across countries and within them. Even in countries with weak protection of property and shareholders' rights, some firms have high returns on investment, and may have difficulties financing their investment. Thus, we hypothesize that in CEE countries for firms with attractive investment opportunities, the returns on investment are greater than the firms' costs of capital.

We now discuss some conventional hypotheses about investment performance by owner identities in CEE countries. In CEE countries, a common view is that firms controlled by foreign investors have easier access to external finance and Western markets, and that they benefit from low-cost management know-how transfers from abroad. On the other hand, we cannot necessarily expect agency problems in firms under foreign control to be less severe than in domestically-controlled firms. Foreign firms are also susceptible to high managerial discretion and the crucial question concerns the differences in *degree* of their agency problems. Thus, we can expect less severe asymmetric information problems in firms under foreign control compared to the domestic firms, but we cannot make any predictions about their agency problems without information about the ultimate owners of foreign firms. We thus test for firms under foreign control if investment performance is better than in firms under domestic control.

Similar considerations can be presented for firms where dominant shareholders are financial institutions. The financial owners may mitigate the asymmetric information problems between managers and external capital markets, but they themselves may also suffer from agency problems. Furthermore, financial institutions are a rather heterogeneous group of investors (for example banks, mutual funds, insurance companies and so on). Thus, we test for any systematic difference in investment performance of firms controlled by financial institutions in general and by banks and non-bank financial owners in particular, but make no predictions.

State-owned companies before their privatization are a part of the emerging transitional ownership structures. After the collapse of planning, state-owned firms faced daunting restructuring tasks to adjust to the new semi-market conditions. Most state-owned firms were used to soft budget constraints. We shall test whether these firms preserve their inefficient investment behaviour even in late transition years. Alternatively, one might expect that the development of legal and financial systems during transition has gradually increased the fiscal discipline and budget constraints at least for state-owned firms in most advanced transition economies joining the EU. We shall test for firms under state control if investment performance is poorer than in firms under private control.

Domestic holding companies (ex-privatization funds) have ownership structures similar to corporate pyramids. Pyramid structures consist of a chain of owners with an ultimate owner who has control over all firms in the chain. The literature reveals that the typical agency issues include expropriation of small shareholders through income shifting (Morck et al., 2000), tunnelling (Johnson et al., 2000), and large family shareholder entrenchment. In some CEE countries, domestic-controlled firms with formal headquarters in offshore zones have emerged. Anecdotal evidence suggests that companies with offshore owners have been involved in capital flight. We expect *re-distribution* activities to be prevalent in these firms. Thus, we hypothesize that for firms controlled by 'transitional owners', investment performance is poorer.

3. METHODS AND DATA

Studies usually apply Tobin's q (defined as the ratio of market value of a firm to replacement costs of the firm's capital stock) to control for a firm's investment opportunities. However, Tobin's q reflects the average return on a firm's capital, but relevant for investment is the *marginal* return on capital. The methodology introduced by Mueller and Reardon (1993) and applied by Gugler et al. (2004) addresses these issues. It uses estimates of marginal q to measure investment performance.

Let I_t be a firm's investment in period t, CF_{t+j} the cash flow this investment generates in $t+j$, and i_t the firm's discount rate in t.[5]

$$PV_t = \sum_{j=1}^{\infty} \frac{CF_{t+j}}{(1+i_t)^j} \tag{18.1}$$

We can then take PV_t from (18.1) and the investment I_t that created it, and calculate the ratio of pseudo-permanent return r_t to i_t, a ratio that we call q_{mt}

$$PV_t = \frac{I_t r_t}{i_t} = q_{mt} I_t \tag{18.2}$$

If the firm had invested the same amount I_t in a project that produced a permanent return r_t, this project would have yielded the exact same present value as the one actually undertaken. The market value of the firm at the end of period t can be defined as

$$M_t = M_{t-1} + PV_t - \delta_t M_{t-1} + \mu_t \tag{18.3}$$

where δ_t is the depreciation rate for the firm's total capital as evaluated by the capital market, and μ_t is the market's error in evaluating M_t. Subtracting M_{t-1} from both sides of (18.3) and replacing PV_t with $q_{mt} I_t$ yields

$$M_t - M_{t-1} = q_{mt} I_t - \delta_t M_{t-1} + \mu_t \tag{18.4}$$

That q_{mt} is a marginal q can easily be seen from (18.2) and (18.4) by contrasting it with (average) Tobin's q. Tobin's q is the market value of the firm divided by its capital stock and equals the ratio of the return on its total assets to its cost of capital.[6] Thus, it is a measure of *average* return on capital. Marginal q equals the change in the market value of a firm divided by the change in its capital stock (investment) that caused it.

Two key features of q_{mt} are worth noting. First, its use as a measure of performance obviates the need to calculate company costs of capital. Equations (18.2) and (18.4) define the *ratio* of a company's return on investment to its cost of capital, which is precisely the statistic needed to test hypotheses about agency problems. Second, the procedure for calculating q_{mt} allows for different degrees of risk across companies. The stock market will demand a greater future stream of cash flows from an investment of 100 before it raises the market value of a high-risk company by 100, than it demands of a low-risk company. The assumption of capital market efficiency implies that the error term in (18.4) has an expected value of zero, and thus that equation (18.3) can be used to estimate both $*_t$ and q_{mt} under the assumption that they are either constant across firms or over time, or both. Dividing both sides of (18.4) by M_{t-1} yields

$$\frac{M_t - M_{t-1}}{M_{t-1}} = -\delta + q_m \frac{I_t}{M_{t-1}} + \frac{\mu_t}{M_{t-1}} \tag{18.5}$$

Equation (18.5) is our basic equation for estimating returns on investment by both countries and ownership categories. Equations (18.4) and (18.5) incorporate the assumption that the market value of a firm at the end of year $t-1$ is the present discounted value of the expected profit stream from the assets in place at $t-1$. Changes in market value are due to changes in assets in place as a result of investment and depreciation. To calculate q_{mt}, one needs an estimate of the depreciation rate of a firm's total capital, δ, where the value of this capital is measured by the market value of the firm. The depreciation rate depends on the composition of tangible and intangible assets in total market value, and these will differ across industries. We assume that industry depreciation rates are constant over time, and use a variant of equation (18.4) to estimate a separate δD.

To estimate (18.5) we need data on the market value of each firm and its investments. The market value of a firm at the end of year t, M_t, is defined as the market value of its outstanding shares at the end of year t plus the value of its outstanding debt. The market value of the firm equals the market value of common equity (share price at the end of the fiscal year times common shares outstanding) plus the book value of total debt (the sum of total short- and long-term debt). An accurate estimate of the market value of debt requires knowledge not only of the associated coupon and maturity structure, but also of the credit quality of each component. Because such information is not available from standard data sources, we use the book values. Since the firm's market value reflects the market's evaluation of the firm's total assets, we wish to use an equally comprehensive measure of investment. Accordingly we define investment as

$$\begin{aligned} I = {} & \text{After tax profits} + \text{Depreciation} - \text{Dividends} \\ & + \Delta\text{Debt} + \Delta\text{Equity} \end{aligned} \tag{18.6}$$

where ΔDebt and ΔEquity are funds raised using new debt and equity issues.

All financial variables are deflated by the consumer price index and are expressed in real 1999 US dollars.

The data are taken from the 2005 version of the Amadeus data set. Amadeus contains ownership, accounting and market data on 1464 non-financial public companies listed in Eastern Europe. We also use the latest versions of Osiris and COMPUSTAT data sets as complementary sources of financial data. Market data are also collected from local stock exchanges in CEE countries and from company websites. In Eastern Europe, most public companies are not actively traded and the quality of information they provide is poor. After excluding companies for which investment and market values were not available for all of the period 1999–2003 and the obvious outliers in the data, the number of companies reduces to 151. These are the non-financial companies in CEE countries whose shares were most traded on local stock exchanges, had the highest degree of information disclosure to the general public, and were likely to be included in country stock exchange indexes in Eastern Europe. Thus, our sample is biased toward the 'blue chips' in the region.

4. COMPANY INVESTMENT IN TRANSITION ECONOMIES

Table 18.1 presents the results of estimating equation (18.5) by constraining all companies in a country to have the same return on investment relative to the cost of capital (q_m). We allow for individual industry depreciation rates defined by 2-digit NACE. The estimated returns on investment are 77 per cent of company costs of capital in the pooled group of CEE countries. This is consistent with our first hypothesis that corporate governance and legal systems in CEE countries are too weak to provide protection of shareholders' rights against managerial opportunism, and thus the marginal returns on investment of the average firm are less than its cost of capital.

Among the countries in Central Europe, the worst performer was the Czech Republic with a q_m of 0.64; Hungary (0.75) was in between; and Poland had a q_m of 1.20. The highest returns on investment were for Slovenia ($q_m = 1.59$), Estonia (1.20) and Poland. However, there is no evidence that corporate governance systems in these countries are sufficiently stronger than in other CEE countries. One possible explanation for these results is that Slovenia, Estonia and Poland had better investment opportunities over the period 1999–2003 than other European transition

Table 18.1 Returns on investment (q_m) by country

Eastern Europe	q_m	t-value	Obs.	Firms	Western Europe	q_m
Czech Republic	0.64	6.34	143	38	Austria	0.71
Hungary	0.75	5.89	59	16	Germany	0.57
Poland	1.20	5.22	94	36	France	0.57
Slovakia	0.81	4.35	24	8	Denmark	0.65
Slovenia	1.59	5.19	32	12	Finland	0.96
Estonia	1.25	1.13	18	10	Sweden	0.65
Latvia	0.66	13.44	24	8	Great Britain	0.85
Lithuania	0.64	3.06	11	4	Ireland	1.10
Bulgaria	0.89	5.73	31	10		
Romania	0.70	4.83	12	6		
Croatia	0.79	2.78	9	3		
Transition economies	0.77	10.44	456	151	Anglo-Saxon legal system	1.02
CEE-5 countries[1]	0.84	8.30	348	110	Scandinavian legal system	0.78
Baltic states	0.64	10.47	53	22	German legal system	0.74
Accession countries[2]	0.69	5.1	51	19	French legal system	0.59

Notes:
1. The group of CEE countries includes Czech Republic, Hungary, Poland, Slovakia and Slovenia.
2. The group of accession countries includes Bulgaria, Romania and Croatia. The table presents the results of estimating equation (18.5) by constraining all companies in a country to have the same return on investment relative to the cost of capital (q_m). We allow for individual depreciation rates defined by 2-digit NACE. The equation has an adjusted R^2 of 0.58. The number of observations is 457. All t-values are robust to heteroscedasticity (White, 1980).

Source: Authors' calculations. The estimates for Western Europe are from Gugler et al. (2004, Table 18.2).

economies. The hypothesis that for firms with attractive investment opportunities the returns on investment are greater than the firms' costs of capital possibly fits their data better.

The right side of Table 18.1 presents estimates of q_m for Western European countries.[7] There are some obvious difficulties in such a comparison. First, our sample includes mainly public companies *actively* traded on local stock exchanges in Eastern Europe, with most being included in the country stock indexes, while the Gugler et al. (2004) study includes virtually all public companies in Western Europe. Another possible bias is due to the different sample periods studied; 1993–2003 in our study and 1985–2000 in the study of Gugler et al. (2004). These problems aside, the preliminary evidence suggests a convergence of investment performance between the new EU members and EU-15 countries. Estimates of q_m for most transition countries are comparable to those for the Germanic (0.74) and Scandinavian legal systems (0.78). The *average* firm in Eastern Europe has an investment performance (q_m) lower than in the Anglo-Saxon countries with their strong shareholders rights' protection, but at the same time has a higher q_m than in EU countries with French-origin legal systems (for example France, Greece, Italy, Portugal, Spain).

The ownership structures of non-financial public companies in CEE and Western European countries are summarized in Table 18.2. Ownership concentration is high in most CEE countries with the median largest shareholder owning around 50 per cent of outstanding shares. Countries with the lowest ownership concentration are Poland (largest median shareholding of 31.29 per cent), Slovenia (36.75) and Hungary (39.95). After about 15 transition years and a number of policy actions to develop active capital markets of the Anglo-Saxon type, the emerging ownership structures in Eastern Europe are nevertheless converging on the model of concentrated ownership typical for countries in Continental Europe.

Ownership concentration of non-financial public firms in the pooled group of CEE countries (49.9) is slightly higher than in the Continental European countries (40.74), but is quite a bit higher than in Anglo-Saxon countries like Great Britain (11.99), and the United States (14.43). There are some well-known explanations for the high ownership concentration observed in countries with civil law systems. The key arguments are based on the predictions of the 'law and finance' literature – in countries with weak shareholders' rights protection, large shareholdings become an essential corporate governance mechanism for monitoring managers, substituting the disciplining role of the large shareholder for that of the market for corporate control. This seems a plausible explanation for the degree of ownership concentration in the transition countries.[8]

Table 18.2 also describes the identity of the largest *direct* shareholders in CEE countries using a typical classification scheme for the key ownership categories in developed economies: individual/family, financial firm, non-financial firm, the state and dispersed ownership. We follow the approach applied in the studies of Western Europe and identify the controlling owner as the largest shareholder holding 20 per cent or more of the outstanding shares. Firms controlled by a bank, mutual fund, pension fund, a domestic private (ex) privatization fund, insurance company, or other financial institution are categorized as financial firm-controlled. In most CEE countries, non-financial firms are the prevailing largest shareholders. The second most important largest shareholders are the state (Czech Republic, Slovenia) and financial institutions (Slovakia, Estonia), while for Poland

Table 18.2 Ownership concentration and identities in Eastern and Western Europe

Country	No. firms	Mean largest holder	St. dev. largest holder	Median largest holder	Family holdings	Financial holdings	Non-financial holdings	State holdings	Dispersed holdings
Czech Republic	38	63.55	22.04	54.2	0	0.105	0.553	0.316	0.026
Hungary	16	35.27	22.57	39.95	0	0.25	0.312	0.062	0.375
Poland	36	34.25	19.32	31.29	0.055	0.167	0.444	0.055	0.278
Slovakia	8	58.27	28.21	51.81	0	0.25	0.625	0.125	0
Slovenia	12	40.91	23.74	36.75	0	0	0.375	0.375	0.25
Estonia	10	56.56	20.51	55.25	0.1	0.2	0.6	0.1	0
Latvia	8	52.30	18.42	47.2	0.285	0	0.715	0	0
Lithuania	4	34.76	18.43	47.2	0	0.25	0.25	0.25	0.25
Bulgaria	10	61.1	25.6	75	0	0	0.70	0.30	0.1
Romania	6	47.5	13.04	52	0.167	0	0.333	0.125	0
Croatia	3	52.13	29.13	62.34	0	0.67	0	0	0.33
European transition countries	151	47.92	24.68	49.9	0.044	0.154	0.463	0.176	0.154
Continental Europe	594	42.05	25.41	40.74	0.152	0.164	0.425	0.039	0.219
Great Britain	439	16.23	13.85	11.99	0.086	0.082	0.109	0.000	0.723
United States	1760	19.85	14.80	14.43	0.292	0.089	0.113	0.001	0.505

Note: The controlling owner is defined as the largest shareholder holding 20 per cent or more of the shares outstanding. Firms controlled by a bank, mutual fund, pension fund, a domestic private (ex) privatization fund, insurance company or other financial institution are categorized as financial holdings.

Source: Authors' calculations. Data for the non-transition economies are from Gugler et al. (2004, Table 18.3).

and Hungary the second most important ownership category is dispersed ownership (no shareholder holds as much as 20 per cent of the outstanding shares). The emerging ownership categories of non-financial public companies in Eastern Europe are rather similar to the typical ownership identities in Western Continental Europe. In the pooled group of CEE countries, 46 per cent of firms are controlled by non-financial firms, followed by firms controlled by financial institutions and companies with dispersed ownership (both with 15.4 per cent), while for the Continental European countries the most important category of king of controlling shareholders is also non-financial firms (42 per cent of firms), followed by firms with dispersed owners (21.9), and firms controlled by financial institutions (16.4).

In Table 18.3 we focus on some ownership categories which are more typical in post-communist countries than in Western Europe. One may argue that in countries with weak corporate governance systems and higher ownership concentration as in CEE, the 20 per cent criterion for identification of the controlling party is too low. Therefore, we have also applied a 50 per cent or more cut-off to identify the majority owner.[9] The left part of Table 18.3 presents the results. In the pooled sample of CEE countries, 48 per cent of companies have a majority owner with a non-financial firm being the majority shareholder in around a quarter of the companies, and the state in about 15 per cent. Foreign owners (foreign state, foreign financial institutions, foreign holding groups, foreign firms, and foreign individuals) are the largest shareholders in 33 per cent of the companies in our sample. Foreign majority participation is concentrated in Hungary (56 per cent of majority owners), Slovakia (33), the Czech Republic (32), and Poland (30).

Financial institutions are typically not majority owners in non-financial public companies in CEE (0.07 per cent of firms). However, the real *participation* of financial institutions in ownership structures is underestimated using both the 20 and 50 percentage criterion to identify the controlling shareholder. In the right side of Table 18.3, we identify additional ownership categories focusing on the presence of financial owners in the ownership structures of public companies in CEE. Firms in which bank(s) only or bank(s) and other financial institutions hold ownership stakes are classified as firms with bank owners. The similar criterion is applied for firms with non-bank owners. These are firms with non-bank financial institutions in their ownership structures. Finally, companies with financial owners are those with at least one financial institution owning their outstanding shares. Financial institutions hold ownership stakes in 58 per cent of CEE non-financial public companies in our sample. Respectively, for banks this figure is 27 per cent, while for

Table 18.3 Majority shareholders, financial institutions and transitional owners

Country	No. firms	Majority owner	State majority owner	Non-financial majority owner	Foreign largest owner	Financial majority owner	Financial owners	Bank owners	Non-bank owners	Transitional owners
Czech Republic	38	0.710	0.289	0.368	0.316	0.053	0.237	0.026	0.210	0.263
Hungary	16	0.437	0.062	0.187	0.562	0.187	0.875	0.375	0.5	0.062
Poland	36	0.222	0	0.194	0.305	0.028	0.639	0.305	0.334	0.167
Slovakia	8	0.5	0.125	0.25	0.333	0.125	0.833	0.5	0.333	0.083
Slovenia	12	0.375	0.25	0.125	0	0	0.75	0.25	0.5	0.625
Estonia	10	0.7	0.1	0.3	0.4	0.1	0.9	0.8	0.1	0.2
Latvia	4	0.286	0	0.286	0.5	0	0.25	0	0.25	0
Lithuania	8	0.25	0.25	0	0.5	0	0.75	0.5	0.25	0
Bulgaria	10	0.80	0.20	0.40	0.1	0	0.3	0.3	0	0.6
Romania	6	0.667	0.5	0.167	0.167	0	0.5	0	0.5	0.5
Croatia	3	0.667	0	0	0	0.667	1.00	0.667	0.333	0.333
Transition countries	151	0.478	0.147	0.243	0.333	0.073	0.581	0.269	0.312	0.206

Notes: *Financial owners*: companies with financial owners are those that have at least one financial institution owning their outstanding shares. *Bank owners*: companies in which bank(s) only or bank(s) and other financial institutions hold ownership stakes. *Non-bank owners*: companies in which non-bank financial institutions hold ownership stakes. *Transitional owners*: companies in which the state, privatization funds, domestic holding companies (some of them ex-privatization funds), insiders (managers and employees), and offshore owners (owners registered in offshore zones) hold ownership stakes.

Source: Authors' calculations.

the non-bank financials (mutual funds, insurance companies, for example) it is 31 per cent. This evidence suggests a massive participation of financial institutions in the ownership structures of non-financial public companies in Eastern Europe. It varies by country with the highest estimates for Estonia (90 per cent of companies), Hungary (88), Slovakia (83), and Poland (64). In the Czech Republic, the corresponding figure is a fairly moderate 24 per cent.

We also identify a specific ownership category labelled 'transitional owners'. It includes such diverse owners as the state, privatization funds, domestic holding companies (some of them ex-privatization funds), insiders (managers and employees), and offshore owners (owners registered in offshore zones). All of these ownership categories are specific for the post-communist transformation from state to market, and we expect them to have a different investment behaviour. The 'transitional owners' held ownership stakes in about 20 per cent of the companies with a significant participation in Slovenia and the Czech Republic.

Table 18.4 presents estimates of returns on investment (q_m) by ownership categories. All ownership categories have returns on investment less than their costs of capital. This is strong evidence for the importance of managerial discretion and weak corporate governance structures in CEE countries. However, significant differences exist in the magnitudes of over-investment by ownership groups.

We test the hypothesis that foreign owners mitigate asymmetric information problems between company managers and external capital markets. This hypothesis was partly corroborated. A company under control by a foreign owner has a *relatively* better investment performance than the other firms in our sample, but its returns on investment are still only 92 $(0.73 + 0.19)$ per cent of its cost of capital.

The overall effect of the financial owners on company investment performance is negative but statistically insignificant using a 20 per cent cut-off (column 1), and significantly negative using a 50 per cent cut-off (column 2). When we separate the financial institutions into banks and non-banks, however, the differences are striking (column 3). Banks have a positive and significant effect on returns on investment, increasing q_m by 16 per cent, while non-bank financial institutions (mutual funds, for example) have an opposite effect. They decrease q_m by 20 per cent and this difference from the overall average (0.77) is also statistically significant. The estimates suggest an effective role of banks in decreasing agency problems. The non-bank financial institutions do not seem to play this role, however.

The coefficients for both the state and 'transitional' owners are positive but small and statistically insignificant. They do not corroborate the more

Table 18.4 Returns on investment (q_m) by ownership categories

Types of owners	I	II	III	IV	V
Non-financial[1]	0.25	0.14			
t-value	3.52	1.63			
Financial	−0.15	−0.22			
t-value	−1.38	−1.88			
State	0.08	0.06			
t-value	0.69	0.52			
Dispersed	−0.139	0.02			
t-value	−0.95	0.24			
Bank owners[2]			0.16		
t-value			2.68		
Non-bank owners			−0.20		
t-value			−3.32		
Non-financial owners			0.04		
t-value			0.67		
Foreign[3]				0.19	
t-value				1.69	
Transitional[4]					0.09
t-value					0.71
q_m	0.73	0.79	0.77	0.73	0.76
t-value	12.15	16.66	8.78	8.78	9.92
Obs.	415	415	426	426	426
Adj. R^2	0.57	0.57	0.57	0.55	0.55

Notes:
The table reports the effect of ownership categories. We interact the ownership dummies with the investment term on the right-hand-side of equation (18.5), and include them along with investment in the specifications. All t-tests are based on White (1980) standard errors. The equations include industry and year dummies (not reported).
(1) Specification I uses 20 per cent cut-off and specification II uses 50 per cent cut-off for identification of owners.
(2) In specification III, for bank owners and non-bank owners, see Table 18.3, Note. Companies with non-financial owners are those that have no financial institution owning their outstanding shares.
(3) In specification IV, foreign owners are defined as the largest owners with foreign origin.
(4) In specification V, for transitional owners, see again Table 18.3, Note.

Source: Authors' calculations.

pessimistic expectations about the inefficient behaviour of these owners. The estimates suggest the hardening of budget constraints for the state and a decrease in the opportunities for primitive accumulation of capital and redistribution of funds for the other transitional ownership categories.

5. DISCUSSION

Most studies on financial integration have focused on the convergence of legal systems, capital markets and law enforcement between the EU-15 countries and CEE. In this chapter, we found that the investment performance (q_m) of the average public non-financial firm in CEE is fairly similar to the corresponding estimates for countries with Germanic and Scandinavian legal systems. The investment performance of CEE companies was better than that of the average firm in EU countries with French-origin legal systems (for example France, Greece, Italy, Portugal, Spain), but worse than in the Anglo-Saxon countries. Thus, this chapter provides evidence for a *functional* convergence of public non-financial companies in CEE countries to those in the West.

Our research supports previous studies of ownership structures in the CEE region. We show that ownership concentration of non-financial public firms in the pooled group of CEE countries is slightly higher than in the group of continental European countries and much higher than in Anglo-Saxon countries like Great Britain, Ireland or the United States. The ownership categories of non-financial public companies in Eastern Europe are similar to the ownership identities in Western Continental Europe. In the pooled group of CEE countries, 46 per cent of the firms are controlled by non-financial firms, followed by firms controlled by financial institutions and companies with dispersed ownership, while for the Continental European countries the prevailing controlling shareholders are also non-financial firms (42 per cent), followed by firms with dispersed owners and those controlled by financial institutions.

We paid special attention to the role of non-bank financial institutions and banks as shareholders in CEE and their effects on investment performance. We identified not only firms whose largest shareholders are financial institutions, but also the group of companies with *any* financial institution (bank, mutual fund, insurance company and so on) owning their outstanding shares. The overall effect of financial owners on investment performance is negative; however, companies with bank owners have higher returns on investment by 20 per cent, while companies with non-bank financial institutions (mutual funds, for example) as shareholders show opposite results. These estimates suggest an effective monitoring role of banks as *minority* shareholders in mitigating agency problems.

For the other ownership categories, companies under control by a foreign owner have *relatively* better investment performance than the average firm in our sample, but their returns on investment are still less than their cost of capital ($q_m = 0.92$). The estimates for the state and the other 'transitional' owners do not corroborate the more pessimistic conventional views. The results suggest a hardening of budget constraints for the state and the other transitional owners over the late transition period (1999–2003).

NOTES

* Dennis C. Mueller is Professor at the University of Vienna; Evgeni Peev is Visiting Professor at the University of Vienna and Senior Research Fellow at the Institute of Economics, Bulgarian Academy of Sciences. The authors thank Zsuzsanna Fluck for her valuable comments. The research in this article was supported in part by a Marie Curie Intra-European Fellowship within the 6th European Community Framework Programme.

1. There is a handful of papers on investment behaviour in transition economies (see for example Lizal and Svejnar (2002) for firms in the Czech Republic during the 1992–98 period; Budina et al. (2000) for Bulgarian firms over the period 1993–95; Konings et al. (2002) for firms in Poland, the Czech Republic, Bulgaria and Romania during 1994–99).
2. For dividend payments, see La Porta et al. (2000); Faccio et al. (2001); for returns on investment see Mueller and Yurtoglu (2000); Goergen and Renneborg (2001); Gugler et al. (2004).
3. See for example Perotti and Gelfer (2001) for Russia; Durnev and Kim (2003) for an international comparative study; Peev (2004) for methodological problems.
4. See for example Pistor (2000).
5. This methodology was developed by Mueller and Reardon (1993).
6. Let M be the market value of a firm, K its total assets, ra the return on these assets, i its cost of capital, π profits, and q Tobin's q. Then $q = M/K$, $M = \pi/i$, and $\pi = raK$. Substituting first for π and then for M, we get $q = (raK/i)/K = ra/i$.
7. Gugler et al. (2004).
8. However, one must mention an important caveat when measuring ownership concentration in both EU-15 and CEE countries. The usual estimates are based on the share of the direct largest shareholder, but the major unresolved issue is rather who are the actual ultimate owners; see for example Mueller et al. (2003) for Bulgaria.
9. This 50 per cent criterion is typical in many studies of ownership structures in transition economies.

REFERENCES

Berglöf, Erik and Patrick Bolton (2002), 'The great divide and beyond: Financial architecture in transition', *Journal of Economic Perspectives*, **16** (1), 77–100.

Berglöf, Erik and Anete Pajuste (2003), 'Emerging owners, eclipsing markets? Corporate governance in Central and Eastern Europe', in P.K. Cornelius and B. Kogut (eds), *Corporate Governance and Capital Flows in a Global Economy*, Oxford: Oxford University Press.

Budina, Nina, Harry Garretsen and Eelke de Jong (2000), 'Liquidity constraints and investment in transition economies: The case of Bulgaria', *Economics of Transition*, **8**, 453–75.

Durnev, Art and E. Han Kim (2003), 'To steal or not to steal: Firm attributes, legal environment, and valuation', William Davidson Working Paper Number 554.

Faccio, Mara, Larry Lang and Leslie Young (2001), 'Dividends and expropriation', *American Economic Review*, **91**, 54–78.

Goergen, Marc and Luc Renneboog (2001), 'Investment policy, internal financing and ownership concentration in the UK', *Journal of Corporate Finance*, **7**, 257–84.

Gugler, Klaus, Dennis C. Mueller and B. Burcin Yurtoglu (2004), 'Corporate governance and the returns on investment', *Journal of Law and Economics*, **47** (2), 598–633.

Johnson, Simon, Rafael La Porta, Florencio Lopez-de-Silanes and Andrei Shleifer (2000), 'Tunnelling', *American Economic Review*, **90** (2), 22–7.

Konings, Jozef, Marian Rizov and Hylke Vandenbussche (2002), 'Investment and credit constraints in transition economies: Micro evidence from Poland, the Czech Republic, Bulgaria and Romania', LICOS Discussion Paper 112.

La Porta, Rafael, Florencio Lopez-de-Silanes, Andrei Shleifer and Robert W. Vishny (2000), 'Agency problems and dividend policies around the world', *Journal of Finance*, **55**, 1–33.

Lizal, Lubomir and Jan Svejnar (2002), 'Investment, credit rationing and the soft budget constraint: Evidence from Czech panel data', *Review of Economics and Statistics*, **84** (2), 353–70.

Morck, Randall K., David A. Stangeland and Bernard Yeung (2000), 'Inherited wealth, corporate control, and economic growth', in Randall Morck (ed.), *Concentrated Corporate Ownership*, Chicago: University of Chicago Press.

Mueller, Dennis C. and Elizabeth Reardon (1993), 'Rates of return on corporate investment', *Southern Economic Journal*, **60** (2), 430–53.

Mueller, Dennis C. and B. Burcin Yurtoglu (2000), 'Country legal environments and corporate investment performance', *German Economic Review*, **1** (2), 187–220.

Mueller, Dennis C., Helmut Dietl and Evgeni Peev (2003), 'Ownership, control and performance in large Bulgarian firms', *Journal for Institutional Innovation, Development and Transition*, **7**, 71–88.

Peev, Evgeni (2004), 'Theory of the firm, corporate governance and determinants of investment in transition economies: Methodological notes', University of Vienna, mimeo.

Perotti, Enrico C. and Stanislav Gelfer (2001), 'Red barons or robber barons? Governance and investment in Russian financial-industrial groups', *European Economic Review*, **45**, 1601–17.

Pistor, Katharina (2000), 'Patterns of legal change: Shareholder and creditor rights in transition economies', *European Business Organizations Law Review*, **1**, 59–100.

White, Halbert (1980), 'A heteroskedasticity-consistent covariance matrix estimator and a direct test for heteroskedasticity', *Econometrica*, May, **48** (4), 817–38.

19. Ownership competition in the European transition arena: towards a viable restructuring?

Diana Pop and Julien Le Maux*

1. INTRODUCTION

The structural reforms and institutional changes performed in the former socialist countries in the last two decades have removed the M&A frontier that used to divide continental Europe. Over several years, the transition process was shaped by the transfer of state assets into private property. The pace of capital transfer was shaped by both the initial conditions for and the sequencing of privatization. It is now broadly documented that acquisitions could be accommodated more easily in countries that gave the green light for privatizations early on (Hungary, Poland and the Czech Republic). The entry strategies adopted by foreign investors varied from joint ventures to acquisitions of controlling stakes, sometimes even 100 per cent of the company capital, based on the business climate in Eastern Europe economies and the propensity of authorities to open capital to investors. Controlling the capital of companies was a necessary condition (albeit not a sufficient one) for imposing the rate of restructuring and for advancing the development of those countries.

After 15 years of transition a broad consensus has emerged around the positive effect of privatization on company restructuring. The aggregate results of many studies investigating the antinomy between state and private ownership in Central and Eastern Europe (CEE) emphasize the superior abilities of private investors in improving the companies' performance[1] (Konings, 1997; Smith et al., 1997; Frydman et al., 1999; Claessens and Djankov, 2002). However, the economic implications of the capital transfer into private hands were generalized based on an asymmetric analysis favouring the transition leaders (for example, the Czech Republic).

This chapter aims to contribute to the debate on the achievement of restructuring objectives in the CEE countries by enlarging the scope of analysis on recent data of Croatian and Romanian listed companies. In this respect, we focus on the expertise mix of different blockholders sharing the control of public companies along three dimensions: the ownership concentration, the distribution of voting power among large shareholders, and the identity of owners. The objective of our approach is to assess whether the private owners were able to commit to a viable restructuring[2] by assuring a prevailing growth in the European transition arena. Following the argument of disciplinary role assumed by dominant shareholders, we are interested in finding out whether the internal governance is effective as would be revealed by the persistence of positive effects identified by previous studies on the transition economies.

The remainder of the chapter is organized as follows. Section 2 presents the configuration of the internal governance mechanism, by investigating the main post-privatization regulations affecting the concentration and interactions among shareholders. In section 3 we justify the extension of the previous research on the role of ownership structure in transition economies. Section 4 describes the sample selection procedure, as well as the restructuring and corporate governance variables. Section 5 studies the effects of ownership concentration and the distribution of voting power among large shareholders on the economic performance of public companies. Section 6 summarizes our findings and concludes.

2. CORPORATE GOVERNANCE: STYLIZED FACTS FROM CROATIA AND ROMANIA

Having reformed ownership rules for small firms before the critical regime change, Croatia was counted among the advanced reformers in terms of the EBRD's Transition Indicators at the beginning of 2000, with an average transition indicator comparable with that of the new EU countries. With a Performance Indicator of 2.8, Romania was classified as an intermediate reformer by contrast. Nevertheless, the two countries were assigned comparable Governance and Restructuring and Securities Markets & Non-bank Financial Institutions indicators. Four years on, there was little obvious further reform progress. The governance and the quality of financial institutions improved from 2.3 to 3 for Croatia, while they remained unchanged for the Romanian economy.[3]

Although the governments proposed different privatization schemes, refined analysis of the development of financial markets (Berglöf and Pajuste, 2003) proved that the early laggards have recovered the initial discrepancy. Ownership has become concentrated either following privatization transactions or subsequent purchases on the capital market. The typical case of the Romanian experience, as presented in Telegdy et al.

(2002) and Brown et al. (2004), provides additional support for this assertion. In the current context, the monitoring performed by active large shareholders is considered the only viable option available in young markets (Berglöf and Pajuste, 2003). The other options, such as disciplinary market for corporate control, proxy fights, shareholders' litigation, have limited impact as long as much progress has to be done for promoting an enforceable legal system.[4]

The exposure of public companies to market judgement and the new wave of harmonizing the national regulations on acquisitions according to the European standards offer new directions for analysing the control system designed by privatization. The European authorities proposed to member and ascending states that they would adopt takeover regulation in a way that would 'prevent patterns of corporate restructuring from being distorted by arbitrary differences in governance and management cultures' (see Directive 2004/25/EC, §3).

The need for a Corporate Governance Code and straightforward rules regarding the transfer of property among private investors has become stringent since there is an enhanced demand of shareholders for transparency and efficient monitoring of listed companies. The corporate governance objectives have also been defined as a function of the peculiarity of control structures driven by acquisition decisions. Consequently, the form and scope of regulations have emerged as a natural answer of authorities to investors' concerns regarding the property rights of minority shareholders, as well as the fair competition for control. Under the pressure of consolidation of control, every country imposed mandatory rules, whenever some capital thresholds are exceeded. From this point of view there are two remarkable differences among the takeover regulations of the two countries.

The first one regards the disclosure requirements imposed upon shareholders of public companies. Croatian companies must report their ten major shareholders, irrespective of the size of their holdings. In Romania, between 2000 and 2003, ownership of 5 per cent of capital or more qualified investors as a 'significant shareholder' and put them under an obligation to disclose their identity. According to takeover literature,[5] the secret accumulation of capital directly on the market represents the main source of gain for acquirers, whenever free rider behaviour of the target company's shareholders or competition threatens the success of acquisition. Consequently, the decision of market authorities related to disclosure thresholds influences the gain sharing between the acquirer and the target's shareholders.

The second particularity, as subtle as the previous one, is related to the preoccupation for promoting the protection of minority shareholders via mandatory bid rules. The Croatian Corporate Takeover Procedures Act (2002) establishes a minimum threshold for making a public offer at 25 per cent of the total number of votes in joint-stock companies. If further acquisitions of shares of the same issuer were to entitle an investor to more than 75 per cent of shares carrying voting rights, he or she has to publish a new takeover bid. In Romania the rules have been changed several times since the promulgation of the first takeover procedure in 1996. For several years there were only two bid thresholds: 33 per cent and 50 per cent. The market law and the takeover regulation from 2002 stipulate two further obligations for investors whose shareholdings exceed 75 per cent and 90 per cent of the voting rights of a public company. In the latter case, the major shareholder has to buy out all the remaining shares and transform the company into a privately-held company.[6] Detailed information about the public offers' characteristics are presented in Pop (2006).

It seems obvious that the Croatian regulation has a more dissuasive effect on prospective riders, as the market may identify even the small shareholders (less than 5 per cent) and the first threshold for making a public offer is set at 25 per cent of capital compared with 33 per cent in Romania. However, in both countries obligations for acquirers have been set in order for the private investors' interests not to bind those of the state. Requiring an equal treatment for all the shareholders of a company means eliminating any control premium. Such a rule could impair the state's objectives, such as selecting strategic investors or negotiating favourable terms with prospective buyers. Consequently, the Croatian Privatization Fund is exempted from the obligation to publish a takeover bid if the issuer is notified about the intention of the state authorities to sell the surplus of shares exceeding 25 per cent within the period for which such an obligation is created (see the Croatian takeover law, §7). Similarly, in Romania, the acquisition of a majority position within the privatization process exempts the investor from the obligation to make a public offer for the remaining shares.

Since the governance principles were designed in response to the evolving agency problems, we naturally address the question of whether the internal mechanism of corporate governance, that is the ownership structure, has had any effect on company performance.

3. RELATED LITERATURE: PERFORMANCE AND OWNERSHIP CONCENTRATION

In order to justify our empirical approach we refer to two strands of literature. First, our interest in further research on restructuring is based on the conclusions of the literature on privatization. Comprehensive analyses on the command of private owners distinguish a positive relation between the post-privatization performance, on one hand, and the owner type (Claessens et al., 1997; Konings, 1997; Smith et al., 1997; Weiss and Nikitin, 1998; Claessens and Djankov 1999b; Frydman et al.,1999; Earle and Telegdy, 2002; Walsh and Whelan, 2001; Cull et al., 2002; Grosfeld and Tressel, 2002), or ownership concentration (Claessens, 1997; Claessens and Djankov, 1999a, 1999b; Earle et al., 2005), on the other hand. Such an influence is expected especially in the countries suffering from the poor legal environment (La Porta et al., 1998), where the concentrated ownership is considered a disciplinary device for managers' behaviour.

However, the main hypotheses regarding the role of ownership cannot ignore the studies investigating the effect of blockholder regimes on the valuation of companies in developed countries. We consider that this distinction is very important since the complexity of shareholding arrangements leads to an opposite conclusion on the performance-ownership concentration relationship. Particularly, the results reported in the studies investigating this topic in Western European economies reveal that the value increases if control, irrespective of its nature (management control or large shareholders' control), is contestable. Lehmann and Weigand (2000); Volpin (2002); Boubaker (2003); Cronqvist and Nilsson (2003); Maury and Pajuste (2005) find that the concentration of capital, as well as the majority holdings of large shareholders, adversely influence the market value of companies. This negative relation is explained by the decreased risk run by large shareholders, notably due to financial engineering such as pyramids, cross-holdings, controlling coalitions and dual-class shares.

This brief survey on the role of ownership structure shows that on the new capital markets, any result is a priori possible. First, since the privatization programmes of these countries have not yet been fully achieved and the restructuring still represents a challenge, a positive relation between performance and private ownership could be expected. Second, the emergence of agency problems within public companies would justify a value discount due to the expropriation of minority shareholders. Finally, the reduced transaction costs on those markets allow the investors to choose the degree of concentration maximizing the firm value. According to Demsetz (1983) and Demsetz and Villalonga (2001), if the market forces affect both the performance and the ownership structure, there is no reason to find a deterministic relation between the two measures. Under these circumstances, only a new empirical investigation could clarify how the recent changes have influenced the restructuring pattern in the European emerging countries.

4. EMPIRICAL STRATEGY

4.1 Sample Selection

To study the efficiency of internal governance mechanism, we investigate the relationship between company performance and various measures of ownership. The final sample was constructed using a three-step selection procedure. First, from the overall companies listed in 2003 on the Bucharest, Varazdin and Zagreb Stock Exchanges (hereafter BSE, VSE and ZSE respectively) we exclude those operating in financial and regulated utilities sectors. Second, we selected only the industrial companies that have ownership information over the period 2000 to 2003. The Romanian ownership data were provided by BSE registry while the Croatian ones are available on the official site of the National Security Commission (hereafter Crosec). For the companies thus selected we computed the return on assets and other control variables by comparing several data sources: Amadeus, Romanian Ministry of Finance, Crosec, BSE, VSE, ZSE. Our final (balanced) samples include 484 and 188 company-year observations for Croatia and Romania, respectively.

4.2 Restructuring Variables

The previous studies on transition economies employed different performance measures. A first class of explained variables is based on information on company activity. The operational performance, like the main objective of a sound management, is a function of productivity determinants: value-added on employee or capital and output (Smith et al., 1997; Weiss and Nikitin, 1998; Estrin et al., 2001; Grosfeld and Tressel, 2002; Brown et al., 2004). Another type of approach is to consider that restructuring is synonymous with employment change (Walsh and Whelan, 2001; Claessens and Djankov, 2002). Finally, Hanousek et al. (2004) use accounting information (profit, sales, operational cash flow) while Earle et al. (2005) consider financial ratios (return on assets, financial return) as proxies for company performance.

In order to appraise the restructuring achievements we employ the return on assets (ROA) ratio. Descriptive statistics of the sample corporations are provided in Table 19.1.

4.3 Corporate Governance Variables

The corporate governance variables include ownership concentration and ownership interaction measures, dummies for each type of owner, as well as combinations of these variables.

Table 19.1 Descriptive statistics

	Croatia				Romania			
	2000	2001	2002	2003	2000	2001	2002	2003
ROA	−1.70	−1.55	−1.24	−0.84	10.09	6.16	5.87	2.83
	(−0.44)	(0.04)	(−0.01)	(0.12)	(8.26)	(5.86)	(3.43)	(3.51)
CONC	64.25	65.46	66.71	69.01	73.61	74.55	76.25	77.77
	(70.78)	(73.93)	(75.69)	(77.15)	(73.05)	(74.94)	(76.81)	(81.28)
HIX	2,544	2,817	2,929	3,197	3,427	3,605	3,960	4,359
	(2,188)	(2,462)	(2,552)	(2,758)	(2,913)	(3,155)	(3,515)	(4,016)
CONTEST	1,460	1,769	1,920	2,168	2,323	2,431	2,849	3,248
	(837)	(945)	(930)	(1,013)	(1,734)	(2,097)	(2,192)	(2,668)
OWN1	40.88	43.27	44.20	46.33	52.17	53.61	57.30	61.24
	(39.41)	(42.31)	(42.36)	(47.70)	(51.65)	(53.02)	(55.97)	(60.67)
SIZE	52,591	51,844	62,342	76,320	30,730	33,027	35,865	45,430
	(23,786)	(21,893)	(26,387)	(33,114)	(13,521)	(16,476)	(18,135)	(26,479)
FATA	0.69	0.69	0.69	0.66	0.51	0.55	0.54	0.56
	(0.72)	(0.71)	(0.73)	(0.70)	(0.52)	(0.53)	(0.51)	(0.58)
LEV	0.40	0.41	0.41	0.43	0.41	0.40	0.43	0.40
	(0.39)	(0.40)	(0.39)	(0.41)	(0.47)	(0.37)	(0.38)	(0.32)
ΔSALES	0.04	0.06	0.25	0.31	0.12	0.16	0.15	0.34
	(0.00)	(0.06)	(0.21)	(0.23)	(0.04)	(0.10)	(0.12)	(0.18)
STAF	687	708	709	695	1,682	1,624	1,510	1,388
	(390)	(396)	(406)	(366)	(1,186)	(1,113)	(986)	(811)

Notes: The descriptive statistics reported in this table comprise year-end mean and median values (in parenthesis) of reported variables: ROA, the ratio between gross profit before extraordinary items and total assets; CONC, the sum of significant shareholders' stakes; HIX, the sum of squares of the significant shareholders' stakes; CTST, the sum of squares of the differences between any two successive stakes of significant shareholders; SIZE, the value of total assets in thousand USD; LEV, the ratio between the debt value and total assets; ΔSALES, the percentage change in sales in the current year relative to the previous one; FATA, the ratio between the fixed assets and total assets; STAF, the number of employees. The Croatian sample consists of 121 industrial firms listed on VSE and ZSE at JDD tier. The Romanian sample comprises 47 industrial firms listed on BSE at first and second tiers.

Source: Authors' calculations.

The post-privatization ownership structure is expressed by the Ownership Concentration Index (CONC) and Herfindahl Index (HIX) that are constructed with respect to the shareholdings exceeding 5 per cent of capital. In order to measure the severity of agency problems between the major and minority shareholders we use a variation of the Herfindahl Index, as in Maury and Pajuste (2005), as the sum of squared differences between any two successive stakes. We have also taken into consideration the size of the largest shareholder in absolute values, on the one hand, and the mandatory bid thresholds established by national takeover regulations, on the other hand. The last analysis is performed by either employing dummy variables or piecewise-linear terms following the specification proposed by Himmelberg et al. (1999). The Romanian sample was divided into three classes reflecting the 33 per cent and 50 per cent thresholds, while the Croatian one was split in four different groups based on the 25 per cent, 50 per cent and 75 per cent thresholds.

The idiosyncrasy of corporate governance is emphasized by analysing six groups of investors: the State Ownership Fund, industrial companies, financial institutions, investment trusts, individual shareholders and employees.[7] Lehmann and Weigand (2000) consider that the type of control (internal vs. external control) depends on the identity of shareholders. The large external shareholders (diversified industrial companies, investments funds) are interested in hiring professional managers while families exercise the control directly.

The privatization strategy has varied among countries not only in connection with the methods of capital transfer (direct sales, voucher privatization), but also in connection with the structure of portfolio to be sold in a specific period of time. The forerunners placed the emphasis on early big-ticket transactions while the others preferred to postpone the sale of 'crown jewels'. Generally, state ownership is associated with inefficiencies that motivate *ipso facto* the whole privatization process. Nevertheless, the effect on performance is a function of the state authorities' goals: on the one hand, a negative influence is expected if the state continues to provide social protection, re-acquires shares in industrial companies or cancels previous transactions; on the other hand, a positive effect can be inferred when actions to restructure the bad performers are taken before the sale of the state block.

The control stake of an industrial company can also have a two-sided effect. If the institutional and legal frameworks limit the profit or assets transfers within the group, one expects to find a positive relation between the industrial property and performance. In the opposite case, the tunnelling effects encouraged by group structures could instigate a decrease in company performance.

The role played by financial institutions is not axiomatic. At the beginning of transition when the limited monitoring encouraged corruption, the banking organizations developed atypical relations with industrial companies (Hanousek et al., 2004). However, Grosfeld and Tressel (2002) consider that the decision to convert the outstanding debts into shares could influence only the shareholder structure of weak companies. Claessens et al. (1997) present arguments in line with the monitoring hypothesis of Jensen and Meckling (1976) when the banks both indirectly control and finance the company.[8]

The 'investment trust' category comprises the investment funds emerging within privatization as well as other foreign entities that are active acquirers specialized in investments in emerging markets (for example, Broadhurst Investment Limited). The role played by those investment funds is hard to establish. In particular, the mass privatization scheme of the Romanian government offers an interesting agency setting. By political decision, five domestic private funds were established as privatization vehicles. In the early stage of transition, their role was to dissociate the absolute state property. A part of their holdings was targeted at distributing free shares to citizens within the mass privatization programme. At the same time, they collected privatization vouchers by counter-offering their own shares. For a long period these funds were rather pseudo-private investors: on the one hand, they represented state instruments within the public companies; on the other hand, the diversification achieved after the accomplishment of mass privatization motivated them to change their status into investment trusts having their own investment objectives. Nowadays in either country the funds that emerged through privatization are listed on the stock exchange.[9]

The empirical investigations on the family shareholdings show that the individual shareholders generally have an owner-manager quality (Faccio and Lang, 2002; Cronqvist and Nilsson, 2003; Maury and Pajuste, 2005). Boubaker (2003) finds a positive relation between this ownership category and firm performance and suggests that the expropriation of minority shareholders in that case is lower. Conversely, Cronqvist and Nilsson (2003) present two channels for transmission of a negative influence: (1) suboptimal investments; and (2) expropriation of the other classes of owners through management decisions.

Finally, the employees' shareholdings are generally associated with insider ownership. However, the role of employees in company restructuring is controversial. The main reason for proposing that they share equity is to give more insights into their company and so more incentives to commit to the restructuring objectives. In reality their expertise in monitoring management is limited. In many cases, the employees' representative colludes with managers. In other cases, there is a coordination problem inside the association if the voting scheme establishes that every member has one voting right.[10]

5. EMPIRICAL RESULTS

The general form of the panel regression is:

$$\begin{aligned} ROA_{it} = {} & \beta_1 OWNERSHIP_t + \beta_2 SIZE_t + \beta_3 FATAmean_t \\ & + \beta_4 FATAhigh_t + \beta_5 LEV_t + \beta_6 LEV_t^2 \\ & + \beta_7 \Delta SALES_{t/t-1} + \beta_8 STAF_t + \beta_9 YEAR_t \\ & + \beta_{10} Industry_i + u_{it} \end{aligned}$$

where the subscript i=1, . . ., 168 identifies individual firms and t=2000, . . ., 2003 represents the years. The firm size (SIZE) is measured by the logarithm of total assets expressed in thousand US dollars at the end of the financial year. The fixed assets ratio, compounded by dividing the value of fixed assets by total assets, is split into three groups reflecting the 60 per cent and 80 per cent thresholds: $FATA_{low}$, $FATA_{med}$ and $FATA_{high}$. The financial leverage (LEV) is the ratio between the debt value and total assets. The sales growth (ΔSALES) is the percentage change in sales year-on-year. We have also accounted for the number of employees at the end of the financial year (STAF). The industry dummies were established based on the NACE primary codes.

Various specifications of this empirical model were estimated by the OLS method with or without the inclusion of fixed effects.[11] In order to identify the heterogeneity of agency settings we perform the estimations separately on the two samples, 'Croatia' and 'Romania'. In several cases we also control for the non-linear effect by considering the squared value of the governance or control variables.

The descriptive statistics presented in Table 19.1 provide evidence on the different patterns of ownership concentration followed by Croatian and Romanian firms. Even if the main large shareholders jointly control more than 50 per cent of the equity and the rhythm of concentration is comparable between the two samples, a striking difference exists in the case of the power of major shareholder. On average, in Croatian companies the largest shareholders did not have the majority over the 2000–2003 period, while in the Romanian listed companies the major shareholder had exerted *de jure* control from the beginning of the analysed period. Generally, we observe that even if concentrated according to the overall index, the control of Croatian companies is shared by many large shareholders while in the Romanian context the ownership has rarely been divided among more than three blockholders (non-reported result).

The results of the OLS regressions are presented in Table 19.2. Intercept terms, year and industry dummies are included in all of the specifications but they are not reported for space reasons.

According to pooled specifications, the coefficients of the 'CONC', 'HIX', 'CONTEST' and 'OWN1' variables (Tables 19.2 and 19.3) are negative and strongly significant for the two sub-samples, which means that the higher the capital concentration or the holdings of major shareholders, the less efficient are the controlled companies. According to the governance theory, are more likely resources to be diverted when the major shareholders, especially the largest one, have discretion on the company's decisions. The negative sign of the contestability index coefficient shows that the higher the discrepancy between successive voting powers, the larger the scope for diverting resources and consequently the lower the performance. These findings are in line with those of Maury and Pajuste (2005).

When we control for firm heterogeneity, the only previous result that remains robust is that concerning the non-linear effect of ownership concentration on the performance of Romanian companies. In contrast, by including the fixed effects, some estimated coefficients change their sign, as is the case of the HIX, CONTEST and OWN1 variables reported to explain the performance of Romanian companies. Himmelberg et al. (1999) explain the sign and significance changes between pooled and fixed effects estimations by offering some insights on the complexity of contractual environment. Failing to take into account the influence of characteristics specific to firms on the ownership concentration decisions could bias the final conclusions.

In order to identify a consistent effect we compare the coefficients of the Ownership and Herfindahl Indices for pooled specifications. By placing more weight on the largest shareholder, we find for the Croatian sample that the negative effect is more important if the ownership of the largest shareholder is more important compared to other significant shareholders. Conversely, the performance of Romanian companies decreases if the capital is shared by several blockholders: the HIX coefficient in that case is –2.71 compared with that of –7.88 obtained when equal weights are given to all shareholders. Taken together, the reported results so far confirm an intuition: in Romania, the additional blockholdings have a dampening effect on the performance of companies whereas in Croatia, the opposite effect is realized.

Lehmann and Weigand (2000) argue that the location of control rights could matter for the development potential of companies. For this reason we additionally control for the identity of the largest shareholder. In a first specification we consider dummy variables for each of the six classes, and then we investigate this issue by interacting the ownership variable with

Table 19.2 Panel regressions on the relation between ROA and ownership concentration

	Croatia pooled			Romania pooled			Croatia firm effects			Romania firm effects		
	(1)	(2)	(3)	(4)	(5)	(6)	(7)	(8)	(9)	(10)	(11)	(12)
CONC	−0.546			−7.889			−0.118			6.956		
	(0.046)			(0.023)			(0.616)			(0.135)		
HIX		−0.600			−2.711			0.178			2.062	
		(0.006)			(0.022)			(0.537)			(0.066)	
CTST			−0.417			−1.231			0.333			0.973
			(0.054)			(0.037)			(0.302)			(0.075)
SIZE	2.125	2.115	2.133	1.768	1.131	0.965	6.644	6.730	6.743	−1.369	−1.245	−1.050
	(0.000)	(0.000)	(0.000)	(0.060)	(0.167)	(0.246)	(0.003)	(0.004)	(0.003)	(0.497)	(0.535)	(0.600)
$FATA_{med}$	−2.355	−2.228	−2.358	−6.760	−6.622	−6.724	1.847	1.908	1.956	−4.839	−4.750	−4.802
	(0.004)	(0.007)	(0.004)	(0.000)	(0.000)	(0.000)	(0.221)	(0.207)	(0.198)	(0.000)	(0.001)	(0.000)
$FATA_{high}$	−2.814	−2.627	−2.911	−20.163	−20.995	−20.913	0.756	0.706	0.729	−14.444	−14.185	−14.194
	(0.014)	(0.018)	(0.008)	(0.000)	(0.000)	(0.000)	(0.834)	(0.843)	(0.837)	(0.002)	(0.003)	(0.003)
LEV	3.433	2.960	2.596	−31.000	−27.651	−27.298	2.490	2.354	2.694	8.588	8.277	8.212
	(0.463)	(0.531)	(0.584)	(0.004)	(0.014)	(0.016)	(0.830)	(0.839)	(0.816)	(0.419)	(0.436)	(0.440)
LEV^2	−20.522	−19.919	−19.828	−4.539	−6.525	−6.703	−19.546	−19.464	−19.757	−28.509	−28.232	−28.222
	(0.000)	(0.000)	(0.000)	(0.689)	(0.587)	(0.584)	(0.115)	(0.117)	(0.113)	(0.001)	(0.001)	(0.001)
ΔSALES	0.951	1.021	1.004	4.402	4.456	4.521	0.881	0.880	0.870	4.242	4.138	4.126
	(0.745)	(0.731)	(0.734)	(0.027)	(0.026)	(0.024)	(0.617)	(0.618)	(0.621)	(0.001)	(0.001)	(0.001)

Table 19.2 (continued)

	Croatia pooled			Romania pooled			Croatia firm effects			Romania firm effects		
	(1)	(2)	(3)	(4)	(5)	(6)	(7)	(8)	(9)	(10)	(11)	(12)
STAF	−0.001	−0.001	−0.001	0.000	0.000	0.000	−0.001	−0.001	−0.001	0.001	0.001	0.001
	(0.108)	(0.096)	(0.085)	(0.742)	(0.507)	(0.469)	(0.336)	(0.321)	(0.314)	(0.624)	(0.623)	(0.604)
Adj. R^2	0.303	0.305	0.302	0.561	0.560	0.557	0.553	0.553	0.554	0.691	0.692	0.692

Notes: The pooled and fixed effects specifications reported in this table all model the economic performance ROA, as a linear function of the indicated variables. The independent variables are: CONC, the logarithm of the sum of significant shareholders' stakes; HIX, the logarithm of the sum of squares of the significant shareholders' stakes; CTST, the logarithm of the sum of squares of the differences between each two successive stakes of significant shareholders; SIZE, the logarithm of total assets; LEV, the ratio between the debt value and total assets; SALES, the percentage change in sales year-on-year; $FATA_{med}$ dummy, equals 1 if the fixed assets ratio is between 0.6 and 0.8; $FATA_{high}$ dummy, equals 1 if the fixed assets ratio is between 0.8 and 1.0; STAF, the number of employees. Intercept terms, year dummies and industry dummies are included in all regressions, but not reported. Probability values resulting from White Heteroskedasticity-Consistent Standard Errors & Covariance correction are reported in parentheses.

Source: Authors' estimations.

identity indicators. In Croatia, companies controlled by another industrial company, a financial institution or an individual investor perform, on average, better that those belonging to the state portfolio. Conversely, the presence of diffused investment trusts has a negative impact on the firm value. The last result makes us think that funds invest in listed firms for diversification reasons and they are less likely to commit to restructuring objectives. However, any further increase of the ownership of the largest shareholder has a negative effect on the performance, irrespective of the type of investor: the most important effect is observed for the state fund and investments trusts (pooled specifications, Tables 19.3 and 19.4).

For the Romanian case, we obtained a surprising result. Compared with the companies still controlled by the state, entities whose largest shareholder is an industrial company perform, on average, worse. We expected industrial companies to be the main entities interested in restructuring. We assign this result to agency problems likely to emerge in these cases, especially to the 'tunnelling' activity. Besides, the findings of the approach aiming at investigating the effect of ownership changes for each type of blockholder reinforce the result inferred when we use dummy variables as proxies for the type of owner. The companies where the state property decreases perform less well than their competitors.[12] This is the only concluding result obtained for the Romanian panel.

To study the impact of takeover regulation on the restructuring pattern we conduct a similar analysis taking into account the legal thresholds established by the mandatory bid rule. In that case the results (not reported for space reasons) are mitigated. For Croatia, we found that the companies having a shareholder with more than 75 per cent of capital have a lower performance compared with companies with dispersed shareholdings. Anyway, once the threshold of 75 per cent is exceeded, any further concentration implies a better performance. This result makes us think that squeeze-out offers are more likely to occur in good companies.

In order to eliminate the bias stemming from the correlation between ownership composition and initial performance, we analyse how the changes in performance are affected by changes in ownership (Weiss and Nikitin, 1998; Earle et al., 2005). For this purpose, we calculate the changes in performance as a difference between ROA at the end of the current year relative to the ratio computed at the end of the previous year. The results of this final approach are presented in Table 19.5.

It is well known that, if there is no material change of ownership structure, the estimated coefficients of governance variables are biased toward zero. As the main objective of privatization was to transfer the capital from the state to private investors we expect to see changes in the distribution of voting power among shareholders rather than in the overall capital concentration.

Table 19.3 Panel regression on the relation between ROA and ownership of largest shareholder

	Croatia pooled			Romania pooled			Croatia firm effects			Romania firm effects		
	(1)	(2)	(3)	(4)	(5)	(6)	(7)	(8)	(9)	(10)	(11)	(12)
OWN1	−1.071	−0.895	0.994	−3.113	−1.707	3.131	0.617	0.612	−2.191	2.936	3.075	2.549
	(0.011)	(0.015)	(0.566)	(0.066)	(0.387)	(0.883)	(0.361)	(0.417)	(0.305)	(0.053)	(0.072)	(0.864)
$OWN1^2$			−0.307			−0.641			0.472			0.072
			(0.301)			(0.822)			(0.279)			(0.973)
IND		2.544	2.620		−5.691	−5.634		1.033	1.025		−6.486	−6.501
		(0.005)	(0.003)		(0.021)	(0.023)		(0.278)	(0.282)		(0.179)	(0.191)
FIN		2.009	2.030		−3.340	−3.290		0.135	0.190		−2.172	−2.162
		(0.066)	(0.062)		(0.332)	(0.343)		(0.926)	(0.896)		(0.597)	(0.594)
TRUST		−1.481	−1.519		−1.117	−1.068		1.171	1.274		−3.268	−3.265
		(0.087)	(0.082)		(0.720)	(0.735)		(0.321)	(0.284)		(0.523)	(0.524)
FAM		5.115	5.187		−0.016	0.097		1.066	0.755		−11.226	−11.208
		(0.000)	(0.000)		(0.998)	(0.987)		(0.446)	(0.591)		(0.021)	(0.021)
ESOP		1.363	1.294		−2.389	−2.421		−0.915	−0.418		−2.526	−2.507
		(0.356)	(0.393)		(0.399)	(0.390)		(0.437)	(0.706)		(0.405)	(0.409)
SIZE	2.120	2.207	2.216	1.087	1.517	1.516	6.721	6.694	6.756	−1.185	−1.869	−1.866
	(0.000)	(0.000)	(0.000)	(0.183)	(0.099)	(0.100)	(0.004)	(0.003)	(0.003)	(0.555)	(0.353)	(0.356)
$FATA_{med}$	−2.285	−2.068	−2.131	−6.789	−6.772	−6.767	1.922	2.037	2.023	−4.742	−4.151	−4.149
	(0.005)	(0.016)	(0.014)	(0.000)	(0.000)	(0.000)	(0.203)	(0.192)	(0.197)	(0.001)	(0.003)	(0.003)
$FATA_{high}$	−2.707	−2.273	−2.315	−21.000	−17.650	−17.534	0.690	0.627	0.575	−14.141	−13.499	−13.498
	(0.014)	(0.033)	(0.030)	(0.000)	(0.000)	(0.000)	(0.846)	(0.861)	(0.873)	(0.004)	(0.005)	(0.005)
LEV	2.670	0.205	−0.049	−28.085	−24.479	−24.653	2.462	2.764	2.974	8.262	8.788	8.790
	(0.573)	(0.966)	(0.992)	(0.013)	(0.040)	(0.040)	(0.831)	(0.808)	(0.794)	(0.437)	(0.427)	(0.429)
LEV^2	−19.773	−16.951	−16.706	−6.131	−8.737	−8.645	−19.549	−19.986	−20.138	−28.261	−28.739	−28.736
	(0.000)	(0.002)	(0.003)	(0.616)	(0.488)	(0.494)	(0.116)	(0.107)	(0.106)	(0.001)	(0.002)	(0.002)

ΔSALES	1.021	0.837	0.809	4.461	4.968	4.987	0.874	0.946	0.977	4.124	4.080	4.078
	(0.730)	(0.777)	(0.784)	(0.026)	(0.011)	(0.012)	(0.620)	(0.581)	(0.572)	(0.001)	(0.002)	(0.002)
STAF	−0.001	−0.001	−0.001	0.001	0.001	0.001	−0.001	−0.001	−0.001	0.001	0.001	0.001
	(0.093)	(0.293)	(0.274)	(0.509)	(0.731)	(0.736)	(0.312)	(0.325)	(0.330)	(0.627)	(0.810)	(0.809)
Adj. R^2	0.305	0.336	0.336	0.555	0.570	0.567	0.553	0.548	0.548	0.693	0.693	0.690

Notes: The specifications reported in this table all model the economic performance ROA, as a linear function of the indicated variables. The independent variables are: OWN1, the logarithm of the stake held by the largest shareholder; IND dummy, equals 1 if the largest shareholder is an industrial company; FIN dummy, equals 1 if the largest shareholder is a financial institution; TRUST dummy, equals 1 if the largest shareholder is an investment trust; FAM dummy, equals 1 if the largest shareholder is an individual; ESOP dummy, equals 1 if the largest shareholder is the employees' association; SIZE, the logarithm of total assets; LEV, the ratio between the debt value and total assets; ΔSALES, the percentage change in sales year-on-year; $FATA_{med}$ dummy, equals 1 if the fixed assets ratio is between 0.6 and 0.8; $FATA_{high}$ dummy, equals 1 if the fixed assets ratio is between 0.8 and 1.0; STAF, the number of employees. Intercept terms, year dummies and industry dummies are included in all regressions, but not reported. Fixed effects are included where indicated, but not reported. Probability values resulting from White Heteroskedasticity-Consistent Standard Errors & Covariance correction are reported in parentheses.

Source: Authors' estimations.

Table 19.4 Panel regression on the relation between ROA and the ownership of the largest shareholder by identity

	Croatia pooled	Romania pooled	Croatia firm effects	Romania firm effects
	(1)	(2)	(3)	(4)
SOF_{own1}	−1.723	−1.380	0.623	3.304
	(0.000)	(0.492)	(0.379)	(0.074)
IND_{own1}	−0.835	−2.240	0.929	2.221
	(0.036)	(0.228)	(0.154)	(0.122)
FIN_{own1}	−0.965	−1.909	0.667	2.865
	(0.039)	(0.393)	(0.430)	(0.109)
$TRUST_{own1}$	−2.127	−0.902	0.855	3.065
	(0.000)	(0.670)	(0.215)	(0.204)
FAM_{own1}	0.070	−1.262	0.984	0.607
	(0.889)	(0.659)	(0.215)	(0.770)
$ESOP_{own1}$	−1.233	−1.791	0.315	2.852
	(0.014)	(0.377)	(0.568)	(0.113)
Adj. R^2	0.345	0.568	0.549	0.691

Notes: The specifications reported in this table all model the economic performance ROA, as a linear function of the corporate governance and other control variables. The reported independent variables are: SOF_{own1}, the logarithm of the stake held by State Ownership Fund, as the largest shareholder; IND_{own1}, the logarithm of the stake held by industrial companies, as the largest shareholder; FIN_{own1}, the logarithm of the stake held by financial companies, as the largest shareholder; $TRUST_{own}$, the logarithm of the stake held by investment trusts, as the largest shareholder; FAM_{own1}, the logarithm of the stake held by individuals, as the largest shareholder; $ESOP_{own1}$, the logarithm of the stake held by employees and insiders, as the largest shareholder. Other control variables, intercept terms, year and industry dummies are included in all regressions but not reported. Fixed effects are included where indicated but not reported. Probability values resulting from White Heteroskedasticity-Consistent Standard Errors & Covariance correction are reported in parenthesis.

Source: Authors' estimations.

The ΔHIX coefficients are negative and statistically significant for the Croatian sample in either specification. The idea is that the larger the additional capital concentration (especially in the hands of large shareholders), the less probable becomes the threat of market for corporate control, and consequently the larger the scope for minority shareholders' expropriation, the more control has been gained. For Romania, the empirical results strengthen the idea that the model has to be structured in order to control for the endogeneity bias. As in the case of fixed effects estimations, we find that increasing the weight of the largest shareholder as well as the scope of its influence creates more economic value thanks to better performance.

Table 19.5 Panel regression on the relation between changes in ROA and changes in ownership concentration

	Croatia pooled				Romania pooled				Croatia firm effects				Romania firm effects			
	(1)	(2)	(3)	(4)	(5)	(6)	(7)	(8)	(9)	(10)	(11)	(12)	(13)	(14)	(15)	(16)
ΔCONC	−0.002*				0.075				−0.004*				0.072			
	(0.812)				(0.382)				(0.787)				(0.439)			
ΔHIX		−0.002*				0.001				−0.002*				0.001		
		(0.004)				(0.007)				(0.000)				(0.003)		
ΔCTST			0.000				0.001				0.000				0.001	
			(0.492)				(0.064)				(0.203)				(0.095)	
ΔOWN1				−0.011				0.093				−0.021				0.091
				(0.647)				(0.094)				(0.422)				(0.175)
ΔSIZE	6.061	6.050	6.033	6.046	−3.893	−3.536	−3.983	−3.838	7.246	7.173	7.187	7.210	−3.971	−3.827	−4.062	−3.899
	(0.016)	(0.017)	(0.017)	(0.017)	(0.053)	(0.079)	(0.030)	(0.050)	(0.022)	(0.023)	(0.025)	(0.023)	(0.057)	(0.063)	(0.038)	(0.057)
ΔLEV	−17.96	−17.87	−18.03	−18.03	−17.32	−17.50	−18.04	−17.64	−15.10	−15.18	−15.28	−15.33	−16.26	−16.68	−17.08	−16.59
	(0.010)	(0.011)	(0.010)	(0.010)	(0.034)	(0.032)	(0.024)	(0.029)	(0.049)	(0.048)	(0.047)	(0.046)	(0.009)	(0.007)	(0.005)	(0.007)
ΔSALES	2.326	2.448	2.325	2.328	6.356	6.274	6.559	6.353	2.630	2.753	2.623	2.628	5.840	5.538	6.123	5.867
	(0.356)	(0.346)	(0.356)	(0.356)	(0.029)	(0.030)	(0.014)	(0.025)	(0.167)	(0.160)	(0.169)	(0.169)	(0.049)	(0.060)	(0.022)	(0.040)
ΔSTAF	−0.025	−0.025	−0.024	−0.026	−4.457	−3.726	−4.603	−4.387	−0.016	−0.017	−0.014	−0.018	−4.018	−3.980	−4.530	−4.106
	(0.078)	(0.078)	(0.091)	(0.065)	(0.178)	(0.263)	(0.154)	(0.182)	(0.782)	(0.773)	(0.816)	(0.757)	(0.225)	(0.225)	(0.178)	(0.225)
R^2	0.084	0.086	0.084	0.084	0.207	0.210	0.222	0.214	0.154	0.157	0.156	0.155	0.262	0.267	0.274	0.267

Notes:
The pooled and fixed effects specifications reported in this table all model the change in economic performance ΔROA, as a linear function of the indicated variables. The independent variables are: ΔCONC, the change in the sum of significant shareholders' stakes in the current year relative to the previous one; ΔHIX, the change in the sum of squares of the significant shareholders' stakes in the current year relative to the previous one; ΔCTST, the change in the sum of squares of the differences between each two successive stakes of significant shareholders in the current year relative to the previous one; ΔOWN1, the change in the level of ownership of the largest shareholder in the current year relative to the previous one; ΔSIZE, the change in the value of total assets in the current year relative to the previous one; ΔLEV, the change in the leverage in the current year relative to the previous one; ΔSALES, the percentage change in sales year-on-year; ΔSTAF, the change of the number of employees in the current year relative to the previous one. Intercept terms, year dummies and industry dummies are included in all regressions, but not reported. Probability values resulting from White Heteroskedasticity-Consistent Standard Errors & Covariance correction are reported in parentheses.
* $\times 10^{-3}$

Source: Authors' estimations.

Our approach gives an important insight into some observable corporate characteristics that could also asymmetrically drive the economic results in the two analysed countries. In all the reported specifications, firm size has a positive and highly significant effect on the performance of Croatian companies. This kind of influence is expected if large firms are able to benefit from economies of scale or have access to financing sources thanks to a better and longer connection with the funds providers. In a challenging environment, the creditors should play an active monitoring role that would be translated into a positive relationship between leverage and assets performance. In the vast majority of cases, the non-linear effect identified for this variable shows that, beyond a certain limit, the bankruptcy threat outweighs the beneficial effect of debt, as an effective monitoring device. Filatotchev and Mickiewicz (2001) explain that, in the case of emerging economies, the negative impact of leverage on the firm's value could be due to the possible collusion between the dominant shareholder and debt holders.

In Romania, companies having a lot of fixed assets are the worst performers, *ceteris paribus*. If the assets can no longer be used to secure borrowings, their stand-alone value becomes irrelevant. A lot of fixed assets reveal potential agency costs related to over-investment. In addition, the need for restructuring is higher in the over-capitalized companies, which could place additional pressure on the current performance. The SALE variable, as a proxy for firm growth, exhibits a positive and significant sign in all reported variations of the general model. Our findings are in line with the investment literature stating that, under common circumstances, companies with more investment opportunities are more likely to see their performance improve.

Concerning the macroeconomic environment, we found that the deterioration of overall conditions after 2000 adversely affected all industrial companies. The non-reported year dummies keep their negative and significant sign in various specifications.

Summarizing our findings, the performance – as the objective of the growth-oriented restructuring – depends not only on the composition of ownership and the industrial features of companies but also on the business environment designed by the national privatization programme.

6. CONCLUDING REMARKS

In this study we try to reveal the patterns of agency relationships within Croatian and Romanian public companies by revisiting the capital concentration topic several years after large-scale privatization. For this purpose, we analyse the economic performance based on various corporate governance indicators between 2000 and 2003.

The differences identified between the two countries reveal that some recent constraints imposed to limit the discretion of large shareholders, and thus to protect the small investors, were established in line with the objectives of domestic privatization programmes. The strategy of the Croatian authorities was to split the ownership among many large shareholders, while the Romanian government opted to allocate large blocks to strategic investors. Takeover rules were adapted in line with these objectives. Acquiring control is more expensive in Croatia since the first threshold is set at 25 per cent of capital (compared with 33 per cent in Romania) and the transparency rules sometimes require very small shareholders (even under 1 per cent at times) to be identified. The results we obtained for the Croatian sample show that the scope of agency conflicts increases if more power is given to a single shareholder, and that company resources are better managed if additional large shareholders comparable in size can monitor the largest shareholder.

Conversely, the Romanian companies seem to perform better if the largest shareholder holds a comparatively large stake. Sometimes, a single dominant shareholder's room for manoeuvre would be restricted by the privatization contract terms, rendering the monitoring by the other large investors less effective. Surprisingly, when we control for the owner's identity, we obtain no relevant result defending the enhanced management capacity of private ownership. Previous analyses comprising almost all privatized companies (Earle and Telegdy, 2002; Brown et al., 2004) report results that are in contrast to ours. Nevertheless, if increasing the ownership concentration is expected mainly in the case of private shareholders, the results obtained by regressing changes in performance on changes in ownership variables give support to such an intuition. However, the return on assets, as a proxy for restructuring, depends on the unobserved firm heterogeneity and time-specific effects.

Integration into the European structures doubtless means common standards, but also competitiveness. Considering only the common features of industrial firms (such as concentrated ownership) when valuing the practice of corporate governance in new ascending countries, as well as ignoring macroeconomic conditions, offers only a partial picture of the problems confronting those economies. Our results provide additional support to the idea that there is no smooth path to growth goals: the transfer of ownership is not a panacea for restructuring and it cannot fully substitute for a sound legal environment.

NOTES

* Diana Pop, Laboratoire d'Economie d'Orléans: Rue de Blois, BP 6739, 45067 Orléans, Cedex 2, France Tel: +33-(0)2.38.41.70.37, Fax: +33-(0)2.38.41.73.80, e-mail: Diana.Pop@univ-orleans.fr. Julien Le Maux, Université Paris 1 Sorbonne. We are grateful to Zsuzsanna Fluck, Hubert De La Bruslerie, Xavier Galiègue, Georges Gallais Hamonno, and Christophe Hurlin for helpful comments and suggestions. We should also like to thank Ivan Kolar (Varazdin Stock Exchange) and Razvan Pavel (Bucharest Stock Exchange), for helping us with data.

1. For a comprehensive survey on the restructuring topics in all the transition economies, see Djankov and Murrell (2002).
2. According to Pohl et al. (1997) the enterprise restructuring is viable only if it is continuous, that is if the profitability can be preserved in a dynamic environment.
3. Nevertheless, according to other indicators, Romania has made much progress.
4. Analysing competition policies in the European transition economies, Vagliasindi (2001) shows that, in 1999, Romania had one of the most effective overall implementations of competition policy. Nevertheless, among the 'institutional', 'advocacy' and 'enforcement' dimensions, the enforcement category of this indicator is much higher in Croatia than in Romania.
5. The reader can refer to Burkart (1999) who provides a resourceful guide on economics of takeover regulation.
6. In 2004, the market authority revised the market law once again by closely referring to the European Directive. Relative to previous texts, there is no mention of the 75 per cent threshold, and the obligation to unquote a public company is raised to 95 per cent. Besides, the acquirer must not make another takeover bid in the next 12 months counted from the closing date of the previous public offer. Without providing clear directions concerning different classes of shares, the new legislation requires the mandatory bid to be addressed separately to each class of shares.
7. When the small shareholders who emerged within the mass privatization are classified into a homogeneous class, we recalculate the shareholder structure only in function of the other groups. In reality, dispersed shareholders could not play collectively a pivotal role in order for considering this class as a blockholder.
8. Analysing the peculiarity of Czech privatization, Claessens et al. (1997) show that the shareholdings of investment funds backed by banks, exceeding 10 per cent, have a positive influence on the company performance if that bank was also the company's fund provider.
9. Earle and Telegdy (2002) provide evidence about the positive effect of these entities on the productivity during five years after the Romanian mass privatization.
10. For Romania, Earle and Telegdy (2002) report a positive effect of inside shareholdings that is significant at conventional levels.
11. The Haussman test rejected the null hypothesis for the Croatian samples, while for the Romanian one it proves that the observed variables are correlated with firm effects. Anyway, the fixed effects specification is reported for the last sample too, knowing that the coefficients estimated in that case are not biased.
12. The positive coefficient (3.30; $p=0.07$) of the state variable is interpreted in this way in order to follow the logic of privatization.

REFERENCES

Berglöf, Erik and Anete Pajuste (2003), 'Emerging owners, eclipsing markets: Corporate governance in transition', in Peter K. Cornelius and Bruce Kogut (eds), *Corporate Governance and Capital Flows in a Global Economy*, Oxford: Oxford University Press, pp. 267–304.

Boubaker, Sabri (2003), 'Ownership-control discrepancy and firm value: Evidence from France', Institut de Recherche en Gestion and Ecole Supérieure des Affaires and Paris XII University working paper.
Brown, David J., John S. Earle and Almos Telegdy (2004), 'Does privatization raise productivity? Evidence from comprehensive panel data on manufacturing firms in Hungary, Romania, Russia and Ukraine', Upjohn Institute staff working paper no. 04-107.
Burkart, Mike (1999), 'Economics of Takeover Regulation', SSE working paper.
Claessens, Stijn (1997), 'Corporate governance and equity prices: Evidence from the Czech and Slovak Republics', *Journal of Finance*, **52** (4), 1641–58.
Claessens, Stijn and Simeon Djankov (1999a), 'Ownership concentration and corporate performance in the Czech Republic', *Journal of Comparative Economics*, **27** (3), 498–513.
Claessens, Stijn and Simeon Djankov (1999b), 'Enterprise performance and management turnover in the Czech Republic', *European Economic Review*, **43** (4–6), 1115–24.
Claessens, Stijn and Simeon Djankov (2002), 'Privatization benefits in Eastern Europe', *Journal of Public Economics*, **83** (3), 307–24.
Claessens, Stijn, Simeon Djankov and Gerhard Pohl (1997), 'Ownership and corporate governance: Evidence from the Czech Republic', World Bank policy research working paper no. 1737.
Cronqvist, Henrik and Mattias Nilsson (2003), 'Agency costs of controlling minority shareholders', *Journal of Financial and Quantitative Analysis*, **38** (4), 695–719.
Cull, Robert, Jana Matesova and Mary M. Shirley (2002), 'Ownership structure and the temptation to loot: Evidence from privatized firms in the Czech Republic', *Journal of Comparative Economics*, **30** (1), 1–24.
Demsetz, Harold (1983), 'The structure of ownership and the theory of the firm', *Journal of Law and Economics*, **26** (2), 375–90.
Demsetz, Harold and Belén Villalonga (2001), 'Ownership structure and corporate performance', *Journal of Corporate Finance*, **7** (3), 209–33.
Djankov, Simeon and Peter Murrell (2002), 'Enterprise restructuring in transition: A quantitative survey', *Journal of Economic Literature*, **40** (3), 739–92.
Earle, John S. and Almos Telegdy (2002), 'Privatization methods and productivity effects in Romanian industrial enterprises', *Journal of Comparative Economics*, **30** (4), 657–82.
Earle, John S., Csaba Kucsera and Almos Telegdy (2005), 'Ownership concentration and corporate performance on the Budapest Stock Exchange: Do too many cooks spoil the goulash?', *Corporate Governance*, **13** (2), 254–64.
Estrin, Saul, Jozef Konings, Zbigniew Zolkiewski and Manuela Angelucci (2001), 'The effect of ownership and competitive pressure on firm performance in transitions economies: Micro evidence from Bulgaria, Romania and Poland', CEPR discussion paper no. 2985.
Faccio, Mara and Larry H.P. Lang (2002), 'The ultimate ownership of Western European corporations', *Journal of Financial Economics*, **65** (3), 365–95.
Filatotchev, Igor and Tomasz Mickiewicz (2001), 'Ownership concentration, "private benefits of control" and debt financing', Centre for the Study of Economic & Social Change in Europe working paper no. 4.
Frydman, Roman, Cheryl Gray, Marek Hessel and Andrzej Rapaczynski (1999), 'When does privatization work? The impact of private ownership on corporate

performance in the transition economies', *Quarterly Journal of Economics*, **114** (4), 1153–91.
Grosfeld, Irena and Thierry Tressel (2002), 'Competition and ownership structure: Substitutes or complements? Evidence from the Warsaw Stock Exchange', *Economics of Transition*, **10** (3), 525–51.
Hanousek, Jan, Evzen Kocenda and Jan Svejnar (2004), 'Ownership, control and corporate performance after large scale privatization', William Davidson Institute working paper no. 652.
Himmelberg, Charles P., Glenn R. Hubbard and Darius Palia (1999), 'Understanding the determinants of managerial ownership and the link between ownership and performance', *Journal of Financial Economics*, **53** (3), 353–84.
Jensen, Michael C. and William H. Meckling (1976), 'Theory of the firm: Managerial behavior, agency costs and ownership structure', *Journal of Financial Economics*, **3** (4), 305–60.
Konings, Jozef (1997), 'Competition and firm performance in transition economies: Evidence from firm-level surveys in Slovenia, Hungary, and Romania', CEPR discussion paper no. 1770.
La Porta Rafael, Florencio Lopez-de Silanes, Andrei Shleifer and Robert W. Vishny (1998), 'Law and finance', *Journal of Political Economy*, **106** (6), 1113–55.
Lehmann, Erik and Juergen Weigand (2000), 'Does the governed corporation perform better? Governance structures and corporate performance in Germany', *European Financial Review*, **4** (2), 157–95.
Lins, Karl V. (2003), 'Equity ownership and firm value in emerging markets', *Journal of Financial and Quantitative Analysis*, **38** (1), 159–84.
Maury, Benjamin C. and Anete Pajuste (2005), 'Multiple large shareholders and firm value', *Journal of Banking and Finance*, **29** (7), 1813–34.
Pohl, Gerhard, Robert E. Anderson, Stijn Claessens and Simeon Djankov (1997), 'Privatization and restructuring in Central and Eastern Europe: Evidence and policy options', World Bank technical paper no. 368.
Pop, Diana (2006), 'M&A market in transition economies: evidence from Romania', *Emerging Markets Review*, **7** (3), 244–60.
Smith, Stephen C., Beom-Cheol Cin and Milan Vodopivec (1997), 'Privatization incidence, ownership forms and firm performance: Evidence from Slovenia', *Journal of Comparative Economics*, **25** (2), 158–79.
Telegdy, Almos, John S. Earle, Victor Kaznovsky and Csaba Kucsera (2002), 'Corporate control: A study of firms on the Bucharest Stock Exchange', *Eastern European Economics*, **40** (3), 6–27.
Vagliasindi, Maria (2001), 'Competition across transition economies: An enterprise-level analysis of the main policy and structural determinants', EBRD working paper no. 68.
Volpin, Paolo F. (2002), 'Governance with poor investor protection: Evidence from top executive turnover in Italy', *Journal of Financial Economics*, **64** (1), 61–90.
Walsh, Patrick Paul and Chiara Whelan (2001), 'Firm performance and political economy of corporate governance: Survey evidence from Bulgaria, Hungary, Slovakia and Slovenia', *Economic Systems*, **25** (2), 85–112.
Weiss, Andrew and Georgiy Nikitin (1998), 'Performance of Czech companies by ownership structure', Davidson Institute working paper no. 186.

PART VI

Banking and financial stability: potential pitfalls

20. Deposit interest rates, asset risk and bank failure in Croatia[1]

Evan Kraft and Tomislav Galac

1. INTRODUCTION

During the 1980s and 1990s, financial liberalization became an almost universally accepted policy prescription. Large numbers of countries eased licensing, deregulated interest rates and dismantled systems of directed lending. However, banking system crises, first in the southern cone of Latin America in the early 1980s (Diaz-Alejandro, 1985), and later in the US (White, 1991; Kane, 1989), Scandinavian countries (Nyberg and Vihriala, 1994; Vihriala, 1996) and a large set of emerging market economies, raised questions about the links between financial liberalization and instability (for cross-country econometric evidence see Demirgüç-Kunt and Detriagache, 1998, 1999). While there are strong arguments and some evidence to argue that financial liberalization is beneficial in the long-term (Allen and Gale, 2003; Ranciere et al., 2003) there is much controversy about the medium-term costs and the optimal approach to regulation under liberalized conditions.

A crucial component of financial liberalization is the liberalization of interest rate setting. With the lifting of Regulation Q in 1980 in the United States, intellectual fashion moved against the regulation of deposit interest rates. However, in the decade that followed the lifting of regulation Q, the US experience provided considerable anecdotal evidence about the negative effects of unlimited freedom to set deposit interest rates. Some aggressive banks used high deposit interest rates to fund their risky lending strategies. And the high deposit interest rates of these banks created a negative externality by forcing less risk-loving banks to raise their deposit rates to retain deposits, thus squeezing bank profits and creating a secondary impulse for less risky banks actually to increase the riskiness of their portfolio. Despite this, deregulation of deposit interest rates became a standard element of the financial liberalization package adopted by large numbers of countries.

Keeley (1990) argues that the increase in risk-taking following deregulation in the United States was the result of the combination of unrestricted competition with fixed-premium deposit insurance. Increased competition erodes franchise value. Under fixed-premium deposit insurance, this increases the attractiveness of added risk, since greater probability of failure is not reflected in higher premia and thus does not increase the extent of losses suffered by the owner under failure. At the same time, added risk implies higher earnings under favourable outcomes, and thus increases the bank's capital conditional upon survival. Keeley demonstrates that US banks with greater market power maintain higher market-value capital–asset ratios and enjoyed lower interest rates on large, uninsured certificates of deposit. Reversing this, the erosion of franchise value caused by deregulation would lead to higher deposit interest rates.

More recently, Jeitschko and Jeung (2005) question Keeley's argument that lower capital–asset ratios necessarily lead to higher risk-taking. They model a double moral hazard problem, where bank managers are subject to moral hazard as shareholders' agents, and banks are subject to moral hazard as agents of the deposit insurer. This model leads to various cases regarding the relationship between capitalization and risk, with both high and low capitalization possibly associated with higher asset risk.

Hellman et al. (2000) provide a theoretical argument to show that, in an environment with only capital adequacy regulation and no regulation of interest rates, banks may have an incentive to bid up deposit interest rates so as to gain the funding to 'gamble' (increase asset risk). Their set-up does not seem to be vulnerable to the Jeitschko and Jeung critique, because gambling occurs when competition lowers the discounted present value of returns on prudent investments below that on the gambling asset. In other words, in the Hellman et al. model, gambling will occur when competition is strong enough on the asset side to depress returns *and*, at the same time, the elasticity of deposits is high, banks discount the future very strongly and the short-term returns to gambling are relatively high. It is true that, *ceteris paribus*, higher capitalization would decrease the incentives for gambling in the Hellman et al. model (the opportunity cost of failure is higher), but a bank with high capitalization might still gamble if deposit elasticity was sufficiently high, the banks' time discount was sufficiently high and the return on gambling was sufficiently lucrative.

Hellman et al. argue that only a combination of capital adequacy regulation and deposit interest rate limitations can implement the Pareto-optimal allocation under all circumstances. Capital adequacy regulation alone tends to fail when competition is strong, that is precisely in deregulated banking systems. Hellman et al. consider systems with and without deposit insurance, but they only consider fixed-premium insurance, and acknowledge that 'sophisticated fee schemes can be used to reduce moral hazard'.

This leaves open the question of whether the levying of risk-adjusted deposit insurance premia could eliminate incentives to excessive risk-taking. Chan et al. (1992) argue that both incentive and information problems make fairly priced deposit insurance infeasible. This question has been hotly debated since then, but the thrust of the literature seems to lean against the feasibility of completely eliminating risk-taking via risk-adjusted deposit insurance premia (see, for example, Flannery, 1991; John et al., 1991; Crane, 1995; Kupiec and O'Brien, 1998; and Freixas and Rochet, 1998. Galac, 2005, provides an overview). Based on this, we hold that risk-adjusted premia, although possibly desirable, cannot be a panacea that wholly eliminates the problem of 'market-stealing' increases of deposit interest rates to fund 'gambling'.

Notwithstanding the important qualification introduced by Jeitschko and Jeung (2005), all this points to a possible connection between 'excessive' competition in the deposit market and increases in risk-taking, particularly under conditions where the future is heavily discounted, and deposit supply is highly elastic. The transition countries of Central and Eastern Europe provide an interesting laboratory to test these arguments. Starting in the early 1990s, these countries rapidly liberalized their banking markets, removing restrictions on entry, asset composition and interest rates. And, in the turbulent and poorly regulated conditions of transition, opportunities for making fortunes overnight – and therefore time discounts – were unusually high. For this reason, the experience of such countries may help confirm whether the US experience of the 1980s was typical.

In this chapter, we examine the experience of Croatia, which enacted rather liberal regulations regarding entry, asset composition and interest rates in the early 1990s. After the end of the wars surrounding the break-up of former Yugoslavia, Croatia experienced rapid growth in the number of banks, strong deposit growth and substantial increases in deposit interest rates in the period 1995–98. This buoyant period was punctuated by the failures of numerous medium-sized banks in 1998 and 1999.

Our argument is that high deposit interest rates helped fund the expansion of risk-loving banks, and in fact were a fairly reliable signal of increased bank asset risk. In this chapter, we will focus on the second part of the argument, providing a set of predictive models of bank failures. These models show that high deposit interest rates were in fact the most significant variable predicting bank failures. That is, high-risk banks – the ones that eventually failed – often offered higher deposit interest rates than low-risk banks.

Regarding policy implications, while we note that the first-best policy would be to use high deposit interest rates as a signal of increased risk, and to initiate appropriate corrective action at such banks, we argue that, when supervision capabilities are weak and/or legislation prevents adequate, timely corrective action, some form of market-conforming regulations to prevent 'market-stealing' via increased deposit interest rates may be an appropriate safeguard.

The chapter proceeds as follows. Section 2 provides a brief overview of the liberalization of the banking market in Croatia in the 1990s and the dynamics of growth and crisis. Section 3 presents models of failure and elucidates the role of deposit interest rates in failures. Section 4 provides a discussion of policy options and conclusions.

2. LIBERALIZATION, GROWTH AND CRISIS IN THE CROATIAN BANKING SECTOR

The liberalization of the banking system in Croatia started while Croatia was still part of the former socialist Yugoslavia in 1989–90. A new banking law was enacted, allowing relatively free entry, and interest rates were deregulated. Bank supervision was established, but its effectiveness in the early years was limited.

Liberalization took place under conditions of war, accompanied by high inflation and sharp declines in output. A macroeconomic stabilization programme implemented in October 1993 succeeded in bringing inflation under control, and real GDP growth began in 1994. Decisive military actions in May and August 1995, and the signing of the Dayton Peace Agreement in neighbouring Bosnia and Herzegovina in November 1995 and the Erdut Agreement in late 1996 ended the period of conflict and brought about a sharp decline in political risk.

The number of banks grew rapidly, even during the war, rising from 22 in 1991 to some 60 in 1997 (see Table 20.1). In addition, by 1997, 36 savings

Table 20.1 Banking and macroeconomic overview

	1990	1995	1996	1997	1998	1999	2000	2001	2002	2003
Number of banks	22	54	58	60	60	53	46	44	46	42
Foreign banks	0	1	5	7	10	13	20	24	23	19
Foreign bank assets share	0	1.0	1.0	4.0	6.7	39.9	84.1	89.3	90.2	91.0
Real GDP growth, %		6.8	6.0	6.8	2.5	−0.9	2.9	4.4	5.2	4.3
Inflation, %		3.8	3.4	3.8	5.4	4.4	7.4	2.3	1.9	1.7

Source: Croatian National Bank.

banks, with limited licences, were also operating. Deposits began growing steadily in 1995. Growth came partly as a result of the return of deposits placed in foreign banks by Croatian citizens during the war. In addition, growing confidence in the banking system began to attract deposits held 'in mattresses'.

In particular, 1996 witnessed a substantial increase in deposit interest rates at some banks. Interest rates on domestic currency deposits rose dramatically in late 1995 and early 1996 (see Figure 20.1). However, it should be noted that these deposits accounted for a very small portion of the total. Interest rates on foreign exchange (FX) deposits, the bulk of deposits, rose substantially later in the year. A number of banks offered interest rates on deposits in Deutschmark exceeding comparable rates in Germany by some 800 to 1000 basis points (see Kraft, 1999, for details).

Deposits grew explosively in this period, with annual growth rates exceeding 50 per cent through most of 1996 and all of 1997 (see Figure 20.2). Both kuna and FX deposits grew rapidly.

At the same time, lending surged, reaching a peak growth rate of 44 per cent in 1997. Such rapid growth suggested the presence of increased risk-taking, and indeed, in 1998, several bank failures occurred. The failures continued into 1999, with a total of 16 banks accounting for approximately 20 per cent of 1997 total banking assets failing in 1998–99. Deposit growth came to a halt, and aggregate deposits actually fell during the height of the crisis in February–May 1999. During the crisis, there were signs of a reallocation of deposits towards the foreign banks, as some domestic banks experienced substantial withdrawals.

The crisis was overcome through a combination of bankruptcies, lender-of-last resort actions by the central bank, and a turnaround in the

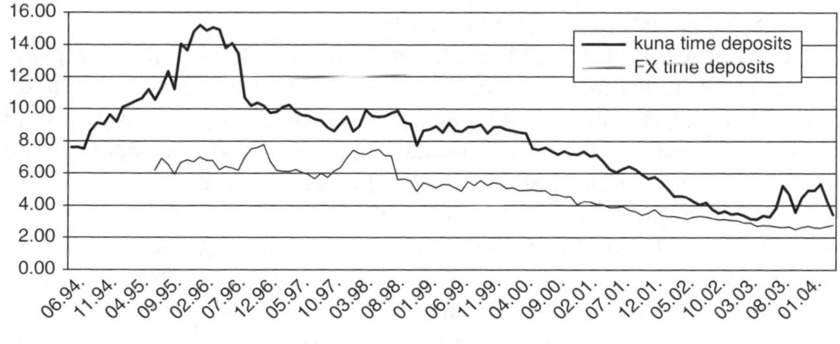

Source: Croatian National Bank.

Figure 20.1 Average bank deposit interest rates

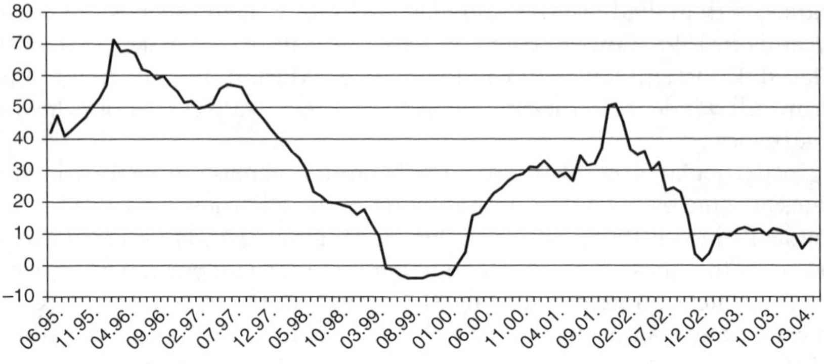

Source: Croatian National Bank.

Figure 20.2 Rate of growth of non-transactions deposits (in per cent, year on year)

macroeconomic situation starting in the second half of 1999. The sale of four banks that had been seized by the government to foreign strategic partners in late 1999 and early 2000 helped further consolidate the situation.

3. DEPOSIT INTEREST RATES AND THE CAUSES OF BANK FAILURES

Most research suggests that bank failures occur as a result of credit boom and bust cycles (see Logan, 2000), recklessness and fraud, and poor management. All other frequently cited reasons can be classified as belonging to the latter category (see Honohan, 1997).

The empirical literature on leading indicators of bank failures suggests that leading indicators can be roughly categorized into five classes: CAMELS[2] grades, international agencies' ratings, market prices of bank stocks and subordinated debt, (standard) balance sheet and income statement financial ratios, and other (non-standard) measures of bank risk and financial strength.

In the case of Croatia in the 1990s, the first three types of indicators cannot be used owing to lack of data. Only one Croatian bank had been rated by an international agency prior to 1998, and only a few banks have ever had their stocks or bonds listed on the market. Also, there is no market for certificates of deposit. Furthermore, even though the interbank market is active in Croatia, it is concentrated on trading in very short-term instruments whose prices carry little information on individual banks' risk premia. Finally, the Croatian National Bank, which supervises commercial banks, had not introduced CAMELS grades prior to the banking failures studied here.

The remaining two classes of potential explanatory variables for our bank failure prediction model are standard balance sheet and income statement ratios and other non-standard indicators of banks' financial condition and risk profile. The indicators most commonly found in empirical studies can further be categorized according to specific risks or strengths that they measure or proxy.[3] We included most of these indicators in our initial analysis, and added some additional ones to measure or proxy specific risks faced by Croatian banks of the mid-1990s (for more information see the detailed discussions of these risks in Kraft, 1999; Šonje and Vujčić, 1999; and Jankov, 2000).

We compiled a list of 38 potential explanatory variables for bank failure prediction, including 33 ratios, 2 interval values and 3 dummies. The three dummies are: new (founded after 1989), foreign (founded as a foreign subsidiary), and 'too big to fail' (by our own expert judgement). Two interval-type variables, to be used for robustness checks, are total assets and total off-balance sheet assets. The remaining 33 'ratios' include standard financial ratios for banks, such as return-on-average assets and Basel-type capital adequacy ratios, but also a number of less standard measures and 'quasi-ratios' (see Appendix Table 20.A1).

Choice of the dependent variable required making several expert judgements. The first decision was whether to include both distressed and failed banks. Since the definition of distress is intrinsically subjective, and in practice often based on perceived levels of the very variables that are included in the candidate explanatory variables list, we chose to consider those banks that eventually entered into a bankruptcy or a liquidation process (14 banks) or had been taken into state receivership and rehabilitated at taxpayers' expense (2 banks). Exceptionally, we also consider one bank as failed that does not formally meet these criteria, but is known to have been insolvent in 1999–2000.[4]

A second, related decision was to extend the time horizon for failure of bankrupt and liquidated banks, since most actually entered into bankruptcy or liquidation only after the 1998–99 crisis period, owing to the unusually slow legal process of bank closure in Croatia. To be precise, we labelled as failed all banks operating at the beginning of 1998 that ceased operations before 2003 due to observable effects of the banking crisis. This gives us a sub-population of 17 failed banks from 1998 to 2002.

Similarly, we extended the independent variable data set to three years before the crisis started (in other words, to 1995), to evaluate the predictive power of our models at three different forecast horizons. We did this because we held a prior belief that some risky bank behaviour would show persistence (that is, its measure or proxy will enter the best model at every lag), while some other behaviours could reasonably be related to failure even if they happened only once (that is deadweight of one year's overly risky investment or chronic illiquidity at the onset of crisis).

Since all of the failed banks were in operation by 1996, and all but one were in operation by 1995, all of the failed banks are included in our analysis. Two foreign-owned subsidiaries that only started their operations in 1997 and the one foreign branch established were excluded from the analysis, since their operations were unusual enough to produce extreme outliers on most candidate variables. This resulted in a sample of 17 failed and 40 surviving banks. Also, since not all candidate variables were measured in all three years of interest, and some banks started operating during this period, not all variables that are measured in all three years have observations on all banks for all years.

Our model building strategy was severely limited by the small size of our bank population. With only 17 failed banks, cross-section logit models containing just one regressor and the constant would be acceptable statistically, and models with two regressors would be pushing the boundaries.[5] These limitations led us to split the analysis into two parts: first, using univariate non-regression methods we tried to find variables that would best discriminate between failed and non-failed banks, and then, second, we analysed all possible two-variable logit failure models as a further check.

We began by testing for normality using the Kolmogorov–Smirnov test with Lilliefors' significance correction, and the Shapiro–Wilk test for variables with less than 51 observations (results available from the authors). The tests found that normality could be rejected at the 5 per cent significance level for 30 of the 35 variables tested. Even among the five variables for which normality could not be rejected, normality could not be rejected for two forecast periods for only two variables, and there were no variables for which normality could not be rejected for all three forecast periods.

Having concluded that by and large the explanatory variables are non-normally distributed, we then used the non-parametric Mann–Whitney U-test (see Table 20.A2 in the Appendix) for the difference in medians between the group of failed banks and the group of survived banks. At the 10 per cent (two-tailed) significance level, the test found four variables that had statistically significant differences in medians for every forecast horizon. It found an additional three variables that were statistically significant at two out of three horizons, and seven variables that were significant at only one horizon. The seven variables significant at more than one horizon (that is persistent features of failed banks) and their group medians with respect to the dependent variable are shown in Table 20.2.

DR represents the annual average of monthly volume-weighted average deposit rates on new or renewed foreign currency denominated deposits. LIQ is the annual average of daily ratios of non-borrowed excess reserves to required reserve deposit base. CAR (capital adequacy ratio) is just a year-end standard Basel I-type regulatory capital-to-risk-weighted assets ratio. RLAR is a year-end risky loans-to-total assets ratio, where risky loans are defined as large and very large loans (with both categories clearly defined by regulation) plus total exposures to connected parties. Computed analogously to DR, the LR variable represents the loan rate on domestic currency-denominated new loans. The only income statement indicator among the selected variables, OHER is the year-end proportion of overhead expenses in total expenses. Finally, the only balance-sheet variable in the selected group, CM (currency mismatch indicator) is the ratio of total foreign currency assets and foreign currency deposits.

These variables represent the persistent features most closely associated with the observed bank failures. They also offer hope of explaining why

Table 20.2 Best persistent univariate predictors of bank failure

Forecast horizon	Group	DR	LIQ	CAR	RLAR	LR	OHER	CM
3-year	F=0	3.9	0.1			24.5	47.8	103.1
	F=1	6.4	−0.1			26.4	52.6	99.3
	Total	4.4	0.0			24.9	50.2	101.0
Mann–Whitney U-Test p		0.0001	0.0035			0.1330	0.2755	0.4294
2-year	F=0	3.2	12.7	35.4	3.8	21.6	52.7	95.4
	F=1	7.4	−13.3	20.2	10.2	26.2	49.9	86.4
	Total	4.4	8.2	31.2	5.5	22.7	50.6	95.1
Mann–Whitney U-Test p		0.0000	0.0009	0.0126	0.0533	0.0143	0.0752	0.0494
1-year	F=0	3.0	13.2	26.8	2.9	15.0	55.9	74.2
	F=1	5.8	−2.3	15.2	11.5	18.7	43.4	57.0
	Total	3.5	8.4	24.4	3.6	16.2	50.9	72.6
Mann–Whitney U-Test p		0.0001	0.0002	0.0024	0.0455	0.0066	0.0396	0.0347

Source: Authors' calculations.

'natural' candidate predictors of bank failures – low profitability, high levels of bad assets, and rapid growth – are not useful for explaining 1998–99 bank failures in Croatia. Looking back to Table 20.2 it is easy to see that the first four variables all have the expected relative values ('signs') at all lags. Thus, the failed banks as a group have higher deposit rates, lower non-borrowed excess reserves, lower capital adequacy and higher levels of risky loans. They also have higher loan rates at all lags, which is consistent with the anecdotal evidence that these banks attracted riskier clients and at the same time mispriced their risk. This contrasts with the more prevalent cross-country finding that low spreads are strongly associated with bank failures (Rojas-Suarez, 2001), perhaps because sudden appearance of fierce competition for deposits raises deposit rates, thus squeezing margins and causing failures of the most inefficient banks.

The remaining two variables, OHER and CM, are both insignificant at lag *t*-3, and for the other two forecast horizons their relative values are difficult to interpret.

Returning to the first four variables, each highly significant and with expected and persistent sign, it is worthwhile to explore possible causal relationships between them and bank failure. The most likely explanation of the causality between high deposit rates and bank failures has already been suggested earlier in this chapter: aggressive banks used high deposit rates to fund their excessively risky business strategies, which eventually led them to failure. The negative relationship between the narrow measure of liquidity (provided by the non-borrowed reserves ratio) and the failure variable can be explained by a temporary failure of the domestic money market during the early stages of the banking crisis, or in a wider context, by the poor liquidity of all economic agents preceding the 1999 recession that made it difficult for illiquid banks to raise funds in those times of need (Šonje et al., 2001). Alternatively, one could cite De Juan in saying that, for banks, chronic illiquidity is almost always a sign of (hidden) insolvency (De Juan, 1996).

Deposit rates and narrow liquidity are by far the most significant univariate predictors of bank failure in our sample, with Mann–Whitney U-test significance levels well below 1 per cent. The other two important variables are capital adequacy and risky loans. Finally, loan interest rates can be interpreted as a measure of negative client selection. They are also highly significant at the first two lags, and only mildly insignificant at lag *t*-3, which makes them a good predictor of bank failure as well.

Having analysed the individual variables that best distinguish between failed and non-failed banks, we proceed to select the 'best' (most parsimonious) two-variable logit models separately for each of the three forecast horizons. The rationale for treating the forecast horizons separately is that the size of the information set available to us for each of the horizons grows as the forecast horizon gets shorter (both due to the availability of new variables, and due to the possibility of using past data). Thus, it is a priori expected that shorter forecast horizons will yield better predictions, which should aid us in the interpretation of the results. The results of this exercise provide further confirmation of an unusually strong connection between deposit rates and bank failures. The model with the lowest SIC statistic[6] was chosen as the 'best' forecasting model for each forecast horizon. The best models are presented in Table 20.3.

The DR variable entered the best model for each of the forecast horizons. More importantly, the two other variables that improved the model fit when added to the DR variable support the thesis developed so far in this chapter: the CRAG variable (measure of the annual growth rate of bank's loan portfolio) entered with a positive sign at the 3-year and the 2-year forecast horizon and the MM variable (the standard liquidity ratio of short-term assets and short-term liabilities) entered with a negative sign at the 1-year forecast horizon. The second best individual predictor of bank failure, the variable LIQ (a non-standard liquidity measure) also entered the second and the third best models for both the 2-year and the 1-year forecast (not shown here). The strong relationship between DR and LIQ as predictors of bank failure in Croatia in the absence of other high-quality predictors has been already documented and interpreted in earlier studies (Kraft, 1999).

Furthermore, it seems that the deposit rate variable DR is not only the best individual predictor of 1998–99 failures of Croatian banks, and the only predictor that is persistently important at all three forecast horizons, but it also dominates other predictors in 'best' two-variable logits for longer horizons, as is evident from the relatively low Wald statistics on the CRAG variable. This result is strikingly similar to the findings of a study of bank failures during the mid-1990s in the Czech Republic (Hanousek, 1999). In the previous version of this chapter (Kraft and Galac, 2004), models with higher SIC values but more reliable parameter estimates were selected as the 'best' for each horizon, but that does not change the main conclusion: at each horizon, the best model always contains the DR variable (see Table 20.4). Moreover, the top 65 specifications out of the total of 4186 specifications tested (for all three horizons), by the value of their SIC statistic, contain the DR variable, and only two out of the top 100 specifications do not contain the DR variable.

Finally, we verified that the DR variable measures a unique characteristic of bank behaviour in the 1995–97 period by estimating the DR-only

Table 20.3 The 'best' logit specifications

3-year forecast

Optimal cut-off =0.41 – 0.62	B	S.E.	Wald	Sig.	95.0% C.I. for EXP (B)	
					Lower	Upper
Intercept	−7.08	2.00	12.54	0.00	−10.99	−3.16
'dr 95'	1.17	0.38	9.44	0.00	0.42	1.92
'crag 95'	0.02	0.01	2.63	0.11	0.00	0.03
Maximized Log-likelihood =		−14.39				

* *Total obs. =45, Failed=15; Total error=15.6%, for failed=26.7%, for survived =10.0%*

2-year forecast

Optimal cut-off =0.32 – 0.54	B	S.E.	Wald	Sig.	95.0% C.I. for EXP (B)	
					Lower	Upper
Intercept	−6.13	1.69	13.22	0.00	−9.44	−2.83
'dr 96'	0.97	0.30	10.36	0.00	0.38	1.57
'crag 95'	0.02	0.01	1.86	0.17	−0.01	0.04
Maximized Log-likelihood =		−14.77				

* *Total obs. =47, Failed=16; Total error=12.8%, for failed=25.0%, for survived =6.5%*

1-year forecast

Optimal cut-off =0.69 – 0.75	B	S.E.	Wald	Sig.	95.0% C.I. for EXP (B)	
					Lower	Upper
Intercept	−2.82	1.64	2.97	0.08	−6.03	0.39
'mm97'	−0.04	0.01	6.31	0.01	−0.06	−0.01
'dr 95'	1.12	0.35	10.20	0.00	0.43	1.81
Maximized Log-likelihood =		−15.83				

* *Total obs. =47, Failed=15; Total error=12.8%, for failed=40%, for survived=0%*

Source: Authors' calculations.

Table 20.4 The best and second-best logit models

3-years ahead		2-years ahead		1-year ahead	
SIC	Model	SIC	Model	SIC	Model
39.99	dr 95 + crag 95	40.88	dr 96 + crag 95	43.02	mm97 + dr 95
42.97	obsag 95 + dr 95	41.79	dr 96 + liq95	45.85	dr 95 + liq97
43.59	dlr 95 + dr 95	41.88	dr 95 + liq96	46.09	dr 96 + liq97

Source: Authors' calculations.

model for each forecast horizon and for each of the five control variables (balance sheet size BS, off-balance sheet size OBS, foreign subsidiary dummy FOR, too-big-to-fail dummy TBTF, and new bank dummy NEW). As expected, including any of the size variables in the regressions was fruitless. Their individual Wald statistics were highly insignificant, while the overall model fit did not change. Also, all interactions between the DR variable and the three dummies were highly insignificant, as were the main effects of the dummies in those regressions.

These findings strongly suggest that high bank deposit rates in the 1995–96 period are the most powerful predictors of bank failures during the 1998–99 banking crisis in Croatia. Other bank characteristics that are possibly associated with those bank failures are strong credit growth in the 1995–96 period, and low liquidity in the 1996–97 period. These findings strongly support the thesis developed in this chapter about the connection between high-risk bank strategies funded by high-yield deposits and subsequent bank failures.

4. CONCLUSIONS

The findings in this chapter lead us to the following conclusions:

1. The link between high deposit interest rates and portfolio risk predicted by theory is confirmed in Croatia. Although deposit interest rates are not the only predictor of failure, they are in fact the best predictor of failure in the Croatian case.
2. At the same time, the Croatian case shows the inability of newly created supervisory authorities to effectively limit risk-taking. In fact, we believe that supervisors did not have a good handle on how much risk individual banks were taking, nor on the quality of banks' loan portfolios. In a situation where bank supervision is undeveloped, or where

liberalization has put greater demands on supervision than it is able to bear, deposit interest rates may be a very useful tool to focus supervisory attention.

3. Monitoring and controlling deposit interest rates seems much easier than monitoring and controlling overall portfolio risk, and this makes the Hellman–Murdock–Stiglitz suggestion of limiting deposit interest rates tempting. However, one should not be naive about banks' ability to get around such regulation. Only the implementation of a comprehensive reporting framework for interest rates like the US Annual Percentage Rate (APR) can prevent banks from offering higher interest rates to customers than they report to the authorities. Usually, drafting, passing and enforcing such regulations takes time; in Croatia, for example, such regulations were introduced well after the banking crisis.

Furthermore, even if one has a uniform system of interest rate reporting in place, risk-loving banks may find other ways to steal market share. These methods most likely will be less transparent than simply offering higher deposit rates.

Finally, one could argue that there is nothing wrong with banks offering high interest rates, if the supervisory authorities use this as a sign of possible increased portfolio risk that triggers enhanced supervisory attention and, if necessary, prompt corrective action. The real problem is not that risk-loving banks offer high deposit interest rates, but that they make bad loans that eventually bring down the bank. It is not clear that limiting deposit interest rates will cut off funding for high-risk projects, or substantially decrease the risk appetite of unsound banks. Thus, it may be more effective to use high deposit interest rates as a signal that helps prioritize the use of scarce supervisory resources in a newly liberalized context, than to try to administratively limit deposit rates and perhaps derive a false confidence that bank risk-taking has been limited. However, in a situation in which bank supervision is very weak, and prompt corrective action powers do not exist or are very limited by legislation, deposit interest rate limitation might be better than nothing.

APPENDIX

Table 20.A1 Definition of variables

Type	No. Code	Description	Measured risk	Expected sign
Dependent	FNAR	Narrow failure indicator: bankrupt, liquidated, rehabilitated	–	–
Dummy	1 NEW	Founded after 1989 indicator	Control	+
	2 FOR	Founded as foreign daughter indicator	Control	–
	3 TBTF	Too big to fail by expert judgement indicator	Control	–
Interval	4 BS	Total balance sheet size	Control	–
	5 OBS	Total size of off-balance sheet items	Control	+
Ratio	6 CAR	Basel 1 capital adequacy ratio	Capital strength	–
	7 RLAR	Very risky loans / total BS assets	Risk-aversion	+
	8 RIAR	Very risky investments / total BS assets	Risk-aversion	+
	9 ROBAR	Uncollateralized off-bs assets / total BS assets	Risk-aversion	+
	10 RMBAR	Mortgage backed BS&OBS claims / total BS assets	Risk-aversion	+
	11 NPAR	Non-performing BS&OBS assets / total BS assets	Asset quality	+
	12 IMPAR	Impaired BS&OBS assets / total BS assets	Asset quality	+
	13 CM	Foreign currency assets / fc deposits	Foreign exchange	–
	14 MM	Short term assets / st deposits	Liquidity	–
	15 SDI	1 – Sum (sector ass. square) / Total ass. square	Sectoral	–
	16 NCSSR	Non-core sources / sources	Liquidity	+
	17 FAAR	Fixed assets / assets	Liquidity	+
	18 PIAR	Permanent investment / assets	Liquidity	+
	19 AARER	Accruals&arrears / revenues&expenses	Liquidity	+
	20 ROA	Return on end-year assets	Profitability	–
	21 ROE	Return on end-year equity	Profitability	–
	22 PAR	Provisions / assets	Asset quality	+/–
	23 PCR	Provisions / equity	Asset quality	+/–
	24 LTIAR	Long-term investment / assets	Liquidity	+
	25 LDR	Loans / deposits	Liquidity	+

Table 20.A1 (continued)

Type	No. Code	Description	Measured risk	Expected sign
	26 DLR	Deposit placements / loan sources	Liquidity	+
	27 MGPPR	Money & gov. paper / core sources	Liquidity	–
	28 NIM	Net interest margin	Efficiency	–
	29 OHAR	Overhead exp. / assets	Efficiency	+
	30 OHER	Overhead exp. / expenses	Efficiency	+
	31 OBBR	Off-bs assets / bs assets	Control	+/–
	32 BSAG	Annual balance sheet growth rate	Growth	+
	33 OBSAG	Annual off-balance sheet growth rate	Growth	+
	34 LR	Interest rate on credits in national currency, ann. avg.	Adverse selection	+
	35 DR	Deposit rate on foreign currency savings, ann. avg.	Moral hazard	+
	36 SPR	LR-DR	Efficiency	–
	37 LIQ	Non-borrowed excess reserves / req. res. deposit base	Liquidity	–
	38 CRAG	Annual loan growth rate	Growth	+

Source: Authors' compilation.

Table 20.A2 *Mann–Whitney U-test results for initial predictors*

Variable	Year (2 × 1-sided p-value)				Total
	94	95	96	97	
DR		0.000	0.000	0.000	0.0
LIQ		0.003	0.001	0.000	0.0
CAR			0.013	0.002	0.0
RLAR			0.053	0.045	0.1
LR		0.133	0.014	0.007	0.2
OHER		0.276	0.075	0.040	0.4
CM		0.429	0.049	0.035	0.5
PIAR		0.253	0.179	0.116	0.5
CRAG		0.143	0.383	0.060	0.6
ROBAR			0.364	0.320	0.7

Table 20.A2 (continued)

Variable	Year (2 × 1-sided p-value)				Total
	94	95	96	97	
MBAR			0.443	0.250	0.7
BSAG		0.131	0.204	0.530	0.9
MM		0.320	0.259	0.287	0.9
SDI		0.416	0.320	0.191	0.9
LTIAR		0.440	0.332	0.215	1.0
OHAR		0.500	0.496	0.072	1.1
ROA		0.606	0.020	0.453	1.1
AARER		0.322	0.475	0.329	1.1
NPAR			0.541	0.760	1.3
MGPPR		0.792	0.202	0.364	1.4
PAR		0.108	0.303	0.958	1.4
IMPAR			0.577	0.855	1.4
NCSSR		0.905	0.530	0.078	1.5
NIM		0.855	0.051	0.625	1.5
OBSAG		0.069	0.745	0.729	1.5
PCR		0.226	0.794	0.542	1.6
SPR		0.815	0.495	0.407	1.7
RIAR			0.917	0.821	1.7
DLR		0.259	0.653	0.930	1.8
ROE		0.984	0.057	0.875	1.9
LDR		0.776	0.799	0.519	2.1
OBBR		0.428	0.866	0.931	2.2
FAAR		0.706	0.807	0.986	2.5
OBS	0.168	0.751	0.794	0.979	2.7
BS	0.304	0.937	0.650	0.903	2.8
Total	**0.472**	**12.586**	**13.461**	**15.213**	**41.7**

Source: Authors' calculations.

Table 20.A3 Correlations among final predictors

Y = 1997

CRAG	LIQ	DR	LR	OHER	OHAR	NCSSR	CM	RLAR	CAR	
1.00	**0.34**	**−0.09**	**−0.29**	**0.06**	**−0.05**	**−0.09**	**−0.20**	**−0.28**	**0.25**	**CRAG**
	0.01	0.52	0.03	0.63	0.69	0.49	0.14	0.03	0.06	
	1.00	**−0.42**	**−0.38**	**0.39**	**−0.02**	**−0.20**	**0.23**	**−0.34**	**0.55**	**LIQ**
		0.00	0.00	0.00	0.89	0.13	0.09	0.01	0.00	
		1.00	**0.55**	**−0.49**	**0.15**	**0.30**	**−0.47**	**−0.04**	**−0.18**	**DR**
			0.00	0.00	0.28	0.03	0.00	0.77	0.19	
			1.00	**−0.18**	**0.10**	**0.25**	**0.10**	**0.07**	**−0.11**	**LR**
				0.19	0.46	0.07	0.45	0.58	0.43	
				1.00	**0.30**	**−0.19**	**0.52**	**−0.11**	**0.48**	**OHER**
					0.02	0.15	0.00	0.43	0.00	
					1.00	**0.09**	**−0.07**	**0.06**	**0.13**	**OHAR**
						0.49	0.61	0.68	0.32	
						1.00	**−0.04**	**0.13**	**−0.06**	**NCSSR**
							0.78	0.33	0.67	
							1.00	**0.07**	**0.32**	**CM**
								0.60	0.02	
								1.00	**−0.44**	**RLAR**
									0.00	
									1.00	**CAR**

Y = 1996

LIQ96	DR96	LR96	OHER96	NIM96	ROE96	ROA96	CM96	RLAR96	CAR96	
1.00	**−0.31**	**−0.24**	**0.37**	**0.12**	**0.12**	**0.26**	**0.38**	**−0.28**	**0.63**	**LIQ96**
	0.03	0.08	0.01	0.39	0.40	0.06	0.00	0.04	0.00	
	1.00	**0.51**	**−0.43**	**−0.10**	**−0.08**	**−0.04**	**−0.28**	**0.05**	**−0.08**	**DR96**
		0.00	0.00	0.49	0.56	0.81	0.05	0.74	0.56	
		1.00	**−0.19**	**0.28**	**0.17**	**0.17**	**0.07**	**0.12**	**−0.16**	**LR96**
			0.16	0.04	0.22	0.21	0.61	0.38	0.26	
			1.00	**0.04**	**−0.29**	**−0.14**	**0.30**	**0.00**	**0.51**	**OHER96**
				0.79	0.03	0.30	0.03	0.98	0.00	
				1.00	**0.29**	**0.41**	**0.44**	**−0.15**	**0.09**	**NIM96**
					0.03	0.00	0.00	0.28	0.52	
					1.00	**0.91**	**0.12**	**−0.53**	**0.00**	**ROE96**
						0.00	0.37	0.00	0.99	
						1.00	**0.21**	**−0.52**	**0.18**	**ROA96**
							0.13	0.00	0.17	
							1.00	**−0.10**	**0.44**	**CM96**
								0.48	0.00	
								1.00	**−0.39**	**RLAR96**
									0.00	
									1.00	**CAR96**

Y = 1995

LIQ95	DR95	OBSAG95	
1.00	**−0.30**	**0.14**	**LIQ95**
	0.04	0.35	
	1.00	**0.00**	**DR95**
		0.98	
		1.00	**OBSAG95**

Note: * shaded areas mark correlations significant at the 10-per cent (2-tailed) significance level.

Source: Authors' calculations.

NOTES

1. The authors would like to thank, without implicating, Dubravko Mihaljek, Velimir Šonje, Helmut Elsinger, Adalbert Winkler, Carsten Detkens, Egon Zakrajšek and Phillip Hartmann for helpful comments and suggestions. All remaining errors are the responsibility of the authors. The views expressed herein do not necessarily represent the views of the Croatian National Bank.
2. CAMELS – Capital Assets Management Earnings Liquidity Sensitivity to market risk.
3. See for example Logan (2000), Gonzalez-Hermosillo (1999), Hanousek (1999) and Rojas-Suarez (2001).
4. The bank was found to be insolvent by central bank examiners. A central bank administrator was appointed, and the announcement of his appointment led to a bank run. The bank was temporarily closed, and then recapitalized by government payment of back interest on certain government securities held by this bank and others. Later the bank was sold.
5. According to Hosmer and Lemeshow (2000), in most cases samples with at least ten observations per coefficient to be estimated in the least represented group are required to achieve standard (95 per cent) confidence levels for parameter estimates of logit models. In our case, we are three observations shy of this for the simple regression models, since our least represented group has 17 members. However, Peduzzi et al. (1996) argue that stable parameter estimates in binary logit models require at least five observations per coefficient estimated for the least represented group. With 17 failures, we then have two observations more than that minimum requirement when we estimate models with three coefficients.
6. In an earlier version of this chapter (Kraft and Galac, 2004) only good univariate predictors for each forecast horizon from Table 20.2 were considered for inclusion in the logit model for that horizon. The approach adopted in this chapter corrects the obvious weaknesses of such approach: (1) omission of indicators of possibly relevant past bank behaviour; (2) omission of potentially useful bivariate indicators with no univariate predictive power; and (3) possible over-parameterization. The SIC statistic selection criterion used in this chapter can be expressed in a standard form as SIC = $-2 \times$ Max. log-likelihood + $\times$ (Ln(N), where N is the number of observations (due to some missing data, it slightly varies with model specification), while k is the number of predictors (for two-variable logits it is fixed to value of three).

REFERENCES

Ahec-Šonje, Amina (1999), 'Navješcujući indikatori valutnih i bankarskih kriza: Hrvatska i svijet', *Privredna kretanja i ekonomska politika*, No. 75, pp. 31–85.

Allen, Franklin and Douglas Gale (2003), 'Competition and financial stability', *Wharton Financial Institutions Center Working Paper Series*, 03–26, September.

Chan, Yuk-Shee, Stuart Greenbaum and Anjan Thakor (1992), 'Is fairly priced deposit insurance possible?', *Journal of Finance*, **47** (1), 227–45.

Crane, Roger (1995), 'Fairly priced deposit insurance and bank charter policy', *Journal of Finance*, **50** (5), 1735–46.

De Juan, Aristobolo (1996), 'The roots of banking crises: microeconomic issues' in Ricardo Hausmann and Liliana Rojas-Suarez (eds), *Banking Crises in Latin America*, Washington, DC: Inter-American Development Bank, pp. 81–102.

Demirgüç-Kunt, Asli and Enrica Detragiache (1998), 'The determinants of banking crises in developing and developed countries', *IMF Staff Papers*, **45** (1), 81–109.

Demirgüç-Kunt, Asli and Enrica Detragiache (1999), 'Financial liberalization and financial fragility', in Boris Pleskovic and Joseph Stiglitz (eds), *Annual Bank Conference on Development Economics 1998*, Washington, DC: World Bank, pp. 303–31.

Diaz-Alejandro, Carlos (1985), 'Good-bye financial repression, hello financial crash', *Journal of Development Economics*, **19** (1–2), 1–24.

Estrella, Arturo, S. Park and S. Peristiani (2000), 'Capital ratios as predictors of bank failures', *Federal Reserve Bank of New York Economic Policy Review*, **6** (2), 33–52.

Fischer, P. Klaus and H. Smaoui (1997), 'From financial liberalization to banking failure: starting on the wrong foot?', *CREFA Working Papers*, WP 97-03.

Flannery, Mark (1991), 'Pricing deposit insurance when the insurer measures bank risk with error', *Journal of Banking and Finance*, **15** (4–5), 975–98.

Freixas, Xavier and Jean-Charles Rochet (1998), 'Fair pricing of deposit insurance. Is it possible? Yes. Is it desirable? No.', *Research in Economics*, **52** (3), 217–32.

Galac, Tomislav (2005), 'Does Croatia need risk-based deposit insurance premia?', *Croatian National Bank Surveys*, S-10, February.

Gonzalez-Hermosillo, Brenda (1999), 'Determinants of Ex-Ante Banking System Distress: A Macro-Micro Exploration of Some Recent Episodes', *IMF Working Paper* 99/33.

Gourinchas, Pierre-Olivier, Rodrigo Valdés and Oscar Landerretche (2001), 'Lending booms: Latin America and the world', *National Bureau of Economic Research Working Papers*, Working Paper No. 8249, April.

Hanousek, Jan (1999), 'Predicting bank failures in transition. Lessons from the Czech Bank crises of the mid-nineties', *CERGE-EI Discussion Papers*, No. 15, October.

Hellmann, Thomas, Kevin Murdock and Joseph Stiglitz (2000), 'Liberalization, moral hazard in banking and prudential regulation: Are capital requirements enough?', *American Economic Review*, **90** (1), 147–65.

Honohan, Patrick (1997), 'Banking system failures in developing and transition countries: Diagnosis and prediction', *BIS Working Papers*, No. 39, January.

Hosmer, D.W. and S. Lemeshow (2000), *Applied Logistic Regression*, New York: John Wiley & Sons.

Jankov, Ljubinko (2000), 'Banking sector problems: causes, solutions and consequences', *Croatian National Bank Surveys*, S-1, March.

Jeitschko, Thomas and Shin Dong Jeung (2005), 'Incentives for risk taking in banking', *Journal of Banking and Finance*, **29** (3), 759–77.

John, Kose, Teresa John and Lemma Sembet (1991), 'Risk-shifting incentives of depository institutions: A new perspective on federal deposit insurance reform', *Journal of Banking Finance*, **15** (4–5), 895–915.

Kane, Edward (1989), *The S&L Insurance Mess; How Did It Happen?*, Washington, DC: Urban Institute Press.

Keeley, Michael (1990), 'Deposit insurance, risk and market power in banking', *American Economic Review*, **80** (5), 1184–1200.

Kraft, Evan (1999), 'Croatia's second banking crisis', *Third Conference on Enterprises in Transition*, Split, Croatia: Split Faculty of Economics, May.

Kraft, Evan (2004), 'Foreign banks in Croatia: Reasons for entry, performance and impacts', *Journal of Emerging Markets Finance*, **3** (2), 153–74.

Kraft, Evan and Tomislav Galac (2004), 'Deposit interest rates, asset risk and bank failure in Croatia', in *Proceedings of the 65th Anniversary Conference of The Institute of Economics, Zagreb*, Zagreb: The Institute of Economics.

Kraft, Evan and Ljubinko Jankov (2005), 'Does speed kill? Lending booms and their consequences in Croatia', *Journal of Banking and Finance*, **29** (1), 105–22.
Kupiec, Paul and James O'Brien (1998), 'Deposit insurance, bank incentives and the design of regulatory policy', *Federal Reserve Board of New York Economic Policy Review*, **4** (3), 201–11.
Logan, Andrew (2000), 'The early 1990s small bank crisis: Leading indicators', *Financial Stability Review*, Bank of England, December, pp. 130–45.
Nyberg, Peter and Vesa Vihriala (1994), 'The Finnish banking crisis and its handling (an update of developments through 1993)', *Bank of Finland Discussion Papers*, 7/94.
Peduzzi, P., J. Concato, E. Kemper, T.R. Holford and A. Feinstein (1996), 'A simulation of the number of events per variable in logistic regression analysis', *Journal of Clinical Epidemiology*, **99**.
Ranciere, Romaine, Aaron Tornell and Frank Westermann (2003), 'Crises and growth: A re-evaluation', *National Bureau of Economic Research Working Papers*, 10073, October.
Rojas-Suarez, Liliana (2001), 'Rating banks in emerging markets: What credit agencies should learn from financial indicators', *Institute for International Economics Working Papers*, 01–6, May.
Šonje, Velimir (1997), 'Banks at the crossroads', *National Bank of Croatia Surveys*, No. 4, September.
Šonje, Velimir (1999), 'Financial crises: A never-ending story', *Croatian National Bank Discussion Papers*, D-1, January.
Šonje, Velimir and Boris Vujčić (1999), 'Croatia in the second stage of transition 1994–1999', *Croatian National Bank Working Papers*, W-1, December.
Šonje, Velimir, Michael Faulend and Vedran Šošić (2001), 'Nelikvidnost: razotkrivanje tajne', *Istraživanja hrvatske narodne banke*, I-9, May.
Vihriala, Vesa (1996), 'Credit growth and moral hazard: An empirical study of the causes of credit expansion by the Finnish Local Banks in 1986–1990', *Bank of Finland Discussion Papers*, 10/96.
White, Lawrence (1991), *The S&L Debacle: Public Policy Lessons for Bank and Thrift Regulation*, New York: Oxford University Press.

21. Investigating the early signals of banking sector vulnerabilities in Central and East European emerging markets

Kadri Männasoo and David G. Mayes*

Most of the Central and Eastern European countries (CEECs) have experienced severe banking problems over the 1990s. These economies have been vulnerable to external shocks coupled with financial liberalization and economic restructuring. The purpose of our research is to establish whether these problems for banks are primarily a function of the unique difficulties of transition or whether they reflect similar factors to those recorded in the lead-up to financial problems elsewhere round the globe. Most of the existing research on the factors that help explain the occurrence of these problems deals with Asian or South American banking difficulties. Moreover, some extensive cross-country studies, Hardy and Pazarbasioglu (1998), for example, deliberately refrain from including Central and Eastern European transition countries because they feel that these former socialist transition economies suffered a special range of problems that make them non-comparable with most of the other countries.

It is normally argued that the CEECs have faced twin problems. They have started from state banks dominated by directed lending. Such banks have had to switch to a risk-based approach and acquire the expertise necessary to run such a system successfully in a competitive environment. Many such banks were technically insolvent on market-based criteria, that is without unlimited state support, and hence needed to be recapitalized. At the same time the opening up of the economy to market forces tends to render many of the previous enterprises uncompetitive in their present activities. This results in a major contraction in the economy and the revelation of a substantial stock of non-performing loans.

The authorities are similarly unprepared for this environment, both in being able to prepare banks for the rigours of the new regime or in detecting problems and assisting in their solution. Major fiscal pressures from declining revenues and increased unemployment compound the difficulty and inhibit recapitalization. If this were not enough there has normally been a bout of high inflation as the whole structure of prices tries to adjust in a period of shortage. In many cases this results in a two-stage problem. In the first instance the banks are overwhelmed by the scale of the macroeconomic pressures on the whole range of their customers. In the second, their fragility, lack of experience and the pressure for success among a substantial number of new entrants leads to further problems, exacerbated by any external shocks.

In this chapter we seek to explore how the experience of banks across the CEECs conforms to this pattern. We anticipate that initially economy-wide problems will dominate as the cause of distress, while later the difficulties will become more bank- and regime-specific and hence more reminiscent of the experience in other countries. After the second shake-out it appears that many of the CEECs have banking and regulatory structures similar to those of their Western European counterparts, assisted by considerable foreign ownership.

1. THE FRAMEWORK FOR ADDRESSING THE PROBLEM

It is inevitable that comparative studies of emerging markets should be dominated by concerns over the data. As a result such cross-country studies tend to focus more on macroeconomic data than on other factors as they are more readily available and prima facie compatible. In these papers, GDP growth, inflation, exchange rate movements and the terms of trade serve as the warning signals of banking problems, as they all indicate sources of pressure on bank income flows and balance sheets. These broad-based macro indicators can sometimes be complemented with a set of aggregate banking sector variables such as credit to the private sector, deposits and banking sector foreign reserves.[1] Detailed differences aside, the general conclusions of macro data-driven studies are consistent and intuitive. In brief the results reaffirm that a deteriorating macroeconomic situation and underlying instabilities precipitate banking crises. These results have much in common with the findings for OECD countries, as is illustrated in Mayes et al. (2001, Chapter 2) for the Nordic countries.

Demirgüç-Kunt and Detragiache (1998) focus on a further potential trigger of financial fragility that is relevant for our study, namely, financial liberalization. Although financial liberalization as it is traditionally viewed – removal of interest rate controls in their case – is a more minor shift than the transition economies faced, it is nevertheless a regime change and hence instructive. Their results indicate that financial liberalization exerts a negative effect on the stability of the financial sector that is additional to those from adverse macroeconomic developments and related vulnerabilities to balance-of-payments crises. A strong institutional environment can, however, alleviate the adverse impact of liberalization on the financial system (Demirgüç-Kunt and Detragiache, 1998). Unfortunately the study does not include the CEECs.

Notwithstanding the valuable insights from previous studies there is little evidence on how authorities such as central banks and supervisory agencies could make use of financial fragility indicators in order to safeguard the stability of the banking system as a whole. Similar problems exist in finding clear evidence on why some banks survive the adverse macroeconomic conditions and external shocks whereas others fail. There are several studies mainly based on US and a few Latin-American countries' banking data (for example Gonzalez-Hermosillo et al., 1997; Gonzalez-Hermosillo, 1999), which try to explore specific banking sector indicators (CAMELS[2] framework) which can serve as valuable early warning signs of banking distress. The particular value of these studies lies in recognition of these factors, which can be addressed by appropriate banking regulation and adequate supervision. The degree of fragility of individual banks is closely linked to the overall propensity to banking crisis (also due to contagion effects), in which the bank-specific factors play an important role in systemic stability.

2. SPECIFICATION OF THE MODEL

We follow the normal framework of assuming that bank distress, d, depends upon three groups of variables: macroeconomic conditions, m; the financial structure of the economy, s; and factors related to the condition of individual banks, b.

$$d = f(m, s, b).$$

2.1 Definition of Bank Distress

There is a considerable debate over how best to measure banking distress or fragility. In order to make our work comparable we employ well-known indicators that can be applied to the data available on individual banks in the CEECs during the period since 1996. Studies of early warning systems that rely on macro-level data (such as Demirgüç-Kunt and Detragiache, 1998, 1999; and Hutchison and McDill, 1999) are mainly based upon the Caprio and Klingebiel (2003) and Lindgren et al. (1996) datasets of systemic and borderline banking crises. Given conceptual ambiguity and data limitations the criteria they use for defining a crisis employ a combination of events, such as forced closure, merger or government intervention in the operations of financial institutions, runs on banks, or the extension of large-scale government assistance. However, neither study relates explicitly to the CEECs.

The choice of indicators of individual bank distress normally covers measures of non-performing assets, problem loans and solvency. Non-performing loans have often been used as the crisis threshold, because they are the best indicator of near term failure (Gonzales-Hermosillo, 1999). Hutchison and McDill (1999) claim that a bank run is very likely to be preceded by deterioration in the quality of assets, but this is difficult to measure, because direct market indicators of asset value are usually lacking. There is no one generally accepted or easily attainable measure of the existence of 'problems' so we have to be somewhat pragmatic in our choice. Gonzales-Hermosillo et al. (1997) define fragile banks as those with non-performing loans of more than 6–8 per cent of total loans. Demirgüç-Kunt and Detragiache (1998) define a crisis period as one in which the non-performing loans of the banking system are more than 10 per cent of total assets. Rojas-Suarez (1998) classify as 'crisis' banks whose non-performing loans to total loans are greater than the average for the system as a whole during 'tranquil' periods plus two standard deviations.

Since we have bank-specific data it makes more sense to focus on measures we can obtain directly. Therefore rather than conditioning on institutional measures such as the existence of government support, recapitalization or other such interventions, we apply a modified version of the Gonzales-Hermosillo (1999) coverage ratio, which is the ratio of equity capital and loan reserves[3] minus non-performing loans to total assets. The advantage of the coverage ratio is that it takes into account reserves and equity capital, which could cover the amount of the problem loans.[4] Instead of total assets we use the larger of net loan provisions or impaired loans as the denominator. In order to account for bank capital cushion and the potential losses from non-performing loans, the crisis for a bank is defined as a situation where the ratio of equity and loan reserves surplus is less than the higher of net loan provisions or impaired loans. We label this as a 'distressed' bank. Banks with negative or zero equity are labelled as 'insolvent'.[5]

$$\text{Equity} \leq 0 \text{ or}$$

$$\left(\frac{Equity + [loan\ reserves - Max(net\ loan\ provisions,\ impaired\ loans)]}{Max(net\ loan\ provisions,\ impaired\ loans)} < 1 \,\middle|\, equity > 0;\ net\ loan\ provisions > 0 \right)^{6}$$

Our definition of 'problem' banks thus encompasses the institutions that are insolvent and institutions that are at increased risk due to high actual or potential loan losses eroding the capital. The latter category of banks might be called distressed, because, while their own funds cover the loan losses in the current period, they would not withstand the same magnitude of losses next period, holding the equity level constant. This gives us a three-way categorization of: sound, distressed and insolvent banks.

2.2 Early Warning Indicators

The choice of early warning indicators of impending problems that can be used in analysis is heavily constrained by the data available. The wider the sample of countries, the narrower will be the choice. As set out in Table 21.1, indicators of the probability of failure for an individual bank can be divided into: those that are bank-specific; those that characterize the banking sector through externalities or contagion factors; and macroeconomic factors that affect all banks. The latter two normally apply equally to all banks, although their exposures differ.

Overall there is no universal set of indicators used across previous studies, although there is more communality over broad-based macro variables, such as GDP, exchange rate and inflation indexes, which have better cross-country comparability and availability. By contrast the set of bank-specific variables varies a great deal across the studies available on a cross-country basis. Even ostensibly similar bank-specific variables may not be very comparable across countries as the accounting regulations and supervisory rules can be very different.

The basis for comparison of bank-specific variables used in Table 21.1 is fairly limited and relies mostly on US, Mexican and Columbian data.[7] However, there is also a study by Berg and Hexeberg (1994) of Norwegian banks, which serves as a good comparison here. Five categories of variables are distinguished (expected signs in parenthesis): Liquidity/assets (–); Capital/assets (–); Loans/assets (+); Deposits/assets (+/–); Interest + fee income/assets (+). All of these are conventional measures of bank strength.

The papers dealing with US and Latin-American banks, despite regional proximity, do not always have consistent results for the same indicators. While in general a high liquid assets ratio is expected to imply a reduced probability of bank distress, the result for Californian banks indicates the opposite, and for Mexico and Columbia the coefficients, although with the intuitively correct sign, turned out to be statistically insignificant. The same applies to bank deposits-to-assets ratios and lending indicators, which have opposite and even statistically significant coefficients for

Table 21.1 Metastudy summary

BANK-SPECIFIC VARIABLES	Liquid assets ratio	Capital-asset ratio	Loan-to-assets ratio	Bank deposits ratio[8]	Interest and fee income to total assets
Berg and Hexeberg; 1994 Norway: 1987–91 (annual, incl.≈20 banks)	n.a.	−***	Loan growth +**	+	n.a.
Gonzalez-Hermosillo et al., 1997 Mexico: 4q1991–4q1995	−	−	n.a.	+**	n.a.
Gonzalez-Hermosillo, 1999					
US:					
SW (1986–93)	−**	−***	−*	−***	+***
NE (1992–93)	−***	−***	+**	−***	n.a
California (92–93)	+	−***	+	−**	n.a
Mexico (1994–95)	−	−***	+**	+*	+
Colombia (1982–87)	−	−	+	+	+**
MACROECONOMIC AND BANKING SECTOR VARIABLES	**Economic activity (GDP or income growth)**	**Financial deepening (Loans to GDP)**	**Average annual growth of CPI**	**Depreciation**	**Real interest rate**
Gonzalez-Hermosillo et al., 1997 Mexico: 4q1991–4q1995	−exp	+**	+ exp	−	+
Demirgüç-Kunt and Detragiache, 1998, 1999: Panel of 65 countries 1980–95	−***	+**	+**	+	+***
Hardy and Pazarbasioglu, 1998 38 country panel, 1980–97	−***	−** Lag(2) +*	+** Lag(2) −**	−** Lag(2) +	+*** Lag(2) +**
Hutchison and McDill, 1999: 67 country panel, 1975–97	−**	−	+	+	+

Table 21.1 (continued)

BANK-SPECIFIC VARIABLES	Liquid assets ratio	Capital-asset ratio	Loan-to-assets ratio	Bank deposits ratio[8]	Interest and fee income to total assets
Gonzalez-Hermosillo, 1999					
US:					
SW (1986–93)	–**	–***	n.a	n.a	+***
NE (1992–93)	–***	–	n.a	n.a	–
California (92–93)	–***	+	n.a	n.a	–
Mexico (1994–95)	n.a.	+**	n.a	+	+
Colombia (1982–87)	n.a	+***	n.a	n.a	n.a

Notes:
Dependent variable:
(1) Berg and Hexeberg, 1994: **Problem bank** is considered as a bank seeking assistance from an insurance fund.
(2) Gonzalez-Hermosillo et al., 1997: **Bank Failure** – Occurrence of bank intervention in form of financial assistance, recapitalization etc.
(3) Gonzalez-Hermosillo, 1999: **Bank Failure** – the incidence of intervention; **Distress** – Coverage ratio i.e ratio of capital equity and loan reserves minus non-performing loans to total assets.
(4) Demirgüç-Kunt and Detragiache (1998, 1999); Hutchison and McDill (1999): Definition of (systemic) **financial crisis** based on Caprio and Klingebiel (1996) and Lindgren et al. (1996). For an episode to be classified as crisis at least one of following conditions must apply: NPL to total banking sector assets above 10%; Ratio of NPL to total assets greater than 2% of GDP; The cost of rescue operation at least 2% of GDP; Large scale nationalization; Extensive bank runs; Emergency measures applied such as deposit freezes, prolonged bank holidays, deposit guarantees.
* statistical significance at 10%, ** statistical significance at 5%, *** statistical significance at 1%. *Exp* – expected sign.

Source: Authors' compilation.

different bank samples. Extensive lending in the form of higher loan-to-assets ratios or loan growth ratios seems to be more predominantly a trigger of a crisis, with the sole exception of the US Southwest. The most convincing result is for the capital-to-asset ratio which is consistently negatively correlated with crises across different samples and studies. Taken together, the degree of heterogeneity is not a good omen for using this approach on the CEECs.

The results for macroeconomic indicators are in better conformity, moreover the studies under consideration incorporate large cross-country samples all over the world. However, we can see that the results also vary here, as some studies come up with conflicting evidence. According to most studies financial deepening seems to increase vulnerability, however there are exceptions. It is not immediately apparent what result we should expect. Financial deepening is a sign of economic maturity so a negative sign would be plausible.

The same ambiguity applies to currency depreciation as a possible precipitator of banking problems. Here, the ambivalent results might stem from cross-country differences in monetary policy (inflation targeting versus exchange rate targeting), country comparative competitive advantages, the level of financial deepening or general stability and maturity of the economic environment. In any case the impact would depend on how well the banks and their customers were hedged, itself a feature of financial deepening. Fortunately, given the aim of our study, the largest weight is carried by bank-specific variables, which can serve as valuable predictors of emerging vulnerabilities. Hence, the main source for vulnerability indicators is the balance sheet and income statement information. The bank-specific view is complemented by several indicators reflecting the macroeconomic environment and structural developments.

One critical issue is the time effect of signalling variables, as this plays a major role when considering the high likelihood of endogenous feedback. Due to likely endogeneity the warning variables might behave counter-intuitively depending on the time lag before the incidence of distress, and perhaps a generalized method of moments (GMM) or some other means of coping with simultaneity will be required.

3. THE EMPIRICAL STUDY

3.1 The Data

Much of the novelty of the present chapter is attributable to the underlying data. The study uses macro- and microeconomic variables drawn from Bankscope, IFS and Eurostat for 21 CEECs including all new EU member states and candidate countries and several republics of the former Soviet Union including Russia over the years 1996–2003. The full list is shown in Table 21.2.

Owing to missing entries the initial sample of 684 banks and 2787 observations was reduced to about 900 observations and 300 banks from 17 countries in the econometric analysis.[9] The following descriptive analysis, except for the table of average values of early warning indicators,[10] however, employs all data for which the bank status could be identified, or 2787 observations.

Table 21.2 Countries included

Albania	Belarus
Bulgaria	Bosnia-Herzegovina
Croatia	Czech Republic
Cyprus	Estonia
Hungary	Latvia
Lithuania	FYR of Macedonia
Malta	Moldova
Poland	Romania
Russian Federation	Slovakia
Slovenia	Turkey
Ukraine	

Table 21.3 shows the crisis episodes for the full data set, indicating that 1999 was the year of greatest banking problems; 40 occurrences (14 insolvent, 26 distressed) in 15 different countries. Weighted by the severity of banking problems (insolvency or distress), the countries, which faced the largest number of bank stress incidences over the period 1996–2003, were Poland, Croatia, Turkey, Russia, the Czech Republic and Slovakia. The systemic impact of bank distress, as measured by the number of problem banks from the whole sector and the share of assets from the banking sector total, indicates that broadly the same countries, except Russia, were the most affected. However, Malta and Cyprus also indicated a relatively high level of stress from a systemic perspective.

Despite the fast restructuring process leading to high diversity in economic and political achievements across CEE countries there are no remarkable differences in bank-specific variables between the new EU members and the rest of the CEECs (see Figure 21.1). The only statistically significant exception is the loan-to-assets ratio, which was higher for problem banks in EU countries but lower for unsound banks in the non-EU sample. This is probably a feature of the immature lending markets, where banks with a larger lending portfolio exhibit a greater resemblance to banks in developed economies and are thus also more market-oriented.

In contrast to bank-specific variables there is more diversity in the macroeconomic variables between the EU and non-EU sub-samples. While higher concentration is indicated by the Herfindahl index for problem banks in the non-EU sample, the opposite of low banking market concentration is coupled with banking problems in EU sample countries. A high

Table 21.3 Distribution of bank problems over countries and years in the CEEC 1996–2003

year	crisis	Albania	Belarus	Bosnia-Herz	Bulgaria	Croatia	Czech Rep	Cyprus	Estonia	Hungary	Latvia	Lithuania
1996	sound	n.a.	2	2	5	30	15	4	7	8	14	3
	distress	n.a.	0	0	2	0	3	0	0	0	1	0
	insolvent	n.a.	0	0	1	0	2	0	0	0	0	2
1997	sound	2	1	4	11	36	14	4	7	10	15	6
	distress	0	1	2	4	1	5	1	1	1	2	1
	insolvent	0	0	0	0	0	0	0	0	0	0	0
1998	sound	1	3	12	19	30	13	5	3	8	13	8
	distress	0	0	0	0	3	4	1	1	0	1	0
	insolvent	0	1	0	0	0	0	0	0	0	1	0
1999	sound	3	6	12	18	30	15	6	4	12	13	7
	distress	0	0	3	1	2	2	1	0	0	2	0
	insolvent	2	0	0	0	1	0	0	0	0	0	0
2000	sound	5	6	15	20	29	15	7	4	14	17	8
	distress	0	0	1	1	7	1	1	1	0	1	1
	insolvent	0	0	0	0	0	0	0	0	0	0	0
2001	sound	4	10	13	21	29	14	10	3	11	13	9
	distress	0	0	1	0	5	1	0	1	0	0	0
	insolvent	0	0	1	0	0	0	0	0	0	0	0
2002	sound	5	10	16	24	26	14	7	4	12	16	9
	distress	0	0	0	0	5	1	5	0	0	0	0
	insolvent	0	0	0	0	0	0	0	0	0	0	0
2003	sound	3	6	12	22	30	14	7	5	9	19	9
	distress	0	0	0	0	6	0	3	1	0	0	0
	insolvent	0	0	0	0	0	0	0	0	0	0	0
1997–2003	sound	23	44	86	140	240	114	50	37	84	120	59
	distress	0	1	7	8	29	17	12	5	1	7	2
	insolvent	2	1	1	1	1	2	0	0	0	1	2
Observations total		25	46	94	149	270	133	62	42	85	128	63

year	crisis	Macedonia	Malta	Moldova	Poland	Romania	Russian Fed	Slovakia	Slovenia	Turkey	Ukraine	Total
1996	sound	6	4	6	28	1	36	11	16	10	6	214
	distress	0	0	0	1	1	1	2	0	0	0	11
	insolvent	0	0	0	1	0	0	0	0	0	0	6
1997	sound	6	5	6	32	5	39	14	22	12	11	262
	distress	0	0	0	2	0	0	2	0	0	0	23
	insolvent	0	0	0	1	0	0	1	0	1	0	3
1998	sound	4	6	5	29	8	25	10	15	14	15	246
	distress	0	0	1	3	0	0	3	1	0	2	20
	insolvent	0	0	0	1	0	2	2	0	1	0	8
1999	sound	7	4	9	28	9	56	9	17	27	25	317
	distress	2	1	0	6	1	1	2	0	2	0	26
	insolvent	0	0	0	2	1	5	1	0	2	0	14
2000	sound	9	4	9	26	14	95	12	17	25	25	376
	distress	0	1	0	11	2	0	1	0	0	0	29
	insolvent	0	0	0	0	1	3	1	0	1	0	6
2001	sound	10	4	10	26	16	114	15	15	16	30	393
	distress	0	2	0	12	0	0	1	0	7	0	30
	insolvent	0	0	0	0	0	0	0	0	1	1	3
2002	sound	10	2	10	19	17	118	14	12	20	29	394
	distress	1	3	0	14	1	1	0	1	5	0	37
	insolvent	0	0	0	0	0	0	0	0	0	1	1
2003	sound	11	3	6	19	16	76	14	13	24	22	340
	distress	0	3	0	12	0	0	0	1	2	0	28
	insolvent	0	0	0	0	0	0	0	0	0	0	0
1997–2003	sound	63	32	61	207	86	559	99	127	148	163	2542
	distress	3	10	1	61	5	3	11	3	16	2	204
	insolvent	0	0	0	5	2	10	5	0	6	2	41
Observations total		66	42	62	273	93	572	115	130	170	167	2787

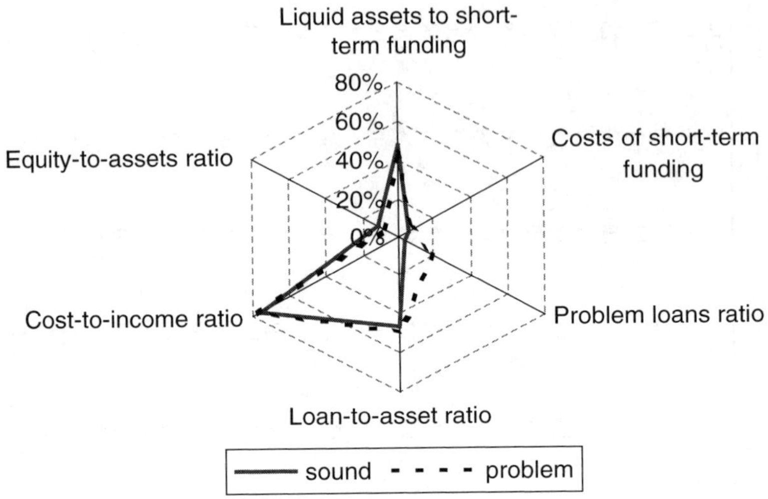

(a) EU 10

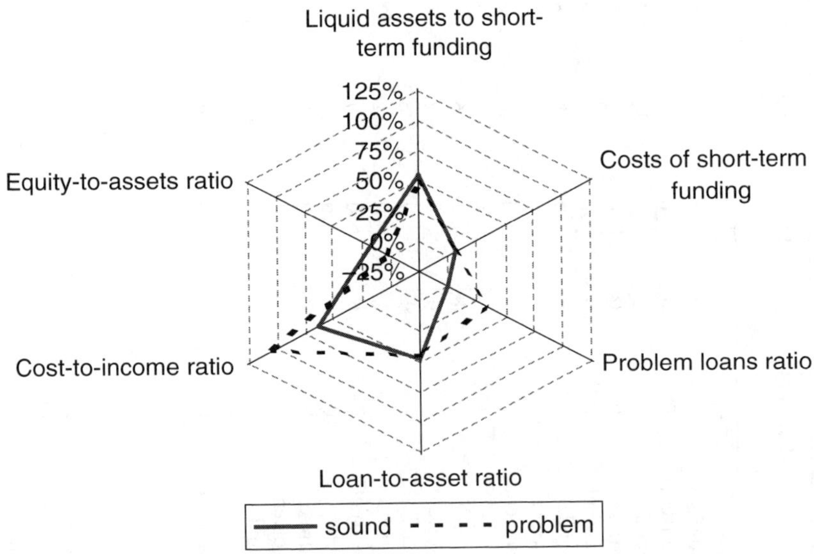

(b) non-EU CEECs

Source: Authors' calculations.

Figure 21.1 *Bank-specific variables of sound and unsound banks in EU-10 and non-EU CEECs*

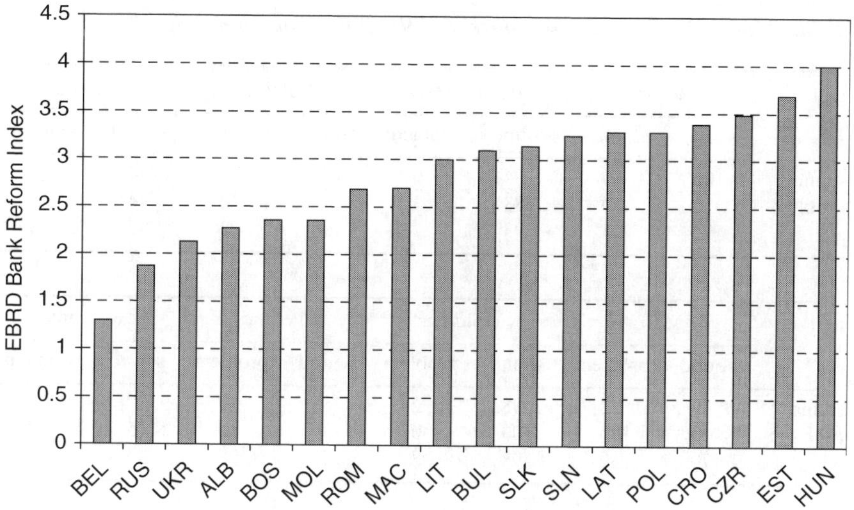

Source: EBRD Transition Report 2004.

Figure 21.2 EBRD Banking Sector Reform Index, average 1998–2004

Herfindahl index in the non-EU sample also corresponds to a high share of public-owned banks. This indicates that the higher the banking concentration, the less efficient and market-oriented is the banking environment. Where a CEEC belongs to the EU group, a less concentrated bank sector tends to be associated with bank failures. Weak monetary policy seems to be more an issue for non-EU countries' banking stability. Both the currency shock (sharp depreciation) and high inflationary pressures tend to be more important triggers of banking problems.

In general, the average indicator levels for sound and problem banks across countries vary a great deal, so no universal threshold level can be found that adequately signals the vulnerabilities over the whole sample of countries. This might also be taken as one further argument in favour of using differences instead of levels for the explanatory variables in the logit model described below.

The sample countries can also be compared according to EBRD banking sector reform index (Figure 21.2). Unfortunately no observations are available for Cyprus, Malta and Turkey. In general the new EU members demonstrate better advancement in banking reforms than other participants in the study. The exceptions are Croatia and Bulgaria, which belong to the frontline of transition countries in respect of banking sector reforms.

Table 21.4 Bank transition matrix 1996–2003 (in percentages)

$t+1$	Belarus		Bosnia-Herz		Bulgaria		Croatia	
	sound	problem	sound	problem	sound	problem	sound	problem
sound	100	0	94	6	100	0	94	6
problem	50	50	88	13	78	22	24	76
all	97	3	93	7	98	2	87	13

$t+1$	Malta		Moldova		Poland		Romania	
	sound	problem	sound	problem	sound	problem	sound	problem
sound	88	12	98	2	88	12	97	3
problem	0	100	100	0	20	80	75	25
all	70	30	98	2	72	28	95	5

Source: Authors' calculations.

Another interesting insight into the pattern of bank problems in different sample countries can be found from the bank transition matrix (Table 21.4). In the whole sample of 21 countries the historical conditional probability of a sound bank remaining in a prudent state was about 96 per cent against the probability of 4 per cent falling into difficulties and become unsound. About half of the problem banks[11] eventually recovered, whereas the rest remained unsound over the next year.

The highest chance (15 per cent) of a sound bank becoming a problem bank was found in Estonia. However, none of the problem banks remained unsound over the next period, they either closed down or improved. This might imply some differences in the way in which the market operated as Estonia only had distressed, but not insolvent banks in the sample period. The probability of falling into problem bank status was also relatively high in Cyprus, Malta and Poland. The transition matrix also demonstrates the persistence of bank problems. The highest likelihood for an unsound bank retaining its vulnerable status was in Malta, where none of the banks recovered once they had fallen into the problem category. This, however, has to be interpreted in the light of the small number of banks in Malta and the fact that none of the problem banks was badly insolvent. The bank problems were also highly persistant for Poland, Croatia, Cyprus and Slovakia.[12]

Czech Rep		Cyprus		Estonia		Latvia		Lithuania	
sound	problem	sound	problem	sound	problem	sound	problem	sound	problem
95	5	87	13	85	15	94	6	98	2
56	44	44	56	100	0	86	14	67	33
88	12	79	21	87	13	93	7	96	4

Russia		Slovakia		Slovenia		Ukraine		Total	
sound	problem	sound	problem	sound	problem	sound	problem	sound	problem
100	0	97	3	98	2	99	1	96	4
67	33	44	56	50	50	100	0	46	54
99	1	88	12	97	3	99	1	91	9

3.2 Model Specification

We use the binomial fixed-effects panel logit model to explore the relationship, which can be expressed with the following general specification:

$$E(y_{ijt}|x, \beta, c) = \beta' x_{ijt} + c_j$$

The dependent variable y denotes the bank status and is equal to 0 or 1 for sound and problem banks respectively. x is a set of early warning indicators having indexes $i = 1, \ldots, N$; $j = 1, \ldots, K$; $t = 1, \ldots, T$ and where $N \approx 300$ banks in the panel; $K = 17$ countries in the panel; $T =$ years (1996–2003).

In theory we have a choice of models of discrete dependent variables, largely between logit and probit, which are the most commonly used in empirical research on financial crisis and early warning systems. The important distinction from our point of view is that the probit model is based on the normal distribution, whereas the logit model applies the logistic distribution. The logistic distribution has fat tails compared to the normal distribution and therefore tends to be more appropriate for modelling financial data, which are often leptokurtic. Furthermore, Gonzalez-Hermosillo et al. (1997) claim in testing for several functional forms, including Weibull, normal and exponential distributions, that the logistic distribution best matches with the features of banking crisis data in Mexico. Similarly, they refer to earlier studies that found that the logistic distribution best describes the banking difficulties in the United States for the period 1985–1992. However, in large samples the two models should give broadly similar results.

Another issue which favours the logit specification is that the probit model does not lend itself well to the fixed-effect treatment, as there is no feasible way of removing the heterogeneity. With a large number of cross-sectional units, as in our study, the estimation of fixed effects is intractable in probit (Greene, 1995). In contrast to probit, logit enables treatment of fixed effects. The fixed-effect treatment in the current study is needed for extracting country-specific time-constant features.

The maximization of a conditional likelihood function (Chamberlain, 1980) requires sufficient statistics for the group-specific parameters. Therefore only those countries enter the estimation that have both distressed and sound banks recorded in the sample period. The partial effects from fixed-effects logit estimates are not straightforward. The logit coefficients on explanatory variables give the log-odds ratio, that is, $\log\{\Lambda(x_t\beta + c)/[1 - \Lambda(x_t\beta + c)]\} = x_t\beta + c$. Hence the partial effects on the response probabilities cannot be estimated without knowing c, whose distribution is unrestricted and thus hard to know (Wooldridge, 2002).

In order to test how well the logit model fits the data it is simplest to look at the maximum likelihood measure. Intuitively, a better measure of model explanatory power is the likelihood ratio index (LRI), whose value is bounded by 0 and 1. The closer LRI is to 1 the better the goodness of fit. The first model we use, with predominantly first differences, gives an LRI of 0.71 and the model based on second differences has an LRI value of 0.696. These are relatively promising results.

$$LRI = 1 - \frac{\ln L_{ur}}{\ln L_o} \quad 0 < LRI < 1$$

Where restricted log-likelihood is:

$$\ln L_o = n[P \ln P + (1 - P)\ln(1 - P)]$$

The key consideration in choosing between a random effects (RE) and fixed effects (FE) approach is whether c_i and x_{it} are correlated. Hausman (1978) proposed a test based on the difference between random effects and fixed effect estimates. Since FE is consistent when c_i and x_{it} are correlated, but RE is inconsistent, a statistically significant difference is interpreted as evidence against the random effects assumption. However, the Hausman test needs strict exogeneity, whereas correlation between x_{is} and u_{it} for any s and t causes both FE and RE to be inconsistent. Applying the Hausman test, however, did not show a statistically significant difference between random effects and fixed effect specifications of the model. Nevertheless, the theoretical arguments and maximum likelihood measures indicate that the fixed-effects model seems to be a more appropriate specification given the aim of the study.

Bank-specific variables from financial statements are closely interlinked, which causes estimation problems from high collinearity if several are included. To cope with the problem two methods were applied. First the factor loadings were calculated and employed in order to filter out the dominating variables of similar nature, that is the most representative efficiency variable from different proxy-measures. Second, since it is not immediately apparent what the appropriate metric is, the inverse values of the variables were used instead of original ratios.

To overcome problems of endogeneity in using bank-specific variables, because the financial variables from bank accounts might be itself a reflection of crisis, the explanatory variables are modelled in differences and not in levels. Statistically significant explanatory variables (in difference form) were in turn tested for exogeneity. For this purpose the simple procedure described by Wooldridge (2002) was used.[13] As a result the one-year-ahead values of differences of loan–asset ratio, equity–investments ratio and cost–income ratio turned out not to be exogeneous. Hence, for these variables only the two-year-ahead or lagged difference values can be used in order to avoid misleading results due to endogeneity.

4. RESULTS

The results from the fixed-effects panel logit model (Table 21.5) indicate that macroeconomic variables tend to give a signal earlier than most financial variables.[14] This might be because the two-year lags are too long for many volatile bank-specific indicators. The Wald test, however, strongly rejects the joint hypothesis that both the bank-specific variables and the macroeconomic variables are irrelevant for explaining the crisis probability.[15]

Variables in all categories of bank conditions offer some degree of explanation of ensuing crisis although market risk is the weakest. Problem loans not surprisingly stand out as the clearest indicator of subsequent distress. The only other bank characteristic that offers some clear explanation looking two years ahead (column 2) is the cost–income ratio, demonstrating that inefficiencies can have a detrimental effect on bank soundness.

With only a one-year horizon (column 1) several variables act as indicators. The solvency ratio indicates a clear path, being negative throughout the period leading to distress. However, in a sense solvency indicators are not so much early warning signs, as actual results of bank long-term

Table 21.5 Panel logit model results

Indicators	One-year ahead	Two-years ahead
LIQUIDITY		
Short-term liabilities and deposits to liquid assets i.e. inverse liquidity ratio	0.22 d*	0.21 dL
	(1.58)	(1.45)
Interest expenses to short-term funding	6.07 d**	−0.64 dL
	(1.93)	(−0.27)
Bank deposits to all deposits	−0.00 d	−0.03 dL
	(−0.01)	(0.19)
CREDIT RISK		
Loan–asset ratio	−1.57 dL	0.01 dL
	(−1.11)	(0.01)
Problem loans ratio	8.82 d***	1.47 dL***
	(5.89)	(2.65)
SOLVENCY		
Equity-to-assets ratio	−9.78 d***	−0.29 dL
	(−4.32)	(−0.11)
MARKET RISK		
Equity investments to assets ratio	−1.98 dL	4.09 dL
	(−0.27)	(0.71)
Trading–income ratio	−0.02 d	−0.00 dL
	(−1.33)	(0.28)
EFFICIENCY AND PROFITABILITY		
Cost–income ratio	0.15 dL	0.38 dL*
	(0.58)	(1.76)
Assets divided by interest and fee income – inverse moral-hazard	0.09 d**	0.03 dL
	(2.13)	(1.07)
MACROECONOMIC AND STRUCTURAL INDICATORS		
Private lending to GDP	−3.84 d	5.76 dL*
	(−1.13)	(1.64)
GDP real growth	−7.99	−16.00 L***
	(−1.21)	(−3.19)
CPI growth	−5.40	1.95 L
	(−1.39)	(0.72)
EURIBOR_3mth	0.13 d	0.36 dL**
	(0.71)	(2.40)
Exchange rate change (domestic currency/$)	106.28	−262.80 L*
	(0.61)	(−1.66)
Herfindahl sector concentration index	−0.00 d	−0.00 dL
	(−1.33)	(−1.11)

Table 21.5 (continued)

Indicators	One-year ahead	Two-years ahead
Share of state-owned banks	−3.02 L*** (−2.79)	−0.01 L2 (−1.10)
MODEL STATISTICS		
Log Likelihood	−203.19	−232.74
Likelihood ratio index	0.74	0.69
AIC	440.371	556.0785
BIC	522.3298	577.3324
Observations (distress)/banks/countries	917 (121)/303/17	900 (117)/302/17

Notes:
z-values in parentheses.
Albania, Belarus, Bulgaria and Hungary were dropped due to no crisis observations in model sample.
d indicates first difference, L, one lag and, L2, two lags.
*, **, *** indicate significance at the 10%, 5% and 1% levels respectively.

Source: Authors' calculations.

mismanagement. Nevertheless, Sundararajan et al. (2002) have claimed that banks with higher equity need to borrow less to support a given level of assets and thus have lower interest expenses, which results in higher net interest and net income.

The liquidity measures tend to have intuitively correct signs. The inverse liquidity ratio is positively correlated with banking problems in both the one-year and two-years ahead models. Interest expenses on funding increase immediately before crisis, while they have been decreasing further ahead of the crash. The inverse moral hazard indicator shows that vulnerable banks have low profitability in the pre-crisis year. The loan–assets ratio does not indicate any clear pattern, although it tends to be lower in the pre-crisis year, which is rather counter-intuitive.

The interpretation of market risk indicators is more ambiguous, as it was the only risk component that turned out to be jointly insignificant. Therefore no conclusions can be drawn based on the coefficients on equity–investments ratio or trade–income ratio.

Our two bank structure indicators offer some support to traditional hypotheses. The negative sign for the Herfindahl index, although the coefficient is insignificant, suggests that low banking sector concentration might lead to more frequent occurrences of bank failure. The behaviour of the financial deepening measure, proxied by private lending to GDP, is also intuitive. A crisis is correlated with financial deepening *ex ante* and financial contraction at the time of the crisis. The share of state-owned banks indicates that privatization or a higher proportion of private banks has been accompanied with crisis episodes in the transition countries. However, it appears that this positive correlation of private banks with distress incidences falls primarily in the non-EU group of CEECs (see Appendix Table 21.A1).

The macroeconomic variables point in the expected directions, although mainly two years ahead rather than just one year. Declining GDP growth and instabilities in the external and domestic environment lead to a higher likelihood of crises. Rises in Euribor-3M interest rates raise the costs of funding, which precipitates financial problems for many CEECs. Pre-crisis inflationary pressures and the eventual drop also belong to a story of crisis. Slowing currency depreciation seems to trigger banking problems two years ahead but the sign is reversed only a year ahead. Depreciation on its own puts pressure on both banks' balance sheets and those of their borrowers if loans have been taken out in foreign currency. There is a delay before payments are due and this bites. This might indicate loose monetary control in the preceding period and restrictive monetary policy *ex post*, which leads to eventual stress in the banking sector.

Given the individual statistical insignificance of many predictive variables and unobserved effects characteristic of the logit model, which does not allow for good interpretation of partial effects, we need to explore the patterns of the proposed early warning indicators in explaining bank distress further. A simple first step is to look at the model's predictive power. Table 21.6 summarizes the in-sample predictive properties of the model estimates. Missing observations in the estimated model means we have 121 crisis observations from 17 CEECs. The in-sample predictive power of the model seems encouraging. In seven countries the in-sample prediction of crises was perfect, although it was coupled with a somewhat higher degree of noise. The model worked best in the case of Latvia, Moldova, Russia and Lithuania. The only countries where the estimates did not pick up any crisis were Slovenia and Ukraine. The in-sample predictive performance in picking up the crisis episodes was also relatively weak for Poland, Turkey and Croatia. The in-sample estimation revealed that the model over-predicts problems for Estonia and Malta, whereas it was insufficiently sensitive in capturing banking problems in Poland, Croatia, Slovakia and Turkey. The model's poor performance for Poland might be largely due to a stringent national definition of sub-standard loans, that is loans overdue 30 days instead of the common international and EU definition of overdue 90 days.[16] Therefore the threshold for defining bank distress for Poland is too low.

The second step was to run an out-of-sample test and see how well the model manages to recognize the crises of 2003 based on the estimates from

Table 21.6 Model predictive power (in-sample)

In-sample crisis probability						
	Overall predictive power	Crisis occurrence	Type I error	Probability of missing crisis	Type II error	Probability of issuing wrong signal
Bosnia-Herzegovina	97%	9%	33%	3%	0%	0%
Croatia	80%	24%	84%	20%	0%	0%
Czech Republic	83%	8%	33%	3%	16%	15%
Cyprus	86%	23%	0%	0%	18%	14%
Estonia	62%	14%	0%	0%	44%	38%
Latvia	98%	5%	0%	0%	2%	2%
Lithuania	92%	3%	0%	0%	8%	8%
Macedonia	93%	7%	0%	0%	7%	7%
Malta	75%	50%	13%	6%	38%	19%
Moldova	91%	4%	0%	0%	9%	9%
Poland	64%	39%	94%	36%	0%	0%
Romania	94%	6%	50%	3%	3%	3%
Russian Federation	98%	1%	0%	0%	2%	2%
Slovakia	85%	12%	60%	7%	8%	7%
Slovenia	96%	4%	100%	4%	0%	0%
Turkey	86%	16%	86%	14%	0%	0%
Ukraine	95%	2%	100%	2%	4%	4%
Total	87%	13%	69%	9%	5%	4%

Source: Authors' calculations.

the years 1996–2002. There were 21 crisis episodes out of 186 observations in 2003. These were concentrated in six countries: Croatia, Cyprus, Estonia, Malta, Poland and Slovenia.

As shown in Table 21.7 the model managed to recognize banking problems in two out of the six countries: Cyprus and Estonia,[17] but it also extracted a high degree of noise. The model failed to pick up any of the crises in Poland, Slovenia, Malta and Croatia. This is a similar result to the in-sample prediction, which also highlighted the model sensitivity for Estonia and Cyprus, and its weakness in identifying problems predominantly in Poland, Slovenia and Croatia. For the 11 countries that did not experience banking problems in 2003 the wrong signal was extracted only once for Russia (type-II error 3 per cent) and three times for Romania (type-II error 33 per cent). In general the results tend to be weaker for banking sectors in highly regulated markets.

Given the limitations of descriptive statistics and the logit model the research could be further elaborated by employing duration models or

Table 21.7 Model out-of-sample predictive power

Out-of-sample crisis probability 2003						
	Overall predictive power	Crisis occurrence	Type I error	Probability of missing crisis	Type II error	Probability of issuing wrong signal
Croatia	76%	24%	100%	24%	0%	0%
Cyprus	75%	50%	0%	0%	50%	25%
Estonia	75%	25%	0%	0%	100%	75%
Malta	48%	48%	100%	48%	0%	0%
Poland	48%	48%	100%	48%	8%	4%
Slovenia	92%	8%	100%	8%	0%	0%
Total	76%	11%	86%	10%	16%	14%

Source: Authors' calculations.

conducting bank survival analysis. Gonzalez-Hermosillo et al. (1997) and Gonzalez-Hermosillo (1999) have successfully employed the logit technique and survival models in parallel. As claimed by Hardy and Pazarbasioglu (1998), the formerly socialist transition economies suffered a special range of problems that make them non-comparable with most of the other countries. The source for these non-comparabilities is mainly related to institutional factors, such as privatization and liberalization, enactment of new banking regulations and reforms in the monetary system. Therefore, further analysis of banking vulnerabilities could incorporate a wider range of indicators reflecting the major institutional changes during the transition process and a broader background for the differences in the development of the banking sector across the sample countries.

5. CONCLUSIONS

Using panel data at the bank level, it is possible to find bank-specific, bank sector structure and macroeconomic variables that are able to predict vulnerabilities in the CEE countries' banking sector over the period since 1996. Macroeconomic variables tend to perform better in predicting a couple of years ahead, as they are more persistent compared to the more volatile financial variables. However, the financial variables have more to say about the crisis pattern, explaining how both the causes and the reactions contribute to a crisis or its avoidance. The measures of bank sector structure have a limited effect also reflecting both contributory factors and responses.

Not surprisingly the indicators are interrelated and while individual factors may be weakly determined, their joint effect is clear. Bank sector structure variables indicate that the sector becomes more fragile as state ownership declines and the sector becomes more fragmented.

There are some interesting differences between the ten new EU members and the rest of the observed CEECs. Although these two groups had broadly similar patterns of differences between the sound and problem banks, the high loan-to-assets ratio in the EU sample was associated with problem banks, whereas the same was characteristic of sound banks in the non-EU sub-sample. Similarly, although not statistically significant, the higher trade–income ratio was a feature of distressed banks in the EU group, while being rather the indicator of prudent institutions for the non-EU group. With the macroeconomic variables, the non-EU banks turned out to be more vulnerable to inflationary pressures and exchange rate movements.

The in-sample and out-of-sample predictions with the model had relatively encouraging results. In-sample, it managed to predict all distress episodes in seven countries out of the 17 studied in detail. Out-of-sample prediction for 2003 revealed that the model was able to capture the bank-distress incidences in two countries out of six. In the remaining countries the number of incidences are either over- or under-estimated, so weakness in prediction does not appear to lie in any particular direction. The estimates tend to be over-sensitive for Estonia and Cyprus, in which cases all the distress episodes were identified but further problems were suggested that did not actually occur. On the other hand the occurrence of unsound banks in Poland, Croatia, Turkey, Malta and Slovenia was underestimated.

APPENDIX

Table 21.A1 Mean level of warning indicators for sound (0) and unsound (1) banks in country comparison

		New EU members (444 observations, o/w 79 crisis episodes)										
INDICATORS	crisis	Czech Rep	Cyprus	Estonia	Hungary	Latvia	Lithuania	Malta	Poland	Slovakia	Slovenia	EU
Liquidity												
Liquid assets to	0	61%	39%	35%	44%	52%	44%	56%	50%	55%	37%	47%
short-term funding	1	40%	31%	36%	–	56%	53%	29%	48%	36%	50%	44%
	all	61%	36%	35%	44%	53%	45%	41%	49%	53%	38%	47%
Costs of short-	0	7%	5%	4%	6%	3%	3%	4%	8%	7%	5%	5%
term funding	1	8%	4%	4%	–	3%	3%	4%	7%	10%	5%	6%
	all	7%	4%	4%	6%	3%	3%	4%	8%	7%	5%	6%
Bank deposits to	0	53%	8%	20%	26%	20%	39%	15%	162%	22%	19%	54%
customer deposits	1	22%	3%	13%	–	32%	3%	11%	44%	17%	19%	32%
ratio	all	50%	7%	19%	26%	21%	38%	13%	116%	21%	19%	50%
Credit Risk												
Problem loans	0	–9%	4%	6%	4%	3%	4%	3%	3%	4%	4%	3%
ratio	1	27%	18%	12%	–	23%	14%	12%	20%	30%	17%	20%
	all	−6%	7%	7%	400%	4%	5%	7%	10%	7%	5%	6%
Loan-to-asset	0	34%	55%	57%	54%	37%	46%	38%	50%	39%	54%	46%
ratio	1	50%	61%	59%	–	29%	27%	52%	49%	50%	49%	49%
	all	35%	58%	58%	54%	37%	46%	46%	49%	40%	54%	46%
Market Risk												
Equity	0	0.4%	0.2%	0.5%	0.3%	0.9%	1.3%	0.7%	1.0%	0.3%	2.2%	1.0%
investments ratio	1	0.6%	0.1%	0.2%	–	2.8%	0.4%	0.8%	1.9%	0.5%	0.3%	1.4%
	all	0.5%	0.2%	0.5%	0.3%	1.0%	1.2%	1.6%	1.3%	0.3%	2.1%	1.2%
Trade–income	0	156%	160%	160%	141%	76%	249%	57%	223%	312%	105%	168%
ratio	1	48%	22%	156%	–	25%	57%	44%	412%	152%	220%	284%
	all	148%	129%	160%	141%	74%	244%	51%	297%	291%	109%	189%

Efficiency and Profitability												
Cost–income ratio	0	98%	67%	74%	72%	89%	87%	62%	64%	82%	64%	76%
	1	62%	91%	71%	–	127%	79%	55%	76%	94%	76%	77%
	all	95%	71%	74%	72%	90%	87%	56%	69%	84%	64%	76%
Moral hazard i.e interest and fee income to total assets	0	8%	6%	8%	9%	8%	7%	5%	11%	8%	8%	8%
	1	10%	5%	8%	–	13%	9%	5%	9%	12%	8%	9%
	all	8%	6%	8%	9%	8%	7%	5%	10%	9%	8%	8%
Capital												
Equity to assets ratio	0	7%	8%	10%	9%	9%	13%	8%	13%	10%	11%	10%
	1	5%	7%	9%	–	−10%	7%	7%	9%	0%	8%	7%
	all	7%	7%	10%	9%	9%	12%	8%	12%	9%	10%	10%
Macroeconomic and sectoral variables												
Herfindahl-banking sector index	0	1760	2797	4150	3610	1929	2734	3711	1222	1802	1927	2137
	1	1743	2856	4707	4033	2009	2505	3306	1085	1875	2068	1819
	all	1758	2809	4217	3615	1934	2719	3614	1189	1812	1931	2094
State-owned banks share	0	4%	23%	0%	8%	4%	17%	12%	30%	21%	34%	20%
	1	4%	4%	0%	–	5%	38%	0%	26%	41%	22%	21%
	all	4%	19%	0%	8%	4%	17%	6%	28%	23%	33%	20%
Real GDP growth	0	2%	3%	6%	4%	6%	6%	1%	4%	4%	4%	4%
	1	1%	3%	7%	5%	5%	5%	−1%	3%	4%	3%	3%
	all	2%	3%	6%	4%	6%	6%	1%	4%	4%	4%	4%
Loans to private sector GDP	0	54%	113%	25%	31%	19%	13%	110%	26%	45%	34%	39%
	1	66%	117%	26%	24%	13%	11%	113%	27%	52%	37%	47%
	all	55%	113%	25%	30%	18%	13%	111%	26%	46%	34%	40%
Average annual growth of CPI	0	3%	4%	8%	11%	5%	3%	3%	7%	7%	8%	6%
	1	2%	3%	6%	19%	6%	15%	2%	5%	8%	7%	5%
	all	2%	4%	8%	11%	5%	4%	3%	7%	7%	8%	6%
Average annual rate domestic/USD	0	0.02%	0.01%	0.00%	0.04%	−0.01%	−0.06%	−0.02%	0.04%	0.01%	0.06%	0.02%
	1	0.03%	−0.14%	0.01%	–	0.02%	0.00%	−0.02%	0.01%	0.09%	−0.04%	0.00%
	all	0.02%	−0.03%	0.00%	0.04%	−0.01%	−0.06%	−0.02%	0.03%	0.02%	0.06%	0.01%

Table 21.A1 (continued)

		Non-EU members (473 observations, o/w 42 crisis episodes)												
INDICATORS	crisis	Albania	Belarus	Bosnia-Herz	Bulgaria	Croatia	Macedonia	Moldova	Romania	Russia	Turkey	Ukraine	non-EU	Total
Liquidity														
Liquid assets to	0	102%	33%	64%	66%	58%	58%	51%	60%	47%	60%	51%	55%	52%
short-term funding	1	–	–	44%	–	51%	26%	33%	49%	68%	52%	33%	49%	46%
	all	102%	33%	63%	66%	57%	58%	52%	59%	47%	58%	51%	54%	64%
Costs of short-	0	5%	10%	2%	2%	5%	4%	7%	12%	6%	20%	7%	7%	6%
term funding	1	–	–	2%	–	5%	5%	14%	11%	9%	20%	8%	8%	7%
	all	5%	10%	2%	2%	5%	4%	7%	12%	6%	20%	7%	7%	7%
Bank deposits to	0	0%	30%	16%	11%	18%	18%	26%	23%	47%	24%	27%	30%	41%
customer deposits	1	–	–	4%	–	21%	11%	112%	2%	15%	10%	19%	19%	28%
ratio	all	0%	30%	15%	11%	19%	17%	30%	22%	47%	21%	26%	29%	39%
Credit Risk														
Problem loans	0	1%	5%	5%	3%	7%	7%	7%	4%	−16%	6%	7%	−1%	1%
ratio	1	–	–	28%	–	30%	28%	19%	23%	15%	57%	2%	33%	24%
	all	1%	5%	7%	3%	13%	9%	8%	5%	−16%	15%	6%	2%	4%
Loan-to-asset	0	0%	57%	50%	41%	50%	45%	50%	41%	49%	35%	51%	47%	47%
ratio	1	–	–	50%	–	46%	56%	61%	42%	30%	28%	54%	44%	47%
	all	0%	57%	50%	41%	49%	45%	49%	42%	49%	33%	51%	47%	47%
Market Risk														
Equity	0	–	0.3%	0.7%	0.6%	0.9%	4.9%	1.1%	1.0%	2.2%	2.2%	1.2%	1.6%	1.3%
investments ratio	1	–	–	0.6%	–	2.4%	28.8%	0.2%	0.4%	0.2%	1.2%	0.4%	2.5%	1.8%
	all	–	0.3%	0.7%	0.6%	1.3%	5.5%	1.1%	1.0%	2.2%	2.0%	1.1%	1.8%	1.5%
Trade–income	0	3%	352%	1002%	350%	89%	105%	35%	61%	202%	742%	78%	243%	209%
ratio	1	–	–	177%	–	196%	309%	26%	43%	47%	89%	155%	166%	243%
	all	3%	352%	929%	350%	115%	119%	35%	60%	201%	635%	79%	236%	213%

Efficiency and Profitability														
Cost–income	0	30%	74%	59%	74%	63%	55%	51%	72%	63%	76%	57%	64%	69%
ratio	1	–	–	92%	–	112%	38%	50%	60%	–	131%	103%	103%	85%
	all	30%	74%	63%	74%	75%	55%	53%	71%	63%	80%	57%	66%	71%
Moral hazard i.e	0	8%	14%	6%	6%	8%	7%	13%	16%	9%	24%	12%	10%	10%
interest and fee	1	–	–	7%	–	7%	11%	16%	18%	8%	26%	10%	11%	10%
income to total assets	all	8%	14%	6%	6%	7%	8%	14%	16%	9%	24%	12%	11%	10%
Capital														
Equity to	0	2%	14%	14%	18%	15%	25%	24%	19%	19%	11%	18%	17%	14%
assets ratio	1	–	–	5%	–	8%	11%	18%	11%	−4%	−22%	0%	3%	6%
	all	2%	14%	13%	18%	13%	25%	24%	18%	19%	6%	17%	16%	13%
Macroeconomic and sectoral variables														
Herfindahl-	0	5422	5404	1363	1419	2132	3309	1863	3567	2357	1343	1057	2175	2161
banking sector	1	5999	9173	1336	2517	2507	2742	2530	3905	2505	1222	1122	2385	2052
index	all	5468	5568	1361	1485	2174	3284	1874	3592	2361	1328	1058	2187	2151
State-owned	0	59%	62%	23%	19%	14%	1%	10%	45%	44%	34%	11%	27%	24%
banks share	1	–	–	30%	–	11%	2%	0%	50%	42%	33%	12%	20%	20%
	all	59%	62%	23%	19%	13%	1%	9%	45%	44%	33%	11%	27%	23%
Real GDP growth	0	6%	5%	8%	3%	4%	2%	2%	2%	5%	3%	4%	4%	4%
	1	9%	10%	14%	−5%	4%	3%	−7%	2%	5%	0%	3%	3%	3%
	all	6%	6%	9%	3%	4%	2%	2%	2%	5%	3%	4%	4%	4%
Loans to private	0	4%	10%	43%	18%	41%	20%	20%	9%	15%	20%	13%	21%	27%
sector GDP	1	3%	12%	45%	28%	44%	20%	14%	8%	14%	19%	12%	27%	39%
	all	4%	10%	44%	18%	41%	20%	19%	9%	15%	20%	13%	21%	28%
Average annual	0	6%	99%	2%	7%	4%	3%	18%	41%	27%	58%	16%	23%	17%
growth of CPI	1	0%	68%	5%	1%	4%	0%	8%	41%	54%	54%	9%	25%	13%
	all	5%	98%	2%	6%	4%	2%	18%	41%	28%	57%	16%	23%	17%
Average annual	0	0.00%	1.11%	−0.02%	0.00%	0.01%	−0.01%	0.24%	0.26%	0.13%	0.48%	0.12%	0.14%	0.09%
rate	1	–	–	0.07%	–	0.02%	0.00%	0.16%	0.42%	0.66%	0.74%	−0.01%	0.18%	0.07%
domestic/USD	all	0.00%	1.11%	−0.01%	0.00%	0.02%	0.00%	0.24%	0.26%	0.13%	0.53%	0.12%	0.14%	0.08%

NOTES

* Kadri Männasoo, Bank of Estonia, David G. Mayes, Bank of Finland. The views expressed here are those of the authors and may not coincide with any held by Eesti Pank or Suomen Pankki. We are grateful to David Llewellyn, Helmut Elsinger and participants of the OeNB's 2005 Conference on European Economic Integration for comments.

1. Both levels and rates of change are important determinants. Rapid increases in lending can weaken quality, and rapid reductions in deposits or reserves are indicators of a loss of confidence.
2. CAMELS – Capital Assets Management Earnings Liquidity Sensitivity to market risk.
3. Loan reserves are held against actual and potential loan losses and, as such, are set aside from the normal definition of capital.
4. Depending on the scope of non-performing loans definition Gonzales-Hermosillo (1999) applies a coverage ratio threshold of zero for US banks and a threshold of 1.5 for Mexican and Colombian banks.
5. Banks whose data on impaired loans are not available, but the net loan provisions are negative, given the positive equity, are considered as prudent. The maximum of impaired loans ratio or provisions ratio is used in order to employ more observations and alleviate the problem of incomparability in provisions definitions across sample countries.
6. In our sample, banks with negative equity may not be insolvent if they are branches of a foreign bank.
7. This meta-analysis summary table is far from a complete survey and should be rather considered as an illustration, not a conclusive statement of the similarities and differences across present literature.
8. Proxy for interest-sensitive funding.
9. The panel drop-out properties did not justify the weighting of remaining panel members.
10. For better comparability with logit analysis the average country values of early warning variables include only these more than 300 banks included in the econometric model.
11. The transition matrix cannot take into account those banks which disappeared from the database.
12. The caveat here is that the transition matrix is sensitive to the choice of sample period, whereby these countries, which suffered more banking sector problems in the beginning of the observation period, have a lower probability of a sound bank becoming a problem bank and a higher likelihood of problem banks recovering. Also the data availability and quality play an important role as the banks with missing data drop out of the matrix.
13. In the first step the explanatory variable of interest is regressed against the rest of the explanatory variables. In the second step the residuals from the OLS are substituted into the logit estimation. If the t-statistic of the residual turns out to be statistically significant the variable of interest is not exogenous.
14. All banks, whether or not encountering distress or insolvency, are included in the estimation.
15. For bank-specific variables the $\chi^2(10) = 36.16$ and Prob $> \chi^2 = 0.0001$. For macroeconomic variables the $\chi^2(6) = 18.30$ Prob $> \chi^2 = 0.0055$.
16. Definition of substandard loans was brought in line with EU standards in January 2004.
17. The model recognized 3 episodes of bank distress out of 21. Two incidences were picked up for Cyprus and one incidence for Estonia.

REFERENCES

Bankscope database: 2005.

Berg, S.A. and B. Hexeberg (1994), 'Early warning indicators for Norwegian banks: A Logit analysis of the experiences from the banking crisis', *Norges Bank Working Paper*, 1994/01.

Caprio, G. and D. Klingebiel (1996), 'Bank insolvencies: Cross-country experience', *World Bank Policy Research Working Paper*, 1620, July.

Caprio, G. and D. Klingebiel (2003), 'Episodes of systemic and borderline financial crises', World Bank.

Chamberlain, G. (1980), 'Analysis of covariance with qualitative data', *Review of Economic Studies*, vol. **XLVII**, pp. 225–38.

Demirgüç-Kunt, A. and E. Detragiache (1998), 'Financial liberalization and financial fragility', *IMF Working Paper*, 98/83.

Demirgüç-Kunt, A. and E. Detragiache (1999), 'Monitoring Banking sector fragility: A multivariate Logit approach with an application to the 1996–97 banking crises', *World Bank Policy Research Working Paper*, 2085.

EBRD (2004), Transition Report.

Gonzalez-Hermosillo, B. (1999), 'Determinants of ex-ante banking system distress: A macro–micro empirical exploration of some recent episodes', *IMF Working Paper*, 99/33.

Gonzales-Hermosillo, B., C. Pazarbasioglu and R. Billings (1997), 'Determinants of banking system fragility: A case study of Mexico', *IMF Staff Papers*, **44** (3), 295–315.

Greene, W.H. (1995), *Econometric Analysis*, New Jersey: Prentice-Hall.

Hardy, D.C. and C. Pazarbasioglu (1998), 'Leading indicators of banking crises: Was Asia different?', *IMF Working Paper*, 98/91.

Hausman, J.A. (1978), 'Specification tests in econometrics', *Econometrica*, **46**, pp. 1251–71.

Hutchison, M. and K. McDill (1999), 'Are all banking crises alike? The Japanese experience in international comparison', *NBER Working Paper*, No. 7253.

IFS database: IMF 2005.

Lindgren, C.-J., G. Garcia and M.I. Saal (1996), *Bank Soundness and Macroeconomic Policy*, Washington, DC: International Monetary Fund.

Mayes, D.G., L. Halme and A. Liuksila (2001), *Improving Banking Supervision*, Basingstoke: Palgrave.

Rojas-Suarez, L. (1998), 'Early warning indicators of banking crises: What works for developing countries?' Inter-American Development Bank.

Sundararajan, V., C. Enoch, A. San José, P. Hilbers, R. Krueger, M. Moretti and G. Slack (2002), 'Financial soundness indicators: Analytical aspects and country practices', *IMF Occasional Paper*, 212.

Wooldridge, J.M. (2002), *Econometric Analysis of Cross Section and Panel Data*, Cambridge MA: MIT Press.

22. Financial integration through the interbank market: stability and welfare implications[1]

Falko Fecht and Hans Peter Grüner

1. INTRODUCTION

Financial integration in the euro area is still lagging behind expectations. Comparing the integration of different financial markets in the euro area, Baele et al. (2004a) conclude that the most integrated financial market is the money market. Government and corporate bond as well as equity markets are reasonably integrated, while the market for loans to the private sector – in particular short-term loans – remains largely segmented. This contribution assesses the welfare and stability implication of a risk-sharing that is mainly achieved through the interbank market. It also discusses how recent structural developments in the euro money market affect this welfare assessment. In section 2 we briefly take stock of the financial integration process that the euro area has witnessed so far. Section 3 gives an overview of the risks that might be associated with a financial integration that is to a large extent limited to the interbank market. In this light section 4 describes the recent structural trends in the interbank market and section 5 analyses how these structural changes in the interbank market affect the costs and benefits of this limited degree of financial integration. Finally, section 6 concludes.

2. FINANCIAL INTEGRATION IN THE EURO AREA

The financial integration in the euro area has been more or less limited to wholesale financial markets. With the introduction of the euro, interest rate differentials on government bonds have been marginalized. Similarly, country-specific factors driving corporate bond spreads became negligible compared to the role they played prior to 1998. Even though this development is largely driven by the macroeconomic convergence process it certainly also reflects the improved cross-border substitutability of these securities, as, for instance, emphasized by Pagano and von Thadden (2004). Studying the correlations of equity returns in the euro area, Adjaoute and Danthine (2004) also find support for a significant increase in cross-country return correlations suggesting an improved integration of stock markets in EMU-member countries.[2]

In contrast, according to the very comprehensive study of the integration process in European banking by Barros et al. (2005), banking – particularly retail banking – markets remained rather local and were more or less unaffected by European financial integration. This is broadly reflected in the low level of cross-border loans to non-banks in the euro area relative to total bank lending to non-banks in the euro area. According to the ECB's banking structure reports, this ratio remained virtually unchanged at around 5 per cent over the period from 1997 to 2005.

The cross-border market penetration by branches and subsidiaries of foreign banks shows the still very limited degree of integration in the retail banking market. While until 2001 credit institutions from the European Economic Area (EEA)[3] increased their number of branches and subsidiaries in other euro area countries, part of this development was reversed by the end of 2004. Moreover, as can be seen from Table 22.1 the overall number of branches and subsidiaries of foreign banks in euro area countries remains virtually unchanged since the introduction of the euro. Similarly, according to Table 22.2 the assets of branches and subsidiaries

Table 22.1 Number of branches and subsidiaries of foreign banks in euro area countries

	1997	1998	1999	2000	2001	2002	2003	2004
Branches								
from other EEA countries	349	368	405	433	467	460	446	475
from non-EEA countries	155	148	138	130	111	105	102	96
Subsidiaries								
from other EEA countries	360	374	373	405	412	388	365	345
from non-EEA countries	256	252	227	215	198	187	174	162
Branches and subsidiaries								
from other EEA countries	709	742	778	838	879	848	811	820
from non-EEA countries	411	400	365	345	309	292	276	258
Foreign branches in total	504	516	543	563	578	565	548	571
Foreign subsidiaries in total	616	626	600	620	610	575	539	507
Foreign branches and subsidiaries in euro area countries in total	1120	1142	1143	1183	1188	1140	1087	1078

Source: ECB (2005a).

Table 22.2 Assets of branches and subsidiaries of foreign banks in euro area countries relative to overall assets of euro area banks (in %)

	1997	1998	1999	2000	2001	2002	2003	2004
Branches								
from other EEA countries	3.49	3.53	3.37	3.65	3.49	3.34	3.17	3.54
from non-EEA countries	1.46	1.09	0.75	0.75	0.93	0.80	0.74	0.68
Subsidiaries								
from other EEA countries	5.76	6.27	6.76	7.66	8.89	9.06	9.11	9.78
from non-EEA countries	1.78	1.47	1.39	1.52	1.49	1.34	1.32	1.33
Branches and subsidiaries								
from other EEA countries	9.24	9.80	10.13	11.32	12.39	12.40	12.28	13.31
from non-EEA countries	3.24	2.55	2.14	2.27	2.42	2.14	2.06	2.00
Foreign branches in total	4.95	4.62	4.12	4.40	4.42	4.14	3.91	4.21
Foreign subsidiaries in total	7.53	7.73	8.15	9.18	10.38	10.40	10.43	11.10
Foreign branches and subsidiaries in euro area countries in total	12.48	12.35	12.27	13.58	14.80	14.54	14.34	15.32

Source: ECB (2005a).

Table 22.3 Numbers of mergers and acquisitions in the euro area banking sector

	2001	2002	2003	2004	2005
Domestic M&As	58	56	57	41	16
Inter-EEA M&As	18	20	7	9	6
M&As from third countries	6	1	4	2	0

Source: ECB (2005a).

of banks from other EEA and non-EEA countries as a percentage of total assets of the euro area banking industry increased only slightly over the last eight years.

Furthermore, the remarkable consolidation in the euro area banking sector did not contribute to a more integrated retail banking market. This development was mainly driven by domestic merger and acquisition (M&A) activity, with very few significant cross-border mergers and acquisitions observed. Particularly in recent years after showing a small peak in 1999 and 2000, the cross-border consolidation process decelerated again and faded completely in 2005 (see Table 22.3).

In contrast, the euro area interbank market can be deemed to have been a fully integrated market virtually from the introduction of the euro. According to Hartmann et al. (2001) differentials in the overnight interest rate observed right after the changeover to the unified monetary policy implementation framework were barely noticeable. Baele et al. (2004b) also report that the cross-sectional standard deviation of secured lending rates at both 1-month and 12-month maturities among euro area countries completely vanished at the beginning of 1999. Furthermore, as reported in ECB (2005a) cross-border interbank loans of euro area credit institutes increased steadily over the past nine years as a percentage of their total interbank loans outstanding. While in 1997 only slightly more than 20 per cent of interbank credit was granted to foreign banks, by mid-2005 more than 30 per cent of loans to other monetary financial institutions was provided to banks from another euro area country.

3. INTERBANK MARKET INTEGRATION AND THE RISK OF CONTAGION

Consequently, most of the cross-country risk sharing in retail business has to be achieved over the interbank market.

Interbank claims are typically short-run deposits or loans, respectively. The fact that they are debt contracts with an associated default option implies that they are comparably efficient in dealing with problems of asymmetric information between the borrowing and lending bank, for instance, given costly state verification problems *à la* Townsend (1979). Following Allen and Gale's (2000) application of the Diamond and Dybvig (1983) argument to the interbank market, the option to withdraw interbank deposits can ensure a truthful revelation of unobservable bank-specific liquidity needs and allow for an efficient mutual insurance against regional, that is bank-specific liquidity shock. Thus the particularities of interbank claims might qualify them to deal with the potentially severe asymmetric information problems arising in cross-border financial relations.

However, these contractual arrangements that might be very effective in dealing with such informational asymmetries bear the risk of financial contagion. The mutual exposure between banks might be an efficient insurance mechanism against idiosyncratic shocks and allowing for an optimal cross-country risk sharing. But as shown by Allen and Gale (2000) and Freixas et al. (2000) in the event of a regional liquidity shock that cannot be compensated by excess liquidity holdings in other regions, this interrelation over the interbank market provides a channel of financial contagion across borders. The default or deposit withdrawal of one market participant can trigger a domino effect in the banking sector that causes large parts of the integrated financial system to default. Consequently while the interbank market might be an efficient way to deal with regional liquidity risks and allow for an optimal cross-border sharing of these risks, integration through the interbank market bears some costs because it is inefficient in dealing with aggregate shocks.

4. DEVELOPMENTS IN THE EURO AREA INTERBANK MARKET

Probably the most pronounced development in the euro area interbank market since the introduction of the euro has been the increasing importance of secured interbank business. The turnover in secured lending and borrowing in the money market has far more than doubled since 2000. At the same time unsecured interbank borrowing and lending only increased by an average annual rate of around 4 per cent (see Figures 22.1 and 22.2).

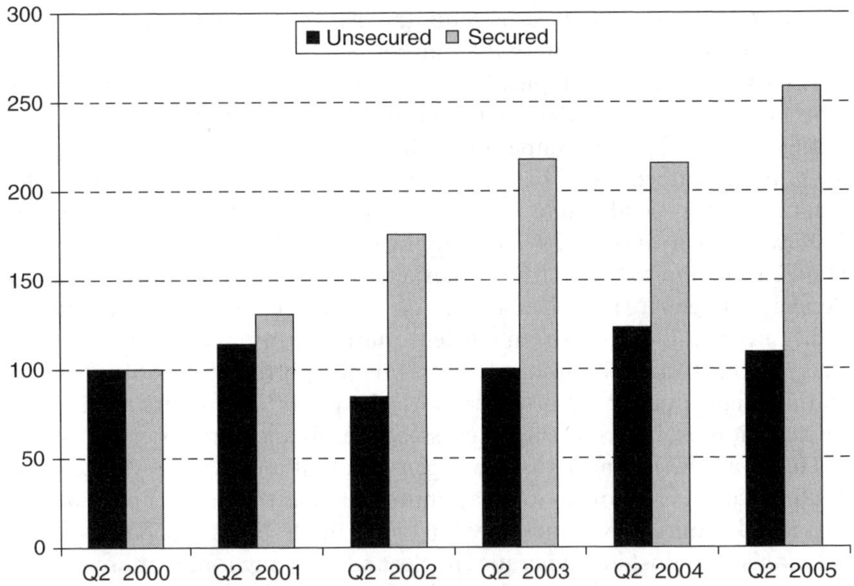

Note: The respective turnovers for Q2 2000 are taken as the base.

Source: ECB Money Market Study, 2005.

Figure 22.1 Developments of secured and unsecured lending in the euro area money market

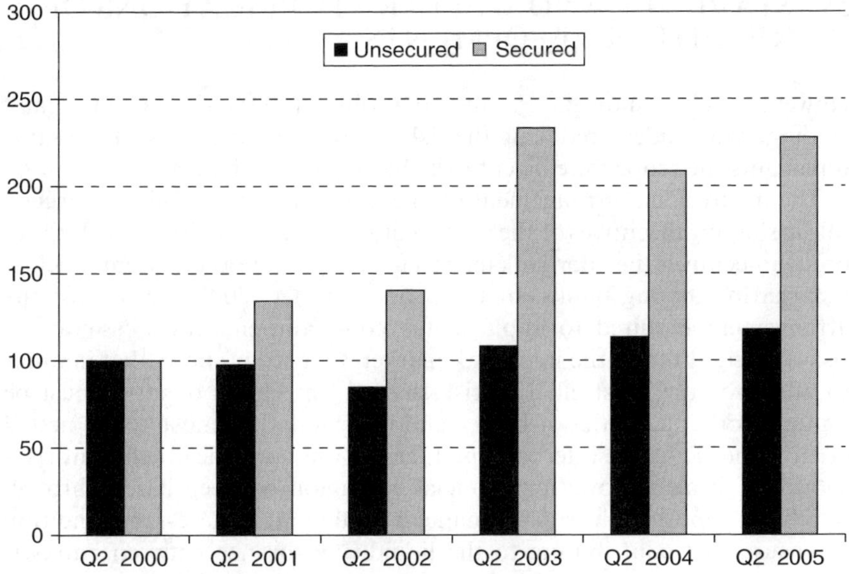

Note: The respective turnovers for Q2 2000 are taken as the base.

Source: ECB Money Market Study, 2005.

Figure 22.2 Developments of secured and unsecured borrowing in the euro area money market

According to the literature on financial contagion in the interbank market outlined in section 3, this development should be highly welcome. An increasing fraction of secured interbank borrowing and lending reduces the negative spillovers of a collapse of one institute. It thereby limits the risk of financial contagion in an integrated interbank market or as the ECB puts it: 'The increasing share of secured transactions can be seen positively from a financial stability point of view, as it shows that market participants have a preference for limiting their credit risk exposure' (ECB, 2005b, p. 65).

Consequently, as the fraction of secured interbank lending and borrowing gains importance, the cost of financial integration – or more precisely the costs of financial integration being limited to an integrated interbank market – seem to vanish. The risk of cross-border financial contagion through an integrated interbank market can be contained. Thus according to this view financial integration would become a free lunch: it only allows for an improved cross-border risk-sharing without incurring any costs of negative spillovers.

5. STABILITY AND WELFARE IMPLICATIONS OF RECENT DEVELOPMENTS

However, as we show in Fecht and Grüner (2005) secured interbank lending, while indeed reducing the risk of contagion perhaps, at the same time limits the scope for efficient risk-sharing among banks.

The institutional arrangement of the interbank market plays a crucial role in shaping incentives of the participating financial institutions. Without proper incentives the interbank market fails to provide a constraint-efficient risk-sharing among banks. In Fecht and Grüner (2005) we derived the arrangement required to implement a constraint-efficient cross-country risk-sharing through the interbank market. Our study shows that in order to allow for the most efficient risk-sharing, interbank deposits must be junior to other liabilities of banks, and interbank debt must not be netted at any time. Thus the interbank market can only provide an efficient risk-sharing if it also allows for financial contagion between banks through interbank deposits. The risk of financial contagion is a necessary condition to ensure that contributing to the liquidity insurance between banks is *ex-post* incentive-compatible.

The role of interbank market rules is to ensure that banks only withdraw financial claims in times of extraordinarily high liquidity needs. However, there may be incentives to free-ride on other banks in good times as well. This problem is mitigated if the unconditional withdrawal of funds raises the expected costs of a default of the respective trading partner. These expected costs are higher if interbank loans are junior to household claims. Thus, banks' ability to mutually insure each other against regional liquidity shocks is inevitably linked to the risk of financial contagion.

There are good reasons to assume that constraint-efficient interbank deposits do not allow all benefits to be captured from international risk-sharing. First, institutions for international risk-sharing should also enable banks to share the benefits of excessive liquidity. The corresponding institutional arrangements require decisions from banks that go beyond simply deciding whether to liquidate their assets with another bank or not. In Fecht and Grüner (2005) we argue that these more complex mechanisms that use a larger strategy space essentially reflect a merged bank and not what is usually labelled an interbank market.

Second, with a sufficiently liquid interbank market, banks may be tempted not to withhold enough liquidity. In particular in a large common economic area, an individual bank may be capable of inducing an economy-wide financial crisis by relying on liquidity provision by other banks through the interbank market. The result may be that all banks hold too little liquidity and that depositors are not offered the best investment opportunities.

Financial institutions which are active across borders are instead likely to properly internalize the adverse effect of too small liquidity holdings. The same holds for a bank that emerges from a large international merger.

Incentives to free-ride on other banks' liquidity holdings will be larger when more regions are covered by a single interbank market (we elaborate on this issue in Fecht et al., 2006). Therefore we expect that the welfare loss ensuing from limited financial integration is larger when the area that is covered by the interbank market is larger.

6. CONCLUSION

European financial integration is to a large extent limited to the integration of the interbank market. In this chapter we argue that neither secured nor unsecured interbank lending is an efficient means of integration. While an unsecured interbank market brings about risks of cross-border financial contagion, a secured interbank market might prevent an efficient cross-regional insurance. So integration through the interbank market is not a perfect substitute for cross-border direct lending or cross-country bank mergers. Accordingly, despite financial integration of the interbank market there remains a substantial cost of heterogeneous financial regulation of banks across Europe.

NOTES

1. The views expressed in this contribution do not necessarily reflect those of the Deutsche Bundesbank or of the European Central Bank.
2. In an earlier study Fratzscher (2002) also reports evidence for improved integration of European stock markets.
3. EU-15 plus Norway, Iceland and Liechtenstein.

REFERENCES

Adjaoute, K. and J.-P. Danthine (2004), 'Equity returns and integration: Is Europe changing?', *Oxford Review of Economic Policy*, **20**, 555–70.

Allen, F. and D. Gale (2000), 'Financial contagion', *Journal of Political Economy*, **108**, 1–33.

Baele, L., A. Ferrando, P. Hördahl, E. Krylova and C. Monnet (2004a), 'Measuring European financial integration', *Oxford Review of Economic Policy*, **20**, 509–30.

Baele, L., A. Ferrando, P. Hördahl, E. Krylova and C. Monnet (2004b), 'Measuring financial integration in the euro area', *ECB Occasional Paper*, 14.

Barros, P., E. Berglöf, P. Fulghieri, J. Gual, C. Mayer and X. Vives (2005), 'Integration of European banking: The way forward', Monitoring European Deregulation, CEPR.
Diamond, D. and P. Dybvig (1983), 'Bank runs, deposit insurance, and liquidity', *Journal of Political Economy*, **91**, 401–19.
ECB (2005a), *EU Banking Structure*, October 2005.
ECB (2005b), *Financial Stability Review*, December 2005.
Fecht, F. and H.P. Grüner (2005), 'Financial integration and systemic risk', *CEPR Discussion Paper*, 5253.
Fecht, F., H.P. Grüner and P. Hartmann (2006), 'Welfare effects of cross border financial integration', mimeo.
Fratzscher, M. (2002), 'Financial market integration in Europe: On the effects of EMU on stock markets', *International Journal of Finance and Economics*, **7**, 165–93.
Freixas, X., B. Parigi and J.-C. Rochet (2000), 'Systemic risk, interbank relations, and liquidity provision by the Central Bank', *Journal of Money, Credit and Banking*, **32**, 611–38.
Hartmann, P., M. Manna and A. Manzanares (2001), 'The microstructure of the euro money market', *Journal of International Money and Finance*, **20**, 895–948.
Pagano, M. and E.-L. von Thadden (2004), 'The European bond markets under EMU', *Oxford Review of Economic Policy*, **20**, 531–54.
Townsend, R.M. (1979), 'Optimal contracts and competitive markets with costly state verification', *Journal of Economic Theory*, **20**, 265–93.

23. Contagion risk in financial networks

Ana Babus*

1. INTRODUCTION

A notable feature of the modern financial world is its high degree of interdependence. Banks and other financial institutions are linked in a variety of ways. These connections are shaped by the choices banks have, and by institutional constraints. Despite their obvious benefit, the linkages come at the cost that shocks which initially affect only a few institutions can propagate through the entire system. Thus, the decisions financial institutions take when incurring mutual exposures influence the stability of the system. Since these linkages carry the risk of contagion, an interesting question is whether banks are choosing a degree of interdependence that sustains systemic stability. This chapter addresses this issue. In particular, we study how banks set up their cross-institutional holdings and investigate the implications for contagion risk.

There are different possible sources of connections between banks, stemming from both sides of the balance sheet. We focus here on linkages resulting from the direct exposures between banks acquired through the interbank market. Cross-holdings of deposits connect banks in a network that facilitates the transfer of liquidity from those that have a cash surplus to those with a cash deficit. This network is characterized by the pattern of interactions between banks, as well as by the amount of interbank deposits that represent the links. In this chapter, we investigate the size of interbank deposits transferred between banks, while keeping the network structure fixed. More precisely, we are interested in the effects different network structures have on banks' decisions on the size of interbank deposits. The same connections make the banking system prone to contagion. Moreover, the risk of contagion increases with the size of interbank deposits, as we will show in this chapter. Hence, it is important to assess the optimality of banks' decisions when the system is exposed to an exogenous bank failure.

Recently, there has been a substantial interest in looking for evidence on contagious failures of financial institutions resulting from mutual claims.

Most of these papers use balance sheet information to estimate bilateral credit relationships for different banking systems. Subsequently, the stability of the interbank market is tested by simulating the breakdown of a single bank. Upper and Worms (2004) analyse the German banking system. Sheldon and Maurer (1998) consider the Swiss system. Cocco et al. (2003) present empirical evidence for lending relationships existent in the Portuguese interbank market. Furfine (2003) studies the interlinkages between US banks, while Wells (2002) looks at the UK interbank market. Boss et al. (2004) provide an empirical analysis of the network structure of the Austrian interbank market and discuss how stable it remains when a node is eliminated. In the same manner, Degryse and Nguyen (2004) evaluate the risk that a chain reaction of bank failures would occur in the Belgian interbank market. These papers find that the banking systems demonstrate a high resilience, even to large shocks. Simulations of the worst-case scenarios show that banks representing less than 5 per cent of total balance sheet assets would be affected by contagion on the Belgian interbank market, while for the German system the failure of a single bank could lead to the breakdown of up to 15 per cent of the banking sector in terms of assets. In this chapter, we advance an explanation for this apparent stability of the financial systems, in an attempt to fill the gap between the relatively sceptical theoretical models and the good news brought by the empirical research.

The theoretical papers which study banking contagion paint a more pessimistic message. There are two approaches in this string of literature. On the one hand, there are a number of papers that look for contagious effects via indirect linkages. Lagunoff and Schreft (2001) construct a model where agents are linked in the sense that the return on an agent's portfolio depends on the portfolio allocations of other agents. Similarly, de Vries (2005) shows that there is dependency between banks' portfolios, given the fat tail property of the underlying assets, which carries the potential for systemic breakdown. Cifuentes et al. (2005) present a model where financial institutions are connected via portfolio holdings. The network is complete as everyone holds the same asset. Although the authors incorporate in their model direct linkages through mutual credit exposures as well, contagion is mainly driven by changes in asset prices. These papers all share the same finding: financial systems are inherently fragile. Fragility arises not only exogenously, from financial institutions' exposure to macro risk factors, as is the case in de Vries (2005). It also evolves endogenously through forced sales of assets by some banks that depress the market price, inducing further distress to other institutions, as in Cifuentes et al. (2004).

The other approach focuses on direct balance sheet interlinkages. For instance, Freixas et al. (2000) consider the case of banks that face liquidity needs as consumers are uncertain about where they are to consume. In their model the connections between banks are realized through interbank credit lines that enable these institutions to hedge regional liquidity shocks. The authors analyse different market structures and find that a system of credit lines, while reducing the cost of holding liquidity, makes the banking sector prone to experiencing gridlocks, even when all banks are solvent. Dasgupta (2004) also discusses how linkages between banks represented by cross-holdings of deposits can be a source of contagious breakdowns. Fragility arises when depositors receiving a private signal about banks' fundamentals may wish to withdraw their deposits if they believe that enough other depositors will do the same. To eliminate the multiplicity of equilibria Dasgupta (2004) uses the concept of global games. The author isolates a unique equilibrium which depends on the value of the fundamentals. Eisenberg and Noe (2001) take a more technical approach when investigating systemic risk in a network of financial institutions. First the authors show the existence of a clearing payment vector that defines the level of connections between banks. Next, they develop an algorithm that allows them to evaluate the effects small shocks have on the system. Another interesting issue is addressed by Leitner (2005). The model constructed in this paper shows that agents may be willing to bail out other agents, in order to prevent the collapse of the whole network.

The paper that is most closely related to ours is by Allen and Gale (2000). They assess the impact of degree of network completeness on the stability of the banking system. Allen and Gale show that complete networks are more resilient to contagious effects of a single bank failure than incomplete structures. In their model, though there is no aggregate shortage of liquidity, the demand for cash is not evenly distributed in the system. This induces banks to insure against such regional liquidity shocks by exchanging deposits on the interbank market. The interbank market is perceived as a network where the banks are nodes and the deposits exchanged represent links.

Our chapter uses the same framework as Allen and Gale (2000) to motivate interactions on the interbank market. We also look at the effects different network structures have on the stability of the banking system. There are, however, important differences. First and foremost, we endogenize the amount of deposits that banks exchange on the interbank market to hedge their liquidity shocks. That is, we create an environment that gives banks the opportunity to take actions. Given a chosen allocation of interbank deposits, we investigate the implications on the fragility of the banking system.

Allen and Gale (2000) study the banking system in which correlations exist between the shocks in the liquidity demand that affect different regions. In this set-up the authors do not need to model interbank deposits as the result of banks' decisions. We extend their analyses and look at the banking system without building in any correlations between liquidity shocks. In particular, we introduce uncertainty about which regions have negatively correlated shocks. The uncertainty created this way generates for each bank a set of choices for interbank deposits. In addition, we incorporate in our model one very important feature of real world banking systems. That is, relations between banks, in general, and deposit contracts, in particular, are private information. Our setting captures this aspect and allows a link that exists between two banks not to be observed by the other banks in the system. Thus, we analyse the decisions that banks take when exchanging deposits if these two sources of uncertainty are present.

We show that when the network is incomplete, banks decide on an allocation of interbank deposits that is unlikely at the level that minimizes contagion risk. This is no longer the case when the network becomes complete. In a complete network banks choose the degree of interdependence such that contagion risk is minimum. Allen and Gale (2000) find that in an incomplete network the losses caused by contagion are larger than in a complete network. Nevertheless, the level of interbank deposits in a network was such that the losses were minimal for the respective structure. We reinforce their result by showing that incomplete networks have an additional effect. That is, an incomplete network causes banks to decide on an allocation of deposits that may be suboptimal. A complete network, however, provides the right conditions for banks to choose the optimal degree of interdependence.

The model is based on a framework introduced by Diamond and Dybvig (1983). There are three periods $t = 0, 1, 2$ and a large number of identical consumers, each endowed with one unit of a consumption good. *Ex ante*, consumers are uncertain about their liquidity preferences. Thus, they might be early consumers, who value consumption at date 1, or late consumers, who value consumption at date 2. The consumers find it optimal to deposit their endowment in banks, which invest on their behalf. In return, consumers are offered a fixed amount of consumption at each subsequent date, depending on when they choose to withdraw. Banks can invest in two assets: there is a liquid asset which pays a return of 1 after one period and there is an illiquid asset that pays a return of $r<1$ after one period or $R>1$ after two periods. In addition, liquidity shocks hit the economy randomly, in the following way. Although there is no uncertainty about the average fraction of early consumers, liquidity demand is unevenly distributed among banks in the first period. Thus, each bank experiences either a high or a low fraction of early consumers. To ensure against these regional liquidity shocks, banks exchange deposits on the interbank market in period 0.

Deposits exchanged this way constitute the links that connect the banks in a network. This view of the banking system as a network is useful in analysing the effects that the failure of a bank may produce. If such an event occurs, the risk of contagion is evaluated in terms of the loss in value for the deposits exchanged at date 0. It becomes apparent that contagion risk depends on the size of these deposits. When deciding on the size of deposits, if the probability of a bank failure is small, banks display a natural order of preference. They base their actions on two principles. They first ensure that they meet their liquidity demands in period 1, no matter what distribution of liquidity shocks is realized. Subject to that, they minimize the risk by diversification.

The chapter is organized as follows. Section 2 introduces the main assumptions about consumers and banks and describes the interbank market as a network. We discuss the linkages between banks and how contagion may arise, in section 3. In section 4 we show how banks set the interbank deposits and investigate if they are at the level that minimizes contagion risk for different degrees of network connectedness. Section 5 considers possible extensions and ends with some concluding remarks.

2. THE MODEL

2.1 Consumers and Liquidity Shocks

We assume that the economy is divided into six regions, each populated by a continuum of risk-averse consumers (the reason for six will become clear in due course). There are three time periods, $t=0, 1, 2$. Each agent has an endowment equal to one unit of a consumption good at date $t=0$. Agents are uncertain about their liquidity preferences: they are either early consumers, who value consumption only at date 1, or they are late consumers, who value consumption only at date 2. In the aggregate there is no uncertainty about the liquidity demand in period 1. Each region, however, experiences different liquidity shocks, caused by random fluctuations in the fraction of early consumers. In other words, each region will face either a high proportion p_H of agents that need to consume at date 1 or a low proportion p_L of agents that value consumption in period 1. There are $\binom{6}{3}$ equally likely states of nature that distribute the high liquidity shocks to exactly three regions and the low liquidity shocks to the other three. One may note that this set of states of the world does not build in any correlations between the liquidity shocks that affect any two regions.

To sum up, it is known with certainty that on average the fraction of early consumers in the economy is $q=(p_H+p_L)/2$. Nevertheless, the liquidity demand is not uniformly distributed among regions. All the uncertainty is resolved at date 1, when the state of the world is realized and commonly known. At date 2, the fraction of late consumers in each region will be $(1 - p)$ where the value of p is known at date 1 as either p_H or p_L.

2.2 Banks, Demand Deposits and Asset Investments

We consider that in each region i there is a competitive representative bank. Agents deposit their endowment in the regional bank. In exchange, they receive a deposit contract that guarantees them an amount of consumption depending on the date they choose to withdraw their deposits. In particular, the deposit contract specifies that if they withdraw at date 1, they receive $C_1 > 1$, and if they withdraw at date 2, they receive $C_2 > C_1$.

There are two possibilities to invest. First, banks can invest in a liquid asset with a return of 1 after one period. They can also choose an illiquid asset that pays a return of $r < 1$ after one period, or $R > 1$ after two periods. Let x and y be the per capita amounts invested in the liquid and illiquid asset, respectively. Banks will use the liquid asset to pay depositors that need to withdraw in the first period and will reserve the illiquid asset to pay the late consumers. Since the average level of liquidity demand at date 1 is qC_1, we assume that the investment in the liquid asset, x, will equal this amount, while the investment in the illiquid asset, y, will cover $(1-q)\ C_2/R$.[1]

Banks are subject to idiosyncratic shocks that are not insurable. That means that, with a small probability π, a bank may fail in either period 1 or 2. This event, although anticipated, will have only a secondary effect on banks' actions for reasons that will become clear in section 4.

2.3 Interbank Market

Uncertainty in their depositors' preferences motivates banks to interact in order to ensure against the liquidity shocks that affect the economy. These interactions create balance sheet linkages between banks, as described below.

At date 1 each bank has, with a 50 per cent probability, either a liquidity shortage of $(p_H - q)C_1$ or a liquidity surplus of $(q - p_L)C_1$. We denote by z the deviation from the mean of the fraction of early consumers, which in turn makes the liquidity surplus or shortage of a bank equal to zC_1.[2] As in the aggregate, the liquidity demand matches the liquidity supply, all the regional imbalances can be solved by the transfer of funds from banks with a cash surplus to banks with a cash deficit. Anticipating this outcome, banks will agree to hedge the regional liquidity shocks by exchanging deposits at date 0. This way, a contract is closed between two banks that gives the right to both parts to withdraw their deposit, fully or only in part, at any of the subsequent dates. For the amounts exchanged as deposits, each bank receives the same return as consumers: C_1, if they withdraw after one period, and C_2 if they withdraw after two periods.

Banks' portfolios now consist of three assets: the liquid asset, the illiquid asset and the interbank deposits. Each of these three assets can be liquidated in any of the last two periods. However, the costliest in terms of early liquidation is the illiquid asset. This implies the following ordering of returns:

$$1 < \frac{C_2}{C_1} < \frac{R}{r} \tag{23.1}$$

An important feature of the model is that the swap of deposits occurs *ex ante*, before the state of the world is realized. Note, however, that this prevents cases when lenders may wield monopoly power. For instance, in an *ex post* market for deposits, lenders might take advantage of their position as liquidity providers to extract money from banks with a shortage of liquidity. To avoid this unfavourable situation, banks prefer to close firm contracts that set the price of liquidity *ex ante*.

An interbank market, as introduced above, may be very well described as a network. The network can be characterized by the pattern of interactions between banks, as well as by the amount of interbank deposits that represent the links. In this chapter, we investigate how banks choose the size of interbank deposits, while keeping the network structure fixed. In particular, we are interested in the effects that complete and incomplete networks have on banks' decisions when setting the level of interbank deposits. In order to illustrate the effects of incomplete structures, we restrict our analysis to regular networks (we introduce definitions below). Thus, each bank in the network is a node, and each node is connected to exactly $n < 6$ other nodes. This means that each bank may, but need not, exchange deposits with n other banks. Note that we do not model explicitly how these connections are formed. Since the contracts are bilateral, and thus the amounts exchanged between any two banks are the same, the network is *undirected*. Next, we introduce some important definitions.

A *network* g is a collection of ij pairs, with the interpretation that nodes i and j are linked. A network is *regular of degree n* (or n-regular) if any node in the network is directly connected with n other nodes. The *complete network* is the graph in which all nodes are linked to one another. Any two nodes connected by a link are called *neighbours*.

We now discuss the incomplete information structure. We incorporate in our framework a very important feature of real world banking systems.

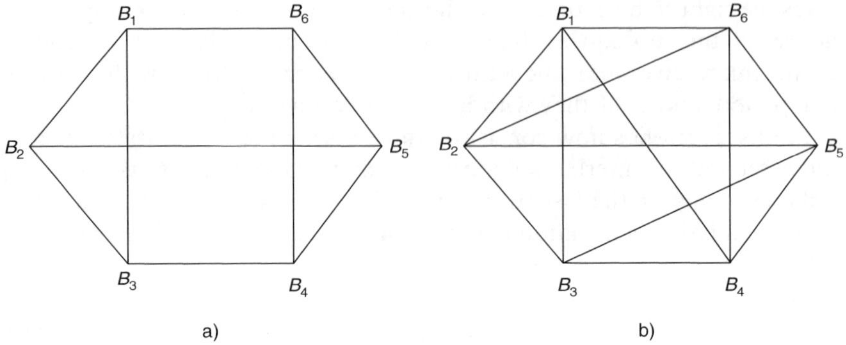

Figure 23.1 *n-regular networks: a)* n = *3; b)* n = *4*

Namely, banks have incomplete information on the network structure. Although it is common knowledge that the network is *n*-regular, banks do not know the entire network architecture. Thus, they do not observe any linkages in the network beyond their own connections. For instance, B_1 in Figure 23.1 knows his set of neighbours: B_2, B_3 and B_6. Nevertheless, it cannot observe how they are connected either among themselves, or to the other banks in the system.

For the purposes of our analyses we consider different values of n. However, since modern banking systems are highly connected, we reasonably assume that $n \geq 3$.[3] In other words, each bank is connected to at least half the other banks in the system. At the same time the markets are not always complete structures. In a possible interpretation, in a single country interbank market all the banks are connected to all the other banks. Connections outside the home country are nevertheless rather scarce.

3. CONTAGION RISK

3.1 Balance Sheet Linkages

The main goal of our chapter is to study which degree of interdependence arises between banks and the implications for the fragility of the banking system. The interdependence stems from two sources. First, there is a system-wide dependence that is reflected in the size of z, the liquidity shortage or surplus of any bank. The larger z, the higher is the degree of interdependence. Second, there is pairwise dependence that is given by the size of deposits exchanged between any two banks. Since we assume z to be fixed, for the moment, we focus on explaining pairwise dependence and its potential contagious consequences.

An *allocation rule for deposits* is a mapping from the set of links to the real numbers $a{:}g \rightarrow R$ that specifies the amount exchanged as deposits between banks i and j at date 0. For simplicity we use the following notation $a(ij) = a_{ij}$. As in the previous section we considered that deposit contracts are bilateral, we have $a_{ij} = a_{ji}$, thus bilateral interbank deposits.

We say that an allocation rule is *feasible* if in period 1 deposits can be withdrawn such that there will be no bank with a liquidity surplus or a liquidity shortage. Formally, let d_{ij} represent the amount transferred from i to j in period 1, for any pair ij, and N_i be the set of neighbours of bank i, for any i. Then, an allocation rule is feasible if, for any bank i and for any neighbour j of i, there exist d_{ij} and d_{ji} such that $|\Sigma_{j \in N_i} d_{ji} - \Sigma_{j \in N_i} d_{ij}| C_1 = zC_1$ and $0 \leq d_{ij}, d_{ji} \leq a_{ij}$.[4]

Lemma 1 *For an n-regular network with $n \geq 3$ there always exists a feasible allocation rule.*

Proof This holds true as in an n-regular network, when $n \geq 3$, there is always a path between every pair of nodes. A path is a sequence of consecutive links in a network. Moreover, it can be shown that the length of this path is 2 at most. A general proof is available on request.

The proof of Lemma 1 shows in fact that there exists a feasible allocation for any connected network. A regular network with a degree larger than half the number of nodes is a particular case of connected network.

Corollary 1 *A feasible allocation ensures that no bank will have a liquidity surplus or a liquidity shortage in period* 2.

In period 2 each bank will have a fraction of $(1 - p)$ late consumers where p has been realized for each region in period 1. Thus, the transfer of deposits between any banks i and j will simply be reversed.

3.2 Losses given Default

In order to evaluate contagion risk we need to introduce a measure that quantifies it. For this purpose, we apply the same procedure as the empirical literature on contagion: we consider the event of a bank failure and analyse its implications for the banking system. In our model, the failure of a bank will occur in either period 1 or 2 with a small probability π. The risk of contagion is then evaluated in terms of *loss-given default* (LGD), which expresses the excess of nominal liabilities over the value of the assets of the failed bank. In our setting, LGD will be given by the loss of value a bank incurs on its deposits when one of its neighbour banks is liquidated.

This measure focuses only on the loss associated with a direct link between two banks. It ignores any aspects related to the indirect effects the failure of a bank might have on the system. For instance, it does not capture the problems that arise when a bank that is a liquidity supplier fails.

Another aspect worth mentioning is that the failure of a bank might have contagious effects only if this event is realized in period 1. Once each bank reaches period 2, straightforward calculations show that the value of its assets is sufficiently large to cover all its liabilities. Hence, there is no loss in value for deposits, and LGD will be 0.

To calculate LGD we need to determine the value of the assets of the failed bank. If a bank fails, its portfolio of assets is liquidated at the current value and distributed equally among creditors. Now, recall that a bank portfolio consists of three assets. First, banks hold an amount of x per capita invested in a liquid asset that pays a return of 1. Second, banks have invested an amount y per capita in an illiquid asset that pays a return of $r<1$ if liquidated in the first period. Finally, there are interbank deposits summing up to $\Sigma_{k\in N_i} a_{ik}$ that pay a return of C_1 per unit of deposit. On the liability side, a bank will have to pay its depositors, normalized to 1 and at the same time to repay its interbank creditors, which also add up to $\Sigma_{k\in N_i} a_{ik}$. This yields a new return per unit of good deposited in a bank i equal to $\bar{C}_i = [(x + ry + \Sigma_{k\in N_i} a_{ik} C_1)/(1 + \Sigma_{k\in N_i} a_{ik})] < C_1$.[5] The LGD of bank j given that bank i has failed is easy now to express as[6]:

$$LGD_{ji} = a_{ji}(C_1 - \bar{C}_i) = a_{ji} \frac{C_1 - x - ry}{1 + \Sigma_{k\in N_i} a_{ik}} \qquad (23.2)$$

In the next section we will present how banks set the allocation rule and discuss the optimality of their decisions in terms of LGD.

4. DEPOSITS ALLOCATION AND THEIR OPTIMALITY

4.1 Network Structures and Uncertainty

To understand how banks set the allocation rule in period 0, it is important to realize that they make their decisions under uncertainty. It thus becomes necessary to characterize the environment in which they act.

In an incomplete network, there are two sources of uncertainty. On the one hand, there is no prior information about the distribution of liquidity shocks. That is, any of the $\binom{6}{3}$ states of the world that allows a high liquidity demand in any three regions and a low liquidity demand in the remaining three is equally likely. This further implies that there is no *ex ante* correlation between the fractions of early consumers in any two regions.

The lack of correlations between liquidity shocks is converted, for any bank i, into uncertainty. First, there is uncertainty about how many neighbours from N_i will be affected by a different liquidity shock than i at date 1. And second, there is uncertainty about who these neighbours are. Note that the first type of uncertainty depends on the network degree of completeness n and disappears when the network is complete. That is because the condition $n \geq 3$ guarantees that each bank has at least $n-2$ neighbours that will face a different liquidity demand in period 1.

Example 1 Suppose that the network degree is $n=3$. Then a bank might have, as regarded from period 0, one, two or three neighbours that may experience a different fraction of early consumers than itself in period 1.

Moreover, any of the banks in the neighbouring set of a bank I, is equally likely to experience a different liquidity shock than i.

On the other hand, any link that connects two banks is private information for the respective institutions. Even though it is common knowledge that each bank i has n links, which nodes are at the end of these links is only known by i.[7] This sort of incomplete information generates uncertainty about the minimum number of links that will connect banks of a different type. Banks are said to be of a different type if they experience different liquidity shocks in period 1. In particular, a bank is of type H if it faces a high liquidity demand and a bank is of type L if it faces a low liquidity demand.

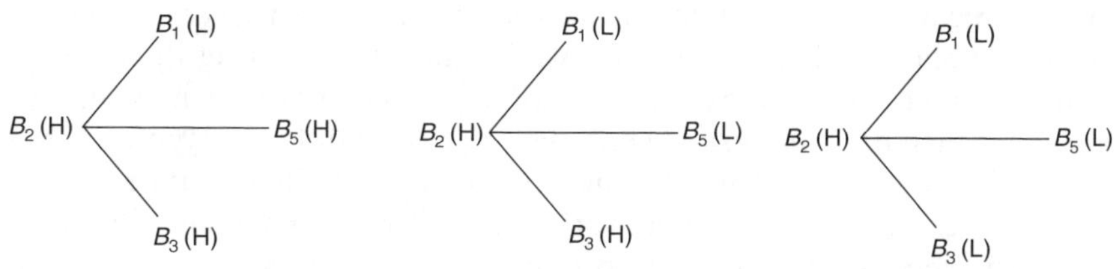

Figure 23.2 Uncertainty about the number of neighbours of a different type

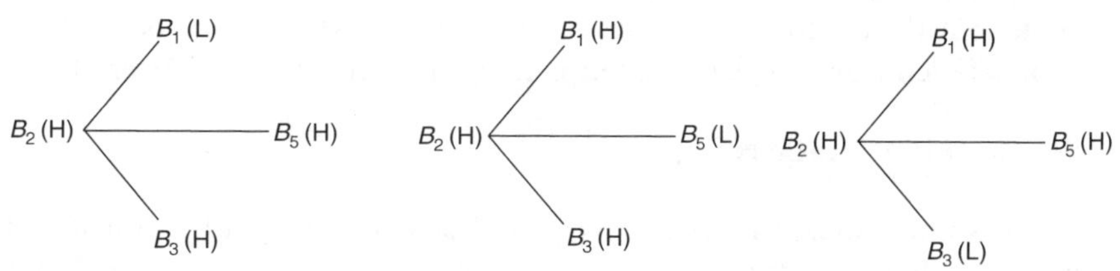

Figure 23.3 Uncertainty about which neighbours are of a different type

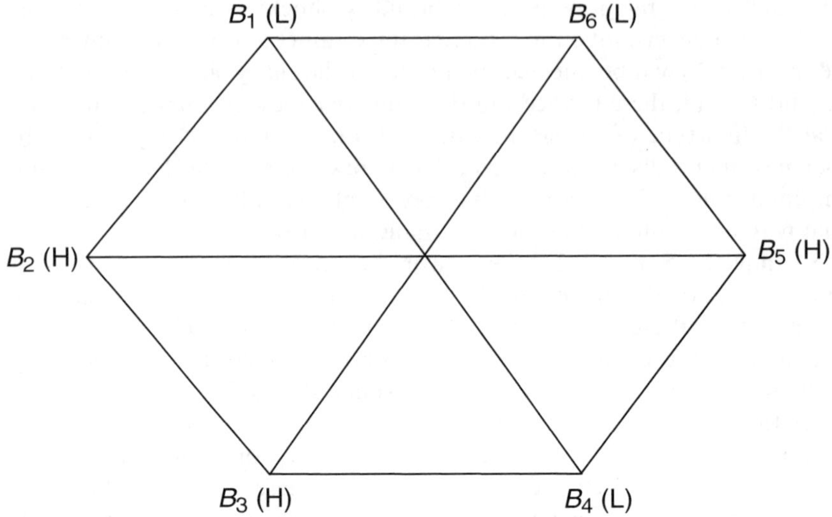

Figure 23.4 The role of incomplete information

Example 2 Suppose that $n = 3$ and the network g is represented as in Figure 23.4.

For this structure, in period 1, there will be at most two banks, each having exactly one neighbour that experiences a different fraction of early consumers, regardless of the states of the world realized. Hence, for any state of the world realized there will be at least five links that connect the H nodes and the L nodes. From the perspective of any bank i, however, it seems possible that each bank has exactly one neighbour of a different type, and thus the minimum number of links connecting nodes of a different type is three.

In the case of a complete network, banks' environment simplifies considerably since most of the uncertainty is resolved. When the network is complete each bank will have with certainty three neighbours of a different type than itself. Moreover, every node is linked to every other node and thus there will be exactly nine links connecting the H nodes and the L nodes, for any state of the world that is realized. The only uncertainty that banks have to consider concerns which of their neighbours will be of a different type.

4.2 Deposit Allocations

Liquidity imbalances that occur in period 1 can be solved by the transfer of funds from banks of type L to banks of type H. For this transfer of funds to be possible, banks have to set the allocation rule properly in period 0. When deciding on the size of deposits, if the probability π of a bank failure is small, banks have a natural preference ordering. They base their decisions on two principles. First, they ensure that they hedge the regional liquidity shocks, no matter what state of the world is realized in period 1. That is, after the transfer of funds takes place, each bank's cash holdings will exactly match the liquidity demand. And second, given that the first criterion is met, they take into account the possibility that a bank failure occurs in period 1 and minimize the risk of contagion by diversification.

In order to meet the first criterion, the interbank system is considered to be at date 1 in the state when each bank has exactly $n-2$ nodes of a different type. Note that uncertainty about the state of the world allows *one bank* to have exactly $n-2$ neighbours of a different type, while uncertainty about the network structure allows *all the banks* to have each exactly $n-2$ neighbours of different type. Thus, the allocation of deposits that ensure the transfer of liquidity from L nodes to H nodes, for any state of the world is that allocation that permits the transfer when each bank has exactly $n-2$ neighbours of a different type. To satisfy the second criterion, banks need to divide z, the amount they will borrow (lend), among the $n-2$ neighbours of a different type. Moreover, each bank takes into account that any of their neighbours can be of a different type than itself.

To summarize, banks choose an allocation of deposits such that they minimize the *loss-given default* associated to each link they have, for the *worst-case scenario*.[8] We consider the *worst-case scenario* to be the state of the world for which each bank has exactly $n-2$ nodes of a different type. Since for any pair ij, LGD_{ij} is decreasing in a_{ij}, the minimization problem yields an equilibrium allocation of deposits exchanged at date 0 between any two banks of $z/(n-2)$.

Proposition 1 *Let g be an n-regular network of banks, with $n \geq 3$. The allocation rule for deposits that sets $a_{ij} = z/(n-2)$, for any pair of banks $ij \in g$, is feasible.*

Proof To show that an allocation rule for deposits is feasible, we need to show that for any bank i and for any neighbour j of i there exists an amount of deposits that can be transferred such that there will be no bank with either a liquidity surplus or a liquidity shortage. Transferring $z/(n-2)$ between banks of a different type and 0 otherwise, insures the feasibility property. A complete proof is available on request.

4.3 Optimality

We examine the optimality of the allocation rule that banks choose in terms of LGD. Moreover, we discuss whether banks' decisions are optimal *ex post*, after the state of the world has been realized. It is clear that *ex ante* banks choose the best allocation of deposits given the information available.

We are interested in establishing whether the *ex ante* optimal allocation will also be optimal *ex post* and when this is the case.

Given that banks choose an allocation rule for deposits that sets $a_{ij} = z/(n-2)$, the loss of any bank i given the default of any neighbour j of i is derived as follows:

$$LGD^*_{ij} = \left(\frac{z}{n-2}\right)\frac{C_1 - x - ry}{1 + (nz)/(n-2)} = z\frac{C_1 - x - ry}{n - 2 + nz}$$

The following proposition relates the optimality of LGD^* to the degree of network completeness.

Proposition 2 *Let g be an incomplete n-regular network (that is $n=3,4$) and consider any realization of the liquidity shocks that allows at least one bank to have minimum $(n-1)$ neighbours of a different type. Then there exists a feasible allocation of deposits a_{ij} such that $a_{ij}[(C_1 - x - ry)/(1 + \Sigma_{k \in N_i} a_{jk})] < LGD^*_{ij}$, for any pair $ij \in g$.*

Proof The following corollary hints on how the proof develops; a complete proof is available on request.

Proposition 2 tells us that the allocation of deposits that banks choose is suboptimal *ex post*, for any realization of the state of the world that is *not* the worst-case scenario. In other words, when the network is incomplete, banks' decisions do not always set the degree of interdependence such that the corresponding losses are minimal.

Corollary 2 *For $n=3$, the allocations of deposits $a_{ij} = 3z/5$, for any pair $ij \in g$, satisfies proposition 2. When $n=4$, the allocations of deposits that satisfies proposition 2 is $a_{ij} = 3z/8$.*

Proposition 2 discusses the case for $n=3,4$ and the next corollary treats the case of complete networks. We briefly explain what happens for $n=1,2$. A network degree larger than 3 insures that the network is connected. For $n<3$, however, the network structure could be characterized by 'islands'[9]. Moreover, the liquidity demand and the liquidity supply in the separate islands might be mismatched. This would create uncertainty about the aggregate fraction of early consumers as well. Anticipating this outcome, banks might decide not to exchange deposits in the first place.

Corollary 3 *Let $\tilde{g}$ be the complete network. Then, there is no feasible allocation of deposits a_{ij} such that $a_{ij}[(C_1 - x - ry)/(1 + \Sigma_{k \in N_i} a_{jk})] < LGD^*_{ij}$, for all pairs $ij \in \tilde{g}$.*

To clarify, there is no allocation of deposits that reduces the loss of one bank without increasing the loss of another bank. The intuition behind corollary 3 relies on the fact that in a complete network the worst-case scenario is realized for any distribution of the liquidity shocks.

This result is particularly important since it states that the complete network is the only network where the *ex ante* optimal decisions of banks are optimal also *ex post*. The complete network thus provides the conditions for banks to choose the optimal degree of interdependence. This occurs for two reasons. First, a limited 'horizon of observability' allows banks to maintain incorrect beliefs about the true state of the world. Second, these incorrect beliefs cause banks to take decisions that are the best response to their incorrect beliefs, but that would not be best responses under full information.

5. CONCLUDING REMARKS

The problem of contagion within the banking system is a fairly debated issue. The main contribution this chapter brings is endogenizing the degree of interdependence that exists between banks. In particular, we investigate how banks set the size of exposures towards each other, when the structure of the network that connects them is fixed. Given a chosen allocation of interbank deposits, we investigate what the implications are on the fragility of the banking system. We compare the outcome of banks' choices across different degrees of network completeness, in order to see for which network structures the interconnectivity level is optimal. In an incomplete network the losses caused by contagion are larger than in a complete network, as we knew from Allen and Gale (2000). In addition, an incomplete network generates an environment of uncertainty that determines banks to take decisions that *ex post* turn out to be suboptimal. It is, indeed, usually the case that in an incomplete information setting the *ex ante* optimal decisions of agents are not also *ex post* optimal. The point our chapter raises is that it is exactly in an incomplete network where this setting of incomplete information is created. We show that in a complete network the uncertainty is resolved and, this way, the *ex ante* optimal decisions of banks are optimal also *ex post*. Thus, we conclude that a complete network favours an optimal degree of interdependence.

In the end we discuss the robustness of our results and draw a parallel with the empirical research on contagion. Our model extends naturally to more than six regions. To see why this is the case, recall that what drives the results is banks' loss-averse behaviour. Banks choose an allocation of deposits that ensures them liquidity for any realization of the states of the world. More precisely, they set the allocation rule such that contagion losses are minimal in the worst-case scenario. When the network is incomplete, the allocation of deposits set this way turns out to be suboptimal for any realization of the state of the world that is not the worst-case scenario. In a complete network, however, the allocation of deposits always minimizes contagion risk since any state of the world will yield the worst-case scenario. This feature of complete networks versus incomplete networks is independent of the actual number of nodes (regions).

The message this chapter transmits is rather optimistic. When the network is complete, banks have the right incentives to choose the degree of interdependence for which the contagion risk is minimal. This result can be interpreted in the light of the empirical research on contagion, which consistently finds that the banking system demonstrates a high resilience to shocks. Recall that we use the same tool as the empirical papers to assess contagion risk. At the same time, the analyses performed in these papers are usually limited to a single country interbank market, where the network is likely to be complete. Our model can thus account as an explanation to support the empirical evidence.

NOTES

* Erasmus Universiteit Rotterdam, P.O. Box 1738, 3000 DR Rotterdam, The Netherlands, email: babus@tinbergen.nl. I am grateful to Casper G. de Vries for useful suggestions and for his support. I would also like to thank Marco van der Leij for numerous discussions on the topic. All remaining errors are my own.

1. This allocation maximizes the expected utility of consumers, see Allen and Gale (2000).
2. Since $q = \frac{p_H + p_L}{2}$, than it must be that $(p_H - q)C_1 = (q - p_L)C_1$.
3. The cases $n = 1$ and $n = 2$ will be discussed briefly later in the chapter.
4. Note that $d_{ij} \neq d_{ji}$ in period 1. That is because when the state of the world is realized in period 1, liquidity will flow from banks that have an excess to banks that have a deficit. Hence, the network becomes directed in period 1.
5. Equation (23.1) ensures that the inequality holds.
6. In principle $LGD_{ji} \neq LGD_{ij}$ since it may be that $\Sigma_{k \in N_i} a_{ik} \neq \Sigma_{k \in N_k} a_{jk}$.
7. This motivates our choice of six banks. In a four-bank setting, if n is common knowledge, each bank can make inferences and accurately guess the network structure.
8. These loss-averse actions are entirely consistent with the usual behaviour of banks. The use of VaR measures in practice is sufficient evidence to support the assumption of loss aversion.
9. For $n = 2$ the network could be structured in two 2-regular components. For $n = 1$ there is no connected network structure.

REFERENCES

Allen, F. and D. Gale (2000), ‘Financial contagion’, *Journal of Political Economy*, **108**, 1–33.

Boss, M., H. Elsinger, S. Thurner and M. Summer (2004), ‘Network topology of the interbank market’, *Quantitative Finance*, **4**, 1–8.

Cifuentes, R., G. Ferrucci and H.S. Shin (2005), ‘Liquidity risk and contagion’, *Journal of European Economic Association*, **3**.

Cocco, J., F. Gomes and N. Martins (2003), ‘Lending relationships in the interbank market’, *Working Paper*, London Business School.

Dasgupta, A. (2004), 'Financial contagion through capital connections: A model of the origin and spread of bank panics', *Journal of European Economic Association*, **2**, 1049–84.
de Vries, C. (2005), 'The simple economics of bank fragility', *Journal of Banking and Finance*, **29**, 803–25.
Degryse, H. and G. Nguyen (2004), 'Interbank exposures: An empirical examination of systemic risk in the Belgian banking system', Discussion paper, Center for Economic Research, Tilburg University.
Diamond, D. and P. Dybvig (1983), 'Bank runs, deposit insurance and liquidity', *Journal of Political Economy*, **91**, 401–19.
Eisenberg, L. and T. Noe (2001), 'Systemic risk in financial systems', *Management Science*, **47** (2), 236–49.
Freixas, X., B. Parigi and J.C. Rochet (2000), 'Systemic risk, interbank relations and liquidity provision by the Central Bank', *Journal of Money, Credit and Banking*, **32** (3), 611–38.
Furfine, C. (2003), 'Interbank exposures: Quantifying the risk of contagion', *Journal of Money, Credit and Banking*, **35** (1), 111–28.
Lagunoff, R. and L. Schreft (2001), 'A model of financial fragility', *Journal of Economic Theory*, **99**, 220–64.
Leitner, Y. (2005), 'Fragile financial networks', *Journal of Finance*.
Sheldon, G. and M. Maurer (1998), 'Interbank lending and systemic risk: An empirical analysis for Switzerland', *Swiss Journal of Economics and Statistics*, **134**, 685–704.
Upper, C. and A. Worms (2004), 'Estimating bilateral exposures in the German interbank market: Is there a danger of contagion?', *European Economic Review*, **48** (4), 827–49.
Wells, S. (2002), 'U.K. interbank exposures: Systemic risk implications', Financial Stability Review, Bank of England.

24. Does corporate mobility enhance corporate governance?

Zsuzsanna Fluck and Colin Mayer*

1. INTRODUCTION

This chapter investigates the determinants of incorporation and reincorporation decisions of firms when there is regulatory competition between states in a union. Understanding how companies choose their place of incorporation is fundamental for understanding the dynamics of new enterprise creation and corporate mobility in the European Union. This chapter is based on Fluck and Mayer (2005), which presents a formal theory of corporate governance, freedom of reincorporation and competition in law in a model of agency problem between firms' management and shareholders. It is an informal discussion of the issues considered there, and for a more formal demonstration of the results presented here, the reader is referred to that paper.

Article 48 of the Treaty of Rome granted companies incorporated in one member state of the European Union (EU) the right to operate in any other. The right was challenged by some member states that sought to impose the traditional Continental European doctrine of the 'real seat'. This requires companies to incorporate where their headquarters or substantial activities are located. It is only recently with the Centros, Überseering and Inspire Art judgements of the European Court of Justice that the principle of freedom of establishment has been reaffirmed (Baelz and Baldwin, 2002).

In the US, where companies have the freedom to incorporate and also the freedom to reincorporate in any state, there has been an active debate on whether competition between states encourages 'runs to the top or bottom' in standards of corporate legislation. According to one school of thought, in seeking to maximize shareholder value, companies choose to incorporate where states impose the highest standards (Romano, 1985, 2002, 2005a, 2005b). According to another, states are forced to adopt progressively more lax standards to attract and retain corporations, and competitive deregulation ensues (Bebchuk, 1992). There is a third line of argument, which suggests that there is not much competition at all (Kahan and Kamar, 2002;

Bebchuk and Hamdani, 2002). Some states, for example Delaware, develop the administrative and legal expertise that encourages companies to adopt their legislation, and prevents others from competing with them. A fourth view argues that states operate under a federal umbrella that limits the relevance of variations in their legislation (Roe, 2003).

2. CONTROL OVER INCORPORATION AND REINCORPORATION

A firm's choice of corporate governance structure is fundamentally different from any other product or factor market decision. In choosing their legal forms, companies are not just buying in normal factors of production, they are determining the allocation of control of companies between managers and shareholders and between shareholders and other parties, such as employees. They are defining the nature of the company as reflected in the control rights of different parties. Competition between legal systems is not therefore the same as competition in product or factor markets. Account has to be taken of the change in the nature of the corporation as it moves as well as the relative efficiency of legal systems in assisting the corporation in attaining its productive objectives.

In Fluck and Mayer (2005) we provide a first examination of the merits and deficiencies of competition for incorporation in the context of a model in which there are conflicts between shareholders and managers in choice of investment strategy, what we term project selection. Moving between regulatory regimes allows companies to match the governance systems to their productive requirements. For example, some entrepreneurial activities benefit from the delegation of authority from shareholders to managers running firms, whereas other more traditional activities may require more active oversight by shareholders. However, legal systems will also determine the allocation of control rights over reincorporation decisions themselves. So the choice of corporate form will itself reflect the allocation of authority over choice of state of incorporation. Therefore, the fundamental question is: who makes the choice of legal system and incorporation/reincorporation – managers or shareholders?

Whether selection of governance arrangements is on balance beneficial depends on the extent to which adverse spillovers can be avoided. Where they can, the governance structures will allow activities that otherwise would be discouraged to be undertaken. Allocation of control over choice of governance, incorporation and reincorporation of firms therefore impacts the technology choice of firms and technological specialization of countries. The allocation of control over firms' reincorporation decisions determines the corporate governance choice *ex ante* and the outcome of competition between legal regimes *ex post*.

3. CONVERGENCE OF LEGAL REGIMES

Since managers value discretion and private benefits of control, when they have control over the reincorporation decision of their firms, they will select the least restrictive, most manager-friendly governance structure for their companies. If states compete for reincorporation, then competitive deregulation and 'runs to the bottom' ensue. If shareholders decide on the original place of incorporation and managers have effective control over the reincorporation decision of their companies, then reincorporating the company in a different jurisdiction will destroy shareholder value.

Hence we predict that when managers have full control over the *ex post* reincorporation decision, then either all states 'run for the bottom' or there will be no competition between states for corporations. The states may replicate the most business-friendly state if replication is costless. If, on the other hand, replicating the legal institutions is costly, then our view coincides with that of Kahan and Kamar (2002), namely, when managers have control over the reincorporation decision *ex post*, then the dominant position of a single state among states in the charter market (in the case of the United States the state of Delaware) is evidence of a lack of regulatory competition between states. This conclusion is also supported by Bar-Gill et al. (2002) model of competition for incorporation by states where establishing legal institutions is costly and one particular state (Delaware) has a first-mover advantage.

When shareholders have partial or full control over incorporation and reincorporation decisions of their companies then they will match the governance structure of their firm with the activities to be performed and will incorporate or reincorporate in countries whose regulatory systems best assist the corporation in attaining its productive objectives. Hence, when control over reincorporation is allocated to shareholders or when shareholders have an effective veto over the reincorporation decision of their firm, regulatory competition between states does not lead to convergence in legal regimes and the diversity of corporate governance regulations in the union will prevail.

A social welfare comparison of regimes yields further interesting insights. From the social welfare perspective, the shareholders' governance structure choice is too restrictive. As shown in Fluck and Mayer (2005), it never coincides with the social-welfare maximizing governance structure choice. While aiming to alleviate the agency problem between shareholders and management, shareholders excessively limit managerial discretion at the expense of creativity and innovation. The manager's choice of governance regime, in contrast, does coincide with maximum social welfare under certain conditions, and managerial control over reincorporation then maximizes social welfare. Where managerial private benefits are high in relation to returns to shareholders or where private benefits are modest but there is little divergence of interest between shareholder and manager, then the social welfare maximizing level of corporate governance corresponds with that selected by management and runs to the bottom are welfare maximizing. Otherwise managerial control over reincorporation may increase or decrease social welfare from what it is under shareholder control. In the latter case social welfare can be improved by granting reincorporation rights to one party and veto rights to the other party.

In summary, single governance systems are optimal and can be achieved in a union by conferring reincorporation rights on management where technologies with high private benefits and/or low divergence of interests between management and shareholders prevail. Technologies with lower private benefits and greater divergence of interests require multiple governance systems. But even here, the optimal level of governance does not correspond to that of shareholder value maximization since this invariably fails to reflect managerial interests adequately. Thus while in some cases it is beneficial to confer full reincorporation rights on management, it is never optimal to confer full rights on shareholders. Management should at least be granted the right to reincorporate in less stringent governance regimes subject to a shareholder veto to prevent uncompensated reductions in welfare from taking place.

It is interesting to relate our theory on reincorporation decisions to the recent literature on firms' cross-listing decisions (Pagano et al., 2002; and Reese and Weisbach, 2002). While there are certain similarities between incorporation/reincorporation and listing decisions, there are also major differences. First of all, incorporation decisions are made by private companies, whereas cross-listing decisions belong to public companies. These two types are substantially different as pointed out in Pagano et al. (1995) and in Becht et al. (2006) among others. Even though reincorporation decisions are relevant for both, a private company considering reincorporation in another country is not necessarily willing to bear the cost of going public in that country. Furthermore, even for a public company reincorporation can accomplish objectives that cross-listing cannot. For example, if a company would like to adopt a less restrictive governance structure than its home country, it can do so by reincorporating in another country but not by cross-listing in that country (at least not without de-listing from the home market). If the goal is to adopt a tighter governance structure, then cross-listing and reincorporation can both be the means to attain it (Reese and Weisbach, 2002). This is so because cross-listing in addition to the home market can only tighten a company's governance structure but cannot relax it. As Fluck and Mayer (2005) demonstrate, under certain conditions relaxing a company's governance structure is socially desirable.

4. INCORPORATION AND TECHNOLOGICAL SPECIALIZATION

Regulatory competition therefore can lead to two opposite outcomes: either runs to the bottom occur and legal regimes will converge, or a diverse set of governance regimes will prevail. In the first case there is no technological specialization by states. The second case, in contrast, will allow the matching of technologies with their optimal governance regimes and activities that otherwise would be discouraged will be undertaken.

Suppose that the set of feasible technologies differs across countries, as some countries may have an edge in certain technologies that are difficult to replicate. This may be due, for example, to geographical characteristics, natural resources, economies of scale, and education and training of the labour force. Then when shareholders set up a new firm, they will choose their firm's technology and governance structure to maximize shareholder value subject to the constraints they face. If the shareholders can hold the future governance structure of the firm unchanged, then their choice of technology will be the one that maximizes shareholder value under their governance structure choice. Otherwise, the shareholders will rationally anticipate the possibility that the manager may reincorporate their firm in another jurisdiction and they will take this into account when making the technology choice *ex ante*. In other words, shareholders' willingness to set up a new company and endow it with capital will depend on the allocation of control rights over the *ex post* reincorporation decision.

When setting up a new company, shareholders rationally anticipate that *ex post* the manager will reincorporate their firm in a country with a less stringent, more manager-friendly governance structure and this reincorporation will result in a loss of shareholder value *ex post*. To minimize their losses, founding shareholders will adopt technologies that guarantee them the highest shareholder value under the least restrictive governance structure, or will pass up the investment opportunity. Therefore, when the manager has full control over the reincorporation decision *ex post*, then the technology that produces the highest shareholder value under the least restrictive, most manager-friendly governance structure will squeeze out all other technologies.

Interestingly, this run for the bottom in regulation gives rise to a run for the top in technological competition. When the manager has full control over the reincorporation decision *ex post*, then founding shareholders will invest more in high-tech or creative industry technologies and will be more likely to start new companies in innovative high-tech sectors, or in sectors with high asset specificity.

Since shareholders rationally anticipate that the manager will reincorporate their firm in the most manager-friendly state, shareholders may possibly choose this state with the most manager-friendly governance structure *ex ante* as the state of incorporation for their company. If this is the case, then reincorporation will not take place, and it will appear as if the shareholder value maximizing governance structure and the most manager-friendly governance structure coincide. However, this governance structure is not an unconstrained maximizer of social welfare, since the technology choice was constrained by anticipation of the *ex post* reincorporation decision.

One can link this finding to the recent debate on regulatory competition between states in the United States (Romano, 1985, 2005a, 2005b; Bebchuk, 1992; Bebchuk and Ferrell, 2001; Bebchuk and Hamdani, 2002; Daines, 2001; Kahan and Kamar, 2002; Roe, 2003). On one side of this debate (see Romano, 1985, 2005a, 2005b), it is frequently argued that incorporation in Delaware, the state that grants broad managerial discretion in its application of the business judgement rule, maximizes shareholder value. For example, Daines (2001) reports higher Tobin's q for firms incorporating in Delaware and interprets it as implying that incorporating in Delaware increases shareholder value. Since Tobin's q is a proxy for firms' growth opportunities, Daines' evidence can also be interpreted that companies with high growth opportunities more frequently incorporate or reincorporate in Delaware, which is in line with our prediction. However, our theory further implies that incorporating or reincorporating in Delaware does not necessarily imply overall shareholder value maximization due to the endogeneity and the time inconsistency of the technology and the governance structure choice. Consequently, our theory can reconcile Daines' evidence with Bebchuk's and Hamdani's (2002) view that a single state's dominant position in the charter market can be sustained in the absence of overall shareholder value maximization.

Finally, when shareholders have partial or full control over the *ex post* reincorporation decisions of their firms, then states will choose different corporate governance structures and there will be technological specialization across states within the union. This prediction is consistent with the observed diversity of governance structure choices in US practice and the relationship between firms' technology and governance structure documented by Klein (2002) in the context of audit committees and by Gillan et al. (2003) in the context of board characteristics, bylaws and charter provisions.

5. NEW ENTERPRISE CREATION

In Fluck and Mayer (2005) different control allocations over the reincorporation decisions of firms have different social welfare implications for new enterprise creation *ex ante*.

Shareholders will be better off when they have partial or full control over the *ex post* reincorporation decision than under the manager's control. However, the comparison for managers is indeterminate. *Ex post* the manager is better off when he has full control over the firm's reincorporation decision. Nevertheless, since shareholders rationally anticipate the manager's *ex post* reincorporation decision when setting up their firm *ex ante*, having full control over the *ex post* reincorporation decision may actually make managers worse off overall. Hence, the comparison of the upsides created by the two regimes is also indeterminate, that is neither the manager's full control nor the shareholders' full or partial control regime dominates or is dominated in terms of the overall value created.

However, the downside of the manager's choice regime can be more severe than the downside of the shareholders' choice regime. This is because both parties may be worse off under the manager's control of reincorporation than under shareholders' choice of reincorporation. The shareholders are worse off because the manager does not maximize shareholder value and the manager might be worse off under the manager's control over the *ex post* reincorporation decision because shareholders take into account the allocation of reincorporation rights in their *ex ante* technology choice.

Interestingly, however, social welfare can be improved by granting reincorporation rights to one party and veto rights to the other party. Since a possible venue to facilitate transfers from managers to shareholders is the market for corporate control, a combination of strong shareholders' rights and an active market for corporate control can potentially improve on social welfare maximization, productive and allocative efficiency.

6. THE GOVERNANCE STRUCTURE CHOICE OF STATES

Given the nature of regulatory competition, how do states within a union choose their governance regimes? To answer this question, first consider the impact of a state's choice of corporate governance regime on its existing companies, and then on new enterprise creation and incorporation within states.

6.1 Impact on Existing Companies

Under the manager's control of reincorporation, a country's choice of governance structure does not matter. Whether or not a company will stay or reincorporate elsewhere depends on the governance structure choices of other states in the union. The only way for any state to prevent exodus of its existing companies is to adopt the least restrictive, most manager-friendly governance structure.

A country's governance structure choice is also irrelevant when shareholders have full control over the *ex post* reincorporation decision of their company. In this case, shareholders of an existing company will reincorporate their company in the country whose governance structure maximizes shareholder value given their firm's technology. When shareholders have full control over the *ex post* reincorporation decision of their companies, then states can prevent reincorporation of their existing companies by adopting shareholder value maximizing governance structures. This will lead to technological specialization across states within the union.

When shareholders have partial control over the *ex post* reincorporation decision of their firm and a state adopts corporate governance regulations that are more lax than the shareholder value maximizing one, then both managers and shareholders will favour reincorporation but in different jurisdictions. Managers would like to reincorporate their firms in another country with less restrictive governance regime but shareholders will veto any such attempt. Shareholders, in contrast, would like to reincorporate their firms in another country that grants more shareholder rights, but managers will veto it. Only when a country's governance regime is more restrictive than the shareholder value-maximizing governance structure choice can the two parties agree where to reincorporate. Hence, when the manager and shareholders have joint control over the *ex post* reincorporation decision of their company, then governance structure choices by states that are no more restrictive than the shareholder value maximizing one will prevent reincorporation of existing companies. This includes the social welfare maximizing governance structure choice.

6.2 Impact on new Enterprise Creation and Incorporation

When setting up a new enterprise, founders anticipate future reincorporation decisions and position their new enterprise to maximize shareholder value *ex post*. For this reason when the manager is in full control over the *ex post* reincorporation decision of his firm, then a state's corporate governance regime choice will not matter for incorporation decisions of new enterprises. Similarly, when shareholders have partial or full control over the reincorporation decision of their firm, their state's governance structure choice will be irrelevant, since founding shareholders will incorporate their firm in the country whose governance structure maximizes shareholder value over all technologies.

To illustrate the decision-making of shareholders, suppose that a state adopts a governance regime to maximize social welfare for its existing companies. Then, all the new firms in the state will incorporate elsewhere. If all other states do the same, then different companies will incorporate in different states and the states' objective of maximizing social welfare over their set of technologies will fail. Hence, the only governance regime that can induce start-up companies to incorporate in their home state is the one that maximizes shareholder value. But this policy is only successful under the legal regime of partial or full reincorporation control by shareholders.

6.3 Overall Impact

Consider now the joint impact of states' corporate governance choices on existing and new enterprises. When either party has full control over reincorporation, then no state can achieve social welfare maximization of its existing and new enterprises by adopting any governance regime. The only governance structure choice that can keep existing and new enterprises in the jurisdiction of the home country is the shareholder value maximizing choice but only if shareholders at least share control in reincorporation decisions. When the manager has full control over the *ex post* reincorporation decision, then no such governance structure choice exists.

When the manager and shareholders have joint control over the *ex post* reincorporation decision, then a state can achieve social welfare maximization of its existing companies *ex post*. However, social welfare maximization fails beyond the scope of existing companies. If a country adopts the social welfare maximizing governance structure, then none of its start-ups will choose to incorporate in their home state.

Hence, there is a distinct life-cycle pattern associated with each regime of reincorporation control. Start-up companies and mature companies will be incorporated in different states and they will do so even if *ex post* reincorporation is correctly anticipated.

7. CONCLUSION

The central principle that has emerged is that freedom of establishment and competition between states in corporate legislation is in principle beneficial. It allows companies to match their governance arrangements to their corporate activities. It promotes economic activity that could not be sustained in the absence of legislative diversity.

Our theory highlighted the potential conflicts that freedom of mobility creates between different stakeholders of the firm. We have focused on the conflict between managers and shareholders and demonstrated that because shareholders select technologies ahead of employing managers, they take account of the impact of governance arrangements on managers' choice of effort. We argue that shareholders should be granted effective veto powers over reincorporation proposals that they deem to be undesirable. Principles of delegation to management can be retained, Pareto improvements ensured and wealth-diminishing moves can be averted. However, in the presence of other stakeholders, there may be other conflicts. In Fluck and Mayer (2006) we focus on the extent to which competition between legal regimes allows companies to reincorporate to weaken the claims of creditors. Similar issues can arise in relation to other stakeholders, such as employees, as well as different classes of investors.

Harmonization at the federal level of regulatory competition between states may be required where there are externalities that would otherwise promote competitive deregulation. However, it comes at a price in terms of diversity in governance arrangements and the matching of governance with corporate activities. This is particularly significant where a variety of governance arrangements are required to support commercially viable activities or where there is uncertainty about what constitutes the optimal form of governance, and experimentation is required to identify it. Harmonization should therefore be targeted specifically at the source of the externality, allowing legislative choice and competition to be retained elsewhere.

NOTE

* Zsuzsanna Fluck: Department of Finance, Eli Broad Graduate School of Management, Michigan State University, East Lansing, MI 48824, USA and The William Davidson Institute (email: fluck@bus.msu.edu); Colin Mayer: Peter Moores Professor of Finance, Saïd Business School, University of Oxford, Park End Street, Oxford, OX1 1HP, UK (email: colin.mayer@sbs.ox.ac.uk).

REFERENCES

Baelz, K. and T. Baldwin (2002), 'The end of the real seat theory (sitztheorie): the European Court of Justice decision in Überseering of 5 November 2002 and its impact on German and European company law', *German Law Journal*, **3** (12).

Bar-Gill, O., M. Barzuza and L. Bebchuk (2002), 'The market for corporate law', *Harvard Olin Discussion Paper*, No. 377.

Baysinger, B. and H. Butler (1985), 'The role of corporate law in the theory of the firm', *Journal of Law, Economics and Organization*, **28**, 179–91.

Bebchuk, L. (1992), 'Federalism and the corporation: the desirable limits on state competition in corporate law', *Harvard Law Review*, **105** (7), 1443–510.

Bebchuk, L. and A. Ferrell (2001), 'A new approach to takeover law and regulatory competition', *Virginia Law Review*, **87**, 111–64.

Bebchuk, L. and A. Hamdani (2002), 'Vigorous race or leisurely walk: reconsidering the competition over corporate charters', *Yale Law Journal*, **112**, 553–615.

Becht, M., C. Mayer and H. Wagner (2006), 'Corporate mobility comes to Europe: the evidence', *Working Paper*, ECARES.

Burkart, M., D. Gromb and F. Panunzi (1997), 'Large shareholders, monitoring and the value of the firm', *Quarterly Journal of Economics*, **112**, 693–728.

Daines, R. (2001), 'Does Delaware law improve firm value?', *Journal of Financial Economics*, **62**, 525–58.

Fluck, Z. (1999), 'The dynamics of the management–shareholder conflict', *Review of Financial Studies*, **12**, 379–404.

Fluck, Z. and C. Mayer (2005), 'Race to the top or bottom? Corporate governance, freedom of reincorporation and competition in law', *Annals of Finance*, **1** (October), 349–78.

Fluck, Z. and C. Mayer (2006), 'Creditor's rights, corporate mobility and the value of debt', *Working Paper*, Michigan State University.

Gillan, S., J. Hartzell and L. Starks (2003), 'Explaining corporate governance: boards, bylaws, and charter provisions', *Working Paper*, University of Delaware.

Judgment of the European Court of Justice (Second Chamber) of 10 July 1986. Case: D. H.M. Segers v Bestuur van de Bedrijfsvereniging voor Bank- en Verzekeringswezen, Groothandel en Vrije Beroepen. Case No: Case 79/85.

Judgment of the European Court of Justice 27 September 1988. Case: The Queen v H.M. Treasury and Commissioners of Inland Revenue, *ex parte* Daily Mail and General Trust plc. Case No: Case 81/87.

Judgment of the European Court of Justice 9 March 1999. Case: Centros Ltd v Erhvervs- og Selskabsstyrelsen. Case No: Case C-212/97.

Judgment of the European Court of Justice 5 November 2002. Case: Überseering BV v Nordic Construction Company Baumanagement GmbH (NCC). Case No: Case C-208/00.

Judgment of the European Court of Justice 30 September 2003 Case: Kamer van Koophandel en Fabrieken voor Amsterdam v Inspire Art Ltd. Case No: Case 167/01.

Kahan, M. and E. Kamar (2002), 'The myth of state competition in corporate law', *Stanford Law Review*, **55**, 679–749.

Klein, A. (2002), 'Economic determinants of audit committee independence', *Accounting Review*, April, 435–52.

Pagano, M. and P. Volpin (2005a), 'The political economy of corporate governance', *American Economic Review*, **95** (4), 1005–30.

Pagano, M. and P. Volpin (2005b), 'Managers, workers, and corporate control', *Journal of Finance*, **60** (2), 841–68.
Pagano, M., F. Panetta and L. Zingales (1995), 'Why do firms go public?', *Journal of Finance*, **53**, 27–64.
Pagano, M., A. Röell and J. Zechner (2002), 'The geography of equity listing: why do companies list abroad?', *Journal of Finance*, **57**, 2651–94.
Perotti, E. and E.-L. Von Thadden (2002), 'The political economy of bank and market dominance', *Working Paper*, University of Lausanne.
Reese, W. and M. Weisbach (2002), 'The protection of minority shareholders' interests, cross-listing in the United States and subsequent equity offerings', *Journal of Financial Economics*, **66**, 65–104.
Roe, M.J. (2003), 'Delaware's competition', *Harvard Law Review*, **117**, 590–646.
Romano, R. (1985), 'Law as a product: some pieces of the incorporation puzzle', *Journal of Law, Economics and Organization*, **1**, 225–83.
Romano, R. (2002), *The Advantage of Competitive Federalism for Securities Regulation*, Washington, DC: AEI Press.
Romano, R. (2005a), 'Is regulatory competition a problem for corporate governance?', *Oxford Review of Economic Policy*, forthcoming.
Romano, R. (2005b), 'The states as a laboratory: state competition for corporate charters', in A. Gerber and E. Patashnik (eds), *Promoting the General Welfare: American Democracy and the Political Economy of Government Performance*, Brooking Institution, Washington, DC, forthcoming.
Wymeersch, E. (2003), 'The transfer of the company's seat in European Company Law', *ECGI Law Working Paper*, No. 08/2003 and 40 CMLR 661.

PART VII

Capital market integration and capital mobility in new EU member states

25. Equity market integration of new EU member states

Lorenzo Cappiello, Bruno Gérard, Arjan Kadareja and Simone Manganelli

1. INTRODUCTION

This chapter studies integration between new EU member states and the euro zone. We employ a factor model for market returns which distinguishes between global and local components. The simple model we consider allows us to adopt an intuitive measure of integration: the higher the amount of return variance explained by the global factor relative to the local components, the higher the degree of integration. As shown by Cappiello et al. (2006) there is a direct relationship between this measure of integration and return correlation. If the correlation between two markets increases, the integration indicator should rise as well.

Return co-dependences are estimated with the 'co-movement box' methodology introduced by Cappiello et al. (2005). This approach possesses, *inter alia*, two advantages. First, contrary to standard correlation measures, it is robust to time varying volatility and departure from normality. Second, it offers a simple and intuitive visual measure of integration. The co-movement box methodology provides a long-term average of the co-dependence between any two financial market returns across two distinct sub-periods.

We analyse returns on equity market indices. We find that the degree of integration of the new EU member states with the euro zone (and in particular with Germany, which we chose as a benchmark for the euro area) has increased in their process towards EU accession. We also find that, for the three new EU member states with the largest economies and most developed financial markets, the Czech Republic, Hungary and Poland, return co-movements between themselves and with Germany increase significantly over the sample period. For the four smaller countries, Cyprus, Estonia, Latvia and Slovenia, we document that the degree of co-movements remains low and/or unchanged throughout the sample. This suggests that although all these countries have experienced tremendous development in their financial markets, they exhibit different degrees of integration and a different speed of convergence with the euro zone.

This chapter is structured as follows. Section 2 provides a brief literature review that leads us to motivate the use of a particular integration indicator. We also derive a relationship between this indicator and correlation measures. In section 3, we explain the empirical methodology. Section 4 contains a brief description of the data and main developments in new EU member state equity markets. In section 5 we discuss the empirical results, while section 6 concludes.

2. MEASURING INTEGRATION

Consider first a closed economy with an efficient local financial market. In such an economy, firms' cash flows and equity returns depend on local factors only. Consider, in contrast, fully open economies, without barriers to trade and financial transactions. In such a world local firms' equity returns are a function of not only domestic but also foreign factors. As a consequence, when a country moves from being closed to an open status, the impact of global factors on domestic firms' cash flows should increase. Therefore the transition to an open economy regime should be accompanied by an increase in co-movements in equity prices.

Against this background, we express asset returns in a national market, r_{it}, in terms of a global factor and a number of local factors. Next, we adopt as a measure of integration the share of variance explained by the common factor. In general the higher this share, the higher the degree of integration. If markets are perfectly segmented, the variance explained by the global factor is equal to zero. On the other hand, if markets are perfectly integrated, all the local factor loadings will be equal to zero and most of the variation will come from the global factor.[1]

It is possible to show that there is a precise relationship between standard correlation measures and our integration indicator. In particular, correlation is proportional to the amount of the total variance explained by the global component. If two markets, i and j, are integrated, the correlation between returns on an asset in market i and j will increase.

3. THE EMPIRICAL APPROACH

We evaluate correlations adopting the 'co-movement box' framework developed by Cappiello et al. (2005) (see Figure 25.1).

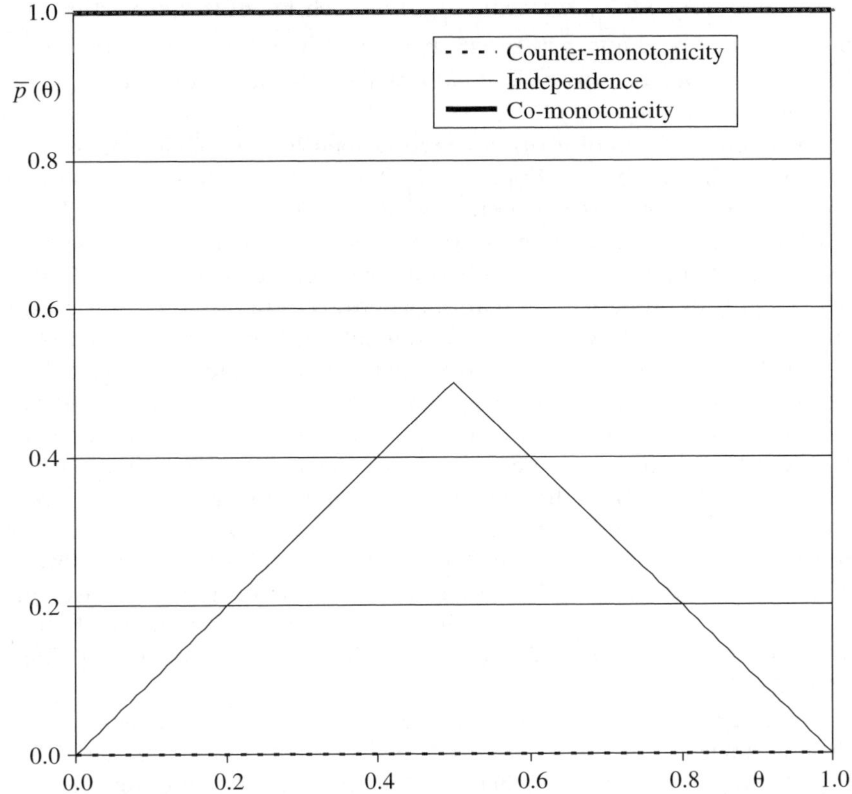

Note: This figure plots the probability that an asset return r_{it} falls below (exceeds) its θ-quantile conditional on another asset return r_{jt} being below (above) its θ-quantile, for $\theta < 0.5$ ($\theta \geq 0.5$). The case of perfect positive correlation (co-monotonicity), independence, and perfect negative correlation (counter-monotonicity) are represented.

Source: Cappiello et al. (2005).

Figure 25.1 The co-movement box

Tests for changes in co-movements are usually conducted by correlations estimates. However, these tests are sensitive to heteroskedasticity (see, for instance, Forbes and Rigobon, 2002) and departure from normality. Therefore, a simple comparison between correlations over time could lead to spurious results. The co-movement box methodology, instead, is robust to time-varying volatility and departure from normality.

Let $\{r_{it}\}_{t=1}^{T}$ and $\{r_{jt}\}_{t=1}^{T}$ denote the time series returns of two different markets. Let $q_{\theta t}^{r_i}$ be the time t θ-quantile of the conditional distribution of

r_{it}. Analogously, for r_{jt}, we define $q^{r_j}_{\theta t}$. For each quantile θ, we estimate a conditional probability $p_t(\theta)$ that, at time t, the returns on market i are below (or above) its θ-quantile, conditional on the same event occurring in market j.

The characteristics of $p_t(\theta)$ can be conveniently analysed in what we call the co-movement box (see Figure 25.1). The co-movement box is a square with unit side, where $p_t(\theta)$ is plotted against θ. The shape of $p_t(\theta)$ will generally depend on the characteristics of the joint distribution of the time series returns r_{it} and r_{jt}, and therefore for generic distributions it can be derived only by numerical simulation. There are, however, three important special cases that do not require any simulation: 1) perfect positive correlation, 2) independence and 3) perfect negative correlation. If two markets are independent, which implies $\rho_{ijt} = 0\ \forall t$, $p_t(\theta)$ will be piece-wise linear, with slope equal to one, for $\theta \in (0, 0.5)$, and slope equal to minus one, for $\theta \in (0.5,1)$. When there is perfect positive correlation between r_{it} and r_{jt} (i.e. $\rho_{ijt} = 1\ \forall t$), $p_t(\theta)$ is a flat line that takes on unit value. Under this scenario, the two markets essentially reduce to one. The polar case occurs for perfect negative correlation, i.e. 0 $\rho_{ijt} = -1\ \forall t$. In this case $p_t(\theta)$ is always equal to zero: when the realization of r_{jt} is in the lower tail of its distribution, the realization of r_{it} is always in the upper tail of its own distribution and conversely (for a more formal description of the model see Cappiello et al., 2005).

This discussion suggests that the shape of $p_t(\theta)$ provides key insights about the dependence between two asset returns r_{it} and r_{jt}. In general, the higher $p_t(\theta)$ the higher the co-dependence between the two time series returns.

While the conditional probabilities of co-movements can be used to measure the dependence between different markets, the interest of the researcher often lies in testing whether this dependence has changed over time. Market integration is an important case in point. It is possible to test for changes in integration by evaluating if the conditional probability of co-movements between two markets increases, for instance, after institutional changes. In the present application we estimate $p_t(\theta)$ over two different periods. When the conditional probabilities for these two different periods are plotted in the same graph, differences in the intensity of co-movements can be identified directly. In particular, an upward (downward) shift of these curves would be consistent with an increase (decrease) of integration.

The framework of the co-movement box can be used to formalize this intuition. Let $p^B(\theta) \equiv B^{-1}_{t<\tau} p_t(\theta)$ and $p^A(\theta) \equiv A^{-1}_{t\geq\tau} p_t(\theta)$, where B and A denote the number of observations before and after a certain threshold date τ, respectively. We adopt the following working definition of increased integration:

Definition 1. (Integration) Integration increases if

$$\delta(0,1) = \int_0^1 [p^A(\theta) - p^B(\theta)]d\theta > 0.$$

$\delta(0,1)$ measures the area between the average conditional probabilities $p^A(\theta)$ and $p^B(\theta)$.

Constructing the co-movement box and testing for differences in the probability of co-movement requires several steps. First, we estimate the univariate time-varying quantiles associated to the return series of interest, using the Conditional Autoregressive Value at Risk (CAViaR) model developed by Engle and Manganelli (2004). Second, we construct, for each series and for each quantile, indicator functions which are equal to one if the observed return is lower than this quantile and zero otherwise. Finally, we regress the θ-quantile indicator variable of returns on market j on the θ-quantile indicator variable of returns on market i, interacted with time dummies which identify periods of greater integration. These regression coefficients will provide a direct estimate of the conditional probabilities of co-movements and of their changes across regimes.

4. DATA

The empirical analysis is carried out on returns on equity market indices. All returns are denominated in local currencies. We compare the equity indices of Germany, which constitutes our euro area benchmark, with those of a selected number of new EU member states, Cyprus, the Czech Republic, Estonia, Hungary, Latvia, Poland and Slovenia.

Stock exchanges for the countries under consideration are approximately open over the same hours during the day, virtually ruling out any non-synchronous effect. Nevertheless, asynchronicity may arise because there are instances in which markets are closed in one country and open in another, as national holidays and administrative closure do not fully coincide. To adjust for these non-simultaneous closures, we include only the returns for the days on which the markets under analysis were open that day and had been open the day before. Hence the daily returns we investigate are synchronous, avoiding the confounding effects that non-synchronous returns can have on the measurement of integration.

Equity returns are continuously compounded and computed from Global Financial Data indices, which are market-value-weighted and include dividends. The daily data set covers the period from 12 January 1993 to 2 August 1998 and from 2 January 2001 to 12 November 2004. We exclude data from August 1998 to December 2000 since the Russian crisis and the stock market bubble burst may induce spurious results.

4.1 Developments in Equity Markets

Equity markets of new EU member states developed along two different lines. The Czech Republic adopted mass privatization schemes, whereas Estonia, Hungary, Latvia, Poland and Slovenia first established a legal framework for trading and next listed the enterprises. By and large, the second approach yielded better outcomes, as the first one resulted in a loss of confidence caused by the delisting of unsuccessful companies (see Caviglia et al., 2002).

The importance of the stock exchanges can be measured by the market capitalization as a percentage of GDP. At the end of 2001, Central European countries and Estonia had a stock market capitalization of 20 to 30 per cent of GDP, whereas Cyprus reported about 70 per cent, and the remaining countries less than 10 per cent. With the exception of Cyprus, these percentages are well below the euro area levels: at the end of 2001 the stock market capitalization for Germany was approximately equal to 60 per cent of its GDP. In our sample, the three largest stock markets are Poland, the Czech Republic and Hungary. Their relative stock market capitalization approximately reflects the respective countries' GDP weight in the region.

5. EMPIRICAL RESULTS

We compute the probabilities of co-movements over two sample periods. For equities we distinguish between a pre-convergence (before July 1998) and a convergence period (after January 2001). An increase in integration in the second period would be reflected by an upward shift in the probability of co-movements.

Figure 25.2 shows the GDP-weighted averages of the estimated co-movement probabilities between new EU member states and Germany over the two sub-samples under consideration. In Figure 25.2a, which plots the probability averages relative to all countries, we observe an increase in the probability of co-movements during the convergence period. This is consistent with an increase in the degree of integration. Interestingly, before 1998 these markets were virtually independent *vis-à-vis* Germany, probably because they were relatively new and had weak economic and financial ties with Western Europe and Germany in particular.

Figures 25.2b and 25.2c present the breakdown of these average co-movements by the economic size of the new member states. Most of the

(a) Germany vs. all new EU member states

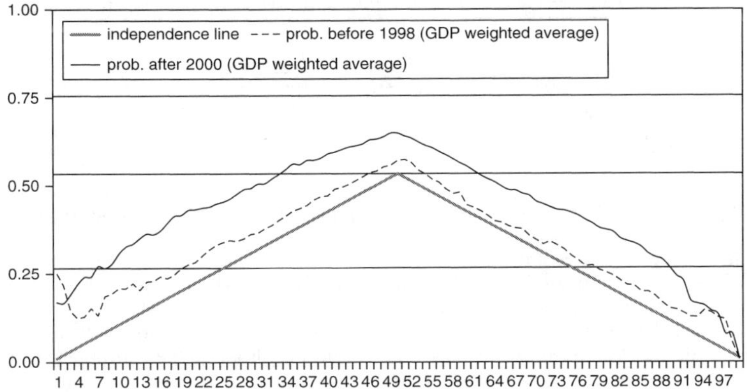

(b) Germany vs. large new EU member states (Czech Republic, Hungary and Poland)

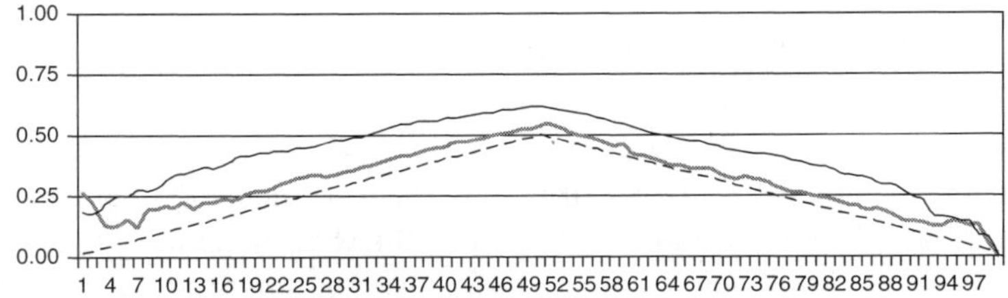

(c) Germany vs. small new EU member states (Cyprus, Estonia, Latvia and Slovenia)

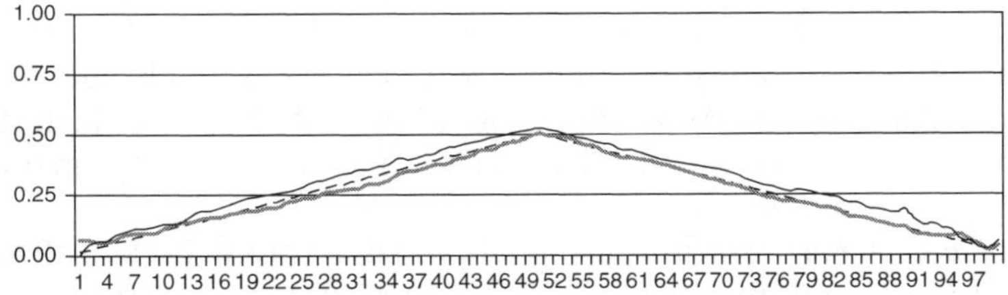

Notes: Figures 25.2a–c plot weighted average estimated conditional probabilities of co-movements between equity market index returns of selected new EU member states and Germany over two periods. The first sub-sample covers the pre-convergence period (January 1993 to August 1998), and the second the convergence period (January 2001 to November 2004). The probability of co-movement of each new EU member state *vis-à-vis* Germany is weighted by the fraction of its GDP relative to the total new EU member state GDP.

Source: Authors' calculations.

Figure 25.2 Weighted average conditional probabilities of co-movements between equity market index returns of selected new EU member states and Germany over the pre- and the post-convergence periods

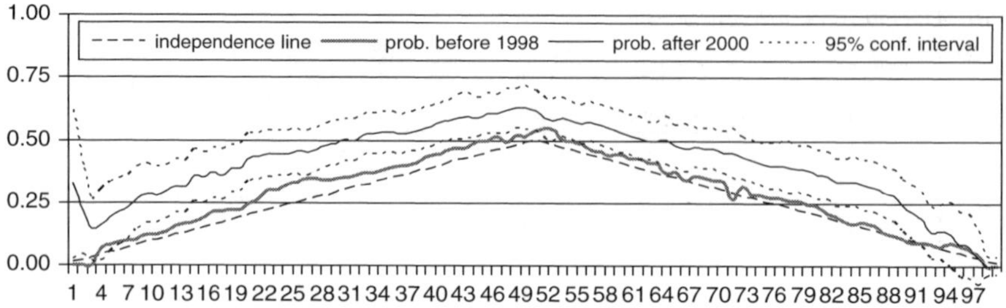

Notes: Figure 25.3 plots the estimated conditional probabilities of co-movements between returns on Czech and German equity market indices over two periods. The first sub-sample covers the pre-convergence period (January 1993 to August 1998), the second the convergence period (January 2001 to November 2004). The dashed lines denote the two standard error bounds around the estimated co-movement likelihood in the convergence period.

Source: Authors' calculations.

Figure 25.3 Czech Republic vs. Germany

increase in co-movements is mainly driven by the large new member states (Czech Republic, Hungary and Poland) which make 85 per cent of the total GDP in the region. Small new member states, instead, remain independent versus Germany also in the convergence period. This could be explained by institutional factors, the sheer size of the economy, the geographical distance and weak economic linkages with Germany.

These results are confirmed by country-pair analyses, which include 95 per cent confidence bands. As an illustration, Figure 25.3 plots estimated probabilities of co-movements for the Czech Republic *vis-à-vis* Germany across the two sub-samples.

Qualitatively similar conclusions can be inferred from Figure 25.4, where we analyse the probabilities of co-movements among new member states. Figure 25.4a is supportive of an overall increase in the degree of integration. As before, most of it is due to the increase in co-movements of large new member states, while small countries remain virtually independent even during the convergence period. The probabilities of co-movements before and during the convergence period for the large countries are much higher than the corresponding probabilities which we observe when comparing Germany with large new EU member states (see Figure 25.2b). The relatively high probabilities of co-movements during the pre-convergence period may be explained by economic linkages which go back to the communist era. Country-pair analyses once again confirm this outcome. A particularly striking case is that of Hungary and Poland

(a) All new EU member states

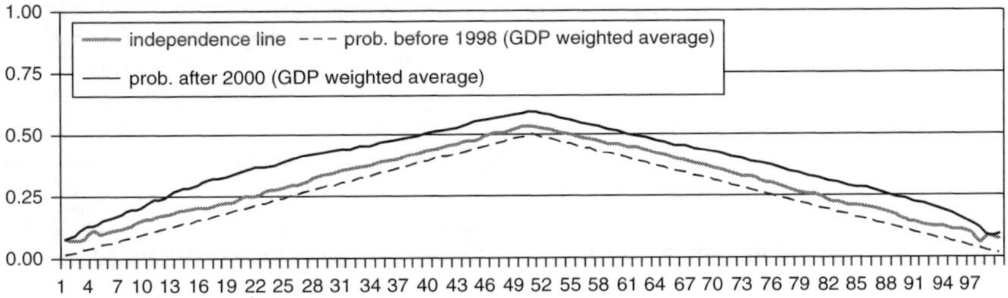

(b) Large new EU member states (Czech Republic, Hungary and Poland)

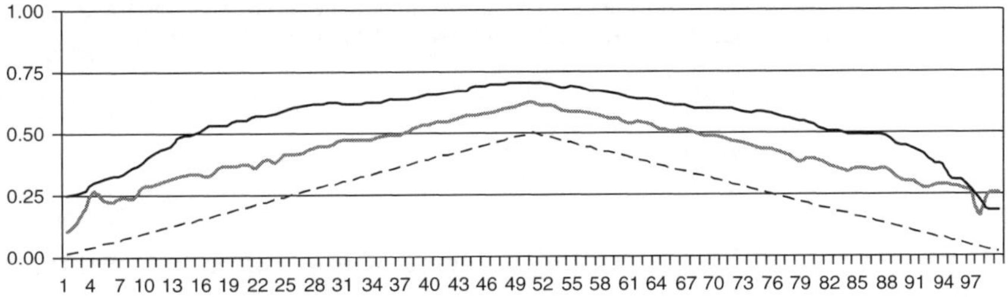

(c) Small new EU member states (Cyprus, Estonia, Latvia and Slovenia)

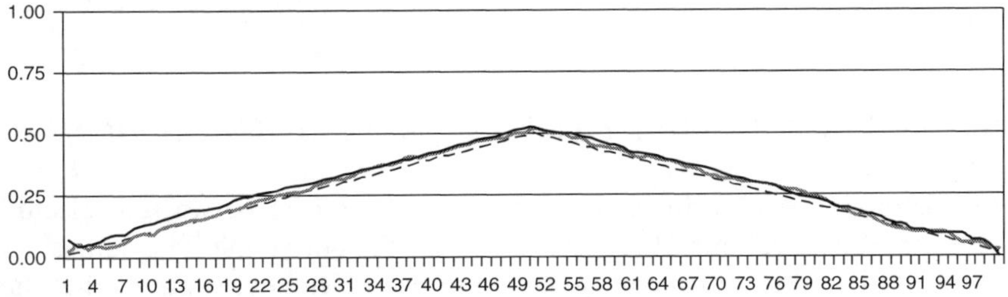

Notes: Figures 25.4a–c plot weighted average estimated conditional probabilities of co-movements between equity market index returns of selected new EU member states over two periods. The first sub-sample covers the pre-convergence period (January 1993 to August 1998), the second the convergence period (January 2001 to November 2004). The probability of co-movement between each country pair is weighted by the fraction of that GDP country pair relative to the sum of all possible country pairs' GDP.

Source: Authors' calculations.

Figure 25.4 Weighted average conditional probabilities of co-movements between equity market index returns of selected new EU member states over the pre- and the post-convergence periods

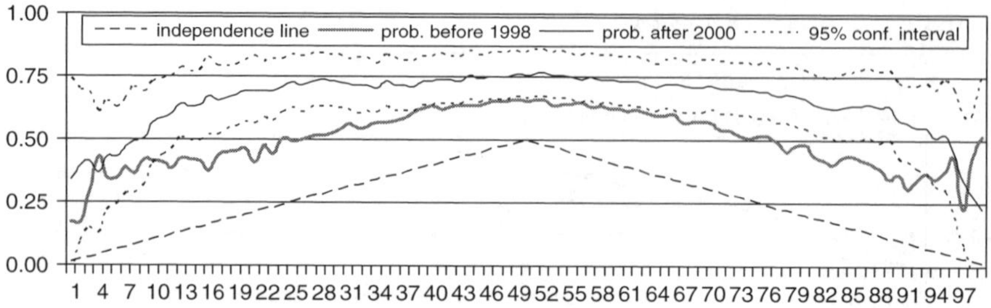

Notes: Figure 25.5 plots the estimated conditional probabilities of co-movements between returns on Hungarian and Polish equity market indices over two periods. The first sub-sample covers the pre-convergence period (January 1993 to August 1998), the second the convergence period (January 2001 to November 2004). The dashed lines denote the two standard error bounds around the estimated co-movement likelihood in the convergence period.

Source: Authors' calculations.

Figure 25.5 Hungary vs. Poland

(Figure 25.5), which suggests a high degree of integration between these two economies.

Formal tests, not reported here, of whether the level of co-movements change significantly between pre- and convergence periods broadly confirm the graphical results.

6. SUMMARY OF RESULTS AND CONCLUSIONS

In this chapter we evaluate the degree of integration between a selected number of new EU member states and with the euro zone. The analysis is conducted on returns on equity market indices. Evidence suggests that the degree of integration between the new EU member states and Germany, which we choose as a benchmark for the euro area, has increased in their process towards EU accession. A more refined investigation, however, indicates that most of the observed increase in integration was driven by the three new EU member states with the largest economies and most developed financial markets, the Czech Republic, Hungary and Poland. For the four smaller countries, Cyprus, Estonia, Latvia and Slovenia, we find that the degree of integration between themselves and with Germany was close to zero during the mid-1990s and remains low and/or unchanged afterwards. Institutional factors, the sheer size of the economy, geographical distance and weak economic linkages with Germany could be responsible for these results. Although all the considered countries have experienced tremendous development in their stock markets, their degrees of integration and speed of convergence with the euro zone differ quite markedly.

NOTE

1. Bekaert and Harvey (1997) investigate the impact of world factors on emerging market country returns by considering (amongst others) the proportion of the country returns variance due to world factors. The main difference between our approach and theirs is that while Bekaert and Harvey use a switching regime GARCH model to estimate variances and co-variances, we use a non-parametric approach to estimate co-movements directly.

REFERENCES

Baele, L., A. Ferrando, P. Hördahl, E. Krylova and C. Monnet (2004), 'Measuring financial integration in the euro area', *ECB Occasional Paper*, No. 14.

Bekaert, G. and C.R. Harvey (1997), 'Emerging equity market volatility', *Journal of Financial Economics*, **43** (1), 29–77.

Cappiello, L., B. Gérard and S. Manganelli (2005), 'Measuring comovements by regression quantiles', *ECB Working Paper Series*, No. 501, July.

Cappiello, L., B. Gérard, A. Kadareja and S. Manganelli (2006), 'Integration of new EU member states', *ECB Working Paper Series*, forthcoming.

Caviglia, G., G. Krause and C. Thimann (2002), 'Key features of the financial sectors in EU accession countries', in C. Thimann (ed.), *Financial Sectors in EU Accession Countries*, European Central Bank.

Engle, R.F. and S. Manganelli (2004), 'CAViaR: Conditional autoregressive value at risk by regression quantiles', *Journal of Business & Economic Statistics*, **22** (4), 367–81.

Forbes, K.J. and R. Rigobon (2002), 'No contagion, only interdependence: Measuring stock market comovements', *Journal of Finance*, **57** (5), 2223–61.

26. The integration of the Czech, Hungarian and Polish bond markets with the euro area bond market – a déjà vu of the Club-Med convergence plays?

Thomas Reininger and Zoltan Walko[1]

1. INTRODUCTION

Between late 2000 and mid-2003 government bond yields and yield spreads to the euro area declined substantially on the three largest and most liquid government bond markets among the new EU member states (the Czech Republic, Hungary and Poland: 'NMS-3'). Market participants were quick to assume 'convergence play', similar to that observed in the second half of the 1990s in the run-up to the introduction of the euro in the high-yield EU countries (Greece, Italy, Portugal and Spain: 'Club-Med'). However, the trend reversed in the second half of 2003 and subsequently yield spreads rose sharply until August/September 2004. This raised the questions whether yield convergence was over for the time being and, more generally, to what extent the bond markets of the euro area and the NMS-3 were already integrated.

In this chapter we intend to answer the question concerning how far integration of government bond markets in the Czech Republic, Hungary and Poland with the euro area has already advanced and whether a convergence play similar to that in the Club-Med during the second half of the 1990s is taking place. By employing different econometric techniques, we intend to contribute to the better understanding of the role of euro area yield movements for yield movements on the three most liquid bond markets in the Central and Eastern European (CEE) region.

In very general terms, financial market integration is an important issue as it has been found to enhance economic growth by a more efficient allocation of financial resources (for example: Levine et al., 1999; Klein and Olivei, 1999; Bekaert et al., 2003; or Giannetti et al., 2002). With respect to the euro area, recent years have seen an abundance of literature on the integration of the euro area financial markets. This literature has demonstrated that integration had started in some market segments already prior to euro adoption, and the process intensified and got broader based following 1 January, 1999. At the same time, integration has differed across market sectors over the past few years (for example Giannetti et al., 2002, Baele et al., 2004). Literature is much less numerous with regard to the integration of CEE financial markets with the euro area. This literature is in part devoted to the descriptive analysis of the integration of financial markets in general (for example: Stirbu, 2004; ECB, 2004; Reininger et al., 2002; Benoit et al., 2001; Köke, 2001; Lanoo and Salem, 2001; Reininger, 2001). Beyond a descriptive approach, early contributions came from Kähler (2001) and MacDonald (2001) with respect to the integration of CEE stock markets. The integration of CEE money and bond markets with the euro area has attracted increased attention only more recently (Hermann and Jochem, 2003; Crespo Cuaresma and Wójcik, 2004; Pungulescu, 2003; Dvorak and Geiregat, 2004; IMF, 2003; Crespo Cuaresma et al., 2004).

2. MEASURES OF BOND MARKET INTEGRATION

Several measures of bond market integration have been developed in the literature (see for example Adam et al., 2002; Baele et al., 2004).

In terms of *quantity-based measures*, the share of non-domestic bond holdings is seen as the most commonly used indicator of integration. This follows from the assumption that economic agents are able to access foreign financial markets more easily when these are increasingly integrated. An application of this measure to the NMS-3 can be found in Reininger et al. (2002).

Yield-based (price-based) measures, which focus on yield levels, are used to test whether the law of one price holds – in the case of bonds, by a comparison of yield levels (that is measuring the spread between the local bond yield and a benchmark bond yield). In so far as liquidity and credit risk differences exist between the local and the benchmark market, the interpretation of the yield-based measure must take into account these differences and their evolution over time.

News-based measures, finally, which focus on yield changes, investigate to what extent changes in local bond yields are driven by common rather than local news. When bond markets are fully integrated, this common news should to a large extent translate into yield changes of local bonds. However, due to – *inter alia* – differences in credit risk and liquidity across bond markets, common news cannot be expected to fully explain changes in local bond yields. Nevertheless, the explanatory power of common news can be expected to increase along with deepening bond market integration. News-based measures test bond market integration according to the following formula:

$$\Delta R_{i,t} = \alpha + \beta \Delta R_{b,t} + \varepsilon_t$$

where $\Delta R_{i,t}$ denotes the change in the bond yield of country i in period t, $\Delta R_{b,t}$ the change in the benchmark bond yield in period t.

Increasing integration requires that (i) the intercept term α (which measures the impact of local news) converges towards zero, (ii) the slope coefficient β (which measures the impact of common news) converges to one and (iii) the proportion of the variance of the local yield changes explained by the common factor (the r-squared) increases also towards one.

Thereby, the close relationship between the slope coefficient β and the correlation coefficient (which equals the square root of r-squared) should be borne in mind:

$$\rho_{x,y} = \beta \frac{\sigma_x}{\sigma_y},$$

This relationship implies that an increase in the correlation coefficient between two variables may reflect either an increase in the slope coefficient or a change in the differential between the standard deviations of the two variables, or a mixture of these two. In order to achieve full integration, not only the slope coefficient, but also the volatility differential of the yields has to converge to one.

It has been extensively demonstrated in the literature (for example Engle, 1982; Bollerslev, 1986) that in many financial time series the magnitude of residuals can be related to the magnitude and variance of past residuals. While such autoregressive conditional heteroscedasticity (ARCH) in itself does not necessarily render the results of standard linear estimation invalid, ignoring ARCH effects may result in loss of efficiency of the estimators. Since econometric tests (on the basis of the Ljung-Box Q-statistics of squared residuals) confirmed that ordinary least squares (OLS) regressions in our samples may be affected by heteroscedasticity, we estimated all regression equations as GARCH models. As to the methodology, we estimated generalized autoregressive conditional heteroscedasticity (GARCH) models with all possible combinations of up to five (in order to take into account possible weekday effects) statistically significant ARCH and GARCH terms and chose the one with the best Akaike information criterion value.

Yet using GARCH models instead of OLS has the disadvantage that the 'relationship triangle' between the correlation coefficient, the regression beta and the volatility differential does not hold strictly any more. However, this relationship is still applicable with respect to the direction of change in the variables, meaning that both a higher regression beta or a higher volatility differential support a higher correlation coefficient (*ceteris paribus*).

The further analysis in this chapter assesses the integration of the NMS-3 bond markets on the basis of both the yield level-based (price-based) and the news-based measure. For regression analysis, GARCH models are applied, unless otherwise mentioned.

3. THE CLUB-MED 'CONVERGENCE PLAY'

Yield spreads, measured by the yield on ten-year government bonds, decreased impressively in Italy, Portugal and Spain during the four years prior to the launch of the euro at the beginning of 1999, and in Greece during the three years prior to euro adoption at the beginning of 2001.

The bulk of the spread narrowing occurred prior to the last one or two years before euro adoption, and spreads declined only modestly thereafter. At the time of introducing the euro, Italy, Portugal and Spain had spreads of around 20 basis points over Germany, Greece around 60 basis points over the euro area.

In line with the theoretical postulation, the compression of yield spreads was only one part of the story. At the same time, the 30-day rolling correlation between daily yield changes in the Club-Med and in Germany tended to rise, albeit fluctuating in a relatively wide range throughout the period. At the end of 1998, the three first-wave euro area Club-Meds showed a correlation coefficient of around 0.7–0.8. The relationship between Greek and German government bonds was slightly weaker at 0.6–0.7 at the end of 2000. Interestingly, the development of the correlation coefficient during the last two years prior to euro adoption showed some similar patterns in the three first-wave Club-Meds and Greece, despite the two years difference in time. Particularly interesting is the sharp drop in the Spanish and Greek correlation coefficients around two months prior to euro adoption.

Looking into the two 'components' of the correlation coefficient, the increase in the correlation coefficient may have been induced by an increase in the sensitivity of Club-Med yield changes to changes in DEM yields (measured by the regression beta) and/or by a change in the relative volatility pattern (measured by the standard deviation differential). Visual observation of the development of the regression betas (in 30-day windows) and the relative (30-day) volatilities compared to German ten-year yields gives evidence that the increase in the correlation coefficient was primarily driven by a decrease in Club-Med yield volatility relative to Germany, especially during the last year prior to euro adoption. At the same time, the magnitude of the impact of one basis point change in German yields on Club-Med yields did not increase in general during the observation period.

This finding is also supported by regression analysis based on GARCH models. For this purpose we regressed daily changes in Club-Med ten-year government bond yields on changes in German ten-year yields, on changes in the local-currency three-month money market interest rate and on changes in the implied local-currency 3 $\times$ 6 Forward Rate Agreement (FRA; the three-month rate in three months' time)[2] during four (Greece: three) distinct one-year periods prior to euro adoption. The economic rationale for the inclusion of the money market variables in the equations was the assumption that they incorporate all available information about the domestic economy and expectations thereof. We ran bivariate regressions on each of the three explanatory variables, and two multivariate regressions (one including all three explanatory variables, and one including only the statistically significant variables from the former).

With regard to the bivariate regressions[3] of changes in Club-Med ten-year government bond yields on changes of German ten-year government bond yields, the correlation between changes in Club-Med ten-year yields and changes in German ten-year yields, as suggested by the r-squared of the respective regressions, increased significantly in the course of the four years prior to euro adoption and reached relatively high levels in the last year before adopting the euro (0.4–0.7). By contrast, the development of the sensitivity of changes in Club-Med yields to changes in German yields (measured by the regression betas) varied across countries. While the regression beta rose in Greece, it was directionless in Portugal and decreased in Spain and Italy. In the last year prior to euro adoption, the betas in the four countries lay between 0.47 and 0.69. In line with this finding, the volatility differentials between German and Club-Med yield changes rose sharply during the four-year period: while Club-Med yield volatilities were considerably above German yield volatility at the beginning of the period, the situation reversed by the last year prior to euro adoption, and German yield volatility was by around 20 per cent higher than Club-Med yield volatility.

The intercept terms in the regressions of changes in Club-Med yields on changes in German yields were negative throughout the period, but their (absolute) value was very small right from the beginning and, in addition, tended towards zero, implying a very minor (and declining) relevance of local news for yield developments.

Not surprisingly, the results of the bivariate regressions of changes in Club-Med ten-year government bond yields on changes of the respective local-currency money market rates showed a weakening relationship between Club-Med ten-year yield changes and both changes in local-currency three-month money market rates and changes in 3 × 6 FRAs (measured both by r-squared and regression betas). By the last year prior to EMU, the r-squared of these regressions was close to zero and the significance of most of the beta coefficients weakened over time (in some cases even turning insignificant). This clearly indicates a declining relevance of local news.

The multivariate regressions showed a similar pattern. The explanatory power of these regressions increased over the four years (with a setback two years before euro adoption in Italy and Portugal). The r-squared stood at between 0.46 and 0.71 in the last year before EMU. The size of the beta coefficients of changes in German bond yields developed quite similar to those in the bivariate regressions over the four years, apart from Italy where the coefficient did not exhibit a decline. The coefficients stood at between 0.46 and 0.66 in the last year prior to euro adoption. At the same time, the significance of the beta coefficients of the domestic money market indicators generally weakened and the coefficients also became small (0.08–0.15) in the last year prior to euro adoption.

The integration of the Club-Med bond markets with the German bond market continued following euro adoption. Although spreads continue to exist between ten-year government bond yields in the Club-Med and in Germany (at around 15–30 basis points), the explanatory power (as measured by r-squared) of German yield changes rose to around 0.95 in Spain, Italy and Portugal, and reached 0.75 in Greece in the fourth year after euro adoption (both in the bivariate and the multivariate regressions).[4] The beta coefficients of these regressions rose to very close to one in Spain, Italy and Portugal, and reached 0.8 in Greece. In addition, Club-Med yield volatility became roughly equal to the volatility of German yields. The intercept terms in the regressions were insignificant. The explanatory power of (euro area-wide) money market indicators remained low after euro adoption in the bivariate regressions. Interestingly, though, the beta coefficients of these indicators regained significance in the bivariate regressions and also the coefficients increased compared to the last pre-euro years. This would suggest that the common monetary policy has exerted a larger influence on bond yields in the Club-Med than the national monetary policies did in the run-up to euro adoption. However, this finding is not confirmed by the multivariate regressions, in the majority of which the money market indicators were insignificant.

Overall, we found two important characteristics of the first-wave convergence play, that is the yield convergence of the Club-Med countries: first, convergence on the basis of the yield level-based measure for integration (yield spread compression); and, second, a high degree of convergence on the basis of the news-based measure for integration. While the convergence process did not satisfy all three conditions of bond market integration according to the news-based measure for integration (as the slope coefficient between changes in German and Club-Med yields did not fully converge to one before euro adoption), it contained a diminishing influence of local news and a substantial increase in correlation as a result of declining volatility of Club-Med yield changes relative to the volatility of German yield changes, with higher yield volatility in Germany than in the Club-Med in the last year prior to euro adoption. The integration of bond markets has continued after euro adoption, and now Club-Med yields are moving roughly in tandem with German yields and exhibit similar volatility patterns. As such, our results are in line with the prevailing literature on bond market integration in the euro area.

4. CONVERGENCE OF NMS-3 BOND YIELDS SINCE 2000

4.1 Summary Results of the Regressions for the Bull and Bear Sub-periods

Based on the development of ten-year government bond yield spreads in the NMS-3 versus the ten-year benchmark yield in the euro area, the period since late 2000 can be divided into four sub-periods: a first 'bull period' with rapidly falling yield spreads (from Q4 2000 to Q4 2002/Q2 2003), a 'bear period' with gradually rising yield spreads (from Q1/Q3 2003 to Q3 2004), a period of relative spread stability between the two, and a second 'bull period' (from Q3 2004 to Q1 2005) (see Figure 26.1).

The bull and the bear periods were specified individually for the three countries in the following way (see Table 26.1).

In the following we present the summary results of the analysis of developments during the full period and during the two bull periods and the bear period.[5] To this end we performed similar regressions for the NMS-3 as for the Club-Med. However, we included daily changes in J.P. Morgan's EMBI-plus Performing Spread as an additional explanatory variable to capture the potential impact of changes in global investor sentiment towards emerging markets on the NMS-3 local currency bond markets. Subsequently, we compare the results of the regressions for the NMS-3 and the Club-Med. Finally, we investigate whether NMS-3 bond yields tend to be more responsive to euro area yield changes during periods of sharp euro area yield movements compared to tranquil periods.

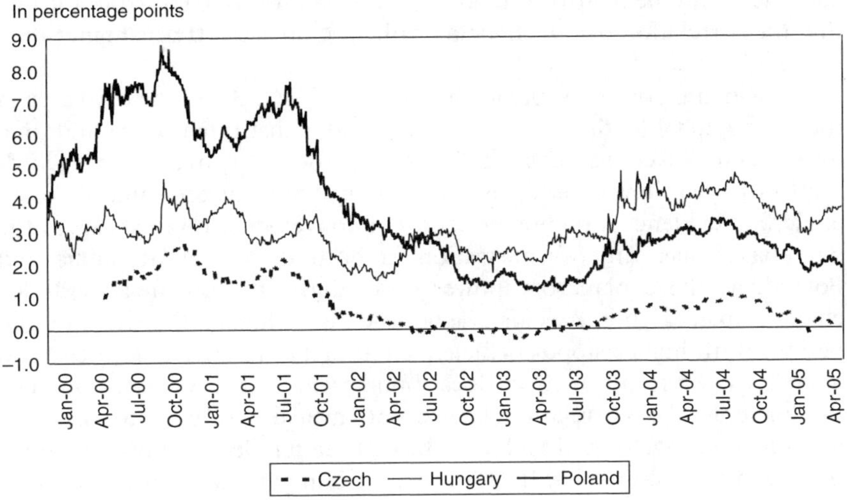

Source: Bloomberg.

Figure 26.1 NMS-3 10Y government bond yield spreads vs. Germany

Table 26.1 Bull and bear periods

	Bull period 1 (falling spreads)		Bear period (rising spreads)		Bull period 2 (falling spreads)	
	start	end	start	end	start	end
Czech Republic	07-Dec-00	27-Nov-02	26-Mar-03	09-Sep-04	09-Sep-04	10-Mar-05
Hungary	18-Oct-00	01-Apr-02	16-May-03	10-Sep-04	10-Sep-04	09-Mar-05
Poland	13-Oct-00	05-May-03	09-Jul-03	05-Aug-04	05-Aug-04	09-Mar-05

The narrowing of yield spreads between the NMS-3 and the euro area between 2000 and 2002/03, that is in the first bull period, constituted convergence according to the yield level-based measure of bond market integration. However, we could not find evidence that this was accompanied by a high degree of convergence on the basis of the news-based measure of bond market integration, as the explanatory power of changes in euro area yields for changes of local bond yields in the three markets was rather low as a result of both the slope coefficients and the yield volatility differentials. Only in the Czech Republic had changes in euro area yields at least a clearly higher explanatory power than domestic money market rates or changes in global sentiment towards emerging markets. Both the slope coefficient and the relative euro area yield volatility contributed to the fact that the correlation of Czech yields with euro area yields was higher than in the other two countries.

The widening of yield spreads between the NMS-3 and the euro area in the period 2003/04, that is in the bear period, constituted per definition a lower degree of convergence, in fact some process of divergence, according to the yield level-based measure. Interestingly, at the same time, we could find evidence for a higher degree of convergence on the basis of the news-based measure of integration in both the Czech Republic and Poland, as the explanatory power of changes in euro area yields for changes in local bond yields was considerably higher than in the bull period. Both higher slope coefficients and higher relative euro area yield volatility (as a result of lower local bond yield volatility) contributed to this higher level of correlation. Hence, both measures of bond market integration (yield level-based and news-based) again failed to show a uniform picture in these countries. By contrast, for Hungary, both measures indicated that the degree of bond market integration was lower in 2003/04 than in 2000/02. Although the slope coefficient was higher in Hungary, as well, the explanatory power of euro area yield changes continued to be very weak, as the volatility of Hungarian yield changes was markedly higher during the bear period (implying lower relative euro area yield volatility). In Hungary, but to a lesser degree also in Poland, the importance of local news (indicated by the coefficient of domestic money market indicators as independent variables) was higher in the bear period than in the bull period (higher explanatory power as well as significant and larger beta coefficients).

In the second bull period since 2000, that is in the second period of narrowing in yield spreads between the NMS-3 and the euro area, which took place in 2004/05, the higher degree of convergence according to the yield level-based measure was accompanied by the maintenance of a considerable, albeit moderately smaller degree of convergence on the basis of the news-based measure of bond market integration only in the Czech Republic. In Poland and Hungary, the explanatory power of changes in euro area yields for changes in local bond yields was very low, as the drop in the slope coefficient more than offset higher relative euro area yield volatility, which resulted from lower local bond yield volatility. In Hungary, but not in Poland, the importance of local news in the second bull period remained at roughly the same considerable level as in the bear period, coupled with sharply higher values of the regression betas.

4.2 Comparison of Yield Convergence in the NMS-3 to the earlier 'Convergence Play' in the Club-Med

In the NMS-3, the 'convergence play' in the first bull period had only the substantial narrowing of yield spread levels in common with the Club-Med convergence process in the run-up to euro adoption, while the degree of convergence according to other measures, like in particular the news-based measure, was vastly lower than the historical values in the Club-Med countries.

Comparing the regression results for the NMS-3 with those for the Club-Med (on the basis of the bivariate regressions), euro area yield changes explained a much smaller portion of the variation in yield changes in the NMS-3 in both the bull and the bear periods than German bond yield changes did in the Club-Med during the last year before euro adoption.

Looking at the whole observation period, in the NMS-3, the highest r-squared was found in the Czech Republic during the bear period at 0.29, while in the Club-Med the lowest r-squared amounted to 0.4 (Greece) and the highest to 0.7 (Italy) during the last year before euro adoption. On the other hand, the Czech value is higher than or equal to the Club-Med values two or three years before euro adoption (with the exception of the Italian value three years before euro adoption).

Hungary and Poland showed significantly lower values than the Czech Republic. Poland during the bear phase was best-off with an r-squared of 0.08, but this value is lower than the Club-Med values during each of the last four years (Italy, Spain) or three years (Portugal) or two years (Greece) before euro adoption. Moreover, this moderate degree of explanatory power of euro area yield changes for Polish yield changes was not achieved on a sustained basis, as r-squared was close to zero in the second bull period. While the sensitivity of Polish bond yield changes to changes in euro area yields in the bear period (regression beta of 0.45) was only modestly lower than the values found for the Club-Med in the last year prior to euro adoption (between 0.47 and 0.69), the combination of relatively low r-squared and relatively high beta coefficient reveals the difference in relative volatility compared to the benchmark. While the standard deviation of daily yield changes was lower in the Club-Med than in Germany by 15 to 20 per cent during the last year prior to euro adoption, the volatility of Polish yield changes exceeded euro area yield volatility by a large margin. However, as the volatility of Polish yield changes decreased considerably between the first and the second bull period, relative euro area volatility in Poland increased to a level comparable to the corresponding Club-Med values three years (Portugal, Spain) or two years (Greece, Italy) before euro adoption.

A slope coefficient in the midst of the Club-Med range in the last year prior to euro adoption (between 0.47 and 0.69) could be found only for Czech yield changes. In addition, this relatively high level of Czech regression beta could be found for both the bear and the bull periods, in particular for the second bull period. Moreover, relative yield volatility in the Czech Republic (that is euro area versus Czech Republic) in the bear period was at levels comparable to Club-Med levels in the last year prior to euro adoption. In the second bull period, relative yield volatility was somewhat smaller but still comparable to or better than Club-Med volatility two to three years before euro adoption. Moreover, it was not far below one and it did not result from an increase in Czech bond yield volatility, but rather from a decline in euro area bond yield volatility that was not matched by a further decline in Czech bond yield volatility.

All in all, the Czech Republic achieved a degree of bond yield convergence on the basis of the news-based measure of integration quite close to that in the Club-Med countries in the bear period, that is at a time when its yields were diverging on the basis of the yield level-based measure. Moreover, in the second bull period, that is when yields were converging again to the euro area, the Czech Republic maintained a degree of convergence on the basis of the news-based measure which was still relatively close to the historical pattern in the Club-Med countries.

However, the fact that the correlation coefficients were comparatively higher in the bear period than in the first bull period in the Czech Republic deserved further analysis. For this purpose, in a first step, we explored the relationship between NMS-3 10Y yield spread levels versus the euro area and the co-movement of yield changes by plotting spread levels against the r-squared in GARCH regressions of changes in NMS-3 yields on changes in euro area yields (in distinct quarterly steps from Q1 2000 to Q1 2005). On this basis (Figure 26.2), we could observe a clear negative relationship between these two variables (that is higher r-squared at lower levels of the yield spread) for the Czech Republic. A modest negative relationship could be observed also for Poland. By contrast, a clear relationship did not seem to exist during this period in Hungary. Furthermore, the figure shows that at comparable levels of yield spreads, the r-squared of the regressions were at similar levels in the Czech Republic, Hungary and Poland, and that Hungarian and Polish yield spreads have not yet fallen to levels which were associated with significantly higher r-squared in the Czech Republic. This may be an indication of a non-linear relationship between spread levels and the explanatory power of the regressions.[6] However, a more in-depth exploration of these issues goes beyond the scope of this chapter.

Then, turning more precisely to the issue of the change in the correlation coefficient in the Czech Republic over time from the period of spread

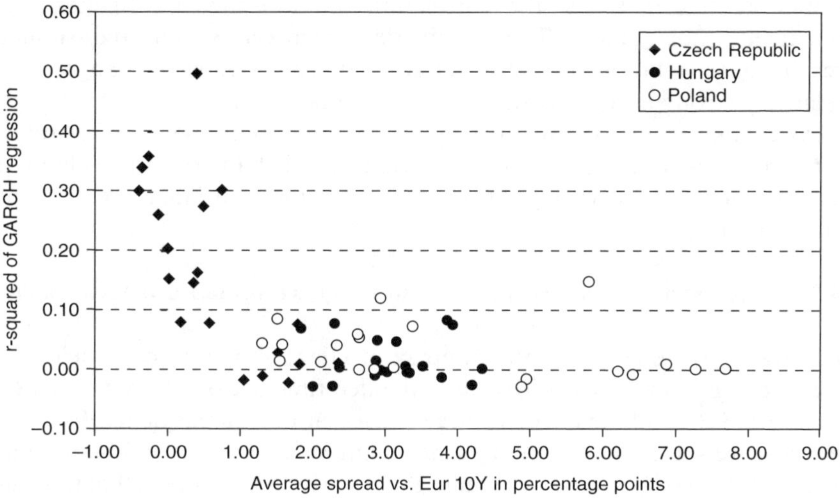

Figure 26.2 Relationship between NMS-3 10 Y government bond yield spreads vs. EUR 10 Y and the explanatory power of changes in EUR 10 Y yields for changes in NMS-3 10 Y yields

tightening to the period of spread widening, a closer look at the values for the Czech Republic shows that the explanatory power of changes in euro area yields for changes in Czech yields had started to increase already during the first bull period, and it stayed at relatively high levels in particular at the beginning of the bear period, when the spreads were at still comparatively low, albeit moderately widening levels.

In a next step, we aimed at a more disaggregated view over time by performing GARCH regressions for the NMS-3 for annual periods between 2000 and 2004 to explain changes in 10-year government bond yields, similarly to what we did for the Club-Med. However, in addition to the explanatory variables used in the equations for the Club-Med, we included daily changes in J.P. Morgan's EMBI-plus Performing Spread as an additional explanatory variable to capture the potential impact of changes in global investor sentiment towards emerging markets on the NMS-3 local currency bond markets. Looking at the development of the correlation over the years on the basis of the bivariate regressions, the previous observation is confirmed in particular in the Czech Republic. The correlation increased markedly from 2001 to 2002, that is within the bull period, and further (but more moderately) from 2002 to 2003, which comprises the tranquil period and the initial phase of the bear period. From 2003 to 2004, which mostly covered the second part of the bear period when spreads were already at somewhat higher levels, the correlation did not increase further, but remained rather stable. The multivariate regressions delivered similar results for the relationship between Czech and euro area yield changes. The relatively strong and increasing role of euro area yield changes for Czech yield changes was accompanied by a weak role of money market rates, forward rates and international emerging market factors in explaining changes in Czech 10-year yields (r-squared of the bivariate regressions of close to zero).[7]

4.3 Reaction of NMS-3 Bond Yields to Large Moves in Euro Area Yields

Having observed only a limited impact of changes in euro area yields on yield changes in the NMS-3 during extended time periods, we investigated how NMS-3 yields reacted to large moves in euro area yields. For this purpose we sorted the dataset by daily changes in euro area yields and separated three sections: euro area bull episodes with the smallest (that is negative) 10 per cent changes in ten-year euro area yields, euro area bear episodes with the largest 10 per cent (that is positive) changes in ten-year euro area yields, and euro area tranquil episodes in between the two. Then, we ran an OLS regression of changes in NMS-3 yields on euro area yield changes in the three sections separately. Depending on data availability, the number of observations varied between the three countries.

These regressions[8] confirmed that changes in euro area yields did not significantly affect changes in NMS-3 yields in euro area bull episodes: none of the slope coefficients in the bull period was statistically significant and the r-squared were very low.

By contrast, Czech ten-year yields seem to react to large upward movements in the euro area ten-year yields (slope coefficients of 0.59). Nevertheless, the r-squared was relatively low at 0.06. Also Hungarian yields seem to react to large upward moves in euro area yields, though their slope coefficient (0.37) was significant only at the 10 per cent significance level and the r-squared amounted to only 0.02.

In tranquil periods of euro area government bond yields, Czech and Polish bond yields seem to follow euro area yield movements, with slope coefficients of 0.42 and 0.34, respectively. However, again the explanatory power of these equations was low, in particular in Poland, as it was in Hungary.

5. SUMMARY AND CONCLUSIONS

In this chapter we analysed to what extent NMS-3 bond markets have become integrated with the euro area bond market since 2000, applying both yield level-based and news-based measures of bond market integration. For benchmarking purposes, we first analysed the yield convergence process in the Club-Med countries in the run-up to euro adoption. There, we found that the compression of yield spreads (compared to Germany) was accompanied by an increase in the correlation between government bond yield changes in these countries and in Germany. However, the higher correlation was primarily attributable to a decline in relative yield volatility in the Club-Med rather than to a one-to-one transmission of German yield changes. We also observed that bond market integration further accelerated following euro adoption, and now yields in the Club-Med move roughly in tandem with German yields.

For the NMS-3 we found that the role of euro area yield changes seems to be roughly comparable with that of German yield changes in the bond market integration of the Club-Med countries in the last year before euro adoption only in the Czech Republic. The results for Poland showed weaker integration with the euro area than the level of integration was in the Club-Med two (Greece) to four (Italy, Spain) years prior to euro adoption. The integration of the Hungarian bond market with the euro area was the smallest among the three countries.

The fact that the correlation of yield changes between Hungary and Poland on the one hand and the euro area on the other hand remained weak resulted from both partly low regression betas and partly high volatility of bond yields in these countries compared to that in the euro area (implying low relative euro area volatility). However, it should not be left unmentioned that the volatility of bond yields in Poland decreased considerably between the first and the second bull period, implying higher relative euro area volatility. Such a development took place also in Hungary between the bear period and the second bull period.

Further research should focus on the question of why the Czech Republic's bond market is at a more advanced stage of convergence to and integration with the euro area bond market according to the news-based measure than its peers. One possible explanation hints at the fact of the comparatively lower average level of yield spreads. According to this view, changes in the benchmark yield might have a more dominant impact if the level of the yield spread is low.

The lower average spread levels may also play a role in the following explanation, which points at the fact that the Czech bond market shows a lower degree of integration than the Hungarian and Polish bond market according to the quantity-based measure of bond market integration. Foreign investors held around 30 per cent of outstanding marketable government debt in Hungary and around 20 per cent in Poland at the end of 2004, while in the Czech Republic, this share was much lower at around

10 per cent. This difference may result from the lower average level of yield spreads of Czech bonds, which probably implies a comparatively weaker incentive for foreign investors to invest. In turn, one cannot exclude that the greater role of large foreign investors (relative to the relatively small total market size) has contributed to higher bond yield volatility in Poland and above all in Hungary. For instance, these investors may react more sensitively to signs of policy inconsistency.

Finally, it would be worth investigating to what extent higher yield volatility was related to, or even emanated from, higher exchange rate volatility. For instance, in as far as foreign investors play an important role for bond yield volatility, exchange rate volatility could be affected in parallel. Also, exchange rate uncertainties (in particular of foreign investors) could lead to higher bond yield volatility.[9] If so, not only euro adoption itself, but also progress in monetary integration that leads to more stable exchange rates may be seen as a way to foster financial integration in terms of lower yield volatility differentials.

The still relatively weak integration of the Polish and the Hungarian bond market with the euro area can be looked at from different angles. From the point of view of investors, the weak correlation offers alternative investment facilities and opportunities for risk diversification. From the point of view of monetary policy, weak correlation between the local bond market and the euro area bond market means that domestic monetary policy impulses may be transmitted into the financial system with a lower degree of external noise.

However, there is no room for complacency. Although the NMS-3 bond markets have so far become only relatively loosely integrated with the euro area, we found evidence that the Czech and – to a lesser degree – the Hungarian ten-year bond yields tend to follow large upward moves in the ten-year yield in the euro area. Hence, external disturbance (contagion) cannot be excluded altogether, and this may temporarily interfere with domestic monetary policy as well. Moreover, the NMS-3 are heading towards the adoption of the euro in the medium term. Once in the euro area, the closest possible integration of their bond markets with the euro area will be essential for a smooth transmission of the impulses of the single monetary policy into the NMS-3 economies. Fortunately, in this respect the example of the Club-Med indicates that both the run-up to euro adoption as well as euro adoption itself can be expected to deepen the integration of NMS-3 bond markets with the (current) euro area.

APPENDIX

Table 26.A1 Regression of changes in Club-Med 10Y yields on changes in DEM 10Y yields

		T–4	T–3	T–2	T–1	T+1	T+2	T+3	T+4
Spain – bivariate	r-squared	0.15	0.22	0.26	0.47	0.64	0.76	0.90	0.96
	Beta	**0.68**	**0.75**	**0.53**	**0.47**	**0.85**	**0.85**	**0.96**	**1.00**
	t-stat	8.48	12.90	11.09	26.87	30.66	35.28	68.13	78.81
Spain – multivariate (only significant terms)	r-squared	0.26	0.34	0.37	0.48	0.64	0.77	0.90	0.96
	Beta	**0.66**	**0.44**	**0.52**	**0.46**	**0.87**	**0.80**	**0.96**	**1.00**
	t-stat	6.98	7.82	11.29	26.85	26.78	33.14	68.13	78.81
	Std. deviation over LC 10Y	0.53	0.73	0.93	1.24	1.00	1.14	1.01	0.98
Greece – bivariate	r-squared	..	–0.02	0.30	0.40	0.54	0.60	0.73	0.75
	Beta	..	**–0.30**	**0.80**	**0.50**	**0.82**	**0.88**	**0.84**	**0.80**
	t-stat	..	–4.34	12.72	14.16	23.53	32.10	35.15	22.36
Greece – multivariate (only significant terms)	r-squared	..	0.19	0.35	0.46	0.54	0.60	0.73	0.75
	Beta	..	**–0.18**	**0.82**	**0.48**	**0.82**	**0.88**	**0.81**	**0.80**
	t-stat	..	–2.06	22.14	17.51	23.53	32.10	36.96	22.36
	Std. deviation over LC 10Y	..	0.54	0.69	1.19	0.97	1.02	1.03	1.08

Table 26.A1 (continued)

		T–4	T–3	T–2	T–1	T+1	T+2	T+3	T+4
Italy – bivariate	r-squared	0.17	0.40	0.22	0.70	0.83	0.79	0.90	0.94
	Beta	**1.19**	**1.03**	**0.80**	**0.69**	**0.87**	**0.80**	**0.93**	**0.96**
	t-stat	10.29	10.57	14.21	44.25	37.96	33.60	81.85	67.01
Italy – multivariate (only significant terms)	r-squared	0.51	0.72	0.44	0.71	0.83	0.80	0.90	0.94
	Beta	**0.67**	**0.63**	**0.62**	**0.66**	**0.87**	**0.77**	**0.95**	**0.96**
	t-stat	7.78	22.06	13.42	55.35	37.96	30.66	60.90	67.01
	Std. deviation over LC 10Y	0.39	0.56	0.66	1.16	1.08	1.13	1.01	1.02
Portugal – bivariate	r-squared	0.07	0.23	0.10	0.50	0.08	0.18	0.77	0.93
	Beta	**0.51**	**0.57**	**0.33**	**0.54**	**0.50**	**0.44**	**0.95**	**1.02**
	t-stat	5.97	12.52	13.07	20.17	9.66	19.91	41.45	58.55
Portugal – multivariate (only significant terms)	r-squared	0.06	0.24	0.12	0.51	0.08	0.18	0.77	0.93
	Beta	**0.44**	**0.54**	**0.36**	**0.54**	**0.50**	**0.44**	**0.95**	**1.05**
	t-stat	5.07	11.68	7.44	22.38	9.66	19.91	41.45	67.69
	Std. deviation over LC 10Y	0.55	0.83	0.98	1.20	0.82	0.90	1.00	0.94

Notes: For Greece, EUR 10Y yields were used (synthetic up to the end of 1998). Bold figures for the beta coefficient in the bivariate regressions mean that this coefficient was significant at the 5% level. The reported results for the multivariate regressions are those of the second-stage multivariate regressions, which included only those variables that were significant at the 5% level in the first-stage multivariate regressions. Bold figures for the beta coefficient in the (second-stage) multivariate regressions mean that this coefficient was significant at the 5% level. 'Std. deviation over LC 10Y' denotes the standard deviation of 10-year DEM (or EUR) bonds relative to the standard deviation of 10-year local currency bonds in the individual Club-Med countries.

Table 26.A2 Regression of changes in NMS-3 10Y yields on changes in EUR 10Y yields: Bull and bear periods

Changes in LC 10Y on changes in EUR 10Y		CZK			HUF			PLN		
		Bull1	Bear	Bull2	Bull1	Bear	Bull2	Bull1	Bear	Bull2
Bivariate	r-squared	0.09	0.29	0.21	0.01	0.00	0.01	0.01	0.08	0.00
	Beta	**0.46**	**0.54**	**0.57**	**0.17**	**0.34**	0.08	**0.26**	**0.45**	**0.24**
	t-stat	7.86	29.61	7.30	2.17	4.16	0.51	3.83	6.20	2.38
Multivariate (only significant terms)	R-square	0.12	0.29	0.23	0.04	0.21	0.21	0.03	0.17	0.07
	Beta	**0.39**	**0.54**	**0.52**	**0.19**	**0.31**	0.14	**0.24**	**0.40**	0.25
	t-stat	7.54	29.61	5.79	2.01	3.60	0.90	3.75	6.17	1.79
	Std. deviation over LC 10Y	0.68	1.10	0.81	0.52	0.32	0.50	0.31	0.56	0.72
Changes in LC 10Y on changes in LC 3M		CZK			HUF			PLN		
		Bull1	Bear	Bull2	Bull1	Bear	Bull2	Bull1	Bear	Bull2
Bivariate	r-squared	0.02	0.00	0.03	0.00	0.19	0.17	0.02	0.05	–0.01
	Beta	**0.25**	0.05	0.25	–0.01	**0.25**	**0.48**	**0.16**	**0.31**	–0.02
	t-stat	4.75	0.78	0.92	–0.21	27.70	6.36	4.73	4.44	–0.23
Multivariate (only significant terms)	r-squared	0.12	0.29	0.23	0.04	0.21	0.21	0.03	0.17	0.07
	Beta	n.s.	n.s.	n.s.	n.s.	**0.20**	**0.34**	**0.18**	n.s.	n.s.
	t-stat	n.s.	n.s.	n.s.	n.s.	11.48	3.02	5.14	n.s.	n.s.
	Std. deviation over LC 10Y	0.56	0.39	0.64	0.61	1.78	0.74	0.81	0.65	1.08

Table 26.A2 (continued)

Changes in LC 10Y on changes in LC 3×6FRA		CZK			HUF			PLN		
		Bull1	Bear	Bull2	Bull1	Bear	Bull2	Bull1	Bear	Bull2
Bivariate	r-squared	0.05	0.00	0.04	0.00	0.15	0.17	0.00	0.13	0.00
	Beta	**0.27**	**0.13**	0.25	0.03	**0.15**	**0.49**	**0.09**	**0.37**	–0.06
	t-stat	5.41	2.44	1.60	0.99	8.31	7.92	3.12	6.32	–1.67
Multivariate (only significant terms)	r-squared	0.12	0.29	0.23	0.04	0.21	0.21	0.03	0.17	0.07
	Beta	**0.27**	n.s.	n.s.	n.s.	**0.07**	**0.23**	0.06	**0.26**	n.s.
	t-stat	6.14	n.s.	n.s.	n.s.	2.93	2.03	1.86	5.31	n.s.
	Std. deviation over LC 10Y	0.67	0.57	0.95	0.73	1.65	0.92	1.00	0.85	1.23

Changes in LC 10Y on changes in EMBI + Performing Spread		CZK			HUF			PLN		
		Bull1	Bear	Bull2	Bull1	Bear	Bull2	Bull1	Bear	Bull2
Bivariate	r-squared	–0.01	0.00	0.02	0.02	0.00	0.00	–0.01	0.01	0.05
	Beta	**0.00**	0.00	**0.00**	**0.00**	0.00	**0.00**	**0.00**	**0.00**	**0.00**
	t-stat	–5.89	0.36	2.37	3.48	0.52	1.97	–2.44	2.97	4.75
Multivariate (only significant terms)	r-squared	0.12	0.29	0.23	0.04	0.21	0.21	0.03	0.17	0.07
	Beta	**0.00**	n.s.	**0.00**	**0.00**	n.s.	n.s.	n.s.	n.s.	**0.00**
	t-stat	–5.09	n.s.	2.67	3.35	n.s.	n.s.	n.s.	n.s.	2.75
	Std. deviation over LC 10Y	327.88	198.74	98.98	277.85	57.21	61.44	138.79	107.55	87.50

Note: Bold figures for the beta coefficient in the bivariate regressions mean that this coefficient was significant at the 5% level. The expression "n.s." (not significant) in the multivariate regressions means that the respective variable turned out to be insignificant in the first-stage multivariate regressions, which included all variables. The reported results for the multivariate regressions are those of the second-stage multivariate regressions, which included only those variables that were significant at the 5% level in the first-stage multivariate regression. Bold figures for the beta coefficient in the (second-stage) multivariate regressions mean that this coefficient was significant at the 5% level. "Std. deviation over LC 10Y" denotes the standard deviation of 10-year EUR bonds relative to the standard deviation of 10-year local currency bonds in the individual NMS-3 countries.

Table 26.A3 Regression of changes in NMS-3 10Y yields on changes in EUR 10Y yields: Annual periods

	CZK	2000	2001	2002	2003	2004
Bivariate	r-squared	0.00	0.04	0.21	0.29	0.30
	Beta	0.07	**0.24**	**0.54**	**0.35**	**0.61**
	t-stat	0.60	2.41	9.21	10.93	17.17
Multivariate	r-squared	–0.03	0.05	0.25	0.33	0.30
	Beta	n.s.	**0.21**	**0.61**	**0.40**	**0.59**
	t-stat	n.s.	2.43	13.05	13.40	11.82
	Std. deviation over LC 10Y	0.79	0.59	0.85	1.28	0.85
	HUF	2000	2001	2002	2003	2004
Bivariate	r-squared	0.00	0.01	–0.02	0.01	0.00
	Beta	–0.03	0.15	–0.05	**0.34**	**0.33**
	t-stat	–0.27	1.54	–0.83	5.81	2.64
Multivariate	r-squared	0.07	0.05	0.00	0.27	0.13
	Beta	n.s.	0.17	n.s.	**0.41**	**0.32**
	t-stat	n.s.	1.74	n.s.	6.19	3.09
	Std. deviation over LC 10Y	0.41	0.63	0.59	0.39	0.32
	PLN	2000	2001	2002	2003	2004
Bivariate	r-squared	0.00	0.01	0.02	0.04	0.05
	Beta	0.02	**0.39**	**0.21**	**0.22**	**0.26**
	t-stat	0.09	3.35	2.14	5.13	2.86
Multivariate	r-squared	–0.01	0.01	0.05	0.11	0.13
	Beta	n.s.	**0.39**	n.s.	**0.25**	**0.33**
	t-stat	n.s.	3.35	n.s.	5.45	3.67
	Std. deviation over LC 10Y	0.20	0.27	0.39	0.76	0.57

Note: Bold figures for the beta coefficient in the bivariate regressions means that this coefficient was significant at the 5% level. The expression "n.s." (not significant) in the multivariate regressions means that the respective variable turned out to be insignificant in the first-stage multivariate regressions, which included all variables. The reported results for the multivariate regressions are those of the second-stage multivariate regresssions, which included only those variables that were significant at the 5% level in the first-stage multivariate regressions. Bold figures for the beta coefficient in the (second-stage) multivariate regressions mean that this coefficient was significant at the 5% level. "Std. deviation over LC 10Y" denotes the standard deviation of 10-year EUR bonds relative to the standard deviation of 10-year local currency bonds in the individual NMS-3 countries.

NOTES

1. Oesterreichische Nationalbank. The opinions expressed in this chapter are those of the authors and do not necessarily represent the views of the Oesterreichische Nationalbank. We would like to thank Jesús Crespo Cuaresma (University of Vienna) for his econometric support and comments on the chapter. The full version of this chapter can be obtained from the authors upon request.
2. Due to data availability issues, we did not use quoted 3 × 6 FRAs but calculated them from outright three-month and six-month money market rates.
3. Detailed regression results can be obtained from the authors upon request.
4. Detailed regression results can be obtained from the authors upon request.
5. A detailed description of the findings from these regressions can be obtained from the authors upon request.
6. It should be noted, however, that the regressions for Spain, Italy and Portugal had higher r-squared (in the magnitude of 0.2–0.4) at significantly higher spread levels (2.4–3.3 percentage points) three years prior to euro adoption.
7. Similar to the bull and bear periods, the explanatory power of euro area yield changes for changes in Hungarian and Polish yields was very small (close to zero). Similarly, three-month money market rates and forward rates contributed little to explaining Polish ten-year yield changes. The explanatory power of three-month money market rates (and hence of local factors) was relatively high in 2004 in Hungary (0.12), while the regression on forward rates delivered relatively large r-squared in 2003 (0.27) and 2004 (0.09). The EMBI spread did not help explaining yield movements in any of the three countries.
8. Regression details can be obtained from the authors upon request.
9. However, our preliminary calculations show that on the one hand the magnitude of exchange rate expectations (defined as the expected percentage changes in the exchange rate versus the euro) is relatively strongly correlated with NMS-3 yield spreads versus the euro, but on the other hand changes in the exchange rate expectations do not have a significant explanatory power for changes in NMS-3 government bond yields or yield spreads versus the euro.

REFERENCES

Adam, K., T. Jappelli, A. Manichini, M. Padula and M. Pagano (2002), 'Analyse, compare, and apply alternative indicators and monitoring methodologies to measure the evolution of capital market integration in the European Union', Centre for Studies in Economics and Finance, Department of Economics and Statistics, University of Salerno.

Angeloni, I. and M. Ehrmann (2003), 'Monetary policy transmission in the euro area: Any changes after EMU?', *ECB Working Paper*, No. 240, European Central Bank.

Annaert, J. and M.J.K. Ceuster (2000), 'Modelling European credit spreads', Research Report, University of Antwerp, UFSIA.

Baele, L., A. Ferrando, P. Hördahl, E. Krylova and C. Monnet (2004), 'Measuring financial integration in the euro area', ECB, *Occasional Paper Series*, No.14, European Central Bank.

Bekaert, G., C.R. Harvey and C. Lundblad (2003), 'Does financial liberalization spur growth?', http://www0.gsb.columbia.edu/faculty/gbekaert/Does_financial_liberalization.pdf.

Benoit, Anne, Walter Demel and Thomas Reininger (2001), 'Market structures and development: Main features of the markets', in Michael Schröder (ed.), *The New Capital Markets in Central and Eastern Europe*, Berlin: Springer Verlag.

Bollerslev, T. (1986), 'Generalized autoregressive conditional heteroskedasticity', *Journal of Econometrics* 31.

Bollerslev, T., R.Y. Chou and K.F. Kroner (1992), 'ARCH Modeling in Finance. A Review of the Theory and Empirical Evidence', *Journal of Econometrics*, **52**, 5–59.

Crespo Cuaresma, J. and C. Wójcik (2004), 'The monetary independence hypothesis: evidence from the Czech Republic, Hungary and Poland', National Bank of Poland research paper, *Bank i Kredyt* No. 1/2004.

Crespo Cuaresma, J., B. Égert and T. Reininger (2004), 'Interest rate pass-through in EU acceding countries: the case of the Czech Republic, Hungary and Poland', in D. Masciandaro (ed.), *Financial Intermediation in the New Europe,* Cheltenham, UK and Northampton, MA: Edward Elgar.

Dvorak, T. and C.R.A. Geiregat (2004), 'Are the new and old EU countries financially integrated?', working paper, http://www.williams.edu/Economics/wp/geiregatdvorak2004.pdf.

Engle, R.F. (1982), 'Autoregressive conditional heteroskedasticity with estimates of UK inflation', *Econometrica*, **50,** 987–1008.

European Central Bank (ECB) (2003a), 'Recent developments in financial structures of the euro area', *Monthly Bulletin*, October.

European Central Bank (ECB) (2003b), 'Recent developments in spreads between euro area government bond yields', *Monthly Bulletin*, November.

European Central Bank (ECB) (2004), 'Bond markets and long-term interest rates in non-euro area member states of the European Union and in accession countries', November.

Feldman, R.A. and N. Wagner (2002), 'The financial sector, macroeconomic policy and performance', *EIB Papers*, **7** (2).

Giannetti, M., L. Guiso, T. Jappelli, M. Padula and M. Pagano (2002), 'Financial market integration, corporate financing and economic growth', Final Report, *European Commission Directorate-General for Economic and Financial Affairs Economic Paper*, November.

Gujarati, D.N. (1995), 'Basic econometrics', 3rd edn, McGraw-Hill.

Hartmann, P., A. Maddaloni and S. Manganelli (2003), 'The euro area financial system: structure, integration and policy initiatives', *ECB Working Paper*, No. 230, European Central Bank.

Hermann, S. and A. Jochem (2003), 'The international integration of money markets in the central and east European accession countries: deviations from covered interest parity, capital controls and inefficiencies in the financial sector', *Discussion Paper* 07/03, Economic Research Centre of the Deutsche Bundesbank.

International Monetary Fund (IMF) (2003), *Global Financial Stability Report*, September.

Kähler, Jürgen (2001), 'The information efficiency of the stock markets in Central and Eastern Europe', in Michael Schröder (ed.), *The New Capital Markets in Central and Eastern Europe*, Berlin: Springer Verlag.

Klein, M. and G. Olivei (1999), 'Capital account liberalization, financial depth and economic growth', *NBER Working Paper*, 7384.

Köke, Jens (2001), 'The role of institutional investors in equity and bond markets', in Michael Schröder (ed.), *The New Capital Markets in Central and Eastern Europe*, Berlin: Springer Verlag.

Lanoo, Karel and Tanja Salem (2001), 'The emerging regulatory framework for banking and securities markets in the CEECs', in Michael Schröder (ed.), *The New Capital Markets in Central and Eastern Europe*, Berlin: Springer Verlag.

Levine, R., N. Loayza and T. Beck (1999), 'Financial intermediation and growth', *World Bank Policy Research Working Paper*, 2059.

MacDonald, Ronald (2001), 'Transformation of external shocks and capital market integration', in Michael Schröder (ed.), *The New Capital Markets in Central and Eastern Europe*, Berlin: Springer Verlag.

Pungulescu, C. (2003), 'Measuring financial integration in the European Monetary Union: An application for the East European accession countries', E-journal, September, http://venus.ci.uw.edu.pl/~rubikon/forum/crina.htm.

Reininger, Thomas (2001), 'Future adjustments in the banking systems', in Michael Schröder (ed.), *The New Capital Markets in Central and Eastern Europe*, Berlin: Springer Verlag.

Reininger, T., F. Schardax and M. Summer (2002), 'Financial system transition in Central Europe: The first decade', *SUERF Studies* No. 16.

Santillan, J., M. Bayle and C. Thygesen (2000), 'The impact of the euro on money and bond markets', *ECB Occasional Paper*, No. 1, European Central Bank.

Stirbu, C. (2004), 'Financial market integration in a wider European Union', *HWWA Discussion Paper*, 297.

Thimann, C. (ed.) (2002), *Financial Sectors in EU Accession Countries*, European Central Bank.

27. International capital mobility and current account targeting in Central and Eastern European countries

Matthias Köhler*

1. INTRODUCTION

In May 2004, the Czech Republic, Hungary, Poland, Slovakia and Slovenia (hereafter: CEEC-5) joined the European Union (EU). Since a prerequisite for accession to the EU was the adoption of the *acquis communautaire*, the CEEC-5 have to join the euro area in the coming years. Since monetary policy in a monetary union is made by a single central bank, this central bank cannot take account of differences in financial structure and differences in the degree of financial integration. These differences might lead to an asymmetric transmission of monetary shocks in an enlarged euro area. This has already been a topic of recent research. The papers of Cecchetti (2001), Jarocinsk (2004), Schmitz (2004) and Köhler et al. (2006), however, only focus on the effect that different financial structures across the EU have on the transmission of monetary shocks.

This chapter represents an attempt to fill this gap and to measure the degree of financial market integration in the CEEC-5 and to compare their degree of integration with that of the euro area in order to see if differences in the degree of international capital mobility might cause asymmetric responses to monetary shocks in an enlarged monetary union. The remainder of this chapter is organized as follows. In section 2, we will present different measures of financial market integration, and then we will use one of these indicators in sections 3 and 4 to measure the degree of capital mobility econometrically. Since current account policies affect the degree of financial market integration, we will analyse the extent to which these policies were used in the CEEC-5 and to what extent they have influenced the degree of international capital mobility in sections 5 and 6. Section 7 concludes.

2. MEASURING FINANCIAL MARKET INTEGRATION

Financial market integration implies that all frictions have been removed that discriminate between economic agents in their access to and the investment of capital on the basis of their location (ECB, 2003, p. 54). Based on this definition of integration three concepts can be distinguished to measure the degree of financial market integration.

Quantity-based indicators measure the degree of financial integration according to the volume of international transactions. Since these indicators only measure the degree of internationalization and not the degree of integration of financial markets, indicators have to be used that analyse the efficiency of the financial sector, which depends upon the level of competition in financial markets. Such indicators are based upon the law of one price and are called price indicators. According to these indicators, financial markets are perfectly integrated into the world capital market if the nominal and real interest rate parity holds.[1] A further indicator that combines quantity-based indicators and price indicators is the Feldstein–Horioka test, which is named after Feldstein and Horioka (1980), who used it to measure the degree of international capital mobility of 16 OECD countries. The idea behind this indicator is that in closed economies domestic investment is limited by domestic savings. Saving and investment rates are hence expected to be highly correlated if financial markets are separated from the world capital market. In order to test their hypothesis, Feldstein and Horioka regressed the domestic savings rate on the domestic investment rate for a cross-section of 16 OECD countries averaged over the period from 1960 to 1974 (hereafter: aggregate savings regression).

$$(I/Y)_i = \alpha + \beta(S/Y)_i + \varepsilon_i, \tag{27.1}$$

where i is a country index, (I/Y) the domestic investment and (S/Y) the domestic savings rate, ε a random error term with zero mean and constant variance. The beta coefficient measures the degree of capital mobility and is also called Feldstein–Horioka coefficient. According to Feldstein and Horioka, financial markets are perfectly integrated into the world capital market if the Feldstein–Horioka coefficient is insignificantly different from zero. In this case, domestic investments do not depend on domestic savings, since they are completely financed by the worldwide pool of capital. Financial markets are conversely perfectly separated from the world capital market if the Feldstein–Horioka coefficient is one. In this case, domestic investments are completely financed by domestic savings and a drop of the domestic savings rate leads to a proportional decline of the domestic investment rate. A lower Feldstein–Horioka coefficient thus indicates a higher degree of international capital mobility. Since Feldstein and Horioka determined saving retention coefficients of 0.87 for gross and 0.93 for net domestic savings rates, they rejected the hypothesis of perfect capital mobility and concluded that 'the evidence strongly contradicts the hypothesis of perfect capital mobility and indicates that most of incremental saving tends to remain in the country in which the saving is done' (Feldstein and Horioka, 1980, p. 321).

This conclusion sparked off a great discussion about the validity of the Feldstein–Horioka criterion to measure the degree of financial market integration. Critics of the econometric techniques argue that the degree of international capital mobility is biased toward lower international capital mobility because of the endogenity of real interest rates and saving rates (Feldstein and Horioka, 1980; Harberger, 1980; Murphy, 1984). Critics of the interpretation of the Feldstein–Horioka coefficient, as the degree of international capital mobility, argue that this coefficient does not measure the degree of international capital mobility, since domestic savings and investment rates are highly correlated even in the case of perfectly integrated capital markets due to productivity and population effects, the existence of an intertemporal budget constraint and current account targeting policies of the government and the central bank (Artis and Bayoumi, 1990; Bayoumi, 1990; Coakley et al., 1995; Feldstein and Horioka, 1980; Sinn, 1992; Summers, 1986). Taking this criticism into account and applying the Feldstein–Horioka test to other countries and periods, however, has not solved the Feldstein–Horioka paradox.

Buch (1999) was the first to use the Feldstein–Horioka approach to measure the degree of international capital mobility in Central and Eastern European countries. In her seminal paper on capital mobility and EU enlargement, she estimated the degree of financial integration for a panel of Central and Eastern European countries (Czech Republic, Estonia, Hungary, Poland and Slovenia). As a benchmark she used three Southern European countries (Greece, Portugal and Spain). Buch concluded that the Central and Eastern European countries have reached almost the same degree of capital mobility as the three Southern European countries and hence 'that membership in the EU was unlikely to boost capital market integration to a significant degree and to trigger huge capital inflows' (Buch, 1999, p. 28).

This chapter extends the approach by Buch in three ways. First, we include Slovakia and 11 euro countries in the sample to compare the degree of capital mobility of the CEEC-5 with that of the euro area. The advantage of this approach over that of Buch is that we can analyse if the

CEEC-5 still have to integrate further into the euro area financial market to ensure an efficient monetary policy in an enlarged monetary union. Second, we increase the sample size by the period from 1998 to 2003. This allows us to test the hypothesis of Buch that EU membership is not likely to increase the degree of capital mobility according to the Feldstein–Horioka criterion. Third and last, we analyse the effect of current account targeting policies on the degree of financial integration. These policies might have biased the degree of financial integration of the Central and Eastern European countries toward lower international capital mobility, since many governments might have targeted the current account to prevent unsustainably large current account deficits.

3. SAVING RATES, INVESTMENT RATES AND THE CURRENT ACCOUNT

The recession in the CEEC-5 at the beginning of the transformation period led to the decline of domestic investment and savings rates. Since mostly domestic savings rates dropped faster than domestic investment rates, the CEEC-5 faced a lack of domestic capital. This lack was financed by foreign capital, which increasingly flew into Central and Eastern European countries, attracted by stable exchange rates and a great number of investment opportunities. Higher growth in the middle of the 1990s further worsened the current account balance, because it often went hand in hand with higher investment rates. In most cases, these current account deficits could be financed by the import of foreign capital. This capital was pulled out again as these economies slipped into recession and investor confidence in the sustainability of the exchange rate regime diminished. In particular, countries that had attracted high volumes of short-term portfolio investments in the past were vulnerable to capital outflows and had to devalue their currency following high pressure on the exchange rate target of the central bank. These currency crises often entailed severe financial and economic crises.

The countries reacted differently to these shocks, some adopting even harder exchange rate regimes and some letting the exchange rate float without interventions. Common to all countries was the adoption of savings programmes that were targeted at reducing the current account deficit.

Czech Republic

After the economic recovery in 1992 and 1993, investment and saving rates increased. However, since saving rates did not rise as fast as investment rates, domestic investment had to be financed by foreign capital. Due to the import of capital, the Czech Republic recorded current account deficits in the following years, which peaked in 1996 and 1997 with a deficit of more than 12 per cent. As these deficits became unsustainable, speculative attacks on the Czech Koruna were launched, which led to a currency and banking crisis, forcing the Czech central bank to abandon its exchange rate target in May 1997. As a result of a savings programme of the Czech government, higher private savings and lower investment rates following the recession of the Czech economy, the deficit dropped to 6 per cent in 1998 and 1999. As the economy recovered, investment rates rose again and caused a temporary rise of the current account deficit to 8 per cent in 2000, until it could be reduced to 5 per cent in 2002.

Hungary

The transition to a market-based economy started with a recession, which led to a decline of saving and investment rates. Since the saving rate dropped faster than the investment rate, Hungary reported a current account deficit of nearly 10 per cent in 1993 and 1994. This deficit dropped to almost 5 per cent after the government launched a savings programme in May 1995 that increased domestic savings without influencing the investment rate. Following lower saving rates in the succeeding years and constantly high investment rates, the deficit rose again to more than 8 per cent in 2000 until it could be reduced to less than 6 per cent in 2003.

Poland

As a result of a recession at the beginning of the transformation period saving and investment rates dropped significantly. Since the investment rate started to recover earlier than the saving rate, Poland recorded a current account deficit of more than 6 per cent in 1993. This deficit dropped to less than 5 per cent in 1995 due to higher domestic savings until it rose to almost 12 per cent between 1997 and 1998 because of increasing domestic investments. Because of higher budget deficits between 1998 and 2001 aggregate savings decreased and foreign capital had to be imported to finance domestic investments. In 2000, the current account balance improved due to lower investment rates following a downturn of the Polish economy, although aggregate savings decreased in this period as well. Owing to constant saving and investment rates in the following years the current account stabilized at a deficit of less than 7 per cent.

Slovak Republic

After a large current account deficit in 1993, a decline of the domestic investment rate and a rise of the saving rate led to an almost balanced current account. Since then the saving rate remained relatively stable, whereas the investment rate rose to 35 per cent between 1996 and 1998 following a rise of private investment and an increasing budget deficit. The current account deficit consequently rose to 13 per cent in 1996 and peaked in 1998 with a deficit of 14 per cent. These deficits were mainly financed by short-term foreign debt, which made the country vulnerable to speculative attacks of foreign investors on the Slovak Koruna. These attacks, together with a rapid outflow of foreign capital, led to a currency and current account crisis in 1998, which forced the National Bank of Slovakia to give up its exchange rate target. After the crisis, the government launched a programme to increase public savings. However, lower private saving rates more than compensated the public savings increase and aggregate savings further decreased. Only because of declining investment rates could the current account deficit be reduced to nearly 7 per cent in 2000, but not for long. Following an investment boom the current account deficit rose again to more than 13 per cent until it could be lowered to 5 per cent in 2003 as the boom came to an end.

Slovenia

The saving and investment rates remained relatively stable in relation to the other CEEC-5 countries. In 1991, Slovenia recorded a current account surplus, which, however, soon evolved into a current account deficit due to lower saving and higher investment rates. At the peak of the investment boom in 1999 and 2000, the deficit reached almost 8 per cent. As a result of an economic downturn investment rates declined and saving rates rose, leading to a current account deficit of less than 4 per cent in 2003.

4. INTERNATIONAL CAPITAL MOBILITY IN THE CEEC-5: THE FELDSTEIN–HORIOKA APPROACH

In order to measure the degree of financial market integration of the CEEC-5 into the world capital market econometrically, we use the Feldstein–Horioka approach. Because of the lack of long time-series data, the degree of financial integration is estimated only for the group and not for each country separately. This panel approach has the advantage that information from cross-sectional and time-series data is used to estimate the relationship between saving and investment rates. The time-series properties could then be interpreted as capturing short-run dynamics of savings and investments, while the cross-sectional estimates reflect the long-run relationship between saving and investment rates (Obstfeld, 1995). The panel has been estimated with Ordinary Least Squares (OLS), which is the standard estimator in the literature on the Feldstein–Horioka approach.[2]

To compare the degree of capital mobility with the euro area states, we also analyse the saving–investment correlations of Austria, Belgium, Finland, France, Germany, Greece, Ireland, Italy, the Netherlands, Portugal and Spain (hereafter: euro area-11).[3] If the Feldstein–Horioka coefficient of these countries is significantly smaller than in Central and Eastern Europe, the euro area-11 are more integrated into the world capital market. In an enlarged euro area, monetary shocks might then cause asymmetric reactions in the CEEC-5.

Equation (27.1) is estimated for annual data for the reform period (1989 to 2003) and for the entire period (1980 to 2003) (hereafter aggregate savings regression). In order to remove serial correlation from the residuals, autoregressive terms are used as additional regressors. To account for unobserved time-invariant differences for each cross-sectional unit, the equation is furthermore estimated with country-specific dummy variables. The regression results are presented in Table 27.1. The regressions confirm

Table 27.1 Domestic saving and investment correlations

	CEEC-5		Euro area	
	1980–2003[1]	1989–2003	1980–2003[2]	1989–2003
		Levels		
S/Y	0.41***	0.32***	0.55***	0.47***
	(0.05)	(0.06)	(0.05)	(0.05)
CZ	0.21***	0.23***		
	(0.01)	(0.01)		
HU	0.16***	0.18***		
	(0.01)	(0.01)		
PL	0.15***	0.16***		
	(0.01)	(0.01)		
SLK	0.21***	0.23***		
	(0.02)	(0.02)		
SL	0.16***	0.18***		
	(0.01)	(0.01)		
AR(1)	0.69***	0.81***	1.03***	1.12***
	(0.10)	(0.12)	(0.05)	(0.08)

Table 27.1 (continued)

	CEEC-5		Euro area	
	1980–2003[1]	1989–2003	1980–2003[2]	1989–2003
AR(2)	–0.18**	–0.31***	–0.25***	–0.41***
	(0.10)	(0.11)	(0.06)	(0.08)
H_0: $(S/Y) = 1$	127.77***	105.24***	73.09***	98.41***
Obs.	72	58	240	163
R^2	0.80	0.82	0.88	0.88
DW	1.83	2.08	1.77	1.85
		First difference		
$D(S/Y)$	0.41***	0.36***	0.56***	0.52***
	(0.05)	(0.06)	(0.05)	(0.05)
H_0: $(S/Y) = 1$	96.75***	85.60***	61.83***	65.47***
Obs.	67	55	229	163
R^2	0.41	0.44	0.52	0.44
DW	2.00	2.21	1.70	1.90

Notes:
1. ***, **, * indicate significance at the 1, 5 and 10 per cent level, standard errors in parenthesis.
2. The intercept coefficients of the euro area-11 have not been reported but are available from the author on request.

Equation (27.5) below is estimated for annual data for the reform period (1989 to 2003) and for the entire period (1980 to 2003) as OLS panel regression with cross-section weights. The regression is estimated with autoregressive terms (AR) to remove serial correlation from the residuals and with country-specific dummy variables to account for unobserved time-invariant differences for each cross-sectional unit. (S/Y) is the aggregate saving retention coefficient. CZ, HU, PL, SLK and SL denote the individual country intercepts of the Czech Republic, Hungary, Poland, Slovakia and Slovenia.

Source: International Financial Statistics (2005) and own calculations.

the conclusions we draw from the descriptive analysis of saving and investment rates in the previous section, since the Feldstein–Horioka coefficient is 0.41 (with a standard error of 0.05) over the entire period and 0.32 (0.06) over the reform period, indicating that the financial markets of the CEEC-5 are neither perfectly integrated into nor perfectly separated from the world capital market. A Feldstein–Horioka coefficient of 0.41 means that 41 per cent of domestic investments are financed by domestic savings. To analyse if the degree of international capital mobility increased between 1980 and

2003, Wald tests were used. These tests do not reject the hypothesis that the coefficients are significantly different. The degree of capital mobility in Central and Eastern Europe thus seems to have significantly increased over the reform period.[4]

To find out if the CEEC-5 have already reached the same degree of international capital mobility as the euro area countries, we ran the Feldstein–Horioka regression for the euro area-11 as well. The regression results are also presented in Table 27.1. The saving retention coefficient of the euro area-11 for the entire period is 0.55 (with a standard error of 0.05) and that for the reform period 0.47 (0.05). These estimates are close to the coefficients Buch (1999) estimated for Southern Europe. To find out if the coefficients over the entire and the reform period are significantly different, Wald tests were performed. These tests reject the hypothesis that the coefficients are not significantly different. The degree of international capital mobility in the euro area-11 thus seems to have increased over the reform period. To find out if the CEEC-5 are more integrated into the world capital market than the euro area-11, the same tests were used. These tests do not reject the hypothesis that the coefficients over the total and the reform period are significantly different from each other. The degree of financial integration thus seems to be higher in the CEEC-5 than in the euro area-11.[5]

A problem with panel data regressions is that the time-series used might be non-stationary, since the regression of a non-stationary variable on another non-stationary variable leads to spurious results when these series are not co-integrated (Granger and Newbold, 1974). In this case, the results obtained from the panel regression above would be biased, and any inference about the degree of financial integration meaningless. Following Buch (1999), we estimated equation (27.1) therefore in first differences as well. The regression results are presented at the bottom of Table 27.1. As expected, taking differences worsens the fit of the regression. The R^2 of the regression over the entire and the reform period drops considerably. The Feldstein–Horioka coefficients of the total and the CEEC-5 sample regressions are, however, still highly significant and insignificantly different from the coefficients of the panel regression in levels. For comparison purposes, we estimated equation (27.1) in first differences for the euro area-11 as well. The regression results are also reported at the bottom of Table 27.1. The Feldstein–Horioka coefficients are slightly higher than those estimated in levels. Wald tests, however, reject the hypotheses that the coefficients of the first-difference regression are significantly different from the coefficients in the levels regression.

To summarize, panel data regressions over the entire period and the reform period in levels as well as first differences indicate that the degree of capital mobility increased between 1980 and 2003 both in the CEEC-5 and in the euro area-11. Hypothesis tests furthermore reveal that the degree of international capital mobility is already higher in the CEEC-5 than in the euro area-11. These results might be explained with the removal of capital controls and further barriers that limit the import and export of capital following accession to the OECD and the preparation for accession to the EU. Another reason is the need for capital to finance the transformation from a centrally-planned to a market-based economy in the CEEC-5. Owing to the underdevelopment of the financial markets in these countries and the small capital stock, these countries have to import foreign capital to finance domestic investment. The euro area-11 countries conversely have a well-developed financial market and a larger capital stock, and hence rely less on the import of foreign capital to finance domestic investments than the CEEC-5.[6] The results also confirm the hypothesis of Buch (1999) that 'the central and eastern European countries have already reached the same degree of integration into the world capital market like the member states of the EU and that the accession process would likely not boost capital market integration to a large extent and to trigger huge capital inflows' (Buch, 1999, p. 28).

What is problematic is that the panel approach only measures the degree of capital mobility for a group of countries and not for each country separately. The degree of capital mobility might therefore have been biased by a small number of highly integrated countries even though most countries in the panel are largely separated from the world capital market. Another problem of the Feldstein–Horioka approach is that the estimates of the Feldstein–Horioka coefficients might have been biased by current account targeting policies of the governments in the CEEC-5.

5. THE FELDSTEIN–HORIOKA APPROACH AND CURRENT ACCOUNT TARGETING

As noted in section 2, the approach by Feldstein and Horioka (1980) to measure the degree of financial integration is criticized, since it can be biased by current account targeting policies of the government. To make the relationship between fiscal policies and the current account clear, we will start with the current account identity according to which the current account balance is equal to the difference between domestic savings and domestic investments:

$$CA = S - I, \tag{27.2}$$

where CA is the current account balance, S domestic savings and I domestic investment. Since domestic savings can be decomposed into private and public savings, the identity above can be rewritten as:

$$CA = S_G + S_P - I, \qquad (27.3)$$

where I is private investment, S_P private and S_G public savings. Since the amount of public savings depends upon the revenues and expenditures of the government, equation (27.3) can be rearranged to:

$$CA = (T - G) + (S_p - I), \qquad (27.4)$$

where T is government revenues and G government expenditures. As illustrated by equation (27.4) the fiscal budget might act as an adjustment variable, since the government can balance the current account by adjusting its budget to the difference between private savings and investments. If a country has higher investment than private saving rates, the government has to increase its savings by reducing government expenditures and/or by raising taxes to balance the current account. If domestic savings on the contrary exceed domestic investments, the government has to increase its debt to balance the current account. For that reason, the correlation of the spread between private savings and investments and the fiscal budget is expected to be negative in perfectly integrated capital markets, if the government has targeted the current account.[7]

The correlation between the fiscal budget and the spread between private savings and investment, however, might also be negative, even if the government has not targeted the current account. Feldstein and Bachetta (1989) addressed this problem in their paper on international capital mobility and argued that the negative correlation might also have been caused by the crowding out or crowding in of private investment in a world of immobile capital. In such a world, the domestic interest rate is completely determined by the domestic demand for and the supply of capital. An increase of government expenditures consequently causes the domestic interest rate to rise and to crowd out domestic investments, whereas a reduction of government expenditures causes the interest rate to decrease and to crowd in new investments. Thus, even in a world of perfectly immobile capital, the government budget and the difference between private savings and investment can be negatively correlated.

To find out whether the regression results of the panel regressions above are biased by fiscal policies, we regress the private and the public saving rate on the domestic investment rate for the period between 1980 and 2003 according to Feldstein and Bachetta (hereafter private savings regression).[8]

$$(I/Y)_{it} = \alpha_i + \beta_1(S_P/Y)_{it} + \beta_2(S_G/Y)_{it} + \varepsilon_{it}, \tag{27.5}$$

where i is a country and t a time index. (S_P/Y) is the private saving rate, (S_G/Y) the public saving rate defined as the difference between public revenues and expenditures and ε is a random error term with zero mean and constant variance. To allow for time-invariant differences between each cross-section unit, equation (27.5) is estimated with country-specific dummy variables. Autoregressive terms are used to remove autocorrelation. Since some of the CEEC-5 countries launched government savings programmes to reduce the current account deficit, we expect the public saving retention coefficient to be statistically significant and the private saving retention coefficient to be significantly lower in this regression than in the aggregate savings regression. This indicates that fiscal policies have significantly biased the degree of capital mobility in the CEEC-5 toward lower capital mobility in the aggregate savings regression. The regression results are presented in Table 27.2.

The regression model fits the data very well and all variables are, as expected, highly significant. The private saving retention coefficient over

Table 27.2 Private and public saving and investment correlations

	CEEC-5		Euro area	
	1980–2003[1]	1989–2003	1980–2003[2]	1989–2003
		Levels		
S_P/Y	0.35***	0.32**	0.52***	0.44***
	(0.06)	(0.14)	(0.05)	(0.05)
S_G/Y	0.45***	0.66***	0.59***	0.48***
	(0.12)	(0.24)	(0.07)	(0.06)
CZ	0.22***	0.24***		
	(0.01)	(0.03)		
HU	0.17***	0.19***		
	(0.01)	(0.03)		
PL	0.19***	0.20***		
	(0.01)	(0.02)		
SLK	0.21***	0.23***		
	(0.02)	(0.03)		
SL	0.17***	0.18***		
	(0.01)	(0.02)		
AR(1)	0.80***	0.81***	1.01***	1.09***
	(0.14)	(0.15)	(0.06)	(0.09)
AR(2)	–0.41***	–0.44***	0.23***	–0.38***
	(0.13)	(0.13)	(0.06)	(0.08)

Table 27.2 (continued)

	CEEC-5		Euro area	
	1980–2003[1]	1989–2003	1980–2003[2]	1989–2003
H_0: $(S_P/Y) = 1$	105.79***	21.96***	70.66***	97.62***
Obs.	53	44	209	132
R^2	0.74	0.72	0.88	0.89
DW	1.99	2.23	1.86	1.97
		First difference		
$D(S_P/Y)$	0.23*	0.21	0.55***	0.49***
	(0.11)	(0.13)	(0.05)	(0.06)
$D(S_G/Y)$	0.40**	0.53**	0.64***	0.57***
	(0.15)	(0.21)	(0.07)	(0.06)
H_0: $D(S_P/Y) = 1$	41.25***	34.27***	56.26***	66.15***
Obs.	59	48	198	132
R^2	0.13	0.12	0.55	0.49
DW	1.79	1.89	1.82	2.14

Notes:
1. ***, **, * indicate significance at the 1, 5 and 10 per cent level, standard errors in parenthesis.
2. Luxembourg was excluded from the regression due to a lack of data on public savings. Data on public savings for the period between 1999 and 2003 were not available for Austria, France, Germany, Greece and Portugal. The intercept coefficients of the euro area-11 have not been reported but are available from the author on request.

Equation (27.5) is estimated for annual data for the reform period (1989 to 2003) and for the entire period (1980 to 2003) as OLS panel regression with cross-section weights. The regression is estimated with autoregressive terms (AR) to remove serial correlation from the residuals and with country-specific dummy variables to account for unobserved time-invariant differences for each cross-sectional unit. (S_P/Y) and (S_G/Y) are the private and public saving retention coefficients. CZ, HU, PL, SLK and SL denote the individual country intercepts of the Czech Republic, Hungary, Poland, Slovakia and Slovenia.

Source: International Financial Statistics (2005) and own calculations.

the entire period is 0.35 (with a standard error of 0.06) and that of the public sector 0.45 (0.12). For the reform period, the respective coefficient for the private sector is 0.32 (0.14) and 0.66 (0.24) for the public sector. Since the private saving retention coefficients are smaller than in the aggregate savings regressions, the degree of capital mobility seems to have been biased by government fiscal policies in the CEEC-5. In particular, in the reform period the development of the domestic investment rate seems to have been significantly influenced by the development of the public saving rate. The public saving retention coefficient in this period almost adds up to unity with the private saving retention coefficient, indicating that the government has almost perfectly offset the gap between private savings and investments. Wald tests, however, do not reject the hypothesis that the private saving retention coefficients in the aggregate and the private savings regression are identical. The degree of international capital mobility of the CEEC-5 thus does not seem to have been significantly biased by government policies although the public saving retention coefficients are highly significant. The results of the regression for the euro area-11 also indicate that the degree of financial market integration has been biased toward lower capital mobility by government policies, since the Feldstein–Horioka coefficients of the aggregate savings regressions are higher than the coefficients in the private savings regression. The respective coefficient for the private sector is 0.52 (with a standard error of 0.05) for the entire period and 0.44 (0.05) for the reform period. The respective public saving retention coefficients are 0.59 (0.07) and 0.48 (0.06). Wald tests, however, reject the hypothesis that the coefficients of the private savings regression are significantly different from those in the aggregate savings regression. These tests thus again indicate that the degree of international capital mobility has not been significantly biased by government policies although public savings rates are significantly correlated to the domestic investment rate.[9]

Following Buch (1999), we estimated equation (27.5) also in first differences to take account of the potential non-stationarity of the time series. The regression results are presented at the bottom of Table 27.2. As for the aggregate savings regression, taking differences worsened the fit of the regression. The Feldstein–Horioka coefficients of the entire and the reform period for the CEEC-5 and the euro area-11 are, however, still (weakly) significant. Wald tests reject the hypothesis that the private and public saving retention coefficients for the first-difference regression are significantly different from the coefficients in the levels regression.

To summarize, neither the private savings regression for the CEEC-5 nor for the euro area-11 indicate that the degree of capital market integration was significantly biased by fiscal policies between 1980 and 2003. The significance of the public saving retention coefficients, however, also indicates that the public saving rate was correlated to the investment rate. Yet this cannot be taken as evidence for current account targeting policies of the government, since significant public saving retention coefficients are both consistent with a crowding out of private investments in the case of low capital mobility and current account policies in the case of high capital mobility. The private savings approach is hence appropriate to control for the influence of fiscal policies on the degree of international capital mobility, but inappropriate to find out if governments targeted the current account. We consequently have to apply other econometric techniques to analyse if the governments in Central and Eastern Europe used fiscal policies to balance the current account.

6. CURRENT ACCOUNT TARGETING IN THE CEEC-5

If governments systematically adjust revenues and expenditures to the difference between private savings and investments to balance the current account, a country cannot infinitely run current account deficits or current account surpluses. For that reason, if the governments in the CEEC-5 successfully targeted the current account between 1980 and 2003, the current account time series cannot be non-stationary. This hypothesis can be tested by analysing the statistical properties of the current account time series of the CEEC-5.

To do the test, we first generate the current account series according to equation (27.2) as the difference between the domestic saving and the domestic investment rate. Then we performe Augmented Dickey-Fuller (ADF) tests of these series to test for the existence of a unit root. If these tests indicate that the current account series are non-stationary, governments did not target the current account. Table 27.3 presents the results of these tests for the period between 1980 and 2003.

Table 27.3 ADF tests of the current account balance

	Level		First differences		Degree of integration
	Specification[1]	t-value[2]	Specification	t-value	
Czech Republic	0C1	–3.33**	0C1	–2.84*	I(0)
Hungary	0C0	–1.66	0C0	–4.82***	I(1)
Poland	0C0	–1.51	0C0	–4.27***	I(1)
Slovak Republic	0C1	–3.36**	0C1	–2.83*	I(0)
Slovenia	0C0	–2.73*	0C0	–7.86***	I(0)

Notes:
1. Trend, constant, lag length.
2. ***, **, * indicate significance at the 1, 5 and 10 per cent level. Sample period: 1993 to 2002 for the Czech Republic, 1980 to 2003 for Hungary and Poland, 1993 to 2003 for Slovakia and 1991 to 2003 for Slovenia.

Source: International Financial Statistics (2005) and own calculations.

The ADF tests come to different conclusions about government influence on the current account. While the ADF tests of the Polish and the Hungarian current account indicate that these series are non-stationary, the tests of the Czech, the Slovakian and the Slovenian current account balance indicate that these series are stationary. These results have two different implications: first, the non-stationarity of the Polish and the Hungarian current account series indicates that the governments in these countries did not target the current account. Second, the stationarity of the current account series in the Czech Republic, Slovakia and Slovenia indicates that the governments in these countries might have adopted current account targeting policies to balance the current account. It has, however, to be noted that the current account can also be stationary due to changes in the private saving rate and the investment rate. A stationary current account hence cannot be taken as evidence for current account targeting policies in these countries. Yet the ADF results might be interpreted as an indication that these policies might have been used in these countries to prevent unsustainable current account balances. They furthermore do not contradict the observations we made in section 3, since the Czech Republic and Slovakia launched government saving programmes after the currency crises in 1997 and 1998 to reduce the current account deficit. The test results for Hungary and Slovenia, on the contrary, are more difficult to interpret, since the Slovenian current account is stationary although no current account targeting policies have been observed in section 3. The stationarity of the current account might, however, have also been caused by changes in the domestic private saving and investment rate. The ADF result for the Slovenian current account therefore does not contradict our initial observations. Only the test result for Hungary is contradicting. Since the Hungarian government adopted savings programmes in May 1995 to reduce the current account deficit, we would expect the Hungarian current account series to be stationary. The ADF test results, however, indicate the opposite. This might be interpreted as evidence against the adoption of current account targeting policies or at least as evidence for the inability of the Hungarian government to sustainably influence the current account balance.

To check the robustness of these results, we also ran Kwiatkowski, Phillips, Schmidt, and Shin (KPSS) tests (Kwiatkowski et al., 1992). This test differs from the ADF test in that it tests the null hypothesis that the series is stationary, whereas the ADF test assumes that the series is non-stationary. The test results confirm the ADF test results for the Czech Republic and Slovakia as well as for Slovenia. Yet for Hungary and Poland the KPSS test comes to different conclusions about the stationarity of the current account series. This might indicate that the unit root test results are not robust and hence have to be interpreted with caution. The small sample period for which data about saving and investment rates are available might be a reason for this. It might also explain the conflicting result we obtained for the Hungarian current account balance.

7. CONCLUSIONS

Different degrees of financial integration might lead to an asymmetric transmission of monetary shocks in an enlarged euro area. The motivation of this study was to measure the degree of financial market integration in the CEEC-5 and to compare their degree of integration with that of the euro area in order to see if differences in the degree of international capital mobility might cause asymmetric responses to monetary shocks in an enlarged monetary union.

According to the analysis of saving and investment correlations, neither the CEEC-5 not the euro area-11 are perfectly integrated into the world capital market. Yet both country groups could significantly increase the degree of international capital mobility between 1980 and 2003. The empirical analysis has furthermore shown that potential asymmetric responses to monetary shocks cannot be expected in an enlarged euro area due to a lower degree of financial market integration in the CEEC-5, since the Central and Eastern European countries have already reached a higher degree of financial integration in quantitative terms than the euro area-11.

Since the CEEC-5 experienced high current account deficits between 1980 and 2003, many countries adopted government savings programmes to reduce the current account deficit. These policies might have biased the degree of international capital mobility. To control for these policies, we also estimated the Feldstein–Horioka equation with private and public saving rates. The results indicate that the degree of capital mobility has not been significantly biased by fiscal policies. However, they also reveal that public savings are significantly correlated to the domestic investment rate. Since the standard Feldstein–Horioka approach is not suitable for detecting current account targeting policies in the CEEC-5, we tested the statistical properties of the current account time series on the basis of unit root tests. These tests reveal that in particular those CEEC-5 countries targeted the current account that suffered from current account crises in the past. Yet robustness checks and the small sample period indicate that the results of these tests have been taken with caution and cannot be interpreted as evidence but rather as an indication for the adoption of current account targeting policies in these countries.

NOTES

* Centre for European Economic Research (ZEW), Mannheim, Germany. E-mail: koehler@zew.de. The author would like to thank Michael Schröder, Andreas Schrimpf, Thomas Pfahler and the participants at the Conference on the Channels of European Integration in Warsaw and the Conference on European Economic Integration 2005 in Vienna for helpful comments and suggestions.

1. Herrmann and Jochem (2003a and 2003b) recorded deviations from covered and uncovered interest rate parity in the Czech Republic, Hungary, Poland and Slovakia. According to the covered and uncovered interest rate parity condition, the financial markets in these countries are thus not integrated into the European financial market.
2. See Coakley et al. (1998) for a survey article on the literature about the Feldstein–Horioka approach and capital mobility.
3. Luxembourg has been excluded from the sample because it constitutes an outlier owing to its characteristics as a small country with a huge financial marketplace. Investment rates have been calculated by dividing the sum of gross fixed capital formation and changes in inventories by GDP. Saving rates have been calculated according to the current account identity as the sum of gross investment and the balance of the current account divided by GDP. Because of a lack of data, saving and investment rates could have been calculated for the Czech Republic and Slovakia only for the period between 1993 and 2002 and 1993–2003 respectively, as well as for Slovenia for the period between 1990 and 2003. Data on Polish and Hungarian savings and investment rates were available for the entire period. All data have been taken from IFS (2005).
4. Test and regression results that have not been reported are available from the authors at request.
5. To find out if the common market and the euro has significantly changed the relationship between savings and investments in the euro area-11, we introduced intercept and slope dummy variables. These dummy variables take a value of one in the period of the Common Market (1992–2003) and after the introduction of the euro (1999–2003) and zero in the other period. The Common Market slope dummy turned out to be highly significant in the levels regression over the entire period, indicating a higher degree of international capital mobility in the period of the Common Market. The Feldstein–Horioka coefficient is, however, still higher than in the CEEC-5. Probably due to the small number of observations, the euro dummy variables remained insignificant. We found no evidence for the insignificance of the relationship between saving and investment rates as observed by Adam et al. (2002) for the period between 1995 and 2000. Yet intercept and slope dummy variables indicate a break in the relationship between saving and investment rates after 1994, which might be attributed to the implementation of the common market. The results of these regressions have not been reported but are available on request.
6. The effect of country size on the degree of international capital mobility has been analysed by Harberger (1980) and Murphy (1984). They have divided the Feldstein and Horioka (1980) sample according to country size into two different sub-groups to see if the degree of capital mobility is related to the size of the country. Their results indicate that smaller countries have a significantly lower Feldstein–Horioka coefficient than the group of large countries. They interpret this as evidence for the existence of a 'country effect' that biases the degree of international capital mobility.
7. Summers (1986) has tested this relationship by regressing the difference between savings and investments on the government deficit to prove that the Feldstein and Horioka paradox can be explained by current account targeting. He interpreted his results as evidence for this policy and criticized the interpretation of the Feldstein–Horioka coefficient as an indicator of the degree of international capital mobility.
8. Artis and Bayoumi (1990) have estimated monetary and fiscal reaction functions to find out if the current account was a policy target of the government and the central bank. Their results suggest that the current account has been targeted by the central bank and

not by governments, and hence that states mainly use monetary instead of fiscal instruments to influence the current account.

9. To find out if structural breaks in the relationship of private and public saving and investment rates in the euro area-11 occurred as a result of the Common Market and the euro, we again used dummy variables for the period of the Common Market and for the period after the introduction of the euro. The regression results indicate that the degree of financial integration has increased after the implementation of the Common Market, since the slope dummy turned out to be significantly negative over the entire period, indicating a higher degree of capital mobility in the euro area-11 over the period of the Common Market. In contrast to the aggregate savings regression, the euro slope dummy variable for the private sector saving retention coefficient turned out to be significant over the entire period and indicates a higher degree of international capital mobility after the introduction of the euro. This conclusion has not been confirmed for the reform period regression probably because of the short sample period. The Feldstein–Horioka coefficient is, however, still higher than in the CEEC-5. As in the aggregate savings regression, dummy variables indicate a break in the relationship between private sector saving and investment rates after 1995 which might be attributed to the Common Market. Yet the regressions do not indicate that saving and investment rates are not significantly correlated as observed by Adam et al. (2002). The results of these regressions have not been reported but are available on request.

REFERENCES

Adam, Klaus, Tullio Jappelli, Annamaria Menichini, Mario Padula and Marco Pagano (2002), 'Analyse, compare, and apply alternative indicators and monitoring methodologies to measure the evolution of capital market integration in the EU', *Working Paper*, Centre for Financial Studies in Economics and Finance, University of Salerno.

Artis, M.J. and Tamin Bayoumi (1990), 'Global capital market integration and the current account', in M.P. Taylor (ed.), *Money and Financial Markets*, Cambridge and Oxford: Blackwell, pp. 297–307.

Bayoumi, Tamin (1990), 'Saving–investment correlations', *Working Papers*, **37**, International Monetary Fund, Washington, District of Columbia, pp. 360–87.

Buch, Claudia M. (1999), 'Capital mobility and EU enlargement', *Review of World Economics*, **135** (4), 629–56.

Cecchetti (2001), 'Legal structure, financial structure and monetary policy', in Deutsche Bundesbank (ed.), *The Monetary Transmission Process*, Palgrave.

Coakley, Jerry, Farida Kulasi and Ron Smith (1995), 'Current account solvency and the Feldstein Horioka puzzle', *Working Paper*, 8/95R, Birkbeck College, London.

Coakley, Jerry, Farida Kulasi and Ron Smith (1996), 'Savings, investment and capital mobility in LDC', *Working Paper*, 10/96, Birkbeck College, London.

Coakley, Jerry, Farida Kulasi and Ron Smith (1998), 'The Feldstein Horioka puzzle and capital mobility: A review', *International Journal of Finance and Economics*, **3**, 169–88.

Dickey, D.A. and W.A Fuller (1979), 'Distribution of the estimators for autoregressive time-series with a unit root', *Journal of the American Statistical Association*, **74**, 427–31.

ECB (2003), 'The integration of Europe's financial markets', in European Central Bank (ed.), *Monthly Bulletin*, October, pp. 53–66, Frankfurt.

Feldstein, Martin and Phillipe Bachetta (1989), 'National saving and international investment', in B.D. Bernheim and J.B. Shoven (eds), *National Saving and Economic Performance*, Chicago: University of Chicago Press.

Feldstein, Martin and Charles Horioka (1980), 'Domestic saving and international capital flows', *The Economic Journal*, **90**, 314–29.

Granger, C.W.J. and P. Newbold (1974), 'Spurious regressions in econometrics', *Journal of Econometrics*, **2**, 111–20.

Harberger, Arnold C. (1980), 'Vignettes on the world capital market', *The American Economic Review*, **70**, 331–37.

Herrmann, S. and A. Jochem (2003a), 'The international integration of money markets in the central and east European accession countries: deviations from covered interest parity, capital controls and inefficiencies in the financial sector', *Discussion Paper*, 07/03, Economic Research Centre of the Deutsche Bundesbank, Frankfurt.

Herrmann, S. and A. Jochem (2003b), 'The international integration of foreign exchange markets in the central and east European accession countries: speculative efficiency, transaction costs and exchange rate premiums', *Discussion Paper*, 08/03, Economic Research Centre of the Deutsche Bundesbank, Frankfurt.

International Financial Statistics CD ROM (2005), in International Monetary Fund (ed.), New York.

Jarocinsk, Marek (2004), 'Responses to monetary policy shocks in the East and the West of Europe: A comparison', mimeo.

Köhler, Matthias, Judith Hommel and Matthias Grote (2006), 'The role of banks in the transmission of monetary policy in the Baltics', Discussion Paper, 06-005, Centre for European Economic Research, Mannheim.

Kwiatkowski, Denis, Peter C.B. Phillips, Peter Schmidt and Yongcheol Shin (1992), 'Testing the null hypothesis of stationary against the alternative of a unit root', *Journal of Econometrics*, **54**, 159–78.

Murphy, Robert (1984), 'Capital mobility and the relationship between saving and investment rates in the OECD countries', *Journal of International Money and Finance*, **3**, 327–42.

Obstfeld, Maurice (1995), 'International capital mobility in the 1990s', in P.B. Kenen (ed.), *Understanding Interdependence – The Macroeconomics of the Open Economy*, Princeton, New Jersey: Princeton University Press.

Schmitz, B. (2004), 'What role do banks play in monetary transmission in EU accession countries?', *Working Paper*, Center for European Integration Studies, Bonn.

Sinn, Stefan (1992), 'Saving–investment correlations and capital mobility: On the evidence from annual data', *The Economic Journal*, **102**, 1162–70.

Summers, Lawrence H. (1986), 'Tax policy and international competitiveness', *Discussion Paper*, 1256, Harvard Institute of Economic Research, Cambridge, Massachusetts.

PART VIII

Complementing the academic view: perspectives from key financial market players

28. Financial institutions as a driving force of integration

Josef Christl

Notwithstanding the fact that a benign legal, regulatory and political environment is a crucial catalyst, overall financial integration has to be seen as a process primarily driven by market forces and by decisions made in the private sector. Commercial banks are an important driving force in this process of financial integration, which should deliver measurable benefits in the form of better and cheaper access to capital and higher growth for the non-financial sector as well as to the financial sector itself of the economies involved. Let me explain this in more detail:

1. Doing business in a single and integrated financial market, which is much larger than the domestic market, helps – maybe not all, but at least the big international – banks to realize economies of scale and scope (European Commission, 2005a). The resulting improvement in cost efficiency may translate into better profitability, unless another consequence of financial integration, namely more intense competition, mitigates or even eliminates this effect. But in the latter case, higher cost efficiency enables banks to survive in a world that is getting more and more competitive.
2. Banks with cross-border business benefit from the harmonization of the legal framework that financial integration necessitates. Doing business in many different countries is complex, difficult and costly if banking regulation and supervisory practices differ a lot, which many European banks have experienced. A better harmonized regulatory and supervisory framework in Europe significantly reduces the cost of compliance for these market participants (European Commission, 2005a, 2005c).
3. The same is true for the harmonization of regulations for accounting and auditing, as credit monitoring and risk assessment should become more harmonized and hence cheaper.
4. Financial integration offers banks better tools and a wider range of instruments for risk management, thus reducing their vulnerability to the different types of shocks.

5. Financial integration also changes the nature of banks' business. For example, the introduction of the euro has given a boost to securities markets, in particular to the non-financial corporate bond market. As a result, the income structure of banks is changing, with fee incomes gaining significance. In a similar vein, growing securitization allows banks to broaden and deepen their customer relations without adding new loans to their balance sheets and hence with relatively lower capital requirements.
6. Last but not least, commercial banks are active in the integration process, not only through everyday business, but also because they are intensively involved in the process of shaping the framework of European financial integration (for example through the Financial Services Action Plan of the European Commission or its more recent White Paper on financial services policy for the years 2005–2010).

European financial integration has definitely accelerated with the introduction of the euro (ECB, 2004). Financial integration is today most advanced in wholesale and capital-related activities, while retail markets, such as loans to households and small and medium-sized enterprises are – not surprisingly – lagging behind (ECB, 2005a). There still exist several types of barriers, stemming from differences in the nature of competition, such as the proximity to clients, bank–customer relationships and access to soft information, but also stemming from different tax regimes, supervisory practices, governance issues and so on, which put a break on the process of financial integration (European Commission, 2005c). As a case in point, currently less than 5 per cent of total bank loans to non-monetary financial institutions are granted across borders to customers in other euro area countries (European Commission, 2005b; ECB 2005d; see Figure 28.1). Thus, there seems to be considerable room for expanding. Moreover, mergers of credit institutions in the euro area have mainly taken place within national boundaries. The presence of large pan-European banking groups in euro area countries through branches and subsidiaries is relatively limited. For example, the share of foreign branches and subsidiaries accounts for only 15 per cent of the euro area banking market (ECB, 2005d).

The banking markets in the Central and Eastern European countries exhibit significant differences compared to the euro area pattern.

In terms of size, all major segments of the financial sector are considerably smaller in the Central and Eastern European countries than in the EU-12, not only in absolute euro terms, but also in relation to GDP. One may expect the ratios of financial assets to GDP to rise as a result of real catching-up and the further deepening of financial intermediation.

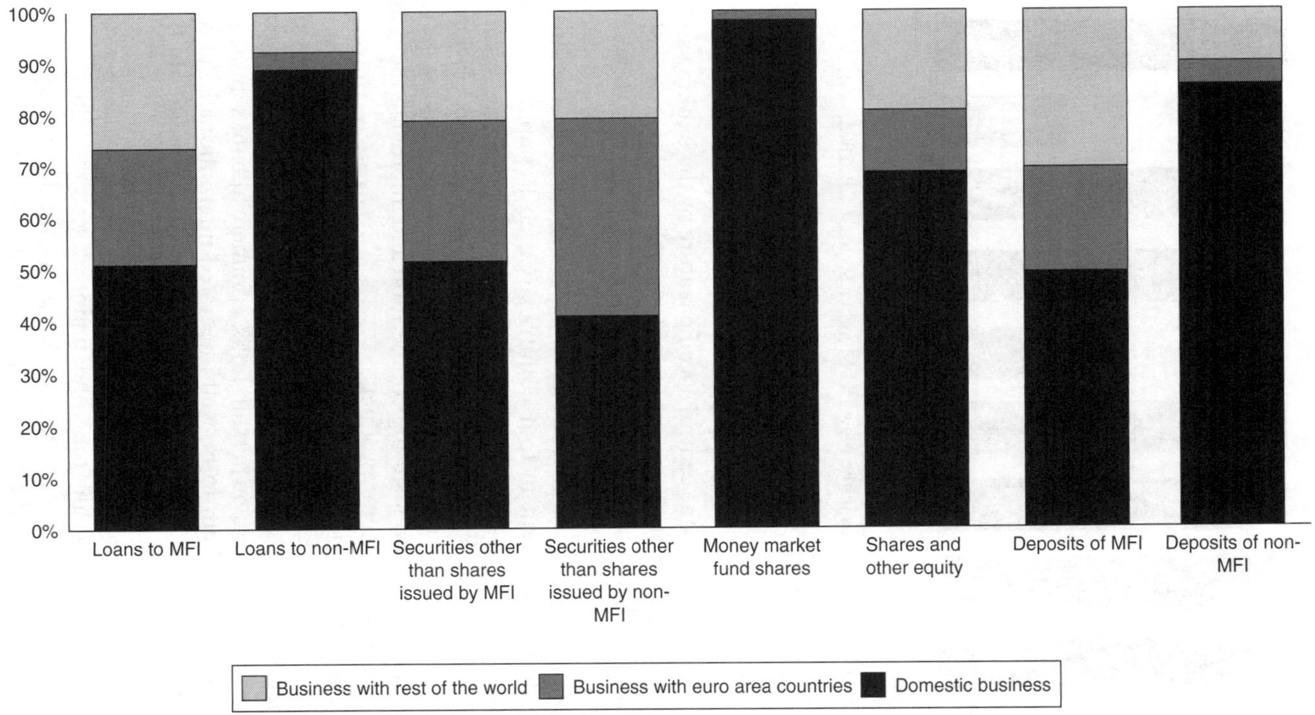

Source: ECB.

Figure 28.1 Balance sheet of the euro area banking sector as of September 2005

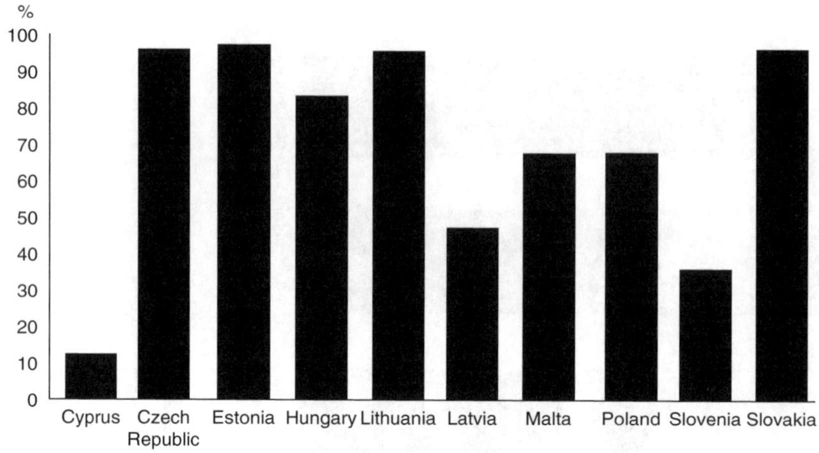

Source: The Banking Structures in the New EU Member States, ECB, 2005.

Figure 28.2 Asset share of foreign-owned banks

In terms of ownership, one central specific feature of the banking sector in most Central and Eastern European countries is the predominant role of foreign-controlled banks (see Figure 28.2). For example, foreign ownership in the banking sector in the eight new EU member states from the region varies between 36 per cent (Slovenia) and 97 per cent (Estonia), with this share exceeding 90 per cent in four countries (Czech Republic, Estonia, Lithuania and Slovakia). As has been demonstrated in empirical research, foreign ownership has significantly contributed to increased efficiency, better management and risk assessment tools in the CEE banking sector, while at the same time also fostering competition and improving the range and quality of financial sector products.

In addition to having been targets in cross-border mergers and acquisitions in the past, large CEE-domiciled banks have more recently started to expand abroad themselves.

Also, in addition to these ownership links, commercial banks in the new member states (NMS) seem to be well integrated internationally, as suggested by the relatively high share of external assets and liabilities in their total balance sheet value.

With respect to the financial structures, a look at the relative size of the different segments within the total financial sector confirms some similarities between the NMS and the euro area, like the dominant position of the banking sector (including its role as an investor in the domestic debt

Table 28.1 Key financial structure data for old and new EU member states

	EU-12	NMS-8
	% of banking assets	% of banking assets
Banking assets (1)	**100%**	**100%**
o/w: domestic loans total	**60%**	**60%**
o/w: domestic loans to the corporate sector	**18%**	**26%**
o/w: domestic debt securities	**15%**	**19%**
o/w: domestic equity securities	**4%**	**1%**
Domestic debt securities (2) (outstanding nominal value)	**42%**	**53%**
o/w: issued by non-financial corporate sector	**6%**	**3%**
Domestic equity securities (3) (market capitalization)	**20%**	**33%**

Source: National central banks, ECB, Eurostat.

securities market) and the larger size of the debt securities market compared with the equity market.

At the same time, there exist three important differences that should be kept in mind (see Table 28.1).

First, the share of domestic loans to the corporate sector is higher in the NMS than in the euro area. Conversely, the share of loans to households is smaller, but rising fast.

Second, the relative size of the corporate debt securities market is much smaller in the NMS than in the euro area. However, given the upswing of the corporate debt securities market in the EU-12 since the start of the common currency area, one can expect that this difference will diminish in parallel to the progress in monetary union.

Third, the relative size of the equity market is bigger in the NMS than in the euro area. However, the large equity market capitalization is mainly the result of the listing of large privatized companies and of the increase in the equity prices over the past few years, rather than attributable to the amount of equity issued to raise capital.

The banking sectors in Central and Eastern Europe also differ significantly from the euro area in terms of profitability (ECB, 2005b). For example, bank profitability in the five Central European new member states of the EU (NMS-5) was in 2004 considerably higher than in the euro area (measured by both ROE and ROA). Return on equity in the euro area ranged between 3.9 per cent in Germany and 15.4 per cent in Ireland, while in the NMS-5 it ranged between 11.5 per cent in Slovenia and 24.9 per cent in Hungary. Return on assets in the euro area ranged between 0.1 per cent in Germany and 0.8 per cent in Spain, while in the NMS-5 it ranged between 0.6 per cent in Slovenia and 1.9 per cent in Hungary. This higher profitability stemmed primarily from higher net interest income in the NMS-5, which was more than twice the level observed in the euro area. In addition, the cost-to-income ratio was already slightly lower in the NMS-5 than in the euro area in 2004, representing an important improvement compared to the results of 2003.

This already provides a first indication of ongoing progress in efficiency in the CEE banking sectors. However, recent empirical work (Rossi et al., 2005) on banking efficiency in Central and Eastern Europe provides a more differentiated picture. The major conclusions which can be drawn from this analysis can be summarized as follows.

First, the banking sectors of the NMS-8 and Romania present significant levels of cost and profit inefficiency, indicating that on average banks operate relatively far below the cost- and profit-efficient frontiers.

Second, inefficiencies are above the levels usually encountered in EU-15 countries, which implies some potential for improvement as well as future competition.

Third, efficiency levels vary considerably across countries. Statistical tests on the significance of these mean differences show that the variations in efficiency levels are significant in almost all cases.

Fourth, the profit efficiency scores are well below the cost efficiency levels: CEE banks seem to fare much better on the cost than on the profit side. It should, however, be noted that given the potential reward of maintaining or expanding market share in a rapidly growing market, banks have less incentive to maximize profits by fully utilizing their discretionary pricing power.

Finally, looking at the evolution of efficiency for the overall sample of banks, a positive and significant increase of cost and profit efficiency can be found over time. However, the improvement is not equally spread across countries.

All in all, the picture of banking efficiency in CEE countries is brightening: comparatively low efficiency levels seem to converge towards higher EU-15 efficiency levels. Given earlier results according to which interest margins were gradually declining, this is all the more important, as efficiency increases are vital for maintaining the aforementioned profitability in the CEE banking markets.

Foreign banks which decided to 'go East' benefit significantly from these higher profitability ratios in Central and Eastern Europe. I would like to demonstrate this on the example of Austrian banks. A striking feature of the importance of the CEE business segment for Austrian banks is the fact that it accounts for only 14 per cent of the balance sheet total, but at the same time generates about 24 per cent of operating income, more than 22 per cent of operating expenses and thus 25 per cent of total profits (before taxes, but including any extraordinary items). Over time, the share of the CEE business segment has been increasing considerably, although the profit generated by the non-CEE business (that is mainly Austrian-related business) of Austrian banking groups has substantially improved as well. For instance, in 2004, profit before tax increased by 48 per cent year-on-year in the non-CEE business segment. However, as profit jumped by 61.3 per cent in the CEE business, its share in the total profits of Austrian banking groups rose further, from 23 per cent in 2003 to 25 per cent in 2004. When examining this significance of business in CEE for the Austrian banking sector, one has to consider that the item 'Central and Eastern European business' in the groups' consolidated balance sheets and results covers not only the Austrian bank subsidiaries in these countries but also the Austrian headquarters' direct cross-border business with clients in this region. For instance, a noteworthy part of this direct cross-border business takes place in the treasury departments of the headquarters.

Financial integration confronts the management of commercial banks with crucial strategic decisions. Key questions which have to be answered include:

- the necessity or possibility of regional expansion (to expand or not to expand?),
- the direction of regional expansion (which is the right destination?),
- the timing of regional expansion (early entry or late entry?),
- the form of regional expansion (better to undertake a green-field investment or buy an existing bank? establish a subsidiary or a branch?),
- the question about centralization or decentralization within a banking group with respect to decision-making structures or to the location of whole business fields and so on.

Despite having the same prime objective of being as profitable as possible, commercial banks differ from one another in their response to these questions. The answers may depend on their historic background, their overall business strategy, their financial possibilities, their corporate culture, but also on the acting persons and sometimes maybe even on luck. A select round of financial market practitioners from the premier league of European banking and investment share their success stories and recipes for a successful future in the following chapters. Their hands-on accounts are meant to complement the academic views proposed in this book.

REFERENCES

European Central Bank (ECB) (2004), 'Measuring financial integration in the euro area', *Occasional Paper Series*, No. 14.
European Central Bank (ECB) (2005a), 'Indicators of financial integration in the euro area'.
European Central Bank (ECB) (2005b), 'EU banking sector stability'.
European Central Bank (ECB) (2005c), 'Banking structures in the new EU member states'.
European Central Bank (ECB) (2005d), 'EU banking structures'.
European Commission (2005a), White Paper: Financial Services Policy 2005–2010.
European Commission (2005b), 'Financial Integration Monitor 2005', Commission Staff Working Document.
European Commission (2005c), 'Cross-border consolidation in the EU financial sector', Commission Staff Working Document.
Rossi, S., M. Schwaiger and G.Winkler (2005), 'Managerial behavior and cost/profit efficiency in the banking sectors of Central and Eastern European countries', *OeNB Working Paper* 96, March, Oesterreichische Nationalbank.

29. UniCredit's strategy in Central and Eastern Europe

Alessandro Profumo

The merger between the Italian UniCredit Group and the German HypoVereinsbank (HVB), which indirectly also involves Bank Austria Creditanstalt (BA-CA) and more than 30 subsidiaries in the region of Central and Eastern Europe (CEE), has created one of the biggest European players. Formally, the UniCredit-HVB Group was established on 18 November 2005. The deal was settled and UniCredit-HVB shares were listed on the Frankfurt stock exchange on 23 November 2005; so the group really started from that day.

The new UniCredit Group has a market capitalization of roughly EUR 59 billion (mid-December 2005), which makes it the fourth-largest banking group at the European level. With total assets of EUR 780 billion, a client pool of more than 28 million and 7000 branches (on a pro-forma basis) it is a leading player in its Western markets. It has a 5 per cent market share in Germany, a 10 per cent market share in Italy and an 18 per cent market share in Austria.

The Group is also the undisputed leader in the CEE region. With more than EUR 70 billion in total banking assets controlled and 2800 branches in 16 countries (on a pro-forma basis, 2004), it is double the size of the second international player in the market. The CEE network is also quite successful. The simple sum of all assets, net profit and revenues of the participating banks in the region shows that roughly EUR 84 billion of assets generate almost EUR 1.2 billion of net profits and almost EUR 5 billion of net revenues (see Figures 29.1 and 29.2).

The CEE is a region offering enormous opportunities and it is also where the internationalization strategy of the group started back in 1999. While the challenge of creating the first truly European bank goes beyond CEE borders, I shall concentrate only on that region in this chapter. My contribution covers four parts: what is the region for us today?; our targets and strategies; what are the main challenges we are seeing?; lesson learnt and next steps.

UniCredit

Banks	Total Asset (€/m)
• Bank Pekao	14,528
• KFS/Kocbank	7,478
• Yapi Kredi	14,571
• Zagrebacka Banka	8,358
• Bulbank	1,860
• Zivnostenska Banka	1,527
• Unibanka	1,266
• Unicredit Zagrebacka	672
• Unicredit Romania	324
• Yapi Moskow	74
• Kocbank Azerbaijan	27
• Pekao Ukraine	9
Total	48,919*

HVB Group

Banks	Total Asset (€/m)
• IMB	2,654
• HVB Latvia	303
• HVB Ukraine Bank	147
• HVB Lithuania Branch	435
• HV Estonia Branch	n/a
Total	3,539*

Bank Austria Creditanstalt

Banks	Total Asset (€/m)
• BPH	13,200
• HVB Hungary	3,839
• HVB Czech Republic	4,689
• Splitska Banka	2,807
• Ion Tiriak Bank	625
• HVB Biochim	1,000
• HVB Slovakia	1,683
• HVB Romania	1,057
• BACA Slovenia	1,251
• Hebros Bank	314
• Eksimbanka	156
• HVB BiH	379
• HVB Serbia	194
• Macedonia (Rep.Office)	n/a
Total	31,194*

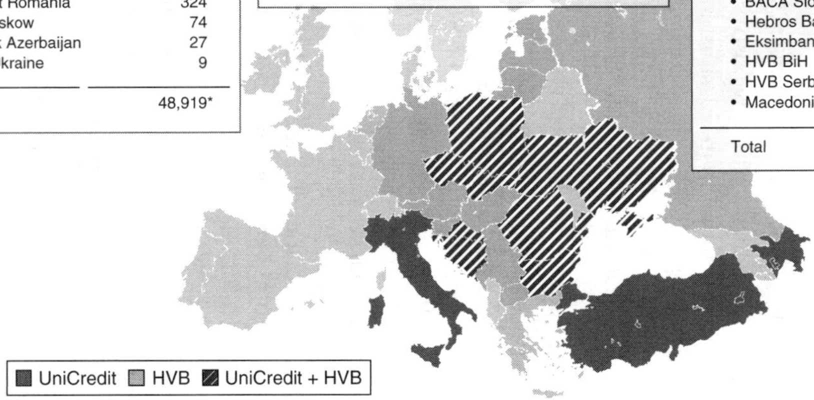

Notes:
Numbers converted with 31st December 2004 exchange rate; figures are 100% ownership.
* Sum of countries may differ from Total because of netting off of consolidated item (e.g. Pekao Ukraine is consolidated within Pekao Group; Unicredit Zagrebacka consolidated within Zagrebacka Banka) and minor companies. All figures are 100%.

Source: Banks' Annual Report and Investor Relations.

Figure 29.1

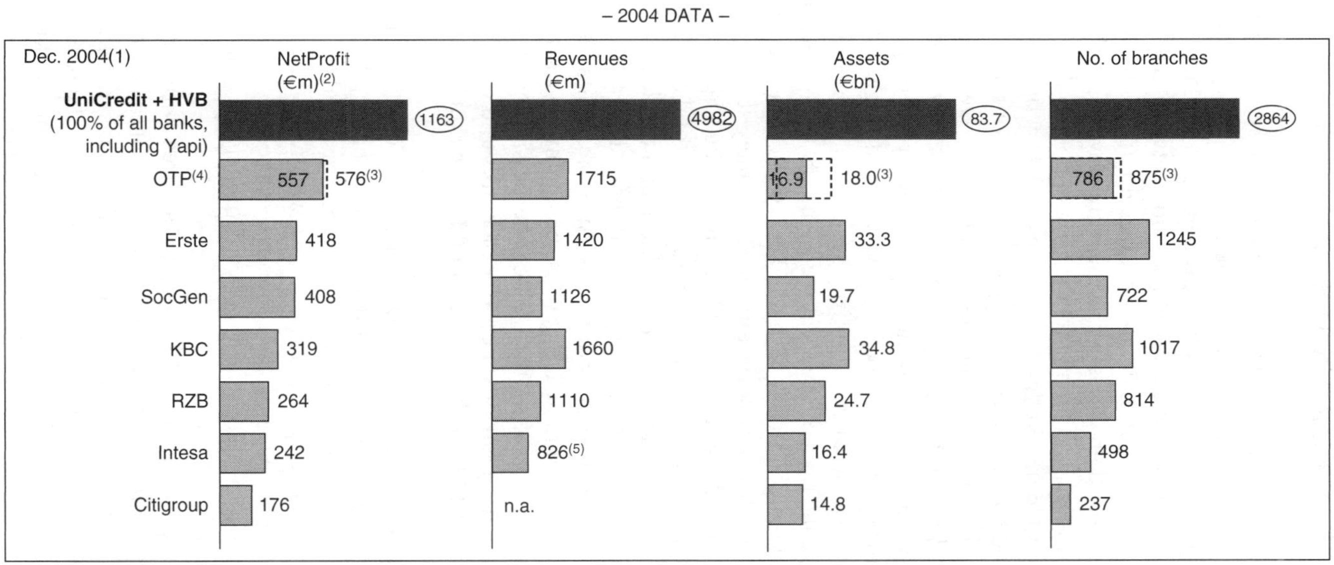

Notes:
1. 100% of total assets and profit after tax for controlled Companies (stake > 50%) and share owned for non controlled companies; 100% of branches and employees; for details please refer to the methodological notes.
2. After tax, before minority interest.
3. Including proforma recently acquired Novabanka.
4. Including OTP's subsidiaries.
5. Data on total revenues refer to contribution to Intesa's consolidated result.

Source: UCI-FBD Economic Research; numbers calculated using average exchange rate except for Unicredit.

Figure 29.2

WHAT IS THE REGION FOR US TODAY?

First of all, the CEE countries are an extremely good opportunity. The region is a huge market in terms of size and people. Risks are low and decreasing (which is key, given the huge differences between CEE and the United States, for instance when it comes to yield spreads between government bonds). Growth prospects continue to be excellent in traditional banking and in new segments and products, while there are new geographies to be gradually exploited. Figure 29.3 highlights the growth potential of the CEE region, comparing total loan and deposit volumes and growth rates in Germany, Italy, Austria and CEE. In terms of assets, the CEE countries are half as big a market as Italy, but in terms of asset and GDP growth, they outpace the EU-15 by far. Real GDP growth in CEE is close to three times that in the EU-15. And the ratio of loans and deposits as a percentage of GDP is rather low, which means that the expected growth is quite high. What is also important is that today a mere three countries account for more or less 70 per cent of the total revenue pool of the area (see Figure 29.4). To have a strong foothold in these three countries – Russia, Turkey and Poland – is essential for leveraging on economy of scale, and therefore a key strategy.

As UniCredit, we first entered the region in 1999, through the acquisition of a controlling stake in Bank Pekao and have since invested a total of EUR 2.7 billion, excluding the acquisition of Yapi Kredi Bank and the deal with HVB/BA-CA (see Figure 29.5). In the six years since 1999 we have built up a huge amount of assets. On top of that, both Bank Austria Creditanstalt and HVB had a strong tradition in the CEE market, being among the first relevant international players operating there since the beginning of the transition process. Consolidating our own network of banks and the CEE activities of Bank Austria and HVB thus means building the undisputed regional leader.

We have been successful in our regional growth plan, but while becoming a regional leader, we have also managed to be an international-local bank in the region. We have a strong regional network, but we are also perceived as a local bank in each market. We really believe we have to be local and behave as local, serving the need of the economy, as the only way to remain profitable in the medium to long term is by adequately supporting the regional economic growth.

What is important to note is that the CEE region is an area with a very high complexity, a rapidly changing environment for sure – think enlargement, the single currency, the integration of international financial markets. There are challenges in integrating different banking models in the region, in integrating different cultures and languages, different ways of thinking and behaving. Integration is our key theme – it is not homogeneity at which

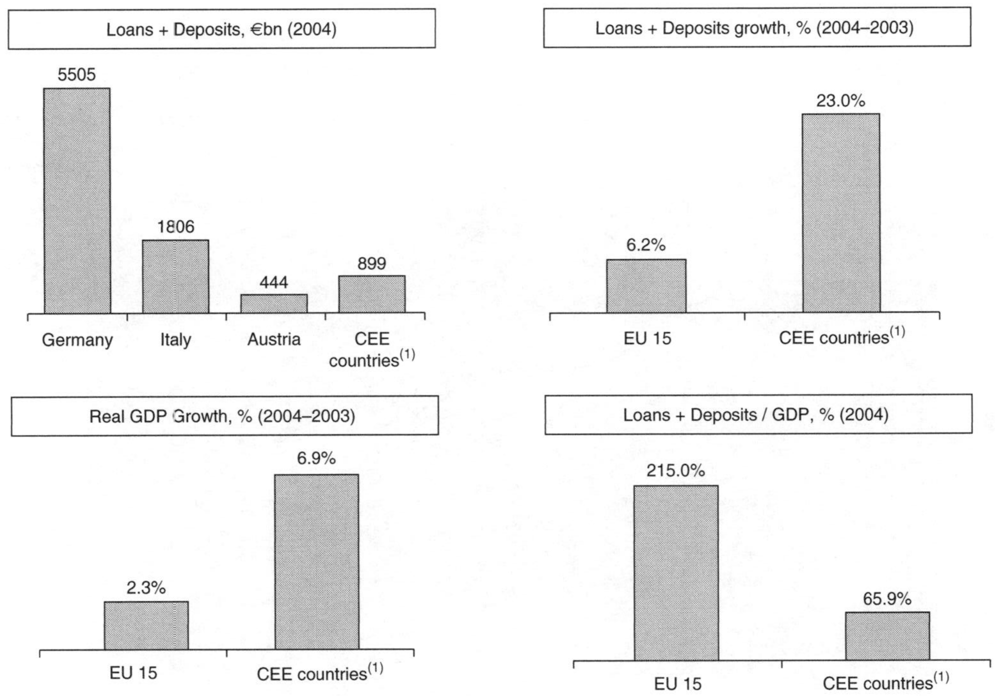

Note: (1) All UCI, BACA, HVB CEE countries with the exception of Greece and Netherlands.

Source: New Europe Research Network.

Figure 29.3

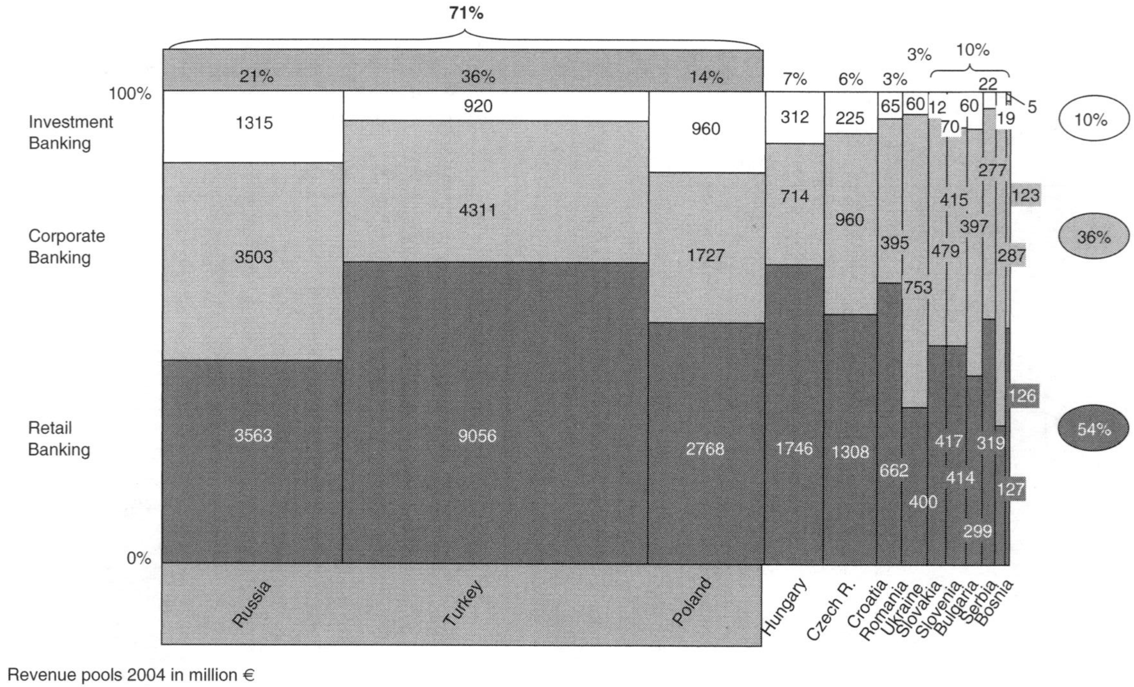

Note: Percentages on top of chart reflect share of country in total CEE revenue pools.

Source: National banks; Economic Research Department BA-CA; BCG analysis.

Figure 29.4

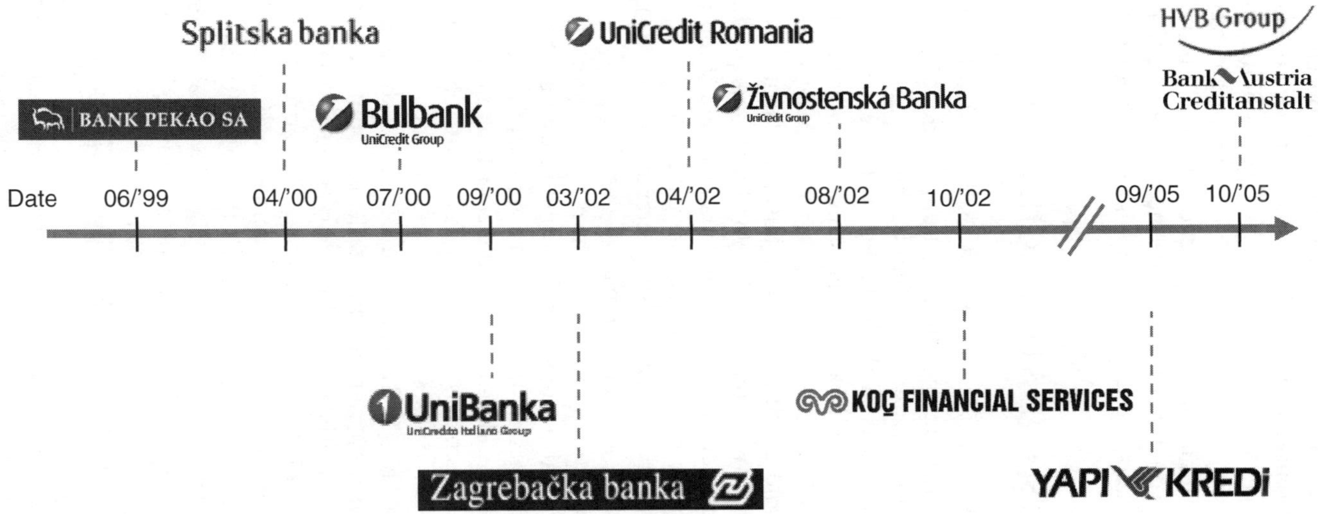

Figure 29.5 *Total investment of ca. 2.7 €/bn excluding Yapi and HVB/BACA*

we are aiming; there is a difference between the two concepts. And last but not least there is a repositioning in the market, and we are making efforts to preserve and enhance our corporate social responsibility, which is about how we manage our business processes to produce an overall positive impact on society. This includes many practical effects, for instance, the type of products we have on the shelves, how we incentivize people, how we work in terms of budget and so on. This concept is really important.

OUR TARGETS AND STRATEGIES

First of all, the CEE business strategy of the UniCredit/HVB group is to consolidate the number one position, exploiting regional strength and the group's strength. Think about investment banking, where we hold a strong foothold in CEE and generate the highest growth rate in terms of revenues.

Second, we strive to achieve and maintain a relevant competitive position in some key business areas: assets under management, mortgages, consumer credits and credit cards – two businesses that we consider as a whole – and leasing. We also aim to develop high value products for corporate and large corporate entities: cash management, transactional services, derivative business, trade finance and real estate.

Third, we want to leverage our existing strengths to new geographies. In some countries, we are after all still relatively small.

Fourth, we want further growth in revenues from large corporates, treasury sales, multinational customers in CEE and investment banking.

We have a differentiated strategy from country to country, because in some countries we are already the leader and thus need to defend our market share and reach cost efficiency. Poland, Croatia, Bulgaria and Bosnia-Herzegovina are cases in point. Then there are countries where we are already relatively big. In Turkey we have a market share of 11 to 13 per cent, depending on how market share is defined. But we expect further growth in terms of growth volumes and market share. Apart from Turkey, Slovakia is also in this category. Then there are countries where we want to achieve a 10 per cent market share. At the time of writing, we had a share of between 6 and 9 per cent in the Czech Republic, Romania, Slovenia, Hungary, Russia, Serbia-Montenegro and Ukraine. Finally, there are countries where we have to develop a growth/entry strategy, because we have a very small presence – or where we need to reshape the overall strategy. In those countries – Latvia, Lithuania, Macedonia, Estonia and Azerbaijan – the focus remains on a specific segment.

Figure 29.6 shows the 11 countries in which we are among the top five players (see flags). Our role in each of the local markets means that we have

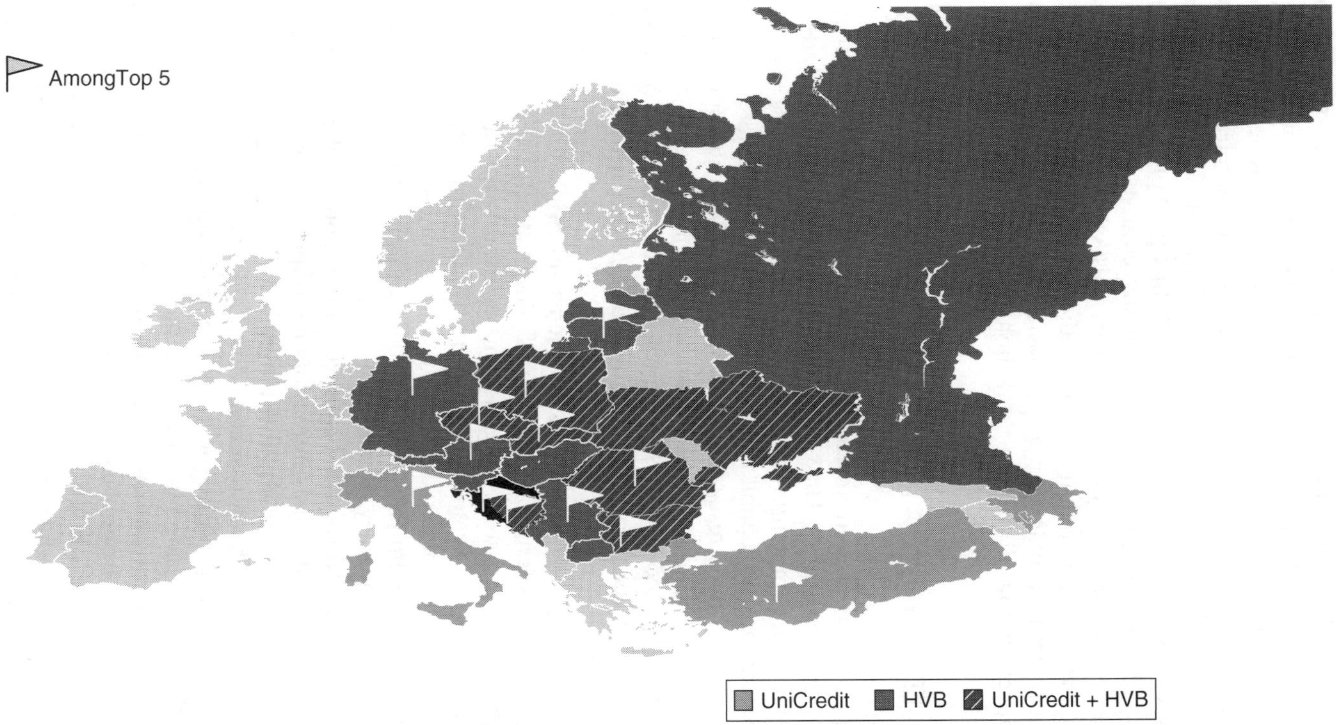

Source: UniCredit-NE Research Network based on local banks' financial statements, central banks and press releases.

Figure 29.6

a strong responsibility towards all our stakeholders: our customers, our employees, our communities and our shareholders. The customers after all pay our salaries and ultimately define our success. But without well-trained, motivated, and I would say, happy employees we would not be able to serve our customers well, so they are our most valuable asset. The local communities where all work are the engines of economic growth. And the shareholders, as 'the milestone for a private company' complete the picture – or the 'four-leg table': unless any of the four legs work well you cannot be successful in the medium or long term. Without happy shareholders, for instance, a company usually changes its ownership structure, which in turn has an impact on how all the other stakeholders are served.

WHAT ARE THE MAIN CHALLENGES BEFORE US?

The first challenges come from the market. We see some very clear trends in terms of revenue drivers. The volumes are going up, whereas spreads are going down and competition is increasing, which puts a pressure on revenue generation and capability. On the positive side, from a revenue perspective, we are seeing a reshaping in terms of the mix between retail and corporate customers, and an increase in the share of fee-based income (at the cost of interest income). And we expect an increase in terms of market penetration for the banking system, which is again a positive driver for revenue generation.

With regard to lending risk drivers, the increasing brightening of macroeconomic scenarios is dampening credit risk. The relatively low level of corporate indebtedness is also positive in terms of risk. At the same time, the expected growth of the retail loan portfolio will drive up credit cost, and the high growth of lending volumes will in one way or other deteriorate the asset quality in the medium term. The important thing in this respect is to have a very strong monetary system.

Then there is the challenge of being truly international. We have learnt from our experience that to be international, it is quite important to have a specific mindset. To become a global player is for sure a big opportunity, but it is also a very tough job that can add exponential complexity to your ordinary business. There are no shortcuts, so you cannot try to escape problems, and there are no standard solutions that you may take off the shelf. We have learnt some lessons in globalizing our banking business, and we have witnessed some of our clients who successfully moved from domestic to international markets. But we have also seen failures from which we can surely conclude that, first, going abroad is no cure for problems at home; second, changing the perimeter per se is not a winning strategy; and third, going abroad only for growing revenues or volumes is not necessarily a good idea. For us today it is not always important to be big. What is important is to be successful in terms of value appreciation on the capital we are asking from our shareholders.

LESSON LEARNT AND NEXT STEPS

We have learnt a lot in recent years and we are now preparing for the big challenges ahead. The lessons we have learnt are summarized below:

It is important to be prepared in terms of organization, much more than in terms of financial strength, namely to be prepared to face the size and approach of global competitors.

It is important to understand that individual customers and individual markets are very different; one must be ready to manage complexity. At UniCredit, managing diversity is one of our key competencies.

We have to understand our competitors and always need to benchmark ourselves against the best players.

We have to make sure that we master local markets; in other words, it is essential for us to have domestic markets. We do not want only to delocalize – we want to be successful market by market.

It is important to balance the cost-to-service equation to provide real value for customers.

We need to build on our strengths and when necessary find a strong local partner. For instance, in Turkey it was important for us to be there with a local partner, because it was clear to us that the Turkish market will consolidate. It is quite important to be humble and to understand where you can be alone and where you need someone else with whom to join forces.

Another key theme is to de-average the strategic approach for different countries or different times. At the same time it is important to develop a specific organization/governance model for global businesses. We have some global business; for instance we make a point of managing consumer credit in order to be successful in the different geographies.

It is also essential to develop a win–win strategy with all the stakeholders. Let me recall the local communities which are key stakeholders, because without social legitimacy you cannot be successful as a company.

Last but not least, we are well advised to build a truly international management team and to strive at developing a real international multi-business network. At UniCredit, we have always tried to balance local talents and experienced expatriates to have the best blend of competencies. We strive to manage existing talents and to recruit and develop future ones. We invest in knowledge transfer both at home and in the hosting countries.

For instance, Yapi Kredit has a strong competence in consumer credit. We want to leverage that for the whole group, not only for CEE but also for Italy, Germany and Austria. We create a team of international managers via cross-country assignments. And this is key. We still have some difficulties in moving a Czech colleague to Poland or a Croatian colleague to Italy. But this is essential and we are trying to do that more and more. We are making an effort to recruit local young high potentials and invest in them, for which we have had a specific programme since 2001. We also put an emphasis on managing 'professional families' (such as the 'legal department family') across the group. Moreover, we continually review the compensation/retention systems and align them to the business strategy. In the end, we also invest in sales and sales management skills, which is certainly the key driver for revenue generation.

All in all, we are ready for the big challenges ahead. We are creating the first truly European bank, a piece of history in the European financial market. We have the commitment, the enthusiasm and the adventurous spirit needed to do that.

30. Banking consolidation

Reinhard Ortner

This contribution is meant to highlight a number of trends and phenomena that we have seen in the more recent history of banking consolidation and will conclude with seven theses developed on that basis. In retrospect, we can discern a number of key themes in global banking. In the United States, for instance, there were some 15 000 banks in the mid-1980s and the question was: 'How many will survive?' Well, more than 7000 credit institutions are still in business at the time of writing. Consolidation took place among the big institutions on a regional and national basis. But we expect, and I will come back to that in one of my theses, to see at least one of the bigger US banks leapfrog into Europe.

In Europe we have recently seen a rising acceptance of cross-border transactions. The UniCredit/HVB deal referred to by Alessandro Profumo (Chapter 29) is of course the most spectacular event of this kind in the more recent past, but things have been moving on also in Italy, above all. And there is a growing interest in growth markets, which is one of the reasons why share prices have exploded in the last couple of years. What is the effect of this trend of concentration and consolidation? In 1995 the five top banks in the world had an average market capitalization of less than EUR 20 billion. In 2005, the average was more than EUR 130 billion, seven times as much. And in 1995 eight out of the top 10 banks, one wouldn't believe it looking back, were Japanese, while only one was American. In 2005 only one of the top 10 banks was Japanese, and the American share had jumped to five out of ten.

What are the main aspects of this wave of consolidation? Well, one aspect is clearly scale, which has been the driving force in the United States (and in Europe), but specialization and focus matter as well. With regard to focus, we see two trends in particular, namely a regional focus (Erste Bank or Standard Chartered being cases in point) and a product focus (practised by State Street, MBNA or Julius Bear). Almost weekly we see plans and announcements of attempted or consummated transactions, with a main emphasis on consolidating and strengthening the respective competitive position particularly in the product-driven businesses and on achieving cost synergies.

What we have also seen in the development of bank stocks and financial company stocks is that specialized companies typically command higher valuation multiples than non-specialized companies (if they concentrate on growth markets). So specialist institutions are attractive but expensive targets for consolidators and, as we have seen, growth is at the premium end of the market: investors pay a premium for sustainable bottom-line and top-line growth, which is more likely in a specialist institution.

What are the barriers to intra-European banking consolidation in general (and to consolidation in Central Europe in particular, to which I will come back below)? Overall, we still see a lot of domestic protectionism, which always looks funny when we are looking at another country while, within one's own country, it is a quite natural thing. One barrier is the lack of a European-wide takeover code. Whoever has had to deal with national themes as far as takeovers are concerned knows what I am talking about. Other differences include the absence of a European corporate law, historically different roles of banks in their local economies, different tax regimes (national interest in retaining tax income) and different accounting standards (rules-based vs. principles-based approaches). The real problem of Intra-European banking consolidation, however, remains the old three questions that always determine the success of a merger: 'Who is the CEO?', 'Where are the headquarters located?', and 'What is the name of the new entity?'

What are the strategic alternatives for banks, and in particular, for those that are not in the league of the top 10 banks worldwide? One is clearly a focus on core competencies. In this context we have also seen in the last couple of years, particularly in Central and Eastern Europe, substantial progress of monoliners, that is banks or financial companies that specialize in a single line of products, such as consumer finance, asset management, sometimes mortgage lending and so forth. A monoline or core competence strategy allows companies to grow organically and through incremental acquisition and is based on the hope that the global institutional model will fail due to risk and complexity.

Another strategic alternative has been and will remain to consolidate in the home country and home regions. Of course, not a single European country is large enough to reach an equivalent size to US competitors, so to create a 'Eurobank' is a tough choice. Mergers across borders are clearly what we expect to see more often in the future. And up until now, most of what we have seen in cross-border mergers of any size has been on a regional basis, like in the Benelux countries, or in Scandinavia, or partly between Spain and Portugal, and UK and Ireland, but these were fairly homogeneous areas in terms of culture and banking practices. So cross-border deals, where you enter into different cultures, are a different game.

Finally, another alternative, but not necessarily the first choice for many banks, is the sale to a global competitor.

The most crucial success factor for top performing banks is, ultimately, revenue growth – the top line, which dictates the bottom line success – and not so much the cost–income ratio and rationalization. The product mix heavily influences revenue growth opportunities. Moreover, as has been mentioned before, we see and will continue to see changes in the structure of the business in favour of fee and commission income at the expense of net interest income.

Common characteristics that can explain superior performance are clearly scale relative to the core market(s) and products, and exposure to markets with higher growth rates. That is clearly the explanation why multiples for Central and Eastern European banks have been going up quite enormously in the last couple of years. When Erste Bank bought Česká Spořitelna in 2000 at 1.6 times book price, we were punished both by the share markets and the rating agencies for paying such an extravagant price. Nowadays banks are sold at 3 or 4 times book price and more. Other characteristics include a significant volume of M&A activity that has, on the whole, been perceived as a success by the market. Banks that have a reputation for being good acquirers and consolidators (such as HSBC, RBS) will be well received. At the same time, banks such as Citigroup, UniCredito and DnB NOR are benefiting from low- or nil-premium mergers undertaken to establish the core platform. Finally, the quality of the management team (clear decision-making/governance structures, perceived 'strong' leadership) and product exposure to growth markets (consumer finance, asset gathering) also play a role.

To conclude, let me propose seven theses: first, we have seen an increasing expansion into Central and Eastern Europe; the number of banks against which OTP Bank had to compete in the last couple of transactions is a clear indication that more and more banks feel the pain that they missed the train and now try to catch the train at a time when it is already leaving the station. This process will slow down, simply because there is not very much left to be bought. After all, the ownership of domestic banks by foreign banks is already 90 per cent, and higher in some countries.

Second, in Western Europe I would expect in-the-market mergers to remain the dominant type, because there is a huge requirement for consolidation – in countries such as Germany, where sooner or later there will have to be some movement in the savings banks sector, but also in other countries.

Third, we will see more cross-border mergers.

Fourth, partly as a consequence of that, but also as a sort of second wave of consolidation, we will see further in-the-market mergers and consolidations in the Central and Eastern European banking markets. Some of these markets are still highly fragmented, and I can imagine that a number of players who are in a 'me too' role but are basically niche players today, will sooner or later lose patience with their awkward sandwich position and sell out. At the same time, cross-border mergers in Western Europe can easily trigger transactions in Central and Eastern Europe. Splitska Banka, which evolved from HVB Croatia and BA-CA's Croatian daughter, and Zagrebačka Banka, which entered into a strategic partnership with Unicredit Group and Allianz, are typical examples.

Fifth, I see a new fault line developing in Central and Eastern Europe, namely the question: 'Is it more important to own the production, or is it more important to own the customer relationship?' Right now, very often the classical business model is to have both, that is to have in-house production for one's own clientele. I would expect the perspective to be completely different ten years down the road.

This could lead to what I would call, sixth, a 'de-consolidation and re-consolidation trend'. What I mean by 'de-consolidation' is that banks will have to prove whether and to what extent they want to have production in-house or not. Is it really advantageous to have a life insurance company? Is it necessary to have one's own investment fund company?

And seventh, sooner or later I would expect one of the big American banks to 'do the leapfrog' and buy a consolidator in Europe.

31. Building a Central European exchange alliance

Stefan Zapotocky

The growing regional integration of the Central European economic area would appear to be a good reason for intensifying cooperation among the national exchanges. By working closely together, Central and Eastern European exchanges will be able to reinforce their positions in the Europe of the regions. Exchanges play a significant role in raising equity capital for the regional economies, and the stock market contributes substantially to the economic development of the region of Central Europe.

A Central European exchange alliance, as proposed in this chapter, would help to create a strong international recognition and visibility of the region, including Poland, Austria, Hungary, the Czech Republic, Slovakia and Slovenia as the core area but extending also to Bulgaria, Croatia, Romania and other countries (see Figure 31.1). Such an alliance would assist in strengthening the participating local markets. And it would lessen the dependence on global market players with diverse interests.

With a presumed stock market capitalization of approximately EUR 500 billion by 2008, a homogeneously organized exchange alliance for Central Europe would certainly have an internationally efficient dimension. It would be a solution providing tangible benefits to all concerned – the national economies, shareholders and market participants. All participants would have the possibility to develop the Group and secure the interests of national markets.

Potential economic benefits include an improved macroeconomic performance (higher GDP growth and employment) as well as lower prices for financial services. Shareholders stand to gain from the regional/local perspective in decision-making and the chance to avoid marginalization. Furthermore, a more diversified investment choice, easier access to markets, cost cuttings, and clearing and settlement savings should appeal to intermediaries. Potential benefits for investors include a more diversified investment choice, a more efficient allocation of capital, higher investment returns and improved performance. Issuers, finally, should see greater investment

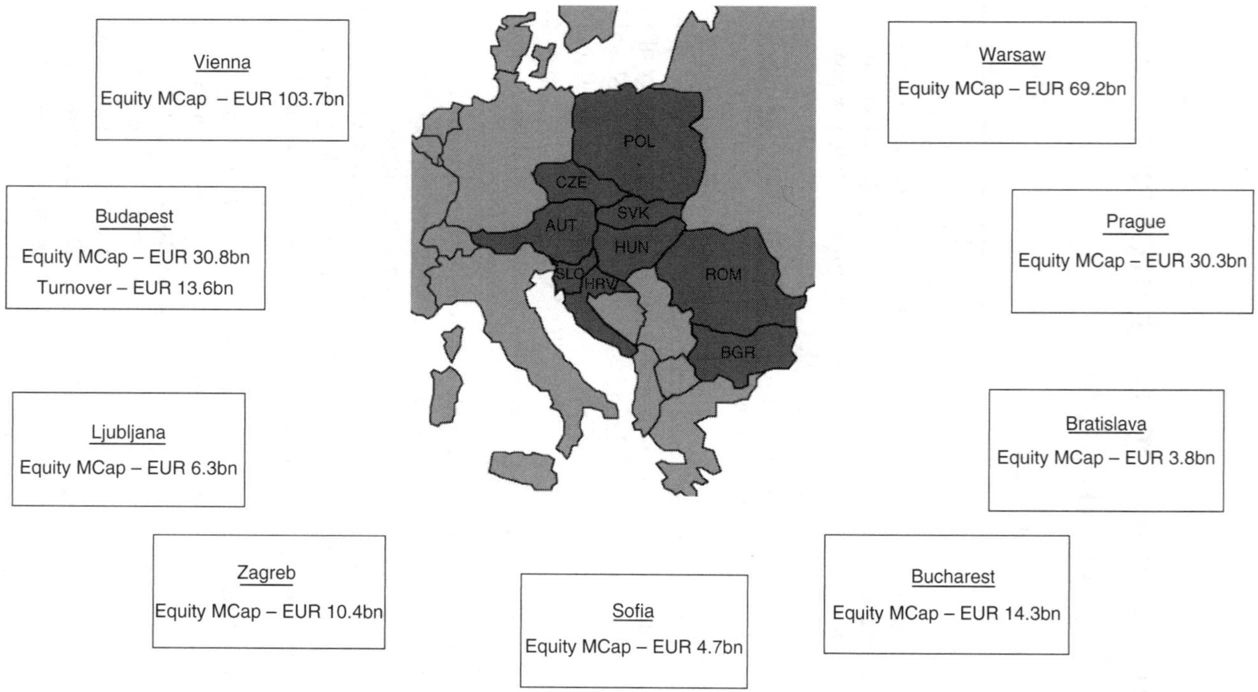

Note: Equity turnover as of the end of September – Electronic Order Book Transactions – single counted (YTD).

Source: FESE, Exchange market statistics.

Figure 31.1 Central European exchange alliance markets

demand, a wider choice of financial instruments, improved equity financing opportunities and a decrease in the cost of capital.

Laying the cornerstone for such a Central European exchange alliance, Wiener Börse, together with a consortium of Austrian banks, acquired a 68 per cent stake in the Budapest Stock Exchange in June 2004; one year later, in May 2005, we got the 'OK' from Brussels. This joint investment will reinforce the position of the two exchanges versus its international competitors. This common stock market is a sound basis that can be enlarged to encompass the entire region of Central Europe.

We have since started an intensive collaboration with the Budapest Stock Exchange (BSE) in the area of data vending: from November 2005, Wiener Börse customers have received data from the Budapest Stock Exchange (cash and derivatives market, indices and market depth) via the already existing datafeed (IDF). This means that since then there has been only one data format and one data source for the data of the two exchanges for the vendors of Wiener Börse. We also intend to establish a common index licencing policy with the Budapest Stock Exchange and to add the BSE indices to our sales products. In the near future, there are plans to cooperate in the formulation and implementation of corporate governance rules, and to harmonize market segments.

Over the medium to long term we hope to cooperate in the areas of connectivity, clearing and settlement, and harmonization of regulations and procedures.

At the same time we are in talks with other Central European exchanges to investigate their interest in building a larger alliance – currently, efforts are concentrating on building up trust and credibility and on openly discussing which options are available. Within the EU, we are primarily interested in cooperation with the exchanges of Warsaw, Prague, Bratislava and Ljubljana. We are also engaged in friendly talks with Bucharest and Zagreb.

All exchanges can join the process! We are interested in partnerships. We believe in the principle of independent regional exchanges that form part of a group of exchanges. The potential is enormous: we expect the regional market capitalization to reach about EUR 500 billion in 2008, compared with EUR 250 billion in 2005.

We are already discussing these ideas with the exchanges in Hungary, Czech Republic, Poland, Slovenia, Slovakia, Russia and Romania. Especially in the area of indices our cooperation with the Bucharest Stock Exchange has set a good example; to this purpose, we signed a joint 'Memorandum of Understanding' (MoU) in December 2004; since March 2005 we have jointly calculated the ROTX index, based on the prices of the most actively traded stocks of the Bucharest Exchange. Our latest project: on 1 December 2005, the Zagreb Stock Exchange and the Wiener Börse signed a cooperation agreement in Zagreb. The aim of this MoU is the closer cooperation of the two exchanges. In the area of index management, the intent is to start collaborating in 2006. And the hope is that more milestones towards building a powerful Central European exchange alliance will follow.

Index